HIGH CRIMES AND MISDEMEANORS

For the third time in forty-five years, America is talking about impeaching a president, but the impeachment provisions of the American constitution are widely misunderstood. In *High Crimes and Misdemeanors*, constitutional scholar Frank Bowman offers unprecedented clarity to the question of impeachment, tracing its roots to medieval England through its adoption in the Constitution and 250 years of American experience. By examining the human and political history of those who have faced impeachment, Bowman demonstrates that the framers intended impeachment to be a flexible tool, adaptable to the needs of any age. Written in a lively, engaging style, the book combines a deep historical and constitutional analysis of the impeachment clauses, a coherent theory of when impeachment should be used to protect constitutional order against presidential misconduct, and a comprehensive presentation of the case for and against impeachment of President Trump. It is an indispensable work for the present moment.

Frank O. Bowman III, the Floyd R. Gibson Missouri Endowed Professor of Law at the University of Missouri, is a nationally recognized authority on criminal law, a legal historian, and a former federal and state prosecutor. He has written extensively on impeachment in legal journals and the popular press, including the *New York Times, Politico,* and *Slate,* where he is a regular contributor. He has provided testimony to both Houses of Congress on multiple subjects including the meaning of "high crimes and misdemeanors" during the Clinton impeachment crisis.

High Crimes and Misdemeanors

A HISTORY OF IMPEACHMENT FOR
THE AGE OF TRUMP

FRANK O. BOWMAN III

CAMBRIDGE
UNIVERSITY PRESS

CAMBRIDGE
UNIVERSITY PRESS

University Printing House, Cambridge CB2 8BS, United Kingdom

One Liberty Plaza, 20th Floor, New York, NY 10006, USA

477 Williamstown Road, Port Melbourne, VIC 3207, Australia

314–321, 3rd Floor, Plot 3, Splendor Forum, Jasola District Centre, New Delhi – 110025, India

79 Anson Road, #06–04/06, Singapore 079906

Cambridge University Press is part of the University of Cambridge.

It furthers the University's mission by disseminating knowledge in the pursuit of education, learning, and research at the highest international levels of excellence.

www.cambridge.org
Information on this title: www.cambridge.org/9781108481052
DOI: 10.1017/9781108646239

First published 2019

Printed in the United Kingdom by TJ International Ltd, Padstow Cornwall

A catalogue record for this publication is available from the British Library.

Library of Congress Cataloging-in-Publication Data
NAMES: Bowman, Frank O., 1955– author.
TITLE: High crimes and misdemeanors : a history of impeachment for the age of Trump / Frank O. Bowman III, University of Missouri School of Law.
DESCRIPTION: Cambridge, United Kingdom ; New York, NY : Cambridge University Press, [2019] | Includes bibliographical references and index.
IDENTIFIERS: LCCN 2018059111 | ISBN 9781108481052 (alk. paper)
SUBJECTS: LCSH: Impeachments – United States – History. | Impeachments – Great Britain – History. | Presidents – United States – Discipline. | Johnson, Andrew, 1808–1875 – Impeachment. | Nixon, Richard M. (Richard Milhous), 1913–1994 – Impeachment. | Clinton, Bill, 1946 – Impeachment. | Trump, Donald, 1946 – Impeachment.
CLASSIFICATION: LCC KF5075 .B69 2019 | DDC 342.73/062–dc23
LC record available at https://lccn.loc.gov/2018059111

ISBN 978-1-108-48105-2 Hardback
ISBN 978-1-108-70376-5 Paperback

*To my wife Robin, helpmeet, sweetheart, and best friend,
without whose patience and support this book
could not have been written.*

Contents

Tables

Acknowledgments

No book of this scope could be written without the active help or patient forbearance of a supportive clutch of friends, family, and colleagues.

I am particularly grateful for much help from many people at the University of Missouri School of Law. First, thanks go to Dean Lyrissa Lidsky and the Law School itself for granting me research leave to finish the book. Throughout the project, I was constantly thankful for the professionalism, insight, and speed of the Law School's library staff. Special thanks go to crackerjack reference librarian Cynthia Shearrer, who found stuff I was looking for faster than I would have thought possible, and suggested sources of whose existence I had no clue, as well as to Randy Diamond, the head of our library, who put all his resources at my disposal.

Thanks to my brilliant law school colleague Paul Litton, and to my brothers, Herbert Bowman and Robert Bowman, lawyers, gentlemen, and scholars both, for reading and giving me invaluable feedback on some of the work. Joel Goldstein provided helpful clarification on the Twenty-fifth Amendment.

The book could not have been written or completed in anything like a timely fashion without the help of my terrific research assistants, Sam Crosby and Taylor Payne. Shawna Quast also did first-rate work on the footnotes.

My editor, Matt Gallaway, and all the rest of the folks at Cambridge University Press have been uniformly splendid in guiding me through the many stages of this project.

Finally, my wife Robin has tolerated long stretches of mental or physical absence with remarkable grace, and encouraged me when I thought the job would never be done. In this, as in all things, I am eternally in her debt.

Frank Bowman

Introduction

My life in the law so far has spanned just over forty years. It is a curious fact, or so it seems to me, that the beginning, the middle, and the current autumn of my career have been defined by national battles over presidential impeachment.

I have often said that Richard Nixon made me a lawyer. In the Watergate summer of 1974, I was a college sophomore who thought he wanted to be a doctor. But I was enthralled by the steadily heightening drama of the struggle between the president and those in the Justice Department, the press, and Congress who were determined to discover whether he had abused the powers of his office and betrayed his trust. I followed every twist and turn of the byzantine legal maneuvering by which the truth was finally extracted. I watched the Senate Watergate hearings and the impeachment hearings in the House Judiciary Committee whenever I could.

I admired all the people one would expect a young idealist to admire. The president's interlocutors, to be sure – Archibald Cox, bow-tied, dignified, relentless special prosecutor; Senator Sam Ervin of North Carolina, avuncular, rapier-sharp, "simple country lawyer" from North Carolina; Congresswoman Barbara Jordan of Texas, brilliant, eloquent, stentorian, too soon taken from us, a woman of color in the vanguard of history; and Peter Rodino, the calm, modest, but dogged, New Jersey embodiment of the best in American politics who chaired the House Judiciary Committee. But I also admired those of the president's own party who did not let their partisan ties to Richard Nixon or the political disaster they feared would surely follow his removal deflect them from finding the facts and acting on them once known – Senator Howard Baker of Tennessee, determined to know what the president knew and when he knew it; Congressman Hamilton Fish of New York who voted to impeach because, "The evidence is clear"; and Senator Barry Goldwater of Arizona, the dean of American conservative Republicans, who, sadly but firmly, walked into the Oval Office and told Richard Nixon that his cause was lost and he ought to go.

I realized that long-ago summer that I was far more interested in what these people, and all those who worked with them, were doing than in the goings-on in any test tube or petri dish or operating theater. I wanted to be a part, however insignificant, of the long story of American law and constitutionalism. So I switched majors from biology to political science, and in 1976 went off to law school.

Two decades or so later, after half a career as a federal and state prosecutor, I became a law teacher. And impeachment came knocking again. William Jefferson Clinton, that charismatic, canny, but deeply selfish man, was under siege from the not altogether imaginary "vast right-wing conspiracy" of Hillary Clinton's nightmares – a brigade of muckraking political lawyers, Independent Counsel Kenneth Starr, and a ferocious new generation of conservative congressmen led by Newt Gingrich. I was asked to write testimony on behalf of a national lawyers' group for the House Judiciary Committee on the meaning of "high Crimes and Misdemeanors." That turned into a law review article, and then another, and over the years into occasional visits to impeachment land whenever the topic raised its head in the national press.

After Clinton escaped conviction in the Senate, stained but astoundingly buoyant, I never really expected to encounter in my lifetime another occasion when impeachment of a president would become a live topic of the American conversation. After all, until 1974, only one American president – Andrew Johnson in 1868 – had been impeached in the two centuries since the adoption of the constitution. From 1974 to date, one president has resigned in the face of certain impeachment and conviction, and another has been impeached and acquitted. A third serious impeachment controversy in only forty years seemed out of the question. Then came Donald Trump.

Mr. Trump's eruption onto the national political scene and his stunning election to the presidency were unprecedented in a hundred ways. One of them was that his distressed political opponents began talking about impeaching him before he ever took office. To be frank, that sort of talk was really quite daft. Whatever Mr. Trump's peculiarities, he won the presidency according to the constitutional rules (even if, as heartbroken Democrats never tire of mentioning, he lost the popular vote by a margin of almost 3 million). Accordingly, he is entitled to an uninterrupted tenure of office unless he dies, is stripped of his powers under the Twenty-fifth Amendment, or is impeached for committing "Treason, Bribery, or other high Crimes and Misdemeanors." Absent compelling proof of the latter – as we will see, always a steep mountain to climb – he was certainly entitled to the benefit of the doubt as he shouldered the burdens of an almost impossible job.

And yet, as time passed, the impeachment talk never waned. Some of the talk is still just partisan resentment. Some of it is still just wishful thinking, a desperate hope of reversing the results of a stunning electoral defeat. But not all the talk has been frivolous. Indeed, as the months march by and Mr. Trump's approach to his office and to American constitutionalism has become clearer, the conversation has taken a more serious turn. I entered the debate first through that quintessentially twenty-first-century expedient of the loquacious intellectual, a blog.[1] For nearly a year, I wrote about the controversies of the day – the Mueller investigation, alleged abuses of the pardon power, possible violations of the emoluments clauses of the constitution, Russian meetings and federal election law, payoffs to mistresses, the gamut. As I wrote, I also read, or reread, the available studies of impeachment. I concluded that, while much ground had been covered over the years, there was no comprehensive treatment of impeachment running from its ancient roots in medieval England through the entire American experience to the present day. Certainly, no one had attempted to write a work that combined a comprehensive scholarly examination of the field with sober analysis of the present political moment. I set out to write that book. Whether I have succeeded, well, you will judge for yourself.

A few introductory thoughts before you plunge in:

There is a lot of history here. There are multiple reasons for that. Impeachment is a mechanism written into the American constitution in 1787 by the crew of renegade Englishmen we have since deified into Founding Fathers. In writing the constitution, they could not help but be influenced by the history and politics of the ancient kingdom they had just left. Their observations about the strengths and weaknesses of Great Britain's parliamentary monarchy infused all the choices they made about both the overall structure and working details of the new government they were imagining. They generally shared Montesquieu's enthusiasm for a government in which power was separated, as in Great Britain it mostly was, between the executive, judicial, and legislative branches. However, they were particularly focused on the problem of how to balance the need for a vigorous executive and an independent judiciary with the fear that either might become abusive, corrupt, or even tyrannical. They saw the legislature as the central organ of a republican government and as the source of necessary checks on the possible excesses of the other two branches. Their immersion in the political culture of the mother country and, for many of them, their deep study of British history, naturally disposed them to think of impeachment, a very old parliamentary institution, as one of those checks. So the first reason we need to know a good deal about British political history is that it informed everything the American Founders did, particularly the choices they made about impeachment.

The second reason for our forced immersion in "olde" parliamentary lore is that, once the framers decided that they were going to put impeachment in the constitution, they also decided, at the very last moment, to define the scope of impeachable conduct with a very "olde" phrase, "high Crimes and Misdemeanors." As we will see, that phrase came from British impeachments. It was first used in Parliament to describe impeachable offenses in the 1300s and became a staple of parliamentary impeachment talk for the next four centuries. Even if you are not already familiar with the furious arguments that swirl around the meaning of these four words, you would immediately grasp that they are not self-explanatory. What, after all, is a "high" crime? Does "crime" in this setting mean crime in the ordinary sense, or just really bad behavior? What does "misdemeanor" mean in this special setting? Surely we are not going to be impeaching people for jaywalking or overtime parking. Does "high" modify "misdemeanor," and if so, what the heck is a "high misdemeanor"? It turns out that "high Crimes and Misdemeanors" is not so much a pair of individual nouns with a single modifier, but a unitary term of art that can be understood only in the historical setting where it arose. As we will discuss at great length in Chapter 4, that is certainly how the men who wrote and ratified the constitution understood it. So we have to go back into history to find out what they meant.

The need for historical knowledge does not end with a foray into the halls of Parliament. It turns out that American colonists before the Revolution and the inhabitants of the new states created after the Declaration of Independence in 1776 knew something about their British constitutional roots. The colonists used impeachment both to rid themselves of troublesome government officials and sometimes to assert the independence of the colonial assemblies from royal government. The new states almost all wrote impeachment into their constitutions and many used it. All that history on this side of the Atlantic was part of the framers' heritage. It affected their thinking about impeachment. So we need to know something about it, too.

Finally, we cannot stop our historical exploration with the Constitutional Convention of 1787 and the impeachment provisions the delegates wrote into the constitution. Although "high Crimes and Misdemeanors" is a term of art derived from British and (some) early American practice, all constitutional language is subject to interpretation through later usage in particular cases, a process that sometimes produces quite radical shifts in meaning. What is more, this particular phrase is more malleable than most because it is mostly just a label for what Parliament and some early American legislatures did as they decided individual cases. They impeached people for this or that, and then called the resulting bag of this-and-that "high Crimes and Misdemeanors." Lawyers call this mode of lawmaking the "common law" method. Put simply, it means that courts, and here legislatures, make decisions in particular cases looking to what they have done in the past for guidance about the best rule, but not being absolutely bound by what they decided before. It is a flexible way of making law, always keeping an eye over one's shoulder for old wisdom while shaping the law to the needs of the present. As we will see, the evidence is very strong that the framers intended impeachments to be decided in just this way.

Therefore, our trip through history must continue. To understand how impeachment should be employed today, we need to examine all the, surprisingly few, times it has been used from the ratification of the constitution in 1788 to the present day. So we will consider the impeachments of federal judges and cabinet officers (actually only one of those, Secretary of War William Belknap), the attempted impeachment of a U.S. senator, and of course the three presidents who have been impeached or nearly so – Andrew Johnson, Richard Nixon, and Bill Clinton.

As we go, we will be looking for patterns and precedents. We will answer questions about who can be impeached, who does the impeaching, what rules there may be about the procedure, and what consequences can be visited on the convicted. We will consider how and by whom investigations of impeachable behavior should be conducted, particularly in the case of presidents. We will think a lot about how impeachment fits into the overall structure of the American national government. We will spend a good deal of time figuring out the kinds of behavior for which an erring official may constitutionally be impeached. We will take especial note of the high procedural barrier the framers erected with the requirement of a two-thirds majority for conviction in the Senate. Finally, we will examine the case for and against impeaching President Donald Trump.

A brief word about how to use this book: of course, like all authors, I fondly hope that you will hurry on from this Introduction and read the entire opus in a single fevered rush. I will give friendly warning, however, that Chapters 2 and 3 may be a little heavy going for those not historically inclined. I think it is all fascinating stuff, and I also think that no respectable constitutional argument about the place of impeachment in the constitution or the meaning of "high Crimes and Misdemeanors" can be made without a solid understanding of what Parliament and pre-1788 Americans were up to. But if you find it all a bit too antiquarian, I will forgive you for dashing through it quickly to get to the chaps assembled at Independence Hall in Chapter 4. After that, if you are really interested in impeachment in America, the rest of the book is pretty plain sailing.

I will offer a final thought before sending you on your way. My study of some 700 years of Anglo-American practice suggests that impeachments have been of three broad types. The first is impeachment as governmental house-cleaning device. The legislature has often used impeachment to force out of office (and in Britain to punish criminally) crooks, swindlers, traitors, petty despots, gross incompetents, and others who infest the middle reaches of government and cannot be induced to go by other means. Most American impeachments have been of this kind – impeachments of misbehaving federal judges with life tenure otherwise removable only by retirement or death. Second, in both Britain and the United States, impeachment is also a political tool, used or threatened as a means of expressing profound legislative displeasure with another branch of government by evicting officials who are the fount or instruments of its policies.

Finally, there is a third, rarer but far more important, class of impeachments. As we will see, impeachment was invented and wielded by the British Parliament through centuries of difficult evolution from absolute monarchy toward the parliamentary democracy that was beginning to take shape in the eighteenth century. It was, from its inception, a revolutionary device. A declaration by the assembled nobles and commons of England that the monarch had limits, that even though the nation was generally loyal to, and deeply reluctant to remove, the king, Parliament would guard against a drift or rush to absolutism by striking at the king's human instruments. These were the great impeachments of British history in which, as Parliament commonly phrased it, the defendant was charged with "the crime of subverting the laws, and introducing an arbitrary and tyrannical government." The essence of these cases was that Parliament was defending its vision of the proper constitutional order. In some cases, these impeachments were genuinely defensive in the sense of sending a sharp and sometimes deadly signal that traditional rights and privileges must not be invaded. In other cases, Parliament's project was more creative. At critical junctures in the nation's history, when fundamental choices about the kingdom path had to be made, Parliament used impeachment to declare in favor of its vision of the constitutional future.

American presidential impeachments by their nature tend to fall into this third category. Great Britain could not impeach its monarch, only his or her minions. In the United States, we can take down the official who is, for an elected time at least, both head of state and head of government. We contemplate that only rarely. We tend to do so when the country is unusually quarrelsome and discontented with itself, when our settled expectations about the constitutional order are shaken, when we fear the shape of things to come, when as Hamlet put it, "The time is out of joint."[2] We are in such a time now. It behooves us to examine, debate, and understand one tool the Founders gave us for defending the constitution.

1

How to Interpret the Constitution's Impeachment Clauses

This is a book about how to interpret and apply the provisions of the U.S. constitution which govern impeachment of the president. Constitutional experts disagree profoundly about the proper mode of constitutional interpretation. Interpretive schools labeled textualism, structuralism, originalism (of several flavors), doctrinalism, prudentialism, living constitutionalism, and others all have their fans. The sheer profusion of approaches would be sufficient reason to begin a book about any part of the constitution with an introduction to the competing interpretive schools.

The need for such a prologue may be even greater in the case of impeachment. Arguments about the correct approach to constitutional interpretation are not confined to obscure law journals or the footnotes in legal briefs. At least in crude form, they have broken into the public consciousness and become defining features of American political ideologies. For decades, a rallying cry of the political right has been a demand for "strict construction" of the constitution, while the left has learned to see the constitution as a "living document." These catch phrases are often no more than expressions of desire for judges and other public officials who will interpret the constitution to produce results consistent with the speaker's policy preferences. And they are, at best, oversimplifications of complex disputes about the tools that can legitimately be brought to bear in deciding close constitutional questions. But they have a powerful visceral political pull. As we will see, impeachment is fundamentally a political process, a contest played out in the quintessentially political forum of the U.S. Congress, but a contest in which the rough boundaries of the playing field and the rules of decision are influenced by the players' beliefs about constitutional meaning. The fact that disagreements over methods of constitutional interpretation are already infused into our elective politics makes it doubly important that a work about impeachment address the methodological dispute squarely and up front.

CONSTITUTIONAL INTERPRETATION AND THE JUDICIARY

The American constitution is, or at least started out as, a document. As first approved in 1787 by the members of the Philadelphia Constitutional Convention, it contained roughly 4,400 words written in the lovely calligraphy of the time on four large sheets of paper.[1] Once this document was ratified in June 1788,[2] its 4,400 words became the framework for governing a country that had existed since at least 1783 when the Treaty of Paris ended the Revolutionary War and recognized American independence,[3] but that had since operated as a partnership of sovereign states loosely bound by the Articles of Confederation.

The document ratified in 1788 is commonly claimed to be the first and oldest written constitution in human history. That is not quite true. Some countries, dating back to Greek city-states, had at least partially written constitutions.[4] Moreover, all the American states had written constitutions before the Philadelphia convention opened.[5] Still, the American constitution can claim pride of place as the first fully written, unitary constitution binding on an entire nation of continental scope.

Of equal importance to its ambition and its geographic reach is the fact that the American constitution was, and was conceived to be, a foundational document in a way that no previous constitution had been, and few subsequent constitutions could be. The Philadelphia delegates were writing the basic organizational rules for an entirely fresh creation, an entity that had not existed in any form prior to the Revolution, and was only slowly coalescing from the thirteen independent colonies of British North America. This made the Philadelphia project distinct from exercises in constitution writing that sought to supplant or modify existing governmental arrangements in nations that had long histories of self-governance under different rules, or nations that, even if they were achieving sovereignty for the first time, had at least long conceived of themselves as nations by virtue of shared ethnicity or culture. In Abraham Lincoln's phrase of not quite a century later, the drafters of the Philadelphia constitution really were bringing forth a "new nation."[6]

Accordingly, once the constitution was ratified, it became – at least for that historical moment – the sole source and repository of fundamental law governing the operation of the national government. The character of the constitutional text as foundational law had immediate consequences. For example, a pervasive criticism of the original constitution was the absence of a guarantee of personal rights as against the central government.[7] That defect was remedied by the addition of the first ten constitutional amendments we know as the "Bill of Rights." Nonetheless, the rights set forth in the amendments are often couched in general terms of uncertain meaning. No "excessive bail" or "cruel or unusual punishments."[8] No criminal punishments without "due process of law."[9] No "unreasonable searches and seizures."[10] A set of rights phrased in this way might have been treated as merely hortatory, but because the rights were adjoined to and treated as parts of the constitution, they immediately became enforceable national law.[11]

Precisely because both the original constitution and its first ten amendments were considered to be law from the outset, questions immediately arose about who had the final authority to interpret that law. This may seem strange to a modern reader accustomed to thinking of the judiciary generally and the U.S. Supreme Court in particular as the natural arbiters of constitutional meaning. But the judicial power we take so much for granted was by no means self-evident in the founding period.

To understand the controversy requires a look at the role of British judges and a glance at the text of the U.S. constitution. Courts in the Great Britain from which the American colonists separated enjoyed considerable authority. They adjudicated facts, interpreted statutes, and made law in the interstitial way characteristic of the Anglo-American common law system.[12] They could in some cases declare actions by the executive branch illegal. But they could not then (and cannot now) declare all or any part of an Act of Parliament invalid as contrary to an antecedent or superior body of constitutional law.[13] One might attribute this deficiency in the power of British judges to the fact that Great Britain has no written constitution against which to measure statutes. That is partly true, but the more fundamental reason is the principle of parliamentary supremacy.

Unlike the U.S. Congress, Parliament does not owe its existence to or measure its powers by a foundational document. Since the Glorious Revolution of 1688–89, when Parliament overthrew King James II and replaced him with the joint monarchs William of Orange and his wife Mary,[14] Parliament has been the sovereign body in British government.[15] The maxim that "Parliament may do anything it wishes" has been said to be "the most fundamental rule of British constitutional law."[16]

The British understand themselves to have a constitution, but, as noted, it is largely unwritten and any part of it can at any moment be changed by a statute enacted in Parliament. Moreover, there are no "super-statutes" that bind later parliaments. Any law or governmental institution can be altered, voided, or abolished by a properly enacted parliamentary statute. The point is not merely that the British have no written constitution against which mere legislative enactments must be measured, but that there is no foundational law, written or traditional, superior to an Act of Parliament. By virtue of their function of interpreting statutes in particular cases, British judges are in a sense partners with Parliament in the ongoing process of making and mending the British constitution. But unlike in the United States, Parliament can pass a new statute legislatively overruling any judicial interpretation with which it disagrees. In short, Parliament always gets the last word if it wants it.

This was the arrangement with which the renegade Englishmen of the Philadelphia convention were familiar.[17] It is true that absolute parliamentary supremacy was one ground of disagreement between the colonists and the mother country in the years leading to the American Revolution. The colonists, when displeased by parliamentary enactments, often protested infringements on what they viewed as their traditional rights as Englishmen,[18] and were dismayed that appeals to what they saw as ancient and immutable principles produced no relief either from Parliament or judges answerable to the crown.[19] Nonetheless, nothing in the new constitution explicitly awarded American judges a different role from that of their British forebears. Article 3 says only that, "The judicial Power of the United

States, shall be vested in one supreme Court, and in such inferior Courts as the Congress may from time to time ordain and establish."[20] Nowhere is the reach of that "judicial Power" defined.

But the status of the written American constitution as fundamental law creates a problem unknown to the British system. In Great Britain, because Parliament is supreme and any new statute supersedes all previous ones, there can never be a question about whether the new statute is rendered invalid because of its conflict with superior foundational law. Judges may be called upon to decide whether a new statute conflicts with an old one, but if conflict is found, the new law prevails. Moreover, if Parliament decides that it disagrees with the judges' reading of the allegedly conflicting statutes, it can simply pass yet another statute with language ensuring that its preferred view carries the day.

By contrast, recognition of the new U.S. constitution as fundamental law created a hierarchy in which the constitution should trump a conflicting later enacted congressional statute. This raised two questions: first, who was empowered to decide whether a new statute really did conflict with the constitution; and, second, if a conflict was found, what happened then? Indeed, the arrangement of the United States as a confederation of semi-sovereign states created yet another level of difficulty in cases where actions by state officials, whether legislative, executive, or judicial, arguably conflicted with the federal constitution.[21]

It seems obvious to us that the answer to these difficulties is that federal judges decide whether statutes or other governmental actions violate the constitution, and that, if federal judges think so, the statute must be voided or the governmental action stopped. But this way of seeing things was not self-evident to the founding generation. Some of the delegates to the Philadelphia convention thought a statute that conflicted with the constitution could be overturned by courts.[22] Others probably disagreed, perhaps viewing Congress as akin to Parliament as the primary locus of sovereignty. The latter group may have thought that, while Congress ought not pass laws contrary to the constitution, it should be presumed that Congress would not do so and that Congress' own view of the constitutionality of its actions was entitled to at least equal weight as the views of judges.

Had this view prevailed, we would now have a very different sort of federal judiciary and probably a very different sort of country. Of course, that is not how things turned out. In 1803, in *Marbury* v. *Madison*, Chief Justice John Marshall wrote that the constitution is a "superior, paramount law," and thus a congressional statute "repugnant to the Constitution is void."[23] Crucially, Marshall claimed for the courts the right to determine whether a statute is inconsistent with the constitution. In his famous phrase, "It is emphatically the province and duty of the judicial department to say what the law is."[24]

Marshall's assertion of judicial authority to assess the constitutionality of statutes also implied a central role for federal judges on any occasion when actions by the federal executive branch or by the states were said to conflict with the constitution.

As natural as this now seems, it was anathema to a good many people we now lump into a homogeneous crowd of "founders." Thomas Jefferson, in particular, raged against Marshall's proclamation of judicial supremacy then and for the rest of his life.[25] Twenty years later, he was still complaining about judges "usurping legislation."[26]

We need not venture any further into the story of how Marshall's original bold claim to judicial power[27] prevailed against Jeffersonian complaints and over two centuries produced the sometimes stunning breadth of modern federal court jurisdiction. It is sufficient to recognize that courts have successfully assumed the role of final arbiters of constitutional meaning on almost every topic. As we will see, impeachment is one of the very few constitutional questions on which judges do not get the last word. But before we consider why that is so and its implications, we must complete our consideration of the effect of judicial supremacy on constitutional interpretation generally.

SOURCES OF CONSTITUTIONAL MEANING

Consider what judges do in the customary setting in which disputes about constitutional meaning arise – the lawsuit. One party sues another and claims that a statute or regulation, or executive branch action, has violated the constitution. In such cases, the meaning of the constitution may be uncontested and only the facts will be at issue. But if constitutional meaning is contested, a judge (and ultimately nine justices) must decide the question. How do they go about that task?

One way to answer this question would be to try to catalogue the various schools of constitutional interpretation. We will not attempt that feat of legal taxonomy here.

In the first place, any attempt to create a definitive list of discrete schools is doomed. The number of entrants in the interpretive melee is too high and their arguments are too dense and interwoven to allow neat assignment to particular teams. Moreover, the words used to describe particular threads in this never-ending argument about the meaning of words keep changing. For example, approaches that focus nearly exclusively on the language of the written constitution, avoiding as far as possible reliance on sources of meaning extraneous to the document, have at various points been labeled "textualist," "interpretivist," and "strict constructionist."[28] And each of those words has different shades of meaning depending on who employs it. Conversely, perhaps the best known term used to brand an interpretive method – "originalism" – has now been claimed by so many different people espousing such disparate approaches that the word is nearly meaningless.[29]

More importantly, this is a book about impeachment, not constitutional theory. Because impeachment is a constitutional mechanism, we need to know something about techniques of constitutional interpretation. But we need not resolve the quasi-theological disputes of constitutional academicians to get where we need to go.

A survey of the major sources to which constitutional thinkers customarily look in interpreting constitutional provisions will do.

Text: The constitution ratified in 1788 is a text. So are all the amendments ratified later. They consist of written words that convey meaning. Therefore, the most obvious source of constitutional meaning is the words of the text. One strain of constitutional interpretation holds that the text is the only indisputably legitimate source of authority on the meaning of the constitution. The most famous modern exponent of this "textualist" view, Justice Antonin Scalia, wrote that judges should "look for meaning in the governing text, ascribe to that text the meaning that it has borne from its inception, and reject judicial speculation about both the drafters' extra-textually derived purposes and the desirability of the fair reading's anticipated consequences."[30]

It is hard to quarrel with textualism, at least if it is viewed as a baseline presumption, a starting point for all constitutional analysis. Not only is the constitutional text America's foundational law, but (although one might not think it given the vast and contentious literature about constitutional interpretation) on most points the text is quite clear and susceptible to only one reasonable interpretation.[31]

Members of the House of Representatives are elected every two years, must be at least twenty-five years old, and must have been a U.S. citizen for seven years.[32] Each state has two senators, who are elected for six-year terms, must be at least thirty years old, and have been a citizen of the United States for nine years.[33] The president serves a term of four years, and must be at least thirty-five years old.[34]

Moreover, on points where a word, phrase, or clause is unclear when read in isolation, it is obviously right to search for meaning in the document read as a whole, including its architecture and the dominant themes ascertainable from that architecture.[35] This is a particularly important point when considering impeachment. As we will see, the impeachment clauses cannot be understood except as part of a set of interlocking decisions about the distribution of power among the government's three constitutionally created branches.

That said, there remain a great many questions to which neither the words being interpreted nor the document *in toto* provide a self-evidently correct answer. Such questions are sometimes minor and technical. Article 1 decrees that a member of the House must "when elected, be an *Inhabitant* of that State in which he shall be chosen."[36] What does it mean to be an "inhabitant" of a state? Is physical presence on election day sufficient? Or must she or he have been present for some designated period before the election? Must one own or lease a dwelling? Must the candidate have a local livelihood?

But sometimes questions about the meaning of constitutional words are quite profound. What is a "cruel and unusual punishment" barred by the Eighth Amendment?[37] Punishment is designed to be distinctly unpleasant. That is its point. In ordinary language, forcing unpleasantness on an unwilling subject is cruel. So what types, or perhaps degrees, of unpleasantness make a punishment constitutionally cruel? Is constitutional cruelty to be measured in absolute terms (no flogging ever), comparative terms (floggings are fine for rape, but not for theft), or historical terms (floggings are fine because they were an accepted form of punishment in 1787)?

The most obvious problem with the more doctrinaire forms of textualism is that the constitution's language is so sparse and the meaning of some passages so uncertain that even an evangelist of textualism like Justice Scalia is routinely forced to reach beyond the words of the document to resolve particular interpretive disputes.[38] Indeed, explanations of how textualism is supposed to work are most notable for their enumerations and prioritization of the sources *outside* the text that are conceded to be permissible in interpreting the text. These sources, in order of presumed authority, include dictionaries and grammatical texts published in the founding period, public statements about the meaning of the contested passage made during the ratification process, private statements by those involved in the drafting or ratification process, and post-enactment history of the provision at issue.[39]

The perceptive reader will immediately notice that, since scarcely any of the hard questions of constitutional law are answerable solely by reference to the text and a couple of eighteenth-century dictionaries, textualism actually decrees that most of the challenging work will focus on mining public and private statements from the founding period for evidence of what the text meant back then. In short, most textualism quickly reveals itself as a particularly dogmatic form of what is generally called "originalism."

Originalism, or what the "founders" meant: As noted above, so many people of such widely differing views now sally forth under the banner of originalism that the term has lost whatever descriptive precision it may once have enjoyed. For our purposes it is sufficient to make several basic points.

First, everyone, whether an avowed "originalist" or not, agrees that the text of the written constitution matters, and almost everybody agrees that where the meaning of the text is plain, that ends the inquiry. Article 2 says that presidents must "have attained to the Age of thirty five Years."[40] Therefore, a twenty-five-year-old person cannot be inaugurated as president, no matter how intellectually advanced or emotionally mature he or she may be.

Second, all originalists, regardless of ideological hue, agree that, after the words themselves, the pre-eminent source for divining the meaning of the written constitution is the contemporary utterances of those who drafted, debated, or voted on the constitutional provision at issue. There is a division of opinion about whose utterances should count (or at least count the most). In the case of the original 1788 constitution, some say that the Philadelphia convention delegates who drafted, debated, and voted on its text are the critical voices. (I will generally refer to those delegates as "framers.") Others say that, because the act of ratification by the states was the event that gave the constitution legal force, what matters is how those involved in the ratification debates understood the text on which they voted.

(These men I will generally call "ratifiers.") But to the extent that this distinction matters in theory, it is almost hopelessly blurred in practice because so many of the Philadelphia framers went straight home and took leading roles in their states' ratification debates. (So if I want to refer to all the players in the process of drafting and ratifying the constitution or one of its amendments, I may bundle them together as "Founders.") Still others focus, not on the views of the particular people who happened to be at either the Philadelphia or state ratifying assemblies, but on what the people as a whole would have understood the constitution's words to mean as the document was going through the national ratification process – an approach designated "original public meaning." (Although, since the best contemporary evidence about what the general population thought will often be what framers or ratifiers said or wrote, it is not altogether clear that original public meaning advances the ball very much.[41])

Third, the vast scrum of folks who call themselves originalists nonetheless divide on the critical question of what to do with evidence of the Founders' understanding of constitutional provisions. For what one might call a strict originalist, the interpreter's job is to figure out what a contested constitutional provision meant to those actively involved in enacting it (or at least to members of the informed public at the time the provision was enacted). Once evidence of the founding understanding yields a persuasive account of the original meaning, the inquiry stops. But for the more expansive breeds of originalist, a persuasive account of the original understanding may be only the beginning of a more complex analysis.

A classic example of the distinction is the application of the Fourteenth Amendment's equal protection clause to the rights of women. Over four decades ago, in a case called *Reed* v. *Reed*,[42] the Supreme Court began laying down a line of precedent establishing that the Fourteenth Amendment bars sex discrimination. As recently as 2010, Justice Scalia unapologetically proclaimed that the amendment does no such thing because, in the 1860s when the amendment was approved, it was directed at post-Civil War discrimination against black freedmen and "nobody thought it was directed at sex discrimination."[43] Justice Ruth Bader Ginsburg, who in her law professor days had written the crucial brief in *Reed*, never pretended that the result she successfully obtained could be justified by reference to the Fourteenth Amendment's original understanding.[44] Nonetheless, prominent originalist Steven Calabresi maintains that originalist principles can be employed to read a guarantee of sexual equality into the equal protection clause.[45] He argues that the Fourteenth Amendment was really a ban on "systems of caste," and the Nineteenth Amendment granting women's suffrage is an implicit condemnation of exclusion of women from the political sphere as a caste distinction.[46]

Who is right about all this does not matter for our purposes. The point is that information about what the people who wrote and ratified a particular constitutional provision said is being used in different ways. For some "originalists," the important question is not only what those who drafted and ratified a constitutional provision thought the words meant, but also how they would have expected the words to be applied in particular cases. For other "originalists," the key is to determine the essential original meaning of the constitutional text and then to apply that meaning to new cases as they arise, regardless of how the framers or ratifiers might have expected the text to be applied in such cases.[47]

Now, if you are just a regular person and not a constitutional scholar, this distinction may not make a great deal of sense. It is one thing to say that only the words of a statute count and that judges can never ask what the creators of the statute meant. That is a defensible position, if for no other reason than that trying to figure out what a multi-headed body like a legislature or constitutional convention meant on any point is a pretty doubtful exercise.[48] But if we concede that it is acceptable to look for meaning in legislative intent (which is really what any form of originalism willing to look beyond the constitutional text is all about), then refusing to consider how a legislature *intended* a statute to apply in foreseeable types of future cases is kind of crazy. After all, when a legislator is drafting or voting on the language in a statute, the choice to select or approve a certain set of words is not an abstract literary exercise. A statute is a string of words selected precisely because legislators expect and intend them to have certain effects when applied to events that have not yet happened.

But we need not resolve this conundrum. For our purposes, it is enough to recognize that a common mode of constitutional argument is citation of evidence of how the constitutional text was understood by those who wrote and ratified it. And for some, an acceptable variant of that mode is informed speculation about how the Founders would have expected the text to be applied to the issue currently under scrutiny. In this book we will devote a good deal of attention to the available evidence about what the drafters and ratifiers of the constitution's impeachment clauses thought they were doing. As we will see, the evidence is patchy – nearly conclusive on some important points and almost non-existent on others. Nonetheless, this is ground that must be mapped because disagreements over original meaning have played a role in every major American impeachment controversy.

Precedent and the common law constitution: Most of the time, the debate about modes of constitutional interpretation is an argument about the kind of evidence *judges* may legitimately use in deciding constitutional issues in court cases. When judges make such decisions, they write opinions explaining why they decided as they did. Future judges then treat prior decisions and the written reasons for them as "precedent" – a guide to constitutional meaning. It turns out that most of what judges, as well as lawyers, legislators, executive branch officials, and the interested public, talk about when they discuss "constitutional law" is not the written constitution, or even such evidence as we have about the written constitution's original meaning, but the web of rules and explanations contained in the vast and growing body of judicial decisions construing the constitution.

Constitutional theorists have spilt a good deal of ink arguing over whether Supreme Court opinions on constitutional subjects are merely *arguments about* the meaning of the written constitution or are themselves *elements of* a constitution consisting not only of the 1788 constitution and its amendments, but also of a constantly evolving body of judicial precedent, congressional enactments, and customary understandings and practices. David Strauss has argued powerfully for this view, embracing the idea of a "common law constitution."[49]

Those of a strongly originalist bent find this sort of talk unsettling, both because it seems to give short shrift to the role of the written constitution as foundational law and because they worry (not without reason) that treating the constitution as an entirely common law construction provides no discernible limits on its meaning, or as Strauss says, "anything goes."[50] I sympathize with such concerns. For me, any sensible approach to constitutional interpretation has to accept the constitutional text as definitive on the easy cases and as a lodestone on harder ones. Nonetheless, the vision of the constitution as an evolving collective enterprise, what Justice Oliver Wendell Holmes called an "organism,"[51] is compelling.

First, it is highly probable that the Founders saw it in precisely that way. After all, the framers and ratifiers of the original constitution were practical politicians and knew perfectly well that the 4,400 words that emerged from Philadelphia did no more than sketch the bare skeleton of a new national government. And they knew, better than anyone, that much of the constitution's language was imprecise or open-ended, often by design. Linguistic clarity is prized by those who interpret the law, but it can be a fatal impediment to compromise between those hoping to pass a law. The skeleton the Founders approved could only acquire flesh and sinew, and the general language they adopted could only acquire useful particularity, through congressional enactments, executive action, and judicial interpretation.

Indeed, if there is one point about the Founders on which we can be reasonably certain it is that none of *them* were "originalists," either in the sense of imagining that the imprecise or open-ended sections of the constitution could have only one acceptable meaning, or in the sense of intending that their views, individual or collective, on the meaning of constitutional language were entitled to sanctified status. Had they wanted the constitutional text to be interpreted primarily by reference to their personal intentions or by a collective original understanding, then both the Philadelphia framers and the state ratifiers would surely have been meticulous in creating and immediately publicizing what we would now call a "legislative history." The Philadelphia convention would have created a set of reports and memoranda about its debates, the resolution of all the major issues, and the rationales for choosing especially contested language. The state ratifying conventions would have done the same. This body of materials would have been widely circulated and would immediately have become the reference point for debates in Congress, in the courts, and among members of the public about what the constitution meant.

Nothing of the sort occurred. Indeed, what happened was almost the exact opposite. The Philadelphia convention met in the strictest secrecy.[52] Major William Jackson acted as secretary and kept an official Journal.[53] The Journal recorded the minutes of the convention and its proceedings as a Committee of the Whole, as well as the text of most of the resolutions debated in the convention and the votes taken on them. But interesting as these materials are, they are terse and often uninformative in the way of organizational minutes down to our own day. Moreover, the Journal was kept confidential until its publication in 1819, thirty-two years after the close of the convention.[54]

In addition to the official Journal, the documentary record of the convention includes notes by eight other delegates,[55] the most famous and extensive of which were made by James Madison. However, the earliest public appearance of any of these notes was 1821 (the Yates notes).[56] At Madison's insistence, his own notes were not published during his lifetime, but appeared for the first time in 1840, four years after his death and more than half a century after ratification. The remaining notes emerged even later.[57] The first compilation of all these materials did not occur until the turn of the twentieth century,[58] and the most authoritative, by Max Farrand, was not published until 1911.[59]

The practices of the state ratifying conventions were even more haphazard. What we know about their proceedings comes from a hodge-podge of notes, journals, newspaper reports, transcripts of speeches, and personal correspondence. Reasonably extensive records exist for only four of the thirteen ratifying conventions: Pennsylvania, Massachusetts, Virginia, and New York. There are fragmentary records for four more: Connecticut, Maryland, South Carolina, and New Hampshire. No records at all exist for Delaware, New Jersey, Georgia, North Carolina, or Rhode Island.[60] The first collection of such records as did exist was assembled by Jonathan Elliot between 1827 and 1830.[61]

Some point to the *Federalist Papers* – the series of newspaper essays written under pseudonyms by Alexander Hamilton, James Madison, and John Jay during the New York ratification debates – as a sort of guidebook to the thinking of the founding generation. They are certainly useful, but they were, after all, not statements of legislative purpose, but advocacy pieces designed to secure votes. As such, they do not necessarily reflect even the private personal views of Hamilton, Madison, and Jay, who in any case disagreed on many things. Moreover, the essays give us the voices of only three men out of the many hundreds directly involved in writing or ratifying the constitution.

This is not to say that all these records are irrelevant. They can help us to understand what the framers, ratifiers, and ordinary Americans of the founding generation thought the constitution meant when first approved. However, the fragmentary form of most of these records and the prolonged, in many cases conscious, suppression of most of them indicate that those closest to the generative act of creating the new government intended that it would take its proper shape, not through the parsing of a text or inquiry into the intentions of its draftsmen, but through the conduct of those charged with building and operating the new institutions imagined in the document. That there would be arguments over the desirability of the new arrangements, over their fidelity to the constitutional design, and over their adaptability to changing circumstances the Founders plainly anticipated. The Founders were not demigods decreeing a flawless new form of government, but Anglo-American politicians, often lawyers, accustomed to muddling toward new and better legal rules and governmental arrangements by the common law process of trial and error and case-by-case accretion of better wisdom.[62]

In any case, that is how things have worked for over two centuries. There have been a handful of important constitutional amendments since the ratification of the Bill of Rights in 1791.[63] But in that period the scope and meaning of the constitution have changed radically due to judicial decisions or the establishment of new norms and expectations as a result of actions by, or interactions between, the legislative and executive branches.

Since *Marbury*, judges have been steadily shaping our constitutional universe, often in ways that do not self-evidently flow from either the constitution's text or any indisputable original intention. In *McCulloch* v. *Maryland*,[64] the Supreme Court decided, again over the vehement objections of Thomas Jefferson and like-minded contemporaries,[65] that the "necessary and proper" clause of Article 1 permitted the federal government to form a national bank, and that the supremacy clause prohibited states from taxing that bank. The result was an expansion of the possibilities of national government without which the needs of a transcontinental nation could not have been met. Beginning with the so-called *Steamboat Monopoly* Case in 1824,[66] the Supreme Court began giving an expansive reading to Article 1's commerce clause, thus permitting Congress to both regulate and encourage economic activity throughout the ever-growing national market.[67]

In the twentieth century, the Supreme Court reexamined the meaning of the post-Civil War Fourteenth Amendment to lay down constitutional decrees that plainly would not have been contemplated by the framers of that amendment. In 1954, *Brown* v. *Board of Education* declared that the equal protection clause prohibited the segregation of black and white children into separate, but supposedly equal, schools.[68] In 1967, *Loving* v. *Virginia* invoked the equal protection and due process clauses of the Fourteenth Amendment to invalidate laws prohibiting interracial marriage.[69]

All these judicial opinions draw their authority from the written constitution, but none of their results are compelled by its text. It is the judicial opinion itself – the result and the reasoning – that we, quite properly, regard as "constitutional law" that not only resolves the question at issue, but is precedent upon which future decisions may be based.

The legislative and executive branches have also created their own forms of precedent. For example, it seems reasonably clear that the reservation to Congress in Article 1 of the power to "declare war"[70] was intended by the Founders to give Congress, not the president, the authority to determine whether the United States should engage in warfare. The power granted the president of acting as "commander in chief" was surely imagined primarily as authority to direct the military after war was declared. Yet even though Congress has not declared war since 1942,[71] the United States has been at war, in the sense of conducting major overseas military operations, in roughly forty of the seventy-four years since the end of the Second World War.[72] Some of those wars were sanctioned by Congress in one way or another. Others were not.[73] Modern presidents have asserted the authority to commit American armed forces to major armed conflicts without prior congressional authorization and Congress has acquiesced to a degree incompatible with any reasonable historical interpretation of the written constitution.

More broadly, the entire post-New Deal administrative state rests on, and continues to generate, a vast body of precedent, some of which is judicial opinions about the administrative state and its decisions, but much of which takes the form of decisions by executive branch administrative agencies and congressional decisions about how to empower or limit the reach of administrative authority. One can argue, and some have, that the entire modern administrative apparatus is unconstitutional, but that horse has long since left the barn and the structure of data collection, policy analysis, rulemaking, administration, and enforcement has assumed quasi-constitutional status.[74]

Perhaps judges or other federal actors ought not to have decided or behaved as they have, and perhaps their decisions ought to have maintained greater fidelity to this or that conception of the written constitution. But it is futile to deny that most of what we now think of as constitutional law is found in the body of judicial, executive, legislative, and normative precedent that accumulated *after* the adoption of the written constitution. In courts, constitutional argument will include a mix of references to the constitutional text, its supposed original meaning, and later interpretive precedent. This book will look to the same sources, including post-enactment precedent, when interpreting the impeachment clauses.

The special case of the impeachment clauses: To this point, we have been discussing constitutional interpretation primarily in its most common setting, the courts. But impeachment is one of the rare components of the constitution about which courts have almost nothing to say. That affects how we should think about interpreting the impeachment clauses.

The first notable distinction between the impeachment decisions of the House and Senate and the judgments of a federal court is that impeachment decisions are not judicially reviewable. A president or other federal official who disagrees with the way Congress decides some matter related to his impeachment almost certainly cannot appeal to the courts.[75] Moreover, there is no requirement that either the House or Senate issue the equivalent of a judicial opinion explaining its decision. Critically, neither house is bound by any decision it made in a prior impeachment case.[76] Indeed, even though legislators commonly look to prior cases for guidance, there is not even a formal presumption of deference to prior decisions. All of which means that there is no impeachment equivalent of the judicial principle of *stare decisis*, according to which prior decisions of the highest court in a jurisdiction create binding, or at least presumptively valid, precedent for later cases.

Moreover, the number of impeachment cases is tiny. There have been only twenty-one actual or attempted impeachments of a federal officer in the last 230 years. (All these cases are summarized in the Appendix at the end of this book.) Sixteen of these were judges, and, as we will see, the standard for impeaching a judge is somewhat different than the standard for a president. Hence, even if legislators and the public at large view past decisions as a sort of persuasive authority, the odds of a prior case having addressed all the issues in a new case are perilously small, and smaller still for presidential impeachments, of which there are only three meaningful examples: Andrew Johnson, Richard Nixon, and Bill Clinton.[77] Therefore, precedent will be of much less help in impeachment than it would be in a case before the courts.

Second, the fact that the final decision about impeachment rests with the elected legislature, not with unelected judges, meshes with the constitutional definition of impeachable conduct. As discussed below in Chapter 4, the constitutional phrase "Treason, Bribery, or other high Crimes and Misdemeanors" has always been understood to describe, in Alexander Hamilton's phrase, offenses "of a nature which may with peculiar propriety be denominated political, as they relate chiefly to injuries done immediately to the society itself."[78] In other words, impeachment is a political judgment made by an elected political body.

And that casts everything we have said so far about modes of constitutional interpretation in a somewhat different light. The political character of both the verbal standard and the final tribunal in an impeachment case does not, of course, eliminate the need for reasonable fidelity to the constitutional text as foundational law, or the interpretive value of what the founding generation understood the text to mean. Nor does it wipe clean the slate upon which our limited impeachment precedents are written. But it does very nearly erase the so-called "counter-majoritarian difficulty" that dogs elastic judicial interpretations of the constitution.[79] Unlike any judicial decision, impeachments are decided by the people's elected representatives who are subject to the democratic checks of con-temporaneous popular opinion and fear of being turned out of office for an unpop-ular choice.

That being so, one should look skeptically at arguments about the impeachability of particular conduct that rely too heavily on involved exegesis of snippets of founding-era evidence or over-analysis of the tiny number of impeachment prece-dents. As we will see, impeachment was designed not as a legal process for punishing individual wrongdoing, but as a means of protecting the republic from the faults, frailties, or skullduggery of high government officers. Accordingly, the imperatives of the present moment, carefully and dispassionately weighed, must be given great weight in the impeachment calculus.

Last word: Precisely because impeachment is in the end a political process, one cannot ignore the fact that methods of constitutional interpretation have become identified with factions in the political realm. Virtually all modern political conservatives at least profess to be "originalists" or "strict constructionists" in the sense of professing to venerate the constitutional text and its understanding by members of the founding generation. Virtually all modern political liberals subscribe to some form of the living constitution school that permits, even encourages, creative interpretation of constitutional language to meet the conditions and exigencies of the modern world. And everyone along the spectrum that runs from the strictest of strict constructionists to the liveliest of living constitutionalists concedes that custom, usage, and sometimes formal decisional precedents inform current understandings of the constitution.

So if one is going to write a book about impeachment that hopes to persuade more than one ideological faction, one must be prepared to employ, and treat seriously, all the customary methods of constitutional interpretation. Happily, even in ordinary cases where judges are interpreting the constitution, I am not a methodological purist. I find assertions that there is one "right" way to approach the constitution tend either to cloak ideological predispositions or devolve into unproductive scholasticism. Instead, I think interpretive methods grounded in text, constitutional structure, history, precedent, and the imperatives of the present moment all have a place in understanding the impeachment provisions of the constitution. And I think that, both as a matter of original intent and of practical politics, the judgment about whether a particular president should be impeached will, at the moment of crisis, turn primarily on whether Congress thinks it is good or bad for the country that he or she should be permitted to remain as chief executive.

So let us begin . . .

2

British Impeachments, 1376–1787

Impeachment is a British invention, created by Parliament beginning in 1376 to resist the tendency of the monarchy to absolutism and to counter particularly obnoxious royal policies by removing the ministers who implemented them. The invention crossed the Atlantic with the British colonists who would one day rebel against the mother country and create an independent United States of America. Both the American colonies and the newly independent American states that sent delegations to the Philadelphia Constitutional Convention of 1787 had employed forms of impeachment adapted from British practice. The debates in Philadelphia about impeachment were framed primarily by American understanding of the strengths and weaknesses of the British model and its applicability to the new government they were inventing.

Even casual students of American impeachment likely know that the phrase "high crimes and misdemeanors," which helps to define the scope of impeachable conduct, was appropriated from British parliamentary usage. However, British influence runs much deeper than that. The basic structure of an American "impeachment" – a set of accusations made by the "lower" house of a bicameral legislature, followed by a trial in the "upper" house – is British, as is the practice of having the case in the upper house prosecuted by members of the lower one called "managers." Conversely, British impeachments traditionally carried very serious penalties, including banishment, imprisonment, and death, a feature the framers of the American constitution consciously and explicitly rejected. In short, one simply cannot understand the American iteration of impeachment without understanding its British antecedent.

This chapter examines the entire arc of British impeachments from 1376 to 1787. It demonstrates that, although British impeachment employed many of the forms of a criminal trial and could produce dire personal punishments of the sort we associate with criminal law, it was, first, last, and always, a political tool in the large sense. Parliament invented and periodically resorted to impeachment as a means of resisting particular objectionable policies of the crown or its ministers, but even more fundamentally as a mechanism for bending the kingdom's basic constitutional order away from absolutism and toward representative government. A study of British impeachments reminds us that, like any other legal mechanism, impeachment will sometimes be employed for petty or ignoble purposes, but it was invented as a mighty weapon against executive tyranny and as a powerful tool for preservation of the constitution (or at least of the legislature's view of what the constitution should be).

That said, the legalistic form of British impeachment mandates an inquiry into the particular types or categories of misbehavior that Great Britain's Parliament found impeachable. Even when Parliament's motive for impeachment was fear that the behavior of the accused endangered the constitution, the House of Commons was obliged to lay out the particulars of its charges and the House of Lords to put them to their proof. Thus, over the centuries, Parliament developed a body of precedent that roughly defined and loosely cabined its impeachment power. To the extent that the framers incorporated British precedent into their model of American impeachment, knowing what Parliament embraced as impeachable conduct helps us to set the baseline minimum for impeachment under the U.S. constitution.

THE ORIGINS OF IMPEACHMENT

Ever since human beings first formed hierarchical societies, they have wrestled with the problem of how to displace powerful people who misbehave. In absolute monarchies (or personal dictatorships), the solution is simple. An absolute ruler's subordinates remain in office at his or her pleasure and are removed, and perhaps punished, when the ruler is sufficiently displeased. The monarch him- or herself can be displaced only by palace coup, national revolution, or external invasion, with all the bloodshed and general inconvenience those remedies imply.

The problem becomes more complicated once political and economic power is dispersed among competing centers of authority. A monarch whose continued reign depends in some measure on the support of powerful hereditary nobles can no longer be quite so arbitrary in his or her treatment of those who hold subordinate positions of authority, many of whom will be those nobles or members of their families. As a result, the nobility gains a voice in the selection and removal of officials who may please the ruler, but displease the nobility. The more centers of power develop external to the monarchy – land-holding lesser gentry, clergy, merchants, bankers, professional lawyers and judges – the more complicated the problem of removal of the powerful becomes. The challenge lies not merely in determining who will have authority to remove an official, but also in the questions of whether removal should be accompanied by additional punishment and what process should be employed in judging each case.

Great Britain began contending with these challenges very early in its history. Magna Carta, now hailed as the Great Charter of English liberties, was actually a peace treaty between King John and his rebellious barons signed in 1215.[1] Most of it dealt with issues of no modern relevance, such as special kinds of rent and taxes called scutage and socage and placement of fish weirs in the River Thames. But several clauses addressed the issue of removal and punishment of officials and persons of rank. The barons wanted protection from royal arbitrariness. Accordingly, multiple provisions of Magna Carta protect the nobility and "free men"[2] generally from punishment, including fines[3] and loss of lands or status, except by "the lawful judgment of his equals."[4] But the barons also wanted to get rid of some of King John's retainers, so the king agreed in Magna Carta itself to turn out of office all the kinsmen and followers of a fellow named Gerard de Athée.[5] This result was no doubt pleasing to enemies of de Athée, but the episode was entirely unsatisfactory as a model for how to deal with troublesome royal officials. A system that requires strapping on your chainmail and rallying the rest of the barons for a rebellion any time that you disapprove of the Chancellor of the Exchequer or the Keeper of the Privy Seal is tiresome in the last degree.

In the centuries following Magna Carta, the national governing body we know as Parliament evolved in fits and starts from ad hoc assemblies of notables such as Simon de Montfort's parliament of 1265[6] into a bicameral legislature consisting of the House of Commons and the House of Lords. From the earliest times, two persistent and cross-cutting themes in the relation between Parliament and the crown were, on the one hand, the determination of the great subjects of the realm to influence the selection, and removal, of royal ministers[7] and, on the other hand, the desire of those same great subjects to ensure that, should they take office under the crown, something akin to due process stood between themselves and removal, ruin, and possibly death, whether at the whim of a capricious monarch or at the hands of the crown's adversaries.[8]

For a good many years, the king could convict and sentence traitors and other malefactors "by record," meaning that he simply recounted what he believed to be the prisoner's misdeeds, and a quasi-judicial body of noblemen or common law judges, or perhaps the king himself, would then pronounce judgment based on what the king had said.[9] But in time it came to be accepted that all criminal proceedings, including those against officials, should be initiated in legal form and tried by a juridical body separate from the crown. In cases involving persons of rank, the mandate of Magna Carta that judgment should be imposed only by a body of one's equals meshed with the natural inclinations of the notables who made up Parliament to confer jurisdiction in such matters on Parliament itself.[10] This innovation ensured that the king could not easily strike against high-placed enemies without the assent (however coerced or grudging) of Parliament. In due course, it also evolved into a weapon Parliament could employ against royal officers or policies of which it disapproved.

One might wonder how parliamentary pursuit of the king's men would be thought an effective means of altering the king's policy. The short answer lies in the modern catchphrase, "Personnel is policy," which recognizes that implementation even of clear directives from an energetic ruler will fail absent loyal, forceful, competent subordinates. But an absolute and hereditary monarchy presents particular problems for the would-be reformer because neither the monarch nor his subordinates are subject to institutionalized limitation or control. In the thirteenth and fourteenth centuries, Parliament gained increased formal authority over lawmaking and the monarch's sources of revenue.[11] Nonetheless, a king resolutely determined to pursue his own course despite parliamentary opposition had considerable power to do so and, the monarchy being hereditary, he could not be removed absent a genuine revolution. Therefore, parliaments displeased by a king's policies, but unwilling to go so far as open rebellion, indulged the fiction that the king was not at fault, but was being misled by incompetent or malicious royal ministers. Parliament found it could hobble unpopular royal policies by removing the minister charged with carrying them out without disrupting the continuity of royal rule. If the most effective executants of a king's policy are removed from the political board, the king's policy will be crippled. If the king's ministers know that pursuit of the king's policies in defiance of the will of Parliament presents a real risk of removal from office and additional painful punishments, their enthusiasm for implementing the king's will is likely to be sensibly diminished.

Another constant thread in the long debate over parliamentary condemnation of erring officials was concern over retrospective punishments. Insofar as Parliament merely acted as the forum in which nobles or servants of the crown were charged and tried for conduct that had previously been defined by statute or common law as illegal, the process presented no conceptual novelty. The principal matters requiring resolution were the roles to be performed by each house, the degree and forms of due process to be afforded the defendants, and the appropriate remedies in the event of conviction. Most of these questions could be resolved by analogy to legal procedures already employed in regular courts. But cases concerning the great and powerful presented a special problem arising from two interlocking features.

First, the misconduct alleged in these cases did not always violate a pre-existing law. For example, in 1388, Michael de la Pole, the earl of Suffolk, and others were charged with "high treason" for, in effect, taking advantage of their privileged access to the young King Richard II to persuade the king to adopt bad policies and to confer a variety of titles and favors on themselves.[12] Allegations of this sort had never previously been denominated as treason.[13] Nonetheless, in a monarchy, the behavior charged against Suffolk – that is, the king's favorites distorting national policy and grabbing wealth and power – is precisely the kind of thing vigilant parliamentarians will be alert to prevent. So it is not surprising that Parliament chose to treat it as treason in Suffolk's case. Moreover, because it will often be difficult to predict, still less to define in advance, the sort of misbehavior, incompetence, or outright knavery that should properly produce scrutiny and perhaps removal of government officials, there was a natural disposition to keep the scope of chargeable conduct indeterminate.

Second, for centuries, the possible penalties for losing a state trial were not limited to removal from office, but included crippling fines, forfeiture of lands and titles, imprisonment, and death (sometimes preceded by the prolonged agony of being hung, drawn, and quartered).[14] In short, these were criminal cases, at least in the sense that the punishments were of the sort otherwise reserved for the most serious criminal offenses. During the medieval and early Renaissance periods, the severity (and occasional finality) of punishments imposed upon those convicted in state trials was scarcely surprising. The losers of political struggles in those eras rarely retired to the country to write their memoirs, but were distressingly apt to respond by arranging a coup, assassination, or insurrection. Accordingly, simple prudence on the part of the winners of these contests dictated that those convicted of state crimes should be disabled from creating future mischief through imprisonment, exile, impoverishment, or death.

Nonetheless, a central principle of the evolving British common law of crimes, expressed in the Latin phrase *nulla poena sine lege,* was that people should not be punished except for violation of pre-existing law.[15] Therefore, British impeachment was always plagued by tension between the suspect legitimacy of retrospective punishment and the pragmatic realization that misconduct by public officials may subvert the proper functioning of government and represent a danger to the state without being criminal or indeed violating any existing law. As long as parliamentary trials produced not only purges from office but severe personal punishment, the process bore a taint of fundamental unfairness.

THE FIRST BRITISH IMPEACHMENTS

The term "impeachment" as a description of one mode of conducting a state trial in Parliament made its appearance in the 1300s. Scholars of the period speak of proceedings against notables accused of public misconduct being initiated using various procedural vehicles: indictment, appeal of felony, original writ, or even by public clamor expressed in the House of Commons.[16] It seems to be broadly agreed that the first true "impeachments" occurred in 1376, during the reign of Edward III in what was known as "the Good Parliament."[17]

These first impeachments set the paradigm for later parliamentary actions against unpopular ministers. At the end of Edward's fifty-year reign, when both the old king and his eldest son, Edward, known as the Black Prince, were ailing, critics of some of the king's favorites moved against them. The opposition's targets included the royal chamberlain, Lord Latimer, the Steward of the Household, Lord Neville, as well as Richard Lyons, William Ellis, and John Peake.[18] The charges brought against them, to which we will return momentarily, were various, but the distinctive feature of the process is that each case was initiated by a formal accusation by the House of Commons followed by a trial in the House of Lords.

Even though these "impeachments" were directed at men who had long enjoyed the favor of the king, the notables in opposition were at pains to avoid the appearance of defying or undermining the authority of the crown. During the impeachments of Lord Latimer and Richard Lyons, the Commons specifically sought and obtained the sick king's approval to proceed in the first instance and at several points thereafter.[19] And the charges were carefully framed to avoid casting blame on the crown, alleging instead that the defendants had in effect deceived the king and misused his delegated authority. Among the charges against Latimer was that he had "notoriously accroached royal power."[20] Likewise, Parliament did not proceed to judgment until receiving assurance that the king was effectively abandoning his former courtiers. Lyons was condemned only after several of the lords testified that the king had disavowed Lyons' claim to have been acting on the authority of the king and his council.[21]

There are two other points of interest for us in these first ancestral impeachments. First, as is true down to the present day in American practice, the lower house not only framed the charges for the upper house, but acted as prosecutors or "managers" in presenting the case for trial.[22] Second, while a good many of the charges against those impeached in 1376 involved corruption of a sort that might have been contrary to some pre-existing law, some of the allegations charged no apparent crime. For example, Lord Latimer was impeached in part for his failure as a military leader to hold the English-occupied French towns of Bécherel and St. Saveur.[23]

After Edward III died, he was succeeded in 1377 by his grandson, Richard II, then only ten years old.[24] In the early years of his reign, there were ongoing disputes between the favorites and ministers of the young king and an opposition party well represented in Parliament. The details are unimportant here. The key developments were that the lords and notables in Parliament used the instrument of impeachment to remove several of Richard's advisors, but when Richard gained political strength thereafter, he attempted to seize royal control over the impeachment mechanism.

In 1386, the Commons brought charges in the form of impeachment against Richard's chancellor, Michael de la Pole, the earl of Suffolk.[25] Three of the charges alleged garden variety corruption – purchasing crown property at a discount or appropriating to himself revenues that ought to have gone to the crown – but several alleged simple incompetence or misconduct in office. Article 3 charged that Suffolk had failed to use parliamentary appropriations for maritime defense to good effect, and Article 7 alleged that Suffolk had bungled the military expedition to relieve Ghent.[26] The Lords convicted Suffolk on some of the charges and, after great pressure was placed on the king, Suffolk was removed from office and imprisoned pending payment of a fine or ransom.[27]

Not content with the removal of Suffolk, the opposition magnates forced Richard to accept a "commission of reform" consisting of fourteen nobles with wide powers to set government policy. Unsurprisingly, Richard acceded only grudgingly and began working to reverse these encroachments on his authority. Among his moves in this direction was a formal set of inquiries directed to the judges of England in 1387, in one of which he asked whether, as a matter of law, his ministers could be impeached without his consent. The judges, perhaps under considerable royal pressure, said Parliament had no such power.[28]

The Lords struck back in 1388 by bringing charges of treason against Suffolk and other supporters of the king using the mechanism of the "appeal." An appeal differed from impeachment in that it was a conventional means of bringing a criminal charge in which an aggrieved party formally accused the wrongdoer and became in effect a private prosecutor. In Suffolk's case, five lords, known to British history as "the Lords appellant," made their charges of treason directly in the House of Lords, with no participation by the Commons.[29] Not only did the House of Lords convict Suffolk and his allies, but they then proceeded to impeach and banish the judges who had previously declared that Parliament lacked the power to impeach without the king's assent.[30] In due course, however, the king slowly regained power relative to dissident members of the nobility. In 1397–98, Richard and his political allies used a combination of appeals and impeachments to charge various of his opponents with treason and other offenses.[31] Several were executed, murdered, or died in prison; others were banished.[32] In the course of these proceedings, Richard was careful to reclaim the right of royal assent to impeachment proceedings.[33] However, his reassertion of authority did not last long. He was deposed by Henry Bolingbroke in 1399 and died in captivity in early 1400.[34]

There were no impeachments in the half-century following the death of Richard II in 1400.[35] But in 1450, William de la Pole, grandson of the Michael de la Pole impeached in 1386 and also bearing the title earl of Suffolk, was impeached by the House of Commons for various supposed offenses connected to his negotiation of King Henry VI's marriage to the French noblewoman, Margaret of Anjou.[36] Before Suffolk could be tried in the House of Lords, the king sought to save him from serious punishment by banishing him on his own authority.[37] This evasive maneuver did Suffolk no good because the ship taking him into exile was captured in the English Channel by brigands, who beheaded him on the side of a longboat.[38] The important point for us in Suffolk's downfall is that it represented a resurrection of Parliament's claim of power to impeach ministers against the wishes of the crown.

Parliament may have reasserted its theoretical power to remove troublesome ministers, but the power then lay dormant in practice for a century and a half until the reign of James I in the first quarter of the seventeenth century. Historians provide various explanations for the interruption, but the basic one seems to have been the weakness of Parliament relative to the crown during this period.[39] Parliament was active in the reign of Henry VIII (1509–47), but primarily as an instrument of the king's will on projects like the reformation of the English

Church.[40] During Elizabeth I's forty-five-year reign (1558–1603), she called parliaments about every five years, but the body was only in session for a total of three years while she was on the throne.[41] Throughout the Tudor period, ministers, high clergy, noblemen, and others were cast out of office and some severely punished or even executed, but these falls from grace were driven primarily by the wishes of the monarch. In any case, as a procedural matter, the crown chose not to reassert control over the impeachment mechanism, but to employ other vehicles for condemning its enemies and erring servants, most notably for our purposes the bill of attainder.

BILLS OF ATTAINDER

A brief explanation of bills of attainder is in order here. Bills of attainder differed from impeachments in several key respects. An impeachment has the form of a judicial proceeding. Formal charges are composed and approved by the lower legislative house and its representatives act as prosecutors before the upper house, presenting evidence in support of the charges. The upper house then acts as judges passing on the question of whether the charges have been proven. By contrast, a bill of attainder is a legislative act, meaning that the subject of the bill can be condemned without any violation of law, or even clearly articulable wrong, having been charged or proven.[42] The bill passes through Parliament like any other, with no necessary provision for those accused to defend themselves. Punishments could be severe, including execution, imprisonment, exile, ruinous fines, and forfeiture of lands and titles.[43] Bills of attainder were often associated with "corruption of blood," which not only stripped the offender of his property and titles, but barred his heirs from inheriting.[44]

During the Wars of the Roses (1455–87),[45] the warring Yorkist and Lancastrian factions used bills of attainder rather than impeachments or appeals to oust and eliminate their opponents.[46] The heyday of attainders was in the reign of Henry VIII, during which 130 regime opponents were attainted and thirty-four executed.[47] Notable victims included Thomas Cromwell[48] and the king's fifth wife, Catherine Howard.[49] Notoriously, Henry secured from the judges of England a declaration that, although it would be bad form, an accused could be attainted by Parliament and executed without any opportunity to be heard in his or her own defense.[50] It was also common to pass bills of attainder posthumously to provide legal justification for seizures or forfeitures of property or the disinheritance of heirs.[51]

Bills of attainder were a very rough business. Not only did they produce draconian punishments that could extend beyond the lifetime of the offender, but their availability as a means of circumventing even the outward forms of legal process for those in bad odor with the dominant power in the state ran contrary to the evolving British dedication to fair procedures. Bills of attainder were not a feature of colonial America, there being no parliament in North America and no occasion for the British parliament to attaint colonists, at least until the American Revolution, after which the issue was moot. However, in the immediate aftermath of American independence, several state governments did enact bills of attainder or their substantial equivalents against unrepentant royalists.[52] These enactments were highly controversial at the time, in part because attainders had garnered such ill fame in British history. The U.S. constitution banned bills of attainder and *ex post facto* laws in Article 1, section 9.[53]

IMPEACHMENT IN THE ERA OF THE STUART KINGS

In Great Britain, impeachment reemerged from its long dormancy during the reigns of the Stuart kings: King James I (1603–25), his son Charles I (1625–49), and his grandson Charles II (1649–51, 1660–85). The uses of impeachment in this tumultuous period are an important key to the American Founders' understanding of the mechanism. The Stuart era was not that far in the historical past for the delegates to the Philadelphia convention and their contemporaries. It was only as far behind them as the period from the American Civil War to the First World War is for us. Moreover, the conflicts between the Stuarts and Parliament helped to define the ideas of eighteenth-century Britons, whether in the home islands or their colonies, about proper constitutional relations between an executive and a legislature.

James Stuart was the son of Mary, Queen of Scots, and a great-great-grandson of King Henry VII of England. He became King James VI of Scotland in 1567 when he was barely a year old after Queen Elizabeth I forced his mother to abdicate in his favor.[54] When Elizabeth died childless in 1603, he succeeded her as James I of England and Ireland, thus placing England, Scotland, and Ireland under one monarch. During the twenty-two years in which he wore the three crowns of the newly consolidated kingdom, he seems to have been a tolerably good ruler,[55] leaving among other legacies the English translation of the Bible we know as the King James Version.[56] Critically for our purposes, James' accession to the British crown coincided with the launch of the English project of settling the east coast of North America. In 1607, the first permanent English colony in the New World set up shop in Virginia (so-called after Elizabeth I, the Virgin Queen) and christened itself Jamestown, in honor of the reigning monarch.[57] From that moment until the new United States declared independence from the parent country in 1776, the histories and collective consciousness of Great Britain and its children across the Atlantic were intimately intertwined.

James I believed firmly in the divine right of kings, a governmental theory he articulated in two learned works, *The True Law of Free Monarchies*[58] and the *Basilikon Doron*.[59] James' theory of kingship claimed not only heavenly sanction for monarchical rule, but also espoused royal absolutism.[60] Parliaments, in particular, he viewed as nothing more than advisors to be consulted or ignored as the ruler deemed best. The authority upon which law itself rested, in James' view, was the royal will and not any legislative assembly.[61] In *The True Law*, he wrote that kings emerged "before any estates or ranks of men, before any parliaments were holden, or laws made, and by them was the land distributed, which at first was wholly theirs. And so it follows of necessity that kings were the authors and makers of the laws, and not the laws of the kings."[62] True to his convictions, James ruled for long periods without convening Parliament; however, he could not raise the funds necessary to support his sometimes extravagant court and pay for various military ventures without occasionally turning to that body.[63] For their part, the notables, grandees, and propertied men of middle station who made up Parliament were concerned about royal finance, foreign policy, and religion. They were determined that the king's spendthrift tendencies should not be financed from their purses.[64] They were at times more bellicose, particularly toward Catholic Spain, than the king;[65] and the majority were devoutly Protestant and deeply suspicious of any real or perceived tendency toward backsliding into papism.

The religious conflicts of the age are of some importance to understanding the tensions between James I, his son Charles I, and their parliaments. Since Henry VIII's divorce from his first wife in 1533 and the separation of the Church of England from Rome-centered Catholicism, England had become firmly Protestant. However, the transition was turbulent. Henry's methods were not gentle and stirred considerable, if fruitless, resentment.[66] From 1553 to 1558, Henry's daughter Queen Mary I tried bloodily, but unsuccessfully, to reverse the English Reformation.[67] Queen Elizabeth I reaffirmed the Protestant character of the Church, but during her long reign, adherents of the old faith remained numerous and hopeful, even among the aristocracy. James I, as a Scot, was himself a Protestant, but he was seen by some as distressingly tolerant of Catholics and he openly sought alliance with Catholic Spain through the marriage of his son Charles to a Spanish princess.

Moreover, the spirit of the Protestant Reformation was always at least somewhat at odds with a theory of divinely sanctioned absolute royal rule of the sort espoused by James.[68] Kings as God's instruments made a certain sense as long as those kings ruled under the sanction of a universal Catholic Church. But wherever the concept of a faith based on scripture accessible to all literate persons supplanted salvation through adherence to the rules of the Church of Rome, the foundations of absolute royal rule softened. If the truth was discoverable through inquiry, rather than attainable only by submission to authority, then automatic acquiescence to the whims of hereditary rulers deserved rethinking. If the path to God ran, as the Protestants claimed, direct from man to his maker and not through ordained intermediaries, then the substitution of kingly intermediaries for priestly ones made poor sense.

As James I's reign progressed, tensions between crown and Parliament increased. Among the leading parliamentarians was Sir Edward Coke, a learned judge and lawyer who believed that the common law of England proceeded from ancient sources and, on some fundamental points, superseded expressions of royal will.[69] This view was not admired by the king's party, and, in 1616, Coke was dismissed from the bench.[70] Coke's leading antagonist among supporters of James and the royal prerogative was Sir Francis Bacon,[71] famous to us as one of the great minds of the age.[72] In 1618, the king appointed Bacon to be Lord Chancellor of England, the highest office of the realm combining executive, judicial, and legislative responsibilities. Three years later, in 1621, James was obliged by extreme financial exigency to call only his third parliament since coming to the throne in 1603.

The parliamentarians ultimately came through with the supplies James required, but they used their leverage to seek reforms of various deficiencies of royal government. Among these were corruption in the system of raising funds for the crown by granting royal licenses and monopolies on certain kinds of trade,[73] and corruption and mismanagement in what were known as courts of chancery which operated under the aegis of the lord chancellor and derived their authority from the royal prerogative rather than the legal precedents that governed the common law courts beloved of Lord Coke.

In March 1621, parliamentary investigators reported that Sir Giles Mompesson, who presided over the licensure of inns and held the gold and silver thread monopoly, had been involved in financial shenanigans.[74] At about the same time, a parliamentary committee investigating the chancery courts discovered that Chancellor Bacon had been accepting generous gifts from litigants in cases over which he presided.[75] Bacon's receipt of bribes cannot have been a great surprise since litigant payments to judges were a common practice of the period, frowned upon by the high-minded, but rarely the source of any official rebuke.[76] In any case, the House of Commons, to what must have been general astonishment, excavated the forgotten impeachment mechanism from under a century-and-a-half of dust and used it, first, to charge Mompesson with various forms of corruption and abuse of authority, and later to charge Bacon with multiple counts of bribery. Mompesson was convicted and banished, after the king himself came down to Parliament to disavow abuses of the royal grants. Bacon, perhaps assuming that the ordinariness of his infraction would spare him any serious punishment, confessed. The Lords convicted him, and King James was either unwilling or unable to save his chief servant, so Bacon was stripped of his offices and condemned to relative penury for the rest of his days.[77]

Three points emerge from these first impeachments of the Stuart period. First, in rediscovering impeachment as a means of removing royal officials and ministers, Parliament signaled its awakening from a long torpor as a serious legislative counterweight to royal authority, or what we would think of as the executive branch of government. Second, impeaching Bacon was part of a larger effort to assert the primacy of law over executive branch absolutism. Finally, the convictions of both Mompesson and Bacon struck blows against the misuse of government office for self-enrichment. All three themes resonate in the present day.

At the close of James I's reign, in 1624, Parliament took another ministerial scalp by impeaching the earl of Middlesex, the Lord High Treasurer. The true reason for

Parliament's enmity may have been the earl's support for James' unpopular pro-Spanish foreign policy, but he was removed on charges of corruption.[78] Though convicted and temporarily imprisoned and stripped of his offices, he was quickly pardoned and restored to grace after King James I died in 1625 and was succeeded by King Charles I.[79]

Charles I inherited his father's absolutist view of monarchy with its attendant disdain for parliaments. That alone would have ensured some tension between the king and the notables who populated Parliament, but Charles seems to have had fewer political gifts than his father[80] and he assumed the throne in an age increasingly disinclined to unquestioning acceptance of claims of authority, whether secular or religious. Tensions between Charles and the parliamentarians eventually produced open warfare, the defeat of the royalist forces by Oliver Cromwell's New Model Army, Charles' capture,[81] imprisonment, and finally, in 1649, his execution.[82] The details of the politics of Charles' turbulent reign are far beyond the scope of this discussion. Instead, we will address only the use of impeachments as a tool in the disputes between king and Parliament.

In 1626, only two years after Charles' accession to the throne, Parliament impeached George Villiers, the duke of Buckingham, who had been a favorite, and possible lover, of James I and remained the closest confidant of the young King Charles I.[83] Buckingham, a man of modest origins, made his way into royal affection through good looks and considerable intelligence and charm. Once firmly ensconced in royal favor, he wielded great personal power and enriched his family and friends liberally with titles, property, and valuable royal concessions.[84] The rapid rise of a social climber like Villiers would have stirred resentment in any case,[85] but he was rendered still less popular by being associated with the unsuccessful and unpopular attempt to marry Charles to the daughter of the Catholic king of Spain,[86] as well as the successful, but also controversial, marriage of Charles to the equally Catholic French princess Henrietta Maria. A number of botched military ventures, including a failed naval assault on the port of Cadiz in 1625,[87] gave Charles' second parliament an excuse to seek Buckingham's impeachment in 1626.

King Charles, who adored Buckingham, prevented the matter from going to trial in the House of Lords by the simple expedient of dismissing Parliament.[88] The charges against Buckingham, which the formal articles of impeachment labeled "misdemeanors, offences, misprisions, and crimes,"[89] are nonetheless revealing for our purposes. They fall into at least six categories: first, acquiring a "plurality of offices" that were beyond the ability of one man to perform; second, buying, selling, or dispensing royal offices and titles for his own benefit or that of his family; third, general misappropriation of royal funds concealed by misuse of the king's personal seal (the "privy seal"); fourth, mismanaging his responsibilities as Lord Admiral of England and Ireland so that trade diminished and piracy increased; fifth, being responsible for the loan of certain English ships to the French king to use against Protestant Huguenots at La Rochelle; and, sixth, suggesting that King James take some useless medicines during his final illness.[90]

Few, if any, of these would have been considered either ordinary crimes or treason against the crown. Unauthorized use of the privy seal, if proven, might have fit into either or both categories. Buying and selling offices may under certain circumstances have violated the law, but it was perfectly legal in many situations and was at worst a venial offense in those days.[91] Moreover, there is no indication that either James I or Charles I disapproved of Buckingham's activities. The charges involving naval matters expressed parliamentary outrage on two points: Buckingham's persistent military incompetence or misfortune; and Protestant parliamentarians' suspicion that the courts of both James I and Charles I were soft on Catholicism. But neither allegation made out either a crime or treason. The business about the medicines was merely a nasty, but almost certainly baseless, insinuation that Buckingham had tried to poison the old king.

In sum, Parliament believed impeachment to be proper for ministers who employed the powers of office for self-enrichment, grossly mismanaged their governmental responsibilities, or betrayed the fundamental interests of the country in dealings with foreign powers. Buckingham's impeachment has been said to have decisively "negatived Charles I's contention that not only was he personally above the law, but also his ministers acting at his orders."[92] But it is not clear that Buckingham's true offenses were violations of law in the conventional sense. They were instead offenses against what the notable personages who made up Parliament perceived to be the proper constitutional relationship between themselves and the crown, and also against parliamentarians' ideas of proper national policy.

Charles managed to forestall further use of impeachments against his ministers for the next fourteen years by keeping parliaments infrequent and short in duration.[93] But in 1640, financial exigencies forced Charles to reconvene Parliament and accede to an Act stipulating that it could not be dissolved without the consent of its members.[94] That body, known as the Long Parliament, remained formally in session until 1660 and did not dissolve even during the war that dethroned King Charles.

When Parliament assembled in September 1640, King Charles was not only in financial distress, but was facing armed rebellion by his Scottish subjects, political chaos in Ireland, and widespread dissension in England.[95] The leaders of the newly assembled legislature, knowing that the king's situation was desperate, were determined to use their leverage to make significant reforms.[96] They resolved to reassert parliamentary control over taxation and revenue. Many of them were concerned that the king's dedication to the Protestant religion was suspect and were distressed at the aggressive hostility of his ecclesiastical appointees such as the archbishop of Canterbury William Laud to the religious reform movement we know as Puritanism. Most fundamentally, the parliamentarians rejected Charles' disposition to personal rule. In modern terms, their quarrel with Charles was a constitutional argument. Charles believed he was anointed by God to govern subject to no lesser authority. Parliament viewed the monarch as a pillar of the state, to be sure, but also as constrained by the law enacted by Parliament in statutes and declared by judges of the common law courts.

In their view of the law, the leaders of the Long Parliament were the intellectual heirs of Sir Edward Coke, who had died in 1634,[97] but whose influence had if anything grown since his falling-out with James I in 1616. Accordingly, they sought to reform the legal system, in particular the practices of two special courts, the Court of Star Chamber[98] and the Court of High Commission,[99] which derived their authority from the royal prerogative rather than from either common or statutory law. The Court of Star Chamber enforced Charles' proclamations, which it held to have the force of law.[100] The Court of High Commission was the highest religious court in England, but also had wide civil jurisdiction. Its powers seem to have been wielded particularly aggressively against Puritans and others disposed to reform of the established Church, a faction increasingly well represented in Parliament.

The parliamentarians abolished the Courts of Star Chamber and High Commission in 1641,[101] but recognized that their program also required the removal or neutering of the king's most powerful ministers and retainers. Accordingly, they deployed impeachments liberally in the first three years of the Long Parliament, bringing at least twenty sets of charges against more than thirty individual defendants.[102] The impeachments of 1640–41 are perhaps of most current significance because they struck both at the king's most able retainers and through them at his theory of kingship.

King Charles' most forceful and energetic secular official was Thomas Wentworth, earl of Strafford.[103] Curiously, before joining the king's party and rising to an earldom, Wentworth had been a member of the House of Commons himself, was an active supporter of the 1628 Petition of Right (which endeavored to set limits on royal power),[104] and had even been imprisoned in the Tower of London for refusing to pay the "forced loans" Charles used early in his reign to finance his government.[105] However, as soon as the Petition of Right passed Parliament and was (grudgingly) accepted by Charles, Wentworth switched sides. Once committed to the king's cause, the earl of Strafford, née Wentworth, became an ardent defender of the royal prerogative and the most effective instrument of Charles' preferred absolutist mode of governance. In Ireland, where he served as the Lord Deputy (essentially the king's viceroy) beginning in 1633, Strafford was particularly aggressive in using prerogative power to sweep away opposition to a program of ruthlessly efficient administration.[106] Recalled to England in 1639, Strafford urged the king to adopt the same sort of unyielding tactics that had proven successful in Ireland. The English proved to be less tractable.

King Charles' most prominent servant among the churchmen was William Laud, consecrated archbishop of Canterbury and thus head under Charles himself of the Church of England. Laud was determined to regularize religious practice and to stamp out dissenters of a Puritan bent. The particulars of his religious project are of less importance than his methods because he shared with Strafford authoritarian instincts and disdain for any law not founded on the will of the king. Laud ruthlessly wielded prerogative courts like the Courts of High Commission and Star Chamber to suppress those he felt to be enemies of true religion or its royal head.[107] For example, in 1637, William Prynne, John Bastwick, and Henry Burton were all sentenced to have their ears cut off for libeling the Church and its bishops.[108]

Laud was a regular correspondent with Strafford and the two commiserated over the impediment to royal government presented by the pestilential common law lawyers and courts. In 1633, just before becoming archbishop of Canterbury, Laud wrote to Wentworth in Ireland and warned him not to expect too much assistance from Laud in his new position because, "the Church it is so bound up in the forms of the Common Law, that it is not possible for me, or for any Man to do that good which he would, or is bound to do."[109] In his reply, Strafford expressed his determination that the king's objectives would not be thwarted by the common law courts, declaring that he would not rest until he saw his royal "Master's power and greatness set out of wardship and above the exposition of Sir Edward Coke and his Year Books."[110] In the ensuing years, both men became, if anything, less tolerant of legalistic opposition to their projects and more committed to the king's absolute authority.

Shortly after Parliament convened in the fall of 1640, the Commons impeached Strafford on charges of high treason. The articles are long, detailed, and at times delve into seemingly trivial matters, but they allege five general theories: first, that Strafford, through both his advice to the king and his personal actions had attempted to "subvert the fundamental laws and government of the realms of England and Ireland, and instead thereof, to introduce an arbitrary and tyrannical government against law";[111] second, that he corruptly enriched himself;[112] third, that he colluded with Catholics to encourage that religion and to secure Catholic support in his "tyrannical designs";[113] fourth, that he mismanaged the unsuccessful military sally against the invading Scots in mid-1640;[114] and, fifth, that he had counseled the king to bring an Irish army to England to make war on his subjects.[115]

Note that these articles include two types of charges prominent in Buckingham's case and other earlier impeachments: abuse of office for self-enrichment and mismanagement of government or military affairs. The novelty in Strafford's impeachment is the charge of promoting tyranny through subversion of law. What makes this allegation particularly striking is that it depended on Coke's view that law exists independent of the will of the king. Everyone knew that all Strafford's actions were taken with the king's sanction in pursuit of the king's policies. Thus, the "arbitrary and tyrannical government against law" Strafford was accused of promoting was the absolute rule of the king administered through unaccountable ministers and prerogative courts. The articles also alleged that Strafford promoted tyranny by encouraging the king to dismiss Parliament.[116] In effect, the Commons charged

Strafford with high treason for putting into action Charles' theory of kingship.[117] Even the charge that Strafford had urged Charles to bring the "foreign" Irish army to England to levy war against the people only makes sense if one believes that a king has no right to use force against rebellious subjects.

All the allegations in Strafford's articles of impeachment were particulars in the overarching capital charge of high treason. As multiple commentators have observed, this necessarily implied the existence of two theories of treason: there could be treasons against the person of the monarch, but also treason against the constitution of the state.[118] John Pym, leader of the Commons, argued when prosecuting Stafford before the House of Lords, that "this crime of subverting the laws, and introducing an arbitrary and tyrannical government, is contrary to the pact and covenant between a King and his people ... the legal union of allegiance and protection." He added that, "to alter the settled frame and constitution of government is treason in any state."[119]

Despite Pym's confident declaration, the Lords hesitated to convict Strafford, in part because Strafford was able to refute the factual basis of some charges and, as some scholars have argued, in part because there was lingering doubt that what Strafford had done amounted to treason as previously defined by law.[120] Twentieth-century lawyer and politician F. E. Smith, Lord Birkenhead, himself a Lord Chancellor of England, maintained that in helping Charles to "substitute arbitrary government for the rule of law" Strafford committed a "high crime" and a "heinous" offense, but not the technical crime of treason because his behavior did not violate the statute defining treason.[121] In the end, for reasons not fully understood, Parliament abandoned the Commons' articles of impeachment and substituted a bill of attainder alleging high treason on the same grounds. It passed both houses. Unlike an impeachment, attainder required the consent of the sovereign, but Charles yielded to pressure, gave his assent, and Strafford was beheaded on May 12, 1641.[122]

The Commons moved against Archbishop Laud at the same time as Strafford. Laud, too, was arrested and impeached by the House of Commons for high treason in December 1640,[123] but he was imprisoned and his trial was delayed until 1644.[124] Several sets of articles of impeachment were prepared against Laud, but both sets mirrored those against Strafford in critical respects.[125] The principal charge, repeated in various forms, was that Laud had committed treason by endeavoring to set up an arbitrary and tyrannical government, destroy Parliament, and subvert the rule of law.[126] The primary difference between the Laud and Strafford impeachment charges was that Laud was alleged to have promoted tyrannical government primarily in the ecclesiastical sphere of the king's sovereignty, while Strafford's transgressions fell in the secular realm.[127]

The technical treason case against Laud was, if anything, weaker than that against Strafford. Laud had no military authority and could not be charged with marshaling foreign armies against the people, and his actions, however brutal, high-handed, and subversive of Parliament and the common law courts, were taken both with the king's sanction and through established institutions like the Courts of Star Chamber and High Commission. Indeed, it was explicitly argued on Laud's behalf that, though the allegations against him may indeed have been "crimes and misdemeanors," they were not in law treason.[128] Nonetheless, Parliament viewed Laud as a dangerous pillar of the king's disposition to absolutism. In late October 1643, the Commons suddenly abandoned the formal impeachment process and drew up a bill of attainder asserting that the charges in Laud's impeachment had been proven, thus meriting his attainder for high treason.[129] Both houses passed the bill in January 1644, rejected as invalid against parliamentary condemnation a pardon of the archbishop the king had issued the previous year, and sent Laud to the executioner.[130]

Charles I's conflict with his Parliament degenerated into the English Civil War (1642–51) and led to his own execution, the kingless Commonwealth of England (1649–60), the Cromwell Protectorate, and finally, in 1660, the restoration of the English monarchy under Charles II.[131] Although Parliament invited the Stuart monarchs back to the throne, it remained protective of its own authority and suspicious of royal overreach. One of Charles II's chief ministers, the earl of Clarendon, a stout monarchist, fell afoul of his political enemies in Parliament beginning in 1663. Two efforts were made to impeach him. The first was widely deemed frivolous, but the second, in 1667, succeeded in driving him from office. The primary charges in the second impeachment involved supposed advice to the king to raise a standing army and govern through it rather than Parliament, seeking money for the crown from France in order to evade parliamentary control of royal finance, and abuses of habeas corpus for sending prisoners out of England and holding them without trial.[132] The parallels to the cases of Strafford and Laud are plain; again the essence of the allegations was that Clarendon was subverting the constraints on monarchy imposed by the elected parliament and the common law. Clarendon's impeachment was technically unresolved because he fled to France before final votes could be taken in the House of Lords, but Parliament thereafter passed a bill of banishment to keep him out of the country.[133]

The final notable impeachment under the Stuart kings was that of the earl of Danby in 1678. Still at loggerheads with Parliament over finance, Charles II authorized Danby to write letters to an intermediary offering the French king British neutrality in the Franco-Dutch war for a huge cash annuity paid to Charles.[134] When the letters leaked, Parliament promptly impeached Danby for treason.[135] The form of the charge was in one respect strikingly similar to those against Clarendon, Laud, and Strafford in that he was alleged to have "endeavoured to subvert the ancient and well established form of government in this kingdom, and instead thereof to introduce an arbitrary and tyrannical way of government."[136] The essence of the complaint was also similar to prior impeachments in that Commons was perturbed that Danby was simultaneously attempting to circumvent parliamentary control over the king's revenue and carrying out a pro-French foreign policy which many parliamentarians believed to be contrary to the country's inter-ests. The Lords were markedly reluctant to convict a minister for treason for carrying out the king's policy, however obnoxious they found that policy to be, but the matter was not resolved because the king prorogued Parliament to stop the proceedings. A later Parliament nonetheless revived the charges and ruled that an attempt by the king to pardon Danby was ineffective against an impeachment.[137] In the end, Danby spent some years in custody before the whole business was dropped.

THE GLORIOUS REVOLUTION OF 1688 AND THE LAST FLURRY OF BRITISH IMPEACHMENTS, 1715–16

The last king of the Stuart lineage was James II. His Catholicism and various of his policies proved to be so obnoxious to leading elements in Parliament and England at large that they invited William of Orange, the statholder of the Netherlands and husband of Mary, James II's daughter, to invade and assume the British crown jointly with Mary.[138] He did so, successfully and largely bloodlessly, in 1688. The removal of James II and the ascendance of William and Mary became known as the "Glorious Revolution."[139] It is important for our purposes primarily because a condition of William and Mary's assumption of the throne was the passage and acceptance by the crown of the Bill of Rights, 1689, that codified increased parliamentary authority at the expense of royal prerogatives.[140] Although the transition would not be complete for many years, the Glorious Revolution is commonly said to be the beginning of constitutional monarchy in Britain. Accordingly, as ministers and officials became less and less agents of the monarchs and more and more the creatures of Parliament, impeachment assumed decreasing importance.

There was a flurry of impeachments in 1715–16 occasioned by the turmoil caused by the death in 1714 of Queen Anne, the daughter and successor of William and Mary,[141] and the accession of George I, a Hanoverian prince who assumed the throne only because he was Anne's closest Protestant relative.[142] Anne's death raised hopes for the restoration of a Catholic monarchy in the person of James Francis Edward Stuart, the "Old Pretender." The result was armed rebellion in Scotland known as the Jacobite Rising of 1715 which was joined by a number of Scottish peers.[143] When the rising failed, seven peers were impeached for high treason and several were executed.[144] Likewise, after George I was installed on the throne, parliamentary critics of the foreign policy pursued under Queen Anne impeached the earl of Oxford, Viscount Bolingbroke, and the earl of Strafford in 1715 for giving "pernicious" advice to the queen to enter into the Treaty of Utrecht in the War of the Spanish Succession.[145]

THE IMPEACHMENT OF WARREN HASTINGS

Once the issue of parliamentary supremacy was settled by the Glorious Revolution and its aftermath, and the issue of Protestant succession was firmly resolved by the accession of George I and the failure of the Jacobite Rising of 1715, impeachment largely disappeared from the British scene. The only notable exception was the impeachment of Warren Hastings, Governor General of India, that, by happenstance, was beginning just as the Philadelphia convention commenced in 1787.

At the time America achieved independence, there had not been an impeachment of a crown official for misconduct in office since 1725,[146] and the practice was on the verge of becoming a mere relic of an earlier age. However, complaints about Hastings' conduct in India had been brewing since his retirement and return to Great Britain in 1785. In April 1786, the great orator, conservative essayist,[147] and supporter of American liberties[148] Edmund Burke presented specific accusations against Hastings in the House of Commons.[149] On May 10, 1787, the Commons approved articles of impeachment,[150] and on May 21, 1787, less than a week before the Philadelphia convention was called to order on May 27, Hastings was arrested and taken before the House of Lords to hear the charges.[151]

Hastings' impeachment trial before the Lords did not begin until February 1788, and it dragged on at irregular intervals for seven years until, in April 1795, he was acquitted on all charges.[152] The *verdict* is unimportant for our purposes because it was handed down long after the American constitution was ratified in 1788, and thus could have had no influence on either the Philadelphia drafters or the state ratifiers of the American impeachment mechanism. But the fact of the Hastings impeachment and the nature of the charges were well known in 1787–88, and would be specifically mentioned in the key exchange between George Mason and James Madison that produced the constitutional definition of impeachable conduct: "treason, bribery, or other High Crimes and Misdemeanors."[153]

Hastings' case was a cause célèbre throughout the English-speaking world, and was of particular fascination to newly independent Americans because it centered on Hastings' conduct as the chief administrative officer of the major British colonial possessions outside the western hemisphere, the growing accumulation of territory that would in time become the Indian Raj. From 1773 to 1785, Hastings had served as the first governor general of British territories and interests in India. The position was created to centralize administration of what was at the time a hodge-podge of territorial possessions, trading concessions, and treaty relationships with indigenous rulers across the Indian subcontinent largely conducted by and through the British East India Company.[154] The company was to modern eyes an anomalous creature, in part a private corporation and trading venture, but in significant part a government with a huge private army drawing its authority from acts of Parliament, grants from or treaties with native Indian rulers, or simple right of conquest.[155] The company's critics viewed it as exploitative and tending to corrupt both the regions it ruled and politics back home.[156] The creation of the office of governor general and Hastings' appointment to that post were part of an effort to restrain the East India Company's excesses and bring its activities and possessions under more direct control by the British government.

Hastings' supporters, both at the time and since, viewed him as an earnest, hard-working, aggressive, and on the whole successful administrator who laid the foundation for British control of India and integration of its possessions there into a system of empire. His critics saw in him the personification of the errors and excesses of imperialism and attributed to him both personal corruption and egregious abuses of authority.[157] The twenty-two articles of impeachment against Hastings charged him with a miscellany of misbehavior,[158] including disregard of instructions from the company's directors,[159] mismanagement of regions under his administrative control (often to the disadvantage of the native population),[160] high-handed or deceitful dealings with local rulers,[161] misconduct of local wars, [162] and allegations of corruption benefiting either Hastings himself or other company officials.[163] A cynic might characterize most of the charges as "behaving like an efficient imperialist." None of the charges could fairly be classed as criminal conduct in any technical sense. Even the allegations of corruption were phrased so vaguely that it would have been impossible to frame them within any existing criminal statute. The essence of the claims against him was abuse of official power. This feature of the articles was so patent that their principal author, Edmund Burke, was obliged to expend his eloquence contending that Hastings' offenses were against natural law or ancestral principles of the British constitution rather than any particular statute. In his opening statement, Burke said the charges against Hastings "were crimes, not against forms, but against those eternal laws of justice, which are our rule and our birthright: his offenses are not in formal, technical language, but in reality, in substance and effect, High Crimes and High Misdemeanors."[164]

Burke's description of Hastings' offenses is important not merely because it confirms, once again, that in British practice impeachable offenses need not have been indictable crimes. In addition, Burke's words, together with other facts about the Hastings case, illuminate a broader point. Note that the Commons voted to impeach Hastings not to remove an obnoxious official from office, nor to hobble the policy of a willful monarch. Hastings had already resigned his office and retired two years before his impeachment. And by 1787, Great Britain was already a parliamentary monarchy in which the personal authority of the king was largely subordinate to the parliamentary majority. Thus, the impeachment of Hastings makes sense only if some other objective was in view.

Certainly one cannot ignore that the move against Hastings had immediate political objectives. For opponents of the government of William Pitt the Younger, Hastings was a convenient whipping boy.[165] But Burke, at least, had larger aims. For him and like-minded others, the Hastings case was an opportunity to establish fundamental points about the nature of the emerging British Empire, the standards of conduct to be expected of government servants of that Empire, and the rights of the Empire's subjects.[166] In this sense, Burke's impeachment of Hastings was a continuance of his arguments before the American Revolution in favor of colonists' enjoyment of the traditional rights of Englishmen. In framing the charges against Hastings, Burke was asserting that the Empire should be a unitary whole in which officials would be subject to central authority and obliged to operate in accordance with the rule of statutory law and natural justice. He was also making bold claims for the rights of British subjects, regardless of national origin. Perhaps the most notable feature of Burke's charges against Hastings is their insistence that the primary victims of Hastings' alleged misbehavior were, not Englishmen or British commercial interests, but the indigenous rulers and inhabitants of India. Burke does not deny that Britain may rule an Empire, but he insists that the peoples under its sway should not be robbed, exploited, or impoverished.

Whether this view carried the day in the Hastings impeachment or in the development of the British Empire after the 1780s is not important for our purposes. The key point is that, at the same moment Americans were redesigning their government in Philadelphia, Burke was using impeachment as a vehicle, not for the chastisement of one man, but to establish basic constitutional principles – and important Americans were aware of his efforts and wanted a similar power for themselves.

LESSONS OF BRITISH IMPEACHMENTS FOR AMERICAN PRACTICE

British impeachment practice is important for students of the American constitution because the framers were conscious heirs to British traditions of representative government, and because at Philadelphia they settled on language to define the scope of impeachable conduct – "Treason, Bribery, or other high Crimes and Misdemeanors" – drawn directly from British impeachment precedents.[167] Whether the framers meant to adopt British language, particularly the phrase "high crimes and misdemeanors," as a term of art tightly restricting the scope of American impeachments by reference to British practice, and if that was their intention, whether we should honor it, are questions for later chapters. For the moment, it is necessary only to ascertain how the British understood impeachment because a proper reading of British precedents helps to set the baseline minimum for the scope of American impeachments. We can fairly draw at least the following conclusions.

Impeachment, Crime, Treason, and Retrospective Punishment

As noted above, a persistent conundrum of British impeachment proceedings arose from the dual character of impeachment. It was a political tool, but it was also criminal insofar as conviction triggered severe personal penalties far beyond mere removal from office. Thus, the combination of growing parliamentary resistance to absolutist royal rule and affinity for government under statutory and common law necessarily implied that even politically dangerous ministers ought not be personally punished for conduct not previously specified as illegal. This tension existed in all British impeachments, but was most acute when treason was among the charges.

Indeed, many parliamentary arguments about retrospective or declaratory treason seem to have been driven primarily by concern about the extreme penalties for conviction on that ground. Those impeached for treason or their parliamentary defenders were often heard to argue that they may well have committed crimes, even serious ones, but not treason.[168] The real issue in many such cases seems to have been that the Commons wanted not merely removal of an obnoxious minister from office, but also his physical and civil death in the form of execution and/or deprivation of lands, titles, and wealth. The technical arguments about whether an accused's conduct fell within previous definitions of treason often seem to be driven by resistance, particularly among the Lords, against the idea that faithful service to an erring king could result not merely in removal from office, but extinction.

For example, it has been argued that the last-minute switch from impeachment to attainder in the 1640 cases of both Lord Strafford and Archbishop Laud and the absence of formal convictions in the House of Lords in later impeachments arose from the Lords' reluctance to impeach officials for treason for conduct not clearly treasonous under existing law. But to draw this conclusion from the Strafford and Laud affairs is to ignore their ultimate fates – in both cases, both houses of Parliament approved bills of attainder based on the same charges contained in the articles of impeachment and condemned the accused to death. Whatever Parliament thought it was doing, it was not forswearing the power to punish as treason conduct that had not expressly been held to be treasonous before.[169]

The general question of whether Parliament could impeach an official for treason based on conduct not unambiguously defined as treason by either statute or existing precedent has been the subject of dense scholarly debate. Raoul Berger concluded in his influential Nixon-era book on impeachment that Parliament had the power to declare what he called "retrospective treasons."[170] Historian Clayton Roberts wrote a biting rebuttal.[171] He noted that, while the Stuart-era House of Commons voted articles of impeachment alleging innovative theories of treason – what he calls "declarative treasons" – for Strafford, Laud, and other officials, these impeachments rarely went to trial in the House of Lords, and never resulted in convictions. Roberts concluded that the Lords were consciously resisting the claim that they had the power to define and punish declaratory treason.[172]

Roberts' argument from parliamentary practice has some force. He cleverly characterizes Berger's emphasis on the treason charges brought by the Commons, as opposed to the inaction of the Lords on those charges, as an argument for the prosecution's view of law as opposed to the view of those who sit as judges.[173] But he falls victim in some degree to the reverse fallacy by relying heavily on contemporaneous arguments from defenders of the impeached officials for explanations of why impeachments did not achieve conviction in the Lords. Moreover, he tends to gloss over the fact that in multiple cases the Lords failed to convict, not because of any principled legal judgment about the nature of treason, but due to events such as the king's dissolution of Parliament (Danby) or the accused's flight from the country (Clarendon). In any event, his insistence that the judgment of the House of Commons on what constitutes an impeachable treason is of no legal weight pushes too far the analogy of parliamentary impeachment to an ordinary criminal trial. In an English impeachment, the actions of both the Commons and the Lords (like those of the American House and Senate) are moved by complex judgments on law, fact, and politics. In England, just as in the United States, the decisions of both the lower and upper house create precedent. The fact is that throughout the seventeenth and early eighteenth centuries the Commons repeatedly impeached ministers, judges, and officials for "declaratory" or "retrospective" treason and secured its objective of politically neutering those impeached, whether by transformation of the impeachment into an attainder, an order of banishment, or the defendant's flight from the jurisdiction.[174] One may disapprove of Parliament's persistent practice of loosely defining treason to achieve political ends, but it is idle to deny that this was their practice.[175]

The potentially grisly result of an English treason conviction had considerable influence on the framers of the American constitution. The framers quite consciously eliminated the tension between the political necessity of a non-electoral mechanism for removing erring officials and the criminal theory rule against retrospective personal punishment by barring bills of attainder[176] and by limiting the consequence of a successful impeachment to removal from office and leaving personal punishment to the criminal courts.[177] In the American setting, the fierce debates over Parliament's power to declare retrospective treasons lose their point, leaving only the question of the kind of behavior that demands removal from office for the good of the nation. Moreover, in the four centuries from 1376 to 1787 a great many British officials were impeached for offenses other than treason. And the most obvious lesson of these cases is that Parliament routinely impeached and often convicted people for conduct that was neither an indictable crime nor a plain violation of any existing law. We have already discussed the duke of Buckingham, impeached in 1626 for, among other things, holding a plurality of offices, mismanaging his office as Lord Admiral, and loaning English ships to the French king to use against Protestant Huguenots;[178] the earl of Strafford, impeached in 1715 for giving "pernicious" advice to the crown to enter into the Treaty of Utrecht in the War of the Spanish Succession;[179] as well as Warren Hastings, impeached for conduct that even his chief accuser conceded were not crimes.[180]

Other examples include:

In 1642, the Commons impeached Sir Richard Gurney, Lord Mayor of London, principally it appears because Gurney made certain proclamations in support of Charles I, attempted to suppress a petition of grievances directed to Parliament, supported another petition critical of Parliament,[181] and failed to transfer certain munitions to a storehouse in London contrary to the orders of Parliament. On the strength of these allegations, Gurney was charged with, among other things, striving to "bring in an arbitrary and tyrannical government."[182] He was convicted, stripped of the mayoralty, disqualified from further office, and cast into prison.[183]

In 1668, Peter Pett, a commoner in charge of the naval shipyard, was impeached for allegedly failing to secure portions of the British fleet from Dutch attack.[184]

In 1701, the earl of Orford, Lord Somers, Lord Halifax, and William, Earl of Portland, were all impeached for advising King William to enter into treaties of which their parliamentary critics disapproved, as well as for garden-variety corruption and, in the cases of Oxford and Somers, playing a role in the granting of letters of marque (a commission to act as a private naval vessel) to William Kidd, who turned pirate as the infamous "Captain Kidd." All were acquitted.[185]

In 1710, an Anglican minister named Henry Sacheverell was impeached and convicted for preaching a sermon at St. Paul's attacking church dissenters and those in government disposed to tolerate them.[186] He was convicted, banned from preaching for three years, and his sermons were ordered to be burnt by the public hangman.[187]

The Meaning of "High Crimes and Misdemeanors" in British Practice

Careful perusal of 400 years of British impeachments convinces me that there was never any precise definition or even well-settled understanding of what constituted impeachable conduct. With increasing frequency beginning in the 1600s, Parliament employed the phrase "high crimes and misdemeanors" at the beginning of articles of impeachment to describe the list of offenses specified in the body of the document. But I find no indication that this phrase, so critical to discussions of the impeachment power under the U.S. constitution, was for the British ever a term of art in the sense of necessarily including or excluding certain kinds of conduct. A reasonable analogy in American practice is the common use of phrases like "unlawfully and feloniously" at the beginning of each count of a criminal indictment ("On or about January 1, 2019, the defendant, Sam Smith, did unlawfully and feloniously" commit whatever crime he is being charged with). This and similar phrases serve no important function in American law. They notify the defendant that the crime is a felony as opposed to a misdemeanor, but even that is superfluous due to the invariable inclusion in the indictment of a citation to the relevant statute. It is the statutory law that makes conduct a felony, not the addition of the descriptor "feloniously" in the indictment charging violation of a statute. Nonetheless, such phrases persist because they are traditional and add a level of solemnity to the accusation.

My sense is that the phrase "high crimes and misdemeanors" served a similar function in British impeachments. The words became traditional. They emphasized the nature and gravity of the accusations in the articles of impeachment. Putting it another way, "high crimes and misdemeanors" was a phrase the drafters of British articles of impeachment habitually used to preface their description of any conduct for which Parliament thought an official should be impeached; it did not refer to a specified set of impeachable offenses from which Parliament was obliged to choose if it wanted to impeach an official. As heirs to the English common law tradition, parliamentarians would have looked to prior impeachments as creating a body of precedent from which they could infer some general principles about the scope of properly impeachable conduct in future cases. But that is as much as they or we could say.

The Scope of Impeachable Conduct in Great Britain

Parliament impeached people for a strikingly wide variety of official misbehavior.[188] It is possible to categorize the offenses charged under a number of general headings and therefore to gain a fair appreciation of the kind of behavior Parliament thought to be impeachable:

Non-Political Impeachments: Armed Rebellion and Ordinary Criminality

A fair number of British impeachment proceedings resulted purely from the ancient requirement that peers of the realm could be tried only by other peers, that is, by the House of Lords. Accordingly, if a hereditary peer was accused either of armed rebellion against the crown[189] or an ordinary felony, the proceedings against him would often be framed either as an impeachment or in some cases as an appeal directly to the House of Lords. Examples of impeachments for armed rebellion include the seven Scottish lords condemned for the 1715 Jacobite Rising[190] and the case of Lord Lovat executed for his role in the 1745 rising.[191] A classic example of impeachment for ordinary criminality is the 1666 case against John, Viscount Mordaunt for unlawfully imprisoning William Tayleur, the surveyor of Windsor Castle, and making "improper addresses" to Tayleur's daughter (a charge later historians have interpreted as raping her).[192]

Corruption

The most common charge in British impeachments, even those in which Parliament's primary concerns were political, was some variant of corruption. From the first impeachments of Lord Latimer and Richard Lyons in 1376[193] right down to Hastings' case in 1787,[194] corruption was an almost invariable theme.[195] Even in the purely political cases, corruption allegations were commonly included in the articles of impeachment.

The essence of all such corruption charges was the misuse of office for private gain. Critically, a good many of the corruption charges were probably not criminal in the technical sense. In pre-modern Britain, public service was not compensated in the formal, regulated way we think of as customary. In large part because the finances of the crown were commonly so irregular that budgeting for standardized salaries was impossible, officeholders were rewarded with varying combinations of salaries, allowances, titles, grants of land, rights to revenue, fees, monopolies, etc. Hence, distinguishing between proper and improper money-making activities was sometimes difficult. Nonetheless, the history of British impeachments illustrates that, even in a system in which public office was expected to produce some private profit, Parliament consistently viewed abuse of the system as impeachable. It was understood that officeholders would make a competency, but violation of formal rules and informal norms in pursuit of excessive self-enrichment was not acceptable.

This idea became even more powerful in the comparatively straight-laced American colonies where it would manifest itself in constitutional provisions such as the foreign and domestic emoluments clauses.[196] For the framers, the connection between the anti-corruption norm[197] undergirding these clauses and the remedy of impeachment was explicit. Bribery is explicitly named as an impeachable offense, and at least one framer explicitly declared that violation of the Foreign Emoluments Clause would be impeachable.[198]

Incompetence, Neglect of Duty, or Maladministration in Office

Another consistent theme of British impeachments was allegations of incompetence, neglect of duty, or maladministration in office. Charges of this sort often arose in connection with military disasters, including the impeachments of Lord Latimer (1376), the earl of Suffolk (1386), the duke of Buckingham (1626), the earl of Strafford (1640), and Peter Pett (1668), but they were hardly limited to that sphere. The charges against Buckingham, Attorney General Henry Yelverton,[199] the Lord Treasurer Middlesex (1624), the earl of Clarendon (1667), Lord Danby (1678), Edward Seymour, Treasurer of the Navy (1680),[200] and, of course, Warren Hastings (1787) were all grounded in part on maladministration, neglect, or sheer ineptitude. And several impeachments were grounded on ministers giving the sovereign bad advice. Great Britain routinely included allegations of this sort under the descriptive heading "high crimes and misdemeanors." As we will see in Chapter 4, the framers rejected the term "maladministration" as a descriptor of impeachable conduct in favor of "high crimes and misdemeanors." In light of ample British precedent including conduct amounting to maladministration within the rubric of "high crimes and misdemeanors," the rejection of the *word* "maladministration" may be less consequential than it is often made to appear.

Abuse of Power

Most British impeachments involved some form of abuse of official power. Most of these can be placed in one of the preceding two categories – corruption or maladministration – insofar as the motive for the abuse was the hope of preferment or monetary gain, or the abuse arose primarily due to incompetence or neglect. Nonetheless, some cases involved abuses that seem to have been moved by simple bloody-mindedness or the enjoyment of exercising unchecked power. Some of the charges in Hastings' case fall in this category. Even more apt are the charge against Viscount Mordaunt for falsely imprisoning the surveyor of Windsor Castle,[201] and a case not previously mentioned, the impeachment of Chief Justice Scroggs for, among other things, "browbeating" witnesses and disparaging them to the jury.[202]

Betrayal of the Nation's Foreign Policy

Another persistent thread in British impeachments is the charge that the impeached minister had pursued a policy at odds with the nation's basic foreign policy interests. Impeachments on this ground were a constant of parliamentary practice beginning with the charges against William de la Pole in 1450 for his role in arranging the marriage of Henry VI to Margaret of Anjou[203] through the 1715 impeachments of Oxford, Bolingbroke, and Strafford for their advocacy of the Treaty of Utrecht,[204] and including the 1787 impeachment of Warren Hastings over fundamental disagreements about the proper relationship of Great Britain to its Indian possessions and the states that abutted them. Over and over again, Parliament employed impeachment to assert an authority independent of the royal executive to define the nation's true foreign policy interests.

Impeachments for betrayal of the country's foreign policy objectives have received relatively little notice among American impeachment scholars, presumably because the only arguably similar American case was the first impeachment of Senator William Blount charged in 1797 with conspiring to assist the British in acquiring Spanish territory in Florida.[205] However, this line of British precedent deserves renewed attention and we will revisit it in Chapter 16 when we consider issues potentially relevant to President Trump.

Subversion of the Constitution and Laws of the Realm

From the first impeachments in 1376, through the tumults of the Stuart period, and right up to the case of Warren Hastings in 1787, Parliament employed impeachment against ministers and officials whose actions threatened its understanding of proper constitutional order. More particularly, Parliament acted repeatedly against those who sought to enlarge or misuse executive/monarchical power at the expense of those elements of society whose interests were represented in Parliament, or were contrary to the legal order established by statutes and the common law courts. The impeachments of Francis Bacon in 1621, the duke of Buckingham in 1626, the earl of Strafford and Archbishop Laud in 1640, the earl of Clarendon in 1667, and the earl of Danby in 1678 are the most notable examples of this category of impeachments. In the cases of Strafford, Laud, Clarendon, and Danby, Parliament explicitly alleged some variant of the charge against Danby that he "endeavored to subvert the ancient and well established form of government in this kingdom, and instead thereof to introduce an arbitrary and tyrannical way of government."[206] And as noted above, the impeachment of Warren Hastings was an effort to extend the traditional constitutional relationships between rulers and ruled in the home islands to the structure of the growing British Empire.[207]

This use of impeachment is of paramount interest at the current moment of American history. It establishes that, at least in British practice, the most important function of impeachment was removal or exemplary chastisement of officials whose behavior presented a threat to constitutional order. In such cases, impeachment need not have been based on discrete incidents of violation of specified laws. Rather, the essence of such cases was a continuing pattern of conduct in opposition to Parliament's conception of proper constitutional arrangements. To employ modern terminology, these impeachments were consciously undertaken either to restore or establish constitutional norms. We will revisit this use of impeachment later in this book.

3

American Impeachments before 1787

The delegates who gathered in Philadelphia in the summer of 1787 and their countrymen who would judge the Constitutional Convention's product were familiar with the institution of impeachment. Not only were they were familiar with its use in the mother country (a point that will be explored in depth in Chapter 4), but Americans had experimented with the procedure both in the colonial period and in the years after independence when the new American states were a loose association operating under the Articles of Confederation. Prior to 1776, there were roughly ten actions against colonial officials that could fairly be called impeachments or near-impeachments,[1] at least two of which, the 1758 case of William Moore in Pennsylvania and the action against Massachusetts Chief Justice Peter Oliver in 1773, were intimately familiar to framers and ratifiers of the constitution. In addition, ten of the original thirteen states included impeachment provisions in their post-revolutionary constitutions and a number of them had already conducted impeachment proceedings by 1787.

American impeachment practice before 1787 predisposed the founding generation to consider impeachment to be an essential component of a republican constitution. However, American experience also offered somewhat conflicting models of impeachment's proper function: on the one hand, a rather prosaic tool for promoting competent administration and fighting garden-variety corruption, and on the other hand, a weapon to be wielded in major conflicts over constitutional structure and authority. This chapter will first consider American colonial impeachments and will then turn to pre-1787 state impeachment provisions and cases.

COLONIAL IMPEACHMENTS, 1607–1776

The stretch of the Atlantic seaboard that became the United States was settled by European immigrants, primarily from Great Britain,[2] beginning with the establishment in 1607 of a colony in Virginia.[3] By 1682, twelve of the original thirteen colonies had been founded,[4] with Georgia following in 1732.[5] For a long time, the governments of these colonies were rudimentary, serving the needs of small, dispersed, agrarian populations on the edge of wilderness. Accordingly, a complex legislative maneuver like impeachment was of little interest or utility. Moreover, the governmental arrangements in the colonies were diverse and experimental, varying according to local experience and the exact relation of each colony to Great Britain.

Speaking broadly, there were four types of government in the first century or so of British North American settlement. Sometimes, for brief periods at the beginning of British migration to a new area, the settlers created forms of self-government with little formal connection to Great Britain. The most famous instance may be the Mayflower Compact, devised in 1620 by the first Puritan settlers of New England when they landed at Plymouth in modern-day Massachusetts.[6] The Compact acknowledged that the settlers would remain subjects of the British crown, but it was a mutual undertaking to create and abide by local governing institutions and laws.[7] Similarly, Connecticut was settled beginning in 1635 by colonists from Massachusetts who maintained allegiance to Britain, but governed themselves under principles formalized in the Fundamental Orders of 1639.[8] However, local self-governance of this sort invariably yielded to formal subjection to British sovereignty and increasing degrees of control by officials in the home islands. So, for example, the second wave of Puritan settlement, beginning with the so-called Winthrop Fleet of 1630, operated under a royal charter issued by Charles I for a Massachusetts Bay Colony.[9] In Connecticut, the Fundamental Orders were superseded by a royal charter in 1662.[10]

Once areas of English settlement received formal status as colonies, their governments were of three general types: proprietary, corporate, and royal.[11] Proprietary governments were, at least at the beginning, quasi-feudal arrangements in which the crown granted ownership of a region to an individual or group in much the same way that kings had traditionally awarded nobles lordship over estates in the British Isles.[12] The colonies of Maryland, Maine, New York, Carolina, and Pennsylvania all began as proprietorial grants by the crown.[13] Proprietors (sometimes called either the "lord proprietor" or "lord proprietary") owned the land and could sell, lease, or bequeath it to their heirs, and they were granted the same kind of governmental authority as feudal lords in Britain.[14] In practice, the authority of colonial proprietors was far less than the feudal model implied. The territories involved were so vast and wild and the powers of the proprietors, who commonly lived in England or at most resided only part-time in their American possessions and conspicuously lacked the private armies characteristic of medieval European magnates, were so weak that relations of substantial social equality between colonists and proprietors soon became the norm.[15] In any case, either by express provision of the proprietary charter or by quickly established custom, the law-making power became shared between proprietors and elected colonial assemblies, while the executive and judicial functions remained in the hands of the proprietors or their local designees, with all remaining ultimately subordinate to the crown.[16]

A second type of British colony was corporate. That is, the authority to settle and administer the affairs of the colony had been granted by the crown, not to a person occupying a feudatory relationship to the monarch, but to a corporation or joint stock company which had, in effect, a contract with the crown.[17] The first successful British colony in North America was created under the aegis of the Virginia Company of London, which in 1606 was granted a charter by King James I to colonize and administer Virginia.[18] Other corporate colonies included Massachusetts, Connecticut, New Hampshire, Rhode Island, and Georgia.[19]

Finally, some colonies were considered "royal" in the sense that they were administered directly by officials of the crown, with no proprietary or corporate intermediaries. Many colonies that began as proprietary or corporate became royal when the original arrangements foundered. By 1776, the majority of the North American colonies were royal in form and all had become increasingly royal in substance inasmuch as royal officials played large roles in the administration of the colonies' affairs.[20]

Although there were significant local variations, in due course the predominant governmental model in the American colonies was a governor appointed by the crown, proprietor, or corporation[21] and a legislature consisting of at least one house popularly elected by eligible colonists and sometimes of an upper house or council appointed by the governor.[22] The judicial function was performed in all sorts of ways depending on the location and the period.[23] Early in the history of English settlement, the colonial assemblies sometimes acted as courts. Sometimes courts were created by legislative enactment and sometimes courts were created and judges appointed by the governor. In some colonies, the governors themselves acted as judges for certain kinds of cases. In Virginia, throughout the colonial period the governor and council acted as a court of general jurisdiction; elsewhere the governor and council commonly served as a court of appeal. Throughout the colonies, the only appeal from the highest colonial appellate body was to the Privy Council in England.[24]

As the populations of the North American colonies increased and their governments became more regularized, they began to experience the sorts of conflict for which the remedy of impeachment seemed suited. As discussed in Chapter 2, in Great Britain impeachment evolved as a parliamentary tool against royal absolutism, objectionable royal policies, or the grievous personal misconduct of royal officials. In the American setting, the analogous problem was how to resist royal, corporate, or proprietary policies of which the legislature strongly disapproved or to remove a misbehaving official appointed by authority of the governor, proprietor, corporation, or crown.

Before considering the particulars of the colonial American impeachments, we should heed the admonition of Hoffer and Hull, the leading authorities on the subject, that the early American colonists will have had only fragmentary information about the particulars of historical British impeachments or even those of the

Stuart era during which they lived.[25] Formal written accounts of parliamentary events were not compiled and published until the early 1680s.[26] These made their way into some colonial libraries and private collections, but access to such materials would have been far more limited than we now think natural. In the 1700s, more such works were written, as for example Hale's *Pleas of the Crown*, first published in 1736.[27] But much of the colonists' information about impeachment will have come in the form of newspapers, letters, personal observation during visits to Great Britain, or tavern and coffeehouse chatter about what were, after all, major components in the political events of their times.[28] For example, the continuing Puritan exodus to New England was sparked in considerable measure by the anti-Puritan repressions of Archbishop Laud.[29] His impeachment in 1640 and later trial would have been closely followed by Massachusetts settlers, and one suspects that his execution in 1644 afforded New World Puritans considerable grim satisfaction.[30]

Moreover, by the eighteenth century, written authorities were multiplying in England at the same time as the upper stratum of colonial society was becoming better educated,[31] and the flow of commerce (and thus information) between Britain and the Americas steadily intensified. As the decades passed, colonial lawyers and other public figures would have had increasing access to detailed information about parliamentary processes generally and impeachments in particular. Despite the relative paucity of written sources, it is nonetheless clear that the colonists had a solid grasp of the essential character of a British impeachment – charges of misconduct against a government official brought by the lower house of the legislature and triable by the upper house with the objective of removing the official from office and, perhaps, of imposing further personal punishments. Moreover, as we will see, with the passage of time the colonists demonstrated an increasingly nuanced appreciation of the constitutional implications of the impeachment mechanism.

The First Colonial Impeachments: Maryland, 1669–83

The first colonial legislative actions designated by their authors as "impeachments" occurred in Maryland in the late 1600s.[32] In 1669, the lower house of the Maryland assembly impeached John Morecroft, a lawyer and one of its members, upon the petition of a merchant named Robert Morris, who seems to have been upset that Morecroft had sued him for libel.[33] However, the upper house dismissed the impeachment both because it was not in proper form inasmuch as the action in the lower house had been initiated by a non-member of the house, and also because the charges (which mostly alleged various forms of legal malpractice) were unsubstantiated.[34]

In 1676, Thomas Truman was impeached for "diverse and Sundry enormous Crimes and Offences" in connection with his command of a bungled joint expedition of Maryland and Virginia militia against the Susquehannock Indians, as part of which he ordered the execution of five Indian leaders held as hostages.[35]

The charges combined allegations of disregarding the instructions of the lord proprietor and violating the law of nations by murdering hostages. The Truman impeachment is notable in that Maryland's lower house specifically opined that they were the "General Inquisitors of this Province and ought to become impeachers of" Truman and that the case should be heard by the lord proprietor and his council, which was effectively the upper house of the legislature.[36] Likewise, the lower house followed the parliamentary practice of appointing managers to present their case in the upper chamber.[37] In council, Truman essentially confessed, whereupon he was convicted and the council asked the lower house to prepare an attainder against him, although that was not done and he was instead merely fined.[38] The analogy between Truman's case and parliamentary impeachments of Lord Latimer for military mismanagement (1376), the earl of Suffolk for bungling the relief of Ghent (1386), the duke of Buckingham for incompetence as Lord Admiral (1626), the earl of Strafford for failure to defend against the Scottish incursion (1640), and Peter Pett's mismanagement of British naval vessels in the face of a Dutch attack (1668) is plain,[39] although Truman's case had the added feature of outright murder in violation of the laws of war.

In the same 1676 session that impeached Truman, the Maryland legislature impeached Charles James, sheriff of Cecil County, for battery and perjury. Apparently, James swore falsely in front of a justice of the peace, induced several others to do likewise, and then assaulted one Edward Pinne. He was convicted and removed from office, but received no other punishment.[40]

In 1681, Maryland once again turned to impeachment in the protracted affair of Jacob Young, employed as an official interpreter by the colonists in their dealings with the Susquehannock Indians. It appears that Young was felt to be too partial to the native inhabitants and was charged, in effect, with treason to the European colonists. However, the assembly felt itself legally unable to pursue a treason charge, perhaps because there were insufficient witnesses. After long deliberation, the lower house impeached Young for "High Misdemeanors." Hoffer and Hull summarize the charges as:

> bringing the proprietary into disrepute among the Indians, urging the Northern Indians to war against the Piscattaway [tribe of Indians] in the province, speaking for the Indians at times likely to cause mischief, failing to mediate between the Northern Indians and other parties according to his instructions as an officer of the government, marrying an Indian, and, in a charge specified when the case came to the upper house, leading raids against the Piscattaway.[41]

Speaking broadly, these allegations amounted to maladministration of the important office of official interpreter, violation of Maryland statutes regarding trade with Indians, and given that Indian tribes were, in law, sovereign nations, subverting or undermining the foreign policy of the lord proprietary and his superior, the king. Young was convicted, but the lower house refused a bill of attainder against him and his ultimate punishment consisted of imprisonment during the lengthy proceedings (1681–83), banishment from the colony (which, as a Delaware native, burdened him very little), and loss of his office as interpreter.[42]

Note that in none of these Maryland cases were serious questions raised about the authority of the lower house of the colonial legislature to bring an impeachment or the authority of the upper house to try one. Disputes over this foundational question of legislative authority would be the sticking point in most of the colonial impeachments of the next century.

Colonial Impeachments in Pennsylvania

The final colonial impeachment of the 1600s was brought in Pennsylvania. Unlike Maryland, where the legislative power of impeachment was apparently implied by the colonists from their knowledge of British practice, the Pennsylvania legislature had an express grant of impeachment authority in the Charter of Liberties issued by Proprietor William Penn in 1682. Articles 19 and 20 provided that the lower house of the legislature (the General Assembly) possessed the power to "Impeach Criminals fit there to be Impeached," while the upper house (the Provincial Council) could determine "Impeachments made by the General Assembly and Judgment of Criminals upon such Impeachment."[43] Penn's inclusion of an impeachment power would have been unusually well informed inasmuch as fourteen years earlier Parliament had unsuccessfully attempted to impeach his father, Sir William Penn, for alleged corruption while Vice Admiral of the Fleet.[44]

The Impeachment of Nicholas Moore, 1685
In March 1685, the General Assembly voted a "declaration" that Nicholas Moore, chief justice of Pennsylvania, had committed "Misdemeanors, Offences & Crimes" and specified his offenses in ten "articles" of impeachment.[45] Moore was an early supporter of Penn's colonization enterprise, forming a joint stock company to capitalize the venture and purchasing 10,000 acres from Penn. Penn rewarded his support by naming him chief justice of the colony, but Moore seems to have been legally untrained, incompetent, and arrogant, a combination that caused rising resentment among Pennsylvanians.[46] The ten articles of impeachment charged him with issuing unlawful writs; scheduling court precipitously and at inconvenient times that prevented fair proceedings; improperly excluding a qualified juror; coercing a jury into changing its verdict; dismissing a case without allowing the complainant time to prepare his case; convicting and punishing two criminal defendants for a felony when none was charged; falsely adjudging a witness guilty of perjury; slandering other judges; missing court sessions; and declaring himself beyond the authority of the Provincial Council.[47]

The impeachment succeeded in removing Moore from his judicial office pending resolution of the case. However, the Assembly and Moore's colonial critics were ultimately denied complete satisfaction. The Council dithered and did not bring the matter to trial, which was also hindered by the refusal of Moore's clerk, Patrick Robinson, to provide the court with the records necessary to prove some of the articles of impeachment. Robinson's defiance, which apparently included verbal slander of the Assembly,[48] resulted in his being held in a form of contempt and excluded from office.[49] Penn refused to endorse formal proceedings in Council on Moore's impeachment and instead appointed his friend to another office.[50] Crucially, however, Moore's colonial opponents achieved their fundamental objective because Moore was removed from office by the original impeachment proceeding and not restored to it by Penn.

The Impeachment of James Logan, 1707

Roughly twenty years after the Moore affair, in 1707, Pennsylvania's lower house once again sought impeachment of a provincial official and favorite of Proprietor Penn. James Logan, born in Ireland in 1674, was a precocious scholar and one-time Anglican clergyman before converting to Quakerism and drawing the attention of William Penn. Penn appointed him to multiple offices in Pennsylvania, including chief steward, commissioner of property, receiver general, and a member of the provincial council.[51] Logan was a stout advocate of the rights of the governor and the proprietor as opposed to the pretensions of the Assembly and other locally elected officials. A dispute over the power to appoint judges led the Assembly first to petition the governor to remove Logan from the council and other offices, and, when that request was ignored, to file thirteen articles of impeachment against him.[52]

The articles were of four sorts. The first two alleged that Logan had tried to undercut the authority of the colonial assembly by inserting provisions in the commission issued by Lord Proprietary Penn to his lieutenant governor in residence in Pennsylvania which: (a) made it impossible to enact laws without Penn's express consent; and (b) conferred on the lieutenant governor a power to dismiss the legislature that was inconsistent with the 1701 Charter of Privileges. Six of the articles alleged mismanagement in Logan's conduct as secretary to the lord proprietary and commissioner of lands in a variety of land transactions. Among these, Article 9 – charging Logan with improperly acting as both proprietary secretary and surveyor general – is resonant of the parliamentary charge against the duke of Buckingham for acquiring a "plurality of offices."[53] The thirteenth article alleged that Logan had interfered in the election for Philadelphia sheriff. The twelfth article is perhaps the most revealing of the general tenor of the conflict between Logan and the Assembly. It charges that "with a wicked Intent to create Divisions and Misunderstandings between [the lord proprietary] and the people" Logan blatantly misinterpreted the language of the Charter of Privileges and the Charter of Philadelphia to deny to the colonists rights plainly set forth in those documents.[54] The echo of British impeachments that held the king harmless by blaming misfortunes on the wickedness of this counselors is clear.

Although the articles sailed through the Assembly, the procedural posture of the business was awkward for Logan's opponents. Even though the Pennsylvania Frame of Government of 1696 maintained the structure of Penn's 1682 Charter of Liberties in giving the Assembly the power to impeach and the Council the power to try impeachments, a new 1701 Charter of Privileges granted the Assembly the "power to . . . impeach criminals," but omitted any reference as to who was supposed to try such cases.[55] The Assembly insisted that the governor and Council retained their authority to do so. But in the end these proprietary organs decided "that they are not qualified to hear and judge of the articles exhibited against the Secretary of an Impeachment, according to the parliamentary Proceedings of England; and being no judicial Court, they cannot oblige him to plead in any Form."[56] Whereupon the matter fizzled out for lack of a venue to try it.

The attempt to bring down Logan is nonetheless illuminating, both because of its political context and the particular charges levied against him. Just as in the Nicholas Moore affair, Pennsylvania's colonial assembly viewed itself as filling the role of the House of Commons in the ancient impeachment ritual. In Logan's case particularly, the Assembly revealed an intimate familiarity with the parliamentary impeachments of the Stuart period by describing Logan's behavior as "high Crimes, Misdemeanours and Offences," and by declaring Logan's "Words, Opinions and Actions" to have been "spoken and done wickedly, falsely and maliciously, to set a Division between the Proprietary and the People of this Province, and to subvert the Law, and to introduce an arbitrary Government."[57] The language and theme of this passage closely track charges in multiple impeachments by Stuart parliaments.[58] Both Parliament and the Pennsylvania Assembly professed loyalty to the royal person, or his designate the provincial proprietor, but accused his subordinates of disserving their master, subverting law, and promoting arbitrary government.

Moreover, despite the fact that Pennsylvania's 1682 Charter of Liberties, 1696 Frame of Government, and 1701 Charter of Privileges all spoke in terms of impeaching "criminals," few, if any, of the charges against Logan (or Nicholas Moore) were indictable crimes. Rather, they were abuses of authority of the sort common in parliamentary impeachments of the Stuart era.[59] The Pennsylvania Assembly plainly viewed its impeachment power as analogous to that of the House of Commons – a remedy against official misconduct and a tool for asserting the rights of the elected legislature against the claims of a royal or proprietary executive.

The Impeachment of William Moore, 1757–59
This view of the role of impeachment persisted among the anti-proprietary faction of Pennsylvania. It was central to a protracted impeachment drama between 1757 and 1759 in which Benjamin Franklin was personally involved and which every other

politically aware Pennsylvanian of the period followed closely. The defendant was
William Moore (no relation to the Nicholas Moore impeached in 1685),
a landowner, justice of the peace, and militia leader granted in 1757
a proprietorial appointment as judge of the Chester County court.[60] Some litigants
in his court soon complained to the Assembly that he had set jury verdicts aside,
delayed execution of judgments, taken double fees, and moreover not paid some of
his own personal debts.[61] After a long period of receiving these complaints, the
Assembly demanded that he give an account of his behavior.

The Assembly's antipathy to Moore may have been moved by more than a desire
to ensure the proper operation of the courts of the colony. From 1754 to 1763, Great
Britain and France were embroiled in a worldwide conflict sometimes called the
Seven Years' War, the North American theater of which is known to us as the French
and Indian War.[62] Britain's military exertions were expensive and it sought contributions from the colonies which, in the not unreasonable view of His Majesty's
ministers, benefited from British military efforts. Some colonists resisted initiatives
to raise money from them, whether by requests for appropriations to colonial
assemblies or by direct taxation. Others opposed the war altogether, disapproved of
particular elements of its conduct, or, in the case of Pennsylvania's Quakers,
declined to participate in the war effort on religious grounds.[63] In Pennsylvania, at
the risk of oversimplifying a complex situation, the Penn family and the proprietary
party were broadly supportive of the war and requests for colonial contributions of
men and money to its prosecution, while insisting that the power to raise militia and
appoint its officers was a prerogative of the crown and resisting the Assembly's efforts
to tax proprietorial property to raise war funding.[64] Significant elements of the anti-
proprietary party in the Assembly found some demands for war funding excessive.[65]
They wanted, at a minimum, greater local control over their own defense and the
exclusive right of the colonial legislature to tax inhabitants to pay for the war.[66] Judge
Moore was allied with the proprietary party in the disputes over the war, a fact that
seems to have enhanced the Assembly's desire to call him to account.

Moore refused to appear before the Assembly, which for its part was unable to
remove Moore directly because he held his judicial office directly from the king.
The Assembly requested the senior proprietary representative present in the
colony, Lieutenant Governor William Denny, to remove Moore.[67] He held an
inquiry at which Moore testified both to his objections to the Assembly's
war policy and his denial of the misconduct allegations.[68] Denny declined
to remove Moore. This would probably have ended the matter had Moore not
been impolitic enough to publish the accusation that the Assembly had manufactured evidence against him. Whereupon, in January 1758, the Assembly
arrested, convicted, and jailed Moore for libel and contempt of the
Assembly.[69] At roughly the same time, the Rev. William Smith, a one-time
protégé of Benjamin Franklin whose politics had increasingly diverged from
Franklin's in favor of proprietary interests, also promoted the publication of

Moore's attack on the Assembly.[70] Smith, too, was arrested for contempt of the Assembly.[71] In January 1758, Smith was tried, convicted, and consigned to jail by the Assembly itself.[72] When the Assembly adjourned for the year, Smith was obliged to be released because he could not be held on the order of the Assembly unless it was in session. However, he feared the new Assembly would renew the case and imprison him again, whereupon he sailed to England to appeal to the Privy Council. It held that the Assembly had no independent judicial power, freeing Smith from the prospect of future incarceration.[73]

Back in Pennsylvania, however, the Assembly still had Moore as an object of its wrath. It had found him in contempt and jailed him, but, like Smith, Moore could be imprisoned for contempt only as long as the 1758/59 legislature was in session. And he retained his judicial office because the lieutenant governor refused to remove him. It is commonly said that the Assembly therefore impeached Moore.[74] Actually, there is some doubt that the Assembly did formally impeach him. I can find no record of formal articles of impeachment having been drafted and voted upon. What seems to have happened is that the leaders of the Assembly elected to treat Moore's contempt conviction as a *de facto* vote of impeachment and Lieutenant Governor Denny took them at their word.[75] In correspondence with Denny, the Assembly repeatedly said it was ready to draw up specific articles of impeachment as soon as Denny agreed to hear the case, but there is no indication that articles were ever drawn.[76]

Regardless, the impeachment case could not proceed because the lieutenant governor declined to try it, claiming he had no power under Pennsylvania law to do so. What ensued was a remarkable debate between the popularly elected Assembly and the proprietary's appointed local executive over the constitutional structure of Pennsylvania, its relation to British institutions, and the place of impeachment in Britain and its colony. In a series of learned exchanges, the Assembly argued that it was expressly granted the power of impeachment by the colony's charter documents and that, both as a matter of logic and of analogy to parliamentary practice, the governor (or governor and council) should stand in the place of the House of Lords to try impeachments or the right of impeachment would be a nullity.[77] Lieutenant Governor Denny responded that the Assembly lacked authority to try impeachments on its own and that he, as executive appointee of the proprietary, had no judicial authority and was not a proper substitute for the House of Lords.[78] The debate ranged widely, covering not only the narrow question of who could try impeachments in Pennsylvania, but the proper role of a popular legislature in a colonial political culture modeled on the parliamentary monarchy of Great Britain.

After multiple salvos from each side, the Assembly having no means of compelling Denny to action, the matter languished. A period was put on Moore's travails in 1759 when his petition to the king for relief was answered by an order of the Privy Council declaring that the Assembly had neither the right to imprison for contempt nor other parliamentary privileges including the right to impeach.[79]

The effort to impeach William Moore had a number of notable features pertinent to an inquiry into how the American constitution's founders would have understood impeachment. First, this was a "political" impeachment, both in its objectives and in its particulars. The colonial legislature was using impeachment as both a tool against individual misconduct and as a means of testing the powers of local popularly elected representatives against the monarchical or proprietary government. While some of the complaints lodged against Judge Moore might have been crimes, the Assembly was explicit in noting to the lieutenant governor that it sought to impeach Moore for "misdemeanours ... some of which are not cognizable in the ordinary courts of justice."[80] In other words, not only was the Pennsylvania Assembly familiar with the procedural niceties of British parliamentary impeachment, but it joined with Parliament in understanding impeachable "misdemeanors" as extending beyond indictable crime to a variety of official misbehavior.[81]

Second, and crucially, the Moore impeachment was well known to at least two Pennsylvania delegates to the 1787 Constitutional Convention – Robert Morris and Benjamin Franklin.[82] Morris was born in England in 1734, but emigrated to the colonies at the age of thirteen. By 1754, three years before the Smith–Moore imbroglio, he had become a partner in a prominent Philadelphia shipping and banking firm[83] and would surely have followed a case that was a *cause célèbre* not only among the colony's small business and political class, but in Britain, as well.[84]

In Franklin's case, we need not rely on that reasonable surmise because he was directly and personally involved. In 1757, Franklin, fifty-one years old and already an international celebrity, was a leader of the anti-proprietary party in the Assembly, which sent him to London as colonial agent.[85] While in London, Franklin was in constant correspondence with leaders of the Assembly and other friends at home. Several surviving letters to and from Franklin relate directly to the Smith–Moore controversy.[86] Moreover, Franklin consulted with the Assembly's representatives who argued Smith's appeal to the Privy Council, he was present at the hearing,[87] and he reported back to Pennsylvania about it.[88]

Franklin's pre-Revolutionary acquaintance with the intricacies of British and Pennsylvania impeachment practice was probably not restricted to the Smith–Moore affair, but likely included the previous Logan impeachment. In 1759, a book titled *An Historical Review of the Constitution and Government of Pennsylvania*,[89] which alludes to the Logan impeachment as part of its larger discussion of Pennsylvania constitutional history,[90] was anonymously published in London, to the apparent dismay of the Penn family. Franklin was widely reputed to be the book's author, he undoubtedly commissioned and contributed to it, and he certainly possessed and read it because he alluded to it in a 1759 letter to Isaac Norris.[91]

Colonial Impeachments in Massachusetts

The Impeachment of Samuel Vetch

Pennsylvania was not the only colony to have employed impeachment in its struggle with royal or proprietary authority. The first colonial impeachment of the 1700s occurred in Massachusetts. In the first decade of that century, Great Britain opposed France in the War of the Spanish Succession (1701–14),[92] a conflict ended by that same Peace of Utrecht so disgraceful in the eyes of many Britons that it produced the impeachments of its advocates Oxford, Bolingbroke, and Strafford in 1715.[93] At the time, France had its own colonial possessions in Canada and trade between English and French colonists was therefore illegal. In 1706, Samuel Vetch and three other merchant adventurers who had been engaging in this profitable, if illicit, commerce were impeached by the General Court of Massachusetts (the lower house of its legislature) for trading with the enemy. The case was complicated by the fact that royal governor Joseph Dudley was suspected, probably correctly, of connivance in the captains' ventures. The facts seemed clear enough, but resolution of the charges was complicated by the legislators' belated discovery that the 1691 Massachusetts charter had deprived the General Court of most of its judicial powers, permitting it to proceed, not with the charge of treason it might have preferred, but only on "High Misdemeanors." The General Court nonetheless impeached the captains and the council convicted them, after which a joint committee of the two houses voted a "bill of punishment" prescribing fines and imprisonment.[94] However, the Board of Trade back in London, perhaps unsettled by the legal irregularity of the process, suggested a new trial before regular courts, and the Privy Council, acting as a court of appeal, simply invalidated the bill of punishment and released the captains.[95]

Impeachment of Chief Justice Peter Oliver, 1774

Almost seventy years later, in 1774, in the midst of the ferment that would shortly produce open warfare between Britain and its American colonies, Massachusetts legislators attempted another impeachment, this time of Chief Justice Peter Oliver. The impetus was a struggle beginning in the 1760s over the independence of Massachusetts judges, a struggle that was itself part of the larger effort by the colonists to secure what they saw as the traditional rights of Englishmen.[96] In constitutional terms, the colonists wanted a judiciary that was independent in the sense that it would issue judgments based on statutes and the common law rather than acting as agents of the royal (or in the colonial case, gubernatorial or ministerial) will. In more pragmatic terms, many colonists wanted judges who would be sensitive to local interests and not slavishly follow the dictates of the royal governor or for that matter all the particulars of English law. One means of ensuring judicial independence is to make removal of judges for political reasons difficult. In Great Britain, this precept was embodied in a provision of the 1701 Act of Settlement which declared that judges' commissions remained valid *quamdiu se bene gesserint* (during good behavior) and that even misbehaving judges could be removed only by a vote of both Houses of Parliament.[97] However, the Act of Settlement was not deemed to apply to the colonies and requests by colonial legislatures for appointment of colonial judges on good behavior, rather than at pleasure of the crown, were repeatedly denied.[98]

Colonial legislatures therefore sought to ensure judicial independence – or at least independence from British officialdom – through local legislative control over judicial salaries. The effect of this legislative tactic on judicial psychology was doubtless enhanced because the legislatures commonly did not pay judges an established salary, but instead voted them annual grants.[99] The colonists recognized that even a judge who owed appointment and continuation in office to royal favor would be attentive to colonial concerns if his salary was set and paid by the colonial legislature. This hard-headed practical calculation about judicial motivations also jibed nicely with the growing insistence of colonial legislatures on control over the collection and expenditure of revenues. The famous slogan, "No Taxation without Representation," protested not only claims of parliamentary power to impose taxes without the consent of locally elected officials, but also embraced an assertion of the colonists' right to determine how and on whom locally raised revenue would be spent.

Until 1773, Massachusetts judges had been paid with annual (and rather stingy) grants voted by the legislature, which was known as the General Court and consisted of a lower House of Representatives and an upper house known as the Council.[100] In 1773, Parliament approved a bill granting colonial judges who held their commissions from the crown annual salaries paid by the British government, rather than by colonial assemblies. In Massachusetts, at least, the amounts designated by Parliament were markedly more generous than the local authorities had been willing to pay. In Boston, tumult ensued, with the General Court on one side, Governor Thomas Hutchinson on the other, and the judges in the middle.[101]

Hutchinson was a man of impeccable Massachusetts lineage but a staunch royalist, who during most of the 1760s served as both lieutenant governor and chief justice of the Massachusetts Superior Court.[102] In 1770, Hutchinson was elevated to the governorship. He first appointed Benjamin Lynde as his replacement in the chief justice's chair, and when in 1772 Lynde vacated the position, Hutchinson turned to his in-law Peter Oliver.[103] As soon as the legislature heard of the new bill granting judges royal salaries, it decried the measure as an assault on judicial independence and its own constitutional prerogatives. And it demanded that all the Superior Court judges declare their intentions – would they take the crown's corrupting gold? Four of the five judges prudently responded that they would accept only the parsimonious allowance from the legislature. Oliver, alone among his colleagues, said he felt bound to accept the royal salary. In his almost plaintive letter to the Assembly explaining his decision, Oliver claimed to have suffered financially for years due to the extreme modesty of the colonial legislators' annual grants and maintained that "without his Majesty's Leave, I dare not refuse [the royal salary] lest I should incur a Censure from the best of Sovereigns."[104]

Unswayed, on February 8, 1774, the House of Representatives voted Oliver's explanation unsatisfactory.[105] Three days later, the House voted out a remonstrance declaring Oliver unfit for office as an "Enemy to the Constitution of this Province" and asking Governor Hutchinson to remove him.[106] Hutchinson denied the remonstrance,[107] whereupon the House asked him to reconsider, this time after consultation with the Council,[108] to whom the House also transmitted the remonstrance.[109] On February 18, the entire House waited upon the governor bringing both their remonstrance and a petition for Oliver's removal.[110] Unsurprisingly, Hutchinson turned the Assembly down flat.[111] The royal governor was hardly likely to dismiss his own judicial appointee for agreeing to accept pay approved by the king in Parliament. Immediately upon receiving Hutchinson's refusal, the House resolved that it would impeach Oliver for "certain High Crimes and Misdemeanors" and appointed a committee to "prepare said Impeachment."[112]

On February 24, the House approved articles of impeachment.[113] The charges were really quite remarkable. The House relied on a claim of "privilege of the English Constitution" of supporting executive and judicial officers of the provincial government "by the free grants of the people." It maintained that the parliamentary enactment paying judges salaries laid a foundation for a "union" of the judiciary and the king's ministers "than which nothing is more to be dreaded by a free people."[114] The articles refer to Oliver's conduct as "high crimes and misdemeanors,"[115] but specify only two supposed offenses. They allege that Oliver's acceptance of an annual salary of £400 from the king is a "continual bribe," and they huffily claim that Oliver's letter explaining his reasons "misrepresented and traduced this government" and sought to alienate the people from the king.[116]

The governor and the legislature then re-enacted the debate that had embroiled Pennsylvania in 1758 in the impeachment of William Moore. The legislature claimed that the governor and council had the power to try an impeachment originating in the lower house, while the governor denied that he had any such power. One key difference was that, in Massachusetts, the council (which had more connections to the popular party than its cousin in Pennsylvania) apparently signaled its willingness to take up the matter. But Governor Hutchinson blocked any impeachment trial in the same way that English kings had sometimes done – by proroguing (dissolving) the legislature.[117]

Hutchinson succeeded in preventing Oliver's impeachment, but could not maintain him in office. The more radical element of the colonists protested violently, threatening Oliver and burning him in effigy.[118] Moreover, the grand jury of Suffolk County refused to serve while Oliver presided.[119] In the end, there was no alternative but for the harassed Oliver to relinquish his duties. He fled Boston in 1776 when the

British evacuated their troops and loyalist citizens, sailing to England from where he never returned.[120]

The Oliver impeachment is notable for the same basic reasons as the Moore case in Pennsylvania. First, to an even greater extent than the Moore affair, Oliver's impeachment was in the purest sense political. Moore's impeachment was an incident in a constitutional struggle between the proprietary and anti-proprietary factions of Pennsylvania, but Moore was reputedly a very bad, perhaps on occasion criminally bad, judge. By contrast, there was no whiff of scandal, corruption, or even ordinary professional incompetence about Oliver.[121] He was, as far as we know, a perfectly fine judge who took a stance at odds with the colonists' deeply held convictions about the governmental arrangements appropriate to free-born Englishmen in America. The specifics of the articles of impeachment make this point limpidly clear. The first alleges acceptance of a "bribe," but the use of the term is merely a rhetorical trick. It can hardly be bribery for an appointee of the British crown to accept the salary decreed by Parliament for his office. The second article, which does little more than express the offended dignity of the Massachusetts legislature, is even less substantial. Note also that the Massachusetts legislators employed the traditional British phrase "high crimes and misdemeanors" to describe conduct with no tincture of ordinary criminality or even technical violation of law. In sum, the dissident colonists seized on impeachment as a legislative tool in a constitutional quarrel. Following the path blazed by parliamentarians of the Stuart era, the Massachusetts legislators sought the ouster of an individual official in order to preserve their conception of liberty against what seemed to them encroaching arbitrary and tyrannical government.[122]

Second, the 1774 Oliver impeachment would have been even more familiar to both the constitutional framers and ratifiers of 1787–88 than the 1758 Moore affair. Not only were Oliver's travails widely publicized and substantially more recent, but important members of the founding generation whose influence extended far beyond Massachusetts were intimately involved.

It is commonly noted that John Adams, Massachusetts patriot, delegate to the Continental Congress, first vice president and second president of the United States, claimed to have originated the idea of dealing with Oliver through impeachment.[123] Whether Adams really came up with the idea is unclear. Certainly, his thinking may have been influenced by Josiah Quincy, his co-counsel in the Boston Massacre trial of 1770, who had written an extensive essay in 1768 examining British impeachment precedents, situating impeachment among the fundamental rights of a free people, and implying that the lower house of the colonial legislature possessed the same inherent authority as the House of Commons to impeach high-placed wrongdoers.[124] Regardless of its truth, Adams' claim of intellectual paternity is not insignificant because he was the primary author of the Massachusetts Constitution of 1780, with its impeachment provisions,[125] and of the 1776 essay *Thoughts on Government*,[126] which also addressed impeachment, both of which documents influenced the shape of the U.S. constitution.[127] Nonetheless, Adams was not a delegate to either the 1787 Philadelphia Convention or the Massachusetts ratifying convention of 1788 because he was serving as the first U.S. ambassador to England.[128]

However, it turns out that a striking number of other Massachusetts men who participated directly in either drafting or ratifying the federal constitution were also directly involved in the Oliver impeachment. Nathaniel Gorham, one of the four Massachusetts delegates to the Philadelphia Convention and later a delegate at the Massachusetts ratifying convention, was among the members of the Massachusetts House of Representatives who voted to impeach Justice Oliver.[129] In addition, first on the official roll of House members voting for Oliver's impeachment were Samuel Adams, notorious revolutionary rabble-rouser, and John Hancock, he of the large signature on the Declaration of Independence.[130] Both were delegates to the Massachusetts ratifying convention and Hancock was its president.[131] In addition to Adams and Hancock, fifteen other men both voted on the impeachment of Justice Oliver and served in the Massachusetts ratifying convention.[132] Another delegate to the Massachusetts ratifying convention, James Bowdoin,[133] had been a member of the governor's council in 1774 during the Oliver affair.[134] Finally, the vice-president of the Massachusetts ratifying convention was William Cushing,[135] one of the four Superior Court judges who avoided impeachment by refusing the royal salary Oliver accepted.[136]

Knowledge of the Oliver impeachment was not confined to Massachusetts. It was covered in the English press[137] and was notorious throughout the colonies.[138]

IMPEACHMENT IN THE NEWLY INDEPENDENT STATES, 1776–1888

On April 19, 1775, scarcely a year after the Oliver impeachment effort sputtered to a close, musket fire crackled across Lexington Green, and then down the road at Concord, and two months later at Bunker Hill.[139] The Englishmen, rebels and loyalists, who had been debating the fine points of legislative and executive power were now saying it with powder and ball. Fighting in Massachusetts produced a new unity among the colonies, which convened a Continental Congress, and on July 4, 1776 declared themselves "free and independent states." The war necessary to secure that independence would last seven years, formally ending only with the Treaty of Paris in 1783, but the rebel colonists treated the 1776 declaration as establishing a new set of free and sovereign states which required new governing arrangements.[140] Therefore, they set about writing constitutions for their new states while the tide of war ebbed and flowed up and down the Atlantic seaboard.

Twelve states adopted constitutions during the war.[141] Of these twelve, ten included straightforward impeachment provisions[142] and an eleventh, Maryland, included impeachment-like sections that permitted legislative removal of judges, but not executive branch officials.[143] Both the near-universality of the new states' adoption of impeachment and the particulars of the procedures they chose are important indicators of the thinking of the founding generation as it approached the task of writing a new national constitution. Fifteen of the delegates to the federal Constitutional Convention in Philadelphia had previously been directly involved in writing their state constitutions, and fourteen of those came from states that had included impeachment in their fundamental charters.[144] Among those who would make up the state ratifying conventions for the federal constitution, many would also have been delegates to their state constitutional conventions.

The fact that almost all the new states gave their legislatures impeachment power is not terribly surprising. Many American rebels conceived of their rupture from Great Britain not as revolution, but as preservation to themselves and their posterity of what they saw as the traditional rights of Englishmen unreasonably ripped from them by capricious English officials and the accident of their distance from the imperial center.[145] Integral to that traditional conception of English rights was the central role of a legislature that represented the interests of the people against the pretensions of monarchs and their ministerial or judicial hirelings. In England, the image of Parliament as the voice of the people was always more than a trifle fictitious inasmuch as the class of eligible voters was tiny and the class interests most vociferously represented even in the House of Commons were not those of the common man. But for the colonists, the centrality of legislative authority and suspicion of executive, and to a lesser extent judicial, power was even more natural given that, since the first settlements in North America, local legislators were the voice of local concerns, while governors and judges were directly beholden to the proprietor, the crown, or the British government at large.[146] The drafters of the new American constitutions were familiar with impeachment as a characteristic defensive power of legislatures against executive overreach or general official misbehavior, through both their knowledge of British history and, in some states, American experience in living memory.

Moreover, the notion of conferring judicial power on legislators, at least for special occasions, did not in those days have the alien flavor that such a thing now would. The idea of a strict separation of legislative, executive, and judicial powers between organizationally distinct branches of government was often cited by the revolutionary generation, and, as we will see, sometimes written directly into state constitutions. Nonetheless, it would remain for Mr. Madison and the other Philadelphia delegates to work out a satisfactory blend of separation of powers and interbranch checks. But that was years in the future. In revolutionary America – a vast territory contested between loyalists trying to maintain the old institutions and rebels trying to supplant them – the primary source of governing authority recognized as legitimate by those on the side of independence would have been the popularly elected assembly. The combination of tradition and wartime necessity made it natural to grant the assembly power to discipline erring officials and, for that matter, others guilty of hewing too close to the Tory line.

TABLE 3.1 *Bodies Responsible for Initiating and Trying Impeachment Proceedings*

State	Date	Initiator	Trier of Fact
Virginia	1776	House of Delegates	General Court (judges)
New Jersey	1776	Assembly	Council
Delaware	1776	House of Assembly	Legislative Council
Pennsylvania	1776	General Assembly	President or vice president and council
North Carolina	1776	General Assembly or Grand Jury of any court of supreme jurisdiction	General Assembly consisted of Senate and House of Commons. Implication is impeachment by General Assembly involved both houses.
New York	1777	Assembly	Special Court: president of Senate, senators, chancellor, judges of Supreme Court
Vermont	1777	General Assembly	Governor or lieutenant governor and council
South Carolina	1778	House of Representatives	Senate and judges not members of House of Representatives
Massachusetts	1780	House of Representatives	Senate
New Hampshire	1784	House of Representatives	Senate

What is most remarkable about the impeachment provisions of the first state constitutions is not that they existed, but the degree to which their details incorporate sophisticated lessons drawn from the successes and failures of both British and American impeachments of the preceding several centuries. To those we now turn.

To assist in the discussion, the most notable features of the states' impeachment architectures are summarized in three tables which identify each state's choice on the following points: Table 3.1 Bodies Responsible for Initiating and Trying Impeachment Proceedings; Table 3.2 Classes of Person Impeachable and Available Penalties; and Table 3.3 Scope of Impeachable Conduct. In addition, the full text of the impeachment provisions of the first American state constitutions is included at the end of the chapter as Appendix A.

Procedural Structure of State Impeachments

Most states adhered to the traditional parliamentary structure of impeachments – the lower house of the state legislature "impeached" or initiated the case and the upper house tried the matter. North Carolina had a unique provision permitting grand juries to initiate impeachments. In Pennsylvania[147] and Vermont,[148] which had unicameral legislatures, the trial court consisted of the executive council presided over by either its

TABLE 3.2 *Classes of Person Impeachable and Available Penalties*

State	Date	Persons Impeachable	Possible Penalties
Virginia	1776	"Governor, when he is out of office, and others offending against the state"	"either for ever disabled to hold any office under government, or be removed from such office *pro tempore*, or subjected to such pains or penalties as the laws shall direct"
New Jersey	1776	Judges, clerks of court, attorney general, provincial secretary, provincial treasurer	"shall be liable to be dismissed"
Delaware	1776	"President [governor], when he is out of office, and within 18 months thereafter, and all others offending against the State"	"either forever disabled to hold any office under government, or be removed from such office pro tempore, or subjected to such pains or penalties as the laws shall direct"
Pennsylvania	1776	"Every officer of state, whether judicial or executive . . . either when in office, or after his resignation, or removal for maladministration"	?
North Carolina	1776	"Governor and other Officers offending against the State"	?
New York	1777	"all officers of the State"	Judgment shall not "extend farther than to removal from office, and disqualification to hold or enjoy any place of honor, trust, or profit under this State. But the party so convicted shall be, nevertheless, liable and subject to indictment, trial, judgment, and punishment, according to the laws of the land."
Vermont	1777	"Every officer of state, whether judicial or executive . . . either when in office, or after his resignation, or removal for maladministration"	"removal" and ?

TABLE 3.2 *(continued)*

State	Date	Persons Impeachable	Possible Penalties
South Carolina	1778	"all officers of the state" [Judges serve during "good behavior," but removable by joint address of house and senate]	?
Massachusetts	1780	"any officer or officers of the Commonwealth"	Judgment "shall not extend further than to removal from office, and disqualification to hold or enjoy any place of honor, trust, or profit under this commonwealth; but the party so convicted shall be, nevertheless, liable to indictment, trial, judgment, and punishment, according to the laws of the land"
New Hampshire	1784	"any officer or officers of the state"	Judgment "shall not extend further than removal from office, disqualification to hold or enjoy any place of honor, trust, or profit, under this state, but the party so convicted, shall nevertheless be liable to indictment, trial, judgment, and punishment, according to the laws of the land"

president or vice president (in Vermont, the "governor" or lieutenant governor"). New York and South Carolina convened special hybrid courts made up of senators and judges. The idea of giving the judiciary a place in impeachment resurfaced in the federal Constitutional Convention, but the only role accorded judges in the final arrangement was the designation of the chief justice of the Supreme Court as the largely ceremonial presiding officer in senate impeachment trials.[149]

Persons Subject to Impeachment and Available Penalties

Five of the state constitutions (North Carolina, New York, South Carolina, Massachusetts, and New Hampshire) provided for impeachment of all state officials, with no express limitation on whether the officer was in the executive, judicial, or legislative branch.[150] Pennsylvania and Vermont limited impeachment to executive

TABLE 3.3 *Scope of Impeachable Conduct*

State	Date	Definition of Impeachable Conduct
Virginia	1776	"offending against the state, either by maladministration, corruption, or other means by which the safety of the state may be endangered"
New Jersey	1776	"when adjudged guilty of Misbehaviour"
Delaware	1776	"offending against the State, either by maladministration, corruption, or other means, by which the safety of the Commonwealth may be endangered"
Pennsylvania	1776	"general assembly ... may ... impeach state criminals"
North Carolina	1776	"offending against the State, by violating any Part of this Constitution, Mal-Administration, or Corruption"
New York	1777	"mal and corrupt conduct in their respective offices"
Vermont	1777	"general assembly ... may ... impeach state criminals"
South Carolina	1778	"mal and corrupt conduct in their respective offices, not amenable to any other jurisdiction"
Massachusetts	1780	"for misconduct and mal-administration in their offices"
New Hampshire	1784	"bribery, corruption, malpractice or maladministration, in office"

and judicial officers. New Jersey specified a limited and idiosyncratic list of impeachable officials. The constitutions of Virginia and Delaware at least implied that anyone, whether in an official position or not, would be impeachable if found to be "offending against the state."

Not all states designated the array of punishment possible upon conviction, but seven restricted penalties for impeachment to removal from office, with five specifying that any punishment beyond removal would have to follow from conviction in a regular court of law. When compared with the British practice from which American impeachment derives, this was a critical innovation, to which we will return below.

The Definition of Impeachable Conduct

The most commonly recurring grounds for impeachment included "maladministration" (five states, or possibly six[51]); "misconduct," "malpractice," or "mal conduct" while "in office," which may mean nothing materially different than "maladministration" (four states); and corruption or "corrupt conduct" (six states). Bribery is mentioned once, as is "Misbehavior."

Both Pennsylvania and Vermont (which copied its impeachment provisions directly from Pennsylvania) speak of impeachment of "state criminals." This phrase implies both that the legislature can act as grand jury and trial court for ordinary crimes and that impeachment is limited to indictable offenses. But we can be fairly sure that the phrase "state criminals" in this context did not carry its apparent meaning. First, the notion of impeachment for "crimes" plainly derived from the language of the Pennsylvania colonial charter documents discussed above, but we know that Pennsylvania's colonists did not read that language as requiring indictable offenses. As demonstrated above, the impeachments of Judge Nicholas Moore in 1685 and James Logan in 1707 were purely political and few if any of the charges enumerated in the articles of impeachment were common law crimes.[152] It is not unreasonable to suppose that the Pennsylvanians who wrote the 1776 constitution employed both traditional Pennsylvania legal language and traditional local inter-pretation of it. Second, if there were any doubt, in 1786, Vermont amended its constitution to eliminate the implication that the legislature should be acting as an ordinary criminal court, specifying that, "No person ought, in any case, or in any time, to be declared guilty of treason or felony by the Legislature."[153] Probably the best reading of the enigmatic phrase "state criminals" would be something like "persons who have gravely offended against the state, especially in some official capacity."

This theme of official conduct presenting a danger to the fundamental interests of the state is explicit in the constitutions of Virginia, Delaware, and North Carolina. Virginia specifies that impeachments should lie against those *"offending against the state*, either by mal-administration, or *other means by which the safety of the state may be endangered."*[154] Delaware adopted nearly identical language.[155] The choice of the word "safety" may be a reflection of the fact that these were wartime constitu-tions and thus that the citizens were concerned, not only about the danger ever-present even in peacetime of the insidious rot of ordinary official misconduct, but about the literal danger of conquest and dissolution by the British army. Nonetheless, the conjunction of the terms "mal-administration [and] corruption" with the phrase "or other means by which the safety of the state may be endangered" suggests a focus beyond the exigencies of war on types of conduct particularly inimical to republican government.

North Carolina's constitution is consistent with this theme, prescribing impeach-ment for "offending *against the State, by violating any Part of this Constitution*, Mal-Administration, or Corruption."[156] The danger most to be feared, as the Stuart parliaments consistently repeated, is conduct that subverts the constitution.

The most striking absence from all these state constitutions is the iconic parlia-mentary phrase "high crimes and misdemeanors," so redolent of fundamental clashes between legislature and executive over matters of power and principle. As we have seen, the political class in the colonies had become careful students of parliamentary history generally and in some cases of the particulars of impeachment precedent. The phrase would not have been strange to them. Their American predecessors, and in the Oliver case they themselves,[157] had deployed it in colonial impeachments. Yet none of the states adopted it. We cannot know exactly why, but it is reasonable to speculate that it was associated in the Americans' minds with the historic clashes between legislature and monarch, and thus felt somehow inappropriate for the new republican world into which they were launching themselves. It may also have been that "high crimes and misdemeanors" carried the implication of conduct for which serious, even fatal, penalties had in British tradition been imposed. As illustrated in Table 3.2, the overwhelming majority of the first state constitutions limited the direct consequences of impeachment to removal from office, leaving any additional punishment to the operation of the ordinary courts. In short, the standards of impeachable conduct adopted by the states suggest that most envisioned *their* impeachments as a fairly routine mechanism of governmental housekeeping, rather than as a species of Sword Excalibur to be unsheathed only on grave constitutional occasions. Or perhaps the drafters of the new state constitutions found "high crimes and misdemeanors" every bit as enigmatic as readers of the American constitution have done since 1787, and they decided to stick to simpler language.

Impeachment Practice in the States, 1776–87

At all events, the young states used impeachment frequently, mostly as a vehicle for dealing with ordinary corruption. Hoffer and Hull suggest that bribery, extortion, and misuse of public funds were the most commonly impeached behaviors.[158] However, a number of cases they list in this category seem more like accusations of disloyalty to the revolutionary cause. For example, the 1778 impeachment of Judge Denny of New Jersey in part for giving bail to a man who had taken an oath to the king was in essence an accusation that the judge himself was disloyal to the revolutionary cause.[159] The New Jersey impeachments of William Clayton on the ground that he "favored persons disaffected to the present government" and Justice of the Peace William Miller for speaking "seditious words and telling people to lay down their arms" fall into the same category.[160] Almost all the true corruption cases would, in modern America, be dealt with as public corruption prosecutions in the ordinary courts. But late eighteenth-century America had not yet invented the institutions with which we now address this problem. There were no regular police forces, no professional prosecutors' offices, and certainly no specialized joint anti-corruption units. Particularly if the offending official was a powerful local figure or perhaps a judge of regional or statewide jurisdiction, the legislature was the only body with the authority to investigate and try such a person. As the capacity of the regular courts and their supporting institutions matured in the years following the revolution, impeachment for garden-variety corruption became less and less necessary. Likewise, once the war was over and questions of loyalty were no longer urgent, impeachment as, in effect, an instrument of revolutionary tribunals disappeared.

Another common ground of impeachment in the new states, particularly for judges, was abuse of authority.[161] Judges in both Great Britain and America have perennially been the targets of impeachment because their discretionary powers are so broad and the means of redress for judicial overreach sometimes so limited.

At least two revolutionary era impeachments or near-impeachments seem to fit into the broad category of being political in the sense of partisan efforts to strike at real or perceived abuses by those of an opposing party holding high office in the state. In 1781, a delegate to the Virginia legislature introduced a resolution to inquire into Thomas Jefferson's conduct as governor, both in regard to his general handling of matters related to the war and in particular to his flight from Virginia's capitol during the British invasion of June of that year. The effort sputtered out, but contemporaries conceived of it as an attempt to impeach.[162] And in North Carolina, a complex dispute over property of former loyalists pitted the judges of the superior court against the state bar and many in the legislature, leading to an unsuccessful attempt to impeach the judges.[163] Hoffer and Hull say of this and similar events that, "they displayed to all Americans who watched state government that impeachment was an appropriate instrument of republican rule."[164]

THE INFLUENCE OF EARLY AMERICAN IMPEACHMENTS
ON THE AMERICAN CONSTITUTIONAL FOUNDERS

As the delegates gathered in Philadelphia in May 1787, the founding generation they represented would have entertained several different models of impeachment. Parliamentary impeachments and almost all of those in the last seventy-five years of the colonial period would have disposed them to see impeachment as a tool of high politics to be wielded against otherwise untouchable men of power, and on some special occasions as a means of preserving or shaping basic constitutional values. Some state constitutional impeachment provisions pointed to this model – particularly Virginia, Delaware, and North Carolina, with their emphasis on conduct that endangered the state or imperiled the constitution. On the other hand, the majority of the state constitutional impeachment provisions point to a more prosaic tool for anti-corruption law enforcement and the everyday governmental management task of rooting out entrenched incompetents. The overwhelming majority of cases brought in the states between 1776 and 1787 fell into this prosaic category. Whether the Philadelphia delegates would adopt one model to the exclusion of the other, look for some middle ground, or dispense with impeachment as a mechanism unnecessary in the novel national government soon to be born remained to be seen.

Nonetheless, there were certainly some auguries in prior American experience that pointed to the result ultimately written into the constitution. First, while there may have been differing conceptions of the value and proper uses of impeachment, both historical memory and experience with post-independence constitution-making and practical governance seem to have established a nearly continent-wide consensus that impeachment belonged in a proper republican government. Certainly, impeachment fitted seamlessly into those views of a proper constitution which placed the legislature at the fulcrum of power. If the constitution that emerged from Philadelphia was one that made the legislature its predominant organ, an impeachment power would surely be included.

Second, it is probably not insignificant that both James Madison, the principal architect of the constitutional structure, and George Mason, the original proponent of including "high crimes and misdemeanors" as the base definition of impeachable conduct, were from Virginia and had played key roles in the adoption of that state's broad impeachment provisions.[165] Nor should it be forgotten that delegates Benjamin Franklin of Pennsylvania and Nathaniel Gorham of Massachusetts had played personal roles in the Moore and Oliver cases in which, at least in patriot memories, liberty-loving legislators brandished impeachment against the agents of autocratic power.

Finally, American experience pre- and post-Revolution demonstrates that Americans had perceived and solved one of the central dilemmas of the British impeachment process. Parliamentary impeachments often struggled with the fact that they were political in purpose, but criminal in effect. That is, the weapon of impeachment was classically employed as a legislative means of counteracting royal power by removal of key official agents of that power. But because British politics, governance, military affairs, and economy were so intertwined and personal, it was long felt that conviction in a state trial must be attended by consequences severe enough – imprisonment, forfeiture of lands and titles, impoverishment, even death – to take the impeached official off the board entirely. Any verdict that left the vanquished defendant with the means to make a political comeback left the victors in future peril.

Given the difficulty of defining in advance the kind of official behavior that might imperil the constitutional order, or at least merit removal from office, parliamentary impeachments were often subject to the objection that the defendant was being tried and punished *as if he were a criminal* for conduct never previously defined as criminal. The combination of a broad, and at times retrospective, definition of impeachable conduct with severe penalties far in excess of mere displacement from office made impeachment morally doubtful and practically difficult.

Americans both before and after the Revolution solved the problem by making impeachment a purely political event in which removal from office was the only punishment that could be imposed absent a separate judicial proceeding conducted under ordinary criminal law rules. In none of the pre-1776 colonial impeachments did the colonial legislatures seek any remedy beyond removal of the offending official. And the same limitation was almost universal in the post-1776 constitutions. This relative lenity was made possible by the character of colonial and early American society and government. Even before independence, government office did not customarily carry with it titles or vast wealth in money or land. With rare exceptions, public office was something one did in addition to however one earned the bulk of one's living. After independence, the resolutely republican framers of the new state constitutions were even more determined to separate office-holding from wealth and power. In state after state, they barred hereditary office-holding, aristocratic titles, and the maintenance of multiple offices.[166] And they prescribed modest salaries for public officials, strictly controlled by the legislature.[167] In such an environment, few if any officeholders on the British, and then American, Atlantic coast were so powerful that prudence required crushing them as an incident of removing them from office.

The Americans' strict limitation on the consequences of impeachment allowed a corresponding relaxation of concern about the breadth of the definition of impeachable conduct. Several of the state constitutions had hardly any definition at all, speaking of "misbehavior," being a "state criminal," or simply offending against the state in some generally dangerous way. Troublesome though this sort of language would be in a criminal setting, it makes perfect sense if the point of impeachment is to protect the commonwealth against bad governance, rather than to inflict personal punishment on an official miscreant.

Perhaps the most obvious influence of the prior American experience with impeachment on the framers of the federal constitution is in this point. Article 1, section 3, is drawn almost verbatim from the constitutions of Massachusetts, New York, and New Hampshire, stating: "Judgment in Cases of Impeachment shall not extend further than to removal from Office, and disqualification to hold and enjoy any Office of honor, Trust or Profit under the United States: but the Party convicted shall nevertheless be liable and subject to Indictment, Trial, Judgment and Punishment, according to Law." As I will argue in Chapter 4, the narrow scope of punishment written into the federal constitution suggests that the framers intended a correspondingly expansive definition of the conduct that merits impeachment.

APPENDIX A

Impeachment Provisions of State Constitutions, 1776–87

Between the Declaration of Independence in July 1776 and the Constitutional Convention in the summer of 1787, twelve states adopted constitutions. Ten of them included explicit provisions for impeachment, and Maryland's document contained provisions for legislative removal of judges and for the lower house to act as a kind of grand jury to inquire into wrongdoing in government and elsewhere. The impeachment provisions of the ten constitutions including them are set out below in the order of adoption of the state constitutions, followed by Maryland's impeachment-like sections.

Virginia, June 1776
The Governor, when he is out of office, and others, offending against the state, either by mal-administration, corruption, or other means by which the safety of the state

may be endangered, shall be impeachable by the House of Delegates. Such impeachment to be prosecuted ... in the General Court, according to the laws of the land. If found guilty, he or they shall be either for ever disabled to hold any office under government, or be removed from such office pro tempore, or subjected to such pains or penalties as the laws shall direct.[168]

[T]he judges of the General Court ... may, in like manner, [be] impeach [ed] ...[169]

New Jersey, July 1776

The Judges of the Supreme Court ... the Judges of the Inferior Court of Common Pleas in the several Counties, Justices of the Peace, Clerks of the Supreme Court, clerks of the Inferior Court of Common Pleas and Quarter Sessions, the Attorney General ... and the Provincial Treasurer ... shall be liable to be dismissed, when adjudged guilty of Misbehaviour by the Council on an Impeachment of the Assembly.[170]

Delaware, September 1776

The president [governor], when he is out of office, and within eighteen months after, and all others offending against the State, either by maladministration, corruption, or other means, by which the safety of the Commonwealth may be endangered, within eighteen months after the offence committed, shall be impeachable by the house of assembly before the legislative council; such impeachment to be prosecuted by the attorney-general or such other person or persons as the house of assembly may appoint, according to the laws of the land. If found guilty, he or they shall be either forever disabled to hold any office under government, or removed from office pro tem, or subjected to such pains and penalties as the laws shall direct. And all officers shall be removed on conviction of misbehavior at common law, or on impeachment, or upon the address of the general assembly.[171]

Pennsylvania, September 1776

The general assembly of the representatives of the freemen of Pennsylvania ... may ... impeach state criminals ...[172]

Every officer of state, whether judicial or executive, shall be liable to be impeached by the general assembly, either when in office, or after his resignation, or removal for mal-administration: All impeachments shall be before the president or vice president and council, who shall hear and determine the same.[173]

The judges of the supreme court of judicature shall ... be commissioned for seven years only, though capable of re-appointment at the end of that term, but removable for misbehavior at any time by the general assembly ...[174]

North Carolina, December 1776

[T]he Governor, and other officers offending against the State, by violating any Part of this Constitution, Mal-Administration, or Corruption, may be prosecuted on the Impeachment of the General Assembly[175] or presentment of the Grand Jury of any court of supreme jurisdiction in this State.[176]

New York, April 1777

[A] court shall be instituted for the trial of impeachments and the correction of errors, under regulations which shall be established by the legislature to consist of the president of the senate, for the time being, and the senators, chancellor, and judges of the supreme court, or the major part of them; except that when an impeachment shall be prosecuted against the chancellor, or either of the judges of the supreme court, the person so impeached shall be suspended from exercising his office until his acquittal . . .[177]

That the power of impeaching all officers of the State for mal and corrupt conduct in their respective offices, be vested in the representatives of the people in assembly: but that it shall always be necessary that two third parts of the members present shall consent to and agree in such impeachment. That previous to the trial of every impeachment, the members of the said court shall respectively be sworn truly and impartially to try and determine the charge in question, according to evidence; and that no judgment of the said court shall be valid unless it be assented to by two third parts of the members then present; nor shall it extend farther than to removal from office, and disqualification to hold or enjoy any place of honor, trust, or profit under this State. But the party so convicted shall be, nevertheless, liable and subject to indictment, trial, judgment, and punishment, according to the laws of the land.[178]

Vermont, July 1777

The General Asembly [sic] of the Representatives of the Freemen of Vermont . . . may . . . impeach State criminals.[179]

Every officer of state, whether judicial or executive, shall be liable to be impeached by the General Assembly, either when in office, or after his resignation, or removal for maladministration. All impeachments shall be before the Governor or Lieutenant Governor and Council, who shall hear and determine the same.[180]

Added in Vermont Constitution of 1786:

No person ought, in any case, or in any time, to be declared guilty of treason or felony by the Legislature.[181]

South Carolina, March 1778

That the form of impeaching all officers of the state for mal and corrupt conduct in their respective offices, not amenable to any other jurisdiction, be vested in the house of representatives. But . . . it shall always be necessary that two-third parts of the members present do consent to and agree in such impeachment. That the senators and such of the judges of this State as are not members of the house of representatives, be a court for the trial or impeachments, under such regulations as the legislature shall establish, and that previous to the trial or every impeachment, the members of the said court shall respectively be sworn truly and impartially to try and determine the charge in question according to evidence, and no judgment of the said court, except judgment of acquittal, shall be valid, unless it shall be assented to by two-third parts of the members then present, and on every trial, as well as on impeachments as others, the party accused shall be allowed counsel.[182]

[A]ll . . . judicial officers [except justices of the peace] shall be chosen by ballot, jointly by the senate and house of representatives, and, except for the judges of the court of chancery, commissioned by the governor and commander-in-chief during good behavior, but shall be removed on address of the senate and house of representatives.[183]

Massachusetts, March 1780

The House of Representatives shall be the Grand Inquest of this Commonwealth; and all impeachments made by them shall be heard and tried by the Senate . . .[184]

The Senate shall be a court with full authority to hear and determine all impeachments made by the House of Representatives, against any officer or officers of the Commonwealth, for misconduct and mal-administration in their offices. But, previous to the trial of every impeachment, the members of the senate shall, respectively, be sworn truly and impartially to try and determine the charge in question, according to the evidence. Their judgment, however, shall not extend further than to removal from office, and disqualification to hold or enjoy any place of honor, trust, or profit under this commonwealth; but the party so convicted shall be, nevertheless, liable to indictment, trial, judgment, and punishment, according to the laws of the land.[185]

New Hampshire, June 1784

The house of representatives shall be the grand inquest of the state; and all impeachments made by them, shall be heard and tried by the senate.[186]

The senate shall be a court with full power and authority to hear, try, and determine, all impeachments made by the house of representatives against any officer or officers of the state, for bribery, corruption, malpractice or maladministration, in office. But previous to the trial of any such impeachment, the members of the senate shall respectively be sworn, truly and impartially to try and determine the charge in question according to evidence. Their judgment, however, shall not extend further than removal from office, disqualification to hold or enjoy any place of honor, trust, or profit, under this state, but the party so convicted, shall nevertheless be liable to indictment, trial, judgment, and punishment, according to the laws of the land.[187]

Maryland, 1776
Declaration of Rights, Article XXX
That the independency and uprightness of Judges are essential to the impartial administration of justice, and a great security to the rights and liberties of the people; wherefore the Chancellor and Judges ought to hold commissions during good behavior; and the said Chancellor and Judges shall be removed for misbehavior, on conviction in a court of law, and may be removed by the Governor, upon the address of the General Assembly; Provided, That two-thirds of all the members of each House concur in such address.[188]
Maryland Constitution (Form of Government), Article X
The House of Delegates ... may inquire on the oath of witnesses, into all complaints, grievances, and offences, as the grand inquest of this State; and may commit any person, for any crime, to the public jail, there to remain till he be discharged by due course of law. They may expel any member, for a great misdemeanor, but not a second time for the same cause.[189]

4

The Founders' Impeachment

In May 1787, an irregular collection of men from up and down the Atlantic coast began to trickle into Philadelphia to discuss the condition of the union of American states. Some reconsideration of the relations among what, since the Declaration of Independence, the Americans had been pleased to call the "United States of America" was plainly necessary. The Articles of Confederation, drafted in haste by the Second Continental Congress during the chaos of the first revolutionary winter of 1776–77 and ratified by all thirteen states in 1781,[1] created a governing compact between the states. But most Americans who wanted to see the thirteen states continue as a single country recognized that the articles were perilously flawed.

The articles insisted that "each state retains its sovereignty, freedom, and independence,"[2] and purported to be no more than "a firm league of friendship" and pact of mutual assistance.[3] The articles created a congress in which each state had an equal vote, but the national Congress could neither levy direct taxes[4] nor compel any state to comply with national law. Remarkably, they provided for no national executive officer or executive departments.[5] The closest approximation to a national executive was a "Committee of the States," consisting of one representative from each state, which was to sit when Congress was in recess and manage the affairs of the federation under the leadership of a presiding officer. But the presiding officer had no special authority and the committee could act only upon a supermajority vote of nine member states.[6] Finally, the articles neither created a national judiciary nor authorized Congress to create national courts, except for cases of piracy and adjudicating prize cases.[7]

The 1783 Treaty of Paris formalizing the Americans' release from Britain's embrace was a moment for rejoicing, but self-governance proved to be an immediate challenge. The national government found it impossible to impose taxes itself or induce the states to pay their share of national expenditures.[8] The states fell to squabbling over boundaries, trade, and much else. Discontents within states led to open violence, most notably Shay's Rebellion in 1786.[9] Foreign powers sought to make separate accommodations with different states, whether for short-term commercial advantage or in the hopes of gaining fragments of the confederation as allies, tributaries, or colonies.[10] In sum, the Articles were a wartime expedient adequate, if barely, for the exigencies of the Revolution, but completely unsuited for the predictable problems of managing a continent-spanning nation.

Not all Americans found this state of affairs insupportable. Some were willing to tolerate the shortcomings of the Articles to preserve state freedom of action. Some imagined the ideal America as populated by a number of independent states or confederations of states. However, those favoring unity realized that change was required. In Congress and among the leadership circles that had met and grown to trust each other across state lines during the war, sentiment grew for a move toward stronger national government. The first formal expression of this sentiment was the Annapolis Convention of 1786, a deceivingly grand name for a September gathering of twelve delegates from five states at Mann's Tavern in Maryland's shoreline capital.[11] Although few in number, the attendees included names that would become legendary in U.S. constitutional history, including Alexander Hamilton, John Dickinson, Edmund Randolph, and James Madison.[12] The primary result of the conference was a resolution drafted by Hamilton calling for a meeting the following May in Philadelphia:

> to take into consideration the situation of the United States, to devise such further provisions as shall appear to them necessary to render the constitution of the Federal Government adequate to the exigencies of the Union; and to report such an Act for that purpose to the United States in Congress assembled, as when agreed to, by them, and afterwards confirmed by the Legislatures of every State, will effectually provide for the same.[13]

Over the next year, the call from Annapolis produced a sometimes grudging agreement by twelve states to send delegations to the Philadelphia meeting (Rhode Island declined the invitation).[14] The reluctance extended beyond the act of agreement to the behavior of the delegates themselves once chosen. The conduct of many of them was at odds with our romantic vision of a committed body debating tensely throughout the summer and united, if not in their vision of what should emerge, at least in their sense of the transcendent significance of the task. In truth, there was considerable uncertainty, even among the delegates, about the precise purpose of the meeting. Some came committed to producing, then and there, an entirely new constitutional design to replace the Articles. Others thought the objective was merely to propose helpful amendments to the Articles. Still others may have thought of the Philadelphia meeting as merely a preliminary round of discussions preparatory to another gathering later. Even those most committed to crafting a governmental framework had the gravest doubts that such a thing could be done, then or later.

Whether for reasons of substance, or just because of the difficulty of traveling long distances in eighteenth-century America, many delegates straggled into

Philadelphia long after the nominal start date of the second week of May, with some arriving as late as July after most of the main work had been done. Others (Alexander Hamilton notable among them[15]) drifted in and out of the convention as the call of personal or business affairs drew them back home. Some delegates left early, either out of disapproval of the impending product or for other reasons, and were not around for the final votes in September. If the framers were demigods, they were an often inconstant and inattentive batch of deities.

Among the first to arrive, on May 13, was George Washington.[16] He and one other delegate, Benjamin Franklin, were the two personifications of the new country in the eyes of the rest of the world. But they projected quite different images: Franklin, the homespun philosopher, wit, man of science, and earthy satyr; Washington, more patrician than the British aristocrats he had defeated in the Revolution, a reincarnation of early Roman virtue triumphant against the decadence of empire. Their joint presence lent the gathering heft, but Washington was the essential man. Any proceeding to which Washington lent his countenance would be warmly viewed by a great fraction of the country.

Franklin's presence, if not indispensable, was also immensely useful. In addition to his international stature, he brought decades of careful study and practical experience in politics, diplomacy, and governance in America, Great Britain, and France. Franklin would say relatively little that summer, confining himself primarily to avuncular nudges toward cooperation and compromise. One subject on which he was vocal, though in his characteristically elliptical way, was impeachment.

Although the mere presence of Washington and Franklin gave the Philadelphia meeting credibility, a bevy of less celebrated figures would do the heavy intellectual work. Some were already well known for their contributions to the early debates over American constitutional structure. John Dickinson, who had been the president of both Delaware and Pennsylvania, chaired the committee which prepared the first draft of the Articles of Confederation.[17] George Mason of Virginia, who would introduce the phrase "high Crimes and Misdemeanors" into the American consti-tution, was renowned as the author of the Virginia Declaration of Rights,[18] adopted in June 1776[19] as the preamble to the Virginia state constitution, which was itself largely drafted by Mason.[20] Mason's declaration of rights was hailed at the time, both in America and abroad, as a towering achievement.[21] Six other states made declara-tions of rights part of their first state constitutions.[22] And Mason's declaration led directly to the American Bill of Rights adopted as the first ten amendments to the constitution.[23]

Far less prominent at the beginning of the convention was another Virginian, the diminutive scholar James Madison. His relatively low profile was signaled by the fact that, although he was the principal author of the so-called "Virginia Plan" that became the basis for much of the debate that summer,[24] it was put forward to the convention by Edmund Randolph, Virginia's governor.[25] Of course, Madison is now hailed as the primary architect of the constitutional structure that emerged from the

Philadelphia meeting. But even his contributions, however significant, were only part of the collective work.

The story of what happened in Philadelphia in the summer of 1787 once enough delegates had gathered to gavel proceedings to order has been often told. The whole saga will not be replayed here. Nonetheless, even though this book is devoted to the single, discrete, and apparently narrow topic of impeachment, one cannot really understand impeachment in the American or any other system unless one first understands the constitutional framework of which it is a part. For example, as we saw in Chapter 2, impeachment was invented by the British as a parliamentary weapon against royal overreach, but was largely abandoned once kings and queens lost their governing authority and Parliament assumed shared sovereignty with the crown and gained practical control over government. Similarly, as we saw in Chapter 3, colonial legislatures adopted the forms of impeachment as a symbolic means of claiming parity with Parliament and as a mechanism to express displeasure with proprietary or royal appointees, but in the new post-revolutionary American states, impeachment became primarily a pragmatic means of fighting corruption and official misconduct in a period when states' legal systems were disrupted by war and slowly organizing themselves during the peace.

Therefore, before we consider the constitution's impeachment provisions, we must survey the structural decisions the framers made about the government as a whole.

CONSTITUTIONAL ARCHITECTURE

The Philadelphia delegates' most basic decision was that the new government would have three branches: legislative, executive, and judicial. To us, this seems such an obvious choice as scarcely to merit comment, but it was not quite so obvious at the time. The empire from which the United States had recently divorced had been mingling the lawmaking, administrative, and adjudicative functions of government for centuries. Indeed, impeachment arose as one weapon in the struggle by Parliament to wrest from the Crown an independent lawmaking power, a recognition of judicial authority resting on common and statutory law rather than royal prerogative, and some means of controlling abuses by the monarch's ministers. Yet the parliamentary government that emerged from the turmoil of the seventeenth and early eighteenth centuries still commingled executive, legislative, and judicial authority.

Where once the monarch had proclaimed complete personal sovereignty, resting on divine ordinance, Parliament was quickly assuming sovereign power itself, and asserting not only supreme lawmaking responsibility, but also both executive and judicial authority. Increasingly, the monarch's chief ministers were simply the leaders of the majority faction in Parliament, who then assumed both legislative and executive power. Likewise, until our own century,[26] the ultimate judicial authority in Great Britain lay in the "Law Lords," a special committee of the House of Lords.[27] The American colonists were conscious of the commingling of functions in Britain's parliamentary model as it existed at the time of the Revolution.[28] But they were also much influenced by the writings of the French philosopher and jurist Montesquieu, who divined from his examination of the British parliamentary system the principle we call the separation of powers.[29] In his 1748 book, *The Spirit of the Laws*, Montesquieu declared that:

> When the legislative and executive powers are united in the same person, or in the same body of magistrates, there can be no liberty; because apprehensions may arise, lest the same monarch or senate should enact tyrannical laws, to execute them in a tyrannical manner.
>
> Again, there is no liberty if the judiciary power be not separated from the legislative and executive. Were it joined with the legislative, the life and liberty of the subject would be exposed to arbitrary control; for the judge would be then the legislator. Were it joined to the executive power, the judge might behave with violence and oppression.
>
> There would be an end of every thing, were the same man, or the same body, whether of the nobles or of the people, to exercise those three powers, that of enacting laws, that of executing the public resolutions, and of trying the causes of individuals.[30]

The first implication of the separation principle for constitution writers was that government should consist of three, largely impermeable, branches. Almost all of the pre-1787 state constitutions were constructed on this model, and more than half explicitly declared separation of powers as a fundamental principle of government. George Mason's Virginia Declaration of Rights proclaimed, "That the legislative and executive Powers of the State should be separate and distinct from the judicative . . ."[31] Six other states wrote separation of powers into their constitutions, not merely as an implicit design principle, but as an expressly stated right of the people.[32]

Clear separation of powers was not a universally accepted tenet. The Articles of Confederation, with neither a distinct executive nor a meaningful judicial branch,[33] retained some defenders, or at least persons who thought that the source of the country's difficulties lay elsewhere than in questions of governmental structure. And several states were operating under constitutions with very muddled allocations of authority. The Pennsylvania constitution of 1776 (copied in large measure by Vermont[34]) provided for a weak group executive consisting of a president and council, the council to be directly elected by the citizens, and the president to be elected by joint vote of the unicameral legislature and the members of the council.[35] Confusing the lines of separation still further, all members of the council automatically became justices of the peace of the commonwealth.[36]

Nonetheless, all the plans for a reconfigured American government advanced in the convention adopted some variation of the tripartite Montesquieu model. The first two proposals were Madison's Virginia Plan and the framework offered by Charles Pinckney of South Carolina,[37] both laid before the convention on May 29, 1787.[38] These were followed several weeks later by the William Paterson propositions (also known as the New Jersey Plan) of June 15[39] and Alexander Hamilton's proposal of June 18.[40] All four were based on a structure of three distinct branches: legislative, executive, and judicial.

Despite this basic similarity, there were significant disagreements about how the three branches should be structured and how they should relate to each other. The framers considered the legislature to be the naturally dominant branch,[41] and thus spent more time and energy on its design than on any other question. The first issue was whether the legislature should consist of one or two houses. The Virginia, Pinckney, and Hamilton plans all proposed a bicameral legislature. Paterson's New Jersey Plan, a product of the small states' fear of any legislative arrangement basing representation on population,[42] would have retained the unicameral legislature of the Articles of Confederation, with each state having a single vote. The impasse between the smaller and larger states over this question was famously resolved by the so-called "Connecticut Compromise," which provided a bicameral legislature with a house of representatives chosen according to population and a senate in which each state would have equal representation.[43]

The adoption of a bicameral legislature is important for our purposes because it opened the door for replication of the procedural model of impeachment drawn from British practice and employed by four of the existing state constitutions[44] in which one house brings charges and another adjudicates them. The path toward this traditional and familiar arrangement was influenced by the final design of the senate. Although the framers resoundingly rejected the preference of Alexander Hamilton and a few others for a government by a new aristocracy,[45] they were suspicious of pure democracy.[46] All the original proposals for a bicameral legislature had a popularly elected chamber and a second chamber chosen by members of the governing class.[47] The compromise that made the Senate a bastion of state power led naturally to the original method of senatorial selection by state legislators.[48] A body selected in this way was conceived not only as representing the interests of the states as quasi-sovereign entities, but also as likely to consist of sober, established persons high in social standing and esteemed by the ruling stratum of their states.[49] The conception of the Senate as a more mature, deliberative body was reinforced by the decision to make senators' terms of office six years, rather than the two selected for members of the House of Representatives. In short, the Senate as it finally emerged had the aura of a republican House of Lords.

The executive, too, was the source of intense debate in Philadelphia. There was no serious disagreement that the Articles of Confederation experiment in purely legislative government had failed and that an executive with at least moderate powers was needed. But the particulars were contested at every point. Hamilton wanted a king,[50] but, recognizing that kings were not much in favor in post-revolutionary America, he urged instead a president for life,[51] insisting that as long as the executive is "subject to impeachment, the term monarchy cannot apply."[52] A proposal for a chief executive who would remain in office "during good behavior," making him, as George Mason observed, the next thing to a king, failed, but only by a margin of six states to four.[53] At the other end of the spectrum, Roger Sherman suggested a president removable at the pleasure of the legislature.[54] Paterson's New Jersey Plan called for a plural executive elected by Congress, ineligible for re-election, and recallable by Congress when requested by a majority of the executives of the states.[55] Pinckney's proposal specified an individual president (to be addressed as "His Excellency") eligible for re-election, [56] while the Virginia Plan permitted, but did not specify, a solo chief executive, who in any case would not be re-eligible.[57]

In the end, of course, the delegates settled on a solo president whose term would be four years and who could be re-elected indefinitely.[58] These two choices profoundly influenced the debate over presidential impeachment. Due to the post-revolutionary fashion for immediate official accountability to the electorate, nine of the twelve states that had adopted written constitutions prior to 1787 prescribed annual elections for governor (or whatever the chief executive officer of the state was called).[59] South Carolina gave its governor a two-year term,[60] and Delaware and New York specified three years.[61] Moreover, with the exceptions of Massachusetts, New Hampshire, and New York, state governors were chosen by their legislatures. Given these arrangements, the need for an extraordinary legislative means of removing misbehaving governors would seem to have been slight, yet nine states wrote into their constitutions impeachment provisions covering governors.[62] The insertion into the national constitution of a president whose term lasted longer than any state governor and who could in theory be reselected indefinitely reinforced the delegates' pre-existing disposition in favor of a mechanism for removing a chief executive gone sour.[63]

This impetus was probably strengthened by the peculiar means ultimately selected to anoint presidents. Throughout the convention summer, the delegates seesawed back and forth between variants of popular election and choice by the legislature. On August 31, the so-called Committee of Eleven retired to consider the question and came back on September 4 with the Electoral College.[64] That misbegotten creation placed the selection of the president and vice president in the hands of a group of "electors" to be chosen by state legislatures, in any manner that seemed to them best.[65] Justified in part on the separation of powers rationale that the president should not be, as state governors generally were, a creature of the legislature,[66] the Electoral College device made the president directly beholden neither to the national legislature nor to the national electorate. The framers imagined the electors as a body of distinguished and experienced public figures who would exercise independent judgment rather than voting automatically for the winner of the popular vote in their states.[67] They saw the electors as a security against the selection of an incompetent or the rise of a popular demagogue because they thought it inconceivable that such a person could pass the scrutiny of the senior statesmen of states holding the majority of electoral votes.[68] That said, to the revolutionary generation accustomed to viewing legislatures as the true locus of sovereignty, the Electoral College created a degree of executive independence that, without a countervailing congressional check, might provoke unease.

Impeachment was the check. Indeed, one little-noticed rationale for the invention of the system of electors was, as Gouverneur Morris put it, "The difficulty of establishing a Court of Impeachments, other than the Senate which would not be so proper for the trial nor the other branch [the House] for the impeachment of the President, if [the President were] appointed by the Legislature."[69] In other words, we have the Electoral College precisely in order that presidents can be impeached by the House and tried by a Senate that had no role in their selection.

Just as important as presidential tenure was the question of presidential power. Here we must tear ourselves free from our twenty-first-century frame of reference. We instinctively assume that the president of the United States is the most important actor in American government, as well as the most powerful person in the world, the nation's paladin and a globe-straddling colossus. The office the framers wrote into the constitution is immeasurably less grand.

Article 2 says that the "executive Power shall be vested in a President of the United States of America."[70] From that simple phrase, modern exponents of the "unitary executive" school derive sweeping claims of presidential authority.[71] But the presidential powers actually enumerated in the constitution were few and, until augmented by time and custom, almost pitifully weak. Even these were often contingent on congressional acquiescence.

For example, the president is designated commander in chief of the army and navy and of the state militias "when called into actual service of the United States."[72] Today this means that the president commands a force of over 2 million[73] armed with weapons that can eradicate human civilization. In 1787, the United States had no standing army at all.[74] Many of those in attendance at the convention opposed the creation of such an army on principle as a danger to liberty,[75] and the reference to state militias expressed the assumption that the bulk of the country's military manpower would remain part-time soldiers whose first allegiance was to their states.

Today, we naturally think of the president as the personal embodiment and ultimate superior of a federal civilian workforce of over 4 million people[76] divided among fifteen cabinet-level departments[77] and a variety of other agencies. In the summer of 1787, there was no executive branch to speak of. By the time George Washington took office as the first president in 1789, there were perhaps 1,000 civilian federal employees spread across the entire eastern seaboard, mostly postal workers and customs officers.[78] The degree of his constitutional authority over those officials was debatable. The constitution says that a president can "require the Opinion, in writing, of the principal Officer in each of the executive Departments, upon any subject relating to the Duties of their respective Offices,"[79] but the president's power to order them to do things nowhere appears. Moreover, the president's power to appoint cabinet officers was made contingent upon Senate approval.[80] It would remain unclear for over a century whether presidents could fire their cabinet appointees without congressional permission. The point was debated heatedly, but inconclusively, during the 1st Congress in 1789, with congressmen who had been delegates to the Constitutional Convention taking different sides of the question.[81] Indeed, as we will see in Chapter 7, President Andrew Johnson's 1868 impeachment turned largely on just this point. As for lesser federal officials, the constitution goes on to say that the power to appoint them can be delegated by Congress to the president, but there is no textual requirement that Congress do so.[82]

The framers gave the president power to make treaties, but only with consent of the Senate.[83] And they allowed that he could "receive Ambassadors and other public Ministers,"[84] implying a role as chief diplomat, but left the extent of his international function otherwise unspecified.

In the framers' minds, perhaps the most significant powers conferred on the president involved his relations with Congress – which, to repeat, they imagined as the paramount organ of government – and to a lesser degree the judiciary. The constitution gave the president a veto over legislation (what the framers called a negative[85]), which could be overridden to be sure, but only by a two-thirds vote of both houses.[86] The president was granted the power to convene Congress, undoubtedly seen as more significant in an age of part-time legislatures,[87] and a very limited power to dismiss it (if the two houses disagreed on a date for adjournment).[88] Finally, the president gained the power to select judges, albeit with the consent of the Senate.[89]

Here we move into the arena of checks and balances, the modifications of Montesquieu's pure separation of powers for which the American constitution is renowned. The architecture of separate, but mutually constraining, governmental branches and state and federal sovereignties is often credited to James Madison, but the question of its paternity is unimportant here. The point is that the final design of the constitution gave the president potentially powerful tools for influencing congressional action, not to mention the authority to determine the composition of the judiciary. Symmetry alone called for some congressional counterweight.

Moreover, the framers were not without pragmatic imagination. They opted for a single executive because they realized that good governance sometimes requires not protracted collective deliberation, but energy, decisiveness, and speed.[90] However, they understood that such qualities applied by an ambitious and powerful personality could fill in the blanks of Article 2 and produce a despotic executive. Both the symmetry of Madison's system and common-sense fear of executive autocracy seemed to require a formal legislative check on the president. The traditional remedy of impeachment came naturally to mind.

THE CONVENTION'S IMPEACHMENT DEBATES

Almost all the discussion about impeachment in the Constitutional Convention concerned the presidency. Judges received a bit of attention, almost exclusively by virtue of the grant of tenure during good behavior. The impeachability of subordinate executive branch officers and even legislators was mentioned in passing. But the focus of the Philadelphia impeachment debate was on the chief executive. Accordingly, the remainder of this chapter will concentrate on impeachment of the president, leaving judges and others for later.

Shall the President be Impeachable?

The first question was whether to make the president impeachable at all. This point was not initially in issue. All four of the draft constitutional structures that framed the summer's debates included impeachment provisions that expressly or impliedly covered the president. The Virginia Plan prescribed "impeachments of any national officer."[91] Pinckney spoke of impeachment of "officers of the United States."[92] Hamilton alluded to impeachment of "governors, senators, and all officers of the United States."[93] Paterson's New Jersey Plan expressly made the executive impeachable.[94] Given that impeachment is a rarely used mechanism, something of a constitutional exotic in both Britain and America, the inclusion of impeachment in every single one of the four outlines of the most important elements of the national governmental structure may seem peculiar. The peculiarity diminishes when we recall that these delegates had been conditioned by study of the British Parliament, American colonial practice, the constitutional ferment leading to the Revolution, and the experience of making and applying their state constitutions to see impeachment as an essential attribute of legislative authority and a necessary antidote to official oppression and corruption.

Nonetheless, the initial unanimity about executive impeachment gave way to some doubt as the delegates firmed up the particulars of the presidential office. The primary points of contention were, first, whether a legislative power of executive removal trenched too far on the principle of separation of powers and, second, whether, given the length of tenure and powers of the president, impeachment was even necessary.

On the first point, Rufus King of Massachusetts went straight to Montesquieu, saying that:

> He wished the House to recur to the primitive axiom, that the three great departments of government should be separate and independent; that the executive and judiciary should be so as well as the legislative; that the executive should be so equally with the judiciary. Would this be the case if the executive should be impeachable? . . . Under no circumstances ought [the president] to be impeachable by the legislature. This would be destructive of his independence, and of the

principles of the Constitution. He relied on the vigor of the executive, as a great security for the public liberties.[95]

King was not alone in this concern,[96] but in the end the pragmatic appeal of Madisonian checks and balances overcame the pure separation principle. For most delegates the need for presidential impeachment depended on their assessment of whether the president's power was sufficiently great to require any formal check beyond the expiration of his term of office. It was generally conceded that if the presidency, like judgeships, was to be conferred "during good behavior," then impeachment was needed.[97] Conversely, if the president were limited to a single term of short duration, some delegates felt he would be unlikely to have sufficient time in office to do any great mischief. With a short term, even if the incumbent were eligible for re-election, the electors could be relied upon to bar a seriously misbehaving chief executive from continuing in office. Thus, the shorter the term, the less the need for impeachment.[98] Conversely, the longer a single term, or the longer the interval between judgments by the electors, the greater the apparent need for a midterm means of removal.[99]

The choice of four-year terms – so very much longer than the norm for state governors – certainly tipped the scales toward keeping presidential impeachment in the constitutional framework. But some delegates remained unconvinced that the presidency they were designing would ever garner sufficient power to present a danger.[100] Some of this complacency can be put down to a simple lack of historical foresight. The delegates failed to anticipate the rise in the twentieth century of the administrative state spawned by the New Deal or the emergence of the national security apparatus born of the Cold War. They certainly did not imagine that Congress would acquiesce in its own defenestration (as it arguably has over the past half-century or so). But they also may have been overconfident in the paper limitations they were placing on the presidency, and they commonly misapprehended how the office would work. For example, Gouverneur Morris at first opposed impeachment as unnecessary on the ground that a president would not be able to operate except through "great officers of state, [such as] a minister of finance, of war, of foreign affairs," who Morris thought would be adequately controlled by being themselves impeachable.[101] But cabinet officers have never been the centers of independent authority Morris seems to have envisioned or as essential to presidential power as Morris supposed.

By Whom Should the President be Impeached and Tried?

Those opposed to presidential impeachment were always something of a rump faction. Once four-year renewable terms were agreed upon, even they subsided and the serious question became by whom presidents would be charged and tried. The necessity of the traditional two-step process placing the charging function in one body and the trial in another was assumed from the beginning. Two of the original frameworks made the point explicit. Pinckney's draft gave the power of impeachment to his lower "House of Delegates" and the trial to the judiciary.[102] Paterson placed the power to initiate in the "executives of the several states" and the power of trial in his proposed unicameral congress.[103] Hamilton allocated impeachment *trials* to courts, implying that they must be initiated elsewhere.[104] In any case, once the delegates began fleshing out the original models, the two-stage system was immediately made explicit. As early as June 2, John Dickinson moved to amend the Virginia plan to specify that the president would be "removable on impeachment *and* conviction."[105] That formulation remained constant for the remainder of the summer,[106] the only question being who would do the impeaching and who the convicting.

The early favorite of many delegates was impeachment by the house and trial by the Supreme Court or some other body of judges. John Dickinson proposed initiating removal whenever requested by a majority of state legislatures, rather than by Paterson's majority of state executives, but the effort to give states direct control over the national executive foundered immediately.[107] Most delegates looked to the Supreme Court as the proper trial venue and that preference persisted throughout the summer.[108] Others were concerned that a court appointed by the president could not be trusted to try him,[109] and preferred alternatives like Hamilton's special panel of chief judges of all the state courts.[110] For months, the convention resisted the obvious analogy of the Senate to the House of Lords. The primary concern seems to have been the separation of powers argument that the executive's continuance in office should not be placed entirely in the hands of the legislature.[111] The great worry of many of the delegates was legislative, not executive, overreach. As Gouverneur Morris said, "Legislative tyranny [is] the great danger to be apprehended."[112] This concern was made more acute by the perception that, even absent the right to decide impeachments, the senate might already be too powerful, with its veto over treaties and executive and judicial appointments.[113] But in the end, the convention accepted the Senate as the trial venue.[114]

What Shall be the Procedures in an Impeachment?

Having decided that the president (and vice president and an undefined group of other "civil officers"[115]) could be impeached in the House and tried in the Senate, the framers provided virtually no further guidance on how such proceedings would be conducted. They specified that when the president is tried in the Senate, the chief justice shall preside.[116] Somewhat curiously, they omitted that specification in the case of a vice president despite the fact that virtually the only constitutionally assigned role for vice presidents is to act as presiding officer of the Senate.[117] And they said nothing about central issues like what form specifications of misconduct should take, who should present the case to the Senate, and what the rules of evidence or burden of proof should be.

Only two procedural rules for the Senate trial made it into the final text: the requirement that when trying impeachments, the senators must "be on oath or affirmation," and the rule that conviction can occur only upon "concurrence of two thirds of the members present."[118] The oath requirement is suggestive and we will return to it when discussing the constitution's standard for impeachable conduct. The two-thirds rule is far more important. Indeed, it is by far the most important component of the entire impeachment structure.

The framers were fond, some might say inordinately fond, of supermajority requirements.[119] They inserted them in the rules for approving treaties,[120] expelling members of Congress,[121] overriding presidential vetoes,[122] amending the constitution,[123] and calling a new constitutional convention.[124] Their choice to insert a two-thirds threshold for conviction on impeachment came late, on September 4,[125] and is a bit surprising given British and state precedent. Parliament required only majorities for both impeachment and conviction. Of the eleven states whose pre-1787 constitutions had impeachment or impeachment-like provisions,[126] only three had supermajority voting requirements for either impeachment or conviction.[127]

Hoffer and Hull argue that adoption of the two-thirds rule for Senate deliberations on impeachments and other selected matters was part of an effort to portray the Senate "as thoughtful and deliberate in its hearing and determining of cases as the House of Lords, without any of the aristocratic trappings of that English body."[128] They may be right. The bottom line, however, is simply that the framers used supermajority thresholds for things they wanted to be difficult. Obviously, they intended to make removing a president through impeachment difficult.

It is reasonable to wonder if the Philadelphia delegates realized how high a hurdle they were setting when they put in the two-thirds requirement. At least some of them still imagined that a national government could be run without what they saw as the horrors of party or "faction." A great deal of Madison's theorizing on the constitution's structure was aimed at diminishing the effects of such phenomena.[129] Although Hamilton in the *Federalist Papers* candidly acknowledged that impeachments would necessarily be heavily influenced by political loyalties,[130] one senses the constitution's designers supposed that public-spiritedness would be sufficiently dominant among public characters that factional loyalty would not prove to be an insuperable obstacle to impeachment in appropriate cases. As we will see in succeeding chapters, that confidence has proven to be justified in the case of judges, but is more doubtful for presidents.

What Shall be the Consequence of Impeachment?

At the same time as the framers were erecting a towering procedural obstacle to impeachment, they limited the consequences of impeachment in ways that should have made it far more palatable. As we observed in Chapter 2, British impeachment could trigger the most severe, even brutal, punishments known to the law – death (sometimes with the added savagery of drawing and quartering), forfeiture of titles and lands, attainder of blood (meaning that the defendant's disabilities passed to his heirs), imprisonment, crippling fines, banishment, and so forth. British impeachments were criminal proceedings in the sense of imposing penalties ordinarily reserved for crime, even if the defendant's conduct was not technically criminal. We saw in Chapter 3 that Americans in their colonies and early state governments civilized this ferocious procedure by limiting the consequence of impeachment to removal from office. Seven state constitutions restricted penalties for impeachment to removal from office, with five expressly providing that any other punishment would have to follow from conviction in a regular court of law.[131]

Using language almost directly quoted from the constitutions of Massachusetts, New Hampshire, and New York, the federal constitution adopted strict limits on punishment, stating that:

> Judgment in Cases of Impeachment shall not extend further than to removal from Office, and disqualification to hold and enjoy any Office of honor, Trust or Profit under the United States: but the Party convicted shall nevertheless be liable and subject to Indictment, Trial, Judgment and Punishment, according to Law.[132]

At the same time, the new constitution banned both bills of attainder and *ex post facto* laws.[133] In tandem, these restrictions eliminated the possibility that Congress could emulate Parliament by acting as an extraordinary court imposing characteristically criminal punishments for conduct never previously defined as criminal. These prohibitions also forestalled the common parliamentary maneuver of switching from an impeachment to an attainder if the defendant's pursuers in the lower house sought execution or other grievous personal punishment, but proof of an acknowledged impeachable offense started to seem doubtful.[134]

This aspect of the impeachment remedy sometimes seems its most underappreciated feature. In the popular imagination, impeachment is often treated as if conviction still leads to drawing and quartering. But it just means loss of a job. Personally devastating, to be sure, particularly if the job is as high-profile as the presidency. But not death, imprisonment, forfeiture, financial ruin, or anything like it. Simply a return to private life. As Gouverneur Morris said, when impeached, a president "should be punished not as a man, but as an officer, and punished only by degradation from his office."[135]

It seems reasonably plain that the framers limited the consequences of impeachment in this way for two reasons: first, as they would prove again with the adoption of the Eighth Amendment's prohibition against cruel and unusual punishments, they conceived of themselves as products of a more enlightened age and had no taste for the grisly and vindictive extremes of English law. They wanted a politics of civility and free exchange of ideas, unburdened by the sometimes deadly consequences that in the English past had attended political failure. More importantly for our purposes, they surely thought that limiting the penalties of impeachment would make its application more palatable. They (and the drafters of most of the new state constitutions) learned from parliamentary practice that severe penalties engender a reluctance to convict. The limitation on the consequences of impeachment was a signal that the range of impeachable conduct should be widened.[136]

"HIGH CRIMES AND MISDEMEANORS": WHAT SHALL CONSTITUTE IMPEACHABLE CONDUCT?

At the same time as the delegates were deciding that the president should be impeachable, by whom, and with what consequences, they were wrestling with a definition for impeachable behavior. That there should *be* a definition written into the constitution seems natural to us, but it is not self-evident. By 1787, the British inventors of impeachment had rubbed along quite well for some 600 years without a written constitution of any kind, and in the four centuries during which impeachment was in fairly regular parliamentary use, impeachable behavior was defined only by reference to precedent. However, the revolutionary generation of Americans was enchanted with written constitutions and convinced of the general principle that legal prohibitions ought to be written down clearly. Eight of the ten pre-1787 state constitutions with impeachment provisions defined impeachable conduct.[137]

It is therefore not surprising that the initial definitions proposed were similar to state constitutional language. On June 2, Hugh Williamson and William Davie, both of North Carolina, proposed impeachment for "mal-practice or neglect of duty."[138] This echoed Madison's offhand suggestion from the previous day of impeachment for "malpractice," [139] and was akin to their own state's formula of "offending against the State, by violating any part of [its] Constitution, Mal-Administration, or Corruption,"[140] as well as similar phrasing in the constitutions of six other states.[141] But it was potentially both broader and narrower than the North Carolina phrase. On the one hand, it seems broader in that "mal-administration or corruption" implies bad purpose or avarice, while the phrase "neglect of duty" seems to embrace mere sloth or negligence. On the other hand, Williamson and Davie omitted North Carolina's idea of impeachment for violating "any part of [its] Constitution," narrowing the reach of their suggestion. The Williamson–Davie formula was provisionally approved and remained the presumptive standard for almost two months.[142]

Sometime in late July, someone on the Committee of Detail, probably John Rutledge of South Carolina, suggested replacing "malpractice or neglect of duty" with "treason, bribery, or corruption." [143] This new language echoed the South Carolina constitution's emphasis on corruption ("mal and corrupt conduct in their respective offices"[144]) and seemed to exclude mere mismanagement or incompetence.[145]

On August 27, the phrase "treason, bribery, or corruption" was approved as the new formula.[146] But on September 4, the Committee of Eleven struck "corruption," leaving only "treason or bribery."[147] We do not really know why the convention's sentiment had migrated so far from the original emphasis on official malpractice toward a narrow limitation to national betrayal and one particular kind of official crime. However, it is reasonable to suppose that the evolution was connected to the fact that virtually the entire impeachment conversation occurred in the context of how to situate the *presidency* in the emerging scheme of separate, but mutually checking, branches. In that context, a broad standard that had proven to be suitable for removing underperforming or venal state judges and statewide officials lent credibility to the concern that easy impeachment would make the president unhealthily beholden to Congress. Nonetheless, the extreme limitation on impeachable conduct proposed by the Committee of Eleven distressed some delegates, particularly George Mason, and set the stage for the exchange that would finalize the constitutional definition.

Madison's notes of September 8 reflect the following colloquy:

The clause referring to the Senate the trial of impeachments against the President, for treason and bribery, was taken up.

Col. MASON: Why is the provision restrained to treason and bribery only? Treason, as defined in the Constitution, will not reach many great and dangerous offences. Hastings is not guilty of treason. Attempts to subvert the Constitution may not be treason, as above defined. As bills of attainder, which have saved the British constitution, are forbidden, it is the more necessary to extend the power of impeachments. He moved to add, after "bribery," "or maladministration." Mr. GERRY seconded him.

Mr. MADISON: So vague a term will be equivalent to a tenure during pleasure of the Senate.

Mr. GOUVERNEUR MORRIS: It will not be put in force, and can do no harm. An election of every four years will prevent maladministration.

Col. MASON withdrew "maladministration," and substituted "other high crimes and misdemeanors against the state."

On the question, thus altered, – New Hampshire, Massachusetts, Connecticut, Maryland, Virginia, North Carolina, South Carolina, (in the printed Journal, South Carolina, no,) Georgia, ay, 8; New Jersey, Pennsylvania, Delaware, no, 3.[148]

On the surface, this passage is distressingly insufficient as an explanation either as to why the convention so blithely adopted "high crimes and misdemeanors" or what they thought it meant. One suspects that a good deal more was said that never made it into Madison's notes, but this is all we have. And, sad to say, the delegates never returned to the question in the week that remained before their adjournment. Still, Madison's summary of Mason's reasons for discontent with "treason and bribery" is one of the richest paragraphs in the whole convention record. If we put Mason's statement here together with statements he, Madison, and others made throughout the convention, and add what we know – and what the delegates would have understood – about the pregnant phrase "high crimes and misdemeanors," we can form a pretty good estimation of what the framers thought they were doing.

We begin with the fact that both Mason and Madison came to the Philadelphia Convention as strong supporters of impeachment as an important constitutional mechanism. Mason had written impeachment into the Virginia constitution of 1776, using language that emphasized the necessity of a remedy that would reach all conduct dangerous to the government – "offending against the state, either by mal-administration, corruption, or other means by which the safety of the state may be endangered."[149] Madison, his fellow Virginian, supported that effort as a young delegate to the Virginia convention and for the remainder of his career, as one source puts it, "thought of impeachment as a necessary part of republicanism."[150]

From the beginning of the Philadelphia Convention to its end, Mason and Madison were the most consistent voices touting the necessity of presidential impeachment, and the scope of the dangers that could be anticipated without it. Both addressed the point in the very first week, Mason more memorably when he said, "Some mode of displacing an unfit magistrate is rendered indispensable by the fallibility of those who choose, as well as by the corruptibility of the man chosen."[151] On July 20, Mason and Madison were again in harness on the question. Mason maintained that "No point is of more importance than that the right of impeachment should continue."[152] Madison thought impeachment "indispensable ... for defending the Community against the incapacity, negligence or perfidy of the chief Magistrate. The limitation of the period of service was not a sufficient security. He might lose his capacity after his appointment. He might pervert his administration into a scheme of peculation or oppression. He might betray his trust to foreign powers."[153]

Thus, when Mason proposed re-expanding the scope of impeachable behavior to include "maladministration," and Madison objected, they were speaking not as adversaries, but as allies in the cause of a strong impeachment mechanism haggling over particulars. Madison, always attentive to checks and balances, wanted to be sure that this necessary check on presidential power did not go so far that it subordinated the president to Congress. But that was a sentiment Mason had voiced himself in June when he coupled his endorsement of impeachment with the admonition that the president should not thereby become "the mere creature of the Legislature."[154] The only question was how to achieve the proper balance.

The first key to understanding Mason's objectives in proposing "maladministration" and Madison's ready acceptance of the substitution of "high crimes and misdemeanors" is a reminder of where the debate over impeachment stood in September and how it related to other decisions the convention had made. By this point, the draft constitution defined treason narrowly as consisting "only in levying war against [the United States], or in adhering to their enemies."[155] The choice to define treason, or any other crime, in the text of the constitution may seem to us strange, but this definition was a conscious repudiation of the expansive and sometimes retrospective definition of treason employed in British impeachments and other state trials discussed above in Chapter 2. Treason trials, in American minds, had too often been an instrument of oppression and accusations of treason too easily employed as a weapon to disable opponents of government.

A narrow definition of treason was a fine idea in isolation (though both Mason and Madison objected to the definition chosen as *too* narrow[156]), but it meant that a definition of impeachable conduct pared down to "treason and bribery" effectively excluded all peacetime wrongdoing except bribery. Bribery itself had a fairly narrow common law definition arguably limited to taking bribes rather than giving them.[157] Thus, "treason and bribery" failed to address official oppression, any betrayal in the foreign policy arena not occurring in time of war, many types of corruption that had been grounds for impeachment in Great Britain and America for centuries, notably including employing the powers of office for self-enrichment and, critically, the central complaint in the most consequential British and early American impeachments – subversion of the constitutional order. So as matters stood when Mason and Madison spoke on September 4, the draft constitution rejected both British precedent and the models provided by state constitutions and covered hardly any of the conduct that a prudent person would want to make impeachable in a president.

Moreover, as of September 4, the draft constitution barred bills of attainder and *ex post facto* laws. Mason alludes to the ban on attainders in a sentence critical to understanding his aims: "As bills of attainder, which have saved the British constitution, are forbidden, it is the more necessary to extend the power of impeachments."[158] Mason shows here that he was a careful student of parliamentary history. He obviously knew about the multiple attempted impeachments where the House of Commons had difficulty in proving treason or some clearly defined common law crime and switched to an attainder instead.[159] Commentators on British practice have sometimes tut-tutted at this maneuver as unjust.[160] Whether the commentators are right about the principle is beside the present point. The critical point is that Mason did *not* disapprove of the old parliamentary attainders. To the contrary, he believed that the ability to shift from impeachment to attainder "saved the British constitution" from dangerous men. Therefore, he argued, given the prohibition of attainders, some substitute must be found if the American constitution was to be protected. The substitute, plainly enough, was an expansive definition of impeachable conduct.

Mason's first suggestion was a reversion to a word – "maladministration" – that he had inserted in Virginia's 1776 constitution and that had been copied into the constitutions of Delaware, North Carolina, Massachusetts, and New Hampshire.[161] Madison then made his checks-and-balances objection that impeachment for "maladministration" would make the president too dependent on the Senate. What happens next, at least according to Madison's notes (the only account we have), is somewhat odd. Elbridge Gerry had seconded the motion to add "maladministration," and no one other than Madison is recorded as objecting to it. Gouverneur Morris says, in effect, "Go ahead, put it in. It will never be used and, anyway, the four-year term limit will deter maladministration."[162] Mason, who was no shrinking violet – he would in the end refuse to sign the constitution because he could not get his way on a number of points – does not seem to have pressed for a vote. Rather, he withdrew "maladministration" and immediately suggested "high crimes and misdemeanors."

There is considerable risk in reading too much into the fragmentary accounts of convention debates. The bits and pieces Madison and others wrote down plainly do not capture everything that transpired among this group of learned, forceful, voluble men. Perhaps Mason perceived that Madison's objection captured the sense of the assembly and elected strategic retreat. But he surely did not come up with "high crimes and misdemeanors" on the spur of the moment, and must have come to the convention hall with that phrase ready as a considered alternative. For his part, Madison seemingly accepted Mason's substitution of "high crimes and misdemeanors" without a murmur, or even a clarifying question. Given that both were Virginians and that the two had been allied since June in promoting the necessity of impeachment, it seems plausible that they had talked about the issue and were in accord on the suitability of "high crimes and misdemeanors" before Mason rose that day.[163]

Whether this speculation has any merit or not, "high crimes and misdemeanors" comes somewhat closer than "maladministration" to capturing the essence of Mason's stated concerns. At this moment in the convention, he was not focused on the garden variety, and often rather tawdry, mid-level corruption and incompetence that had been the subject of most post-revolutionary state impeachment cases. He was instead thinking about the president and conduct that put the governing order at risk: "great and dangerous offenses" and "attempts to subvert the Constitution." Maladministration is a term sufficiently elastic to include such large matters, but it also lends itself to the interpretation both Madison and Mason feared as giving Congress too much authority – essentially any sort of poor performance in office. So maladministration fell out and the universe of impeachable conduct became "treason, bribery, or other high crimes and misdemeanors."

It is worth pausing here to dispel a common misinterpretation of the Mason–Madison impeachment exchange. As pithily asserted by Lawrence Tribe and Joshua Matz, the claim is that, "When the Framers replaced 'maladministration' with 'high Crimes and Misdemeanors,' they sought to narrow – not expand – the class of impeachable offenses."[164] Others have made the same claim,[165] but it is obviously wrong, or at least fatally misleading. The framers never *replaced* "maladministration" with "high crimes and misdemeanors" because "maladministration" was never in any draft of the constitutional text. What the convention was debating on September 4 was whether to leave the current draft language – "treason or bribery" – as it stood or expand it. They expanded it. The choice between "malad-ministration" and "high crimes and misdemeanors" was about how far the expansion should reach.

But the question remains: exactly what did Mason, Madison and the other delegates think "high crimes and misdemeanors" meant? It has been argued, most notably by Raoul Berger over forty years ago, that "high crimes and misdemeanors" was suggested by Mason and adopted by the convention because it was a legal term of art within which the framers intended to cabin the impeachment power.[166] Alternatively, if one adheres to the original public meaning school of constitutional interpretation, one can argue that, regardless of the framers' intentions, "high crimes and misdemeanors" *was in fact* a recognized legal term of art with a meaning discoverable at the time of the founding and thus restricts the scope of impeachable offenses to that meaning. Even if one believes the founding generation's views to be merely useful, rather than dispositive, on interpretive questions, it would be helpful to know what "high crimes and misdemeanors" meant to them and to their contemporaries.

The Influence of British and American Precedents on the Founders' Understanding of "High Crimes and Misdemeanors"

"High crimes and misdemeanors" was indisputably a term of British parliamentary origin. This tempts commentators into one of two errors: either assuming that the former Britons assembled in Philadelphia knew everything that we know about parliamentary impeachment; or seeing impeachment as an antique and peculiarly British mechanism, so foreign to Americans that the founding generation must be presumed to have been ignorant of its particulars absent explicit proofs to the contrary. The better approach lies between these two mistaken poles.

On the one hand, neither the framers nor anyone else in 1787 America – or Great Britain for that matter – could have known everything about British impeachments that we know today. Books of law and parliamentary history that treated the subject were beginning to be written and circulated in America.[167] Blackstone's *Commentaries on the Laws of England*, first published in 1765, and already a standard work in the colonies by the time of the American Revolution,[168] discusses impeachment at length. John Rushworth's eight-volume work, *Historical Collections of Private Passages of State* (1980), is full of impeachments.[169] As are Edward Hyde's *History of the Rebellion and Civil Wars of England* (1731)[170] and David Hume's *History of England*.[171] Hale's *Pleas of the Crown* (1736)[172] and Selden's *Of the Judicature of Parliaments* (1681)[173] mention them. Detailed treatments of particular famous impeachments appeared in pamphlet form. The cases covered by the pamphlets, unsurprisingly, tended to be those with the largest implications for British constitutionalism. Among them were the trials of the earls of Strafford,[174] Danby, and Oxford, Justice Scroggs, the Reverend Sacheverell, and the earl of

Torrington.[175] But no comprehensive compilation of *all* the details of *all* the impeachments and related parliamentary proceedings appeared anywhere until the early 1800s.[176] Two centuries of subsequent research have added greatly to what was publicly available even then.

On the other hand, it would be a far larger error to assume that the framers knew little about British impeachment or the prior uses of "high crimes and misdemeanors," or that they ignored what they knew when writing the term into the constitution.[177] As we have seen in Chapters 2 and 3, impeachments were a prominent, even notorious, feature of the political history of Great Britain throughout the entire period of British colonization of the Atlantic seaboard. No educated colonist who entered adulthood with a basic knowledge of British political history and thereafter maintained a reasonable familiarity with current events back in the home islands could have avoided knowing at least something about British impeachment. From 1621, when Parliament impeached Francis Bacon, who was both Lord Chancellor of England and recognized as one of the great intellects of the age, to the impeachments of the earl of Strafford and the Puritans' nemesis Archbishop Laud in 1640, to the impeachment for treason of the earl of Danby in 1678, to the flurry of impeachments in 1715–16 following the death of Queen Anne, to the Hastings impeachment ongoing in the summer of 1787, and on many occasions in between, impeachment was a recurring feature of political crises in the kingdom of which, until 1776, the colonists felt themselves an integral part.[178]

Therefore, when considering whether the American founders would have been familiar with British impeachment, the proper question is not whether they had researched the specifics of every parliamentary impeachment precedent, but whether they were conversant with the history of parliamentary relations to the British crown. If there is one subject on which we know the American revolutionaries were fixated and deeply learned, it was the interrelation of king and Parliament and the degree to which their own colonial legislatures ought to enjoy the powers and privileges of Parliament.[179]

Of the fifty-five delegates to the Constitutional Convention, thirty-three were trained as lawyers[180] and at least ten were or had been judges.[181] Nine of the thirty-three had studied law in England.[182] To study law in either England or America in the 1700s necessarily meant studying the constitutional arrangements of Great Britain and the interactions between the crown, the courts, and Parliament. Moreover, examination of the personal libraries of a number of the delegates, lawyers and non-lawyers alike, reveals volumes about British constitutional history and practice, including material on British state trials generally, and impeachments in particular.[183] In addition to their personal libraries, the Philadelphia delegates had been given access to the Library Company of Philadelphia, two blocks from the hall in which the convention assembled.[184] We do not know to what extent the delegates used that resource, but its holdings suggest the range of materials available to the founding generation. The Library Company collection included Coke's *Institutes of the Laws of England*, Hale's *Pleas of the Crown*, Hawkins' *Pleas of the Crown*, Blackstone's *Commentaries on the Laws of England*, Edward Hyde's *History of the Rebellion and Civil Wars of England*,[185] and David Hume's *History of England*, all of which covered parliamentary history generally and dealt with impeachment as part of their subject.[186] Other bibliographic sources suggest that, among the colonial governing class, there was considerable access to information about British impeachments.[187] Finally, at the time of the convention, everyone in the English-speaking world was following the impeachment of Warren Hastings, the details of which were published in newspapers across the United States, including in Philadelphia.[188]

The integration of the Americans' general learning about British parliamentary history and their familiarity with a great many parliamentary impeachments is nicely illustrated in Thomas Jefferson's famous 1774 pamphlet, *A Summary View of the Rights of British North America*. In the course of arguing that Parliament maintains such independent constitutional stature that it may not be involuntarily dissolved by the king, Jefferson alludes to the 1387 impeachment of the judges under Richard II,[189] stating:

> One of the articles of impeachment against Tresilian, and the other justices at Westminster Hall, in the reign of Richard the second, for which they suffered death, as traitors to their country, was, that they had advised the king that he might dissolve his parliament at any time; and succeeding kings have adopted the opinion of the unjust judges.[190]

Indeed, the more one reads the literature of the founding era, the more one realizes that knowledge of British impeachment practice was remarkably widespread among the political leadership class of the period.[191]

Likewise, as discussed in Chapter 3, we know that the colonists attempted to use impeachments against royal and proprietary officials. The records of the colonial cases reveal both familiarity with British parliamentary precedents and sophisticated arguments about the roles of legislatures and executive officials and the special place of impeachment in the relationship between them. Several of these cases, particularly the 1758 Moore impeachment in Pennsylvania and the 1774 impeachment of Justice Oliver in Massachusetts, would have been familiar to all the delegates. Moreover, Benjamin Franklin was intimately involved in the Moore affair, and Judge Nathaniel Gorham, the Massachusetts delegate who chaired the Philadelphia Convention's Committee of the Whole, had been a member of the Massachusetts House of Representatives that impeached Justice Oliver for "high crimes and misdemeanors."[192]

What is more, at least fourteen delegates to the federal Constitutional Convention had also been delegates to state constitutional conventions between 1776 and 1780 which adopted impeachment provisions (or in the case of Maryland, removal mechanisms closely akin to impeachment).[193] The debates about how to structure these state impeachment procedures would inevitably have involved discussions about how the parliamentary system from which the new states were separating had handled this process over the centuries. Once the state constitutions were in place, at least seven Philadelphia delegates were involved directly or indirectly in state impeachment proceedings after the war.[194]

In sum, virtually all the Philadelphia delegates would have had a solid familiarity with the impeachment mechanism and its origins, and would have recognized "high crimes and misdemeanors" as a term associated with British impeachments. Some would have known that the phrase had also been used in America, most notably in the Oliver case. They would have had varying degrees of familiarity with the particulars of British impeachments.

Crucially, the framers most active in the convention's impeachment debates had the most intimate knowledge of its history. Mason proved as much with his subtle analysis of the relation between British attainders and impeachments. The depth of his studies (and those of Madison[195]) is further illustrated by the fact that both of them objected to the narrow definition of treason on the ground that it would not reach as far as the 1351 British treason statute of Edward III,[196] the details of which were debated in virtually every British impeachment alleging treason from 1376 onward. Franklin knew Parliament better than any other American, having spent most of his time from 1757 to 1775 in London as agent for Pennsylvania and later other colonies. He was deeply involved in the Moore impeachment of 1758, had an extensive library on parliamentary history, and interjected relevant parallels from European history several times in the discussions of impeachment.[197]

It is thus reasonable to conclude that at least the most knowledgeable among the delegates would have had the same general understanding of the British use of "high crimes and misdemeanors" as we do, albeit without some of the subtleties that access to more complete records affords us. They would have understood that Parliament from very early times used "high crimes and misdemeanors" as a general descriptor for behavior alleged by the House of Commons to be impeachable. They would have recognized that the phrase had no statutory definition. In impeachment debates Parliament never asked, "What does 'high crimes and misdemeanors' mean?" Instead, it asked, "Is this or that behavior by the accused within the power of Parliament to impeach?" Answering the latter question over centuries produced a large body of precedent, some helpful, some quite ambiguous. Here, as in their regular courts, the British were making law case by case through common law methods. The unique parliamentary setting made divining the rule of all these cases even harder than in ordinary courts, but both Britons and Americans would have recognized that in impeachments and other matters Parliament had created its own body of common law, known by the Latin tag, *lex parliamentaria*, to which it was necessary to turn to divine what conduct might be impeachable in Great Britain.[198]

As frustrating as this is to us, it would probably have seemed less so to the framers, particularly the lawyers. They would have understood that "high crimes and misdemeanors" was a term of art only in a common law sense, which is to say that its meaning at any given time is roughly ascertainable, but open for debate depending on one's reading of precedents, and that its future meaning is subject to modification based on changed circumstances. In short, "high crimes and misdemeanors" was, by design, a flexible concept.

Happily, despite the indeterminacy, it turns out that the categories of conduct Parliament classed as "high crimes and misdemeanors" correspond closely to the type of behavior Philadelphia delegates said impeachment should cover. Recall that British impeachments up to 1787 could be grouped into a number of broad categories, including: (i) armed rebellion and other obvious treasons; (ii) ordinary crime by peers triable only in the House of Lords; (iii) corruption; (iv) betrayal of the nation's foreign policy interests; (v) incompetence, neglect of duty, or maladministration in office; and (vi) subversion of the constitution and laws of the realm.[199]

Armed Rebellion and Treason

Under the constitution's narrowed definition, armed rebellion is "treason" and is therefore plainly impeachable. Matching the other categories of British impeachments to the framers' produce requires a bit more reflection.

Crime

Parliamentary "high crimes and misdemeanors" plainly included some indictable crimes, from false imprisonment and rape,[200] to the well-defined treasons, to a plethora of bribery and other financial offenses. In England, parliamentary jurisdiction over many of these offenses was limited to peers of the realm who could not be tried in regular courts. The U.S. constitution prohibits an American aristocracy,[201] so there can be no American peers whose ordinary crimes are triable only by Congress. Nonetheless, the framers made clear that some ordinary crimes are impeachable offenses by providing that any punishment beyond removal from office and disqualification from further federal service could be imposed only through the regular courts.[202] This proviso would not have been necessary unless some impeachable behaviors were crimes over which the regular courts had jurisdiction.

Conversely, Parliament commonly impeached for conduct that was not a statutory or common law crime.[203] This undeniable fact reveals one of the most important points about "high crimes and misdemeanors" as a term of art. *It does not mean what it appears to mean.* The phrase first appeared, not in ordinary criminal law, but in 1386 in the impeachment of the earl of Suffolk.[204] When the phrase was used in parliamentary impeachment practice, the words "high crimes" did not require some especially aggravated subcategory of felony, or indeed any felony at all. The word "misdemeanors" did not mean a common law criminal offense less serious than a felony, or at least it was not limited to such offenses. Instead, the words "crimes and misdemeanors," though they could include indictable offenses, were used more in their colloquial sense of bad behavior. The word "high" signaled seriousness and political character. The whole phrase came to mean nothing more than "the kind of serious bad behavior Parliament has thought worthy of removal and punishment."

Some have made contrary arguments, often relying on Blackstone, who declared that an impeachment is criminal in character and "is a prosecution of the already known and established law."[205] But this means less than it appears. A British impeachment was necessarily criminal in the sense that conviction authorized imposition of characteristically criminal punishments up to and including death. But that did not mean that the charges must involve conduct of a type that violated a criminal statute or constituted a common law crime. And they often did not. Even Blackstone's stricture that impeachments involve "already known and established law" is misleading. In impeachments for the capital offense of treason defendants often claimed that they could not be convicted unless their conduct fell within the statute of Edward III, but as we saw in Chapter 2, those pleas worked only sometimes. As for charges under the more general rubric of "high crimes and misdemeanors," there is no indication that any defendant ever successfully defended based on the argument that his conduct was not criminal.[206] All Blackstone is really saying is that impeachments should not lie except for types of behavior previously established by Parliament as being impeachable. However, that was not a serious limitation inasmuch as Parliament had been impeaching people since 1376 for a wide variety of behavior not conventionally criminal, each new case creating precedent for impeaching on the same or, this being a common law system, analogous grounds thereafter. Because the framers severed impeachment from criminal punishment, "high crimes and misdemeanors" was for them merely a signifier for the kind of conduct Parliament historically found impeachable.[207]

Anyone as familiar with British legal language and parliamentary practice as Mason and Madison were would have understood this point perfectly. Madison illustrated it during the Virginia ratifying convention when he contended that a president who summoned senators from a minority of states to confirm a bad treaty "would be impeached and convicted, as a majority of the states would be affected by his *misdemeanor*."[208] In the impeachment setting, a misdemeanor to Madison was a removable offense against constitutional propriety, but not necessarily a crime. Other members of the founding generation understood the distinction, as James Iredell showed in the North Carolina convention, saying: "If [the president] commits any misdemeanor in office, he is impeachable, removable from office, and incapacitated to hold any office of honor, trust, or profit. If he commits any crime, he is punishable by the laws of his country, and in capital cases may be deprived of life."[209]

Some have suggested that the position of "high crimes and misdemeanors" at the end of the phrase "treason, bribery, or *other* high crimes and misdemeanors" implicates a maxim of statutory construction known by its Latin name, *ejusdem generis*.[210] Put simply, this maxim presumes that items at the end of a long descriptive list should be presumed to be similar to items earlier on the list. That is fair, as far as it goes, but the tough problem whenever this catchphrase is invoked is determining what kind of similarities ought to flow down from the top to the bottom of a list. If we were to apply *ejusdem generis* uncritically here, we might conclude that the most obvious thing about treason and bribery is that they are indictable crimes, and therefore that "high crimes and misdemeanors" must all be criminal, too. But that would require ignoring the fact that in 1787 "high crimes and misdemeanors" was already a term of art that included a lot of non-criminal conduct. To the extent that this maxim is useful in the present case, it is to emphasize the seriousness of all behavior eligible for impeachment. Treason is a betrayal of the whole polity, and capital to boot. Bribery in the case of a government official demonstrates personal unfitness for office and destroys public confidence in governance generally. Thus, impeachable offenses need not be criminal, but ought to be serious in the way treason and bribery are.

As we will see, over the years not everyone understood, or at least chose to accept, the non-criminal parliamentary meaning of "high crimes and misdemeanors." The assertion that impeachment can lie only for indictable criminal conduct is a hardy perennial trotted out in nearly every major impeachment battle of the last two centuries. But that is not what "high crimes and misdemeanors" meant to the framers.

Corruption

Corruption in all its inventive forms was the most common charge in parliamentary impeachments. The primary theme in virtually all such cases was the misuse of public office for private gain, though in many British impeachments, the self-enrichment violated no law.[211] Corruption was plainly a major concern in Philadelphia.[212] Mason spoke of the "corruptibility" of those who would be president as a primary justification for impeachment.[213] Gouverneur Morris specified "corruption" as one of the "few" offences for which he would favor impeachment.[214] Edmund Randolph listed misuse of "public money" among the presidential abuses of power for which impeachment was required.[215] Madison expressed the point most colorfully when he said that impeachment was required because a president "might pervert his administration into a scheme of peculation . . ."[216]

Another variant of the corruption theme in British impeachments was the allegation that an impeached minister sold his loyalty to a foreign power, or in the notable case of the earl of Danby acted as an intermediary in selling the loyalty of the king by helping to arrange a bribe from the king of France to King Charles II of England to secure England's neutrality in the Franco-Dutch War.[217] In Philadelphia, Gouverneur Morris mentioned Danby's case as an example of the need for impeachment to protect against "the danger of seeing the first Magistrate in foreign pay without being able to guard against it by displacing him."[218] Morris later opined that, "No man would say that an Executive known to be in the pay of an Enemy, should not be removable in some way or another."[219]

The convention addressed the fear of direct foreign purchase of presidential favor in the foreign emoluments clause which prohibited any "person holding any Office of Profit or Trust under [the United States]" from accepting "any present, Emolument, Office, or Title, of any kind whatever, from any King, Prince, or foreign State."[220] The intended enforcement mechanism of the emoluments prohibition was impeachment. At the Virginia ratifying convention, Edmund Randolph said that if the president is discovered "receiving emoluments from foreign powers . . . he may be impeached."[221]

For framers concerned about corruption of the new chief executive, "high crimes and misdemeanors" in its parliamentary sense expanded impeachment beyond the tiny sliver of behavior covered by bribery to every sort of corruption, domestic and foreign.

Betrayal of the Country's Foreign Policy Interests

Some British impeachments involved overt corruption in the form of payments from foreign powers. However, British foreign affairs impeachments did not necessarily involve bribery. Instead, a string of British ministers and royal advisors were impeached for using their official powers contrary to the country's vital foreign interests or for inducing the monarch to engage in a foreign policy of which Parliament fundamentally disapproved. The misdeeds included everything from trying to arrange politically disadvantageous or religiously objectionable royal marriages to giving bad advice about unpopular treaties.[222] In each of these cases, Parliament claimed a power to judge for itself the nation's essential international interests and to remove and punish officials who undercut those interests. If these precedents are part of the inherited common law definition of "high crimes and misdemeanors," then Congress assumes analogous authority. Madison seemed to be alluding to something of the sort when he said impeachment is required because the president "might betray his trust to foreign powers."[223] Similarly, at the Virginia ratifying convention, Madison contended that a president who made a treaty that "violated the interest of the nation" and convinced the Senate to ratify it could be impeached.[224] That said, reading into Madison's comments a general right to impeach presidents for grave foreign policy errors is probably straining farther than the content will bear. Moreover, James Iredell in the North Carolina convention was insistent that a president's support of a treaty "deemed unwise, or against the interest of the country" should never be impeachable because one should not be impeached for exercising one's "own judgment," regardless of how flawed it may prove.[225] It is impossible to tell conclusively from contemporary sources what the framers and others of the founding generation thought about this thread of parliamentary precedent.

Incompetence, Neglect of Duty, or Maladministration in Office

The most troublesome British impeachments are those embracing incompetence, neglect of duty, or maladministration in office. Parliament impeached people for this sort of thing for centuries, usually calling it "high crimes and misdemeanors."[226] This fact would have been known to the framers not only through the laborious process of studying individual parliamentary precedents, but through the simpler expedient of reading Blackstone, the most common resource of eighteenth-century Anglo-American lawyers, who said that the "first and principal" of "high misdemesners" [sic] is "the mal-administration of such high officers, as are in public trust and employment ... [which is] usually punished by the method of parliamentary impeachment."[227] Thus, the convention's abandonment of its first formula of "malpractice or neglect of duty," and the later offer and withdrawal of "maladministration" in favor of "high crimes and misdemeanors," pose a conundrum. As used by Parliament, "high crimes and misdemeanors" plainly *included* neglect of duty and maladministration. Therefore, if "high crimes and misdemeanors" is to be interpreted based solely on British precedents, that sort of behavior should be impeachable under the federal constitution. Indeed, the only reason anyone thinks malpractice or neglect of duty or maladministration are *not* covered is because we have the convention record.

It is revealing that at least some delegates to the state ratifying conventions and other contemporary commentators who had not been present in Philadelphia for the *pas de deux* between Mason and Madison, or had not seen the convention record (because it was not publicly available until 1819[228]), commonly assumed that maladministration or something like it was impeachable. At the Virginia convention, George Nicholas is recorded as saying that American impeachment is more powerful than the British sort because "the President himself is personally amenable for his mal-administration."[229] In the Massachusetts ratifying convention, the Reverend Mr. Stillman spoke of impeachment for "malconduct."[230] The anonymous essayist Cassius wrote in the *Virginia Independent Chronicle* that there was no need for a privy council to advise the president because "the president himself is amenable for his conduct, and liable, like any other public officer, to be impeached for bad a[d]ministration."[231]

Remarkably, only two years after the convention, during a debate in the first Congress, Madison himself maintained that the country need have no fear that a president would abuse the power of removing executive branch officials because "he will be impeachable by the House before the senate for such maladministration; for I contend that the wanton removal of meritorious officers would subject him to impeachment ..."[232] It could be, of course, that Madison had simply forgotten his exchange with Mason two years before, or that he was a hypocrite happy to take advantage of the fact that the convention's records were still secret in order to make a current political argument. A more generous explanation is that Madison (and Mason) had always understood that "high crimes and misdemeanors" included some forms of non-criminal official ineptitude or misbehavior, the parameters of which would have to be worked out in practice.[233]

The most obvious factor in such a calculus is presumably seriousness. Both the modifier "high" in front of "crimes and misdemeanors" and the application of the phrase in parliamentary practice are consistent with the notion that impeachment should not be used for petty or insignificant matters. From time to time Parliament did pursue people and conduct that may seem trivial to us, as, for example, the impeachment of the Rev. Sacheverell for an inflammatory sermon.[234] But in virtually every case, the matters that produced British impeachments loomed large in the context of the times.

The seriousness limitation implied in parliamentary practice also resolves the apparent contradiction presented by the convention's abandonment of terms like "malpractice or neglect of duty" and "maladministration" in favor of a term of art that, if we take British precedent seriously, includes some behavior in those categories. There is no necessary contradiction as long as the rule is that non-criminal official incompetence, mismanagement, and the like are not impeachable unless serious enough to pose a genuine risk to important national interests or to establish the defendant's complete unsuitability for office – which in the case of the president by definition threatens a vital national interest.

The proposition that a president is ever impeachable for maladministration, however extreme, is nonetheless controversial. Some scholars (and all defenders of any president in political peril) tend to reject it out of hand. They justify their position through some combination of reliance on the convention record, particularly the Mason–Madison exchange, and agreement with Madison's rationale that impeachment for maladministration would make the president unduly dependent on the legislature. I cannot find these arguments convincing. What we know from the record is that the convention opened by approving impeachment for "malpractice and neglect of duty," swung to the opposite extreme with "treason and bribery" only, flirted for a few minutes with "maladministration," and ended up with "high crimes and misdemeanors," a phrase that traditionally reached non-criminal official ineptitude and neglect. The fairest reading of the convention record is that the framers returned not quite full circle to a more nuanced version of their original position.

Moreover, even if we place Madison's concern about institutional balance at the center of the analysis, that hardly rules out impeachment for the most serious sort of maladministration. If impeachment for any arguably substandard official behavior gives the Senate too much power, a rule that insulates a president from removal regardless of how woeful his inadequacy – as long as it breaks no law – gives the president too much protection and the constitutional order far too little.

Reading "high crimes and misdemeanors" in its British sense also solves a (so-far theoretical) problem often raised by impeachment scholars. Pretty much everyone assumes that a president who, for example, simply stopped coming to work, or refused to sign any bill passed by Congress regardless of content, or refused to organize the defense of the country against invasion, or fired all cabinet officers and refused to name replacements must be impeachable.[235] But unless maladministration in some form is an impeachable offense, then there would be no constitutional remedy in any of these cases. (The Twenty-fifth Amendment would not fit any of these scenarios because it applies only to a president "unable to discharge the powers and duties of his office," not one who refuses to do so.[236]) Reading the parliamentary precedent behind "high crimes and misdemeanors" to permit removal in extreme cases of official neglect or incompetence provides a solid constitutional foundation for impeaching a sufficiently deadbeat president. The touchy question, to which we will return in the final chapter, is how derelict in his or her duties a president must be before impeachment is constitutionally plausible. The work ethic of presidents is variable, as are their decisional styles. Obsessive attention to detail is not necessarily good. Hands-off management limited to guidance only on large issues is not necessarily bad. Is there, nonetheless, some minimum level of engagement constitutionally required of a modern president?

Parliamentary precedents provide no direct help in one circumstance that Madison and others initially wanted to be covered by impeachment – a president who becomes incapable of serving after taking office.[237] This problem is now addressed by the Twenty-fifth Amendment, which is discussed below in Chapter 15.[238]

Subversion of the Constitution

The most important category of British impeachments, both for British history and for understanding what Mason and Madison were about, is the last. Over and over, Parliament impeached ministers for conduct alleged to subvert its conception of proper constitutional order in favor of the "arbitrary and tyrannical" government of ambitious monarchs and their grasping minions.[239] This is the tool Mason wanted for Congress. Recall that at the close of Chapter 3, we noted that before the convention Americans were familiar with two basic models of impeachment: one limited to rooting out ordinary government corruption and eliminating incompetent officials, and the other a tool of high politics to wield against the powerful and sometimes as a means of shaping or preserving constitutional values. When the convention accepted Mason's addition of "high crimes and misdemeanors" to "treason and bribery," it was choosing political impeachment.

Alexander Hamilton recognized the point. In *Federalist 65*, he famously describes impeachable offenses as those "which proceed from the misconduct of public men, or, in other words, from the abuse or violation of some public trust. They are of a nature which may with peculiar propriety be denominated POLITICAL, as they relate chiefly to injuries done immediately to the society itself."[240]

Other prominent members of the founding generation were of the same mind. James Iredell said in the North Carolina ratifying convention:

> The power of impeachment is given by this Constitution, to bring great offenders to punishment. It is calculated to bring them to punishment for crime which it is not easy to describe, but which every one must be convinced is a high crime and misdemeanor against the government. This power is lodged in those who represent the great body of the people, because the occasion for its exercise will arise from acts of great injury to the community, and the objects of it may be such as cannot be easily reached by an ordinary tribunal.[241]

Both Hamilton and Iredell were careful to avoid defining the precise set of offenses that would warrant impeachment. But they were aligning themselves with George Mason in saying that the focus of the impeachment mechanism (particularly for presidents) is on offenses against the community or polity – the society in its political character – that violate public trust. Those reach beyond mere violations of the criminal code to any dangerous assault on the foundations of the political order.

This much is now pretty universally accepted. But Mason's original remarks at the convention suggest something a bit more expansive – and more consequential in the current constitutional moment. Let us go back to them.

> Col. MASON: Why is the provision restrained to treason and bribery only? Treason, as defined in the Constitution, will not reach many great and dangerous offences. Hastings is not guilty of treason. *Attempts to subvert the Constitution may not be treason,* as above defined. *As bills of attainder, which have saved the British constitution, are forbidden, it is the more necessary to extend the power of impeachments.*[242]

This passage is easy to misunderstand because modern Americans read the word "constitution" as referring to the document drafted in Philadelphia and ratified by the states, together with its later amendments. But Mason, Madison, and the rest of the founders were not Americans yet. Or, if so, only barely. They were rebel Englishmen and they had an English understanding of what a "constitution" is. Notice that Mason expressly refers to the "British constitution." Yet the British did not then, and still do not, have a written constitution. To Mason, the word "constitution" referred not merely to a discrete document, but to the entire interlocking network of foundational documents, statutes, common law rules, history, institutional behavior, informal understandings, moral and professional norms, traditions, and popular expectations that make up the political and governmental culture of a nation. When Mason and Madison were debating the impeachment language of Article 1, they were, of course, drafting a document that, once ratified, would become the "Constitution," but they knew the writing was only the bare framework on which the country's real constitution would grow.

Therefore, what Mason (and Madison) wanted was to ensure that impeachment could reach not merely technical violations of the large "C," proper noun, written "Constitution" that they were composing, but also presidential conduct that subverts the small "c" constitution in the broad English sense of a developed set of governing rules and norms. Adoption of the phrase "high crimes and misdemeanors" accomplished that end, in part because there is no other way to read many famous British impeachment cases. The impeachments of the earl of Strafford and Archbishop Laud were expressly premised on the charge that they were subverting law in favor of arbitrary royal government, or as John Pym, leader of the Commons put it, endeavoring "to alter the settled frame and constitution of government."[243] The essence of the case against the earl of Clarendon in 1667 was undercutting parliamentary constraints on the monarchy.[244] The articles of impeachment against the earl of Danby in 1678 quoted the operative language of the Strafford and Laud cases almost verbatim, charging that he "endeavoured to subvert the ancient and well established form of government in this kingdom, and instead thereof to introduce an arbitrary and tyrannical way of government."[245] The articles of impeachment against Warren Hastings alleged "high crimes and misdemeanors," but their instigator Edmund Burke conceded that Hastings' offenses were not crimes in law, but "against those eternal laws of justice, which are our rule and birthright."[246] In short, the offenses of all these men were against Britain's unwritten constitution, or more precisely – and critically – against Parliament's understanding of that constitution.

Even if we did not have the evidence of British practice, the debates in Philadelphia and during ratification would make the point clear. In adopting impeachment provisions that permit removal of a president for "high crimes and misdemeanors," the founding generation conferred on Congress the same power that Parliament had progressively seized for itself. The written constitution granted successive generations of legislators the power to identify for themselves the essential characteristics of the American constitutional system and to defend that system by removing its chief executive officer if he or she, by any individual act, pattern of behavior, or culpable inattention, places it at risk.

5

Impeaching Legislators and Lesser Executive Branch Officials

When the framers wrote that the "President, Vice President and all civil officers of the United States" are impeachable, they conspicuously failed to define "civil officers."[1] Because this clause is in Article 2, which defines the structure and powers of the executive branch, the term plainly applies to executive branch subordinates of the president. Yet there has only been one such impeachment in all of American history, that of Secretary of War William Belknap in 1876, which we will consider at the end of this chapter.[2] Likewise, it was generally assumed, though not expressly written into the constitutional text, that life-tenured federal judges could be impeached, a point to which we will return in Chapter 6. But there was general uncertainty about whether members of Congress were impeachable. Enough people thought the answer was yes that the very first federal impeachment, in 1797–98, was of a senator – William Blount – who had himself been a delegate to the Constitutional Convention.

IMPEACHING CONGRESS: CONSTITUTIONAL TEXT AND WHAT THE FOUNDERS THOUGHT

The ambiguity about the impeachability of legislators stems not merely from the failure of the constitutional text to define "civil officers" and the placement of the clause containing that phrase in Article 2 on the executive branch, but also from the provision in Article 1, section 5, that, "Each House may ... punish its Members for disorderly Behavior, and, with the Concurrence of two thirds, expel a Member." Inasmuch as the principal consequence of a successful impeachment is removal of the offender from office, it seems superfluous to have in the same constitution powers both to expel and to impeach legislators, particularly since expulsion requires action by only one house and impeachment by two.

The pragmatic counterargument is that expulsion does not bar re-entry into Congress by re-election or prevent the offender's later appointment to executive or judicial offices, while impeachment can disqualify the guilty party from any future opportunity to "hold and enjoy any Office of honor, Trust or Profit under the United

States."[3] Therefore, the framers may have intended that this measure of civic self-protection be available against defaulting legislators as well as judges and executive branch officials. The problem is that, even if this would be a sensible interpretation of an ambiguous textual point, neither the text nor the founding-era debates clarify the question.

During the Constitutional Convention, impeachability of legislators was scarcely mentioned. In Philadelphia, Hamilton's proposed model for the new constitution provided for, "The Governour [i.e., the President] Senators and all officers of the United States to be liable to impeachment."[4] But Hamilton's model was never an important part of the convention's deliberations. During a debate midway through the convention on whether presidents should be impeachable, Rufus King argued that neither presidents nor senators, both of whom would face the electorate periodically, should be subject to "intermediate trial, by impeachment."[5] James Wilson, later one of the first justices of the U.S. Supreme Court, said that, if there were to be impeachment of the president, then "Senators who are to hold their places during the same term with the Executive ought to be subject to impeachment and removal."[6] What these two delegates thought at the end of the convention about whether senators *were actually* included among "civil officers" is anyone's guess. Members of the House of Representatives were never mentioned as possible subjects of impeachment, perhaps because their popular election and two-year terms were thought to provide any necessary surety against misbehavior. In any case, nothing more specific was said at the convention about impeaching legislators, leaving the question open.

During the ratification debates, many of the most influential figures seem to have assumed that senators, at least, could be impeached. Indeed, one of the common criticisms of the Senate as proposed was that senators were given too much power and could be held to account only by an impeachment process in which they would act as their own judges. At the Virginia ratifying convention, George Mason complained, "The Senators were to try themselves. If a majority of them were guilty of the crime, would they pronounce themselves guilty?"[7] Patrick Henry made the same complaint: "Are the members of the Senate responsible? They may try themselves, and, if found guilty on impeachment, are to be only removed from office."[8] Edmund Randolph supported the Senate as proposed, and offered as one security against senatorial impropriety that senators "may also be impeached."[9] He was supported in his view of the impeachability of senators, though not in his approval of the constitution, by Richard Henry Lee, a Virginia congressman under the Articles of Confederation, who wrote to Randolph opposing ratification and noting that the Senate would "try all impeachments, either of their own members or of the officers appointed by themselves."[10] The view that senators were impeachable was sufficiently general in the Virginia convention that it included among the proposed amendments attached to its ultimate ratification vote one suggesting, "That some tribunal other than the Senate be provided for trying impeachments of senators."[11]

Worry that the impeachment mechanism gave senators undue control over their own disciplinary proceedings was shared outside Virginia. James Wilson of Pennsylvania supported ratification, but found imperfection in the fact that "when two thirds of the Senate concur in forming a bad treaty, it will be hard to procure a vote of two thirds against them, if they should be impeached."[12] Samuel Spencer in North Carolina and Charles C. Pinckney in South Carolina expressed similar concerns.[13] The North Carolina convention offered a proposed amendment identical to Virginia's for trying the impeachments of senators elsewhere than the Senate.[14]

In *Federalist 66*, Alexander Hamilton responded to the argument that the trial of impeachments in the Senate provided no protection against the specter of the president and the Senate in combination "betraying the interests of the nation in a ruinous treaty."[15] Hamilton did not deny that impeachment of senators is the apparent constitutional remedy for such misconduct. He simply argued that, even though the two-thirds majority required to ratify a treaty could not be relied upon to impeach itself, once skullduggery producing a disastrous treaty was exposed, the Senate as a whole would, as a matter of self-interest, convict the few senatorial ringleaders of the business.[16]

At least one ratifying convention delegate interpreted "civil officers" to extend beyond the Senate into the House of Representatives. Samuel Stillman of Massachusetts declared that, "the constitution provides for the impeachment ... of every officer in Congress, who shall be guilty of malconduct."[17] In sum, if we relied on the convention and ratification debates alone, we would have to conclude that the original public understanding of the question was that senators, at least, were impeachable. But the constitutional text remained tantalizingly obscure, leaving the point open for debate whenever it should be squarely presented for the first time.

THE IMPEACHMENT OF SENATOR WILLIAM BLOUNT, 1797–98

A test case arose remarkably quickly. On July 7, 1797, only nine years after the constitution was ratified, Congressman Samuel Sitgreaves entered the Senate chamber and informed that body that the House had impeached Senator William Blount of Tennessee "of high crimes and misdemeanors."[18]

William Blount was born in North Carolina in 1749, son of a well-to-do landowner and businessman. He aligned with the Patriot side of the American Revolution and served in the Continental Army, chiefly as a paymaster. In 1780, Blount took a seat in the North Carolina House of Commons, and in 1782 was elected as one of North Carolina's delegates to the Continental Congress. Over the next five years, Blount moved back and forth between membership in the Continental Congress and the state legislature. In 1787, he was elected as a member of the North Carolina delegation to the Constitutional Convention; however, he was present for only a few weeks in late June and early July and then again in August. He is counted as among the leaders of the 1788 ratification effort in North Carolina.[19]

So far, his story sounds like many of the other "Founding Fathers." However, Blount's public life and private interests were always intertwined. Like a great many of his contemporaries, Blount was convinced that his fortune was to be made in land speculation in the unsettled portions of the growing American empire.[20] He was at the center of a complex series of legislative maneuvers in the North Carolina legislature and the national congress that ultimately severed North Carolina land west of the Appalachians and transformed it into a "Southwest Territory" that in due course became the state of Tennessee. In 1790, George Washington appointed Blount governor of the territory. Political organization in the area proceeded swiftly so that by May 1796 the new state of Tennessee was admitted to the Union. Blount was appointed one of its first two senators.

Blount's commitment to development of the frontier was not disinterested. He and his brothers managed to lay claim to vast swathes of undeveloped Tennessee land, over 2.5 million acres, which he hoped to sell and make himself rich. Unfortunately, his purchases were often made on credit and a combination of international developments caused western land prices to collapse, placing the Blount family on the brink of ruin. One of the reasons for the fall in land prices was that Spain, which at the time owned Louisiana and with it New Orleans and control of the mouth of the Mississippi, had suffered reverses in its war with France.[21] American frontiersmen feared that the French might secure return of their former territory Louisiana (as indeed they did in 1800[22]) and cut off commercial access to the Gulf of Mexico, which would cripple commerce in the interior.

In order to restore his fortunes, Blount concocted a scheme to give Great Britain control of Louisiana and Florida. The idea was that American militias would attack Spanish military installations at Pensacola, New Orleans, and New Madrid (up the Mississippi River), while the British Navy attacked, or at least blockaded Pensacola and New Orleans.[23] Blount's proposal to the British was that, in return for the territorial gains, they would allow American merchants free access to New Orleans and Mississippi trade. Whether the scheme was merely audacious or plain crazy remains debatable. The British seem never to have had any genuine interest,[24] but Blount was incautious enough to write letters to his co-conspirators in the plot, one of which was turned over to an American military officer in Knoxville, Tennessee, who in turn passed it along to Secretary of State Timothy Pickering. Pickering gave the letter to President John Adams. Adams, not surprisingly, viewed Blount's behavior as outrageous. He sought legal advice from the attorney general, who consulted with other lawyers and concluded that Blount's letter was evidence of a crime. Adams sent the letter to the Senate suggesting that something should be done about it.[25]

On July 3, 1797, Blount returned to the Senate chamber from a walk, whereupon the clerk read the letter aloud, to Blount's undoubted astonishment. Vice President

Thomas Jefferson, performing his role as President of the Senate, asked Blount if he had written the letter. Blount ducked the question and asked for a day to respond, which he was given. The following day, Blount did not return to the Senate, but requested more time to respond. That request was denied and a committee formed to investigate the matter.[26]

On July 5, Blount tried to flee, but was intercepted and his belongings seized. He evaded capture himself but slunk back to the Senate the following day resolved to contest the allegations against him.[27] On July 7, the House voted to impeach Blount and informed the Senate that they would present formal articles of impeachment in due course.[28] On July 8, two senators swore that they recognized Blount's handwriting on the most incriminatory letter, whereupon the Senate found that he had committed a "high misdemeanor, entirely inconsistent with his public trust and duty as a Senator," and voted 25:1 to expel him.[29] Blount posted bail and lit out for Tennessee, from which he never returned during any of the ensuing proceedings.[30] However, before leaving he engaged two remarkably gifted lawyers to act on his behalf.[31]

Jared Ingersoll was the Pennsylvania attorney general and had served as one of Pennsylvania's delegates to the Constitutional Convention, which obviously lent his arguments about constitutional construction special weight.[32] Alexander J. Dallas was Secretary of the Commonwealth of Pennsylvania and the first reporter of decisions of the U.S. Supreme Court.[33] Throughout a protracted investigation by the House and the trial in the Senate, Ingersoll and Dallas represented Blount aggressively.

During the remainder of 1797, the House committee appointed to investigate Blount's affairs pursued its inquiries. In January 1798, it presented five proposed articles of impeachment to the House, which promptly approved them.[34] Article 1 charged that Blount's attempt to help Great Britain conquer Spanish territory was a "violation of the obligations of neutrality, and against the laws of the United States, and the peace and interests thereof."[35] The law to which the article referred was the Neutrality Act 1794, which made it a misdemeanor for "any person . . . within the territory or jurisdiction of the United States [to] begin or set on foot or provide or prepare the means for any military expedition or enterprise . . . against the territory or dominions of any foreign prince or state of whom the United States was at peace . . ."[36]

Part of Blount's plan was to enlist the Creek and Cherokee nations in assaults on Spanish interests. Therefore, Article 2 charged that his actions violated the 1795 Treaty of Friendship, Limits, and Navigation between the United States and Spain, which bound both countries to restrain Indian tribes from attacking the other.[37]

Article 3 alleged that, as part of the scheme to secure Indian cooperation, Blount sought to alienate the Creeks and Cherokees from the official U.S. Indian agent, Benjamin Hawkins. Article 4 maintained that Blount seduced James Carey, the official American interpreter legally assigned to assist Indian agent Hawkins, to help in his scheme of conquest. Finally, Article 5 alleged that, the better to gain the help of the tribes, Blount fomented distrust among them about the process by which boundary lines between U.S. and tribal territories would be set.

Ingersoll and Dallas never seriously contested the factual allegations against Blount. Not only did the Senate have Blount's own letters, but House investigators had secured testimony from several of Blount's confederates. Instead, they rested their case on a series of legal, which is to say constitutional, arguments about impeachment itself. In their formal answer, counsel raised four points:

(1) that this was a criminal prosecution and therefore jurisdiction of the case lay, not in the Senate, but in ordinary courts, and that, at a minimum, the accused should receive rights guaranteed in criminal trials by the Sixth Amendment, particularly the right to a jury;

(2) that none of the articles charged him with committing any "crime or misdemeanor, in the execution of any civil office held under the United States, or with any malconduct in civil office, or abuse of any public trust" – in other words, that all of his conduct was unimpeachable because unconnected with his senatorial office;

(3) that Blount, having been expelled a year-and-a-half before, "is not now a senator" subject to impeachment; and

(4) that senators are not civil officers of the United States.[38]

The claim that impeachments are criminal actions requiring juries was batted about,[39] but never treated seriously by the Senate.[40] The argument that a public official may not be impeached for unofficial behavior presented a more serious question. Blount's conduct may have violated U.S. law, particularly the Neutrality Act, but none of it was done in his official capacity as a senator. His senatorial status doubtless conferred on his overtures to the British and others some credibility that a private citizen would lack, but he never claimed to be acting as an emissary of the American government. Indeed, the whole point of the scheme was to do something he and others knew quite well the national government would disapprove. The question posed by Blount's lawyers was whether a public official should be impeached for a private betrayal of the interests of the government under which he holds office.

Although Senator Blount's lawyers raised this point, they did not press it particularly hard.[41] The reply of the House manager Robert Goodloe Harper nicely summarized the common-sense rebuttal:

> But if, by official offenses, the learned counsel mean offenses committed by an officer, and relating solely to the duties of his office, I must entreat them to reflect on the extent to which their doctrine would lead. Suppose a Judge of the United States were to commit theft or perjury; would the learned counsel say that he shall not be impeached for it? If so, he must remain in office with all his infamy; for there is no

method of removing a judge but by impeachment. It seems to me, on the contrary, that the power of impeachment has two objects: first, to remove persons whose misconduct may have rendered them unworthy of retaining their offices; and, secondly, to punish those offenses of a more political nature, which, though not susceptible of that exact definition where they might be brought within the sphere of ordinary tribunals, are yet very dangerous to the public. These offenses, in the English law, and in our Constitutions, which have borrowed its phraseology, are called "high crimes and misdemeanors."[42]

In the Blount case, the Senate never formally resolved the question of whether arguably private offenses are impeachable when committed by civil officers because they dismissed the impeachment on jurisdictional grounds. Nonetheless, as we will see when we consider judges, Harper's argument for the impeachability of private crime demonstrating unfitness for office has largely prevailed.

Harper's argument implicitly raised another question about the charges against Blount. His circumlocution about "offenses of a more political nature ... not susceptible of that exact definition where they might be brought within the sphere of ordinary tribunals" plainly refers to political misbehavior that does not qualify as an indictable crime. In saying that such conduct is impeachable, he echoes Hamilton in *Federalist 65*,[43] but it is worth considering why he made the point at all.

This requires a closer examination of the Blount charges. The first article, which alleges "violations of the obligation of neutrality," arguably charges a criminal violation of the Neutrality Act of 1794. Some have contended that Blount's conduct did not quite reach the threshold for breach of the Act because he only conspired to set in motion a military expedition that never occurred. This seems to ignore the language of the Act making it a crime even to "begin or set on foot or provide or *prepare the means*" of a prohibited expedition. Likewise, one could have argued that, in 1797, there existed a federal common law of crimes that would permit charging a conspiracy to violate the Act.[44] However, neither Blount's lawyers nor the House managers seemed interested in pursuing this line.

Their disinterest is the more remarkable because none of the final four articles allege that Blount committed any crime. Article 2 asserted that Blount's efforts to stir up Indian attacks on Spain were contrary to the 1795 friendship treaty between the United States and Spain, while Articles 3, 4, and 5 allege various means of subverting U.S. policy toward the Creek and Cherokee nations. All these things were plainly contrary to American interests. Indeed, the whole scheme to hand Florida and Louisiana to the country's former imperial overlords was downright infamous for a U.S. senator. But as traitorous in the colloquial sense as the whole business seemed to Blount's contemporaries (Abigail Adams fumed, "When shall we cease to have Judases?"[45]), the articles charge no crime beyond the violation of the Neutrality Act in Article 1.

It is fair to conclude, both from the fact that the House approved Articles 2–5 and from the desultory arguments on the point in the Senate, that the vast majority of both chambers believed that impeachment extended beyond crime, and even beyond misuse of formal official power, to betrayals of public trust and conduct patently contrary to the national interest. Whether the Blount case counts as "precedent" for that point depends on how one thinks of the idea of precedent in impeachments. If one insists on a conviction to create a precedent affirming the impeachability of particular behavior, the Senate did not convict Blount of anything, and thus no precedent emerged. The better view is that the Senate's choice to resolve the case on other grounds is good evidence that Congress as a whole viewed impeachable conduct as extending beyond indictable crimes.

This left the Senate confronted with two strong jurisdictional arguments: first, that a senator is not a "civil officer" subject to impeachment; and, second, that, even if senators are civil officers, Blount was no longer a senator by virtue of his expulsion and therefore could not be impeached.

The arguments over whether senators are civil officers were technically complicated, and relied almost entirely on close reading of the impeachment clauses and other portions of the constitution.[46] They are of little interest to us here, though we will touch briefly on the question of what it means to hold an "office" or be an "officer" in Chapter 14's discussion of the emoluments clauses. An interesting side note to the Blount arguments was the suggestion that American impeachments should mirror the scope of British parliamentary impeachments and extend beyond federal government officials to the citizenry at large. While it was true that Parliament had impeached private citizens, the proposition that Congress had the power to do so was received coldly and has never been raised since.[47]

The contention of Senator Blount's counsel that a former federal official can no longer be impeached once out of office had strong appeal, not the least of which was the intuition that, with Blount expelled from the Senate and back in Tennessee, the whole thing was moot. The managers responded that an official wrongdoer should not be able to avoid either the stigma of forced removal from office or imposition of a ban on future office-holding by the simple expedient of resigning before Congress can act.

In the end, the Senate chose to terminate its proceeding against Blount, but on which exact ground has always been somewhat in dispute. On January 10, 1799, after several days of private debate, the Senate rejected the following motion:

> That William Blount was a civil officer of the United States, within the meaning of the Constitution of the United States, and, therefore, liable to be impeached by the House of Representatives;
>
>   That, as the Articles of Impeachment charge him with high crimes and misdemeanors, supposed to have been committed while he was a Senator of the United States, his plea ought to be overruled.[48]

The rejection of the motion *in toto* implied either that the Senate thought Blount, as a senator, was not a civil officer, or that his commission of the offenses while a senator did not subject him to impeachment once he stopped being one. On January 14, Thomas Jefferson took the chair of the Senate and announced that the Senate had reached the following final verdict:

> The Court, after having given the most mature and serious consideration to the question, and to the full and able arguments urged on both sides, has come to the decision which I am now about to deliver.
>
> The Court is of opinion that the matter alleged in the plea of the defendant is sufficient in law to show that this Court ought not to hold jurisdiction of the said impeachment, and that the said impeachment is dismissed.[49]

The usual interpretation of this vote is that the Senate decided senators are not civil officers and are thus not impeachable. But others have contended that the verdict could just as easily mean that former officeholders are not within congressional impeachment jurisdiction.[50] I find the conventional interpretation somewhat more plausible, both as a reading of the Senate's two final resolutions and as an assessment of the strength of the two arguments. In any event, no legislator has been impeached since 1799, and despite serious arguments that the Blount decision is wrong,[51] it seems improbable that the effort will ever be made again.

Additional Lessons from the Blount Affair

Beyond its apparent resolution of the bare question of whether legislators may be impeached, the Blount case had several other intriguing features:

Interpretive Authority

Perhaps as interesting as the substance of the charges in the Blount case and the Senate's resolution of the case is the authority on which both sides relied in contesting every point. No one referred to the particulars of the debates in Philadelphia, not even defense counsel Jared Ingersoll, who had been a delegate. No one alluded either to the debates in ratifying conventions or to the pamphlet and newspaper literature of the ratification period. Of course, almost none of these materials had yet been published. The official journal of the Philadelphia convention was published in 1819.[52] Madison's notes of the convention containing the crucial exchange in which Mason offered, first, "maladministration" and then "high crimes and misdemeanors" would not be made public until 1840.[53] The *Federalist Papers* were compiled and published in 1788,[54] but did not receive canonical stature for many years. Still, it is noteworthy that Ingersoll made no effort to employ his special knowledge of the framers' deliberations.

Instead, both sides relied on three sources of authority: arguments from the constitutional text; arguments that combined the text and political or governmental theories presumed to underlie it; and British precedent. Counsel for both sides recognized that the constitutional text was sparse, and sometimes contradictory, but both sides assumed (with varying degrees of enthusiasm) that guidance to the meaning of the constitution in general and the impeachment clauses in particular could be found in British practice and legal vocabulary.

House manager James A. Bayard opened by noting that the constitution has a number of provisions that cannot be understood except by reference to English precedents, and put impeachments among them.[55] Defense counsel Dallas argued against employment of English common law precedents in construing the impeachment power (insofar as they seemed to hurt his client), but then turned around and cited more favorable impeachment precedents at some length.[56]

Ingersoll then rose. Throughout his arguments, Ingersoll cited Magna Carta, Blackstone's *Commentaries*, Hume's *History of England*,[57] and Wooddeson's *Lectures on the Laws of England*,[58] and deployed the substantive and procedural details of British impeachments back to 1321.[59] He mentioned the "statute of 25th Edward III" (the Treason Act 1351) and the controversy over whether Parliament can convict for constructive treasons.[60] In contending that impeachment should lie only for offenses involving the abuse of the powers of office, he cited the impeachments of the duke of Suffolk, the earl of Bristol, the duke of Buckingham, Lord Chancellor Michael de la Pole, Lord Finch, and the earl of Oxford.[61] House manager Harper closed out the arguments by rebutting the defense on the applicability of English precedent, and trotting out his own antiquarian reference to the impeachment of the Rev. Sacheverell for preaching a seditious sermon.[62]

The fact that, not unlike advocates in any age, the combatants either emphasized or disparaged the importance of parliamentary impeachments according to their usefulness does not alter two points: first, in this debate among members of the founding generation, including one of the actual framers (Ingersoll), everyone argued the interpretation of "high crimes and misdemeanors" by reference to British precedents; and, second, all of them had access to plenty of detailed information about those precedents.

Foreign Affairs

Throughout the debates over Senator Blount's impeachment, there was scarcely any discussion of whether his conduct amounted to an impeachable offense. The first article of impeachment alleging a violation of the Neutrality Act 1794 had the advantage of charging a crime, albeit a misdemeanor. None of the other articles even arguably involved crimes, yet Blount's counsel made no effort to seek their dismissal on that ground. The first lesson from the apparent consensus on the impeachability of Blount's conduct is that impeachable offenses include non-criminal behavior involving betrayal of public trust and conduct plainly contrary to the national interest. The fact that Blount's scheme involved relations with foreign nations, both European and Native American, carries further implications.

Blount's scheme violated national foreign policy objectives shared by the executive and legislative branches. President Adams, and Washington before him, favored U.S. neutrality in the ongoing European wars.[63] Before Adams' election, Congress had passed legislation mandating neutrality and specifically barring the sort of buccaneering adventure against foreign states Blount was planning. The friendship treaty with Spain, negotiated by the executive and ratified by the Senate, imposed an obligation on both nations not to stir up hostility against each other among the Indian nations.[64] Similarly, U.S. policy toward the Indian nations, embodied in legislation, was to maintain peaceful relations and to avoid friction by dealing with them only through governmentally authorized agents. Finally, unstated in any treaty or statute, but widely understood, was a general desire to weaken the hold of European powers on lands bordering the United States, particularly land around the vital Mississippi waterway, leaving those territories available for American expansion and annexation.

Blount's adventure ran afoul of all these objectives. If we assume the Senate acquitted Blount on the ground that senators are not "civil officers," then we might also conclude that his impeachment establishes that, under certain circumstances, conduct that undercuts the nation's foreign policy is impeachable. But, as is so often true with impeachment precedent, the extent of this principle is unclear.

THE IMPEACHMENT OF SECRETARY OF WAR BELKNAP

The life of William Belknap was adventurous, colorful, scandalous, and pretty darn interesting. However, most of the interesting parts are beyond our scope. The tale of his impeachment is much more quickly told. Belknap was a New Yorker, a Princeton graduate, and a lawyer who settled in Iowa, was elected to Congress, and, upon the outbreak of the Civil War, raised a unit of Iowa volunteers. He fought with distinction throughout the war and rose to the rank of Brevet Major General. After Ulysses S. Grant was elected president in 1868, General William T. Sherman, under whom Belknap had served, recommended him to Grant as Secretary of War.[65]

In many respects, he may have been a perfectly fine cabinet officer. Unfortunately, so the story goes, he had married as his second wife a woman with lavish tastes that could not be satisfied on Belknap's government salary. Belknap's third wife was the sister of his second, and she, too, seems to have had an affinity for the finer things. Whether the greed was his or theirs, it manifested itself in corruption. The maneuver that led to his downfall was a scheme to sell the post of trader at Fort Sill in the Oklahoma Territory, an extremely lucrative sinecure because the trader received a monopoly on supplying goods to soldiers posted in the area and often to Indians in the region. The details were convoluted: Belknap induced John Evans, the trader legitimately appointed to the post, to pay Caleb Marsh, Belknap's preferred candidate, regular kickbacks, a portion of which was funneled to Belknap.[66]

In February 1876, the Democratic House launched an investigation and discovered the scheme.[67] Impeachment loomed. On March 2, Treasury Secretary Benjamin Bristow told General Grant that Belknap would surely be impeached. Belknap was immediately summoned to the White House, where Grant accepted his resignation. It is generally thought that the purpose of the resignation was to forestall impeachment. It did not. Congress was aware of the resignation, but the House was determined that Belknap should not escape punishment so easily.[68] A committee headed by Congressman Hiester Clymer drew up five articles of impeachment which were passed unanimously by the full House.[69]

The matter went to the Senate for trial.[70] Belknap's lawyers argued that the Senate lacked jurisdiction because their client was no longer in office. By a vote of 37:29, the Senate declared that it did. However, to convict Belknap required a two-thirds vote, which the House managers could not wrangle. In the end, the Senate voted 35:25 for conviction, which failed the two-thirds threshold.[71] Scarcely anyone doubted that Belknap had taken the bribes or that doing so was impeachable.[72] Indeed, Belknap himself does not seem to have contested either point.[73] Instead, many of the senators who voted for acquittal concluded that they lacked jurisdiction. Nonetheless, I am obliged to confess that I think that those who favored asserting jurisdiction had the better argument.[74] The jurisdiction of an ordinary court, civil or criminal, to address claims of malfeasance by a government official is not defeated by the resignation of the official. Such an outcome might make sense in impeachments if the remedy were entirely limited to removal from office. However, that is not the case. The constitution also provides that the Senate may disqualify an offending officeholder from ever again holding "any office of honor, Trust or Profit under the United States,"[75] and there seems no reason in law or logic to allow a malefactor to escape that added debarment with a quick resignation.

The result in Belknap's case has not conclusively settled the jurisdictional question of whether an official can be impeached after resigning from office. On the one hand, in the 1926 proceedings against District Judge George English, the judge resigned after he was impeached and on the day of his Senate trial, whereupon, on the recommendation of the House, the Senate dismissed the impeachment.[76] On the other hand, the House managers were explicit in declaring their view that the judge's resignation "in no way affects the right of the Senate, sitting as a court of impeachment, to hear and determine said impeachment charges."[77] The best reading of the affair is that neither the House nor the Senate was conceding a lack of jurisdiction based on English's resignation, but neither had any interest in spending the time necessary to beat a dead judicial horse.

The Loneliness of Secretary Belknap

The singularity of Belknap's case as the only impeachment of a federal cabinet officer deserves brief comment. Recall that the British Parliament invented impeachment as a means to strike back at royal overreach by attacking ministers of the crown. In Great Britain, impeachments died out in the late eighteenth century as ministers became less servants of the crown and more appointees of the leadership of the dominant faction in Parliament. In that setting, there was no longer a need for Parliament to impeach a minister who had fallen out of favor with the legislature. Instead, the prime minister simply fired the offender. If it was the prime minister who no longer enjoyed the support of a parliamentary majority, out he (or in due course she) went. No messy impeachment required.

Impeachments of cabinet and sub-cabinet level officers have never caught on in America for an analogous reason. Some of the framers imagined that cabinet officers might enjoy a sphere of autonomy by virtue of their senatorial confirmations and thus a status of quasi-independence from the president, which might in turn require impeachment to remove them.[78] That lingered as a theoretical possibility as long as there remained any doubt about the power of the president to dismiss his or her high-level appointees, a question raised in the impeachment of Andrew Johnson and not decided until the twentieth century (and not entirely conclusively even then).[79] But even in the absence of certainty on that point, the issue has almost invariably proven moot. If the president said "Go," appointees went. Any appointee whose continued service was so politically toxic as to provoke a serious effort at impeachment has been shuffled off the stage. In short, the latent legislative power to impeach subordinate executive branch officers has in nearly every case been sufficient to secure removal of officials who became noxious to the legislative majority and whose behavior verged anywhere near an impeachable zone.[80]

This is, after all, exactly what happened to Belknap. As soon as President Grant found out about the corruption allegations against his secretary of war, Belknap got the sack. That the sacking was probably intended to protect Belknap as much as Grant is somewhat beside the point. As soon as impeachment loomed, the offender was out of a job. The only apparent mystery in the Belknap matter is why Congress persisted. The answer was pure politics. Democrats had gained control of the House for the first time since the Civil War. Grant's administration was tainted by corruption. The Democrats wanted to make a large public splash of their discovery of Belknap's tawdry defalcations. No Congress since that time has either moved fast enough or thought it worthwhile to actually impeach a subordinate executive branch official.

Nonetheless, the latent power to do so remains important. Not only is it useful as a signal of legislative displeasure with administration personnel and policy, but the undoubted authority of Congress to impeach subordinate officials carries with it the associated powers of the House to investigate potentially impeachable conduct and of the Senate to try the allegations in articles of impeachment. As we will see in Chapter 8 when discussing Watergate and the travails of Richard Nixon, because impeachment authority is directly and exclusively granted to Congress, the courts have been especially willing to enforce congressional investigative demands in impeachment matters.

6

Impeachment of Judges

Even in a book about impeaching the president some discussion of judicial impeachment is essential. The impeachment of judges received little detailed attention at the Constitutional Convention or in the subsequent ratification debates, but what the Founders did say provides some insight into how they thought the impeachment of presidents should work. More importantly, cases against judges make up almost the entire body of federal impeachment precedent. Of the roughly twenty-one impeachments or near-impeachments in the nation's history, all but five involved federal judges. As we will see, there is a strong argument that the standard for impeaching judges is somewhat different than that for other officers, particularly the president, but no one seriously contends that judicial impeachment cases are irrelevant to presidents. They have been routinely cited as precedent in presidential impeachments and have important lessons to teach.

THE CONSTITUTIONAL TEXT AND THE FOUNDERS' UNDERSTANDING

Recall that judicial independence was a favorite battle cry of the colonists before the Revolution, and that their markers of that independence were tenure during good behavior and salaries paid regularly and not subject to withholding or variation based on political whim.[1] Both these elements were written into Article 3 of the constitution, which decrees that judges "of the supreme and inferior Courts, shall hold their Offices during good Behavior, and shall, at stated Times, receive for their Services a Compensation which shall not be diminished during their Continuance in Office."[2]

The constitution does not specifically refer to the impeachment of judges. Article 2 provides only that, "The President, Vice President *and all civil Officers of the United States,* shall be removed from Office on Impeachment for, and Conviction of, Treason, Bribery, or other high Crimes and Misdemeanors."[3] It is now accepted that "civil officers of the United States" includes judges. But if that is what the framers meant, it was peculiar to insert impeachability of "civil officers" into Article 2, which defines the powers and duties of the executive branch.

Nonetheless, as Rufus King of Massachusetts pointed out during the convention, impeachment or something very like it is a necessary implication of judicial tenure during "good behavior."[4] If judges are entitled to stay as long as their behavior is good, then they must go when their behavior is bad. Thus, there must be a mechanism for deciding what behavior is bad and when a particular judge has behaved that way. The only such mechanism in the constitution is impeachment. The proceedings of the Philadelphia Convention imply, but never expressly declare, that impeachment is the procedure by which judges will be removed.

On August 20, the Committee of Five (also known as the Committee of Detail[5]) was tasked with considering and reporting "a mode for trying the supreme Judges in cases of impeachment."[6] The request was made because, at that point in the convention, the working draft assigned trial of impeachments to the Supreme Court,[7] who could hardly be expected to try themselves if they were impeached. Still, the assumption plainly was that judges *could* be impeached.

On August 27, John Dickinson proposed that judges should hold office "during good behavior," but "may be removed by the Executive on the application [of] the Senate and House of Representatives."[8] Gouverneur Morris objected that such a procedure would amount to removal without trial of judges supposed to have tenure during good behavior.[9] Roger Sherman said that a similar rule prevailed in England.[10] James Wilson replied that the procedure was less to be feared in England due to the unlikelihood of the Lords and Commons agreeing, but that he had no such confidence in an American legislature which might be swayed by "every gust of faction."[11] The motion failed.[12] As a result, the final text gave judges tenure on good behavior, specified that impeachments should be initiated in the House and tried in the Senate, but did not expressly close the circle to say that this procedure applied to judges.

THE CONSTITUTIONAL STANDARD FOR JUDICIAL IMPEACHMENT

If judges are indeed "civil officers" as defined in Article 2, then they, like the president and vice president, are impeachable for "treason, bribery, or other high crimes and misdemeanors." Some have contended that the Article 3 provision that federal judges "shall hold their Offices during good Behavior" means that judges can *also* be removed for forms of bad behavior less serious than the "high" offenses of Article 2.[13] The basic argument is that the differences in length of tenure, power, and constitutional function between the judicial and presidential offices justify different standards of removal.

First, the fact that judges have life tenure means they are not subject to the democratic controls imposed on presidents by regular elections. A president who is just a really bad president will (presumably) be expelled from office after four years. A federal judge who proves to be a really bad judge remains in place until death unless impeachment intervenes. Therefore, one can argue that judges should be impeachable for at least some kinds of poor performance that, in a president, can be efficiently remedied by electoral defeat.

Second, judges are appointed while presidents are elected. The Electoral College scheme, even in its modern variant in which the electors exercise no personal judgment, but simply cast their ballots for the winner of their state's polling, is not perfectly democratic because the results do not always reflect the national popular vote. Nonetheless, in the modern age, the president's legitimacy depends on at least an indirect electoral mandate. A judge's does not. This is not a trivial distinction. Because the tenure of any American president is legitimized only by the ballot box, the mandate conferred by the electorate is not lightly to be repealed. Any effort to undo the results of an election – which is the practical consequence of presidential, but not judicial, impeachments – should be undertaken with great care and only in cases of great need.

Finally, the president's place in the constitutional scheme is far different than that of any judge. Any attempt to remove a president may precipitate a constitutional crisis and certainly threatens a dramatic upheaval in the national government. A change in presidents requires, or at least permits, a reordering of the executive branch and unforeseeable changes in national policy. The removal of a lower federal court judge has no necessary consequence outside his or her own district or circuit, and only modest effects even there. Even the removal of a Supreme Court justice may have no noticeable impact on the court's decisions.

The customary resolution of this problem has been to insist that the textual standard of removable bad behavior by judges is the same as for presidents and other civil officers – "treason, bribery, or other high crimes and misdemeanors" – while conceding that this phrase may apply differently to judges.[14] The questions thus become, first, how the impeachment remedy has been employed in the special case of judges, and, second, what lessons can be drawn from these precedents for impeachment of the president. To provide the answers, we look first at the impeachment in 1805 of Samuel Chase, associate justice of the Supreme Court, because that proceeding set a precedent against removal of judges either for partisan political reasons or for poor professional performance in the form of routine mistakes of law. We will then consider the other fourteen federal judicial impeachments or near-impeachments to find, if we can, some patterns in the misbehavior that has been deemed removable.

THE CASE OF JUSTICE SAMUEL CHASE

The impeachment trial of Samuel Chase opened in the Senate Chamber of the partially constructed Capitol building on February 4, 1805.[15] Presiding over the trial was Vice President Aaron Burr, wanted in both New York and New Jersey for his recent murder of Alexander Hamilton in their famous duel.[16] Luther Martin, formerly one of the Maryland delegation to the Constitutional Convention, led

Chase's defense. Thomas Jefferson, beginning his second term as president, lived down Pennsylvania Avenue in the mansion we now call the White House. And it appears Jefferson set in motion the machinery that brought Chase into the dock.

Samuel Chase was born in Maryland in 1741. He was admitted to the bar in 1761, and elected to the Maryland legislature in 1764. In the years before the Revolution, he was a vocal, energetic, and sometimes quarrelsome advocate of colonial rights and in due course independence. He represented Maryland in the Continental Congress and signed the Declaration of Independence.[17] Chase became a state judge in 1788, and in 1796, George Washington appointed him to the U.S. Supreme Court.[18]

Although Chase initially opposed ratification of the federal constitution on the ground that it lacked a bill of rights, he later became a committed Federalist. He was politically aligned with John Adams during Adams' single term as president, and was notorious as an adversary of Jefferson's emergent anti-Federalist coalition that became known as Republicans. Before considering the particulars of the impeachment case against Chase, a brief primer on the political controversies of the day is required.

Adams' Federalists and Jefferson's Republicans divided over issues domestic and foreign. To oversimplify, the Federalists favored a more politically and financially powerful central government that encouraged manufacturing, and thus to some degree favored northern and urban interests. The Republicans were suspicious of centralized government and economic power, preferred dispersal of political authority to the states, idealized agriculture over other forms of economic activity, and thus to some degree favored southern and rural interests. In foreign policy, the Federalists were sympathetic to an aristocracy of talent and commercial wealth and retained a cautious affinity for Great Britain, despite the recent separation. Republicans laid claim to more radical egalitarian ideals, a political philosophy that, together with gratitude for French support during the American Revolution, disposed them to at least initial sympathy with the French revolutionaries and their new republic.

From 1793 until the Battle of Waterloo in 1815, England was at war with France.[19] The dramatic high points of that long struggle were the great land and sea battles, but the contest was also waged in the less dramatic realm of trade and commerce. Both Great Britain and France needed to supply themselves by seaborne trade, and each sought to cut the ocean lifelines of the other. Americans wanted to trade with both sides and avoid seizure of their vessels and impressment of their seamen. In 1794, John Jay negotiated a treaty with Britain that addressed – one-sidedly in British favor – some of these problems. Despite its deficiencies, President Washington and the Federalists secured its ratification in the Senate as the best deal available, to howls of protest from the Republican opposition.[20] Three years later, in 1797, the Adams administration made diplomatic overtures to the revolutionary French regime aimed at eliminating French naval seizures of American vessels. The ruling Directory refused to see the American envoys, referring them instead to three anonymous officials known to history only as X, Y, and Z. These worthies demanded a bribe of $250,000 for French Foreign Minister Talleyrand and a $10-million loan as preconditions for negotiations. The Americans refused and when news of the demands became public in the United States, outrage was universal.[21]

In this environment, nativism and anti-foreign feeling surged. In 1798, Congress passed the infamous Alien and Sedition Acts. The first extended the period of residence necessary for citizenship and gave the president power to expel undesirable foreigners. The second made it a crime carrying both fines and imprisonment to make defamatory statements about either the president or Congress.[22] The Sedition Act was inspired by the rise of a virulently partisan brand of journalism prone to making scurrilous allegations against those in authority, who at the time were Federalists. The Sedition Act was a particular target of Jefferson and the Republicans. Their ire was no doubt due in part to the fact that prosecutions under the Act were directed primarily at Republican writers, but the Jeffersonians stood on solid ground in labeling the Act a violation of the First Amendment and a blow to the free political discourse necessary to a healthy democracy.[23]

As concern about the possibility of war with France increased, the Federalist-dominated Congress passed another unpopular measure – a property tax intended to finance a strengthened military. A group of German farmers in Pennsylvania, incensed by seizures of property from those who did not pay the tax, banded together under the leadership of John Fries and, weapons in hand, intimidated a federal marshal into releasing prisoners held for tax resistance. President Adams sent troops to quell the farmers, who quickly submitted to superior force. Fries and others were arrested and charged with treason.[24]

The final Federalist assault on Republican sensibilities came in the form of the Judiciary Act 1801. After John Adams lost his bid for re-election to Thomas Jefferson in November 1800, the lame-duck Congress passed a bill that did some very sensible things, but also enabled what Republicans saw as partisan skullduggery. From 1788 to 1801, Supreme Court justices had a dual role. For a few weeks each year, they gathered in the capital city to act as the nation's highest appellate court. The rest of their time was spent "riding circuit," which meant traveling around their assigned geographic region and sitting, customarily in tandem with a local federal district judge, as trial judges on ordinary cases. The Judiciary Act created six new circuit courts staffed by sixteen new judges, thus eliminating the need for high court justices to spend weeks bumping along bad roads and sleeping in doubtful inns, as well as ending the troublesome practice of having the justices sit on appeals of cases where they had themselves been the trial judges. Republicans, however, found the creation of new federal courts an assault on state prerogatives. They were doubly displeased when President Adams and the Federalist Senate quickly filled the new appellate posts (as well as justice of the peace slots also created by the bill) with Federalist appointees. Jefferson was particularly outraged by this effort, as he saw it, to entrench his opponents in the government. The new Congress voted in 1802 to repeal the Act and abolish the judgeships it had created.[25]

Samuel Chase entered into these controversies in three ways: first, because he was an outspoken, almost pugilistic, Federalist partisan even while a member of the Supreme Court; second, because he sat as trial judge in the treason trial of John Fries and in one of the most notorious Sedition Act cases; and, third, because of statements he made when performing another circuit-riding duty – instructing investigative grand juries.

John Fries was first tried for treason in 1799 before Supreme Court Justice Paterson (he of the New Jersey/Paterson Plan in the Constitutional Convention) and District Judge Richard Peters. Fries was convicted, but the case was reversed on appeal due to possible juror bias. The second trial, in April 1800, came on before Justice Chase and Judge Peters. There being no serious issue that Fries had led an armed group against federal authorities, the only question was whether it amounted to treason under the narrow constitutional definition of "levying war against [the United States], or ... adhering to their enemies, giving them aid and comfort."[26]

Before the evidence began, Justice Chase announced that he intended to instruct the jury in a way that brought the conduct of Fries and his confederates within the category of "levying war" against the United States. It was later alleged that he also told counsel that they would be barred from arguing any different definition of the law to the jury. The first of these announcements will seem troublesome to a modern lawyer primarily because Chase had arrived at his legal conclusion without hearing argument from the parties. However, his prohibition against arguing to the jury an interpretation of the law contrary to the judge's instructions will seem entirely appropriate because that is the universal norm in current American practice. Interestingly, it seems that, in the eighteenth century, the norm was reversed and arguing law to juries was, at least in some courts, seen as something approaching a fundamental right. Fries' lawyers were so enraged by Chase's pronouncements that they refused to continue as counsel. However, it seems that, when confronted with vigorous objections to his initial rulings, Chase backed off and offered defense counsel the opportunity to present their legal contentions both to him and ultimately to the jury.[27] The lawyers persisted in their refusal to participate, the defendant refused the offer of other counsel, and the trial proceeded to conviction and sentence of death. (John Adams later pardoned Fries.[28])

These transactions were the subject of the first article of impeachment against Chase.[29] They are peculiar in any number of ways. The most obvious is that, even if Chase's initial proclamation was in error, he offered to correct it and defense counsel imperiously refused to accept the concession. Moreover, if there was error, it was appealable to the Supreme Court. While it is true that such an appeal would have been tainted in the eyes of some by Chase's presence on the high court, the same was true of all appeals in cases in which the justices were riding circuit. In impeaching

Chase for the Fries trial, the House was asserting that judges could be removed merely for making legal errors in the conduct of criminal trials.

In June 1800, several months after the Fries trial, Justice Chase presided in the prosecution of James Callender for violating the Sedition Act with portions of his book, *The Prospect Before Us*. Callender was a political polemicist and an early practitioner of what we might now call yellow or tabloid journalism. For what it is worth, he was an equal opportunity offender who over the course of his career earned the loathing of public figures of all persuasions. The writing that brought him to trial before Justice Chase was an attack on John Adams. Some years later, he was responsible for publicizing the claim that Jefferson had taken his slave Sally Hemmings as his mistress – an allegation universally condemned as baseless slander then and for two centuries thereafter ... which, of course, turned out to be true.[30]

In his book, Callender wrote, in effect, that John Adams "was a professed aristocrat, and that he had proved faithful and serviceable to the British interest."[31] Callender was indicted for seditious libel. According to the later articles of impeachment against him, Justice Chase made a series of errors during Callender's trial, including:

- failing to dismiss a potential juror who had expressed an opinion pretrial about the seditious character of Callender's book;[32]
- excluding a defense witness called to prove the truth of part of one of the allegedly false statements about Adams on the ground that his testimony could not prove the truth of the entire statement;[33]
- requiring defense counsel to submit certain questions in writing, rather than delivering them orally;[34]
- refusing a continuance;[35]
- misinterpreting the Judiciary Act 1786 in a manner that resulted in holding Callender's trial at the wrong term of court;[36]
- using "unusual, rude, and contemptuous expressions toward the prisoner's counsel";[37]
- "repeated and vexatious interruptions" of defense counsel;[38] and
- "an indecent solicitude ... for the conviction of the accused, unbecoming even a public prosecutor."[39]

The first five claims are for errors of law or procedure. Even considered as specifications of error on appeal, they are pretty weak. The determination of whether to exclude a juror for potential bias is always case-specific and subjective, and mere formation of an opinion about a case prior to trial is not necessarily grounds for exclusion.[40] Refusing a continuance is almost never reversible. Whether the Callender trial was held in the proper term was both debatable and immaterial to the outcome. The requirement of submitting written questions was odd and contrary to the presumption of oral interrogation of witnesses, but probably inconsequential in this case. Only the exclusion of the witness for inability to prove all of a contested issue of fact was plainly wrong. (A basic principle of evidence law is that relevance depends on the propensity of evidence to make a contested fact more or less probable, not the capacity of that evidence to wholly prove or disprove something.[41]) But even if all the specifications of legal error had been valid, the defendant had the remedy of an appeal. That, after all, is what appellate courts are for – to correct the inevitable errors of trial judges. If commission of reversible error were the standard for impeachable "high crimes and misdemeanors," every member of the trial court bench would be impeachable at regular intervals and the guarantee of tenure during good behavior would be hollow indeed.

The last three specifications in the impeachment articles relating to the Callender trial amount to a claim of judicial bias against the defendant manifested in intemperate treatment of defense counsel and remarks that might have had a tendency to prejudice the jury against the defendant. Here the House was on sounder footing, at least in principle. The success of the Anglo-American adversarial jury trial model depends on certain norms of judicial behavior, notably including civility to parties, witnesses, and counsel, careful impartiality in applications of the law, and judicial abstention from any conduct suggesting to the jury a judge's opinion about the merits of the case. Judges may have strong personal views, but they ought not to allow those views to affect their legal rulings or their in-court expressions.

Even here, however, some elasticity is plainly necessary. Judges are human. Lawyers can be vexing, sometimes unendurably so. And one party's idea of tyranny and bias may seem to the other party an entirely proper effort to maintain order and apply the law correctly. Still, if impeachment is to impose some limit on judicial behavior less egregious than overt corruption, then legal errors and oppressive conduct ought to trigger a congressional response at least sometimes. The added features in Chase's case were personal and political bias. At Chase's impeachment trial, the House managers introduced evidence suggesting that, prior to taking the bench in Callender's case, he had expressed strong opinions about the libelous character of Callender's book and the necessity of using the Sedition Act to suppress outbursts of that kind.[42] This evidence certainly suggested a bias particular to Callender, but the predisposition that most invigorated Chase's congressional pursuers was his general political allegiance.

Chase was a vocal Federalist. Of the Jefferson administration, Chase had said, among other things, "our republican constitution will sink to a mobocracy, the worst of all possible governments."[43] The Fries revolt was a reaction to unpopular Federalist-sponsored war taxes. Callender had been charged with insulting the Federalist president in violation of the despised Federalist-sponsored Sedition Act. The connection between Chase's political disposition and his courtroom behavior in these cases seemed apparent to Republicans. To Chase's critics, notably including Thomas Jefferson, the link was made express by two interactions between Chase and federal grand juries. This requires a bit of explanation.

As visiting judges of the district courts, Supreme Court justices also sometimes presided over grand juries. Modern federal grand jury practice is a highly regulated affair, in which judges play extremely limited roles.[44] This seems not to have been entirely the case in Chase's time. In June 1800, Chase presided over the grand jury in Newcastle, Delaware. When the jury indicated that they had no indictments to return and wished to adjourn, Chase interjected that he was aware of a printer in Wilmington rumored to be printing seditious material. He declined to allow the jury to disperse, but ordered the local U.S. Attorney to collect the back numbers of the paper and review them for seditious matter.[45] Nothing seems to have come of his request. Chase's behavior, even if unusual, was not illegal. If Chase had said, "I've heard of a murder committed in Wilmington that should be investigated before you adjourn," no one would find his conduct at all troublesome. What makes his conduct suspect to us is that the unconstitutionality of laws criminalizing criticism of the government has long since been settled. What made it suspect to Jeffersonian Republicans was their opinion that the Sedition Act was an instance of Federalist oppression and *ought* to be unconstitutional.

The second grand jury incident was about a speech. At the outset of a grand jury's term, it was (and remains[46]) customary for the presiding judge to address the jurors and give them some basic instructions about their role and the relevant law. In Justice Chase's time, these addresses sometimes ranged far beyond the legally necessary content and became homilies on the rule of law, aspects of American government, and other civic topics. Especially oddly in modern eyes, these addresses were often published for the edification of the local citizenry.[47]

When opening the grand jury session in Baltimore in May 1803, Chase expressed himself vigorously on the subject of judicial independence. He criticized the Republicans' repeal of the Judiciary Act 1801 and their abolition of the federal circuit courts it had created. He also complained about recent modifications to the Maryland state constitution, some of which involved the judiciary.[48] Hearing about this address, Jefferson wrote a letter to Joseph Nicholson, a Maryland congressman, describing Chase's remarks as a "seditious and official attack on the principles of our Constitution" and strongly intimating that the House ought to look into punishing him.[49]

Jefferson's complaint went deeper than annoyance at Chase's outspokenness. He had been aggravated from the outset by the Federalists' maneuver of expanding the judiciary and packing it with their allies immediately before his own accession to office. Some historians have thought that he did not share the vision of judicial independence that actuated the framers' design and imagined the impeachment of Chase to be a prelude to a thorough housecleaning of Federalist judges through the same mechanism.[50] Whether this was the plan or not, the impetus for the action against Chase was plainly political in the general sense. Chase was an outspoken opponent of the president and the party holding the congressional majority. His impeachment tested the proposition that a judge might be impeached for expressing political opinions contrary to the reigning majority of Congress, or alternatively for misusing his judicial authority in ways that could be attributed to his political opinions.

Indeed, some of Chase's congressional adversaries argued expressly for the broadest, and most overtly political, reading of the impeachment power. As Virginia Senator William Branch Giles put it:

> The power of impeachment was given without limitation to the House of Representatives; and the power of trying impeachments was given equally without limitation to the Senate ... A trial and removal of a judge upon impeachment need not imply any criminality or corruption in him ... [but] nothing more than a declaration of Congress to this effect: You hold dangerous opinions, and if you are suffered to carry them into effect you will work the destruction of the nation. We want your offices, for the purpose of giving them to men who will fill them better.[51]

In the end, the House impeached Chase in eight articles, and the Senate acquitted him on all of them. On three, the House managers secured a numerical majority of the Senate, but on none did the majority approach the required two-thirds.[52] The question is what the verdicts mean.

The most significant constitutional lesson of the Chase affair is the rejection of Senator Giles' view of impeachment. Chase was a large, cranky, imperious, sometimes tyrannical judge, irrepressibly outspoken, often offensive, who plainly and publicly set his face against Republicanism. He was in that sense the best possible test case for politicians eager to use impeachment to bring the judiciary to heel. Yet Jefferson and the Republicans could not generate a two-thirds majority against him in a Senate in which they held an advantage of 25:9.[53] Chase's acquittal is generally agreed to stand for the proposition that impeachment should not be employed as a purely partisan weapon, particularly against the judiciary. Justice Rehnquist argues that the failure of the Chase impeachment helped to establish a level of judicial self-confidence that allowed elaboration of the doctrine of judicial review of congressional enactments cautiously advanced two years before in *Marbury* v. *Madison*[54] into a cornerstone of American constitutionalism.[55]

Rehnquist's conclusion seems fair, but close consideration of the Chase impeachment offers a complementary, and somewhat countervailing, lesson about the place of judges in the constitutional scheme. The combination of the framers' guarantee of life tenure and the Senate's acquittal of Chase signaled a powerful dedication to the norm of judicial independence. But the Chase matter was also an admonition to judges – the price of the independence granted by life tenure is abstention from party politics. The charge on which Chase came closest to removal was his anti-Republican harangue in the Maryland grand jury, where the vote was 19:15 for conviction.[56] The judiciary got the message. Since then, federal judges have generally avoided overtly partisan affiliations and rhetoric, and the current *Code of*

Conduct for United States Judges bars judges from participating in "political activity."[57]

The final lesson of the Chase affair seems to be that Congress was reluctant to remove judges for ordinary legal mistakes, or for the kind of intemperance, snappishness, and arrogance to which the judiciary is often prone. As indicated above, part of the hesitation in the case of legal errors doubtless stems from the complexity and indeterminacy of the law, and the availability of appellate relief from the errors of trial judges. That said, the combination of legal error, personal intemperance, and evidence of bias could in a proper case be a winning trifecta. Two of the three counts on which a majority of senators voted to convict Chase alleged that combination in the Callender trial. So the question remains – if what Chase did was not sufficient to impeach and remove a judge, what would be? To answer that question, we turn to the remaining judicial cases.

IMPEACHABLE JUDICIAL CONDUCT

At the end of this book is an Appendix describing briefly the facts, charges, and resolution of each of the federal impeachments or near-impeachments between 1788 and the present. The sixteen judicial cases can be roughly grouped into five categories: treason; corruption in office; incompetence, neglect of duty, or maladministration in office; ordinary crime unrelated to office; and perjury.

Treason

West Humphreys, a federal district judge in Tennessee who went over to the Confederacy, was impeached and removed in 1862 for, among other things, organizing an armed rebellion against the United States and levying war against them (as well as acting as a judge in a Confederate court considered illegal by the United States).[58] His behavior fitted neatly into even the constitution's narrow definition of treason.

Corruption in Office

The vast majority of judicial impeachments have involved official corruption of one kind or another. Alcee Hastings[59] and Thomas Porteous[60] were impeached and removed for taking bribes. Robert Collins was convicted of bribery in the federal court and resigned the day before his impeachment hearing in the House Judiciary Committee was to begin.[61] These three cases were obviously impeachable because bribery is in the constitution as an impeachable offense. Most of the remainder of the corruption cases did not involve bribery *per se*, but instead various means of using judicial office for self-enrichment.

Judge Swayne was impeached (though ultimately acquitted) for submitting false expense reports and using a railroad car owned by a rail company in receivership in his court to take long pleasure trips.[62] Judge Archbald was impeached and convicted for coercing litigants in his court to make favorable deals with him on coal properties.[63] Judge English was impeached, but resigned before a trial could be held in the Senate, in part for colluding with another lawyer to profit from bankruptcy cases before him.[64] Judge Ritter's conviction was based in part on receiving a kickback after awarding his former law partner high fees in a receivership proceeding and on procuring for himself and his family free lodging from a hotel under receivership.[65] In one case, that of Judge Louderback, the unsuccessful impeachment rested less on allegations that the judge directly enriched himself than on claims that he engaged in a variety of official skullduggery that enriched his friends.[66]

None of the corruption allegations against Archbald, English, Ritter, or Louderback specify violations of the criminal law.[67] The Swayne articles did characterize his submission of false expense reports as the crime of false pretenses.[68] Some of the other judges' alleged behavior might today fall somewhere under the expansive provisions of the federal criminal code, but corrupt self-enrichment broadly conceived, rather than a technical violation of the law, was the essence of the claims against them. It is fair to conclude from these cases that using the powers of office to enrich oneself or one's family and associates is among the impeachable "high crimes and misdemeanors," regardless of whether the conduct was technically criminal. The Ritter case also suggests that impeachable misuses of the powers of office are not limited to financial gain. Among the charges against Ritter was that, during the pendency of his impeachment investigation, he agreed to recuse himself from a case in return for a declaration from the Miami city commissioners "expressing faith and confidence in [Ritter's] integrity."[69]

Incapacity, Neglect of Duty, or Maladministration in Office

Eight federal judges have been impeached, though not all were convicted, for various sorts of non-pecuniary official misbehavior. Several impeachments were based on incapacity. Most fall into the category of what one might call conduct unbecoming a judge – arbitrary, overbearing, tyrannical, abusive, or biased treatment of litigants or lawyers.

Incapacity

The first successful judicial impeachment in U.S. history was the 1803 removal of Judge John Pickering of New Hampshire. He was impeached for making a series of erroneous rulings about a seized ship, and of appearing on the bench "in a state of total intoxication, produced by the free and intemperate use of intoxicating liquors," and "in a most profane and indecent manner, invok[ing] the name of the Supreme Being, to the evil example of the good citizens of the United States."[70] Pickering was alleged by his own son to have been insane, but the Senate convicted him anyway.[71]

Drunkenness on the bench also figured in the 1873 impeachment of Mark H. Delahay, a district court judge in Kansas. In an oddly half-baked procedure, the House sent a committee to Kansas to investigate reports about Delahay's conduct. The committee came back convinced that Delahay's "personal habits" – being habitually drunk on the bench – made him unfit for office, but not entirely convinced of allegations of corruption. The House impeached him regardless, but without drawing up actual articles of impeachment. They simply sent a delegation to the Senate to report that they had impeached the judge and would present formal articles in due course. Delahay resigned before that was done, and the matter was dropped.[72]

The best reading of the Senate's verdict on Pickering is that he was removed not because he had committed any crime[73] or was even of an evil disposition, but because he was incapable by virtue of alcoholism or mental illness of doing his job. Similarly, the House impeached Delahay not because he was corrupt or had done anything criminally or civilly wrongful, but because he was a drunk and thus unsuited to his post. The Pickering and Delahay cases suggest that, at least for judges, the phrase "high crimes and misdemeanors" extends beyond misbehavior to types of personal incapacity that prevent performance of the duties of office. Indeed, if prior congressional actions in impeachment cases are precedential in any meaningful sense, that conclusion is inescapable.

This has caused considerable discomfort among some commentators. In his otherwise compelling book on the Chase and Johnson impeachments, Justice Rehnquist acknowledged the pragmatic and constitutional problem presented by a judge who, like Pickering, is obviously incapable. But rather than accepting the plain implication of the Pickering precedent (and the later Delahay case,[74] which he omits to mention), that "high crimes and misdemeanors" extends to incapacity, he tried to devalue the Pickering result by suggesting that the Senate's vote to remove him was politically motivated.[75]

That the case had a political subtext is undeniable. Pickering had been a distinguished jurist and, not incidentally, a strong Federalist. His increasing derangement and frequent intoxication were well known before the incident that precipitated the impeachment effort. Pickering's friends and family apparently tried to convince him to resign to avoid the trauma and humiliation of impeachment. But his more politically attuned Federalist acquaintances apparently dissuaded him, probably because they wanted to block President Jefferson from appointing his successor. In the view of some historians, and of some of Pickering's contemporaries, the effort to remove the insane Pickering was simply the opening gambit in a planned Republican purge of the Federalist-dominated judiciary that would target Justice Chase as its next victim.[76]

None of that, however, changes the fact that Pickering was mad and incapable of performing his judicial duties. Pickering's Federalist supporters argued that incapacity was not an impeachable condition. "High crimes and misdemeanors," they contended, are limited to indictable crimes and Pickering's insanity prevented him from having the kind of culpable mental state necessary for crime.[77] They also insisted that the Senate must determine the question of Pickering's current mental state before turning to the facts of the case because, they said, if Pickering was insane he could not have received proper notice of the trial, which would then be improper.[78] In effect, they were arguing both what modern lawyers would class as insanity (mental state at the time of the offense) and competence (mental state at the time of trial).[79]

Those favoring removal (mostly Republicans) contended that Pickering's insanity may have been brought on by (morally culpable) voluntary intoxication, but more importantly that the judge's inability to perform his duties was the essential point, and therefore that the inability to form a criminal state of mind was irrelevant.[80] In the end, the Senate voted 19:7 for conviction.[81]

Commentators like Justice Rehnquist who disparage or dismiss this result miss the boat in several respects. First, whether "high crimes and misdemeanors" does or does not embrace non-criminal maladministration up to and including incapacity was a fairly debatable point in 1804. As discussed in Chapter 3, the British and American usages of that phrase prior to the Constitutional Convention included maladministration, and many of the framers approved the phrase knowing this to be true. One can go further and argue that Madison and Gouverneur Morris, at least, would have thought that the final impeachment language addressed incapacity since fear of an officeholder becoming incapable after taking office was one of their primary reasons for insisting on impeachment.[82] While the immediate focus of their concern was the president, the actuarial probability of post-inaugural incapacity is obviously greater for a judge with life tenure than for a president who faces the electorate every four years. It must be conceded that an understanding of "high crimes and misdemeanors" embracing maladministration, narrowly or broadly construed, was not universal in the founding generation. At the Philadelphia Convention, Gunning Bedford of Delaware contended that "impeachment would reach misfeasance only, not incapacity."[83] After the constitution was ratified, Pickering's case was by no means the only occasion on which serious, learned persons argued for a limitation to chargeable criminal conduct. The same contention would be made the next year in Justice Chase's trial.[84]

That said, the arguments on the other side were – and in my view remain – more compelling. The argument from English and American precedent for a broad, non-criminal definition of "high crimes and misdemeanors" is powerful. More powerful still is the argument from pragmatism, the best illustration of which is Judge Pickering. Whatever their longer-term motives, the Republicans seeking Pickering's impeachment were seeking to remove an insane person from the bench. The Federalists conceded his insanity, indeed insisted on it, but wanted for political reasons to keep the gavel in the hand of a madman.

Moreover, the emphasis of Pickering's defenders on the unfairness of trying and condemning a person so far out of his wits that he is not responsible for his former conduct was emotionally appealing, but misplaced in this setting. The charge of unfairness would have force if American impeachments were, as British impeachments had been, criminal proceedings that both assigned moral blame and imposed personal punishments beyond simple removal from office. But the particular genius of American impeachments is precisely that they are not criminal trials whose object is to assign blame, but are instead merely a mechanism to protect government from those who ought not hold office.

When the Senate voted to remove Pickering, it was neither oppressing the mentally ill nor defying the constitutional text. It was instead interpreting a debatable point in the text and creating precedent for its application in future cases, in effect, creating a legislative common law of impeachment the same way Parliament had been doing for centuries. The fact that partisan political considerations may have motivated some of the senators' votes is relevant only as a reminder that Congress is not a true court, even when acting quasi-judicially, and thus feels less bound than a court would by its own prior decisions. Nonetheless, prior impeachments are treated as having some precedential effect. The Pickering and Delahay cases,[85] together with the historical evidence about the pre-1787 meaning of "high crimes and misdemeanors," create solid precedent for several propositions: (1) that "high crimes and misdemeanors" need not be crimes; (2) that contrary to the arguments of some commentators, impeachment requires no bad intent, no culpable mental state; and (3) that, at least in the case of judges, incapacity to fulfill the duties of office can be impeachable.

Abusive Behavior

Justice Chase and judges James Peck, Charles Swayne, Robert Archbald, George English, and Harold Louderback were all alleged to have behaved abusively toward parties or their lawyers. In some cases, the abuse seems to have been sheer meanness or an inability to accept criticism. Judge Peck was impeached, but escaped conviction, when he held a lawyer in contempt and jailed him for having the temerity to publish in a local newspaper his reasons for disagreeing with Peck's ruling against his client.[86] Judge Swayne was also charged with five allegedly unjustified and malicious contempt citations against lawyers. The House called the contempt citations in both cases "high misdemeanors."[87] Perhaps indicating the Senate's general indifference to the feelings of the practicing bar, both Judge Peck and Judge Swayne were acquitted on all counts.[88]

In other cases, notably those of judges English and Louderback, the claim (echoing the charges against Justice Chase) was inappropriate partiality to one side or another in violation of a judge's obligation of neutrality.[89] English resigned before the Senate could try him, which creates something of a precedent for the impeachability of judicial bias. But Louderback was acquitted. In any event, the basic thrust of the charges against both men was corruption. It is doubtful that a case would have been mounted against either absent the corruption claims, and it is unknown whether either house would have acted on charges of mere partiality.

These cases confirm the implication of the Chase case that neither capricious petty tyranny nor obvious favoritism toward one side of a case (both judicial sins too familiar to trial lawyers) is likely grounds for removal from the federal bench absent proof of corrupt or improper motive for the behavior. The cases do not rule out pure abusive behavior as an impeachable offense; indeed, such allegations are a routine feature of judicial impeachment articles. But the Senate has never convicted and removed a judge merely for being a bully.

Legal Errors

None of the post-Chase cases rest on allegations of legal mistakes or professional ineptitude (as distinct from incapacity, as in the cases of Pickering and Delahay).[90] In its report on the impeachment of George English in 1926, the Judiciary Committee declared flatly that, "No judge may be impeached for a wrong decision."[91] As stated, that may be unduly dogmatic. Many impeachment allegations charge that judges took official actions, sometimes including rendering legal opinions, contrary to law. But in virtually every such instance, the allegation of legal error is paired with a claim of corrupt motive or judicial intemperance. Examples of the latter include the charges that Judge Swayne "maliciously and unlawfully" held lawyers in contempt.[92] What seems clear is that no judge, certainly no lower court judge whose decisions are amenable to appeal and correction, should be impeached for rendering a legal decision with which a majority of the House happens to disagree.

Ordinary Crimes

A number of judges have been impeached for crimes that, at least arguably, did not directly implicate their judicial office. Judges Halsted Ritter and Harry Claiborne were both impeached and convicted for tax evasion.[93] Samuel Kent's post-impeachment resignation in anticipation of the Senate trial occurred after he pleaded guilty in criminal court to obstructing the investigation into his sexual abuse of two employees.[94]

These cases present something of a conundrum. Judge Kent's sexual predation on his employees obviously had a logical connection to his office because they worked for him. But at first glance it is hard to see anything about sexual abuse of one's employees that is particular to judges. To be sure, the elevated position of a judge might make an abuse victim feel even more vulnerable and less able to complain. Still, power imbalances of that sort are hardly unique to the judiciary. Therefore, one must ask whether Kent's behavior was impeachable only because these were his employees, or whether the same behavior would have been impeachable had the victims been people he knew in other areas of his life. Was the key factor the misuse of judicial status and workplace rank, or simply the heinous character of the behavior?

The question becomes more acute in the Ritter and Claiborne tax evasion cases. Differences between the two illustrate the problem. Ritter failed to report as income money he received from continuing to work on cases after he took the bench, work that violated the Judicial Code. Ritter's conduct can thus be construed as concealing a form of judicial misconduct. But Claiborne just did not want to pay the taxes that the law requires.

The apparent lesson of these three cases considered together is that, for judges, who are the arbiters and public faces of the law, commission of any reasonably serious felony undermines the integrity of the offender in the eyes of the public so greatly that he or she should not be allowed to remain on the bench. Some kinds of relatively minor crimes perhaps need not lead to impeachment. On the other hand, for judges, there seems to be no requirement that the crime be "great" in the sense of threatening the constitutional order. In any event, no special connection between the type of crime and the judicial role is required. Perhaps the best way to put it is that an offense is sufficient to remove a judge if it is serious enough to undermine public confidence in the honesty and integrity of that judge.

Perjury and False Statements

Three judges, Alcee Hastings in 1988,[95] Walter Nixon in 1989,[96] and Thomas Porteous in 2010,[97] were impeached, convicted, and removed for committing perjury or lying under oath. A fourth, Samuel Kent, resigned after being impeached for sexual assault, for obstructing justice by lying to an investigative committee of the U.S. Court of Appeals for the Fifth Circuit, and for making false statements to the FBI. In three of these cases, the lies were told during investigations into allegations that the judge had committed some kind of corruption. Hastings' alleged perjury was committed when he denied guilt during his federal bribery trial (in which he was found not guilty). Nixon was charged with lying to a grand jury investigating his relationship with the father of a drug defendant appearing in Nixon's court. Kent lied during investigations by the Fifth Circuit and the FBI into the sexual assault allegations.[98]

The Porteous matter is distinct. The third article of impeachment against him was making false statements in his personal bankruptcy filing. The bankruptcy occurred while Porteous was a federal judge, but none of the false statements related to his judicial function. The fourth article is unique in alleging that, during his confirmation process as a federal judge, Porteous denied or concealed *past* corrupt behavior as a state judge. The Senate convicted him on all counts, thus establishing an important precedent that conduct prior to assuming office is impeachable.

These three cases also raise a variant of the issue presented by the tax evasion cases. Is perjury impeachable simply because lying under oath is always disqualifying for a judicial officer? Or were these falsehoods impeachable because of their direct relationship to the performance of judicial duties or the process of becoming a federal judge? This is a question to which we will return when discussing the impeachment of President Clinton.

CONCLUSIONS FROM JUDICIAL IMPEACHMENT CASES

A number of conclusions can be drawn from the body of judicial impeachment precedents:

First, all the charges against the judges fit reasonably well into the first four of the categories of behavior that Parliament most commonly found impeachable as "high crimes and misdemeanors": (i) armed rebellion and other obvious treasons; (ii) corruption; (iii) abuse of power; and (iv) incompetence, neglect of duty, or maladministration in office.

Second, the other British categories – (i) ordinary crime by peers triable only in the House of Lords; (ii) betrayal of the nation's foreign policy interests; and (iii) subversion of the constitution and laws of the realm – have not been found useful for judges. The absence of the first two is hardly surprising: American judges are not peers of the realm and have little or no connection with foreign policy. It is, however, noteworthy that no federal judge has been impeached for subverting the constitution. Given that the federal bench has since *Marbury* v. *Madison*[99] laid claim to the final word on what the constitution means, one can readily imagine a Congress sufficiently distressed with the Supreme Court's judgments deciding to reassert primacy over constitutional meaning by impeaching some justices.

This was the thinking (rudimentary though it may have been) behind the movement that produced "Impeach Earl Warren" signs across the country in the wake of *Brown* v. *Board of Education* and other desegregation rulings.[100] The multiple unsuccessful efforts to impeach Justice William O. Douglas, though focused in part on his extra-judicial activities and personal conduct, also had a strong undercurrent of disagreement over constitutional doctrine. For example, one of the complaints against Douglas by then-Congressman Gerald Ford was about a dissent in an obscenity case.[101] In theory, of course, there is nothing inherently anti-constitutional about impeaching judges who deviate sufficiently from the very wide band of societally tolerable readings of fundamental law. Should, for example, a majority of the justices wake up one morning and decide that *Brown* was wrongly decided and that racial apartheid could be reinstated in America, it is hard to argue that impeachment should not be available. Happily, however, no such radical divergence between the court and the citizenry has so far occurred. But if impeachment is constitutionally permissible on that ground in a sufficiently egregious case, then this necessarily means that Congress has some power independent of the judiciary to set the outer bounds of American constitutionalism.

Third, the judicial impeachment precedents support the conclusion drawn from British practice that impeachable offenses may, but need not, be indictable crimes. The Judiciary Committee report on the 1926 impeachment of District Judge George English sums up the consensus view of that period (which has, if anything, been confirmed by nearly another century of practice):

> Although frequently debated, and the negative advocated by some high authorities, it is now, we believe, considered that impeachment is not confined alone to acts which are forbidden by the Constitution or Federal statutes. The better sustained and modern view is that the provision for impeachment in the Constitution applies not only to high crimes and misdemeanors as those words were understood at common law but also acts which are not defined as criminal and made subject to indictment but ... which affect the public welfare. Thus an official may be impeached for offenses of a political character and for gross betrayal of public interests. Also, for abuses or betrayal of trusts, for inexcusable negligence of duty, [or] for the tyrannical abuse of power ... [102]

Hence, to be impeached, judges must commit "treason, bribery, or other high crime and misdemeanors," but what makes particular misconduct "high" is not that it violates some provision of the criminal code, but that it cuts to the heart of the judicial role. That said, when judges do commit actual crimes, because upholding the law and imposing consequences on those who do not is so essential to a judge's function, judges may be impeachable for less serious crimes than non-judicial officers. This may help to explain why two judges have been impeached for income tax evasion, but, as we will see in Chapter 8, the House Judiciary Committee chose not to include Richard Nixon's tax violations in its articles of impeachment.

Fourth, the tough question is how to draw a principled distinction between conduct impeachable for judges and conduct impeachable for presidents. A good way of summarizing what we find in the judicial precedents is that the impeachment standard for judges is not "lower" than for presidents; rather, the standard for each is calibrated to the different expectations we have for that office. [103] For example, judges are expected to be apolitical and impartial. Judges need not be ideological eunuchs. Ideology, after all, is merely one word for the set of philosophical premises one brings to the act of deciding. But judges are expected to abstain both from partisan politics and from making official decisions to favor one political faction over another. Exercising the powers of one's office to favor one's friends and allies or to advance partisan political goals is conduct fundamentally incompatible with the judicial role, and is thus impeachable conduct for a judge. However, the same sort of behavior is often the essence of being a president. Absent violation of some statute, a president will not be impeached for exercising the powers of patronage or using the office to advance a political agenda. The nature of the presidential office is so fundamentally different than the nature of any judgeship that the constitutional standard for impeaching a president should reflect that difference.

Nonetheless, there are certain areas in which reasonable impartiality is expected of both presidents and judges. We expect that neither judges nor presidents will seek or accept bribes for the performance of their official duties, nor employ the powers of their offices in other ways to enrich themselves or their families. Likewise, a president who attempts to use the investigative and prosecutorial powers of the executive branch to shield himself or his family or friends from legal jeopardy, or to harm his political enemies, breaches a critical norm of republican government and would be impeachable for doing so.

Conversely, there are areas of presidential responsibility that have no clear judicial analogue. The conduct of foreign policy, command of the armed forces, supervision of the executive departments, and the exercise of the appointments and pardon powers are all obvious examples. A president may deviate from the law and accepted constitutional norms in all these realms, but we may not be much aided by judicial impeachment precedents in determining whether such deviations amount to impeachable conduct.

7

The Impeachment of Andrew Johnson

On April 14, 1865, one of the great tragedies of American history played out in the box seats to the right of the stage at Ford's Theater in the District of Columbia. John Wilkes Booth, actor and dead-end Confederate sympathizer, imagined that the southern rebellion, already irretrievably defeated by Lee's surrender of the Army of Northern Virginia five days before at Appomattox Courthouse, could be resurrected by assassination. Booth slipped into the box behind President and Mrs. Lincoln, shot the president, jumped to the stage and fled. Lincoln died early the following morning.[1]

Few now remember that Booth's plot also sought to kill Lincoln's vice-president, Andrew Johnson, and Secretary of State William Seward. Seward's attacker stabbed him nearly to death, but Johnson's would-be killer lost his resolve and never made the attempt.[2] On April 15, 1865, Andrew Johnson took the oath of office and became the seventeenth president of the United States. Not quite three years later, in February 1868, Johnson became the first president ever impeached by the House of Representatives.

Johnson's impeachment and his narrow escape from conviction by the Senate was the second truly consequential case in the history of American impeachment. The first was the impeachment and exoneration of Justice Samuel Chase because it was ever after treated as foreclosing the removal of judges for partisan political reasons. But the Chase result was founded in large measure on a pre-existing American commitment to independence of the judicial branch from direct influence by either the legislature or the executive. There was no such taboo in the case of a president. Recall that Madison, Mason, and other founders were leery of making the president a "creature" of Congress, but equally wary of the prospect of executive tyranny. As Hamilton said in the *Federalist*, the kinds of offense characteristic of such tyranny and thus impeachable are by their nature political. Therefore, except in the "easy" case of a president who commits treason or bribery or overt official corruption, an effort to impeach a president for betraying his office or subverting the constitution in other ways will inevitably be a political fight. The question, unresolved by the constitutional text or founding generation debates, was what kind of political considerations would be admissible in an attempt to remove the president.

The battle over Johnson's removal was political in the largest sense. It was a debate over fundamental questions of the separation of powers and even more fundamental questions about the course the nation would chart in the century following the Civil War. At stake were the relative strengths of Congress and the presidency in American government, the relation of states to the national whole, and, most significantly, whether the United States would aggressively refashion itself to provide full equality to millions of newly freed black citizens or whether it would subside into the more comfortable course of maintaining racial apartheid without actual chattel slavery. The conventional verdict on the Johnson impeachment is that the Senate got it right, either because the whole affair was a gross congressional overreach in response to reasonable exercises of executive power, or because Johnson's opponents drafted articles of impeachment that failed to allege impeachable conduct. I am sympathetic to the second of these perspectives. Nonetheless, I believe that Johnson *did* engage in behavior for which he should have been impeached and removed. Moreover, it can fairly be argued that the failure to do so set the stage for – even it was by no means the primary cause of – both the failure of Reconstruction and the rise of Jim Crow.

The effect of the Johnson verdict on the role of the impeachment power as a legislative check on executive authority is far less speculative. By impeaching President Johnson, the House of Representatives claimed a dominant role for Congress in charting the constitutional future of the country. By acquitting him, the Senate shrank from that responsibility. The conventional wisdom is that they were right to do so. Certainly, the Johnson case has long been interpreted as precedent for the proposition that impeachment ought not be used to remove a president over differences with Congress on matters of policy. I disagree, cautiously. Some disagreements about "policy" are in truth fundamental differences about the constitution in the broad sense of that term employed by the framers. The Johnson affair was a missed opportunity to establish the principle that, at rare moments in the country's history, certain presidential constructions of proper constitutional order are so misconceived as to amount to "high crimes and misdemeanors" for which removal is the appropriate remedy.

THE IMPROBABLE RISE OF ANDREW JOHNSON

In background, if not in wisdom or temperament, Andrew Johnson had a great deal in common with Abraham Lincoln. Johnson was born in 1808 in Raleigh, North Carolina, to a laundress and a laboring man who had raised himself in the estimation of his neighbors so far as to become town constable. After his father died, Johnson was apprenticed to a tailor, but ran away and drifted from South Carolina to Tennessee to Alabama and finally settled in Tennessee.[3] Entirely self-educated, he prospered as a tailor, invested in real estate, and went into local and state politics.[4] In 1843, Johnson, who had by that time become both a slave owner and a staunch

Democrat, was elected to Congress, where he served five terms.[5] He voted for all of the provisions of the Compromise of 1850[6] except the elimination of the slave trade in Washington, D.C.

In 1852, having been gerrymandered out of his former House district by Whig opponents, Johnson was elected governor of Tennessee.[7] He secured a second term in 1854 on a strongly pro-slavery platform, and then moved to the U.S. Senate in 1857.[8] In the secession crisis of 1860–61, precipitated by Lincoln's election to the presidency, Johnson planted himself firmly on the side of the Union. He spoke in the Senate against secession and returned to Tennessee in spring 1861 to campaign against the statewide referendum authorizing secession. In the fevered atmosphere of the time, Johnson's stance required not only moral but physical courage. He addressed referendum crowds with a gun on the lectern and, when it passed and carried Tennessee into the Confederacy, Johnson had to flee the state.[9] He returned to Washington and became the only senator from a southern state to remain in office, a lonesome, but also influential, figure as the most prominent southern Unionist.[10]

In March 1862, President Lincoln appointed Johnson military governor of Tennessee to administer the central and western portions of the state reconquered by Union armies.[11] By most accounts, Johnson performed a difficult task competently – administering the areas in Union hands efficiently and with no tolerance for vocal secessionists. He removed the Nashville mayor and city council for refusal to take an oath of allegiance and nullified the election of a secessionist judge. His slogan was, "Treason must be made odious and traitors punished."[12] He was, moreover, no mere blowhard. When Confederate forces under Braxton Bragg marched through Tennessee in September 1862, threatening Nashville, Johnson remained on the spot to fortify the town, swearing he would defend the city and never be taken alive. Johnson stayed. The city held.[13]

On matters of race, Johnson, like many other slave-state Unionists, was a reluctant pragmatist. When Lincoln promulgated the Emancipation Proclamation in September 1862, it purported to free slaves in all the seceding states except Tennessee.[14] Johnson's was a powerful voice for excluding Tennessee,[15] even though its eastern regions remained in rebel hands and Confederate forces continued to threaten restoration of southern control of the entire region until Grant defeated Bragg's army at Chattanooga in November 1863.[16] Nonetheless, Johnson soon saw that slavery was doomed by the war. He emancipated his own slaves in August 1863[17] and, as the presidential election year of 1864 approached, called for abolition in Tennessee.[18]

There are two points about the presidential election of 1864 that seem self-evident to the modern eye, but were not so at the time. The first is that an election was held at all. Perhaps the most reassuring evidence of the durability of the American constitutional system in all of its history is that in the middle of a vicious civil war there seems to have been no thought of suspending the quadrennial national election. Second, if we think about it at all, we now take the re-election of Lincoln – Father Abraham, Old Abe, the single most admired figure in American history – as a foregone conclusion. It was not. Particularly during the first several years of his term, Lincoln was widely disparaged as a weak and even comical figure.[19] Only the accumulating evidence of his fundamental decency, calm competence, firmness in the face of disaster, and unifying eloquence, plus the slow accretion of successes by Union armies beginning with the twin victories of Gettysburg and Vicksburg in July 1863, transformed Lincoln's image among his countrymen. In the winter of 1863–64, the transformation was by no means complete. Many doubted Lincoln could be re-elected. Not a few doubted he would be re-nominated by his own party. Even members of his own cabinet like Treasury Secretary Salmon P. Chase were maneuvering to replace him.[20]

The state of the party itself was in flux. Republicans had first coalesced as a national party in 1856[21] and elected Lincoln as their first successful presidential candidate in 1860. By 1864, the party's identity was blurred. In 1860, Lincoln's undoubted personal antipathy to slavery and his public opposition to its expansion outside its existing domain[22] repelled some who hoped to maintain the national union with slavery undisturbed. Northern Democrats, as well as southern slave-holders, suspected in Lincoln a private disposition to radicalism at odds with his careful public pronouncements about slavery. The war hardened southern views of Lincoln as the chief author of the national calamity. But in the north, the southern states' almost gleeful willingness to plunge the country into fratricidal bloodshed over the mere prospect of future threats to slavery alienated northerners who were either sympathetic or indifferent to slavery as an institution, but were deeply devoted to the United States as an indivisible union. Such persons, War Democrats as they were sometimes called, found themselves in uneasy alliance with Lincoln's party.

The presidential nominating convention that assembled in Baltimore in June 1864 labeled itself National Unionist rather than Republican.[23] It convened not only prewar Republicans, but War Democrats and a variety of other political subspecies unified primarily in their determination to see the rebellion crushed and the Union restored. Lincoln did not attend (because that was not thought seemly in those decorous times). Even his primary political operatives skipped the gathering because, by summer, the tide of the war and of public opinion had turned sufficiently in Lincoln's direction that his nomination was a foregone conclusion.[24] The only undecided point going into the convention was the identity of Lincoln's vice presidential running mate.

The sitting vice president was Hannibal Hamlin of Maine, but Lincoln had no special attachment to him. Estrangements between presidents and vice presidents are not uncommon. And no presidential contender probably likes to dwell over-much on an office that exists only as a hedge against his own extinction, but Lincoln's attitude seems not to have been hostility to Hamlin so much as complete indifference to who would be vice president. Several names were floated as possible alternatives to Hamlin, including Daniel Dickinson of New York, political general Benjamin Butler, and Andrew Johnson. All were War Democrats proposed on the theory that they would expand the ticket's appeal beyond committed Republicans to all who wanted aggressive prosecution of the war. Lincoln was repeatedly entreated for some expression of preference between them. He declined even to hint at a favorite.[25]

Going in to the convention, the betting favorite was probably Hamlin. However, as his stock fell and that of Dickinson rose, Thurlow Weed, New York newspaper editor, power broker, and principal advisor to Secretary of State William Seward, realized that, should Dickinson be chosen, Lincoln might have to dispense with Seward, also of New York, because of an unwritten custom that no two of the major national offices should be held by persons from the same state. Weed therefore threw his support behind Johnson and the deal was done.[26]

THE END OF THE CIVIL WAR AND THE CHALLENGE OF RECONSTRUCTION

The selection of Lincoln's running mate probably seemed of less consequence to the delegates than their ringing endorsement of a platform provision that would have been unthinkable four years before. "Resolved," said the platform's third plank, "That as Slavery was the cause, and now constitutes the strength, of this Rebellion . . . [we] demand its utter and complete extirpation from the soil of the Republic." It went on to favor a constitutional amendment permanently prohibiting slavery.[27]

During the remainder of 1864, Johnson did and said a number of things that seemed to place him in harmony with the sensibilities of the party that had adopted him. Seemingly reconciled to the end of slavery, on October 24, he issued a proclamation as military governor abolishing slavery in Tennessee.[28] He also helped to facilitate a state convention that, in January 1865, passed resolutions revoking the state ordinance of secession and declaring slavery abolished, with both measures to be ratified by later popular referendum.[29]

In a stump speech during the 1864 campaign, Johnson declaimed:

> I say, let the Government go on, and slavery get along the best it can. Give me my country, and, if need be, let all else go. If slavery gets in the way, it must get out and go down. Let "niggers" go, if they get in the way of putting down treason. Before the rebellion, I was for sustaining the Government with slavery; now I am for sustaining the Government without slavery, without regard to a particular institution. Institutions must be subordinate, and the Government must be supreme.[30]

The substance of Johnson's declared policy on slavery was all his new Republican friends could desire. Still, his narrow focus on abolition as no more than a necessary war measure and the use of the pejorative epithet suggested a personal attitude toward the soon-to-be freedmen that cast doubt on his enthusiasm for the emancipation project.[31] A later passage in the same speech foreshadowed even more clearly the controversies that would engulf Johnson and the country once he took Lincoln's chair.

"Negroes, when freed," Johnson said, "have got to work – must work; those who won't work will be subject to vagrant laws or an apprentice system until they are educated to the idea that freedom for anybody of color simply means liberty to work and to enjoy the production of his labor."[32] In one respect, these sentiments were hardly remarkable, particularly for a nineteenth-century Union politician. A standard northern complaint about the antebellum South was precisely that, by conscripting Africans to work for nothing, it enjoyed unfair economic advantages over the northern system of free paid labor. So half of Johnson's argument here was simply that emancipation meant that blacks would be obliged to enter the free labor system like everybody else. But there was a darker subtext, or really two of them. The first was the fear that masses of newly freed black laborers either could not find work, or would not be disposed to work, and would thus become public charges. The second was the casual assumption that free blacks unwilling or unable to find work in a free labor economy should be compelled to work by application of the criminal law or what Johnson euphemistically refers to as an "apprentice system" – meaning forcing unemployed black persons into contractual arrangements that amounted to compelled labor, literal indentured servitude.

In the context of the times, Johnson's approach was perhaps not quite as outrageously oppressive as it now sounds. Union victory in the Civil War and the advent of universal emancipation was going to present a social problem unprecedented in the history of civilization. A population of 4 million enslaved human beings,[33] largely unskilled, and almost all illiterate, whose forced labor was integral to the economy of one-half the country would be released from bondage and simultaneously cut off from their previous means of securing the basic necessities of life. At least in the short term, the black labor force would be woefully bereft of the skills, tools, and capital necessary to earn a living except by manual work.[34] For their part, the former southern owner class needed black labor, but the southern economy was wrecked and white landowners, the former "masters," often had no money to pay wages, even if willing to do so. Some interim arrangements were going to be necessary in the transition from a slave to a free labor system. And to the nineteenth-century mind, the idea of forced apprenticeships did not seem as totalitarian as it now would. After all, Johnson himself was bound out as a child apprentice to a tailor. That he was a minor indentured by a parent while most slaves were adults would not have seemed a meaningful distinction to Johnson. To him and most of his countrymen, even those most sympathetic to the enslaved, blacks were childlike, as unprepared for self-sufficiency as any ten-year-old, and could be treated as such. The fact that Johnson found his own apprenticeship so unpleasant that he fled the state to avoid the last six years of the agreement lends more than a tinge of irony to his enthusiasm for forcibly placing millions of others in a condition he had despised. But he probably would have said that, however uncomfortable, his apprenticeship gave him a trade and might do the same for freed blacks.

The real question was whether the dispensations made for freedmen once the war was over would be temporary and aimed at moving them into a position to compete fairly in a free labor market, or whether they would be subterfuges for maintaining the antebellum status quo of white supremacy and black subordination. The question of black–white relations extended beyond the purely economic sphere. The plight of southern freedmen was not simply a problem in labor economics, but one of deeply rooted cultural, ideological, and indeed religious, attitudes.[35] The white South had convinced itself that slavery was the natural, biblically commanded, condition of the African[36] and had gone to war to prove the proposition. Losing the war had changed few southern minds. If anything, it may have hardened white attitudes. It is a truism of human nature that we most easily resent those we have most wronged. In that atmosphere, even if the most sympathetic transitional economic measures were somehow adopted, black people would find it difficult to make and sustain social gains without the right to participate in the political realm, which inescapably required a right to vote. Black suffrage was, of course, unthinkable and unthought-of in the South as long as the Confederacy survived. It was hardly less controversial in the North. By 1865, only five states, all in New England, allowed free black residents to vote.[37]

During the war, the North had come around to the near-universal conviction that slavery must be abolished, if for no other reason than that it was the foundation of the economic and social system of the traitorous southern planter aristocracy. But that did not mean that white northerners were broadly enthusiastic about accepting former slaves into anything approximating either social or political equality. It was here that Andrew Johnson diverged sharply from the Republican Party, or at least from that wing of it which realized that black people would have to be granted some political rights for their own protection and to prevent the recreation of the practical equivalent of a slave society.

Johnson's personal attitude toward African Americans has sometimes been a matter of dispute. His supporters point to the fact that he emancipated his own slaves in 1863 before there was any legal necessity to do so, as well as to his somewhat impetuous invocation of his powers as military governor to proclaim the abolition of slavery in Tennessee in October 1864. In that proclamation, he announced grandly to the black population that he would "be your Moses" and lead them "through the Red Sea of war and bondage, to a fairer future of liberty and peace."[38] Whether these were merely the gestures of a political opportunist who could see the way the wind was blowing, or whether in 1864 he was genuinely moved by the spirit of liberation that had infused the Union war effort, will remain a mystery.

What is clear is that once the Confederacy collapsed and he was unexpectedly thrust into the presidency, he consistently expressed both personal distaste for black people and the utmost hostility to black participation in American political life. Those who dealt with Johnson privately observed, as one wrote to Congressman Elihu Washburne in 1865, "almost unconquerable prejudices against the African race."[39] In a February 1866 White House meeting with Frederick Douglass and other advocates for freedmen's rights, Johnson rejected the idea of black suffrage and intimated that the best course for blacks in the South was emigration. After Douglass left, he is reported to have said to his secretary, "Those d***-d sons of b***-s thought they had me in a trap! I know that Douglass; he's like any nigger, and he would sooner cut a white man's throat than not."[40] And in his December 1867 message to Congress, Johnson declared that, "in the progress of nations negroes have shown less capacity for government than any other race of people. No independent government of any form has ever been successful in their hands. On the contrary, wherever they have been left to their own devices they have shown a constant tendency to relapse into barbarism."[41]

The political conundrum presented by the postwar South was not limited to race relations. In 1861, the leadership class of the southern states favored secession and led their people into rebellion. Four years later, the rebellion was over, but not because those who began it had a change of heart. To the contrary, the rebellion was ground down in a war of attrition that cost 750,000 lives[42] and half a million wounded (many missing limbs due to the crude surgical methods of the time),[43] imposed huge economic costs,[44] and destroyed much of the infrastructure of the southern states. Surviving southern leaders (mostly) conceded themselves defeated, but even that minimal level of acceptance was not universal. Confederate president Jefferson Davis wanted to fight on even after Lee's surrender until dissuaded of the hopelessness of the project by his aides.[45] Thousands of southerners fled west or south into Mexico or Central America, either because they feared retribution, or refused to live under a Yankee government, or even hoped to rally and renew the fight if circumstances permitted. Confederate cavalry commander Jo Shelby led perhaps 1,000 men across the Rio Grande into Mexico in 1865 intending to form a kind of foreign legion for Mexican emperor Maximilian that could, of course, be directed northward should the opportunity arise.[46]

These facts posed large questions for the victorious North. The first was one of responsibility for the carnage. Southerners and some in the north seemed to want to treat the war as a sort of prolonged sporting contest at the end of which the contestants, winners and losers alike, should just slap each other on the back, say "Well played," and go on as if nothing much had happened and no one was really to blame. As we will see, it is only a modest exaggeration to say that this became Andrew Johnson's position. But, of course, something of immeasurable consequence, a vast and bloody catastrophe, had happened. And, Lost Cause revisionism notwithstanding, one side was to blame. The South had sought to tear the country asunder, and not for laudable or even morally defensible reasons, but in order to keep 4 million people in slavery. As Jefferson Davis insisted, the South's rebellion was not a revolution, but an effort "to save ourselves from a revolution" that would render "property in slaves so insecure as to be comparatively worthless."[47]

The horror of the Confederacy's central organizing principle, the resolve written into its constitution to preserve slavery forever,[48] will have seemed less odious to white Americans north and south in 1865 than it does today. After all, slavery had been a fact of American life since its founding and deep prejudice against black people was nearly universal. Still, even if white northerners were ambivalent about the morality of slavery, they were anything but ambivalent about the morality of fighting a civil war to preserve it. The South had started the war for that purpose and fought that war to its bitter conclusion. The logic of reuniting the country by force necessarily implied that the vanquished would, in the main, have to be restored to full participation in American civic life at some point. But that logic did not require holding the southern leadership class entirely harmless.

The second problem was how to prevent an immediate reopening of hostilities and forestall a future repetition of the recent disaster. In the near term, the Union could not sensibly abandon control of the South's cities, towns, and resources without assurances that the fire of rebellion would not reignite as soon as the army left. In the longer run, it seemed to many in the North that the southern social, economic, and political structure – particularly those aspects involving large-scale plantation agriculture dependent on bound labor held in subjection by violence and dominated by a wealthy, pugnacious leisure class with aristocratic pretensions – was a major cause of sectional conflict. Thoughtful northerners recognized that the danger from the "Slave Power" would not evaporate with the formal legal abolition of slavery if the South was permitted to preserve its prewar social system with cosmetic changes only. If the former Confederate states were allowed to regain immediate full representation in the national government with no change in their social arrangements, no expansion of voting rights, and no constraints on their internal politics, they would inevitably send to Congress a block of unchastened rebels devoted not only to suppressing the rights of freedmen, but also to reviving the sectional influence the South enjoyed before the war. At the least, southern representatives acting in concert with northern conservatives would shortly have blocking power over much necessary congressional action, potentially reviving the tensions that led to war. Prudence suggested not only that some subset of the leaders of the rebellion be debarred from return to office, but that the system they represented be rearranged.

Set against these concerns were others that pointed in the direction of permitting a rapid return to conditions as close to the prewar status quo as possible. Prime among them were northern commercial interests which depended on the resumption of large-scale production of southern crops like cotton, sugar, and tobacco that previously had been grown with slave labor. The northern textile industry, in particular, wanted southern cotton in quantity, but no one yet knew how to produce this extremely labor-intensive crop economically without slave labor or its near approximation.[49] Moreover, the white laboring class north and south was extremely hostile to the idea of competition from millions of freed slaves. For many northerners, therefore, there was much to be said for swallowing their outrage over the war and treating the white south as returning prodigals, rather than as eternal enemies. If slavery in its pure, and most morally troublesome, legal form was removed from the equation, a new south in which blacks were legally free, but practically subordinated into a politically impotent and economically exploited underclass, seemed for many a perfectly acceptable outcome.[50]

In sum, by 1865, everyone agreed that the South must be reconstructed. But the term "reconstruction" meant markedly different things to different people. For some, particularly southerners themselves, it conveyed merely a literal physical rebuilding with minimal social modification. For others, true reconstruction required refashioning southern society along lines less parochial and more national, less aristocratic and racialist and more egalitarian, less agrarian and more industrial and mercantile than that which existed before the war.

THE FAILURE OF "PRESIDENTIAL RECONSTRUCTION"

Had it not been for John Wilkes Booth, Andrew Johnson's views on the post-Civil War world would now be only a matter of antiquarian curiosity. But Booth hit what he aimed at and on April 15, 1865, Johnson's opinions became central. Indeed, in one way at least they were more central then than they would be now. Article 1 of the constitution as it then existed provided that Congress must meet once a year and that it should convene on the first Monday in December unless otherwise provided.[51] In 1865, Congress held a brief special session in March, but then adjourned until December.[52] Lee surrendered in early April and hostilities would sputter on in odd spots through the summer, but by early June the Union had total military control of the entire Confederacy.[53] Therefore, in the first six months of the peace, Congress was not an active participant in the reconstruction and reintegration of the defeated South. The Constitution decrees that a president "may, on extraordinary Occasions, convene both Houses or either of them."[54] It would be hard to imagine an occasion more extraordinary than the end of a four-year civil war, and Johnson could have called Congress back into session and made it a partner in a joint project of postwar rebuilding. He did not. The body that mattered in those crucial first months was the Union Army that held the ground and administered the occupied South, and with Lincoln's death it passed into the command of Andrew Johnson.

The period between the cessation of hostilities in May 1865 and the opening of the 39th Congress in December is sometimes known as "Presidential Reconstruction." A full recounting of the events of those tumultuous months is beyond the scope of this book, but the general outline is as follows.

In December 1863, Lincoln had approved the creation of provisional governments in seceded states brought back under Union military control. The preconditions for recognition of these governments were 10 percent of the prewar electorate signing a loyalty oath and acceptance of the Emancipation Proclamation.[55] Those who signed the oath were also granted pardons for crimes against the United States in connection with rebellion, although the proclamation excluded from eligibility a variety of Confederate government officials and military officers, as well as those who had abandoned U.S. military commissions or certain elective or appointive offices to serve the Confederacy. By May 1865, provisional governments had been established on this basis in Arkansas, Louisiana, Tennessee, and Virginia. Critically, however, none of these governments had extended voting rights to blacks. On May 9, 1865, Johnson moved by presidential proclamation to recognize these four provisional governments as members of the Union.[56]

Across the South, Johnson appointed provisional governors who had at least been opposed to secession before the war, even if they had remained in the South and participated in political life during the conflict. But those governors tended to leave wartime Confederate officials undisturbed or to appoint members of the former ruling elite.[57] The events in Louisiana were typical and profoundly disturbing to many northern observers. There, Johnson supported the efforts of Louisiana Governor James Madison Wells to purge officials previously appointed by Union General Nathaniel Banks and replace them with conservative Unionists and former Confederates. Johnson encouraged the formation of new governments in the remaining Confederate states and recognized those which met minimal qualifications of ensuring that major state offices were held by "loyal" men, ratifying the Thirteenth Amendment abolishing slavery, repudiating Confederate debt, and repealing secession ordinances.[58] A universal theme of all the southern state governments that emerged in the year following the war was the fixed and unyielding opposition to black suffrage, and indeed to any notable improvement in the economic or civic status of freedmen.[59]

The resolve of Johnson's reconstituted state governments to oppose improvement in black status went beyond mere inertia or static obstruction. Across the South, the new governments began enacting "Black Codes." These provided nominal access to previously forbidden freedoms like marriage, property ownership, the right to make contracts, and testify in court, but their primary purpose was to keep the black labor force in a condition as close to slavery as possible. Blacks in South Carolina were forbidden to work as anything but farmers or servants without paying special exorbitant taxes. There and elsewhere blacks who did not work were made criminals by vagrancy laws (just as Andrew Johnson's wartime speech had foretold). Once committed to a labor "contract," blacks could not quit without forfeiting all wages already earned. Some laws made breaking a labor contract punishable by whipping, pillorying, and sale for a year's indentured labor. White employers were prohibited from competing for black labor. And a host of other areas of black lives remained regulated just as they had been before emancipation. Preaching the gospel without a license was in some states made a crime and the special pre-emancipation criminal laws governing slaves and free blacks often remained in effect.[60]

Southern police, militia, and courts used force to keep the black labor force subjugated. Even when the letter of the law should have ensured fair treatment and increased black autonomy, the embedded customs and attitudes of the theoretically dead slave culture ensured that whites and white interests would prevail.[61] As one observer noted about the operation of southern courts, "The admission of Negro testimony will never secure the Freedmen justice before the courts of this state when that testimony is considered valueless by the judges and juries who hear it. It is of no consequence what the law may be, if the majority be not inclined to have it executed."[62] The avowed intention of Andrew Johnson was to keep the United States a white man's country with a white man's government.[63] Southern whites and the state regimes they created in the period when the president was primarily in charge of the reconstruction effort were of precisely the same mind.

The resurgence of former Confederates to power in the South was not limited to state governments. The Johnson administration also opened federal patronage positions, particularly in the Treasury Department, throughout the South to ex-Confederate military officers and civil officeholders, disregarding the Test Oath Act passed by Congress in spring 1865 to prevent precisely this result.[64]

Reports of all these developments caused rising alarm in the North. As Eric Foner puts it, the news from the former Confederacy was "of the white South's inability to adjust to the end of slavery, the widespread mistreatment of blacks, Unionists, and Northerners, and a pervasive spirit of disloyalty."[65] Among those who had given so much to preserve the Union, the rising impression was that "the rebels are all to be let back ... and made a power in the government again, just as though there had been no rebellion."[66] Both at the time and since, it has been broadly recognized that Johnson's policy of leniency toward the defeated white southern leadership and hostility toward newly free black citizens destroyed the possibility of effective and expeditious reconstruction.[67]

"RADICAL RECONSTRUCTION"

The 39th Congress that assembled in December 1865 was dominated by Republicans. Because the war had scrambled party affiliations, a precise count is difficult, but Republicans or like-minded "Unionists" held a majority of approximately 155:46 in the House.[68] In the Senate, the Republicans opened the session with an advantage of 39:11, which by summer 1867 had grown to 43:11 after Tennessee was readmitted to representation in 1866, and Nebraska was admitted as a new state in 1867.[69] Throughout, Republicans and their allies enjoyed two-thirds supermajorities in both houses that, as long as they held together, made their legislation immune to presidential veto and enabled them to propose constitutional amendments for state ratification with no votes from the Democratic minority.[70] This state of affairs existed not only because of Republican triumphs in the 1864 congressional elections, but because no state that had joined the Confederacy was represented.[71] A number of former Confederate states sent representatives,[72] but they were not welcomed. Not only were these purported delegates put forward by state governments whose legitimacy was unresolved, but they were predominantly former Confederate soldiers or officeholders – nine former members of the Confederate Congress, seven Confederate state officials, eight Confederate generals or colonels, and Confederate Vice President Alexander Stephens.[73]

Both the House and the Senate invoked their constitutional power to determine qualifications for membership[74] to exclude the southern delegates.[75] Their right to do so has been contested. Raoul Berger noted that in the twentieth century the Supreme Court determined that exclusion can be based only on the three constitutional qualifications for congressional membership – residence, age, and citizenship.[76] However, Congress' decision to exclude these delegates was not based on the qualifications of the men, but on the status of the entities that sent them. In essence, Congress concluded that the governments of the Confederate states had by the act of rebellion lost the right of participation in the national government, and that Congress, not the president, would determine when and how that right would be restored. Its position was bolstered by Article 1, section 8, of the constitution granting Congress the power to "suppress insurrections"; Article 4, section 4, enjoining the United States to "guarantee to every State in this Union a republican form of government"; and the Supreme Court's 1849 opinion in *Luther v. Borden* holding that "it rests with Congress to decide what government is the established one in a State."[77] While the question of what constituted republican government was debatable, Congress had as good or better a claim to the deciding power as Johnson.[78]

For the moment, neither Congress nor the president was inclined to confront the other directly on this fundamental disagreement about their respective powers over the postwar political order. Initial relations between Johnson and the 39th Congress were reasonably harmonious. Republicans were reassured by the fact that Johnson was known to have been a hard man in opposition to secessionist treason during the Civil War, and his initial message to Congress on December 5, 1865, was moderate and conciliatory. He signaled his position that the southern states had never legally left the Union and therefore that the ordinary business of the country could not constitutionally proceed until they were restored to their prewar representation in national government, but he was not yet dogmatic on the point. Moreover, although he insisted that matters of suffrage must be left to the states, here, too, his tone was not combative.[79] Nonetheless, the events of the previous seven postwar months had convinced the majority in Congress that it needed to act both to prevent the renascence of the Slave Power in a new guise and to protect freedmen and southern Unionists.

The foundation for congressional action to protect the black population was already laid. The Thirteenth Amendment abolishing slavery was passed by the 38th Congress in January 1865, while Lincoln still lived, and was ratified by the necessary number of states on December 6, two days after the 39th Congress convened.[80] Republicans sought to build on this monumental, but incomplete, achievement.

Their first move was to perpetuate a wartime institution – the Freedmen's Bureau – created in 1863 to assist refugees and newly freed slaves. The Bureau was headed by General Oliver O. Howard, with other army generals designated assistant commissioners for each former slave state. The Bureau had 550 local agents, generally army officers. Backed by the power of the Union Army's occupying troops, the agents aided refugees, black and white, gave food aid, built hospitals, and provided medical care. When the war ended, the Bureau did what it could to assist freedmen in the transition out of slavery, organizing schools in some places, working with freedmen to secure reasonable (by the standards of the era) labor contracts, and prevent flagrant abuses.[81] The Bureau had first been given formal legal status by a Freedmen's Bureau Bill signed by Lincoln in early 1865.[82] By its terms, that bill sunsetted a year after the cessation of hostilities.[83] Therefore, at the end of 1865, Republican friends of the Bureau's work introduced a bill continuing the Bureau and its humanitarian relief efforts, granting it power to acquire land for asylums and schools, and, crucially, the power to use military tribunals against persons attempting to deny civil rights to freedmen and others "on account of race or color, or any previous condition of slavery or involuntary servitude."[84] On February 19, 1866, President Johnson vetoed it. He rejected the assertion that military authority was any longer appropriate even in the rebel South now that open war was over, as well as the very idea that the federal government had responsibility for the social welfare or education of any of its citizens. Central to his argument was the complaint that Congress ought not legislate for the South at all until all southern states were once more represented in Congress.[85] At least for the moment, Republicans could not assemble quite enough votes to override Johnson's veto. So they moved on to other legislation.

In March 1866, Congress passed the Civil Rights Act.[86] By any modern standard, and even in the circumstances of the time, it was an exceptionally modest piece of legislation. It decreed that all persons born in the United States regardless of race or color were citizens of the United States and "shall have the same right . . . to make and enforce contracts, to sue, be parties, and give evidence, to inherit, purchase, lease, sell, hold, and convey real and personal property, and to full and equal benefit of all laws and proceedings for the security of person and property, as is enjoyed by white citizens . . ."[87] Section 2 of the Act made it a misdemeanor to deprive another of his rights under the Act, and the balance of the legislation conferred power on federal marshals and courts to enforce the bill.[88] When introducing the Act, Congressman James F. Wilson explained its purpose as limited to private interactions, insisting that it did not confer rights of suffrage, jury service, desegregation of public education, or any other privilege connected with government.[89]

On March 27, President Johnson vetoed the Civil Rights Act. The justifications in his veto message were plausible only if one believed that the Civil War had changed neither the constitutional relationship between states and the nation nor the essential relation between the white and black populations of the country. Johnson could not argue that Congress has no right to regulate admission to American citizenship. The constitution grants Congress the power to "establish a uniform rule of naturalization,"[90] and Congress had been passing laws setting and modifying the requirements for citizenship since 1790.[91] Rather, he contended that Americans possessed two forms of citizenship, one national and one state, and that states had the exclusive right to regulate admission to the latter.[92] More importantly, he argued that states could treat those who are not admitted to state citizenship differently than those who are, even if both classes are national citizens. In some cases, of course, this is right and completely unobjectionable. If a state is to enjoy any measure of sovereign authority, it must be able to define who is entitled to participate in its political sphere and to exclude others from doing so. Similarly, it must be able to make some distinctions in the economic and social realms between those who are affiliated with it and those who are not. If I live in Missouri and have no significant economic or social ties with California, it is both constitutional and entirely fair for California to bar me from voting or holding office there and to restrict those privileges to people who do. Likewise, California need not license me to drive or practice law or probate an estate there unless I meet reasonable requirements of residence or competence or what have you.

But Johnson's vision of state control over state citizenship and its consequences ran far beyond these common-sense conclusions. His contention was that states can deny a person with national, but not state, citizenship virtually every private right and all rights of participation in state government, based on race or some other reason, *and that the national government has no power to intervene.* Practically speaking, Johnson's position was that states could effectively void the Thirteenth Amendment by denying state citizenship to the black national citizens within their borders and then legislate away virtually all their rights and privileges, thus imposing on freedmen a condition that would be slavery in all but name.

To be fair to Johnson, the Civil Rights Act was a significant departure from antebellum norms. But Johnson stubbornly refused to see that the Civil War required new arrangements. The war quashed the notion that the country was a gentleman's club which did not pry into its members' affairs and from which one could withdraw whenever displeased by the company or the management. To pursue the metaphor, the northern members of the national club were, at a minimum, determined that those who tried to withdraw, and nearly wrecked the building in the attempt, could not regain their former privileges without substantial reformation. More importantly, Johnson would not recognize that the universal emancipation decreed by the Thirteenth Amendment fundamentally altered the constitutional landscape and required more than a rebranding of African slavery.

Southerners, originally deeply skeptical of Johnson, began to warm to him, as did conservative northern Democrats. Johnson's emerging position embodied the northern peace Democrat's wartime slogan, "The Constitution as it is, the Union as it was."[93] On April 9, 1866, dismayed by Johnson's steady southern drift, Congress overrode Johnson's veto of the Civil Rights Act, the first time in history that the legislative override power had ever been employed.[94]

On June 18, 1866, Congress took its next step by approving the Fourteenth Amendment and forwarding it to the states for ratification.[95] The amendment guaranteed citizenship to all persons born in the United States regardless of race, and barred states from "abridge[ing] the privileges or immunities of citizens of the United States," denying any person life, liberty, or property without due process of law, and denying any person equal protection of the laws. Once ratified, these provisions would cut the legs from under Johnson's argument that states could deprive national citizens of their rights by controlling admission to the status of state citizen.[96] The amendment also required reapportionment based on the actual number of persons in each state, thus voiding the odious provision of the original constitution that treated slaves as 3/5 persons.[97] It disqualified certain classes of former Confederates from holding federal office without congressional approval.[98] Johnson did not campaign openly against the Fourteenth Amendment, but he let his views be known.[99] He sent a special message to Congress on June 22 expressing reservations. When asked, he advised southern legislatures not to ratify it.[100]

Southern intransigence increasingly took violent forms. In May 1866, in Memphis, a street-fight between off-duty and recently discharged black federal troops and several white policemen escalated into a riot, and then a white assault on black citizens of the town. By the time order was restored, forty-six blacks and two whites were dead, seventy-five other persons were wounded, black women were raped, and ninety-one houses, twelve churches, and four schools were destroyed. No one was prosecuted.[101] On July 30, 1866, in New Orleans, a white mob, aided by local police, assaulted delegates to a reconvening of the state's 1864 constitutional convention. The mob killed thirty-seven black and three white delegates before federal troops intervened. Johnson took no action in response to either massacre. Indeed, in a September speech, he blamed Republicans for provoking the New Orleans violence.[102]

Johnson's vetoes of both the Freedmen's Bureau and Civil Rights Acts and his known opposition to the Fourteenth Amendment, combined with continuing southern resistance to modest efforts to protect freedmen and revise prewar social arrangements, began to convince even moderate Republicans that a more assertive congressional stance would be necessary. On July 3, 1866, Congress passed a reworked version of the Freedmen's Bureau bill. On July 16, Johnson vetoed it again. Congress overrode the veto the same day.[103]

Unchastened, Johnson was determined to take his case to the country. In the midterm elections of 1866, which were largely fought on the question of the Fourteenth Amendment,[104] he abandoned the long-standing norm of presidential abstention from electoral combat by personally campaigning throughout the Midwest, defending his policies and attacking congressional Republicans in the harshest terms. He said that Congress was not really Congress in the absence of delegates from the South and called leaders of the Radical Republican faction traitors or worse.[105] Before launching his tour, he suspended martial law throughout the country, including the South, giving credence to the suspicion that he was re-empowering the rebels preparatory to reopening the armed struggle.[106] Ohio Republican Senator John Sherman wrote to his famous military brother, General Sherman, "I almost fear he contemplates civil war."[107]

The country's verdict in November 1866 was a shellacking for Democrats and by necessary implication for Johnson himself.[108] Republicans gained thirty-seven seats in the House[109] and eighteen seats in the Senate.[110] In the 40th Congress, Republicans would hold 76 percent of House seats and 83 percent of the Senate. These numbers are somewhat misleading because those who called themselves Republicans were distributed widely across the spectrum from moderate to radical. But the message should have been clear – outside the defeated South, Presidential Reconstruction had been deemed a failure and Congress had been invited to apply stronger remedies. Moreover, the combination of Johnson's intransigence and the renewed spirit of southern defiance that it engendered united moderate Republicans with their radical colleagues in the conviction that Congress must act.

President Johnson did not get the message. In December 1866, Congress passed a bill granting suffrage to blacks in the District of Columbia. Johnson vetoed it. Congress overrode him.[111] Moreover, as Johnson's estrangement from Republicans increased, so did his affinity for the southerners he had formerly labeled traitors. By proclamation in May 1865, Johnson had created broad classes of former Confederates disqualified from voting and other attributes of full citizenship who could be restored to favor only by direct application for a presidential pardon.[112] The more Johnson came to view southern whites as his natural constituency, the more pardons he granted. Many in the North were shocked and dismayed by what appeared to be wholesale rehabilitation of the Confederate ruling class.[113]

In February 1867, after much deliberation and horse-trading between the Republican factions, Congress passed the First Reconstruction Act.[114] It began by declaring that there were "no legal state governments or adequate protection for life or property" in the "rebel states" of the former Confederacy (excepting Tennessee). It divided these ten states into five military districts and placed them under martial law, but also specified a path back to recognition as restored states of the Union. Readmission would require: (a) creation of a state constitution drafted and ratified by an electorate consisting of all males over twenty-one regardless of race, excepting certain persons disqualified for participation in the rebellion; (b) recognition in that constitution of universal male suffrage; and (c) ratification by the state of the Fourteenth Amendment.[115] Fuming privately that the purpose of the Act was "to protect niggers" at the expense of southern whites, on March 2, Johnson vetoed the bill. Congress overrode him the same day.[116] On March 23, Congress passed a supplemental bill that filled in details absent in the original.[117] Johnson vetoed the bill and was immediately overridden.[118]

March 2, 1867, also saw two other major legislative developments. First, Congress passed a military appropriations bill with a rider requiring that all presidential orders to the army pass through the General of the Army, then Ulysses S. Grant, whose removal the bill prohibited without consent of the Senate. Though famous for his generosity at Appomattox toward Lee and the defeated Confederate Army, Grant was coming around to the view that stiffer reconstruction measures were required. The Republicans wanted to ensure that Johnson did not nullify their newly stringent approach through his control over the Army.[119]

Second, Congress passed, over Johnson's veto, the Tenure of Office Act,[120] which would soon be at the heart of the impeachment effort. In substance, the Act said that any executive branch officer appointed by the president and confirmed by the Senate was entitled to remain in office until a replacement was nominated and received senatorial confirmation. The bill also said that seven cabinet-level officials, once confirmed, were entitled to remain in office throughout the term of the president who appointed them, unless removed with the advice and consent of the Senate. The tenure bill had two purposes, one general and one very particular. In general, the Republicans sought to prevent Johnson from using his appointment authority to remove Republican executive branch officials and insert opponents of congressional reconstruction policy. The Act not only declared Johnson's appointment power to be limited, but sought to enforce the limit by making violation a crime and categorizing that crime as a "high misdemeanor." The term was almost unknown in ordinary law and was plainly employed to create a compelling case for impeachment should Johnson continue to employ his appointment authority to defeat congressional aims.

Some proponents of the bill also intended it to protect Secretary of War William Stanton in particular. Stanton was a Lincoln holdover critical to congressional Republicans because he was known to be sympathetic to their reconstruction policy and, as head of the War Department, he would be the immediate civilian superior of the army officers charged with administering the newly created southern departments. The effectiveness of the Act in protecting Stanton was in some doubt from the beginning because Stanton had been a Lincoln appointee; to bring him within the scope of the law required arguing that Johnson was not serving a term of his own, but instead filling out the balance of the term to which Lincoln had been elected in 1864.[121]

Despite initially conciliatory statements, Johnson set out to weaken the effect of the new laws. Notably, in June 1867 he secured from his attorney general an opinion that, "the army's supremacy over civil governments was confined to police duties; that commanders could not remove civilian officials; that only those antebellum officeholders who had taken an oath to support the United States Constitution could be disenfranchised for rebellion; and that [election] registrars must accept without question a prospective voter's oath that he had not participated in the rebellion."[122] The effect would have been to allow former rebels to control the southern constitutional conventions and ratification votes. General Grant protested against the opinion and told his subordinates they need not abide by it.[123] In response, in July, Congress passed, as usual over Johnson's veto, a third reconstruction Act clearly subordinating southern provisional governments to the military and toughening voting eligibility requirements to bar more former confederates.[124]

Johnson still would not relent. As soon as Congress adjourned for the summer of 1867, the president suspended Secretary of War Stanton pending the return of Congress to ratify that decision.[125] He persuaded Grant to become interim Secretary of War, and much to Grant's dismay, replaced generals Phil Sheridan and Dan Sickles as heads of southern military departments with generals Johnson thought sympathetic to his reconstruction policy.[126] In December, he made similar moves in two other departments.[127] In September, Johnson issued a revised pardon proclamation, broadening the class of beneficiaries to embrace almost everyone of consequence in the South.[128] Pending Congress' return, the reconstruction effort was increasingly paralyzed by the schism between a Congress determined that real changes would be made and a president whose attitude from the first had been that no real reconstruction was required because the southern states had never left the Union, and that the abolition of slavery should effect no material change in the status of black people in America.[129]

IMPEACHMENT IN THE HOUSE OF REPRESENTATIVES

Radical Republicans in Congress had begun thinking about impeachment as early as 1866.[130] In January 1867, Congressman James Ashley of Ohio introduced an impeachment resolution which was referred to the Judiciary Committee. The resolution was succinct and sounded themes that would resonate throughout the coming struggle. It bears recitation in full:

I do impeach Andrew Johnson, Vice President and acting President of the United States, of high crimes and misdemeanors.
I charge him with a usurpation of power and violation of law:
   In that he has corruptly used the appointing power;
   In that he has corruptly used the pardoning power;

In that he has corruptly used the veto power;

In that he has corruptly disposed of public property in the United States;

In that he has corruptly interfered in elections, and committed acts which, in contemplation of the Constitution are high crimes and misdemeanors.[131]

That summer, the Judiciary Committee considered Ashley's outline and other allegations, but voted 5:4 against recommending impeachment. In November, the Committee reversed itself and by a 5:4 vote forwarded to the full House a report favoring action. It was voted down by a margin of 108:57.[132] At that point, the impeachment effort was dogged by two central problems. The first was the difficulty in overcoming the argument of Johnson's defenders and the constitutionally cautious that impeachment required a direct violation of some particular law.[133] The points on either side of that question were discussed at great length in the Judiciary Committee's November report, with the majority adopting the broad view of impeachment as a political determination requiring neither an indictable crime nor other infringement on existing statutory or common law.[134] But the bulk of Republicans were as yet unwilling to accept the implications of this position. The hesitation over these nice legal points was abetted by state election returns that fall in which northern Democrats made some gains by stoking white disdain for freed blacks.[135]

When the 40th Congress returned for its second session in December 1867, Johnson transmitted what we would now call a State of the Union message that practically dared the legislature to take action. It reiterated his by now familiar argument that the southern states had never ceased their legal existence and must be part of Congress for its enactments to be valid and it utterly rejected black political participation. Of southern freedmen, he wrote, "They are taught to regard as an enemy every white man who has any respect for the rights of his own race."[136] By which he plainly meant that whites had the "right" to remain ascendant over blacks and that it was outrageous and subversive for blacks to believe otherwise. So far, these were merely more dogmatic repetitions of Johnson's favorite themes. But this time he went a threatening step further. He described possible executive responses to legislative actions a president considers unconstitutional and said that some such actions would justify the use of force – in his own words, "civil war" – to resist them. Having made this remarkable declaration, he then added an ominously reluctant caveat: "The so-called reconstruction acts, though as plainly unconstitutional as any that can be imagined, were not believed to be within the class last mentioned [i.e., justifying armed resistance]."[137] The unmistakable implication was that, although the reconstruction acts "were not [in the past] believed" to merit forceful resistance, Johnson might change his mind on the point, and thus future congressional action might cross the line Johnson was so actively mulling. Though couched in language that would allow Johnson to deny any untoward intention, the passage was an unmistakable threat to use force if Congress continued in a direction of which Johnson disapproved.

Within a month, Johnson gave his furious congressional opponents the opening they had been hoping for. The Senate refused to affirm the suspension of Secretary of War Stanton and conveyed its refusal to the president on January 13, 1868. Grant relinquished his interim position to Stanton in accordance with the terms of the Tenure of Office Act. Johnson and Grant got into a public spat over the matter in which Johnson accused Grant of bad faith, deeply offending the general who was not only the most popular man in the country but in many minds the presumptive Republican nominee for president in 1868. On February 21, Johnson formally ordered that Stanton be fired, but Stanton refused to yield either his title or the keys to his office.[138] On February 24, the House voted 126:47 to impeach the president.[139]

On March 5, the House forwarded to the Senate eleven articles of impeachment.[140] The first eight charged Johnson with violating the Tenure of Office Act by firing Secretary Stanton and seeking to replace him with General Lorenzo Thomas. The articles broke the firing down into multiple components: the issuance of the dismissal order (Article 1); the appointment of Thomas as successor (Articles 2 and 3); conspiring with Thomas to replace Stanton unlawfully (Articles 4, 5, and 7); and conspiring with Thomas to seize unlawfully War Department property (Stanton's office and records) (Articles 6 and 8).[141] The need for eight variants of the same charge is unclear, but presumably the drafters wanted to frame the firing as a violation of multiple laws.

Article 9 alleged that Johnson had told General William Emory that the act requiring the president to transmit military orders through General Grant was unconstitutional, but did not claim that Johnson actually gave Emory any orders in violation of the act.

Article 10 alleged that Johnson had cast aspersions on Congress in various ways, framing those aspersions as an effort to subvert the authority of a coordinate branch. They focused particularly on Johnson's repeated claim that a Congress without representatives of the states of the former Confederacy was not a constitutional body. Article 11 was a catch-all summarizing all the previous allegations, with the potentially critical addition of the allegation that Johnson violated his constitutional obligation to "take care that the laws be faithfully executed" by attempting to prevent the execution of the reconstruction acts.[142]

THE SENATE TRIAL OF ANDREW JOHNSON

Having hesitated long in bringing charges against Johnson, the Republicans now brooked no delay. Trial in the Senate, Chief Justice Salmon P. Chase presiding, convened on March 13.[143] A bit more than two weeks were allowed for the composition of pretrial pleadings and the preparation of evidence. The House managers opened their case on March 30.[144]

The managers' task appeared to be deceptively simple. The articles charged the president with violating the Tenure of Office Act and with questioning the constitutional legitimacy of the sitting Congress. Although the managers and the defense explored the nuances of Johnson's actions and his words in excruciating detail, each hoping to extract the last morsel of incriminating or exculpatory inference, the facts were never in serious dispute. He did what he was charged with doing. The managers' problem was that Johnson had plausible arguments that he was within his rights to fire Stanton, either because, as a Lincoln appointee, Stanton was never covered by the Act in the first place or because the Tenure of Office Act was an unconstitutional legislative infringement on executive authority. He had an even more appealing argument that disparaging Congress was an unexceptional example of normal political debate, rude no doubt, but protected by the First Amendment and in any case hardly a high crime or misdemeanor.

The managers and the president's lawyers hammered at each other on these legal points throughout the trial because the composition of the articles necessarily framed the formal case in that way. But to win, the managers had to press their real complaint against Johnson, which was that throughout his presidency he had resisted and undermined the congressional program of southern reconstruction and sided with the former rebels to restore the prewar southern leadership class to power and to maintain freedmen in a condition as close to slavery as possible. Their problem was that, in yielding to the understandable temptation to build a case around a discrete violation of the law, they consigned the central questions of the postwar period – what should be the course of the country in the aftermath of civil war and who had the power to set it – to the periphery of the case. Only Article 11 raised these issues, and it did so only obliquely.

The Tenure of Office Act

The most basic question about the articles based on Johnson's removal of Secretary of War Stanton was whether the firing actually violated the Tenure of Office Act. Johnson's defenders contended that the Congress which passed the Act never intended it to cover cabinet officers generally or Stanton in particular. Although they (and later commentators) raised serious questions about what individual legislators thought their product meant,[145] it seems quite difficult to read the Act as not covering the cabinet. The Act proclaimed that a list of cabinet officers including the Secretary of War "shall hold their offices . . . for and during the term of the President by whom they may have been appointed and for one month thereafter, subject to removal by and with the advice and consent of the senate."[146]

The question of whether Stanton himself was protected by the Act was a different pair of sleeves. Stanton had been a Lincoln appointee; to bring him within the scope of the law required arguing that Johnson was not serving a term of his own, but instead filling out the balance of term to which Lincoln had been elected in 1864.[147]

Notice, for example, that Congressman Ashley's first resolution for impeachment in the preceding year had styled Johnson as "Vice President and acting President of the United States."[148] This was a plausible, if tendentious, view of Johnson's legal status, and also a plausible, if highly contestable, reading of the Tenure of Office of Act. Nonetheless, to impeach a president for violating so debatable an interpretation seems imprudent. In defense of the House Republicans and those who voted to convict on this ground in the Senate, Johnson himself acted as though the Tenure of Office Act bound him in his relations to Stanton up until the point where he crossed the Rubicon and fired Stanton outright. Before that, he followed the procedure specified in the Act of waiting until the Senate was in recess, suspending Stanton, notifying the Senate of his action, and appointing Grant as an interim placeholder pending receipt of the Senate's verdict. From the Republicans' perspective, Johnson's claim that Stanton was not covered was the belated justification of a lawbreaker who simply never thought he would be called to account.

The more profound question about the Tenure of Office Act was whether it was constitutional in the first place. Whether a president has unrestricted authority to dismiss those he appoints to federal service is unaddressed in the constitution and was disputed from the beginning. In the 1st Congress of 1789, the House of Representatives debated for three days the question of whether the constitutional requirement of Senate concurrence in certain presidential appointments implied a senatorial power to withhold consent when a president seeks to remove an appointee.[149] Participants included framers such as James Madison, who argued that the constitution did not permit a senatorial veto over removals, and Roger Sherman and Elbridge Gerry, who argued the reverse. The debate was inconclusive in the sense that no vote was taken on precisely the point at issue.[150] Nonetheless, the majority seems to have concluded that limiting the president's removal power was constitutionally doubtful.[151] Moreover, in the following decades, major constitutional commentators – James Kent, Joseph Story, and others – and a string of attorneys general concurred that the president's removal power was nearly unchecked. Finally, in practice the power had gone unchallenged for eighty years.[152]

All that having been said, the managers had four points on their side. First, the constitutional text was ambiguous, so much so that even the framers sitting in the 1st Congress disagreed with one another on its meaning. Second, whatever practice may have grown up, there had never been an authoritative judgment on the point by the Supreme Court. Third, the passage of the Tenure of Office Act – over the president's veto and thus by more than two-thirds majorities of both houses – represented a far more definitive judgment by the legislative branch than an inconclusive debate by one house. Finally, although the managers did not raise this argument, the judgment of the House in 1789 was based to an important degree on the view, expressed publicly and privately by Madison at the time and shared by many of his contemporaries,[153] that the presidency was a weak office requiring as much protection as interpretation of the constitutional language could give it.

On the issue of presidential power, the Congress of 1789 was necessarily engaged in augury, not analysis. The government outlined in the constitution was then not yet a year old and Madison's arguments about how the constitution ought to be interpreted were based almost entirely on predictions of how the untried experiment would develop. By contrast, the Congress of 1868 had just lived through a bloody four-year lesson in the imperfections of the original constitutional arrangements. They were in the process of remodeling the old structure into something new. They were, I think, as entitled to a fresh look at the constitution's balance between the coordinate branches as the original founding generation.

Abraham Lincoln had saved the Union by proving Madison's prediction about presidential impotence utterly wrong. He had raised and commanded the largest and most lethal armies to that point seen in the history of the world. He had suspended habeas corpus, imposed martial law not only in states formally seceded but in large chunks of nominally loyal border states like Missouri, emancipated most of America's slaves, and done half-a-hundred things barely contemplated by the constitution or positively contrary to it. By the end, his unique character had made him to his generation what Washington had been to the founders: a man whose honesty, personal decency, and unquestioned dedication to the public good made the grant of supreme power unobjectionable. In Andrew Johnson, however, it was not unreasonable for northern Unionists to see a cautionary counterexample. The personal power assumed by Lincoln in the emergency of rebellion, as well as the expanded power of the much enlarged federal establishment created by the war and required to maintain and manage the peace, ought not be entrusted even to an ordinary politician, still less to a man like Johnson – rigid, stubborn, profoundly bigoted against freedmen, and determined to sustain a social order that needed to die.

It is often said that Johnson escaped impeachment because a good many of the senators who voted for acquittal thought the Tenure of Office Act was unconstitutional. Parsing the *post hoc* justifications for such a very political choice is always dicey, but this conclusion is difficult to support with the available evidence. It must be remembered that the seven Republican senators who voted to acquit Johnson had, to a man, voted for the Tenure of Office Act, not once but twice: once on its first passage and again to override Johnson's veto.[154] It seems most unlikely that all, or indeed more than one or two of them, based their acquittal on the proposition that a bill – a contentious, high-profile bill – they had approved only a year before was actually an unconstitutional violation of the separation of powers.

Nonetheless, some senators certainly thought that the Act, because of its peculiar phrasing, did not apply to *Stanton*. Others concluded that either the general constitutionality of the Act or its application to Stanton was sufficiently doubtful that a president should not be impeached for testing it. In the trial, Johnson's defenders framed this issue as one of intent, arguing that conviction required an intention to violate a law conceded by the president to be valid, and insisting that he always intended that the legality of the Stanton firing be resolved in the courts. Some of the acquitting Republicans plainly bought this argument.[155]

Johnson's Attacks on Congress

On the surface, the ninth and tenth articles of impeachment seem inconsequential. Article 9 alleging Johnson told General Emory that the Act requiring to him route orders through General Grant was unconstitutional was both substantively inconsequential and tactically foolish. Johnson offered an opinion, but there was no evidence he had actually given Emory a direct order. Inserting this sort of stuff risked trivializing the whole endeavor.

Article 10 was a different matter altogether. To us, looking back at the safe remove of more than a century, Johnson's verbal assaults on Congress may seem to have been no more than rumbustious political rhetoric. In the circumstances of the period, they were far graver and more dangerous. Johnson's position was that once the southern states ratified the Thirteenth Amendment and formed new governments selected by an electorate consisting of persons enfranchised under the states' own rules (which, of course, excluded blacks), and excluding only an ever-diminishing class of former Confederate officers and officials not pardoned by Johnson, then they were entitled to full representation in Congress and every other perquisite of state sovereignty. Using Johnson's definition, by 1867, all the former Confederate states qualified. Therefore, he stated, a Congress convened without them was illegitimate and its enactments were of no constitutional force.

These were claims of immense consequence. First, Johnson was asserting that he, not Congress, had the right to define the status of the states of the rebellion and the conditions for their readmission to full participation in the national government. Second, by branding Congress and its enactments constitutionally illegitimate, he justified his own unconcealed efforts to undercut congressional reconstruction policy. Third, and most consequentially, Johnson was signaling to the white South that they, too, were justified in resisting "unconstitutional" measures for their reformation. This would be troublesome from a president in any era, but Johnson was encouraging recalcitrance from a section of the southern populace whose stubborn pugnacity had cost 750,000 dead to subdue. This was not mere political rhetoric, not an innocent exercise of First Amendment rights, but was, to borrow a phrase from a famous Union veteran, akin to shouting "fire" in a crowded theater,[156] or perhaps even more aptly to throwing a match into a fireworks factory. Moreover, any effort to excuse Johnson's stump speeches as harmless rhetorical excess was belied by the barely veiled threat of violence in the 1867 State of the Union message.

That said, Article 10 presented two main challenges for the managers. The first was convincing the Senate and the country that the phrase "high crimes and misdemeanors" was not limited to actual crimes, but embraced unindictable offenses against constitutional order. This is a point already familiar from our earlier consideration of British impeachment practice, the views of the founding generation, and the early impeachments of Senator Blount, Justice Chase and the lower court judges. Law and history were entirely on the side of the managers and they mined all of it to great effect.

Manager Ben Butler incorporated into his opening a brief previously prepared for the House that explored British impeachment practice in detail. It cited Blackstone, *Comyn's Digest*, Hale's *Pleas of the Crown*, Howard's *State Trials*, and *Wooddeson's Lectures*, and mentioned by name a great number of the cases addressed above in Chapter 2 in which British ministers, officers, and clergy were impeached for conduct not criminal. The argument surveyed the records of the Constitutional Convention, touched on the practices of the states, and concluded that:

> With these landmarks to guide them, our fathers adopted a Constitution under which official malfeasance and nonfeasance, and, in some cases, misfeasance, may be the subject of impeachment, although not made criminal by act of Congress, or so recognized by the common law of England or of any state of the Union. They adopted impeachment as a means of removing men from office whose misconduct imperils the public safety and renders them unfit to occupy official position.[157]

Notably, it quoted Madison's observation during the 1789 congressional debate over the presidential removal power that, "the wanton removal of meritorious officers would subject [the President] to impeachment and removal from his own high office."[158] The House brief went on to cite copious British and American academic authority that impeachment extends beyond crimes to political offenses. It concluded with an exploration of all the American impeachments to that time, conclusively demonstrating that none of them depended on the doctrine that crime is necessary for impeachment.[159]

The managers' presentation on what we would now call the original understanding of "high crimes and misdemeanors" was so overwhelming that the defense essentially punted on the question. In summation, defense counsel Thomas Nelson waved away all reference to British precedent by declaiming that "this tribunal [the Senate sitting as a court of impeachment] has no exemplar in the history of the world."[160] He skipped nimbly past the records of the Constitutional Convention and made no reference at all to prior federal impeachments. His argument boiled down to the non sequitur that because the Senate proceeding is denominated a "trial" and is presided over by the chief justice, then its subject must necessarily be crime, followed by the bald assertion (unsupported by any authority) that because the framers used the terms "crimes" and "misdemeanors" they could only have meant ordinary crimes and misdemeanors as defined by the common law of the period.[161] It was a half-hearted performance and can have convinced no one not already predisposed in President Johnson's favor.

The weakness in Article 10 was not that it failed to allege a crime, but that it focused purely on political speech rather than official presidential action. As incendiary – and as genuinely dangerous – as Johnson's rhetoric had been, he was not alone among the politicians of the era in hurling accusations of illegitimacy, unconstitutionality, and outright treason. Though many senators doubtless were outraged by Johnson's verbal assaults, it would have been an unusually obtuse legislator who would not have recognized the danger to himself and political debate generally of declaring excessive speech a removable offense. Speech inciting disloyalty and resistance to congressional enactments might make a *part* of a coherent theory of impeachment. But an article alleging speech alone, without persuasive allegations of unconstitutional *conduct*, was doomed to fail once subjected to the searching analysis of a trial. No doubt the Republican managers thought that the requisite conduct was supplied by the charges of violating the Tenure of Office Act, but as we have seen, those charges were always rickety.

The Senate's Verdict and its Reasons

In the end, the effort to impeach Andrew Johnson failed. On May 16, 1868, the Chief Clerk of the Senate called the roll on Article 11, the catch-all thought most likely to succeed. The votes for conviction fell short of a two-thirds majority by the margin of a single senator: thirty-five in favor, nineteen opposed.[162] Because of the huge Republican majority, this meant that seven Republicans – branded by their outraged critics as "the recusants" – voted with all the Democrats to acquit.[163] The recusants were excoriated by many northern Republicans. Dismayed southern Unionists, white and black, foresaw in Johnson's survival the collapse of reconstruction efforts and feared for their own safety. The formerly secessionist white power structure across the South rejoiced.[164]

The reasons for the recusants' votes have been debated endlessly. Partisan politics and personal animosities and ambitions were certainly a large factor in the outcome. First, the Republican Party had secured sweeping triumphs in the national midterm elections of 1866, but suffered some reverses in state elections during 1867. Moderates worried that the Radical approach to reconstruction, particularly its continuing emphasis on black suffrage, might cost Republicans in 1868, and that impeaching Johnson would align the entire party in the public mind with the Radicals.

Second, the issue of who would succeed Johnson was a major sticking point. Johnson had succeeded to the presidency upon Lincoln's death, but at the time there was no provision for replacing a vice president (a problem that would not be remedied until the ratification of the Twenty-fifth Amendment in 1967).[165] Moreover, the succession rules of the time provided that the person next in line should Johnson die or be removed from office was the president *pro tempore* of the Senate, Ben Wade of Ohio.[166] In the political taxonomy of the period, Wade was a true radical – he favored women's rights (including the right to vote), labor rights, high tariffs, and black suffrage.[167] Moreover, he was a brusque, insistent party man who had made enemies both back in Ohio and in the Republican senatorial caucus.

A good many Republicans were apprehensive about installing Wade in the White House even for a short time. Some disliked Wade personally. Others feared that a sharp turn toward more radical reconstruction policies might alienate voters before November. Many were also concerned about how a President Wade could complicate the expected nomination of General Grant as the Republican standard bearer for 1868. Grant's supporters could take some comfort in the expectation that his overwhelming popularity would assure his ultimate success at the convention, but Republicans wanted no internecine squabbles. Moreover, if Wade were interim president, that would give him a powerful claim on at least the vice presidential nomination, and a good number of Republicans in and out of the Senate did not fancy him in that role, either on the merits or because they favored some other candidate.[168]

Many contemporary observers believed that Johnson survived in large part because Wade would have succeeded him.[169] One newspaper declared that, "Andrew Johnson is innocent because Ben Wade is guilty of being his successor."[170] Most modern students of the affair concur that Republican discomfort with Wade was a major factor.[171] It was not that they preferred Johnson to Wade (although a few might have), but that the impeachment trial was drawing to a close in mid-May, the election was less than six months away, and Republicans knew they had an almost sure winner in Ulysses S. Grant. Moreover, some moderate and conservative Republicans had made direct overtures to Johnson, securing pledges, express or implied, that he would appoint General John Schofield, an acceptable moderate, to replace Stanton and not move aggressively in the near term to undercut congressional reconstruction.[172]

Beyond questions of intramural Republican politics, Johnson's congressional opponents made a politically expedient vote easier by choosing to fight the battle on the weakest possible grounds. From its inception, there had been doubt that the Tenure of Office Act covered Secretary of War Stanton, not to speak of the doubt about whether the Act itself was constitutional. Thus, Johnson could claim either that he was legally in the right or not so obviously in the wrong as to merit removal. Violating the Act was, in any case, of only modest national importance, particularly as long as Grant remained General of the Army and could prevent complete evisceration of congressional reconstruction policy. To the extent that Stanton's firing was of constitutional consequence, it was only because Johnson had defied Congress to order his removal and made the firing a test of the scope of executive and legislative authority.

Had the Tenure of Office Act been central to the congressional reconstruction program and had Congress been on firmer constitutional ground in passing it, this might have carried the day. But of all the Reconstruction legislation Congress passed, the Tenure of Office Act was the least consequential and the most constitutionally suspect. Even the bill requiring that presidential orders to the military pass through the General of the Army could be defended on the ground that Congress did not fatally subvert the president's commander-in-chief power merely by insisting that he exercise it through the military chain of command. The Tenure of Office Act severely impaired presidential authority, arguably violated separation of powers principles, was contrary to such precedent as existed, and would have had a permanent effect on the legislative–presidential balance long after the Reconstruction period ended. By contrast, all the rest of the Reconstruction bills were either plainly within Congress' power or, given the unprecedented situation presented by the recent War, arguably so. Certainly, Congress had a better claim to control over these matters than a president acting unilaterally.

THE IMPEACHMENT CASE THAT MIGHT HAVE BEEN

The true rationale for Johnson's impeachment was explained by Thaddeus Stevens at the close of the House debate on adopting the articles:

> When the so-called confederate States of America were conquered and had laid down their arms and surrendered their territory to the victorious Union the government and final disposition of the conquered country belonged to the Congress alone, according to every principle of the law of nations.
>
> Neither the Executive nor the judiciary had any right to interfere with it except so far as was necessary to control it by military rule until the sovereign power of the nation had provided for its civil administration. No power but Congress had any right to say whether ever or when they should be admitted to the Union as States and entitled to the privileges of the Constitution of the United States. And yet Andrew Johnson, with unblushing hardihood, undertook to rule them by his own power alone; to lead them into full communion with the Union; direct them what governments to erect and what constitutions to adopt, and to send Representatives and Senators according to his instructions. When admonished by direct acts of Congress, more than once repeated, he disregarded the warning and continued his lawless usurpation. He is since known to have obstructed the reestablishment of those governments by the authority of Congress, and has advised the inhabitants to resist the legislation of Congress.[173]

Stevens wisely framed the central question as one of basic constitutional authority over the most important problem ever faced by the American republic – how to reunite and reorder the country in the aftermath of civil war. He might have gone further, and did during the Senate trial, to point out that the issue went beyond an arid question of separation of powers to the merits of the competing approaches to reconstruction. Johnson was impeached because he wanted to revive the South as nearly unchanged as possible and to lock freedmen into a status as close to slavery as possible, while Congress insisted that the former rebel leadership must be suppressed, the South reformed, and the freedmen supported on a path to participatory citizenship. The Supreme Court was unwilling to choose between these irreconcilable visions, having held that congressional power to reorganize state governments as a precondition to readmission to the Union was a political question.[174] Therefore, thought Johnson's adversaries, if Congress was to control the composition of the national union and its future course, the president must be impeached.

The problem for Johnson's opponents was that, with the debatable exception of the firing of Stanton, none of Johnson's overt acts in pursuit of his vision of reconstruction were *in themselves* unlawful. They were instead misuses of otherwise lawful authority in pursuit of an objectionable end. Congressman Ashley's impeachment resolution introduced back in January 1867 provided a partial list of particular conduct: abuses of the appointing power, the veto power, and the pardoning power.[175] But the House failed to articulate a theory of impeachment focused on the totality of Johnson's behavior. Instead, it rested its case on inconsequential particulars like the Stanton firing and a couple of speeches, thus allowing Johnson's defenders to focus on minutia.

A better case for Johnson's impeachment would have begun with Thaddeus Stevens' assertion of congressional authority over Reconstruction. It would have placed front and center the throwaway allegation at the end of Article 11 that Johnson violated his constitutional obligation to "take care that the laws be faithfully executed"[176] by actively undermining the legislative mandates of Congress in the various Reconstruction acts. It would have recited the entire panoply of Johnson's obstructive behavior: appointment of officials opposed to the congressional reconstruction program; dismissal of those who supported it; the effort to use the army to institute reconstruction policies at odds with Congress; the failure to use the army or the prosecutors and marshals of the Justice Department to protect the rights, property, and lives of southern freedmen and Unionists; efforts first to destroy and then undercut the work of the Freedmen's Bureau; the increasingly indiscriminate employment of the pardon power to reinstate unrepentant rebels; and the active encouragement of southern resistance to Reconstruction by, among other things, disparaging the legitimacy of Congress and suggesting that force might be a legitimate response to congressional enactments.

In aid of this more comprehensive case, the House could have taken advantage of the impressive constitutional erudition displayed in some of the debates to point out that important framers supported impeachment for abuse of the pardon power in cases of rebellion. Likewise, it could have framed the firing of Stanton and others not merely as a violation of the Tenure of Office Act, but as fitting neatly into Madison's 1789 statement that a president might be impeached for dismissing meritorious officers.

A comprehensive case might also have alleged that Johnson violated his oath to "preserve, protect, and defend" the constitution.[177] Johnson, of course, would have

resented any such allegation profoundly. He saw himself as the pre-eminent champion of the constitution. But he failed to defend the constitution in the large sense by
seeking the hasty restoration of southern governments and institutions that led the
recent rebellion, thus endangering the peace and security of the nation. Moreover,
Johnson's allegiance was to the old constitution, the words on paper and the set of
norms and understandings that predated the Civil War. The war disrupted the old
understandings and plainly demanded new ones. In resisting all evolution, Johnson
was not preserving or protecting, but was in fact endangering the entire constitutional project. Most important, by December 1865, the constitution had important
new words in the form of the Thirteenth Amendment abolishing slavery.
By supporting the subjection of freedmen into a form of peonage, Johnson sought
to undercut the constitution in its new form.

Of course, one can readily see why the Republicans chose a narrower theory for
their impeachment effort. The broad approach outlined here would have been hard
to prove.[178] But more importantly, it necessarily rests on a big claim about the
impeachment power, namely, that if Congress and the president are in irreconcilable disagreement over fundamental constitutional issues implicating the future
direction of the country, Congress may impeach the president in defense of its
constitutional vision. This is not only a big, but a potentially dangerous, claim.
In adopting "high crimes and misdemeanors" as the standard for presidential
removal, the framers certainly did not mean to grant Congress the power to remove
any president with whom it has a constitutional quarrel. And it is often said that no
officer ought to be impeached merely for entertaining an opinion contrary to
Congress.[179] On the other hand, as we have seen, since the 1300s, the phrase has
been used to embrace executive branch conduct that imperils legislative views of
proper constitutional order.[180]

Moreover, unless the constitution is, in the now-hackneyed phrase, a suicide pact,
impeachment must extend to non-criminal constitutional disagreement at least
sometimes. Addressing this very question, House manager Ben Butler offered the
following hypothetical:

> Let it be supposed that with the initiatory steps of the rebellion the President had
> declared that the national Government had no constitutional power to suppress
> a rebellion by force of arms.
>
> Now, whether such an utterance was extorted by fear, or might have been an
> honest, but perverted political theory, or the result of a treasonable purpose to aid
> traitors, would have been in its consequence to the nation all the same if it could
> have controlled the counsels of the nation. This sentiment, believed and acted on,
> would have witnessed the destruction of the Government. Must the nation perish
> because a President honestly believes in the fatal heresy that the Constitution and
> Congress are powerless for self-preservation? If so, the nation must die out of tender
> regard to the political idiosyncrasy of the President. The same fatal error of opinion
> and conduct will be impeachable in one President who knows the right and yet the

wrong pursues, while another, who believes in a fallacy because he loves it, will escape unpunished, though the inherent wrong in principle and effect is the same in both cases.[181]

In short, to say that a president may not be impeached for an honest, but fundamental, disagreement on constitutional principle is to say that Congress would have had no recourse if, in 1861, the White House had been occupied by a president who, quite sincerely, believed states had a constitutional right to secede. Andrew Johnson's view of the constitutional constraints on postwar reconstruction was no less misguided and nearly as consequential for the country's future. Johnson did not merely entertain a difference of opinion with Congress, and he did not merely abstain from action based on that difference of opinion. Rather, he differed fundamentally and irreconcilably with Congress on the most important constitutional questions of the most pivotal era in American history, and he acted forcefully and repeatedly, employing every means at his disposal, to thwart Congress' constitutional vision and to substitute his own. In such a case, Congress had every right to categorize his constitutional errors as "high crimes and misdemeanors" and to impeach and remove him. This is not as radical as it may sound. The two most recent presidential impeachment efforts, those involving presidents Nixon and Clinton, have accustomed us to see the injunction that impeachment is for "great offenses" which, in Hamilton's words, are "political, as they relate chiefly to injuries done to the society itself"[182] as a *limitation* on the impeachment power. But the political character of impeachment also *expands* its reach to conduct with no tincture of criminality that nonetheless damages constitutional order and thereby injures society.

To apply this principle to Johnson's case means not only that Congress can impeach a president for failing to preserve the old order of things, but also when the country stands at a constitutional crossroads and Congress is determined to modify the old dispensation. The old British cases offer ample precedent for this idea. The parliaments of the Stuart era impeached Lord Strafford, Archbishop Laud, and others because they clung to the old model of absolute monarchy, while Parliament, however much it spoke in terms of the immemorial rights of Englishmen, was determined to change the status quo and expand the reach of the common law and the power of the legislature.

If one admits this conclusion in principle, it is a principle that begs for some limitation. Certainly, we can say that impeaching a president based on a difference in constitutional vision with the Congress should be a remedy of last resort. Defining the occasions on which it is appropriate – at least beyond deploying a lot of exclamatory adjectives (great occasions, and so on) – is probably futile. The primary limitations on such a quintessentially political act are themselves political. For example, in Johnson's case, the House opted for a limited theory of impeachment in part because making the broader case would have required articulating the Republican Party's aims for Reconstruction and convincing both the country (or at least the northern section of it) and the Senate that the vision was correct and that defying it was impeachable. The party itself was divided on many points, particularly black suffrage, and any effort to spell out the party's program in articles of impeachment would have been internally divisive and potentially danger-ous in the upcoming 1868 elections. The same difficulty is likely to confront any future effort to impeach a president on a matter of constitutional principle not associated with criminal behavior. Second, once again, the framers' decision to require a two-thirds supermajority for conviction looms large. Even in a Senate where Republicans held 83 percent of the seats and the president was of the opposite party, the managers could not secure two-thirds of the votes.

LESSONS FROM THE JOHNSON IMPEACHMENT

For much of the twentieth century, Johnson's impeachment was seen as a congressional misuse of the impeachment power. The most familiar expression of this perspective is found in John F. Kennedy's ghostwritten book, *Profiles in Courage*, which lauds the selflessness of Kansas senator Edmund G. Ross, the recusant credited with casting the deciding vote against convicting President Johnson. Ross is portrayed as a reasonable man resisting the extremist agenda of Radical Republicans who sought to punish the defeated South. Johnson is cast as a "courageous if untactful Tennessean" who was the true heir of Abraham Lincoln's policy of postwar reconciliation.[183] Even some more recent and better-informed commentators have declared Johnson's impeachment "a gross abuse of the impeachment process" and his acquittal a victory for the proper constitutional balance of power between co-equal branches.[184]

I disagree. First, Johnson's behavior was an egregious example of executive over-reach and defiance of the repeatedly expressed will of a supermajority of Congress, undertaken without even the justification that he was acting in a time of open armed rebellion. The failure to remove Johnson was a significant step along the road that led to today's imperial presidency.

Second, Johnson was wrong about the central issues of his time. He was wrong about the proper relations of states and the federal government; wrong about the proper response of the victorious Union to the defeated rebel South; and most wrong about the path the country needed to chart if it was to move from a society divided by both region and race to an integrated continental union that would fulfill the promise of the war's verdict and the passage of the Thirteenth Amendment of full citizenship for freed African Americans. Although the final failure of Reconstruction in the 1870s was due to many factors, the Senate's refusal to remove Johnson in 1868 undoubtedly contributed to that failure and to the descent into a century of black repression under Jim Crow.

Even strident policy disagreement between a president and the dominant con-gressional party should not ordinarily constitute grounds for impeachment. Both the executive and legislative branches have the power, and responsibility, to interpret the constitution according to their own best lights and to act in accordance with that interpretation. Nonetheless, in case of irreconcilable disagreement on fundamental questions, some choice must be made. Most of the time, the decision falls to the Supreme Court. Sometimes, the points at issue do not fall within the Court's jurisdiction or it will decide to abstain. In the impeachment clauses, the constitution confers on Congress the power, in the last extremity, to choose its fundamental vision of America over the idiosyncratic view entertained by the individual person occupying the presidency. Johnson's conduct merited impeachment because he abused his executive power in the service of a vision that was morally wrong (even if he and many of his contemporaries could not yet see it to be so) and, entirely predictably, endangered the long-term tranquility of the constitutional order. Congress could, entirely constitutionally, have removed him and in doing so charted a different course for the Republic.

8

The Fall of President Richard Nixon

On August 8, 1974, Richard M. Nixon sat behind the desk in the Oval Office of the White House, looked into a camera lens, and announced that he would resign the presidency effective at noon on the following day. Two days before, a delegation of senior Republican lawmakers – House Minority Leader John Rhodes, Senate Minority Leader Hugh Scott, and the dean of senatorial conservatives, Barry Goldwater – visited the president to tell him that impeachment in the House and conviction in the Senate were near certainties. In the Senate, they said, he might secure as few as a dozen not guilty votes. Goldwater discussed the three articles of impeachment recently approved by the House Judiciary Committee, saying that good lawyering might secure acquittal on Articles 1 and 3. When Nixon asked about the second article, alleging abuse of presidential power, Goldwater replied, "I'm leaning that way myself, Mr. President."[1]

President Nixon's resignation was the finale of a two-year saga which began with the famous "third-rate burglary" of the Democratic headquarters in the Watergate apartment complex that lent its name to the crisis and its suffix to every real and imagined political scandal since. Although the formal impeachment process never got farther than committee approval of articles, the Nixon affair is customarily thought of as establishing a range of important precedents. Some have to do with the definition of impeachable conduct, because as we will see, Nixon's opponents accused him of the widest array of misbehavior of any impeachment controversy in American history. But the Nixon case may be most important in what it taught about how presidential conduct is to be investigated.

In the trial of Andrew Johnson, there was never any serious dispute about the facts. Johnson was impeached for his official acts and public speeches. The question was whether what he did was properly impeachable. By contrast, Watergate was a "whodunnit." Or perhaps more aptly a "who-covered-it-up." The big questions from beginning to end were largely about what happened, who ordered it, and who knew about what when. Once the factual questions were answered, the question of the president's impeachability almost answered itself, even if the precise framing of appropriate charges remained a challenge. The hard constitutional questions in

Watergate almost all related to how wrongdoing by a president or presidential aides is to be investigated. Therefore, our discussion of the fall of Richard Nixon will concern in roughly equal measure what the president did, how the press, federal law enforcement agencies, courts, and Congress uncovered it, and how the House Judiciary Committee organized the facts into articles of impeachment.

RICHARD NIXON AND THE PRELUDE TO WATERGATE

Richard Nixon was perhaps the most complex and contradictory figure in twentieth-century American politics. Born in Yorba Linda, California in 1913, the son of a struggling small businessman and a Quaker school teacher, Nixon grew up poor. He nonetheless managed to work his way through Whittier College and attend Duke Law School on scholarship. He served in the Navy in the Second World War. On his return home, he was invited by hometown Republican worthies to run for Congress against a long-time Democratic incumbent, Jerry Voorhis. He won by painting Voorhis as a Communist tool.[2]

In Congress, Nixon gained national fame as a member of the House Committee on Un-American Activities (HUAC) for pursuing Alger Hiss, a State Department official accused of passing diplomatic secrets to a Soviet agent.[3] The affair and Nixon's time on HUAC established one of his public personas. The young congressman was dogged, almost gleefully vicious, in his pursuit of Hiss and in stoking fear of communists everywhere. He and his HUAC colleagues joined with Joe McCarthy in the Senate in exposing suspected "Reds" in government, business, and the arts. The result was the public destruction of thousands of careers and reputations, often for no greater sin than youthful affiliation with the Communist Party or a continuing sympathy to the milder forms of socialism.[4] Of course, as would so often be true with Nixon, there was another side – there were real Soviet communist agents in the United States and, although it would not be proven until the fall of the Soviet Union, Alger Hiss was almost certainly one of them.[5]

Among Democrats and the American left, the Hiss affair branded Nixon as the dark face of Republican politics, a reputation he would carry for the rest of his political life more or less regardless of the substance of his policies. But it also raised Nixon's profile. In 1950, he was elected senator in a race against Democrat Helen Gahagan Douglas, whom he once again branded as a dangerous communist sympathizer. His vocal anti-communism and the hope of drawing western votes put him on the ticket in 1952 as Dwight Eisenhower's vice presidential running mate.[6] During Ike's two terms, Nixon carved out a somewhat larger-than-customary role for himself as vice president. His forte was foreign policy, the field that always interested him most and in the 1950s provided an obvious avenue for expressing his signature hardline anti-communism.[7]

In 1960, Nixon lost a whisker-close presidential election to John F. Kennedy.[8] That was followed in 1962 by a blowout defeat by Democrat Pat Brown in a race for the California governorship. Most people, including Nixon himself, assumed his political career was over.[9] Expressing the self-pity and hostility to the press that were among his least attractive and ultimately most damaging traits, he declared at the post-election press conference, "You won't have Nixon to kick around anymore."[10] Six years later, Nixon was back. He seized the 1968 Republican nomination and won a narrow victory over Hubert Humphrey.

To understand how Nixon traveled from achieving the pinnacle of his ambition in 1968 to the humiliating nadir of his resignation in 1974, one must step back for a brief reminder of the turmoil that enveloped America during Nixon's sojourn in the political wasteland. At the time of Nixon's 1960 defeat by Jack Kennedy, the long post-Second World War economic expansion continued. The Cold War with the Soviets and their allies had begun, but the Korean conflict had ended in 1953, and America was not involved in any shooting wars. The movement for African American civil rights had begun,[11] but was so far rigorously non-violent and seemed largely non-threatening to whites outside the deep South.

And then, from the viewpoint of many Americans, things began to spin out of control. The Cuban Missile Crisis of 1962 allowed a glimpse of civilizational annihilation. In June 1963, Governor George Wallace blocked integration of the University of Alabama until President Kennedy called in the National Guard. In August, Martin Luther King stood before 250,000 people on the Washington Mall and gave his "I have a dream" speech – an inspiration to many, but a disconcerting reminder to some that the Reconstruction struggle at the heart of the Johnson impeachment was to be renewed by black Americans no longer willing to meekly accept second-class status. White resistance to civil rights protests grew increasingly violent. In September, a bomb killed four black girls at the 16th Street Baptist Church in Birmingham, Alabama. In March 1965, State troopers beat marchers on the Edmund Pettus Bridge outside Selma. Civil rights workers were assaulted, jailed, and murdered.[12]

Abroad, the United States was slowly wading into the bloody mire of Vietnam. A small number of "advisors" sent by President Kennedy in 1961 were supplemented with air and naval support. On November 22, 1963, Lee Harvey Oswald assassinated President Kennedy in Dallas. In 1964, Kennedy's successor, Lyndon Johnson, used the "Gulf of Tonkin Incident" to justify full U.S. intervention in Vietnam, and by 1966, 400,000 American troops, largely draftees, were in the country. Casualties mounted. Success was always one more escalation, one more round of bombing away.

The anti-war movement, small at first, grew larger and more strident. Some of the more radical elements moved beyond stridency to violence. The swelling protest against the Vietnam War coincided with other currents of social change: a revolution in sexual mores; the beginnings of modern feminism, then called "women's liberation"; increased tolerance of recreational drugs; weird clothes and long hair; rock music; the first stirrings of the environmental movement; decreasing patience among black people with the slow pace of racial progress, together with the concern that the war was not only crowding out focus on civil rights, but killing a disproportionate number of black men. All these movements coalesced, at least in the eyes of older or more conservative Americans – Nixon's natural constituency – into a frightening kaleidoscope of disharmony and disruption.

In 1968, everything seemed to explode. In January, the North Vietnamese launched the Tet Offensive, a wave of attacks across South Vietnam that were militarily defeated but destroyed any notion that the North was on the verge of collapse. On April 4, James Earl Ray murdered Martin Luther King in Memphis. Black communities in 100 cities across America erupted into rioting. On June 5, Robert F. Kennedy, campaigning for the Democratic presidential nomination, was assassinated in Los Angeles. In July, in Chicago, the Democratic National Convention nominated Hubert Humphrey for president. Outside, Chicago police fought with protesters. Images of the riot were on every American TV screen.[13]

Richard Nixon ran that fall as the calm antidote to chaos. On the one hand, he stood for "law and order" – suppression of rioters and hippies and malcontents. On the other hand, he promised to end the Vietnam War and bring an "honorable peace." The promises of order and peace carried him past Humphrey to the White House.

By most measures, Nixon's first term was a success in navigating the turbulent currents of the time. He was not a vocal advocate of civil rights, but his administration created some of the first affirmative action hiring programs. His administration enforced the civil rights decisions of the courts, while signaling to whites its opposition to measures that imposed integration through measures like forced busing.[14] He worked constructively with the Democratic majority in both houses of Congress on the economy, social programs, environmental policy, medical research, and regulatory regimes like the Occupational Safety and Health Act. In other areas, notably health care reform, his opposition stalled progressive legislative initiatives.

The point is not the details of any of these policy debates, but that Nixon enjoyed a very different relationship with Congress than Andrew Johnson. Although, Nixon, like Johnson, faced two legislative houses controlled by the opposing party, neither the parties nor the Congress itself were comparable to their 1865 manifestations. The Republican and Democratic parties of 1865 were defined primarily by their attitudes toward disunion, race, and the problems of Reconstruction. Their successors of 1974 were much more complicated. We have become accustomed to viewing Democrats as the "liberal" and Republicans the "conservative" party. But in 1974, the Democrats were chock full of white southerners who had inherited their party affiliation and their racial attitudes from their Confederate forebears, while one wing of the Republican Party was anchored among northeastern liberals who were the political heirs of the party of Lincoln. In the 1940s and 1950s, Democrats had been the internationalist party, while Republicans had a more isolationist strain, a polarity that

Vietnam was in the process of reversing. Both parties were ideologically hetero-
geneous coalitions united by geography, ethnicity, history, tradition, and some
through-lines of policy.[15] Accordingly, all presidents of this era were accustomed
to seeking support on some questions from congressional members of the other
party. For their part, members of Congress expected to legislate and therefore to
work with or against any president as the occasion demanded.

President Nixon's greatest challenge, of course, was Vietnam. Nixon was determined to end the conflict on terms that would allow disengagement without the
appearance of defeat. Therefore, the war went on. Casualties mounted. Protests
intensified. Campus unrest was epidemic. In May 1970, National Guardsmen shot
and killed four Kent State University students.[16] National disillusionment with the
war increased.[17] Nixon, who had campaigned in 1968 on ending the war, became its
public face, loathed by the anti-war left. To those less ideologically blinkered, Nixon
defied easy stereotyping. In February 1972, this rabid anti-communist opened diplomatic ties with China, giving birth to the phrase "Nixon to China" as the quintes-
sence of a politician playing against type.[18] He pursued a relaxation of tensions with
the Soviet Union that became known as détente, and in May 1972 signed a strategic
arms treaty.[19]

To bring the North Vietnamese to the bargaining table and secure concessions
that would reassure South Vietnamese allies, Nixon and his advisor Henry Kissinger
on occasions intensified the conflict. In particular, beginning in March 1969, Nixon
ordered bombing inside neutral Cambodia to destroy North Vietnamese forces and
supply routes (and the next year would openly invade Cambodia).[20]
The administration went to great lengths to keep the early raids secret; however,
in May, news of them leaked to the *New York Times*. The administration denied the
reports publicly, but privately informed five senior legislators about the bombings.
Infuriated by the leak, Nixon ordered that the leaker be found and authorized the
FBI to wiretap the most likely suspect, Mort Halperin, a Kissinger aide. This was the
first of a series of FBI wiretaps of people in and out of government justified on
national security grounds, but often launched simply to gather evidence of internal
dissent or political intelligence.[21] Also in 1969, the Nixon White House began using
its own employees to collect political information using wiretaps and other unsavory
methods.[22]

By June 1970, Nixon was increasingly concerned about anti-war and other
dissident organizations. He commissioned the main intelligence agencies to assess
the threat they posed. The agencies proposed relaxing constraints on domestic
intelligence-gathering. In response, a White House aide named Tom Huston
came up with a plan consisting of "surreptitious entries" (warrantless searches),
electronic surveillance, opening mail, and other outrages. President Nixon
approved the plan, but withdrew it five days later following protests by FBI
Director J. Edgar Hoover and Attorney General John Mitchell. However, elements
of the domestic surveillance program proceeded nonetheless.[23]

Nixon also sought to use other government agencies for political or personal ends. The president's aides tried to procure IRS investigations of enemies and IRS consideration for friends. Inquiries were made about the possibility of Department of Justice antitrust investigations of news outlets critical of the president.[24]

In June 1971, the *New York Times* began publishing the so-called Pentagon Papers, a collection of secret government documents leaked by Daniel Ellsberg that exposed the government's knowledge about the poor prospects for success in the Vietnam War. Although the papers related to actions of the Johnson Administration, Nixon was determined to discredit Ellsberg as a leftist radical and also prevent any future leaks.[25] The administration sued the *Times*, and later the *Washington Post* when it took up the story, to prevent further publication of the purloined secrets. In a decision that set the stage for the investigative journalism that would become a hallmark of the Watergate scandal, the Supreme Court ruled unanimously that the government had not overcome the "heavy presumption" against "prior restraint" of the publication even of classified information.[26]

Privately, the White House set up a special internal unit to ferret out leakers and engage in various kinds of political espionage and dirty tricks. Because of its charge to plug leaks, it became known as the "Plumbers unit." Among its first escapades was the warrantless September 1971 burglary of Daniel Ellsberg's psychiatrist in search of damaging information on Ellsberg. The unit also enlisted the CIA to perform a psychological profile on Ellsberg to be used in discrediting him.[27]

As the 1972 election approached, Nixon formed a campaign organization called the Committee to Re-elect the President, famously known by its infelicitous acronym CREEP. In December 1971, G. Gordon Liddy, one of the Plumbers, was named general counsel. Liddy's job was not legal advice, however, but to run a political intelligence operation. While all campaigns have something of the kind, Liddy conceived of his mandate as a form of spy warfare. He drew up a proposal dubbed the Gemstone Project that in its original form envisioned kidnappings, wiretapping, seducing Democratic convention delegates with prostitutes, and other horrors. In January 1972, he took it to Attorney General John Mitchell, who was about to resign to become chair of CREEP, for his approval. Mitchell declined to approve the plan, but astoundingly neither had Liddy arrested nor called the White House to insist that he be fired on the spot. Instead, Liddy left, revised the plan, and finally secured Mitchell's approval in March for a trimmed-down version that, fatefully, included a scheme to burglarize and plant bugs in the Watergate office of Democratic National Committee chair Lawrence O'Brien.[28]

THE WATERGATE BREAK-IN AND ITS AFTERMATH

On June 17, 1972, five men broke into O'Brien's Watergate office. Due to their spectacular incompetence, they were caught. A search revealed their connection to Plumbers unit member E. Howard Hunt (who was at the Watergate, but escaped) and his connection to the White House.[29] The hunt was on, as was the cover-up that would bring down the president.[30]

It bears emphasis that, although President Nixon had already demonstrated a willingness to bend the law for political ends either under the "tent of national security"[31] or out of simple amorality, there is no indication he knew in advance about the Watergate burglary. What is indisputable is that he found out the next day and thereafter both bent and broke the law many times to conceal the White House connection to the crime.[32]

The details of the Watergate cover-up are far too convoluted to be traced in this summary. Some highlights will be sufficient. Perhaps the pivotal moment came only six days after the burglary. On June 23, Nixon ordered his Chief of Staff Bob Haldeman to ask the CIA to intervene with the FBI to stop the burglary investigation and also decided that former Attorney General Mitchell, who had authorized Gemstone, had to be protected. The CIA refused to intervene and the FBI moved ahead with its probe. So the White House decided, with Nixon's approval, to pay hush money to the burglars and to send John Mitchell and Deputy Campaign Manager Jeb Magruder into the grand jury to lie about what they knew.[33]

In November 1972, Nixon won re-election in a landslide over George McGovern. His popular and electoral vote margins were the largest in history, underscoring the bitter irony that all Nixon's secret manipulations and political skullduggery were utterly unnecessary.[34] Nixon never inspired deep national affection, and many on the left cordially despised him. Nonetheless, all but his most bitter adversaries saw him as an adroit politician, cynical no doubt, but generally moderate in instinct, and capable of surprising statesmanship. Unlike Andrew Johnson, he was not wholly estranged from the dominant congressional party. Congressional Democrats, who retained solid majorities in both houses that fall, may not have loved him, but saw him as a president they could work with. Moreover, and also unlike Johnson, Nixon at the beginning of his second term had an inarguable electoral mandate.[35] But the Watergate investigation continued.

On January 30, 1973, Gordon Liddy and James McCord, another CREEP employee, were convicted in federal district court for the Watergate burglary; five other participants had already pleaded guilty.[36] The judge, John Sirica, made plain that his sentencing decisions would turn in part on the defendants' willingness to cooperate in the ongoing investigation. On March 21, White House counselor John Dean met with the president and discussed how to keep the burglars quiet; both money payments and offers of executive clemency were discussed, and money was paid to Howard Hunt the following day.[37] Nonetheless, the containment effort began to fail. At the end of February, L. Patrick Gray, nominated as successor to J. Edgar Hoover as head of the FBI, told the Senate panel conducting his confirmation hearing that White House counselor John Dean had probably lied to FBI investigators about Watergate. In March, McCord wrote a letter to the judge admitting to perjury in the trial and pointing to White House involvement.

The House Judiciary Committee's impeachment report described the effect of these developments within the White House:

> Faced with a disintegrating situation, the President, after March 21, 1973, assumed an operational role in the detailed management of the cover-up. He knew of the previous untruthful testimony of his aides and of his own false public statements. He issued direct instructions for his subordinates to give false and misleading testimony. The President knew that his agents had instructed and were continuing to instruct witnesses on how to testify to protect the cover-up; the President himself so instructed witnesses.[38]

At the beginning of April, Dean began cooperating with federal prosecutors investigating the break-in. On April 27, Acting FBI Director Gray resigned when it came to light that he had helped to destroy files of one of the Watergate burglars. Three days later, White House senior aides Bob Haldeman, John Ehrlichman, and John Dean resigned in the face of increasing public information implicating them in various aspects of the Watergate cover-up.[39]

The daily cascade of courtroom and press revelations about Watergate drew congressional attention. The Senate was the first to act. In February 1973, Senate Majority Leader Mike Mansfield tasked Sam Ervin (D-NC) to form a special investigative committee – the Senate Select Committee on Presidential Campaign Activities.[40] The Senate Watergate Committee, as it became known, convened its first public hearing on May 17. Its televised proceedings riveted the country, and ultimately produced a seven-volume report.[41]

On May 19, newly appointed Attorney General Elliot Richardson appointed Harvard professor Archibald Cox as special prosecutor to pursue the Watergate investigation. In July, former White House appointments secretary Alexander Butterfield told the Senate Watergate Committee that there was a taping system in the White House that recorded virtually all presidential conversations. Special Prosecutor Cox requested, and when the requests were denied, subpoenaed certain of the tapes. Nixon refused to turn them over, claiming executive privilege. The Special Prosecutor secured an order from Judge Sirica compelling disclosure for *in camera* review (meaning that the judge would review the tapes to determine if they were relevant or privileged). Nixon, claiming executive privilege, refused to comply and appealed Sirica's order, but lost in the court of appeals.[42]

In October 1973, events cascaded. First, Vice President Spiro T. Agnew resigned in the face of corruption charges against him dating from his term as governor of Maryland. Under the terms of the recently enacted Twenty-fifth Amendment, Nixon nominated and in November Congress confirmed Gerald Ford, then House minority leader, to fill the vacancy. Meanwhile, the White House had been negotiating with Special Prosecutor Cox over the subpoenaed tapes; it offered to turn over summaries of the tapes with the accuracy of the summaries verified by a single senator. Cox refused to accept anything other than the tapes themselves.

On October 20, Nixon, determined to halt the Cox investigation and prevent release of the tapes, carried out the famous "Saturday Night Massacre." He ordered Attorney General Richardson to fire Cox, and when Richardson refused, fired him. The process was repeated with Deputy Attorney General William Ruckelshaus. Solicitor General Robert Bork agreed to carry out the order. Near-universal outrage erupted.[43] Under intense public pressure, only twelve days after sacking Cox, Nixon appointed a new special prosecutor, Leon Jaworski.[44]

The Cox firing also brought another player onto the board. As soon as the news hit the papers, multiple congressmen introduced resolutions calling for Nixon's impeachment.[45] These were referred to the House Judiciary Committee, then chaired by Congressman Peter Rodino (D-NJ), who began assembling staff to investigate possible grounds for impeachment.[46] In February 1974, the House passed a resolution formally authorizing the Judiciary Committee to investigate whether sufficient grounds existed to impeach the president and to employ subpoena authority in its work.[47]

The Saturday Night Massacre slowed the Justice Department's criminal investigation while Jaworski got up to speed, and postponed the final confrontation between the president's claims of privilege and the engines of the law. But in the end it would prove to have been for naught. The criminal investigation ground on. In January and February 1974, first Nixon campaign aide Herbert Porter, and then Nixon's personal counsel, Herbert Kalmbach, pled guilty to felonies.

On March 1, 1974, a federal grand jury returned an indictment against seven former presidential aides, including Mitchell, Ehrlichman, and Haldeman. The indictment named Richard Nixon as an unindicted co-conspirator, and was accompanied by an extensive sealed report from the grand jury. The report, which was only released in 2018,[48] has been characterized as a "road map" to the critical evidence collected by the grand jury, but without any legal analysis or recommendation about what the House should do. Special Prosecutor Jaworski and the grand jury requested that the report be conveyed to the House Judiciary Committee. Judge Sirica approved that request on March 18.

The national press reported the developments in the courts and in the Senate and House Watergate committees. But it also played an investigative role of its own. Reporters, most famously Bob Woodward and Carl Bernstein of the *Washington Post*, made discoveries that, once published, provided leads to Justice Department and congressional investigators. As but one example, a story by Woodward and Bernstein probably led to Alex Butterfield being asked before the Senate about the existence of a White House taping system. The essence of the Watergate story was sufficiently clear by early 1974 that on June 15, Woodward and Bernstein were able to publish it in book form as the instant bestseller, *All the President's Men*.[49]

In May 1974, the House Judiciary Committee opened public hearings on possible articles of impeachment. Like the Senate Watergate hearings of the previous year, the House hearings drew massive TV audiences. The Committee's hearings rested on a foundation of material disclosed in criminal cases, received from Special Prosecutor Jaworski and the grand jury, published in the newspapers, and transferred from the Senate Watergate Committee. In addition, the Committee and its staff had for months been performing their own independent investigative work, interviewing witnesses and collecting documentary evidence. Over the course of its investigation, the Committee issued a total of eight subpoenas to the White House. The president complied tardily and reluctantly with some requests, and flatly declined to provide some requested documents or any of 147 subpoenaed tapes.[50] In April 1974, the president turned over edited transcripts of some of the requested tapes. Even the redacted transcripts proved to be immensely embarrassing as they revealed a manipulative, often crude, president (the phrase "expletive deleted" appeared so often that it immediately became a national joke) engaged in discussions that were certainly questionable, if not overtly criminal.[51]

Also in April, Special Prosecutor Jaworski requested and Judge Sirica authorized subpoenas for multiple White House tapes. These were not grand jury subpoenas, but trial subpoenas issued pursuant to Federal Rule of Criminal Procedure 17 to obtain evidence for an upcoming trial, in this case that of Mitchell and his co-defendants. Nixon appealed. Jaworski sought an immediate writ of *certiorari* to the Supreme Court, bypassing the court of appeals. On July 24, 1974, in *United States* v. *Nixon*, the Supreme Court held unanimously that the special prosecutor had the authority to bring an action against the president to enforce a subpoena, and that a "generalized assertion of [executive] privilege must yield to the demonstrated, specific need for evidence in a pending criminal trial."[52]

Even before this climactic ruling in the long struggle over the White House tapes, the picture of a presidency deeply enmeshed in crime and cover-up had solidified. The Watergate burglary was, of course, a crime and one authorized by presidential campaign officials, including Attorney General Mitchell. Moreover, it became plain that Nixon himself knew about the burglary almost immediately after it happened and that his closest aides had orchestrated a cover-up that employed bribery, perjury, attempts to misuse the CIA and suborn the FBI, the withholding of documents and tape recordings, and in at least one case the probable destruction of evidence in the form of the infamous 18½-minute gap on a crucial tape recording.[53] For Nixon's defenders, all this could be deplored without actually abandoning Nixon himself as long as it could be framed as misconduct by overzealous underlings acting without presidential direction. During the Senate Watergate hearings, Republican Senator Howard Baker posed his famous question, "What did the President know, and when did he know it?"[54] As more and more information trickled out, and in particular as a larger and larger percentage of the White House tapes were extracted from a reluctant president, it became increasingly clear that the president had known a lot, had known it early, and had been at the center of a conspiracy to conceal the truth and to obstruct justice. Worse, the investigations revealed that the burglary itself was not a freakish aberration by overzealous low-level operatives, but was instead merely one example of conduct by Nixon and his advisors that could be described in no other way than as a pattern of abuse of executive power in disregard of the constitution, laws, and political norms of the United States.

From July 27 to July 30, 1974, the House Judiciary Committee held a series of votes on proposed articles of impeachment. During the course of its investigation, the committee considered not only the events set off by the Watergate burglary, but the president's efforts to use government power against his "enemies," the effort to conceal the secret bombing of Cambodia, possible personal income tax evasion, and other matters. In the end, possible grounds for impeachment were honed down to three articles. The committee was composed of twenty-one Democrats and seventeen Republicans. Article 1, charging obstruction of the Watergate investigation, passed 27:11.[55] Article 2, alleging abuse of power, passed 28:10. Article 3, concerning Nixon's defiance of committee subpoenas, passed 21:17. At least six Republicans voted in favor of each approved article. A proposed article on the bombing failed, as did one charging violation of the domestic emoluments clause and tax evasion, both by votes of 12:26.[56]

Despite the committee's approval of formal articles, President Nixon was at first determined to tough it out through a full House vote and then, if necessary, a Senate trial. The resolution of those around him crumbled when, in compliance with the Supreme Court's order upholding the special prosecutor's subpoenas, the White House released all the subpoenaed tapes. They destroyed any illusion that Nixon had not known what his minions were doing and had not directed the cover-up. One tape in particular, labeled the "smoking gun," captured Nixon directing that the CIA be employed to quash the FBI investigation of the Watergate burglary and established that his motive was politics, not as he had been saying about many of his actions for months, an effort to protect national security.[57] On August 6, 1974, Senator Goldwater and his colleagues went to see the president. Nixon was out of the White House and on a plane west to California three days later.

THE JUDICIARY COMMITTEE'S ARTICLES OF IMPEACHMENT

All three articles of impeachment approved by the House Judiciary Committee against President Nixon were prefaced by the general allegation that he had violated his oath of office "faithfully to execute the office of President of the United States, and, to the best of his ability, preserve, protect, and defend the Constitution" and that he had violated his "constitutional duty to take care that the laws be faithfully executed."[58] None of them alleged a violation of a particular federal criminal statute, even though the facts adduced in support of Articles 1 and 2 made plain that he had committed crimes or conspired with others to do so.

In drafting the articles, the committee followed the blueprint laid out by its staff in a report on "Constitutional Grounds for Presidential Impeachment."[59] The staff reviewed the historical origins of impeachment, the framers' intentions, and all previous American impeachment cases. Of the prior American cases, it observed that all "involved charges of misconduct incompatible with the official position of the officeholder," falling into "three broad categories: (1) exceeding the constitutional bounds of the powers of the office in derogation of the powers of another branch of government; (2) behaving in a manner grossly incompatible with the proper function and purpose of the office; and (3) employing the power of the office for an improper purpose or for personal gain."[60]

Impeachable conduct need not be criminal: the Committee report specifically rejected the contention, pressed by the president's counsel and some members of the committee's Republican minority,[61] that impeachment required a violation of the criminal law. That the president's defenders would take this position is unremarkable – the defense in virtually every American impeachment case has made the same claim. Nonetheless, it is worth dissecting the particulars of the differing approaches to the criminality issue adopted by President Nixon's defenders.

The official White House brief leaned heavily on a supposed difference between the standards of impeachable conduct for judges and presidents, conceding that judges may be impeached for non-criminal misbehavior due to their tenure during "good behavior," but insisting, without any compelling textual or founding-era evidence, that presidents may be removed only for crime. Nixon's lawyers conceded that British parliamentary practice had some interpretive value, but then interpreted the historical evidence selectively. They emphasized the undoubted facts that parliamentary impeachments had the punitive consequences characteristic of the criminal law and that the framers consciously purged American impeachment of those consequences. Of course, the most logical inference from these facts is that, in adopting the parliamentary term of art "high crimes and misdemeanors" while limiting the penalty to removal from office, the framers wanted to preserve the traditional British grounds for impeachment without the traditional sanguinary consequences. This inference was unsatisfactory from President Nixon's perspective because Parliament routinely impeached people for conduct that was neither a statutory nor common law crime. His lawyers sought to evade the natural consequence of their own logic by characterizing British impeachments for non-criminal conduct as "a 17th Century aberration where impeachment was used as a weapon by Parliament to gain supremacy at the expense of the rule of law."[62] As discussed in Chapters 2 and 4, this characterization would have come as a surprise to parliamentarians before and after the seventeenth century who viewed impeachment as a tool for asserting the rule of law against royal authoritarianism, as well as to the framers who insisted on retaining the power of impeachment in the American constitution for the analogous reason of maintaining a check on overweening presidential power.

The minority staff report took a more nuanced approach than the president's counsel. It insisted that "high crimes and misdemeanors" must be criminal, but conceded that "wilful misconduct in office by public men" would have been a crime at common law at the time of the founding.[63] This framing of the issue left open the argument that the president was not impeachable because he had not acted "willfully," without, however, defining what willfulness means.

After Nixon's resignation, the ten Republican committee members who had voted against impeachment composed an explanation of their position. They conceded that the "smoking gun" tape and other evidence had convinced them of Nixon's guilt on Article 1. However, echoing the theme of the Minority Staff Report, they argued that the standard for impeachable conduct ought not include "ineptitude, or unintentional or 'technical' violations of rules or statutes, or 'maladministration' – which would not be criminal; nor could [such conduct] be made criminal consonant with the Constitution, because the element of criminal intent or *mens rea* would be lacking." They insisted that impeachable conduct requires "criminal acts or at least criminal intent."[64]

The minority members had a valid point insofar as they were arguing that neither administrative incompetence within some fairly broad range nor inadvertent nor minor violations of law should merit impeachment. But their contention that impeachable conduct must be attended by "criminal intent" or "*mens rea*" is unsupported by the constitutional text properly understood, or by relevant precedent. Even if it were, the interposition of these terms into impeachment practice would serve no useful function because they do not mean what the congressmen seemed to think they mean. In the criminal law, *mens rea* includes a wide range of mental states. In the case of *mens rea* regarding the harms caused by a defendant's conduct, the law customarily assigns criminal liability to a spectrum of mental states, including purposeful, knowing, reckless, and negligent behavior. The most demanding mental state is purposefulness (sometimes described as intentionality), which requires a subjective desire to cause a particular harm. The least demanding is negligence, which requires only that a reasonable person in the defendant's situation would have been aware of a substantial and unjustifiable risk that harm would occur.[65] A few statutes require an awareness that one is violating the law (a state of mind sometimes described as "willfully"), but most of the time, ignorance of the law or the fact one is violating it is no excuse.[66] In short, even if there were a constitutional basis for insisting that impeachable offenses must constitute a crime or be attended by a criminal state of mind, that would tell us nothing about the exact state of mind required. As a matter of general criminal law, mere negligence would suffice, precisely the position the minority was arguing against.[67]

Implicitly rejecting all the minority's arguments, the Judiciary Committee staff report observed:

> Impeachment and the criminal law serve fundamentally different purposes. Impeachment is the first step in a remedial process – removal from office and possible disqualification from holding future office. The purpose of impeachment

is not personal punishment; its function is primarily to maintain constitutional government.[68]

The Prime Purpose of Presidential Impeachment Is to Protect Constitutional Order

Although a bipartisan majority of the Judiciary Committee rejected the claim that impeachment requires commission of a crime, it agreed that, *for a president*, impeachable conduct must be serious in a way that endangers constitutional order. The Judiciary Committee staff report concluded that, "Impeachment is a constitutional remedy addressed to serious offenses against the system of government. *** [Impeachable offenses] are constitutional wrongs that subvert the structure of government, or undermine the integrity of office and even the Constitution itself ..."

Individual members amplified on this theme. Among those who voted for impeachment, Congressman Conyers wrote that the impeachment remedy "was framed with the intention that it be used only as a last constitutional resort against the danger of executive tyranny."[69] Another group of members declared that, "In these proceedings we have sought to return to the fundamental limitations on Presidential power contained in the Constitution and to reassert the right of the people to self-government through their elected representatives within that Constitutional framework."[70] Congressman Waldie went a step further, echoing some Radical Republicans in the Andrew Johnson controversy in arguing that impeachment is not merely a means of preserving the founding era status quo, but of addressing threats presented by an evolving presidency. "Impeachment of a President," he said, "should not be undertaken to punish a President, but to *constitutionally redefine and to constitutionally limit the powers of the Presidency* when those powers have been dangerously extended and abused."[71] Several members who voted for impeachment did so because the president's conduct, in their view, "violated our guarantees of liberty,"[72] or was a "grave threat to the liberties of the American people."[73] Referring in particular to Article 3 concerning the president's defiance of congressional subpoenas, Congressman McClory observed that the "power of impeachment is the Constitution's paramount power of self-preservation."[74]

The staff report captured the tenor of these sentiments:

> Not all presidential misconduct is sufficient to constitute grounds for impeachment. There is a further requirement – substantiality. In deciding whether this further requirement has been met, the facts must be considered as a whole in the context of the office, not in terms of separate or isolated incidents. Because impeachment of a President is a grave step for the nation, it is to be predicated upon conduct seriously incompatible with either the constitutional form and

principles of our government or the proper performance of constitutional duties of the presidential office.[75]

The full Committee adopted the staff's broad formulation in framing the particulars of the proposed articles.[76]

Article 1: Obstruction of the Watergate Investigation

The basic thrust of Article 1 was simple: Richard Nixon used the powers of the presidency to obstruct the investigation of the Watergate burglary and "to conceal the existence and scope of other unlawful covert activities."[77] The article specified nine ways in which Nixon carried out the obstruction. They merit quotation in full.

The means used to implement this course of conduct or plan included one or more of the following:

(1) making false or misleading statements to lawfully authorized investigative officers and employees of the United States;

(2) withholding relevant and material evidence or information from lawfully authorized investigative officers and employees of the United States;

(3) approving, condoning, acquiescing in, and counseling witnesses with respect to the giving of false or misleading statements to lawfully authorized investigative officers and employees of the United States and false or misleading testimony in duly instituted judicial and congressional proceedings;

(4) interfering or endeavoring to interfere with the conduct of investigations by the Department of Justice of the United States, the Federal Bureau of Investigation, the office of Watergate Special Prosecution Force, and Congressional Committees;

(5) approving, condoning, and acquiescing in, the surreptitious payment of substantial sums of money for the purpose of obtaining the silence or influencing the testimony of witnesses, potential witnesses or individuals who participated in such unlawful entry and other illegal activities;

(6) endeavoring to misuse the Central Intelligence Agency, an agency of the United States;

(7) disseminating information received from officers of the Department of Justice of the United States to subjects of investigations conducted by lawfully authorized investigative officers and employees of the United States, for the purpose of aiding and assisting such subjects in their attempts to avoid criminal liability;

(8) making or causing to be made false or misleading public statements for the purpose of deceiving the people of the United States into believing that a thorough and complete investigation had been conducted with respect to allegations of misconduct on the part of personnel of the executive branch of the United States and personnel of the Committee for the Re-election of the

President, and that there was no involvement of such personnel in such misconduct; or

(9) endeavoring to cause prospective defendants, and individuals duly tried and
convicted, to expect favored treatment and consideration in return for their
silence or false testimony, or rewarding individuals for their silence or false
testimony.[78]

Many of these specifications seem self-evident. For example, Article 1 says that it is
impeachable conduct to lie to law enforcement about a pending criminal investigation, to encourage others to lie to law enforcement or in legal proceedings, or to
bribe witnesses with money or promises of other favors to lie or maintain silence.
These are affirmative acts that are themselves the crimes of false statements, aiding
and abetting false statements or perjury, and witness bribery or witness tampering.[79]
Moreover, the investigations Nixon sought to obstruct all concerned the behavior of
the president himself, his close aides, or persons working to advance his policies or
political interests, and thus could not be dismissed, as President Clinton would seek
to do decades later, as either inconsequential or unrelated to the core functions of
the presidential office.

Even on these obvious points, the Nixon case presented interesting wrinkles.
Specification 9 relates to the fact that Nixon, through intermediaries, repeatedly
dangled the prospect of presidential pardon or commutation to those who could
implicate Nixon or those close to him. Nixon was careful to ensure that no direct
promises were made, but was plain in his directions to intermediaries that hope
should be offered.[80] In short, the Judiciary Committee found that even suggesting
a possible future use of the presidential pardon power as a means to influence
witness testimony is impeachable conduct.

Article 1 goes well beyond active personal obstruction of criminal investigations.
It insists that the president's constitutional obligation to ensure that the laws be
faithfully executed is not merely a reiteration of every citizen's duty not to violate the
law himself, but instead imposes on presidents an affirmative obligation to assist law
enforcement agencies in discovering and punishing crime. Thus, while an ordinary
citizen could not be criminally prosecuted for failing to disclose evidence relevant to
a federal investigation, Article 1 declares that a president can be impeached for
"withholding relevant and material evidence or information from lawfully authorized investigative officers and employees of the United States." Crucially, the
committee plainly considered the president's repeated invocation of "executive
privilege" as an excuse for refusing to produce subpoenaed material to be part of
the pattern of impeachable concealment.[81]

Specification 4 finds impeachable "interfering or endeavoring to interfere with
the conduct of investigations" by both executive branch agencies (the Justice
Department special prosecutor and the FBI) and congressional committees. This
provision raises several important issues.

First, the committee rejected the notion that, as head of the executive branch and its criminal agencies, the president has plenary authority to stop, limit, or impede federal criminal investigations. The committee made plain that a president who employs his authority to interfere with such investigations for illegitimate reasons such as covering up the crimes of his advisors to shield them from conviction and himself from political damage is impeachable for doing so. However, the Nixon case gives little other guidance about the precise limits of permissible and impermissible motives for presidential intervention in law enforcement. The Nixon case also illustrates the difficulties posed by a standard of impeachability that depends on proof of presidential motive. Future congresses are unlikely to enjoy the advantage conferred by tape recordings of all the critical conversations between a president and his minions.

Second, the committee considered both the president's refusal to cooperate with Special Prosecutor Cox and his subsequent firing of Cox to be among the culpable acts that together constituted impeachable obstruction of the Watergate investigations.[82] Here, as in the Johnson case, we find confirmation of Madison's suggestion in 1789 that a president may be impeached for dismissing meritorious officers.[83]

Third, specification 4 asserts that a president may be impeached for impeding investigations by Congress. On the one hand, a president cannot counter this assertion with arguments about the unitary executive. Whatever power a president may have over executive branch law enforcement agencies, he has no claim of authority over congressional inquiries. On the other hand, in this specification, the Committee maintained that the president's duty to execute his own office and defend the constitution includes an obligation to cooperate with legitimate investigations by the separate, if coordinate, legislative branch. This point was made even more explicit in Article 3, to which we will turn presently, charging failure to comply with committee subpoenas.

Perhaps the most striking single specification in Article 1 was number 8, which alleged that the president made or caused to be made, "false or misleading public statements for the purpose of deceiving the people of the United States into believing that a thorough and complete investigation had been conducted." It is not a crime to tell lies to the public (except in highly specialized settings like securities offerings). Nor does anyone seriously expect that every public pronouncement by a political actor will be 100 percent verifiably accurate. Nonetheless, the Judiciary Committee here laid down a marker for future presidents – lies to the public when part of a larger effort to engage in criminality, abuse power, or conceal either may be impeachable.

Article 2: Abuse of Power

Article 2 alleged a pattern of conduct "violating the constitutional rights of citizens, impairing the due and proper administration of justice and the conduct of lawful inquiries, or contravening the laws governing agencies of the executive branch and the purposes of those agencies."[84] Some of the facts supporting this article related to the Watergate cover-up, but its true thrust was that President Nixon had repeatedly tried to use federal agencies to help his friends, hurt his perceived enemies, and gain political advantage.

The committee found that Nixon illegally sought private income tax information from the Internal Revenue Service for purposes such as damaging George Wallace's 1970 Alabama gubernatorial campaign (Nixon saw Wallace as a danger from the right) and attacking Democratic National Committee Chairman Lawrence O'Brien. Such information was also sought on a journalist investigating a campaign fundraiser and various prominent entertainers. The most sweeping request, made two months before the 1972 election, was for IRS data on 575 staff members or supporters of Democratic candidate George McGovern. There were also attempts to induce the IRS to audit persons thought hostile to the president. The IRS successfully resisted most, but not all, of these requests.[85]

The committee further found that Nixon initiated illegal and unconstitutional programs of domestic surveillance, including multiple illegal wiretaps, through the FBI, the Secret Service, and private contractors. Finally, it found that there had been an attempt to enlist the CIA in this effort, but that the agency refused due the lack of jurisdiction over domestic intelligence gathering. Finally, it found that Nixon and his White House staff concealed the records of all these activities from the public and the courts.[86]

The third specification of Article 2 concerned the White House "Plumbers Unit," particularly the effort to discredit Daniel Ellsberg and the burglary of his psychiatrist's office. The committee found that the activities of that unit were illegal and that, despite President Nixon's avowals to the contrary, it served no national security purpose. The committee again emphasized the efforts to conceal these activities as an integral part of the overall abuse of power.[87]

The fourth specification related to obstruction of lawful inquiries "by duly constituted executive, judicial, and legislative entities" into the Watergate break-in, the abuses of power enumerated in the first three specifications of the article, and several other matters. The most notable feature of this section is its assertion that a president can be impeached not only for what he actually knew, but also for failing to take care that the laws be faithfully executed by inquiring about and putting a stop to improper actions by his "close subordinates" of which he "had reason to know."[88] In the terminology of criminal law mental states, the committee found that a president is impeachable for a negligent failure to discharge his duties, or, to use another criminal law concept, for adopting a posture of willful ignorance of improprieties going on all around him. The committee noted that Nixon himself acknowledged this obligation of care. It observed that, in March 1973, John Dean told the president that he would be hurt by disclosures of his subordinates' conduct with respect to

Watergate, and that Nixon agreed, saying: "First, because I am expected to know this, and I am supposed to, supposed to check these things."[89]

Although one can fit Article 2's fourth specification into a criminal law framework of negligence or willful blindness, the real thrust of the Committee's thinking is better understood as a rejection of impeachment as a criminal process. Rather, the committee was saying that, upon taking the oath, a president assumes an array of affirmative obligations – among them upholding the laws and defending the constitutional rights of American citizens – and that sufficiently egregious failures to meet those obligations are every bit as impeachable as carefully meditated wrongdoing. In Nixon's case, even if he could plausibly have denied personal knowledge of the details of his underlings' misdeeds, the misdeeds were so numerous, outrageous, and intimately entwined with his own political interests that failure to find out the details and put a stop to the misconduct was itself impeachable.

The fifth specification of Article 2 alleged a general misuse of the executive power by "interfering with agencies of the Executive Branch," including the FBI, the DOJ Criminal Division, the Watergate special prosecutor, and the CIA. This was in part a recharacterization of earlier allegations of presidential obstruction of justice. But it differed importantly by finding impeachable not only presidential interference with law enforcement agencies that constituted violations of law, but also interference "in derogation of [the agencies'] *purposes and functions.*"[90] This is a crucial distinction. In essence, the committee here declared that law enforcement agencies exist to investigate and pursue, fairly and impartially, legal redress of criminal and civil wrongs and that presidents may neither rein in federal investigators nor unleash them, for personal or political benefit. If they do either, they may be impeachable regardless of whether a particular statute prohibits such behavior.

In its introduction to Article 2, the committee was careful to note that the president's failure to achieve his unlawful or improper objectives "does not make the abuse of power any less serious, or diminish the applicability of the impeachment remedy."[91] The committee quoted Supreme Court Justice William Johnson, who wrote in 1808:

> If an officer attempt an act inconsistent with the duties of his station, it is presumed that the failure of the attempt would not exempt him from liability for impeachment. Should a President head a conspiracy for the usurpation of absolute power, it is hoped that no one will contend that defeating his machinations would restore him to innocence.[92]

Perhaps the most important point about Articles 1 and 2 is that they avoided the central flaw in the Johnson articles of a century before. As John Labovitz, one of the Watergate Judiciary Committee staffers, later wrote, neither of the first two Nixon articles charged an "impeachable offense" in the sense of a single discrete act of gross criminality or constitutional consequence. Instead, each laid out a pattern of misconduct consisting of many acts, consciously performed, over a long period of time, unified by a single illegitimate objective (Article 1 – covering up Watergate and other illegal intelligence operations) or demonstrating a characteristic form of misbehavior (Article 2 – abuse of the power of the presidential office). This structure presented a formidable challenge to the president's defenders because they were unable to nitpick the facts or legalities of a single incident. Beyond this tactical consideration, Labovitz argues, and I agree, that it misconceives the function of impeachment to think in terms of *an* "impeachable offense." Rather, removal of a president will most likely be warranted not for a single act, but for a course of conduct marked by "the very factors – repetition, pattern, coherence – that tend to establish the requisite degree of seriousness warranting the removal of a president from office."[93]

Article 3: Defiance of Judiciary Committee Subpoenas

The third article of impeachment approved by the Judiciary Committee was the simplest, but passed by the narrowest margin: 21:17, on party lines.[94] It charged that the president defied eight subpoenas issued by the Judiciary Committee for documents and recordings by providing either fragmentary responses or, in the case of subpoenaed tapes, no response at all. Of the three approved articles, this raised the most difficult constitutional questions.

The fundamental issue was separation of powers. The constitution grants the House of Representatives "the sole Power of Impeachment."[95] The majority position was that the power of impeachment necessarily implies a power to investigate behavior by members of the executive and judicial branches, which in turn implies a power to compel testimony and evidence. In support of this implied power, the committee cited an early declaration by the House itself and the Supreme Court's 1881 assertion in *Kilbourne v. Thompson* that, "Where the question of . . . impeachment is before [either the House or Senate] acting in its appropriate sphere on that subject, we see no reason to doubt the right to compel the attendance of witnesses and their answers to proper questions, in the same manner and by the use of the same means, that courts of justice can in like cases."[96]

Note that the Committee's assertion of compulsory subpoena power in impeachment investigations is distinct from any power Congress may enjoy in pursuit of a supervisory authority over executive branch actors. The subpoena power in impeachment cases arises directly from an explicit constitutional directive that the House conduct an adjudicative proceeding akin to a grand jury, the success of which is necessarily dependent on the availability of relevant evidence. Without the power to compel compliance with subpoenas and the concomitant right to impeach a president for refusal to comply, the impeachment power would be nullified. As the committee wrote, "Unless the defiance of the Committee's subpoenas under these circumstances is considered grounds for impeachment, it is difficult to conceive of any President acknowledging that he is obligated to supply the relevant evidence necessary for Congress to exercise its constitutional responsibility in an impeachment proceeding."[97]

The minority did not deny that the House and Senate may compel the production of evidence, but argued, that, because the president had claimed that the subpoenas were overbroad, the whole House should have been asked to vote on whether the requested materials were relevant before the president's refusal to comply was deemed impeachable.[98] Although the committee could have adopted this procedure, it seems unnecessarily duplicative. After all, the Judiciary Committee had no independent authority to impeach the president; it was only recommending proposed articles of impeachment to the full House. Had President Nixon not resigned, the articles would have gone to the full House, his supporters would have raised the overbreadth issue, and that body would have decided the question in the course of voting on Article 3.

Nine members of the minority also contended that the committee should have sought judicial enforcement of its subpoenas before basing impeachment on the president's failure to comply.[99] The obvious rejoinder to this argument is that bringing courts into the question would necessarily grant the judiciary an important, perhaps dispositive, influence over the legislative power of impeachment. Suppose that the Supreme Court had ruled that subpoenas seeking information about the burglary of Daniel Ellsberg's psychiatrist were unenforceable because they were beyond the scope of a proper impeachment investigation. Or that it had quashed subpoenas looking for information about the secret, congressionally unauthorized, bombings in Cambodia on the same ground. In either case, the court would be placing a *de facto* limitation on the meaning of "high crimes and misdemeanors" and on the scope of congressional impeachment power. There is no obvious warrant in the constitution for such a judicial role.

The minority also argued that the so-called "executive privilege" of the president to maintain the confidentiality of the advice he receives from his aides ought, at least sometimes, to trump congressional power to compel information relevant to impeachment. This is perhaps the most difficult issue raised by Article 3. On the one hand, the impeachment power would be crippled if presidents could refuse all requests for production based on a blanket claim of privilege. On the other hand, separation of powers principles (and simple common sense) dictate that Congress ought not to be able to compel production and public exposure of all the president's private deliberations merely by raising the banner of impeachment. The final section of this chapter will consider the precedents established during the Watergate affair regarding the reach of both congressional and prosecutorial sub-poena powers in a case implicating impeachment.

Articles of Impeachment Proposed, but Not Approved

The three articles of impeachment approved by the Judiciary Committee all centered on President Nixon's penchant for abusing his presidential authority to gain political advantage in the domestic sphere. However, the committee's inquiry also ranged into foreign policy and personal misconduct.

The Cambodian Bombing

As noted above, in 1969–70, President Nixon authorized airstrikes against targets in neutral Cambodia as part of his ongoing effort to apply military pressure to force North Vietnam to accept peace on politically palatable terms. These strikes have customarily been labeled "secret bombings," but of course they were hardly secret to either the Vietnamese who were their targets or the Cambodians who witnessed and were sometimes killed by them. In fairly short order, they were no secret in the United States either because they were reported in the press. They were nonetheless "secret" in two senses: first, the Nixon administration publicly denied that they were happening; and, second, the military falsified its own records about the strikes either by creating none of the customary reports or by stating in such reports that the strikes occurred in South Vietnam or Laos.[100]

Those who sought impeachment based on these events maintained that "the Constitution vests the power to make war in Congress and implicitly prohibits the Executive from waging an undeclared war." They further argued that "the President, by issuing false and misleading statements, failed to provide Congress with complete and accurate information and thereby prevented Congress from responsibly exercising its powers to declare war, to raise and support armies, and to make appropriations."[101] From a constitutional perspective, these arguments seem ironclad. Although the eighteenth-century European nicety of formally declaring war before starting the shooting may now be outdated, the grant to Congress in Article 1, sections 8 and 9, of powers to declare war, raise and support armies, maintain a navy, make rules for the regulation of the army and navy, and make appropriations for all government activities necessarily imply that Congress is to have material input into both the initiation and conduct of any war in which the United States engages. Whether a president must obtain prior approval before starting hostilities, or as in the case of Cambodia, opening a new front in an ongoing war, is an interesting technical point (and one addressed by the War Powers Resolution 1973[102]), but not germane to the question of whether a president can actively deceive Congress about either proposed or ongoing military operations.

The supporters of this article seem to have been aware that imposing a strict presidential duty of candor enforceable by impeachment would represent a new development in inter-branch relations. However, they argued that "impeach-ment is a process for redefining the powers of the President" and that the imposition of such a duty was necessary to maintain a proper balance between the authority of the executive and legislative branches. Their effort failed. The committee report explained that some members felt that the bombing had been carried out in furtherance of the president's constitutional role as commander in chief and that he had satisfied any notice requirement by informing select members of Congress. Others seemed to feel that passage of the War Powers Resolution made the issue moot.[103] An equally compelling reason for the failure of this article was the reluctance of many members, even those who most disapproved of President Nixon, to diminish the force of the powerful case for impeachment in Articles 1, 2, and 3 by introducing the poisonous politics of the Vietnam War.

Emoluments and Tax Evasion

President Nixon owned two properties, one in Key Biscayne, Florida, and another in San Clemente, California. During his presidency, roughly $17 million of government money was spent on modifications and upgrades to these properties. Some members of the committee believed these outlays violated Article 2, section 1, clause 7, of the constitution that bars a president from receiving any "emolument" in addition to his salary "from the United States or any of them." The president's defenders argued that much of this money was for security and that, as to non-security expenses, Nixon was not aware of the government source of the funds.

Finally, some committee members sought impeachment on the ground that Nixon had committed tax evasion in connection with a supposed gift of his vice presidential papers for which he sought a very large tax deduction. Although there was at least reasonable suspicion that Nixon knowingly mishandled his taxes, it was also arguable that he relied on bad advice from lawyers and tax planners. In short, the evidence was debatable. The larger point for many committee members seems to have been that personal tax evasion "was not the type of abuse of power at which the remedy of impeachment is directed."[104] This somewhat offhand remark in the Committee Report would assume outsize importance during the Clinton impeachment affair a quarter of a century later, suggesting as it did that private crime was not a proper subject for presidential impeachment.

LESSONS FROM THE NIXON IMPEACHMENT INVESTIGATIONS

The truth about Richard Nixon's involvement in Watergate, and about the multiple other abuses of presidential authority during his tenure, emerged through a synergy of American constitutional institutions: prosecutors of the executive branch; trial and appellate judges of the judicial branch; the Senate; the House of Representatives; and the free press protected by the First Amendment. Some details of that cooperative interplay, the issues it resolved, and those issues it left undetermined merit discussion.

The Central Role of Federal Prosecutors

Perhaps the most important pragmatic lesson of Watergate was that serious misconduct by the president or those close to him is nearly impossible to ferret out without the investigative powers of the criminal justice system. The Senate Watergate Committee and the House Judiciary Committee did remarkable work, as did the press, but throughout they built on a foundation laid by Justice Department prosecutors, FBI agents, the federal grand jury, and federal judges. Leon Jaworski later said of the "road map" and accompanying grand jury material he delivered to the House Judiciary Committee: "We succeeded, which was the first [time] in history, to get the courts to permit the grand jury report to go to the House Judiciary Committee because the committee would have had real difficulty in doing its work. Way behind. It hadn't gotten off the ground."[105] It is doubtful that the Watergate scandal would ever have been fully unraveled without prosecutors and their agents employing the ordinary processes of the federal criminal law in an extraordinary situation.

The very first break in the case, the connection of Watergate burglar E. Howard Hunt to the White House, came as a result of the execution of an ordinary search warrant. Thereafter, the inexorable force of the federal investigative mechanism kicked into gear. Search warrants, innumerable interviews conducted by an inexhaustible cadre of trained agents, access to the grand jury's power of subpoena to compel production of testimony and physical evidence, the authority to use the threat of criminal punishment to turn conspirators into cooperating witnesses – all these were at the disposal of Watergate Special Prosecutors Cox and Jaworski. That being so, the result might seem preordained. But, of course, it was not. The outcome was highly contingent on the character of the Justice Department's leadership.

Both Archibald Cox and Leon Jaworski acted in the best traditions of the Department of Justice and the American bar. They did not grandstand or pander to the press, nor did they truckle to the president. Instead, they carefully, respectfully, but firmly, insisted on following the evidence where it led. Even more important, perhaps, was the political courage of Elliott Richardson and William Ruckleshaus, both members of the president's party, who by forcing Nixon to fire them to get to Cox, demonstrated to the country the gravity of the president's assault on the administration of justice. Their principled sacrifice created an outcry far greater than a simple dismissal of Cox would have, and thus created the pressure to replace him. There can be no guarantee that in a future similar crisis the Department of Justice will be led by persons of equal mettle.

A desire to avoid a repetition of the Saturday Night Massacre crisis led Congress, in 1978, to pass a statute creating the office of "Independent Counsel."[106] The law provided that a special group of federal judges could appoint an independent counsel to investigate the president and other named officials upon the application of the attorney general. The independent counsel enjoyed all the powers of regular

Justice Department prosecutors, but was guaranteed virtually complete autonomy from Justice Department supervision. He or she was removable only by the attorney general and only for cause, and removal was appealable to the special court. As we will see in the following chapter on the impeachment of President Clinton, the Office of Independent Counsel solved the problem of improper presidential control over criminal investigations of himself or his aides, but created so many other difficulties that the law was allowed to lapse.

The Federal Grand Jury

A brief word on the role of the federal grand jury is in order. Although in practice grand juries are powerful tools wielded by prosecutors, they are technically neither within, nor entirely controlled by, any of the three constitutional branches of government. They are composed of ordinary citizens bound to an oath of secrecy about the matters presented to them[107] and thus tend to remain individually invisible even in the most monumental cases. Nonetheless, introducing a body of regular folk into the midst of a clash between a president and the law alters the dynamic of the confrontation. In Watergate, Special Prosecutor Jaworski used the grand jury with particular skill. It was the grand jurors who approved inclusion of President Nixon as an unindicted co-conspirator on a criminal indictment. It was they who appeared as sponsors of the report Jaworski convinced Judge Sirica to send to the Judiciary Committee. Of course, the special prosecutor wrote the report and put it before the grand jurors for their consideration. But the fact that it was a grand jury report made any effort to suppress it doubly awkward.

Whether sending the report to the House was technically within the authority of either Jaworski or the court is debatable. The only role assigned to grand juries by the constitution is to determine whether probable cause exists to file felony charges by indictment. Ordinary federal grand juries, unlike those in some states, are not statutorily authorized to issue a report, or indeed to do anything other than hear evidence and approve or reject proposed indictments.[108] The federal rules place strict limits on who may receive grand jury materials and congressional committees are not specified in the rules.[109] Nonetheless, Judge Sirica found evidence of a venerable Anglo-American tradition of grand jury reports, and a respectable number of federal cases approving them in special circumstances. He closed by observing, "We deal in a matter of the most critical moment to the Nation, an impeachment investigation involving the President of the United States. It would be difficult to conceive of a more compelling need than that of this country for an unswervingly fair inquiry based on all the pertinent information."[110]

Sirica's decision, affirmed by the Court of Appeals,[111] provides respectable precedent for use of grand jury materials in impeachment inquiries (a point to which we will return in Chapter 10). But it may be worth noting two points about the posture of the Nixon case. First, President Nixon did not object to releasing the report to the

Judiciary Committee.[112] Second, the committee had not subpoenaed or even requested release of the report; in fact, Judiciary Committee counsel John Doar wrote to Judge Sirica declining to take any position on the proposed release.[113] Accordingly, neither the executive nor Congress threw its weight into the scales. A case in which, for example, the Justice Department did not sponsor the creation or release of a grand jury report, Congress subpoenaed grand jury materials for an impeachment inquiry, and the President sought to quash the subpoena might come out differently.

The Judiciary and "Executive Privilege"

When we think of the "heroes" of Watergate, we most often think of the prosecutors, reporters, and legislators, but the courts played a central role. Watergate was about secrets – secret surveillance, secret uses of presidential power against "enemies," secret payoffs, secret obstruction, and a president's determination to keep all those secrets. The work of the special prosecutors and the Senate and House committees would have been impossible had not the federal judiciary supported the prosecutors' efforts to use the tools of the criminal law to induce cooperation from the president's men and rejected the president's persistent assertion of an executive privilege to keep his misdeeds secret. District Judge Sirica, of course, stands out for his forthrightness, particularly his unapologetic declaration that sentences for Watergate defendants in his court would be dependent on full disclosure of the painful truth. But the appellate courts played a quiet, deliberative, and ultimately central role by issuing opinions that carefully balanced legitimate presidential prerogatives with the imperative of discovering the truth and preventing executive abuse of authority.

In *United States* v. *Nixon*,[114] the Supreme Court enforced a criminal trial subpoena[115] against a claim of executive privilege. The court acknowledged that executive privilege exists, but insisted that determination of its proper scope is a task for the courts, and not the president alone. The court thus denied Nixon's assertion that the president has the sole authority to determine the materials that fall within the privilege. The court said claims of privilege based on the need to maintain military or diplomatic secrets would receive special deference, but that a claim based on a general need for confidentiality must yield to the imperative of obtaining evidence in criminal trials. A trial subpoena is enforceable as long as the requesting party can show that the material sought is (1) relevant, (2) admissible, and (3) specific.[116] The court held that the Watergate special prosecutor had met the requirements for enforcement of a trial subpoena and that the requested material must therefore be disclosed for *in camera* review by the trial judge.[117] In the earlier case of *Nixon* v. *Sirica*,[118] the United States Court of Appeals had reached essentially the same conclusion with respect to grand jury subpoenas.

The limitation of both the Supreme Court and Court of Appeals cases was that they concerned a privilege created by courts for application to the discovery and presentation of evidence in judicial proceedings (or in the case of grand juries, quasi-judicial proceedings). Therefore, strictly speaking, the opinions addressed only the relation between the executive and judicial branches. Congress is not bound by judicial rules of evidence in either its legislative activities or in carrying out the special adjudicative function of impeachment, a fact that left Congress free to claim an unfettered right to presidential materials thought relevant to impeachment and the president free to claim an absolute right to refuse such requests.

In *Senate Select Committee on Presidential Campaign Activities* v. *Nixon*,[119] the U.S. Court of Appeals for the D.C. Circuit confronted these conflicting claims, at least tangentially. The case arose from subpoenas issued by the Senate Watergate Committee seeking White House tapes. The president claimed executive privilege and refused to comply. The Senate Committee elected to sue. This was an interesting choice in itself inasmuch as both chambers have the power to hold in contempt and even incarcerate those who defy its subpoenas. However, this rarely used mechanism would have presented the comic opera spectacle of the Senate Sergeant at Arms attempting to arrest a White House records custodian or even the president himself. So to the courts the Senate went.

The circuit court opinion was notable primarily for its effort to avoid forcing a constitutional showdown. It began by reaffirming that presidents possess a privilege to keep their official conversations private, and that this privilege can be overcome by a sufficient showing of need in criminal matters, including grand jury proceedings. The court ducked the question of whether Congress possesses a general oversight power and, if so, what limitations there might be on that power. Instead, it noted that the House Judiciary Committee was then engaged in an impeachment inquiry and had obtained copies of the particular tapes that were the subject of the Senate subpoena. Therefore, said the D.C. Circuit, the Senate's request was effectively cumulative and thus less compelling than the requests of Justice Department criminal prosecutors made through a grand jury. To the irritation of the Senate, the appellate court upheld the district judge's assertion that he could act as a "court of equity" and pass judgment on how essential the requested materials were to the Watergate Committee's performance of its assigned task.

On the other hand, the circuit court seemingly placed the House impeachment inquiry on a different plane because its "investigative authority ... has an express constitutional source."[120] The court reinforced that suggestion by saying, "There is a clear difference between Congress's legislative tasks and the responsibility of a grand jury, *or any institution engaged in like functions*," the final phrase being a clear reference to the role of the House in an impeachment case.[121] The opinion did not resolve the question of whether federal courts even possess jurisdiction to pass on the propriety of congressional demands for evidence in a presidential impeachment inquiry, still less how claims of executive privilege might fare in such a case.[122]

The House and Senate Committees

Since the fourteenth century, impeachment has been a political act. Though attended by legal arguments, modern American impeachments remain political. Therefore, the tenor and outcome of every impeachment will depend centrally on the political atmosphere of the times and the personalities of the legislators in the cockpit of the fight. Even discounting for the distorting effects of the rapid transformation of the Watergate saga into a national myth of constitutional virtue, the intellectual and moral quality of the individual members of the congressional committees and their collective devotion to discovering the facts, debating their implications, and acting in the public interest continue to astound. Both committees were run fairly, openly, and with the full participation of members of both parties. The staffs were diligent, erudite, and thorough. The hearings were genuine inquiries into the facts for which the members prepared carefully and during which they asked generally perceptive questions and made impressively nuanced arguments. This is not to say that all or any of them were perfect, either in the purity of their motives or the execution of their intentions. Still, collectively, the members of both parties behaved as one would want the elected representatives of a free people to behave. Impeachment can only work, or at least work beneficially, if Congress performs its obligations at something approximating that high standard. As we will see in the next chapter, the Clinton impeachment illustrates how a process designed as the ultimate tribunal of constitutional values can, if conducted by a Congress that has lost touch with basic legislative and civic virtues, degenerate into a ribald spectacle. At the end of this book, we will consider whether Congress in the early 21st Century remains capable of conducting a successful impeachment case against an American president.

The Press

In Watergate, the press played a significant independent investigative role. They dragged facts into the light that assisted the governmental sleuths, as well as maintaining a level of public interest that sustained the special prosecutor and the committees in their confrontations with a resistant President. That much is part of the standard Watergate mythology. In hindsight, however, the press (or the media as we are wont to call it in an age when news less and less often passes through the inky medium of a printing device) performed another critical function, one taken for granted at the time, but now increasingly in doubt. That is, the media of the early 1970s, print and broadcast, not only reported information, but collectively validated a set of facts as being true, or as nearly so as it was possible to determine through honest inquiry. This public "truth" in the sense of a body of generally accepted fact was subject to constant modification and adjustment. Nonetheless, the media shared an ethos in which the existence of objective fact was not in doubt and the mission of the press was to go find it, verify it, and report it before the other fellow.

This is not to say that 1970s media outlets had no political leanings, or that those leanings never affected news judgment. No utopia like that ever existed. Still, it is entirely fair to say that all the major news outlets genuinely tried to keep opinion separate from news, and in the realm of news were committed to getting the facts right, and that the public believed this to be the case. The unstated (and I think at the time largely unthought-of) collective understanding was that news organizations worked hard to scoop each other and they had some biases and they sometimes made mistakes, but that they essentially checked each other's work. If a wire service or major newspaper or major network reported something important and the others did not produce contrary evidence, that something was added to the shared body of fact upon which civic decisions were to be made.

During Watergate, Americans in and out of Congress argued vigorously, some-times bitterly, about the import of the facts that slowly came to light. To the very end, some of President Nixon's diehard supporters insisted that all the damning facts still did not amount to impeachable conduct. But nobody claimed the facts were not facts. There was never a contingent of the media insisting that the Justice Department and congressional investigators were all liars inventing evidence to bring down the President. Nor was there ever a body of members of Congress contending that all media reports of evidence adverse to the President should be ignored as emanating from an incurably biased source. Congress's choices and the public's acceptance of those choices were premised on common facts. Without a shared public understanding of at least the rough outlines of the truth in a politically contentious matter, an exquisitely political institution like Congress cannot function properly. One suspects that this is doubly true in the context of a presidential impeachment investigation. It is an open question, to which we will return later, whether the media environment has now changed so drastically as to effectively forestall any future impeachment premised on contestable facts.

The role of presidential character: As important as were the strengths and weak-nesses of the people and institutions arrayed against the President, Nixon's character, too, was critical. Nixon fired Archibald Cox because he understood the unique danger posed by a federal criminal investigation. Nonetheless, he wilted in the public firestorm that followed the Saturday Night Massacre and replaced Cox with Jaworski, who would prove no less dogged. Had Nixon been more brazen, hunkered down, and flatly refused to authorize any further investigation by the Department of Justice, the full Watergate story might not have emerged and he might have survived his term. The unified opposition of the Republican members of the Judiciary Committee to Article 3 suggests that flat refusal to cooperate with investigations might have worked.

Consideration of Nixon's character is also essential when considering the role of the courts in Watergate. President Nixon obeyed the orders of the courts. He might not have. He might have stood upon an absolutist view of the president's supposed constitutional prerogatives and refused to turn over the tapes or any other damaging material. There, too, Richard Nixon, almost despite himself, remained bound by historical norms and expectations of American political culture. As contemptuous of legal rules as Nixon sometimes was, it does not seem to have occurred to him to deny the authority of law or its institutions. Crook though he proved to be, he retained an instinctive reverence for the presidency and American constitutional government. He is in this respect a cautionary tale. Should there arise a president who has no respect for the criminal justice system or the courts or the Congress as a coordinate branch, then a very different sort of constitutional challenge will ensue.

9

The Strange Case of William Jefferson Clinton

On February 12, 1999, not quite twenty-five years after Richard Nixon climbed into the helicopter that lifted him off the White House lawn and away from the presidency, the U.S. Senate acquitted President William Jefferson Clinton of two articles of impeachment – one charging perjury and the other obstruction of justice. The Clinton impeachment was, in multiple respects, a direct consequence of the social and political conflicts of the Nixon era and of legal reforms enacted in response to Watergate. Yet the two events could not have been more different.

Nixon presided over one of the most turbulent periods of modern American history. The Cold War was at its height, with superpower tensions constant, and nuclear Armageddon a real specter. He inherited a bloody and universally unpopular shooting war he had promised to stop, but felt unable to abandon without a crippling loss of face. Opposition to the war coalesced with the long-overdue resumption of the struggle for African American equality as well as a general reconsideration of social norms to produce widespread, sometimes violent, unrest. Nixon's response to this cascade of troubles was often deft, sometimes generous, occasionally brilliant, but no president in those times could have avoided becoming the personification of policies some Americans loathed. Also, there was a meanness in the man he could never entirely suppress or successfully conceal. The insecure, even paranoid, streak in his personality moved him to step repeatedly outside the boundaries of law and democratic governance to aggrandize presidential power, to strike at perceived enemies, and then to commit even more outrages against constitutional propriety to conceal the original transgressions. Whatever one thinks of Nixon, there can be no question that, just as was the case with Andrew Johnson, the conflicts of the time and the issues raised by the president's conduct were of a type and magnitude suitable for judgment in the tribunal of an impeachment.

By contrast to both Nixon and Johnson, Bill Clinton was president in a happy period of relative peace abroad and prosperity at home. The Soviet Union had collapsed in 1991, effectively ending the Cold War and leaving the United States as the sole global superpower.[1] Clinton's predecessor, George H. W. Bush, waged and won the First Iraq War, but pulled out American ground troops once the Iraqis were driven from Kuwait, leaving Clinton with the limited task of containing any resurgence of ambition by Saddam Hussein.[2] American forces conducted air operations in the Balkan wars arising from the break-up of Yugoslavia, but no American ground forces were engaged and the limited intervention seemed to work. Domestically, the U.S. economy was thriving. Economic growth was up. Unemployment was down. Inflation was stable.[3] The status of black Americans was improving, however incrementally. It was, considered in the round, a singularly fortunate time.

Moreover, Clinton himself was elected and governed as a political moderate. He saw that the Reagan–Bush period from 1980 to 1992 had moved America's political center of gravity somewhat to the right and, as the most politically sensitive and politically talented Democrat of his generation, he adjusted accordingly. He suffered an early reverse with the failure of an attempt to secure healthcare reform, but throughout two terms achieved significant legislative successes on the budget, welfare reform, and deregulation.[4] In virtually every case, Clinton's successful initiatives deviated at least somewhat from liberal orthodoxy. This was in some measure a matter of necessity. The so-called "Republican Revolution" of the first midterm elections of Clinton's presidency gave Republicans control of both the House and Senate for the first time since the 1950s, but Clinton responded by co-opting some aspects of Republican thinking in the service of broadly liberal policy goals. His disposition to chart a course independent of his own party was labeled "triangulation," which at least among Democrats was not a term of endearment.[5]

Nonetheless, this supreme pragmatist became the bête noire of Republican politics, the object of near-fanatical dislike. To the extent there is a rational explanation, it may have some of its roots in the politics of the Nixon era. By the 1990s, most Americans had long since concluded that the Vietnam War was a horrible mistake, but a hardy core of conservatives retained the conviction that it could have been won had cowardly politicians not restrained the military from unleashing total war on North Vietnam, and had hippies, pinkos, and draft-dodging protesters not destroyed America's will to fight. Even conservatives with a more realistic appraisal of the war retained a powerful resentment of those who protested it, particularly privileged youths who, like Clinton, avoided the draft with student deferments,[6] and in the conservative imagination spent the war smoking dope and having unrepentant sex while more patriotic or less economically fortunate young men fought and died in rice paddies.

Clinton spent the Vietnam War years at Georgetown University, Oxford University, and Yale Law School. After a brief stint as a law professor at the University of Arkansas, he launched the political career that raised him from Arkansas attorney general, to Arkansas governor, to president. In the 1980s, few politicians of either party wanted to relitigate the particulars of Vietnam, but Republicans eagerly labeled Democrats as unpatriotic critics of their own country's virtues and historic accomplishments.[7] The twelve years of the Reagan–Bush era made flag-waving, chest-thumping patriotism a litmus test for Republican approval.

Clinton was the first president since Franklin Roosevelt to have had no military service whatever.[8] Instead, he had protested his generation's war (and smoked dope, whether or not he had inhaled).

Moreover, he got along famously with black people and had married a proud and unapologetic feminist, who throughout Bill's political career assumed a larger and more outspoken role than had previously been customary for political wives. It was not lost on older Republicans still smarting from Nixon's removal that Hillary Rodham had been a Judiciary Committee staffer during the impeachment inquiry.[9] One might say that, for Republicans, Clinton was a living exemplar of the battles that had roiled the country in the Nixon years and continued to change society in ways threatening to social conservatives. He was, moreover, always something of a rogue, and not merely in his relations with women. Richard Nixon was "Tricky Dick." Bill Clinton was "Slick Willie."[10] But where Nixon's deviousness always had a mean edge, Clinton had the quality peculiarly common among southern politicians of being a likeable rascal. One suspects that though his louche charm contributed largely to his overall success, it was also a special source of frustration for his Republican adversaries. Judge Richard Posner may have captured it best when he wrote that, "it is not what Clinton says or does, but what he is, that is the provocation."[11]

The Clinton impeachment differed from those of Johnson and Nixon not only in the absence of either a national political crisis or irreconcilable presidential policy differences with the party controlling Congress, but also – one must be candid – in the sheer triviality of the charges leveled against him. The articles of impeachment against him will be dissected with appropriate gravity below, but they amounted to this: the president had a consensual adulterous sexual affair – or perhaps more accurately a series of consensual, but rather grubby, sexual encounters – with a White House intern. He lied about the sex in a civil deposition, and again in grand jury testimony. And he tried to obstruct an investigation into the sex and the lies.

As discreditable as all this was, it had no precedent as the subject of an American impeachment case, before or after the ratification of the constitution. The only case in Anglo-American history even remotely comparable was the impeachment of John, Viscount Mordaunt, in 1666 for unlawfully imprisoning the surveyor of Windsor Castle and raping his daughter;[12] an event even President Clinton's harshest critics would presumably find rather more troubling than whatever Clinton and Ms. Lewinsky got up to in the Oval Office. Which begs the question of how a president's sex life and prevarications about it ended up before the U.S. Senate. Part of the answer must be sought in the collective psychology of the 1990s Republican Party, a subject beyond the scope of this work. But an equally important factor was the existence of the Office of Independent Counsel, without which the Clinton impeachment imbroglio could never have happened.

The remainder of this chapter will consider (briefly) the facts about President Clinton's relationship with Monica Lewinsky, turn (at greater length) to the institution of the independent counsel and how that office pursued Bill Clinton, and conclude with a discussion of the articles of impeachment against Clinton passed by the House but rejected in the Senate. The discussion of the articles will focus particularly on how the Clinton impeachment helped to set a minimum standard for impeachable conduct.

THE PRESIDENT AND THE INTERN

In November 1995, a budget impasse between President Clinton and the Republican Congress produced a government shutdown.[13] As a result, the vast majority of White House employees were furloughed with some of their functions being filled by unpaid interns. One of those interns was Monica Lewinsky, a twenty-two-year-old from Beverly Hills, California. On November 15, Ms. Lewinsky encountered President Clinton in the office of Chief of Staff Leon Panetta and, by her own account, began flirting with him by lifting her jacket to display the top of her thong underwear. As the independent counsel's report would later document with the level of lurid detail that was its special hallmark, the flash of undergarment led to a sexual interlude the same night in a hallway near the Oval Office in which Ms. Lewinsky performed oral sex on Mr. Clinton.[14]

Over roughly the next sixteen months, there were some ten other sexual interludes between the two, all in the White House and all sharing the same hurried, improvisational character. There were also telephone conversations of a lascivious nature. Both parties ultimately denied that there had ever been an act of intercourse.[15]

Ms. Lewinsky apparently conceived of the relationship as having more than a purely physical character. She was distressed when members of the White House staff who had become concerned that she was spending too much time lingering near the Oval Office arranged for her transfer to the Pentagon, and was persistent in her efforts to get reassigned to the White House. At the Pentagon, she made the acquaintance of one Linda Tripp, a much older woman who had also formerly been at the White House, and had taken a strong dislike to President Clinton.[16] Lewinsky confided in Tripp. Tripp repaid the confidence by secretly recording more than twenty hours of their conversations, allegedly at the suggestion of her literary agent, a former Republican political operative named Lucianne Goldberg.[17]

Meanwhile, back down in Arkansas, a woman named Paula Corbin Jones had another kind of beef with Bill Clinton. She maintained that in 1991, while she was a state employee working a conference at the Excelsior Hotel in Little Rock, a state trooper approached her and invited her to meet then-Governor Clinton in his suite. She agreed, but claimed that after entering the room, Clinton made sexual overtures, including the request that she perform oral sex upon him, a request she said she indignantly declined.[18]

Three years later, two years into Clinton's first presidential term, Jones filed a civil lawsuit in federal district court in Little Rock, Arkansas. She alleged several constitutional torts, particularly quid pro quo and hostile work environment sexual harassment, as well as intentional infliction of emotional distress, and defamation.[19] The defamation claim arose from comments Clinton was alleged to have made when reports of the encounter were published in the media.

President Clinton moved to dismiss the action on the ground that a president is immune from civil suit while in office. The district court denied the motion and ordered discovery to proceed, while deferring trial until the end of Clinton's term. The Eighth Circuit upheld the denial of dismissal, but reversed the stay of trial. The U.S. Supreme Court affirmed the Eighth Circuit, rejecting the president's argument that responding to civil actions would materially distract from the performance of presidential duties.[20] The court acknowledged the unique scope of a modern president's power and the unremitting demands on his or her time. Nonetheless, with a comment that, in retrospect, seems almost comically deluded, the court waved these concerns away: "As for the case at hand, if properly managed by the District Court, it appears to us highly unlikely to occupy any substantial amount of petitioner's time."[21]

The Jones case proceeded. Ms. Jones' motivations for filing and maintaining the lawsuit have been much discussed. At the beginning, the impetus may have been entirely personal – some combination of Ms. Jones' own outrage at having been crudely propositioned and later defamed and the indignation of her fiancé (later husband) on her behalf.[22] However, in fairly short order, Clinton's political enemies entered the picture. Author H. Lowell Brown summarizes the transformation of the Jones lawsuit into a political tool this way:

> From its inception, the Jones suit was as much a vehicle . . . for political conservatives to attack and embarrass Clinton as it was to vindicate purported violations of Jones' civil rights. Prior to filing her suit, Jones had appeared at a convention of the Conservative Political Action Committee in Washington, D.C. Jones' expenses had been paid by another conservative group, the Legal Affairs Council. Following the decision of the U.S. Supreme Court allowing the Jones case to proceed against Clinton, an offer was made to Jones to settle the case for $700,000, the amount of damages sought in her complaint. Despite what her attorneys considered to be a "complete victory" in view of the weaknesses of her case on the merits (by that point her defamation claim had been dismissed and there was virtually no evidence that Jones had lost either income or status at her job) Jones rejected the president's offer. Jones' decision was based largely on advice from her media advisor, Susan Carpenter McMillan, and conservative lawyer and media personality, Ann Coulter. Jones' lawyers, Joseph Cammarata and Gilbert Davis, withdrew from the case and

were replaced by lawyers working for another conservative organization, the Rutherford Institute.[23]

The Jones lawsuit and Clinton's entanglement with Monica Lewinsky intersected in November 1997, when Linda Tripp disclosed her recordings of Lewinsky to Jones' civil attorneys. To the lay observer, there would seem to be little connection between Jones' claim that Clinton crudely propositioned her and a consensual, even if adulterous and unseemly, affair with someone else years later. However, two lines of federal legal authority opened the door to inquiries into Clinton's sex life. First, before the adoption of Federal Rules of Evidence 413–415 in 1994, evidence of a party's unrelated prior bad behavior was admissible only under the restrictive limits of FRE 404(b), which generally barred trying to prove that a party had a propensity to do some bad thing. The new rules focused on criminal and civil sexual assault cases opened the door to propensity evidence in such lawsuits. Ms. Jones maintained throughout her suit that Clinton had committed a sexual assault, which permitted inquiry into any prior instance of nonconsensual sex involving Clinton.

Second, Jones' complaint alleged that Clinton had engaged in (a) so-called quid pro quo sexual harassment, meaning that he had either tried to induce her to engage in sex with improper promises of job benefits, or had punished her for refusing to have sex by causing her to suffer some employment detriment; or (b) hostile work environment harassment, which might include suffering adverse employment consequences, but might also include a pattern of unwelcome sexualized workplace behavior by Clinton or others under his supervision.[24] These kinds of claim can be proven by establishing a "pattern and practice" of harassing behavior. Thus, the particulars of any instance in which Clinton engaged in sexual activity with a subordinate might be relevant. Therefore, at the preliminary discovery stages of the Jones lawsuit, the plaintiff was granted fairly wide latitude to inquire into the president's sexual history.

In early December 1997, Ms. Jones' counsel added Lewinsky to their witness list.[25] One can only imagine the dismay reading that name would have evinced in President Clinton. He resolved to keep his sexual dalliances with her secret. That resolution produced two chains of events that ultimately led to impeachment.

First, although the details are contestable, there seems little doubt that Clinton communicated with Ms. Lewinsky and tried to keep her loyal and quiet. Before her eruption into the Jones case, Clinton had promised to help her try to obtain a job in New York City. In particular, he asked his friend Vernon Jordan to make calls on Ms. Lewinsky's behalf.[26] After Lewinsky was identified as a witness, those efforts seem to have accelerated. In January, she received a position at Revlon.[27]

In December 1997, Clinton told Lewinsky that she had been named as a possible witness and shortly thereafter she received a subpoena to testify.[28] In late December, when Clinton became aware that Lewinsky's subpoena included a demand that she produce any gifts she had received from him, Clinton took steps to have Lewinsky return the gifts to his secretary, Bettie Currie.[29] Unsurprisingly, Ms. Lewinsky wanted to avoid testifying. It appears that Vernon Jordan arranged for counsel to represent Ms. Lewinsky, and that attorney suggested she submit an affidavit in lieu of testimony. In the affidavit, executed on January 6, 1998, Lewinsky denied ever having "a sexual relationship with the President."[30] The majority of the Judiciary Committee would ultimately view these activities as a form of obstruction of justice.

Second, on January 17, 1998, President Clinton gave a sworn deposition in the Jones civil case. He was asked whether he had ever had "sexual relations" with Ms. Lewinsky. In a misbegotten effort to ensure specificity on the point, Ms. Jones' lawyer had written out a detailed definition of that phrase that was wordy, confusing, and (if one cocked one's head at just the right angle) could be read to include only circumstances in which Clinton himself made physical contact with a partner for the purpose of "arous[ing] or gratify[ing] the sexual desire" of his partner, but not circumstances in which the partner had physical contact with Clinton in order to gratify him.[31] In short, Clinton could deny having "sexual relations" as defined by maintaining the (probably entirely candid) mental reservation that his only purpose when entangled with Ms. Lewinsky was to please himself and that he did not give a fig about her arousal or gratification. This cynical little evasion might have worked had his only worry been a civil lawsuit. But it failed to account for the misplaced zeal of Kenneth Starr and the Office of Independent Counsel.

THE INDEPENDENT COUNSEL INVESTIGATION: FROM WHITEWATER TO LIES ABOUT SEX

Recall that one result of the Nixon impeachment saga was the enactment of the Ethics in Government Act of 1978 creating the Office of Independent Counsel (OIC).[32] Among the important features of the law were that the independent counsel could be appointed by a special division of the U.S. Court of Appeals for the District of Columbia at the request of the attorney general; that the independent counsel was not subject to operational control by the Justice Department; and that the OIC had a virtually unlimited budget.[33] In 1988, the Supreme Court upheld the law against claims that it violated principles of separation of powers.[34] Uses of the statute were widely criticized, primarily on the ground that OIC investigations tended to become lengthy, expensive, and focused on matters either tangential to their original charter or so inconsequential that regular prosecutors would not have pursued them.[35] Republicans were particularly annoyed by IC Lawrence Walsh's seven-year investigation of the Iran-Contra Affair in which the Reagan administration traded arms to Iran to secure the release of Hezbollah hostages in Lebanon and gain funding for anti-communist guerrillas in Nicaragua.[36]

The statute had a sunset provision requiring periodic congressional reauthorization. In 1992, a Republican filibuster prevented reauthorization of the statute.[37]

However, when Bill Clinton was elected in November 1992, Republican enthusiasm for independent counsels mysteriously revived. In July 1994, an independent counsel reauthorization bill passed Congress with (ironically) the enthusiastic support of President Clinton. Clinton almost immediately found himself in the cross-hairs of an independent counsel.[38] It happened in the following way.

Back in 1978, when Bill Clinton was attorney general of Arkansas, he and his wife Hillary partnered with James and Susan McDougal to borrow $203,000 to buy 220 acres of land in Arkansas' Ozark Mountains. They formed the Whitewater Development Corporation intending to build vacation homes. The development plan never panned out. Instead, it became entangled in the finances of James McDougal and his savings and loan company, Madison Guaranty. In the 1980s, as Bill Clinton moved up the ladder of Arkansas politics, Hillary was a partner at a law firm that did work for McDougal and Madison Guaranty. In 1989, Madison Guaranty collapsed as part of the nationwide savings and loan crisis, causing large losses to the federal guarantee fund. McDougal was charged with fraud (though later acquitted).[39]

In 1992, during Clinton's first presidential campaign, the Federal Resolution Trust Corporation sent a referral to the Justice Department suggesting that the Clintons might have benefited from illegal activities. In June 1993, Deputy White Counsel Vincent Foster filed three years of delinquent Whitewater corporation tax returns. The next month, Foster was found dead in a Washington area park. The police ruled his death a suicide, but rumors spread that somehow he had been connected to the Whitewater business and might have been murdered to keep him quiet.[40]

Clinton's political adversaries clamored for investigations of all these supposedly interrelated matters. Despite the fact that the independent counsel statute had expired in mid-1992, the Justice Department retained the institution of special prosecutor – the office filled during Watergate by Archibald Cox and then Leon Jaworski. In January 1994, with Clinton's support, Attorney General Janet Reno appointed Robert Fiske, a moderate Republican, prominent New York big firm lawyer, and former U.S. Attorney for the Southern District of New York, as special prosecutor to investigate Whitewater. He indicated that he would also investigate Vincent Foster's death. On June 30, 1994, Fiske issued a preliminary report finding that Foster had committed suicide[41] and that there was no wrongdoing by Clinton related to inquiries by the Resolution Trust Corporation into the collapse of Madison Guaranty S&L. The same day, Clinton signed the Independent Counsel Reauthorization Act 1994.[42]

Acting under the provisions of the Reauthorization Act, Attorney General Reno requested the special court to keep Fiske in place to conclude the Whitewater investigation by appointing him special counsel. The special court, headed by Judge David Sentelle, refused, appointing instead Kenneth Starr, a former appeals court judge and solicitor general under President George H. W. Bush.[43] Although

Starr had enjoyed a distinguished legal career, critics noted at the outset and later that he had long been a reliable Republican partisan and he had no prosecutorial experience whatsoever.[44]

Under Starr, the OIC not only revisited issues that Fiske had already resolved,[45] but expanded the scope of its investigations. By the end, it had considered Whitewater, the Foster suicide, allegations of impropriety in connection with the replacement of employees at the White House travel office ("Travelgate"), acquisition by low-level White House staffers of FBI files on former Republican White House staff ("Filegate"), and other stuff. By January 1998, the month in which Monica Lewinsky submitted her false affidavit in the Jones case and Bill Clinton slithered through his civil deposition in the same litigation, the OIC under either Fiske or Starr had been investigating the Clintons for four years. They had so far found nothing on any of the matters then in their jurisdiction, and as Starr ultimately reported to Congress, they never did.[46]

However, on January 12, 1998, five days after Lewinsky submitted her affidavit, and five days before Clinton's scheduled deposition, Linda Tripp approached the OIC and told them that Lewinsky was submitting a false affidavit with the knowledge of Clinton. The next day, the OIC equipped Tripp with a body wire and monitored her lunchtime meeting with Lewinsky. The transcript certainly showed that Lewinsky was prepared to deny falsely that she had a sexual relationship with the president (based partly on the Clintonian rationalization that they had never had intercourse), but she never said her prevarication was requested by Clinton.[47] Regardless, on January 15, lawyers from the OIC obtained permission from the attorney general to seek expansion of their mandate to include the Lewinsky/Jones business. The special court assented. On Friday, January 16, Tripp met Lewinsky for breakfast. FBI agents detained her and secreted her in a hotel room, refusing to allow her to leave or contact her attorney, despite her requests to do so. They also threatened her (and her mother) with prosecution for multiple federal offenses and tried to convince her to consent to electronic monitoring of future conversations with the president. They held her until just before 1 a.m. the following morning, January 17.[48]

A little over nine hours later, Clinton began his deposition in *Jones v. Clinton*. Monica Lewinsky had not agreed to "flip" on the president, but neither did she contact him that morning to tell him that the independent counsel had tapes of her conversations with Linda Tripp. In that respect at least Starr's men had achieved their objectives. Lewinsky was frightened into silence. Bill Clinton would walk into the Jones deposition unaware that recordings of Lewinsky admitting to sexual activity with him existed. So he would lie (or at the least engage in devious pettifogging evasion).

Perhaps the most remarkable aspect of the independent counsel's conduct in the Lewinsky–Clinton affair is this, its beginning. The OIC had been commissioned in January 1994 to investigate what became a spreading miscellany of suspicions about the president. After four years, they had nothing, a dry hole. What they got from Linda Tripp was nothing more than an allegation that a woman had lied about an affair with Clinton, and that Clinton himself might do so at an upcoming civil deposition – as long as nobody warned him in advance that the lie could be disproven. It has been argued that the OIC had an affirmative obligation to prevent a future crime by advising the president of what they knew.[49] Even if one does not go quite that far, their choice to try to flip Lewinsky the night before the deposition and then keep quiet when that failed tells all one needs to know about their motives. They had investigated Clinton for years to no avail. He was their Moby Dick. It is impossible to avoid the conclusion that they wanted him to lie, thus, finally, placing him in their power. Their zeal led in the short term to Clinton's humiliation and impeachment. In the long term, it also contributed largely to his acquittal.

Having maneuvered to increase the odds that Clinton would commit perjury in the Jones case, the OIC intervened in that case with a request that all further civil discovery regarding Lewinsky be stayed because it might interfere with the gathering of evidence in the criminal investigation. Judge Wright granted the motion largely on the basis that the Lewinsky affair was "not essential to the core issues of this case" and that it was quite likely inadmissible "extrinsic evidence" under the Federal Rules of Evidence in any case.[50] On April 1, 1998, the judge dismissed Jones' lawsuit altogether in response to what is called a motion for summary judgment, which means that the judge felt the case to be so weak that a jury should not even hear it.[51] Starr's investigation nonetheless continued. Reflect on this a moment. Having secured jurisdiction to investigate the president of the United States for civil perjury that had not yet occurred, Mr. Starr pursued the matter even after it became clear that the perjury, once it occurred, was about a tangential, and very probably inadmissible, point in a lawsuit so insubstantial that it did not even merit a trial.

The independent counsel's dubious exercise of prosecutorial judgment notwithstanding, President Clinton himself had not only cheated on his wife and sullied his office by taking sexual advantage of the neediness of a woman less than half his age, but lied about it under oath (in substance, even if *perhaps* not in a hypertechnical sense). Of course, in the weeks following Clinton's civil deposition, the OIC could not prove even that. It had tapes of Monica Lewinsky talking about sexual acts with the president, but not as of yet Ms. Lewinsky's testimony. And even if she agreed to turn on Clinton (as she ultimately did), the case would, it appeared, be nothing more than her word against his.

Undoubtedly conscious of the apparent strength of his position, Clinton went on television on January 26 to make his famous protestation of innocence: "I want to say one thing to the American people. I want you to listen to me. I'm going to say this again. I did not have sexual relations with that woman, Miss Lewinsky."[52] Note the stilted phrase "sexual relations," the same words used and narrowly defined by Paula Jones' attorney in the deposition. Perhaps even here Clinton privately rationalized his dishonesty by clinging to the knowledge that these words had been given a special meaning in the lawsuit. But the simple fact is that he sought to deceive the public, a position he brazenly maintained throughout the summer.

In late July 1998, Lewinsky arrived at a cooperation agreement with the OIC. As part of the agreement, she turned over a blue dress that bore a semen stain from Clinton as a result of a sexual encounter in early 1997. As bizarre and just plain creepy as her retention of the garment, unwashed, for over a year was, it broke open the case for Starr and his band. In August, they secured a blood sample from Clinton. It matched. With the dress and the stain and Lewinsky's own testimony, at last they had incontrovertible proof that there had been sex with "that woman."[53]

On August 17, 1998, President Clinton testified before a federal grand jury at the request of the independent counsel. Knowing what the outcome of the testing would surely be, he nonetheless trimmed. He began by admitting to "inappropriate intimate contact" with Ms. Lewinsky, but avoided admitting details, and persisted in claiming that his civil deposition testimony had been literally true.[54] That night, he went on television, admitted a "relationship with Miss Lewinsky that was not appropriate," but still claimed he had told the truth in the Jones case.[55]

Writing about this all these years later, one remains astonished that the matter did not end right there. The president had been caught in a lie (or perhaps several) about adulterous (and extremely tawdry) sex. He had been under oath. And all that was both humiliating and technically felonious. But when considered either in isolation or against the backdrop of six centuries of Anglo-American impeachment precedent, the notion that such conduct met the definition of "high crimes and misdemeanors" or that, as a matter of sound policy, it should be grounds for removing a president seems frivolous, really quite beyond serious contemplation.

Nor would it have been seriously contemplated had it not been for Kenneth Starr. It was he, not Congress, who transformed oral sex in Oval Office anterooms into an impeachment crisis. Starr's authority to transmit information on impeachment was far clearer than Leon Jaworski's had been in Watergate. Jaworski was essentially freelancing when he composed the road map to the grand jury's evidence and requested that Judge Sirica authorize its release to the House Judiciary Committee. By contrast, the independent counsel statute under which Starr operated provided that, "An independent counsel shall advise the House of Representatives of any substantial and credible information which such independent counsel receives ... that may constitute grounds for an impeachment."[56] Armed with this authority, Starr wasted no time. As soon as Clinton's August 17 grand jury testimony was completed and the stain on the dress matched to his blood, the OIC raced to finalize a report recommending that Clinton be impeached. By September 9, the report, 452 pages, with eighteen boxes of supporting documents, was bound and delivered to the House.[57]

The Starr report differed from the Jaworski road map in two important respects. First, Jaworski simply laid out the evidence and supporting documents without interjecting either factual or legal conclusions.[58] Starr's report took precisely the opposite approach. It does not so much describe evidence as press a point of view. It is, in effect, a prosecutor's argument to the congressional jury, assertive in tone, graphic in detail, admitting no room for ambiguity or doubt, and omitting both exculpatory evidence and facts about the conduct of the independent counsel's investigation that would, once revealed, cast doubt on the objectivity of its proceedings.[59]

Second, unlike the Jaworski road map, the Starr report identified specific grounds for impeachment – eleven of them – although all of them boil down to variations of the assertion that Clinton had sex with Lewinsky, lied about it, and tried to cover it up.[60] Remarkably, despite running on for 452 pages, the report provides no analysis of what constitutes an impeachable offense. Its entire treatment of the subject consists of two paragraphs which say, in sum, that a president has an obligation to faithfully execute his or her office and take care that the law be faithfully executed, that he committed perjury and obstruction of justice, and that those are grounds for impeachment.[61]

Starr would doubtless argue that the ultimate determination of what constitutes an impeachable offense lies with Congress, not the independent counsel. That is true, but insufficient. The statute authorizing Starr to report to Congress did not say "report all wrongdoing." It said that the OIC shall report information that "may constitute grounds for impeachment." That reporting obligation could be met in one of two ways. One might, as Jaworski did, simply present facts to the House and leave questions of constitutional interpretation to it. Or one might, as Starr did, recommend particular grounds for impeachment. Having chosen the second course, analogous to recommending that a grand jury indict a defendant on particular charges, an independent counsel assumes, at least in my view, the additional obligations of carefully analyzing the applicability of the constitution's impeachment provisions to the known facts and then explaining that analysis to Congress. Once a prosecutor proposes an indictment to a grand jury, she or he does not merely present facts, but also instructs the grand jury on the government's view of the applicable law. An independent counsel's momentous decision to report possible impeachable conduct to Congress necessarily implies having made a careful legal judgment that provable facts meet the constitutional standard of impeachable behavior, and, I would submit, gives rise to an obligation to show one's work in the sense of describing the constitutional standard and explaining how the facts meet that standard. In his initial report, Starr shirked that basic obligation.[62]

In the end, the Starr report differed from the Jaworski road map in another critical way. Jaworski's transmission was intended to be and remain secret (and it did for over forty years). Starr's report was transmitted as a nominally confidential document, but the House voted to release it publicly within forty-eight hours of receiving it.[63] Although Clinton's humiliation (not to speak of his wife's) at the worldwide exposure of his disgraceful private behavior was no doubt acute, the inquisitorial thoroughness of the report, its obvious relish in every steamy detail, came to be seen by many as reflecting worse on the pursuers than the pursued.

PROCEEDINGS IN THE HOUSE AND SENATE

The House immediately commenced impeachment proceedings by referring the matter to the Judiciary Committee, which held its first executive session on September 18.[64] In another notable difference from the Nixon precedent, the committee held no evidentiary hearings and did no meaningful factual investigation itself, with the exception of sending President Clinton eighty-one "Requests for Admission." Instead, it essentially took the Starr report as a given and devoted all its attention to the constitutional question of whether the facts asserted in the report amounted to impeachable offenses. Indeed, almost all the testimony, oral and written, heard by the committee was from legal academics and commentators.[65]

A key background point about the entire proceeding was that the OIC had made its referral two months before the 1998 midterm elections. This was a breach of the (concededly informal) norm that enjoins ordinary Justice Department prosecutors to avoid seeking indictments or taking other public steps in highly political cases in the period immediately before elections.[66] Once Starr delivered his report, however, Congress had little choice but to act on it. However, the political effect seems to have been the reverse of what one might have expected. Far from recoiling at Clinton's infidelity and prevarication, the public seems to have decided that Clinton was a flawed human being, but a pretty good president, who was being pursued by puritanical fanatics. His popularity actually increased.[67] In November 1998, Republicans *lost* seats in the House and just held even in the Senate, the first time since 1934 that the party out of the White House failed to gain seats.[68]

Strangely undeterred, the Republicans soldiered on. The Judiciary Committee prepared four proposed articles of impeachment. The first charged perjury in the grand jury, the second false deposition testimony and discovery responses in the Paula Jones litigation, the third obstruction of justice, and the fourth refusal to respond to some requests for admission propounded by the House and false answers to others. On December 10, 1998, the committee approved all four.[69] A little more than a week later, the full House approved the first and third articles, but voted down the second and fourth.[70] The vote was almost completely on party lines.

The timing of these proceedings introduced a novel question. The House of Representatives of the 105th Congress impeached Bill Clinton in December 1998 during its lame duck session, and went out of existence at the end of the year. A number of scholars argued that impeachment by a lame duck House did not compel a trial by the Senate of the succeeding Congress.[71] The Senate proceeded anyway.

Clinton's Senate trial began on January 7, 1999.[72] It was a curiously truncated affair, perhaps because everyone knew what the outcome would be. With fifty-five Republican senators and forty-five Democrats, and presidential approval ratings north of a stratospheric 70 percent,[73] the chances of persuading every Republican plus twelve Democrats to vote for conviction were nil. There was a palpable sense of trying to confer a patina of dignity on a distasteful task with a foregone conclusion.

The House managers, Lindsey Graham, Stephen Buyer, Charles Canady, and Henry Hyde, presented no live evidence, relying instead on the record created by Independent Counsel Starr and videotaped depositions of Monica Lewinsky, Vernon Jordan, and White House aide Sidney Blumenthal.[74] Throughout they struggled to distinguish between Clinton's private sexual conduct, which they conceded was "none of our business," and perjury and obstruction about the sex, which they maintained were "public acts" amounting to "willful, premeditated, deliberate corruption of the nation's system of justice."[75]

The managers were handicapped not only by the fact that the American public had already signaled that it did not much care about Clinton's infidelities or his lies, but also by their own seeming hypocrisy. The relentless pursuit of Clinton's peccadilloes by the conservative groups backing the Jones litigation and then by Starr's office had triggered a retaliatory round of snooping into the private lives of Republican legislators that revealed a striking incidence of marital infidelity.[76] Moreover, Republican outrage about lies under oath had been notably muted during Independent Counsel Lawrence Walsh's investigation of the Iran-Contra affair under President Reagan. The Republicans' difficulties were nicely exemplified by Henry Hyde, Chair of the House Judiciary Committee, who was obliged to distinguish Clinton's adultery from his own and Clinton's lies from the Iran-Contra perjuries of the Reagan administration, which Hyde had defended.[77] However logically defensible the distinctions may have been, the need to make them left Republicans open to ridicule.

Clinton's defenders not only pressed on the evidentiary weakness of the two articles of impeachment, but pushed even harder to establish that impeachment of a president is only justified by abuses of the presidential office itself or moral failings so grievous "that the people could not contemplate the notion of a president's remaining in office."[78] Manager Graham conceded that the standard of impeachment for judges is different than that for presidents, that in judging a presidential impeachment the Senate must consider "the impact on society" of deposing a president, and that reasonable people could disagree over whether Clinton's behavior met the constitutional standard of "high crimes and misdemeanors."[79] The prosecution had lost whatever edge it once had.

On February 12, 1999, the Senate voted 55:45 to acquit Clinton on the first article, and split 50:50 on the second, seventeen votes shy of the two-thirds necessary for conviction.[80]

CRIMINAL OFFENSES FOR WHICH PRESIDENTS OUGHT
AND OUGHT NOT BE IMPEACHED

Despite the comic opera denouement of the Clinton case, it raised several important issues of impeachment law and practice. All of the major impeachment controversies before Clinton (and many of the minor ones) involved the question of whether non-criminal behavior is a proper subject of impeachment. Clinton raised the opposite question. Both articles of impeachment approved by the House alleged criminal conduct – perjury and obstruction of justice – and the evidence of his guilt of one or both was strong. Nonetheless, he was acquitted in the Senate. The result implies that there are crimes, even felonies, for which an officeholder, particularly a president, ought not be impeached.

Even before the Clinton controversy broke, the scholarly consensus was that not all violations of criminal statutes are "high Crimes and Misdemeanors."[81] The framers' debates, the original restriction of impeachment by the Committee of Eleven to the crimes of treason and bribery, and the Convention's final choice of moderately expanded language, all demonstrate an intention to exclude some crimes from the category of impeachable offenses.[82] Their judgment was sound. Jaywalking, public drunkenness, and reckless driving are all crimes, and offenses such as hunting without a license in a wildlife refuge are crimes punishable by six months' imprisonment,[83] but a president self-evidently should not be displaced for committing them.[84]

Not even all felonies are necessarily impeachable offenses. For example, punching a "foreign official" in the nose, destroying a document belonging to the estate of a debtor, operating a bus or train while intoxicated, counterfeiting a postage stamp, and obliterating the vehicle identification number of someone else's car are all federal felonies.[85] One doubts that any of these are "high Crimes and Misdemeanors." Thus, not only are some, perhaps many, indictable crimes not impeachable, but there is no pre-existing division in the criminal law itself, such as that between felonies and misdemeanors, which could reliably distinguish impeachable from non-impeachable crimes.

Still, if not all crimes or even all felonies are "high Crimes and Misdemeanors," perhaps the president's unique status should broaden the category of criminal violations that ought to be grounds for impeachment. Article 2 of the constitution vests the executive power of the United States in the president. Section 3 of the same article commands that the president "shall take Care that the Laws be faithfully executed," and section 1 of that article prescribes an oath of office in which the president must swear that he or she will "preserve, protect and defend the Constitution of the United States." The first two articles of impeachment against President Nixon were framed around these provisions. Nixon's offenses were far graver and more numerous than Clinton's, but one can fairly argue that the president's role as chief executive imposes a special obligation of scrupulous adherence to the law.[86] Clinton's congressional opponents extrapolated from that general principle the corollary that the failure to remove a presidential law-breaker from office so endangers the rule of law that the remedy of impeachment ought to be liberally invoked whenever a president commits a significant legal infraction.[87] That argument is subject to several powerful criticisms.

First, impeachment is not the only remedy the law provides against a president who breaks it. Alexander Hamilton said of an officer actually impeached, "After having been sentenced to a perpetual ostracism from the esteem and confidence and honors and emoluments of his country, he will still be liable to prosecution and punishment in the ordinary course of law."[88] The same holds true for those who commit crimes, but are not removed from office on that account. In other words, a refusal to impeach does not mean a refusal to punish. If a president commits crimes for which he or she is not impeached, nothing bars prosecution for those offenses once the president leaves office.[89]

Second, the contention that the president's special Article 2 obligation to uphold the law authorizes presidential impeachment for virtually all serious criminal infractions is at odds with the design of the constitution's impeachment clauses. In effect, the proponents of this view are arguing that the president's constitutional role should render him or her liable to impeachment for *more* kinds and degrees of crime than any other federal officer. But as discussed in Chapter 4, the framers adopted the "Treason, Bribery, or other high Crimes and Misdemeanors" formula in order to strike a careful balance between making the president a creature of the Senate and ensuring adequate legislative control on any executive tendency to authoritarianism. And as detailed in Chapter 6, several centuries of practice suggest that judges, being life tenured, unelected, and less personally essential to the operation of their own branch, are impeachable for less severe infractions than presidents.

There is no inconsistency in the fact that the constitution imposes on the president an obligation of scrupulous adherence to law and simultaneously permits his or her impeachment and removal from office only for great infractions which constitute a limited subset of the crimes for which presidents and paupers alike may be prosecuted and imprisoned. The framers were sophisticated political architects who counted on more than the single and supremely disruptive mechanism of impeachment to regulate presidential behavior. As noted in Chapter 4, they assumed that the primary political check on presidential excesses would be the limited tenure of the post and the power of the electorate to turn presidents out of office for misbehavior. For criminal transgressions both great and small, they expressly contemplated the possibility of ordinary criminal prosecution of presidents.[90]

The view that only a somewhat restricted class of grave crimes warrants removal of a president was manifest in several aspects of the impeachment proceedings against President Nixon. The most obvious of these was the Judiciary Committee's refusal to impeach Nixon on the basis of substantial allegations of income tax evasion, a refusal that contrasts sharply with congressional readiness both before and after 1974 to impeach federal judges on that ground.[91] Clinton's acquittal by the Senate is generally interpreted as confirming the existence of crimes for which impeachment should not be imposed. However, the factual nuances of the evidence and the effect of the behavior of the Independent Counsel Starr dilute the clarity of that conclusion a bit.

The evidence that Clinton committed perjury in the grand jury (Article 1) was legally sufficient, but not terribly compelling.[92] This is not to say that he told the complete truth. He plainly did not. Nonetheless, at the outset of the grand jury session, Clinton conceded that he had engaged in a relationship with Ms. Lewinsky that included "inappropriate intimate contact" and he later admitted some of the particulars. That he minimized his misbehavior and shaded or twisted the facts, particularly in response to questions about the earlier Jones deposition, can hardly be denied. But his lawyers put forward colorable explanations of how most of his challenged statements could be considered technically true.[93] Moreover, grand jury perjury requires a knowing false statement of "material" fact that has some tendency to influence, impede, or hamper the grand jury's investigation.[94] Given that the grand jury was investigating the question of whether Clinton had lied about the Lewinsky affair in the Jones deposition or tried to induce others to do so, questions about those topics were all "material" in a narrowly legal sense. But senators could be forgiven for thinking that, once the OIC secured a confession of the sex, the rest of the salacious detail added little to the jury's understanding and was immaterial in the ordinary human sense, a form of voyeuristic piling on. Finally, Article 1 did not specify exactly which statements it claimed to be lies – as is customary in regular perjury indictments – which added to the sense of partisanship and desperation surrounding the House's case.

The proof that Clinton sought to obstruct justice (Article 2) through the job assistance for Monica Lewinsky (which began before she was identified as a witness in the Jones case), in the return of gifts by Ms. Lewinsky, in the broad hints he gave to his secretary about his remembered interactions with Ms. Lewinsky, and so forth was plausible. But inasmuch as all the people he supposedly influenced, including Lewinsky, denied that they had been improperly influenced or that they had understood him to be trying to influence them, the case was not overwhelming. And the fact remained that all the alleged obstructions occurred in December 1997 or January 1998 at the time Clinton was scrambling to conceal the Lewinski affair from the discovery process *in the Jones civil case*, where, as will be remembered, the judge ultimately concluded that the Lewinski allegations were immaterial and likely inadmissible.

As a result, senators who voted against these articles might have done so because: (a) they did not believe the evidence proved that Clinton lied or sought to obstruct justice; or (b) because they agreed that he lied or sought to obstruct justice, but concluded that the grand jury lies and the Jones obstructions concerned immaterial matters; or (c) they might have concluded that Clinton committed both perjury and obstruction, but that these particular perjuries and obstructions were not sufficiently grave or sufficiently associated with the powers and duties of the presidency to qualify as impeachable conduct.

There were, in addition, two more factors that surely entered into the calculations of some senators, that is, the behavior of the Clintons' political foes who funded the Jones civil lawsuit and the conduct of the independent counsel. We will return to those issues at the close of this chapter.

TOWARDS A WORKING DEFINITION OF AN IMPEACHABLE CRIME

Looking beyond the particulars of the Clinton case, can we devise a working standard for differentiating statutory crimes for which a president should be impeached from those for which he or she should not? Careful consideration of the constitutional text, the founders' remarks, the precedents, and the commentators viewed in the light of reason and common sense suggests certain tentative conclusions:

(a) *The severity of the crime in the eyes of the criminal law.* Although not all crimes – not even all felonies – are impeachable "high Crimes and Misdemeanors," the severity of the crime in the eyes of the criminal law is certainly relevant. Felonies are more serious than misdemeanors. Within the broad class of felonies, Congress has expressed a rough view of the relative seriousness of different felony offenses by assigning different levels of punishment.[95] On balance, a crime for which the criminal law prescribes a sentence of ten years is probably more serious than an offense where the likely punishment is six months. Such distinctions are certainly relevant to an impeachment inquiry.

(b) *The relative importance of the elements of a crime and the circumstances under which it was committed.* Consideration of whether allegedly criminal presidential conduct is also an impeachable "high Crime or Misdemeanor" should not be limited to an abstract assessment of the statutory elements of the crime, but must also take account of the particular circumstances of the case. For example, in the state of Washington, wrongfully appropriating a $5,000 watch misdelivered in the mail is the same statutory crime, first degree theft, as embezzling $5 million from a trust fund for widows and orphans.[96] It will often be the circumstances rather than the label of the crime that determine its true seriousness.

(c) *The relationship between moral gravity and political character.* It is tempting to assert categorically that only those crimes that relate to an official's public duties are impeachable. This was certainly the view of some noted commentators in the first half of the nineteenth century,[97] and a number of prominent constitutional scholars came quite close to this stance during the Clinton impeachment proceedings.[98] While this absolutist position has the merit of simplicity, it is very difficult to maintain, either as a matter of original intent, political theory, or practical politics.

When pressed on the point, almost all modern commentators concede that at least a few really nasty private crimes would certainly result in impeachment. For example, Professor Cass Sunstein told the House Judiciary Committee during the Clinton inquiry:

The basic point of the impeachment provision is to allow the House of Representatives to impeach the President of the United States for egregious misconduct that amounts to the abusive misuse of the authority of his office. This principle does not exclude the possibility that a President would be impeachable for an extremely heinous "private" crime, such as murder or rape. But it suggests that outside of such extraordinary (and unprecedented and most unlikely) cases, impeachment is unacceptable.[99]

Professor Sunstein went on to argue that the criminal allegations against President Clinton – perjury and obstruction of justice as part of an effort to cover up an illicit sexual affair – were not impeachable because the subject matter of the cover-up was private conduct unrelated to the office of the presidency and because the allegations did not fall into the narrow category of "extremely heinous" impeachable private crimes.[100] This argument leapt nimbly over the question of why the allegations against President Clinton were not sufficiently heinous to merit impeachment.

The key to Sunstein's argument is his characterization of impeachable private crimes as particularly "heinous." This may be an accurate characterization, but it fails to explain why even heinous crimes should merit impeachment if "high Crimes and Misdemeanors" embrace only abuses of office. The answer is that certain kinds of egregious behavior, whether connected to the office or not, strip the president of legitimacy and render him or her unfit in the eyes of the country to hold office. Murder and rape are easy exemplars of this truth, but contrary to Professor Sunstein's suggestion, the principle extends beyond such extreme cases. Democratic leadership requires more than an electoral majority and a four-year lease on the White House. American presidential leadership has traditionally depended in significant part on the exercise of moral authority, some inherent in the office of the presidency and some deriving from the character of its occupant. Presidential leadership has also traditionally required integrity, at least insofar as both a president's friends and foes must have reasonable confidence that, at least most of the time, he or she speaks the truth and keeps promises. Thus, presidential leadership has traditionally demanded at least some modicum of virtue, at least to the degree that the president must not violate the basic social norms embodied in the law's proscriptions against very serious criminal offenses. Without some indefinable minimum of these characteristics of moral authority, integrity, and personal virtue, a president's ability to govern is likely to be fatally compromised.

This is not to suggest that the president must be the spotless high priest of the nation's civic religion who must be cast down for any sin. Nor is it to suggest, in the maudlin terms employed by the House managers in the Clinton impeachment, that a president must be removed whenever he becomes a bad role model for "the kids."[101] It is, rather, to endorse the practical view that "high Crimes and Misdemeanors" includes not only crimes that are "political" *in nature*, but also crimes that are "political" *in effect*. While the principal focus of the constitution's impeachment clauses is certainly on offenses involving serious abuses of the powers of office, a president may also be impeached for crimes that so undercut the President's public standing as to gravely impair his or her capacity to perform the duties of that necessarily political office.

Accordingly, what makes a crime, or other presidential behavior, a "high Crime or Misdemeanor," and therefore a proper basis for impeachment, is a combination of moral gravity and political character, which is difficult to define with precision (a point to which we will return in Chapter 10). Some particularly morally reprehensible crimes, including but not limited to the oft-cited examples of premeditated murder and forcible rape, would certainly require impeachment of the president even if committed for entirely private motives in circumstances wholly unconnected with the Office of the President. On the other hand, the more political the crime and the more it involves abuse of the president's official position or subversion of the proper functions of the other branches of government, the less need there will be for showing moral depravity. A president who used illegal wiretaps to obtain information with which to blackmail a congressman into voting for flood and famine relief would be no less impeachable because his motives were good. Such conduct imperils honest constitutional government.

Crimes that are both morally reprehensible and intimately related to the presidential office are the most obviously impeachable (for example, murder of a political rival, or selling military secrets to known terrorists). Beyond such extreme examples, however, the more reprehensible the crime, the more relaxed will be the required nexus to the president's official duties. The more direct the connection between the crime and the president's constitutional functions, the lower the required level of heinousness.

(d) *The model of prosecutorial discretion*: as the previous section emphasizes, the decision about whether to impeach a president is necessarily political. Nonetheless, a useful model for a Congress deciding whether commission of a criminal offense warrants presidential removal is the decisional process by which a public prosecutor decides which of many technically prosecutable offenses and offenders merit the imposition of the moral opprobrium and harsh punishments of the criminal law. Prosecutors must consider: (1) what are the provable facts; (2) whether the facts establish a violation of the law; (3) whether prosecution promotes or disserves the goals of criminal law; and, more broadly, (4) whether the interests of society are best served by proceeding or exercising restraint.

In the case of impeachment, two of the five conventionally articulated rationales for criminal prosecution and punishment – retribution, rehabilitation, deterrence, incapacitation, and reprobation – are absent.[102] The goal of impeachment is neither retribution against nor rehabilitation of the official who commits an offense.[103] However, the impeachment remedy certainly is designed to deter would-be presidential miscreants from abusing their office.[104] Likewise, and perhaps more importantly, impeachment serves a function much akin to "incapacitation" in criminal theory – it is a remedy designed to put the offender in a place where he or she can do no more harm. For the ordinary felon, incapacitation is attained by imprisonment; in cases of presidential impeachment, Congress incapacitates by removal from office. As Joseph Story observed, "an impeachment is a proceeding of a purely political nature. It is not so much designed to punish an offender, as to secure the state against gross official misdemeanors. It touches neither his person nor his property, but simply divests him of his political capacity."[105]

The final justification for criminal punishment, designated above as "reprobation,"[106] but sometimes called by other names such as "denunciation"[107] or "education,"[108] requires a bit of explanation, but is particularly applicable in impeachments. The idea, though different commentators define it a bit differently and find slightly different uses for it in criminal law theory, is that the application of the criminal law in individual cases and across a population of offenders establishes moral boundaries that the society at large internalizes as guides to future behavior. As one author put it, criminal punishment may be viewed as "a teacher of right and wrong."[109] Impeachments, rare though they are, can and should serve precisely this function in the political realm. They define and educate both about the kinds of conduct that are impermissible for public officials and about the nature of the constitutional order itself.

A Congress applying the "prosecutorial discretion" model of impeachment analysis would first ascertain the facts regarding the president's conduct, then decide whether the conduct constituted a "high Crime or Misdemeanor" under the constitution, and finally determine whether to exercise its discretion to impeach or forbear from impeachment. Carrying the analogy to prosecutorial discretion a step further, a Congress considering impeachment of a president whose conduct has reached the impeachable threshold might find it useful to consider:

(i) whether impeachment and removal for the particular conduct at issue is necessary to deter future presidents from engaging in similar conduct;

(ii) whether impeachment and removal for such conduct might deter others prone to engage in such conduct from seeking the presidency in the first place, and whether the country is better off if such persons are deterred from running;

(iii) whether "incapacitation" of the president under scrutiny is necessary for the immediate protection of the republic; that is, whether removal before the natural expiration of the presidential term is necessary in order to prevent more wrongdoing of a similar character;

(iv) whether impeachment of this president serves the reprobative or educative function of reminding the public of settled norms of constitutional order, or in rare cases, of establishing new norms through extraordinary congressional action; and

(v) most importantly, whether the impeachment and removal of this president on these grounds promotes or disserves the country over the long term.

The result of the Clinton impeachment can be explained primarily in terms of the first two stages of prosecutorial discretion analysis. That is, one can conclude that the impeachment effort failed because of lingering doubts about the facts of the case or because not enough legislators were convinced that the charges met the constitutional standard of "high Crimes or Misdemeanors." Indeed, the House's refusal to accept two articles of impeachment recommended by the Judiciary Committee – perjury in the Paula Jones lawsuit and abuse of power – seems to have been based on this kind of analysis,[110] as does the Senate's acquittal on the obstruction of justice charge.

However, Clinton's acquittal may also be an example of the exercise of discretion by the Senate. Some senators may well have believed that the president's conduct met the minimum constitutional threshold for impeachment, but employed something akin to the deterrence and incapacitation rationales enunciated above. That is, particularly in reference to the charge of perjury before the grand jury, they may have concluded that the House managers failed to show either that conviction was necessary to prevent this president, or deter future presidents, from engaging in similar behavior, or that the country either required or desired protection from further misdeeds by President Clinton through his immediate ouster from the presidency.

THE INDEPENDENT COUNSEL AND CONGRESS

As influential as the foregoing considerations may have been, one suspects that President Clinton would have been removed from office had it not been for another factor bearing on the exercise of congressional discretion: a powerful national consensus opposing impeachment which took into account not only the gravity of the statutory violations and the subject matter of the lies and obstructive behavior, but the procedural context in which the occasions for lying and obstruction arose. While the adultery at the heart of the scandal was the president's failing alone, an original sin without which nothing that happened thereafter could have happened, by contrast, the crimes for which he faced impeachment were the lies and evasions about the sin. Those crimes of falsehood were, at least arguably, manufactured for the purpose of destroying the president. They were not "manufactured" in the sense that the president did not commit them. Rather, they were manufactured in the sense that once evidence of the original sin began to surface, the president's opponents – who transparently included not only the unapologetic partisans behind the Jones litigation, but the supposedly neutral professionals employed by the independent counsel – persistently sought to place him in situations where either a lie or the truth would be used as a political weapon against him. The country recoiled from the virulent partisanship that pervaded the whole business, and that, as much as any other consideration, saved Bill Clinton.

This brings us back to the Office of Independent Counsel. The Clinton affair demonstrated most of the well-known deficiencies in the design of the independent counsel statute under which Kenneth Starr was appointed. The statute made it too easy for the Justice Department to hand over its ordinary responsibility to investigate possible public corruption whenever minimally colorable allegations were made against the president, those associated with him, or any one of the large number of officials named in the statute. Indeed, the statute created a situation in which political optics often required referrals for even the most doubtful or trivial matters. Once a referral was made, the independent counsel was given effectively unlimited time, staff, and budget to focus on a single person or allegation, thus removing several of the practical constraints that tend to prevent excessive zeal in ordinary prosecutors' offices. The absence of supervision by the Justice Department's ordinary chain of command exacerbated the risk of independent counsel losing perspective and a sense of proportion.

The inception of the Clinton affair illustrated yet another defect in the statute's design. In the wake of Nixon's Saturday Night Massacre, the natural thought was to place the power of appointment and removal of independent counsel outside the executive branch. Hence, the involvement of the special panel of appellate judges. The most common criticism of this arrangement, urged most vociferously by Justice Scalia,[111] was that it created a prosecutorial entity foreign to the tripartite separation of powers design of the constitution. The more insidious correlate of this complaint is that the statute tempted judges into becoming political actors. The designers of the statute no doubt assumed, based in part on the commendably impartial performance of the judiciary in Watergate, that the new special court would be rigorously impartial in performing its appointive and supervisory functions. As it proved, however, at least one of the special court judges responsible for the Whitewater independent counsel appointment – David Sentelle – was anything but a political neutral and was credibly supposed to have finagled the firing of Robert Fiske and the hiring of Kenneth Starr for overtly political reasons.

Beyond the particular deficiencies of the independent counsel statute, one explanation for the Clinton mess is that the post-Watergate reforms substituted ethical perfectionism enforceable through criminal penalties – a sort of utopian legalism – for the constitutional scheme of controlling both public corruption and factional excesses through political interactions between and factional conflict within governmental branches. Not only did the post-Watergate legal apparatus composed of expanded substantive criminal law and novel politically unaccountable institutions like that of the independent counsel grind out sometimes quite unreasonable political prosecutions on its own, but its existence had indirect effects on the traditional constitutional mechanism of impeachment. The Clinton case is a dismal illustration of the point.

First, the independent counsel's office pursued the president, his wife, and his underlings in directions and to degrees that a politically responsive Justice Department or Congress (controlled by the opposing party though it was) would very likely never have done. It seems beyond dispute, for example, that had Linda Tripp taken her story to the House Judiciary Committee, the very most that might have happened would have been that she and Monica Lewinsky would have been used to create acute political embarrassment for the president. The suggestion that an impeachment inquiry would have been opened on this basis is absurd.[112] Moreover, no congressional committee would have the tools (or the inclination) to wire up Tripp, detain and try to flip Lewinsky, and all the rest of it.

Second, and more critically to the present point, by sticking doggedly to a legalistic view of his mandate, exposing every tawdry detail of the Lewinsky matter, forcing the president into a grand jury perjury trap, and then writing a detailed, adversarial report recommending specific grounds of impeachment, Independent Counsel Starr also trapped Republicans in the legislative branch. Republicans who, without the OIC report, would have enjoyed (and exploited) the president's discomfiture over disclosure of his sexual misadventures but would never have pursued the details, or thought those details a proper basis for impeachment even if they knew them, were now forced into a choice between impeaching the president or seeming to condone both his personal immorality and a provable felony violation of the criminal law.

The post-Watergate reformers sought to cure a perceived weakness in the constitutional system of checks and balances in the face of serious presidential wrongdoing by turning to law to fix politics. They wrote laws delineating the proper conduct of public men and women, and created an extra-constitutional inquisitorial office to ensure the law was enforced even if the heavens should fall. What the reformers forgot is that politics has virtues as well as vices, and that one of those virtues is the instinct to moderation. The framers of the constitution certainly relied on political competition among institutions and factions to produce conflict, in which the self-interest of each institution or faction would be checked by the strivings of its institutional or factional opponents. But the framers also recognized that politics is often home to public-spirited action, and that even narrow calculations of political interest will often counsel in favor of restraint and magnanimity. The trouble with the rule of law is that sometimes, as Mr. Bumble said, "the law is an ass,"[113] knowing neither common sense nor anything else outside itself. Thus, Clinton's congressional tormentors might have justified themselves by arguing that post-Watergate utopian legalism left little room for either political maneuver or broad-minded statesmanship.

There is a good deal of truth in this critique of post-Watergate reforms. But it only partially explains, and cannot excuse, the Clinton–Lewinsky fiasco. Ronald Reagan served under the strictures of the Watergate reforms, and was subject to scrutiny by an independent counsel. Reagan could have been impeached over Iran-Contra, and on more constitutionally substantial grounds than those marshaled against Clinton, but it did not happen. Independent Counsel Lawrence Walsh did not become the head cheerleader and chief witness in the cause of impeachment. The legislators principally responsible for the Iran-Contra investigation decided early on that, whatever else might come, impeachment was not a live option.[114] By contrast, Kenneth Starr, from the moment he sought expansion of his jurisdiction to encompass the Lewinsky affair to his final oral exposition of his written report to Congress, chose at virtually every juncture the most aggressive, confrontational, prosecutorial option available to him. Congressional Republicans, for their part, while they may ultimately have outfoxed themselves by using the cover of the independent counsel statute to defer as long as possible direct responsibility for investigating the Clinton–Lewinsky matter, could undoubtedly have dampened Mr. Starr's enthusiasm for impeachment by signaling privately that an opinionated, adversarial report from the independent counsel would be unwelcome.

In the end, a determinist explanation of the Clinton impeachment will not wash. The post-Watergate reforms certainly set the stage for the Lewinsky imbroglio, but no law forced Kenneth Starr, congressional Republicans, or, of course, Bill Clinton into the self-defeating choices they made.

At the core of the national consensus that saved President Clinton was the belief that, while presidents must obey the law, the impeachment calculus may in the extraordinary case require a judgment about the legal process that unearthed or even induced allegedly unlawful presidential behavior. Impeachment is a political tool whose constitutional function is to remove officials whose presence in office disserves the country. As a political process, impeachment can equally aptly, and equally constitutionally, be used as a vehicle to express disapproval of a method of politics more destructive of the public welfare than the continuance in office of one severely flawed individual.

10

The Scope of Impeachable Presidential Conduct:
General Principles

Having traced impeachment from its medieval English origins, across the Atlantic to the colonial assemblies of British North America, to the first American state constitutions, to the careful deliberations and puzzling verbal stylings of the Constitutional Convention, and thereafter through more than two centuries of American practice, what have we learned? In particular, can we say with confidence what conduct by a president of the United States is impeachable and what conduct is not? Better yet, can we tell when impeachment *can* be used to remove a president and also when it *should* be used? The best answer, the constitutional answer, is that impeachment was designed by the Founders as a mechanism for the maintenance of a healthy politics and the preservation of constitutional governance. The placement of the impeachment power exclusively in the legislative branch and the elasticity of the constitutional language defining the range of impeachable conduct, taken together, mean that *we can impeach a president whenever we should.* The impeachment of presidents is a political act, performed with one eye on history, but ultimately constrained only by the political norms, popular expectations, and factional alignments of the era in which a particular impeachment is attempted. The caveat to that apparently happy conclusion is that, by inserting the procedural obstacle of securing a two-thirds majority in the Senate, the framers made impeachment so politically difficult that even in cases where we both can and should impeach the chief executive, we nonetheless may not.

This chapter summarizes the case for an expansive, flexible impeachment power, leaving for Chapter 16 all the reasons why, particularly in the present moment, its power may prove so hard to wield.

THE IMPORTANCE OF CONSTITUTIONAL STRUCTURE

We begin with the seven basic decisions the framers made about presidential impeachment: (1) presidents can be impeached; (2) Congress decides whether they will be; (3) conviction requires concurrence of two-thirds of the Senate; (4) the consequences of conviction are limited to removal from office and future disqualification from federal office-holding; (5) Congress' decisions on impeachment, conviction, and punishment are final; (6) the constitution contains a definition of impeachable conduct; and (7) the heart of the definition is a term of art of ancient lineage the meaning of which is uncertain, can only be approximated through common law methods of interpretation, and is therefore subject to adjustment based on the challenges of the moment.

Consider first the underappreciated implications of the core fact that presidents are impeachable at all. The average person tends to think of impeachment as a quasi-criminal procedure intended to winkle out and punish executive wrongdoing. It is that, in small part. But from a broader constitutional perspective, impeachment is a recognition of the occasional disadvantages and dangers of a system of fixed quadrennial presidential terms. The framers chose a presidential system over a constitutional monarchy because, though they did not want a hereditary king, they recognized the need for a vigorous executive with democratic legitimacy and a marked degree of independence from the legislature. But in granting fixed terms to a president in whom they combined the roles of head of state and head of government, they surrendered the flexibility of parliamentary systems which are able to remove an unsatisfactory head of government through the simple expedient of a legislative vote of no confidence whenever his or her performance in office is deemed to be inadequate. The American impeachment device is a compromise. It provides a mechanism for political control of the executive through midterm executive removal, but acknowledges the president's status as elected head of a co-equal branch of government by making removal harder than a parliamentary vote of no confidence. The big question is how much harder.

The constitution reveals the framers' ambivalence about the optimal scope of presidential impeachment. On the one hand, the limited punishments for impeachment together with the constitutional ban on the bills of attainder that were a common British alternative to impeachment were plainly intended to make American impeachment easier to contemplate than its sanguinary British progenitor. The framers wanted Congress to use impeachment to protect the constitutional order without legalistic reservations over retrospective punishment of previously undefined offenses or moral qualms about killing, imprisoning, banishing, or impoverishing deficient office-holders. On the other hand, the framers erected one hugely consequential and another largely illusory barrier to impeachment. The big one is the two-thirds requirement for conviction in the Senate. The other is the textual limitation of impeachable conduct to "Treason, Bribery, or other high Crimes and Misdemeanors."

THE IMPORTANCE OF CONGRESS AS FINDER OF FACT
AND ARBITER OF CONSTITUTIONAL MEANING

In practice, the meaning of the constitutional definition of impeachable behavior is heavily influenced by the fact that Congress, not the judiciary, decides what constitutes an impeachable offense and whether a president has committed one. The framers' choice to place the impeachment power – both the initiation of the removal process through the approval of charges and the trial of those charges – entirely in the hands of the elected Congress was not inevitable. Recall that throughout the convention summer the Philadelphia delegates proposed situating the final trial with some body of judges – the U.S. Supreme Court or a special panel of state court judges – and settled on the Senate as the trial venue only at the very end.[1] Siting the trial in the judiciary would have produced a very different process.

For example, in Missouri, the current state constitution places the power to impeach in the House of Representatives and the power to try impeachments in the state Supreme Court.[2] In the only case actually tried under this system, the Missouri Supreme Court held that, "Missouri's constitutional provision [assigning impeachment trials to the judiciary] is a clear acknowledgment that the trial of impeachment charges is essentially judicial in character and is not a political function. This Court can convict only where there is actual misconduct as the law defines it."[3] The court went on to conclude that the judicial character of the trial function effectively limits the extremely broad definition of impeachable behavior in the Missouri constitution – "crimes, misconduct, habitual drunkenness, willful neglect of duty, corruption in office, incompetency, or any offense involving moral turpitude or oppression in office"[4] – so as to restrict impeachable conduct to actual crimes or statutory infractions. The effect of this holding is to read out of the constitution several substantively significant parts of Missouri's constitutional definition of impeachable conduct, notably "misconduct, habitual drunkenness, willful neglect of duty" and "incompetency."[5] The court effectively erased all of the words requiring it to exercise pragmatic political judgment, leaving only the terms that permitted judges to do what they are comfortable with: finding facts and applying existing law.

The Missouri experience suggests that, had the framers consigned the federal impeachment trial function to judges, it would have dramatically altered the system we know. In that alternative reality, the judges might have taken one of three paths.

First, they might have decided to defer entirely to Congress (which in practice would mean the House of Representatives alone) on the question of what kinds of conduct are impeachable "high Crimes and Misdemeanors." In this model, the House would investigate executive misconduct and frame charges in articles of impeachment and the judges would be a mere jury, acting strictly as fact-finders. If the court found that the House managers proved the facts alleged in an article of impeachment, then conviction and removal would automatically follow. The obvious difficulty with such an approach is that it would make the president (and impeached judges, for that matter) extraordinarily vulnerable to perturbations of opinion in the lower house. All that would be required to depose a president would be for a majority of the House to identify some conduct the president had unquestionably performed and designate it a high crime or misdemeanor. Conviction would be unavoidable unless the impeachment court was willing to engage in the equivalent of jury nullification by returning a "not guilty" verdict in the teeth of the evidence.

The judges, accustomed as they are to seeing themselves as the final arbiters of constitutional meaning, would be unlikely to adopt so deferential an approach. Instead, a judicial impeachment court would surely have assumed the power to interpret the constitutional language defining impeachable behavior. In that event, the court would have had two basic options.

On the one hand, it might have adopted the Missouri model, hewing closely to the traditional juridical role and eschewing as far as humanly possible any pretensions to political judgment. A federal impeachment court taking the Missouri approach would interpret the constitutionally operative language narrowly to restrict "treason, bribery, or other high crimes and misdemeanors" to violations of established law. Federal impeachment would have become closely akin to the limited version employed by the first post-Declaration of Independence state constitutions – a housekeeping mechanism for dispensing with official crooks and finaglers of the medium grade.

On the other hand, a federal impeachment court might have reviewed British practice and some of the American colonial precedents and consciously assumed the role now played by the Senate of determining whether facts have been proven *and also* of exercising political judgment on the question of whether the facts proven are of a type and gravity that justify reversing the results of a national election. Granting the Supreme Court, or any body of federal judges, that kind of discretionary political authority would amount to a major alteration of the constitutional balance. It would also present an extreme version of the "counter-majoritarian difficulty" introduced back in Chapter 1.[6] It is one thing for unelected judges to exercise "judicial review" by overturning statutes passed by the elected branches on the ground that such statutes violate the fundamental law of the written constitution. After all, the existence of a fundamental written law necessarily implies the existence of some authority somewhere to assess the compliance of later inferior enactments with the original foundational enactment. It is something else entirely for an unelected Supreme Court to be tasked with the inescapably political task of deciding whether presidential conduct is of a type that threatens constitutional order. Officials who make that sort of decision ought to be politically accountable themselves, which our life-tenured judges are not.

A federal impeachment court in the judicial branch would have differed from the current regime in another pivotal way. As we discussed in Chapter 1, when American courts make decisions, at least on important questions like constitutional interpretation, they customarily write opinions in which they specify what they are holding and why. Moreover, American courts customarily recognize the doctrine of *stare decisis*, the proposition that prior decisions of a jurisdiction's highest court create precedent that binds, or at least presumptively constrains, the decisions of later courts. If the constitution had created a judicial court of impeachment, that court would presumably have issued a judgment and accompanying opinion in each case. Each opinion would contain a reasoned explanation for the judgment based on the customary sources of authority – exegesis of the constitutional text, arguments about original public meaning, analysis of relevant precedents, and so forth. As the body of precedents grew, in theory, some measure of certainty would be achieved, at least on recurring points. Two centuries on, we would now have a body of impeachment law.

But we do not. Not really. As we have seen, Congress does not operate like a court. Impeachment proceedings are often incomplete, leaving their meanings obscure and their value as precedent unclear. The House Judiciary Committee approved articles of impeachment against Richard Nixon, but he resigned before the full House could act, still less the Senate. What is the precedential significance of the committee-approved articles? Judges George English and Samuel Kent were impeached by the House, but then resigned before they could be tried, and the Senate decided not to pursue either matter to trial. Does this mean that the Senate loses impeachment jurisdiction once an officer resigns (a conclusion suggested by the acquittal of the egregiously guilty Secretary Belknap after his resignation)? Or do the English and Kent cases signal nothing more than that the Senate did not want to waste its time on cases that were effectively moot?

Even completed impeachment proceedings produce results that are hard to interpret. Andrew Johnson was impeached by a greater than two-thirds majority in the House and avoided the two-thirds conviction threshold in the Senate by only a single vote. Does that mean the offenses charged against him were not proper constitutional "high crimes and misdemeanors"? Or that the managers did not prove the facts? Or simply that some senators did not want Senate president *pro tem* Ben Wade in the White House? We can use contemporary sources to make reasonable guesses at the answers to some of these questions. But those educated guesses are by nature debatable, and even when it is absolutely plain what Congress decided and why, congressional verdicts and their inferable reasons can never enjoy the same precedential status as a judicial opinion. To Congress, impeachment is fundamentally a legislative act, even if it has adjudicative trappings. Congress neither writes opinions explaining its results nor treats the impeachment decisions of previous congresses as binding on the present one. Moreover, the constitution makes no explicit provision for judicial review of congressional impeachment decisions and the Supreme Court has found such decisions to be effectively unreviewable "political questions."[7] Therefore, there is no "law of impeachment," or at least no "law of impeachable offenses," in the sense we ordinarily think of such a thing.

And yet … the public and the legal academy and even Congress itself act like there is. Every time a presidential impeachment crisis rolls around, legal journals, the public press, and, if the matter gets so far, the Congressional Record are deluged with solemn legal analyses of what does or does not constitute an impeachable offense. Why? The answer lies in the fact that the framers elected to insert a definition of impeachable conduct into the constitutional text. They might not have. They might have aped Parliament or followed the examples of Pennsylvania and Vermont, which in their first state constitutions conferred an effectively unde-fined power of impeachment on the legislature, and left it at that.[8] One could argue that we would all be better off had the framers done the same. This parsimonious approach would have tasked Congress with deciding the most appropriate uses of the impeachment power without warping the process through the distorting lens of the perennially enigmatic "high Crimes and Misdemeanors." However, once a definition was inserted into the fundamental law, Congress became constitution-ally obliged to conform impeachments to it. That created a seemingly ordinary task of constitutional construction. Not surprisingly, in each impeachment season, every-one reaches reflexively for the customary tools used in such a job: parsing the constitutional text; arguing from constitutional structure; probing the framers' intentions; searching for clues to original public understanding; seeking and con-struing analogous precedent; making arguments about policy and the public good.

This is all quite predictable, but also quite peculiar. Congress is not a court. It is not well equipped to entertain or decide constitutional arguments. Indeed, it does not really decide them at all. In impeachment cases, because the impeachment power rests unreviewably in the legislature, no issues other than the outcome of the particular case are ever truly decided. Rather, in Congress, constitutional arguments become merely one type of argument employed to secure an inescapably political decision. Moreover, when the subject is impeachment, even framing constitutional arguments is peculiarly difficult. The framers selected as the operative core of the constitutional definition of impeachable conduct an extraordinarily elastic phrase drawn from a British tradition in which the scope of impeachable conduct shifted with the needs of changing times and the transitory preferences of Parliament. This is a crucial point. The problem is not merely that "high Crimes and Misdemeanors" is an antique phrase of honestly debatable meaning, but that, *considered as prece-dents*, the British impeachments to which the framers and everyone since has been obliged to look in construing the term have deficiencies similar to American congressional impeachment decisions. That is, Parliament was no more definitive in its impeachments than Congress has been, either as to results or explanations. It is true that Parliament, unlike Congress, was accustomed from its inception to serving an expressly judicial function sometimes (impeachment being one such time). Thus, British legal theorists have maintained that, when acting in that mode, Parliament created a special form of common law, the *lex parliamentaria*.[9] But in practice, the supposed parliamentary law on impeachment was no more definite and no more binding on Parliament than its later American cousin is on Congress. Parliament treated its own prior impeachment actions as persuasive authority, a guide for the deliberations of each new generation of parliamentarians, grist for the advocates in each new case, but nothing more.

Put simply, Congress creates no binding precedents for itself, and the constitutional phrase it is bound to construe originates in the practices of the British Parliament which did not do so either. In a formal sense, every impeachment case effectively starts anew as a fresh exercise in figuring out what the impeachment clauses mean and how they should best be applied to the facts and national circumstances at hand. This is what then-Congressman Gerald Ford meant with his famous assertion that, "An impeachable offense is whatever a majority of the House of Representatives considers it to be at a given moment in history; conviction results from whatever offense or offenses two-thirds of the other body considers to be sufficiently serious to require removal of the accused from office."[10]

On the positive side of the ledger, if Congress suffers some handicaps that a court would not in playing this role, it also has a signal advantage in that it faces no "counter-majoritarian difficulty." Impeachment is, in the last analysis, the constitution's ultimate defense against executive evil and error, and the ultimate arbiter of irreconcilable differences between Congress and the executive about the nation's constitutional future. Whether to impeach a president is, by design, a quintessentially political question properly assigned to the most democratically legitimate arm of the national government.

That having been said, the constitutional language defining impeachable conduct matters, as do all the conventional tools for interpreting it. Writing about this question twenty years ago in the aftermath of the Clinton impeachment, I said:

> In the Clinton case ... despite much disagreement over important details, the universally-voiced consensus that the constitutional impeachment threshold is "high" set the general boundaries of the field on which the battle was fought. This consensus, drawn from constitutional language and historical precedent, placed an immensely heavy burden of proof on proponents of impeachment, and represented an immensely valuable psychological bulwark for the President's defenders. Perhaps more important still, the very debate over the constitutional standard – the meticulous dissections of constitutional language and legislative history, the enumeration of precedents rooted in dimly remembered controversies from the Nation's past, and the sometimes mind-numbing disputes of scholars, journalists, and politicians – served an incommensurably valuable function. In the course of debating the meaning of four words – "high Crimes and Misdemeanors" – the Nation wrestled with itself over fundamental questions about the design of the Republic: the proper relationship between the branches of government, the nature of presidential leadership, the connection between private morals and public duties, and the kind of politics appropriate to healthy representative democracy. In the course of deciding the meaning of four words, the country was able to make some decisions about itself.[11]

I continue to think the constitution's language and its historical uses can perform the same functions – setting the terms of debate and suggesting some broad, if ultimately permeable, limits on what behavior is most likely to be accepted as impeachable, and forcing at least the intellectually honest participants in any impeachment controversy to wrestle seriously with the constitution's structure, history, and best future. As physicist Stephen Hawking said in another context, "It's the past that tells us who we are. Without it, we lose our identity."[12]

THE SCOPE OF IMPEACHABLE PRESIDENTIAL CONDUCT

We can say some reasonably definitive things about what the founding generation probably meant by the phrase "Treason, Bribery, or other high Crimes and Misdemeanors" and about how that phrase has been understood and used in the more than two centuries since. Let us begin with the easy stuff.

Treason and Bribery

Treason is unequivocally impeachable. It is also specifically defined in the constitution as "consist[ing] only in levying War against [the United States], or in adhering to their Enemies, giving them Aid and Comfort."[13] There are a number of interesting technical questions about this definition of treason, mostly relating to what it means to adhere to or give "aid and comfort to" the nation's enemies, but the essence of the crime remains actually taking up arms against the United States or assisting sovereign states or entities which do so.[14] In *Federalist No. 43*, Madison explained the inclusion of a treason definition in the constitution, and its narrow scope:

> As treason may be committed against the United States, the authority of the United States ought to be enabled to punish it. But as new-fangled and artificial treasons have been the great engines by which violent factions, the natural offspring of free government, have usually wreaked their alternate malignity on each other, the convention have, with great judgment, opposed a barrier to this peculiar danger, by inserting a constitutional definition of the crime, fixing the proof necessary for conviction of it, and restraining the Congress, even in punishing it, from extending the consequences of guilt beyond the person of its author.[15]

The extremely limited definition of treason of course narrows the scope of impeachment for treason itself, but considered in the context of other moves by the framers, also signals an intention that "other high Crimes and Misdemeanors" should be liberally interpreted to embrace other types of national betrayal. As discussed in Chapter 4, the restriction on treason as a criminally punishable offense was of a piece with the constitution's ban on bills of attainder and *ex post facto* laws; together, these restrictions were aimed at avoiding an American repetition of the tendency of British parliamentary factions to use state trials to kill, imprison, banish, or impoverish their political opponents.[16] George Mason noted the absence of bills of attainder as a potential weakness in the constitution because he thought that mechanism had on past occasions "saved the British constitution," and it was in part because of this perceived weakness that he proposed "high Crimes and Misdemeanors" as the core definition of impeachable conduct.[17]

Only one person, West H. Humphreys, the secessionist judge from Tennessee, has ever been impeached for conduct amounting to treason, and only one of the six articles on which he was convicted alleged levying war against the United States. Five of the other articles of conviction charged other kinds of disloyalty, including inciting revolt, advocating secession, and refusing to hold court once Tennessee passed its secession ordinance.[18] The Humphreys case establishes that one may be a "traitor" to the United States in the colloquial sense of betraying its fundamental interests and values without committing the crime of treason per se, and that this more expanded kind of betrayal may be impeachable as falling within the general rubric of "high Crimes and Misdemeanors."

Bribery is not defined in the constitution. Nonetheless, it was in 1787 and is now a well-recognized crime. The only mildly tricky questions when considering bribery as an impeachable offense arise from the fact that the precise definition of bribery *in the criminal courts* varies over time and jurisdiction. In 1788, at the time of the constitution's ratification, there was not yet a federal bribery statute. Bribery was, however, a common law crime that developed from a narrow beginning as a prohibition on a judicial officer taking "an undue reward to influence his behaviour in his office,"[19] and by the time of American independence had expanded to include executive officers, jurors, and voters in public elections, as well as to giving, and offering to give, such improper rewards.[20] Beginning in 1789, the federal government began enacting bribery statutes, first for customs officers,[21] then judges,[22] and as time went on for effectively all federal officers and employees. At present, the federal code not only prohibits most imaginable forms of giving or taking bribes by federal officers,[23] but also bribery in connection with programs involving federal funds,[24] commercial bribery,[25] and bribery of certain foreign persons and entities.[26]

The judicial construction of some of these statutes has at times been highly technical.[27] However, although none of the American impeachment precedents specifically tests this proposition, it is fair to conclude that bribery for impeachment purposes is not limited by federal statutory law or the case law construing it. From a constitutional point of view, such a limitation would be at best odd and probably unsupportable. If the constitution of 1788 permitted impeachment for bribery as that term was understood by the founding generation, then Congress ought not be able to restrict, and perhaps not materially to enlarge, the reach of the constitutional language by subsequent statutory enactment. A number of the federal judicial impeachment cases rest in their essence on bribery allegations. However, none charge a violation of a particular bribery statute and proving violation of any particular statute has obviously not been thought essential.[28]

The final issue about bribery as impeachable conduct is raised by the modern expansion of public corruption statutes beyond the limits of common law bribery to include things like federal program bribery, private commercial bribery prosecuted as fraud, or bribes to foreign entities under the Foreign Corrupt Practices Act. Had George Mason not prevailed upon his colleagues to add "high Crimes and Misdemeanors" to the description of impeachable offenses, one could imagine a great deal of argument in impeachment cases based on corruption over the precise scope of common law bribery in 1788. As matters stand, corruption that fits the new statutes, but not old-time bribery, can plainly be placed within the ambit of "high Crimes and Misdemeanors." The question in such cases then becomes not whether the conduct alleged is bribery, but whether it is conduct of a sort that merits inclusion in the more general phrase.

High Crimes and Misdemeanors

Almost all American impeachments have been based on conduct categorized as "high Crimes and Misdemeanors" (a fact that validates George Mason's insistence on broadening the definition of impeachable conduct beyond treason and bribery). Therefore, the substantive reach of the impeachment power depends on Congress' interpretation of that phrase. In the remainder of this section, we will review quickly the question of whether commission of a crime is either necessary or sufficient for proof of "high Crimes and Misdemeanors," and then try to discern some general principles for identifying non-criminal presidential conduct that is nonetheless properly impeachable.

Crime is Not Necessary for Impeachment

If there is one point established by eight centuries of Anglo-American impeachment practice, it is that the phrase "high Crimes and Misdemeanors" is not limited to indictable crime. Those tasked with defending officials facing impeachment invariably argue the contrary, but they are, and always have been, wrong. British impeachments were chock full of allegations of and convictions for non-criminal behavior.[29] American colonists before the Revolution, and American states after the Revolution but before 1787, all impeached officials for non-criminal conduct.[30] The framers in Philadelphia had a high degree of familiarity with British impeachment practice and adopted a parliamentary phrase they knew reached beyond the narrowly criminal to political misconduct in a broad sense.[31] The ratifiers in the states repeatedly spoke of impeachment in ways that affirmed their understanding that the constitutional impeachment power extended beyond behavior cognizable in a criminal court.[32] Since 1787, Congress has repeatedly impeached federal officials for non-criminal behavior.[33] All serious modern scholars and commentators are unanimous that "high Crimes and Misdemeanors" need not be crimes.[34]

Crime May Not be Sufficient for Impeachment

It is also plain that not every crime will be a sufficient ground for impeachment.[35] The point is obvious from the constitutional text – only "*high* Crimes and Misdemeanors" count, phrasing that necessarily implies the existence of low (or perhaps just mediocre) crimes that do not. Even crimes the law designates as felonies may not be impeachable "high Crimes and Misdemeanors" in the sense that Congress may not find them sufficiently serious to justify presidential removal. That is the apparent lesson of the Clinton impeachment, and to a lesser degree of the impeachment of Andrew Johnson. Both presidents were impeached by the House for conduct that, if proven in court, would constitute a serious felony-level crime – Johnson, the Tenure of Office Act, punishable by ten years in prison and a $10,000 fine,[36] and Clinton, the federal felonies of perjury and obstruction of justice. The motives of the senators who voted to acquit Johnson were various, but some may have acquitted simply because they thought that violation of the Act was an insufficiently "high" crime.[37] Explanations of Clinton's escape also vary, but as we saw in Chapter 9, the most likely is that, although he almost certainly committed perjury and probably obstructed justice, the Senate acquitted him because enough members concluded that his conduct was insufficiently grave and the circumstances were sufficiently extenuating that removal from office was unwarranted.[38] In short, although it would make life a lot simpler, we cannot determine whether conduct is impeachable simply by showing that it constitutes a felony.

Defining an Oxymoron: Non-Criminal "High Crimes and Misdemeanors"

If indictable crime is neither necessary nor sufficient for impeachment, what are the best arguments to use in determining whether presidential conduct amounts to "high Crimes and Misdemeanors" meriting impeachment, conviction, and removal?

ORIGINALIST ARGUMENTS. By approving the addition of "high Crimes and Misdemeanors" to treason and bribery, the framers broadened the scope of the impeachment power. As explained at length in Chapter 4, the overwhelming evidence is that the Philadelphia delegates and the ratifiers knew that "high Crimes and Misdemeanors" was a term of art from British parliamentary practice that had sometimes been used in American colonial impeachments. The same evidence also establishes that the central figures in the impeachment debates were well informed about the scope and procedures of parliamentary and colonial impeachments. The evidence of the immediate founding period is reaffirmed by the later debates in the first federal impeachment, that of Senator Blount in 1798, in which the advocates, including Philadelphia delegate Jared Ingersoll, relied as a matter of course on British precedent to interpret the constitution's impeachment provisions.[39] Therefore, we may confidently conclude that, in approving "high Crimes and Misdemeanors," the Founders impliedly endorsed two aspects of

British and colonial practice: impeachment for the same general types of conduct which had been the subject of those proceedings; and, critically, an understanding that the phrase was subject to constant redefinition by Parliament using common law interpretive methods in light of the contemporary needs of the kingdom.

The Founders' appreciation of the origins and meaning of the term "high Crimes and Misdemeanors" provides two signals to those of an originalist turn of mind. First, one can examine the work of Parliament and the few cases of pre-constitutional American impeachment and identify classes of conduct that the Founders evidently intended to be impeachable in the American republic. As described in previous chapters, those include: some kinds of ordinary personal crime; official corruption; severe instances of incompetence, neglect of duty, or maladministration in office; abuse of power; betrayal of the nation's foreign policy; and subversion of the constitution and laws.[40] The final parliamentary category – subversion of the constitution and laws of the realm – in itself compels a broad reading of the impeachment power. Deciding what the "constitution" (British or American) consists of and what conduct constitutes an effort to undermine it are inherently imprecise determinations fundamentally political, rather than legal, in character.

Second, parliamentary use of the term "high Crimes and Misdemeanors" as a descriptor of what it had done, rather than a limitation on what it might do, ought to preclude even a devoted originalist from limiting American impeachments to these particular categories. The Founders adopted a British term that embraced not only a list of past cases, but a common law process for defining its future uses.

In any case, one need not rely on inferences from the Founders' familiarity with British practice to confirm their intention to confer substantial discretionary authority on Congress. As discussed in the first part of this chapter, the structural decision to place impeachment entirely in the hands of Congress necessarily made impeachment both political and inescapably discretionary. The Founders were not shy in affirming this point. Over and over, founding era writers spoke of the political character of impeachment and the impossibility of defining its ambit in advance.[41] Likewise, beginning with George Mason's remarks during the constitutional convention debate in which he introduced the phrase "high Crimes and Misdemeanors," the founding generation repeatedly emphasized that the core function of presidential impeachment was preservation of constitutional order against executive overreach, a malleable and expansive grant of authority if ever there was one.[42]

The evidence of what conduct the Founders thought impeachable extends beyond the historical precedents associated with the phrase "high Crimes and Misdemeanors." The Founders offered specific examples of behavior they thought would be impeachable. These generally emerge from notes of debates in Philadelphia or the state ratifying conventions, or in advocacy pieces like the *Federalist Papers*. Because we have so little material of this type related to impeachment, there is a natural tendency to place immense, and probably undue, weight on these sometimes offhand utterances. Still, they are helpful clues to founding era thinking and it would be as wrong to ignore them as to overemphasize them.

Among the specific grounds for impeachment endorsed by notable members of the founding generation were: (1) corruption (a ubiquitous concern[43]); (2) receipt of foreign emoluments,[44] which fits nicely in the parliamentary category of corruption but also represents a violation of a specific provision of the American constitution; (3) abuse of the pardon power,[45] which could represent an unadorned abuse of official authority or, depending on motive, might fit the rubrics of corruption, betrayal of the nation's foreign policy, or even subversion of the constitution; (4) lying to the Senate, at least in particular circumstances, such as communications relating to the approval of treaties,[46] which might be called maladministration, abuse of power, or betrayal of foreign policy interests; and (5) corrupting electors.[47]

One final point about the original understanding of the impeachment power: generally, constitutional arguments from original understanding take the form of saying, "The Framers (or Founders) thought such-and-such a passage meant X. Therefore, we should interpret the passage to mean X." But sometimes it is clear that the framers were uncertain about how to proceed and wrote language based on their best guess about how this novel constitutional structure would work in practice. When their best guesses turn out to be wrong, fidelity to the Founders' purposes may be better achieved by adjusting our understanding of what constitutional language permits. For example, as noted in Chapter 4, the prevailing assumption in Philadelphia was that Congress would be the dominant power in the federal government and that the president was likely to be a relative weakling. That assumption was at the root of the efforts – definitional ("Treason, Bribery, or other high Crimes and Misdemeanors") and structural (the two-thirds Senate majority requirement) – to cabin presidential impeachment.

The framers' prediction about the relative power of Congress and the president was fairly accurate for many years. Certainly, through most of the nineteenth century, the federal executive and legislative branches were, at worst, roughly equal in authority. But since no later than the New Deal, presidential power has grown and relative congressional authority has diminished. As matters now stand, the president dominates the foreign and domestic political landscape, controlling a military of frightening power, an immense national security information-gathering capacity, a large (if currently underused) foreign policy and international aid apparatus, a vastly expanded federal law enforcement establishment, and a huge civilian bureaucracy with its own administrative lawmaking and enforcement mechanism. Meanwhile, Congress can barely perform routine functions like passing a budget. One can fairly argue that much of the current interbranch imbalance stems from Congress' own choices to cede its authority over a wide spectrum of issues. Nonetheless, whatever the explanation, one of the central features of the

Founders' constitutional plan – a system of co-equal branches with each precluded from predominance by institutional checks exercised by the others – is now badly degraded and in some danger of utter collapse. In such circumstances, it is not unreasonable to think that preservation of the Founders' constitutional system might, under the right circumstances, militate in favor of an expanded application of impeachment authority.

ARGUMENTS FROM AMERICAN IMPEACHMENT PRECEDENTS. After over two centuries of experience using the impeachment clauses, we are not limited to originalist arguments about their meaning, but can look to a body of American applications of the constitution's language. The obvious shortcoming of arguments based on American precedents is that there are so few of them overall, and a pitiful three for presidents.

The sixteen judicial impeachments or near-impeachments are useful in the presidential setting primarily in identifying the types of conduct for which impeachment might plausibly be sought for any official. As noted in Chapter 6, American judicial impeachments fall primarily into five of the seven basic categories found in British impeachments generally: treason; corruption in office; incompetence, neglect of duty, or maladministration in office; abuse of power; and ordinary crimes unrelated to office.[48] In addition, four judges were impeached for perjury or official false statements, offenses not found in the British or pre-constitutional American precedents, but in all four instances the perjury was related to other corrupt or criminal conduct.[49] The absence of cases founded in the remaining two traditional British categories – foreign policy concerns or subversion of the constitutional order – highlights the difference in function between judges and presidents and emphasizes the necessity of considering the place in the constitutional scheme of the office from which impeachment seeks to remove an accused.

The last point was particularly evident in the attempted impeachment of Justice Samuel Chase.[50] The motive for his impeachment arose primarily from partisan politics – disapproval by President Jefferson and the dominant Republican congressional majority of Chase's outspoken Federalist opinions – even if the particulars of the charges had little explicit political content. Chase's acquittal is said to stand for the proposition that impeachment should not be used merely to displace officeholders of the party opposed to the congressional majority, a proposition that extends to both judicial and executive branch officials. However, the primary lesson of the Chase case is probably more limited. It may stand primarily for the principle that Congress ought not use the impeachment power to undercut the special constitutional protection afforded judges, who are to hold office during good behavior. If that is the case, Chase's acquittal may be less germane in the case where one political branch – Congress – seeks removal of the head of another political branch – the executive.

The impeachment of Senator Blount in 1798 suggests that conduct short of treason that is nonetheless detrimental to U.S. foreign policy interests can be impeachable. Blount's plot to help the British seize Florida while snatching Louisiana from the Spanish threatened American international relations on several fronts.[51] Of course, Blount was not acting as president when he concocted his buccaneering scheme, which was contrary to the avowed objectives of presidents Washington and Adams and to treaties signed by Congress. Hence, its precedential value in the case of a president is doubtful.

In principle, the three presidential impeachments or near-impeachments should provide the most direct guidance in interpreting "high Crimes and Misdemeanors" as that phrase relates to the chief executive. Those cases are discussed at length in Chapters 7, 8, and 9. We will not repeat their outcomes or lessons here, though we will draw on them throughout the remainder of this book. The point for present purposes is that the presidential impeachment cases, while making better comparators than the impeachments of judges, senators, or cabinet secretaries, in the end provide only somewhat more definitive guidance than any other kind of case. Their facts are inevitably idiosyncratic, as are the political alignments and pressures of their eras. Their results and the reasons for them are no easier to interpret than impeachments of other officers.

It should also be remembered that the results in an impeachment case enjoy no conclusive presumption of correctness. The outcome for Nixon seems self-evidently right. He committed serious felony offenses for corrupt political motives and presented a genuine danger to the constitutional order. But the results in Johnson and Clinton are at least debatable. And, right or wrong, both had costs that a different outcome might have avoided.

For example, the decision not to convict Andrew Johnson in 1868 can be defended both on the contemporary partisan political ground that it kept that crazy radical Ben Wade out of the White House and therefore did not alienate constituencies important to the Republicans in the upcoming presidential election, and on the separation of powers ground that it created a precedent against impeaching presidents for political disagreements with Congress, without which Congress might have gained undue power over the executive. But one can fairly argue that the costs of leaving Johnson in office were very high indeed. Johnson's survival cheered and invigorated the most racially retrograde elements of the defeated Confederate states and surely contributed to, though it was not the unitary cause of, the ultimate failure of Reconstruction and the rise and persistence of the southern Jim Crow apartheid regime. Moreover, the positions that made Ben Wade a crazy radical in the eyes of some of his contemporaries – support for full black political participation, women's suffrage, and the rights of labor – hardly seem so crazy now. Just maybe a Wade presidency would have accelerated progress in all those areas. Indeed, a more congressionally centered government might not be all that bad a thing. The steady migration of power away from Congress and toward the executive has no doubt served the country well on some occasions. But Congress has now shrunk itself to a nearly vestigial body. Would it be so terrible to have the memory of a successful impeachment to stiffen congressional spines and provide a check to the inevitable presidential will to power?

Presidential "High Crimes and Misdemeanors": A Typology

Notwithstanding all the foregoing caveats, one can discern three basic, if sometimes overlapping, types of presidential impeachment justifiable under the constitutional label of "high Crimes and Misdemeanors."

IMPEACHMENT FOR CONDUCT THAT DESTROYS OR GRAVELY IMPAIRS PRESIDENTIAL LEGITIMACY. Impeachment is not personal punishment, but a means of national self-protection. A healthy national government requires a president who is not only capable of performing executive duties, but whose occupancy of the office and choices within it are broadly recognized as legitimate. Presidential legitimacy is of two kinds: personal and political.

As noted in the discussion of the Clinton impeachment, a president's *personal* legitimacy depends on national confidence that the president possesses an indefinable minimum quantum of ability, personal character, and devotion to the constitutional order and the collective good. The presidential oath to "faithfully execute the Office of President of the United States, and . . . preserve, protect and defend the Constitution of the United States"[52] implies, among other things, a commitment to subordinate personal interests to the duties of office. Conduct that casts serious doubt on those aspects of a president's character central to his or her official role may so damage public confidence in a president's integrity and commitment to promoting the national interest that the president can no longer be effective. In such cases, impeachment is warranted. Examples of such behavior include, but are not limited to, the heinous private crimes discussed in Chapter 9, all forms of official corruption, many types of abuse of official power, and, as will be discussed in Chapter 13, a sufficiently pervasive pattern of dissimulation.

By contrast, a president's *political* legitimacy derives from the constitutional process that put him or her in office. A president is legitimate in this sense not because of any personal qualities, but because he or she was elected according to the rules set out in the constitution, or in extraordinary cases, selected under the rules of succession created by statute. Conduct designed to illegally or unethically distort the selection process may so impair a president's political legitimacy that impeachment is appropriate. When the Founders spoke of impeachment for bribing electors, they were thinking of this sort of disqualifying political illegitimacy. Of course, the Electoral College no longer serves its imagined function as a group of wise elder statesmen who would exercise judgment in selecting a president, and is now merely an imperfect means of transmitting the democratic preferences of a state's voters. Therefore, to the extent that presidential legitimacy now derives primarily from the sanction of democratic election, any presidential behavior that seriously interferes with the integrity or fairness of the electoral process ought to be viewed as potentially impeachable.

PROPHYLACTIC IMPEACHMENT. A president's past conduct may so damage his or her personal or political legitimacy that impeachment is called for even if there is no serious risk of similar future misbehavior. Had President Clinton been removed from office, it would not have been to prevent him from lying about adultery again, but because the commission of past perjury fatally impaired his personal legitimacy. If a second-term president were found to have bribed electors, he would be impeached not to prevent a recurrence in a constitutionally impossible run for a third term, but because his political legitimacy would be destroyed for the second one. However, some presidential misbehavior is impeachable because the conduct was not only reprehensible when committed, but gives cause for concern that it will continue and do additional damage to the presidency and the country, unless the president is impeached and removed. This concern was common in the classic British impeachments brought against ministers to prevent the continuation of disfavored policies of the crown or abusive behavior by royal favorites. It can arise in all the major historical categories of impeachment: treason; corruption and bribery; severe incompetence or maladministration; abuse of power; undercutting foreign policy interests; and subverting the constitutional order. American examples include virtually all of the judicial impeachments with the exception of Judge Humphreys, the secessionist from Tennessee whose defection to the Confederacy removed him from the federal bench. The actions against presidents Johnson and Nixon were also markedly prophylactic. The Radical Republicans wanted to remove an implacable opponent of their reconstruction plans. By the end of the Watergate investigation it had become clear that Nixon refused to be constrained by law or constitutional custom in the pursuit of his political aims and the maintenance of his power; he had to be impeached to stop him.

DEFINITIONAL IMPEACHMENT. In one sense, all impeachments are definitional in the sense that they help to define the boundaries of impeachable conduct. But some of the impeachments we have discussed have as their primary purpose defining the important components of the constitutional order itself. The definitional project can sometimes be defensive in the sense of preserving existing constitutional interpretations, institutional relationships, or political norms and values against presidential assault. But a defensive use of impeachment will be definitional insofar as it requires choice about what the essential elements of the constitutional order are and whether preservation of whichever elements the president threatens is essential. After all, the constitution is not a porcelain statue that will either be preserved in its entirety or shattered to bits. It is, rather, an evolving organism. A president who violates norms may be doing so for the best. Congress gets to decide whether that is so, and in the course of deciding to define the constitution as it will be. In moving to impeach Richard Nixon, Congress used impeachment in this essentially conservative way: reaffirming traditional understandings about the rule of law, the necessary integrity of the electoral process, and limitations on presidential power.

Definitional impeachments can be creative, rather than defensive. Most discussions of impeachment assume a president who is alleged to be violating existing norms and a Congress that seeks to preserve them. The reverse might be true, as was the case after the Civil War. President Johnson wanted to pretend that no war had been fought, or at least that the war that was fought wrought no change in fundamental conditions and required no material adjustment in governmental arrangements. It was Congress that saw the dawn of a new age and sought to move in an unprecedented direction. The impeachment of President Johnson was an attempt to define America as rejecting both its past of slavery and a future of racial apartheid, and to define the federal constitutional balance as weighted more to Congress and less to the presidency. The view espoused in this book is that, in the case of irreconcilable conflict between the executive and the legislature over the constitutional future of the country, the legislature has the right to use impeachment to ensure that its view prevails. Another way of putting the point is that there is no unalterable status quo bias in the impeachment clauses. A president who refuses to adjust with the times when adjustment is required to preserve and protect a thriving republic can be impeached just as readily as a president who subverts those existing constitutional norms that the Congress finds essential.

11

Impeachment for Obstruction of Justice

Chapter 10 concluded that the constitution's placement of the impeachment power within the exclusive dominion of the national legislature, combined with its adoption of the venerable common law phrase "high Crimes and Misdemeanors" as the primary verbal descriptor of impeachable conduct, confers upon Congress immense discretion in invoking the impeachment remedy. This chapter and the three following will consider impeachment for particular types of conduct, beginning with obstruction of justice. The discussion in these chapters is written to be general; however, the choice of subjects has inevitably been influenced by controversies swirling around the presidency of Donald Trump at the time this book was written. Accordingly, at some points the argument will be illustrated by facts known or allegations made about Mr. Trump.

Two of the three serious impeachment cases against American presidents – those of Richard Nixon and Bill Clinton – involved obstruction of justice. When we speak of obstruction of justice in the impeachment setting, the term embraces both the narrow technical meaning of a violation of federal obstruction of justice statutes, and, more importantly, the broad general idea of improper interference with the investigative and adjudicative functions of the law. It is hardly surprising that a president would be impeachable for obstruction in either the broad or narrow sense of the term. A president is constitutionally obliged to "take care that the laws be faithfully executed,"[1] and, as head of the executive branch, is formally the country's chief law enforcement officer. The staff of the House Judiciary Committee's Nixon impeachment inquiry identified several broad categories of impeachable conduct, including "behaving in a manner grossly incompatible with the proper function of the office," and "employing the power of the office for an improper purpose or personal gain."[2] If a president, rather than enforcing the laws, seeks to thwart their honest execution, that is grossly incompatible with the function of the office. If the motive for doing so is self-aggrandizement, that is to employ the power of the office for an improper purpose.

Obstruction allegations now commonly swirl around American presidents, even when they do not result in impeachment proceedings. As professors Daniel Hemel and Eric Posner note, as of 2018, "six of the last nine presidents, or their top aides, were embroiled in obstruction of justice scandals. The law of obstruction of justice has evolved into a major check on presidential power, without anyone noticing it."[3] It is worth reflecting a moment on why obstruction allegations are now such a common feature of high-level American political fights.

Most older British and American impeachments involving distortions of the legal system tended to involve the receipt of favors or bribes by an official to exercise legal authority in favor of the giver. Lord Chancellor Bacon was impeached for taking bribes in 1621.[4] American judges Hastings, Porteous, and Collins were removed for receipt of outright bribes, while Judge Ritter took a kickback for awarding a high lawyer's fee.[5] But before Nixon, impeachment cases rarely if ever involved allegations that officials tried to induce witnesses to lie or fail to appear, or tried to bully or cozen law enforcement officers to decline to perform their duties honestly.

The modern surge in obstruction allegations arises from at least two interrelated historical developments, one necessary and generally beneficial, and the other less so. The first development is that, as the country has evolved from the largely agrarian society of the founding generation into a densely populated, highly industrialized, continent-spanning economic and military superpower, webs of law and regulation have been spun to control the resultant concentrations of private and governmental power. Those laws are tended and administered by law enforcement agencies that evolved in tandem with the rest of the burgeoning economic and legal structure – particularly the lawyers of the U.S. Department of Justice working with the investigators of the Federal Bureau of Investigation, the Internal Revenue Service, the Securities and Exchange Commission, and a host of others. Critically, the ethos of these agencies is rigorous enforcement of the law, not (except in happily rare instances) service of any political party. Standing behind these agencies are the courts, which have an even more foundational commitment to impartial enforcement of the law.

In consequence, if a president or his subordinates or political allies misbehave, the federal law enforcement establishment – prosecutors, agents, and courts in partnership – is quite likely to investigate. This is, without doubt, a very good thing. As presidents have accrued ever-greater power to act beneficially in the world, so, too, has their power to do evil grown. The federal law enforcement establishment is a vital check on presidential corruption – as long as that establishment is not itself corrupted, whether by the president, the president's opponents, or its own bureaucratic imperatives. In any case, presidential resistance to such investigations can easily become obstruction of justice, in either the narrow or broad sense.

The second less desirable development is the one we saw in the Clinton investigation of the weaponization of the law for political purposes. In Clinton's case, well-financed political opponents of the president embarked on private litigation designed to embarrass him, litigation that, as we saw, led him to lie under oath and commit other obstructive behavior. Political litigation of analogous sorts has become an increasingly common feature of the political landscape. To take but two current examples, President Trump has been sued by private parties over alleged payments to silence former adulterous girlfriends,[6] and by three different groups over his alleged violations of the constitution's emoluments clauses.[7] The increasing prevalence of political lawsuits against presidents is troubling, regardless of what one may think about any particular president or any particular lawsuit. Although the courts plainly should remain open to those who cannot get redress against the powerful or cannot, as in the case of the emoluments cases, induce Congress to fulfill its constitutional responsibilities, this mode of essentially political combat is often a symptom of institutional dysfunction in the primary constitutional entities. Be that as it may, entanglement in litigation of this kind can produce allegations of obstruction because presidents, like other citizens, are obligated to comply with the rules governing all legal proceedings.

When thinking about impeachment for obstruction, it is critical to remember the general principle evident throughout Anglo-American impeachment cases that proof of commission of a serious statutory crime is certainly helpful to any impeachment effort, but is not dispositive. Hence, proof that a president technically violated one of the federal obstruction statutes is not automatically proof of impeachable conduct, and, conversely, failure to meet all the elements of one of the obstruction statutes does not mean conduct is not impeachable. Indeed, with obstruction of justice as with other categories of presidential misconduct, the impeachable offense may lie in subversion of essential norms, rather than a concrete violation of law. Nonetheless, if allegations of obstruction arise in an impeachment controversy, the debate tends to be framed by the technical requirements of the law. Hence, we will begin with a review of the history and particulars of federal obstruction of justice statutes.

FEDERAL CRIMINAL OBSTRUCTION OF JUSTICE

The phrase "obstruction of justice" is a fairly new label in Anglo-American criminal law. No federal obstruction statute per se existed until 1831, and the two main federal obstruction of justice statutes, 18 U.S.C. § 1503 and 18 U.S.C. § 1512, did not take their present form until the twentieth century.[8] Nonetheless, obstruction in its various forms describes types of misconduct that have long been thought both criminal and impeachable. Section 1503 obstruction originates from older prohibitions against bribing or threatening jurors or court officers to affect cases. It complements the specific ban on bribery in 18 U.S.C. § 201. Section 1512 is a much-expanded bar against witness tampering. Threatening or bribing judges and "endeavor[ing] to dissuade a witness from giving evidence" were all well-known offenses in Blackstone's time.[9] An "attempt to influence a jury corruptly to one side by promises, persuasions, entreaties, money, entertainments, and the like" was the crime of "embracery."[10] All such offenses, ancient and modern, fall under the broad rubric of corruption, albeit these particular crimes are aimed at corrupting the judgments of courts.

Section 1503 Obstruction

A violation of 18 U.S.C. § 1503 occurs if a defendant "corruptly ... endeavors to influence, intimidate, or impede any ... officer in or of any court of the United States, or ... *corruptly ... influences, obstructs, or impedes, or endeavors to influence, obstruct, or impede, the due administration of justice.*" The last phrase is the so-called "omnibus clause" and has been construed quite broadly by federal courts.[11] Nonetheless, the statute is subject to several technical limitations.

First, an obstruction charge may only be brought against a defendant who obstructed a "pending judicial proceeding."[12] The term "judicial proceeding" includes cases that have been commenced before judges, and also, critically, grand jury investigations.[13] A judicial proceeding is pending if a grand jury has been empaneled, has been advised of the existence of the investigation at issue, and has issued subpoenas in the matter.[14] In sum, the minimum requirements for a section 1503 case of obstruction of a criminal investigation are that a grand jury was empaneled at the time of the allegedly obstructive behavior and that one or more subpoenas relating to the investigation were issued under that grand jury's authority.

Second, under section 1503, "The action taken by the accused must be with an intent to influence judicial or grand jury proceedings; it is not enough that there be an intent to influence some ancillary proceeding, such as an investigation independent of the court's or grand jury's authority."[15] Even when there is a "pending judicial proceeding" in the form of an ongoing grand jury investigation, the defendant must know that a grand jury investigation – as opposed to a general inquiry by, say, the FBI or the IRS – is occurring.[16] In addition, a defendant must "know that his corrupt actions 'are likely to affect the ... proceeding.'"[17]

Section 1512 Obstruction

Title 18, United States Code, section 1512 has two relevant subsections. A violation of section 1512(b)(3) occurs if a defendant: "corruptly persuades another person ... with intent to ... hinder, delay, or prevent the communication to a law enforcement officer or judge of the United States of information relating to the commission or possible commission of a Federal offense ..." A violation of section 1512(c) occurs if a defendant: "corruptly ... obstructs, influences, or impedes any official proceeding, or attempts to do so ..."

Charging obstruction under section 1512 can eliminate some of the technical difficulties presented by section 1503, notably the requirements that there be a "pending judicial proceeding" at the time of the obstructive behavior, and that the defendant be aware of the existence of such a proceeding and intend to obstruct it. Section 1512(b)(3) contains no limiting reference to any kind of proceeding; it criminalizes attempts to hinder communication to law enforcement officers or judges of information about crime. Moreover, section 1512(c) uses the term "official proceeding" – which is broader than "judicial proceeding" in that it includes proceedings before judges, grand juries, Congress, and federal agencies.[18] Section 1512(f) specifically provides that in section 1512 prosecutions "an official proceeding need not be pending or about to be instituted at the time of the offense." Finally, section 1512(g) specifies that the government does not have to prove that the defendant knew the official proceeding was before a "judge, court, magistrate, grand jury, or government agency." In short, under section 1512(c), all the government must prove is that the defendant corruptly attempted to obstruct, influence, or impede some official proceeding, either actual or impending.[19]

The $64,000 question under all federal obstruction statutes is whether the official could fairly be said to have acted "corruptly."

"Corruptly": the Culpable Mental State for Obstruction of Justice

"Corruptly" is defined in 18 U.S.C. § 1515(b) to mean "acting with an improper purpose, personally or by influencing another, including making a false or misleading statement, or withholding, concealing, altering, or destroying a document or other information."[20] What does it mean to act "with an improper purpose"? Consider two kinds of conduct: (1) acts that are either illegal in themselves or self-evidently wrongful even if not technically illegal; and (2) acts that would be perfectly legal absent a corrupt motive.

Examples of the first category would be lying to a grand jury,[21] forging a court order in a federal civil action,[22] bribing someone to withhold information from a criminal investigation,[23] or requesting that a witness lie to a court or government agent in support of the defendant's theory of the case.[24] In these cases, the defendant not only acted in ways calculated to affect a proceeding, but employed methods so obviously wrong in themselves that the corrupt intention was plain.

The trickier cases are those in which the defendant's acts are of a type not inherently wrongful, but are made criminal by "corrupt" motive. The Supreme Court considered this sort of conduct in *Arthur Andersen LLP* v. *United States*,[25] which involved the conviction of the accounting firm for destroying audit documents that might be sought by government prosecutors. The Supreme Court reversed that conviction because merely making information unavailable to the government, or persuading another to do so, is not necessarily illegal. For example, a lawyer may, entirely properly, advise a client to withhold documents under a legal privilege. Or a spouse may urge a marital partner to invoke a marital testimonial privilege.[26] A corporation sued by the government surely delays, and may frustrate altogether, the government's case by retaining counsel and defending the action. The jury instruction in *Arthur Andersen* was improper because it omitted any requirement that the act of withholding information be dishonest or wrongful. As one lower court put it, the term "corruptly" is important because it requires "that jurors believe that the defendants were conscious of their wrongdoing."[27]

An analogous problem arises when considering the conduct of government officials. Every day government officials decide to delay, decline, or not investigate thousands of legally sustainable civil and criminal claims. Sometimes these are individual exercises of "prosecutorial discretion" in which government officials balance the equities in particular cases. Sometimes they are policy choices such as not pursuing deportation of some classes of undocumented aliens,[28] not prosecuting federally marijuana vendors operating in states that have legalized medical or recreational use of the drug,[29] or declining to seek legally available penalties against corporate law-breakers.[30] The dividing line between legal behavior and criminal obstruction of justice is the mental state requirement that the defendant act "corruptly," by which is meant dishonestly, wrongfully, or immorally.[31]

Corrupt Purpose and Presidential Power

Some have claimed that a president cannot commit obstruction of justice, at least not by ordering the cessation of a federal investigation or firing the officials running it.[32] Note that this claim goes beyond the assertion that the Justice Department cannot (or as a result of current policy will not) prosecute a sitting president to the flat assertion that these statutes cannot be applied to a president in the exercise of his supervisory authority over federal law enforcement. The argument is that because the president is the sole head of the executive branch, the person to whom all federal criminal prosecutors and agents report, and the person charged by the constitution to take care that the laws be faithfully executed, he or she cannot commit a crime by exercising his or her powers in this field.

To be candid, this argument is not merely wrong, but laughably wrong. The constitution and laws of the United States grant authority to all sorts and grades of officials. The grant does not immunize officials from the legal consequences of abusing their powers. A federal judge is constitutionally empowered to render decisions and legal opinions. If she or he rules for one party because that party paid him or her a bribe, we would not say the judge is immune from prosecution because the power she or he exercised was conferred by law. A U.S. Attorney is empowered to initiate and dismiss criminal prosecutions. If he or she dismisses a case against a defendant as part of a secret bargain in which the defendant promises not to divulge incriminating information about the prosecutor, we would hardly wave that aside on the ground that the U.S. Attorney was merely exercising his or her undoubted discretionary authority. In all such cases, the issue is not whether the official performed an act among his or her official powers, but the reason the act was performed. If the reason was corrupt, the act will likely be illegal. If the act involved impeding legal proceedings, the applicable crime may well be obstruction of justice.

This principle applies no less to presidents than anyone else. The tricky bit is that presidents have more discretionary power and a wider scope of authority than any other constitutional officer. Therefore, decisions which might be illegitimate for many constitutional officers are acceptable for a president. For example, a president could – legitimately – conclude that misconduct by a government official or political figure, though technically prosecutable, ought not be prosecuted because doing so would be harmful to the national interest. Assume (however improbably) that President Roosevelt had been told in May 1944 that General George C. Marshall, then Army Chief of Staff, was suspected of embezzling from the Pentagon's petty cash. Marshall was integral to the war effort and to coordinating the upcoming invasion of Europe. Roosevelt would plainly have been within his rights to quash the investigation. Vindication of the law would and should have taken second place to winning the war.[33]

Likewise, even though there is a well-understood norm of presidential non-interference in Justice Department prosecution decisions, the president is the constitutional head of the executive branch and is entitled to wield personally the same discretionary authority enjoyed by his or her prosecutorial subordinates, or at least to order them to exercise that discretion in accordance with his or her wishes.[34] Thus, a president could determine that the equities of a particular case or the appealing personal circumstances of a defendant were such that the interests of justice would best be served by not prosecuting a provable crime. Presidents have generally avoided such personal intervention at the front end of prosecutions, both because they have many other fish to fry and because of the likely political fallout, but the custom of abstention is no more than a custom that a president could, it seems, lawfully ignore in an individual case – as long as the motive for doing so was not "corrupt."

The dividing line between the ordinary exercise of lawful official discretion and criminal obstruction is whether the official exercised his lawful power over the course of legal processes in good faith – which essentially means using one's best judgment to promote the public interest – or instead acted with an "improper purpose." The calculation of whether there was improper purpose unavoidably involves a judgment about whether the official allowed calculations of private interest to distort or supplant entirely his obligation to employ *in the public interest* his lawful power over legal processes. Thus, when a president – from whom federal prosecutorial authority constitutionally flows – intervenes in the course of federal investigative processes, we cannot avoid inquiring into private motives. Only if the president acts for illegitimate reasons, which prominently include protecting him, his family, or close aides from well-founded investigative efforts, can the president be found to have acted corruptly.

Professors Hemel and Posner conclude that a president's exercise of his discretionary and supervisory authority in the realm of law enforcement is entitled to a presumption of regularity, rebuttable by a showing of corrupt motive, which they define as follows:

> *A president commits obstruction of justice when he significantly interferes with an investigation, prosecution, or other law enforcement action to advance narrowly personal, pecuniary, or partisan interests.* He does not, however, commit obstruction when he acts on the basis of a legitimate and good faith conception of his constitutional responsibilities, even if he receives a personal or pecuniary benefit or incidentally advances his party's interests.[35]

One might quibble with details of this formulation, but it seems as close to a good general rule as we are likely to get.[36] Of course, the subject of this book is impeachment and the legal limits of particular crimes are not co-extensive with the impeachment power. Still, when it comes to obstruction of justice, the dividing line between legitimate and illegitimate presidential conduct runs in roughly the same place for both impeachment and criminal court. A corrupt use of otherwise lawful authority is criminal, and if sufficiently serious, is likely to be impeachable.

OBSTRUCTION OF JUSTICE AS SUBVERSION OF THE JUSTICE SYSTEM

The behavior of Donald Trump two years into his presidency presents some established and some novel features to anyone imagining his impeachment for obstruction of justice. On the one hand, he has engaged in many of the same kinds of behavior that were deemed impeachable for Richard Nixon. Nixon tried to get the CIA to block the FBI investigation of the Watergate burglary and then to convince the FBI itself to back off.[37] Mr. Trump sought privately to convince the FBI in the person of Director James Comey not to proceed in its investigation of a high administration official, National Security Advisor Michael Flynn, suspected of having some knowledge of misdeeds by the Trump campaign.[38] Once special counsel Robert Mueller opened his investigation of alleged collusion between the Trump campaign and Russian operatives, Trump exerted constant pressure on the Justice Department and the FBI to halt or hobble it. Among other actions, Trump, like Nixon, has actively sought to block or impede an investigation into campaign misconduct by firing those in charge of it. Trump first fired Director Comey. He later fired Attorney General Jeff Sessions so he could be replaced by a more complaisant Acting Attorney General, Matthew Whitaker, who had publicly explained how the special counsel investigation by Robert Mueller could be crippled.[39] If Mr. Whitaker's successor, William Barr, or the president himself were either to strangle the Mueller investigation slowly or jump straight to an additional round of firings, the analogy to Nixon's Saturday Night Massacre would be plain. Nixon's famous firings were considered by the House Judiciary Committee to constitute important parts of both the obstruction and abuse of power articles of impeachment against Nixon.[40] In addition, Mr. Trump and his allies have conducted a steady public relations and bureaucratic campaign to undermine and discredit the investigation and anyone associated with it.[41]

As this book is written, it is impossible to say how much further President Trump will travel along the path Nixon ignominiously blazed. Nonetheless, a colorable argument can be (and has been) made that Mr. Trump has already committed obstruction of justice in the formal legal sense and ought to be impeached on that ground.[42] The particulars of that argument will not be pursued in any further detail here. Too much remains unknown.

Regardless of what happens to the Mueller investigation in particular, there is a plain case for impeachment of Donald Trump based on presidential obstruction of justice in a larger sense. A better label for this conduct would be subversion of the justice system as a whole. As noted at the outset of this chapter, a pillar of modern American government is a powerful law enforcement establishment committed to neutral enforcement of the law against anyone, regardless of social or economic status, political office, or partisan affiliation. The continued commitment of that establishment to the ideal of neutrality is indispensable to the perpetuation of the rule of law, which is to say, the rule of the constitution itself. Mr. Trump's most serious transgressions lie, not in his frenetic efforts to stop the Mueller investigation in particular, but in his open and unapologetic efforts to transform the Justice Department and the rest of the federal criminal justice apparatus into a political tool.

Mr. Trump has repeatedly sought to warp the Justice Department and its auxiliaries in two ways. The first we have already mentioned. He wants a Justice Department personally loyal to him that will protect him, his family, and his associates from embarrassing investigations.[43] This is distressing enough. Much more distressing have been his repeated calls for the Justice Department to investigate his political enemies,[44] or indeed anyone who simply criticizes him too severely.[45] Among the most disturbing of Mr. Trump's demands has been the endless harping that Hillary Clinton, his defeated opponent in the 2016 election, should not merely be investigated, but jailed. A staple of his political rallies has been the chant, "Lock her up!"[46]

Even Republican stalwarts like former Attorney General Michael Mukasey have observed that launching criminal investigations of defeated presidential candidates is contrary to American norms and akin to the practices of "banana republics."[47] This is profoundly true. An indispensable feature of successful democracies is the peaceful transfer of power from one elected administration to its popularly chosen successor. Such transfers reliably occur only if the loser of an election knows that the sole consequence of losing is a return to private life. But if the predictable consequence of losing is criminal prosecution by the winner, then losing becomes unthinkable and the contestants are tempted to ever more extreme measures to prevent it. Vicious propaganda, overt corruption, strong-arm tactics, ethnic incitement, all can be rationalized. All are soon normalized. Democracy dies. This is the all-too-common story in the developing world. But regression is perfectly possible among mature democracies like our own. Even threatening to criminalize political failure is not something the United States should tolerate in a president.

The fact that the Department of Justice and the FBI have not, so far, yielded to these calls for political investigations of Trump's political enemies does not alter the point.[48] The words of a president, any president, are powerful signals to the federal bureaucracy he or she heads, about the kind of government behavior he or she desires. If the president calls, repeatedly, for conduct that would be subversive of the rule of law and ultimately of democratic government, it would be unreasonable to expect that his or her subordinates will ignore their superior's demands indefinitely, particularly after repeated demonstrations that those who defy the president pay a professional price. As we saw in Chapter 8, the House Judiciary Committee was emphatic in its assertion that Richard Nixon's failure to achieve his illicit objectives "does not make the abuse of power any less serious, or diminish the applicability of the impeachment remedy."[49]

The larger constitutional danger of failing to respond to Trump's attacks on the justice system extends beyond whatever damage he may do during his term of office. A characteristic feature of Mr. Trump's presidency is that he does things openly and unapologetically that, because they are so obviously contrary to established values, no previous president would have done, or if done, would have done in secret. Although President Nixon maintained an "enemies list" and sought to use federal agencies to discredit or punish some of those on it,[50] the list and Nixon's efforts to employ the government against his political foes were secrets, scandalous when exposed. And they formed a material part of the second article of impeachment against Nixon approved by the House Judiciary Committee.[51]

Trump tweets lists of opponents who are supposed to have committed crimes and encourages his supporters to press for politically motivated prosecutions.[52] Which they dutifully do.[53] The result is that presidential conduct universally assumed to be reprehensible in 1974 has become, for a significant chunk of the electorate and some in the political class, normal, even laudable. Unless the defenders of constitutional order impose some penalty for this kind of presidential behavior, it will be employed again, perhaps next time by a president who is not a blustering reality show impresario, but a coldly competent aspiring tyrant. Impeachment on the ground that a president has attempted, however unsuccessfully, to subvert the justice system would be a paradigmatic defensive definitional impeachment of the sort discussed in Chapter 10.

12

Impeachment for Abuse of the Pardon Power

Article 2, section 2 of the constitution grants the president the "Power to grant Reprieves and Pardons for Offences against the United States, except in Cases of Impeachment."[1] The president can pardon any federal crime, but not state ones. The authority reaches only convictions in a court of law, not senatorial verdicts in impeachment cases. It has been suggested that a president could even pardon him- or herself, but this seems highly unlikely as running contrary to the basic common law principle that a person may not be a judge in his or her own case. The pardon power is nearly absolute in the sense that a pardon, once granted, cannot be voided by either the courts or Congress. Some academics have argued that a pardon can be reviewed and reversed by courts either on due process or separation of powers grounds. Those arguments are almost certainly wrong.[2] However, to say that the pardon power is nearly absolute means only that a pardon, once issued, cannot be undone and the person pardoned cannot be unpardoned. That does not mean that the pardoner – the president – is immune from consequences if he misuses his constitutional authority.

This seemingly simple point was resisted by some supporters of President Trump during controversies over his early uses of the pardon power. In effect, they said, "The constitution grants presidents the power to pardon anyone for anything. So no pardon can possibly be an impeachable offense." This is plainly incorrect. As we saw in relation to obstruction of justice, merely because a president is given a power does not mean that any use of it is permissible. The primary reason the Founders wrote a power of impeachment into the constitution was precisely to permit removal of a president who misuses constitutionally granted authority. For example, the constitution makes the president the "commander in chief of the Army and Navy of the United States."[3] That grant does not make the American armed forces the president's personal Praetorian Guard. If a president were to order the armed forces to bomb the headquarters of the opposing political party, or invade an ally that had offended the president personally, or kill prisoners in violation of international law, or refuse to defend the United States against a foreign invasion, or even allow the armed forces to degrade to a point where their ability to defend the United States and its allies was in question, he or she would plainly be impeachable for a misuse of a constitutionally conferred power. The president's pardon power is no different. Misuse of a constitutionally bestowed power is every bit as impeachable as wrongful assumption of a power the constitution does not grant.

It is absolutely clear that the framers of the constitution believed that a president could be impeached for misuse of the pardon power. During the Virginia ratifying convention for the federal constitution, George Mason expressed concern about the breadth of the pardon clause and, indeed, about the very idea of giving pardon power to the president. He said:

> Now, I conceive that the President ought not to have the power of pardoning, because he may frequently pardon crimes which were advised by himself. It may happen, at some future day, that he will establish a monarchy, and destroy the republic. If he has the power of granting pardons before indictment, or conviction, may he not stop inquiry and prevent detection?[4]

James Madison responded:

> There is one security in this case [a misuse of the pardon power by the president] to which gentlemen may not have adverted: if the President be connected, in any suspicious manner, with any person, and there be grounds to believe he will shelter him, the House of Representatives can impeach him; they can remove him if found guilty . . .[5]

In short, Madison said that the remedy for presidential misuse of the pardon power was impeachment. George Nicholas, another delegate to the Virginia convention, made a similar observation, suggesting that the American constitution was superior to British arrangements because the president was subject to impeachment for preemptive pardons of political allies.[6] Alexander Hamilton wrote in *Federalist No. 69* that if a president tried to use the pardon power to protect his associates from prosecution for treason, the president himself could on that ground be impeached.[7]

These founding era statements are most obviously applicable to any effort by a president to pardon political or business associates or family members under criminal investigation by the Justice Department. Use of the pardon power either to shield a president personally from liability or to shield him from the political repercussions of criminal prosecutions of his intimates or supporters is indisputably an impeachable offense. Even offering, or hinting at the availability of, a pardon for a presidential associate in order to dissuade the associate from cooperation with authorities is assuredly impeachable. This was the essence of the ninth specification of the first article of impeachment against Richard Nixon, which was based on evidence that Nixon conveyed promises or suggestions of the possibility of executive clemency to Howard Hunt, John Mitchell, Jeb Magruder, and John Dean.[8] In effect, pardons of this type are a means of obstructing justice in violation of the president's general constitutional obligation to "take care that the laws be faithfully executed"⁹ and his or her oath "to preserve, protect, and defend the Constitution."¹⁰

As with obstruction of justice, whether a pardon or the promise of a pardon will be impeachable will necessarily turn on motive. In addition to pardons proffered to obstruct justice, a pardon issued in return for money or as part of any other corrupt bargain would be impeachable. A plausible example of this kind of impeachable pardon was President Clinton's pardon of Marc Rich, an indicted, fugitive swindler, on the last day of his presidency.¹¹ The pardon was issued over the strong objections of the U.S. Attorney's Office that indicted Rich and the U.S. Pardon Attorney. Moreover, Rich had arranged for very large contributions to be made to the Democratic Party and the Clintons in particular in the months and years before the pardon was issued. These included $450,000 to the Clinton Library and $10,000 to the Clinton legal defense fund. There was no plausible case for the pardon, either on legal or humanitarian grounds. Thus, the pardon was both objectively unjustifiable and arguably overtly corrupt. It was the sordid capstone to a presidency that, however politically adroit, was irremediably stained by Bill Clinton's degraded personal morals.¹² There was some talk of impeaching Clinton a second time in order to impose the penalty of permanent disqualification from federal office, but the effort understandably never gained much traction.¹³

The class of impeachable pardons may extend beyond those intended to obstruct justice and those awarded for corrupt personal gain to pardons extended to gain partisan political advantage. Alexander Hamilton suggested in *Federalist 74* that the presidential pardon power had a twofold purpose: to provide a means of tempering with executive clemency the sometimes harsh results of rigid application of the law; and as a tool of statecraft.¹⁴ Hamilton's example of the second purpose was the use of a well-timed pardon to potential rebels or insurrectionaries to prevent open conflict. Over the succeeding centuries, multiple presidents have employed pardons and amnesties for reasons of state, often after hostilities to reconcile a divided country or region. Notable illustrations include George Washington's pardons of participants in the Whiskey Rebellion; Madison's amnesties to deserters in the War of 1812; Andrew Johnson's pardons of Confederates after the Civil War (though, as we have seen, there is a less benign view of these pardons¹⁵); and the post-Vietnam War pardons of draft law offenders by presidents Ford and Carter.¹⁶

Neither the mercy nor statecraft rationale for pardons can be extended to the issuance of pardons for partisan political ends. Of course, one must tread carefully here because one person's exercise of mercy or statecraft is another one's partisan political maneuver. Thomas Jefferson pardoned violators of the Alien and Sedition Acts because he thought that the Act was probably unconstitutional and certainly contrary to American principles.¹⁷ But Jefferson had opposed the Acts in the first place and the pardons pleased his political supporters. Barack Obama pardoned or commuted the sentences of hundreds of drug law violators.¹⁸ For many observers, this was a long-overdue and even insufficient reaction to over-criminalization of narcotics offenses. For Obama's harsher critics, it could be portrayed as a pander to his electoral coalition.

Likewise, there is plainly some constitutional room for pure whimsicality in presidential judgment about what offenses deserve executive clemency. Nonetheless, a pattern of pardons issued purely for whimsical or self-aggrandizing purposes would be cause for concern. One could argue that such a pattern has begun to emerge with President Trump – pardons issued almost exclusively (1) to Trump political allies or fellow travelers, (2) to friends or friends of friends, or (3) for the purpose of sending political messages. Trump's pardon of conservative provocateur Dinesh D'Souza[19] and former Arizona sheriff Joe Arpaio[20] plainly fall in the ally and fellow traveler box. In the second category is the pardon of Scooter Libby whose case seems to have been brought to Trump's attention by Victoria Toensing, who with her husband and law partner Joe diGenova is an ardent public defender of Trump and was briefly set to represent him.[21] In the third category is the pardon of Kristian Mark Saucier. Saucier was a sailor convicted of the unauthorized retention of defense information and Trump explicitly compared his treatment to the supposed failure of the Justice Department to prosecute a top Clinton aide.[22] Some have intimated that the Libby pardon also falls in the signaling category inasmuch as Libby was convicted of the kind of crimes, perjury and obstruction of justice, that figure so heavily in the ongoing Mueller investigation.[23]

The common feature of all these pardons is that none was issued following the ordinary Department of Justice and White House review processes created to avoid the actuality or appearance of presidential arbitrariness or favoritism.[24] Likewise, none of them was accompanied by any principled explanation of why the defendant merited an exercise of clemency. All this having been said, impeachment on the ground of merely capricious misuse of the pardon power with hints of self-aggrandizement is in the highest degree unlikely. To be plausible, an impeachment based on pardons alone would have to rest on strong evidence of indisputably improper motives, most likely relating to personal or political self-protection, shielding of corrupt family or associates, or pecuniary corruption. More probable would be a situation like that of President Nixon in which a proposed use of the pardon authority was part of a larger pattern of impeachable behavior.

13

Impeachment for Lying

Lack of candor has been the subject of multiple American impeachments. Four federal judges and President Clinton have been impeached for perjury or official false statements. The House Judiciary Committee approved articles of impeachment against President Nixon on those grounds. The impeachment cases against both Clinton and Nixon were based in part on suborning perjury by others.[1] All the judges and President Nixon were either convicted by the Senate or resigned in the shadow of the impeachment. Accordingly, this type of behavior deserves careful treatment in any modern impeachment discussion. Impeachment for presidential lies is a complex issue. We will consider three categories: (1) criminally indictable falsehoods; (2) unindictable official falsehoods; and (3) chronic or pervasive public falsehoods. In my view, falsehoods in all three categories may be impeachable, particularly if they are part of a larger pattern of undermining constitutional norms.

INDICTABLE FALSEHOODS

Federal law makes a great many kinds of lies indictable felonies. The most well-known category is perjury – knowingly telling a falsehood under oath – before a court, grand jury,[2] or other official tribunal.[3] But it is also a felony to lie to virtually any federal agency as long as the subject matter of the lie is within the "jurisdiction of the executive, legislative, or judicial branch of the Government of the United States."[4] So, for example, if a president were to submit to an interview by the FBI in an investigation of foreign meddling in an American election and were to tell a lie about a matter material to the investigation, that lie would be a felony, regardless of whether the statement was under oath. Similarly, all sorts of unsworn lies told (or written) in commercial settings can be felonies. All federal fraud statutes have as one element a false or fraudulent pretense, representation, or promise.[5]

Many of these felonious lies are proper grounds for impeachment. Judges Alcee Hastings and Walter Nixon were impeached for lying in a federal trial and before a federal grand jury, respectively, both instances of indictable perjury even though their articles of impeachment did not specify violation of a particular federal statute.[6] In the case of a president, it seems plain that lying in the course of a federal investigation into, for example, foreign manipulation of a U.S. election, whether under oath to a grand jury or in an unsworn statement to the FBI, would qualify as an impeachable offense. Such an indictable falsehood would be criminal, consequential, integral to the integrity of the presidential office, and thus squarely in the zone the Founders would have considered impeachable.

But, as discussed at length in relation to President Clinton, not all indictable lies are necessarily impeachable offenses. Not even lies told in the most solemn, legally consequential setting will always be impeachable. The House of Representatives approved an article of impeachment charging that Mr. Clinton committed perjury in front of a grand jury by lying about his sexual relationship with Monica Lewinsky (and about previous allegedly perjurious testimony on the same subject in a civil lawsuit brought by Paula Jones). But the Senate acquitted him of that charge.[7] The consensus view of Clinton's case is that: (a) perjury certainly can be an impeachable offense; (b) Clinton surely lied under oath and pretty certainly committed the crime of perjury; but (c) a majority of senators probably concluded that the peculiar circumstances of his case – lying about a private sexual affair in legal proceedings instituted as an elaborate political trap – made this perjury unworthy of the drastic, politically destabilizing, remedy of removal of a president from office. In short, the Clinton acquittal stands for the proposition that, to merit impeachment and removal, felonious lying will probably have to relate not to purely private acts of immorality, but to matters that either have a solid connection to a president's official function or are efforts to conceal matters that are of grave moral or political consequence in their own right.

Judges Hastings and Nixon lied under oath about their own participation in other crimes of corruption in office, which were both consequential and intimately connected with the judicial office. Presidential lies of a similar sort would be impeachable. Similarly, lying under oath to protect a member of one's family or a political associate from prosecution for a serious crime would, in my view, be impeachable.[8] The first of the articles of impeachment for President Nixon rested in part on this ground – Nixon's false statements to law enforcement had the ultimate purpose of protecting himself, but in many instances their immediate objective was to protect Nixon's aides from criminal liability.[9] A president's obligation to ensure that the laws be faithfully executed bars him or her from lying to protect favored connections from the law's strictures.

OFFICIAL LIES TO THE COURTS AND CONGRESS

The president is the head of one of the three co-equal branches of the federal government, the other two must on many occasions rely on the president's candor to perform their own functions properly. Official falsehoods communicated to the courts will almost invariably be covered by the criminal perjury and false statements statutes, and can be analyzed accordingly. It can be a crime to lie to Congress, even when not under oath,[10] but, except in the case of an actual congressional impeachment investigation, presidents are unlikely to find themselves in the special circumstances required for such criminal liability. The more difficult question is whether non-criminal presidential lies in official communications to Congress might be impeachable.

James Iredell, one of the first Supreme Court justices, speaking of the impeachment clauses during the North Carolina debates about ratifying the constitution, said that, "The President must certainly be punishable for giving false information to the Senate."[11] Although he was speaking of the particular situation in which a president was seeking senatorial approval of treaties or other foreign projects, the general principle he espoused was that the legislature as a coordinate branch of government is entitled to rely on a president's honesty – and can impeach him if he willfully misinforms them on important matters.

There is one historical example of an attempt to impeach a president for lying to congress. Article 5 of the proposed articles of impeachment of Richard Nixon charged concealment of the bombing of Cambodia through the creation of false military documents.[12] The House Judiciary Committee did not approve this article, although as I wrote some years ago, its decision not to do so "probably resulted from a disinclination to inject the explosive politics of the Vietnam War into a case where ample ground for impeachment already existed, rather than a rejection of the principle that the Chief Executive may not intentionally deceive Congress in matters that relate to the legislature's own constitutional duties."[13] It would be entirely consistent with the language and purpose of the impeachment clauses to impeach a president for telling Congress material falsehoods on subjects that could affect legislative action. Falsehoods of this sort could include both personal statements of the president or, as in the case of President Nixon, the submission to Congress of agency testimony or reports the president knew to contain material untruths.

That said, precisely defining the types of presidential statements to the legislature that could plausibly be deemed impeachable is difficult.

Lies to Congress by the President in a Formal, Official Communication

The easiest case would arise if a president were to lie when speaking formally to Congress or one of its committees in person or in writing in an effort to obtain a congressional decision on a matter where congressional action depended on the truth of the president's statement. This is the case that Iredell and, two centuries later, the Nixon-era Judiciary Committee had in mind.

Another historical example of lies of this kind that *might* plausibly have been characterized as an impeachable offense would be the misstatements and omissions by President Johnson and Secretary of Defense Robert McNamara about encounters between U.S. and North Vietnamese naval vessels on August 2–4, 1964, that led to the passage of the Gulf of Tonkin Resolution and, in turn, to deepening U.S. involvement in the Vietnam War.[14]

To cut a long story short, in 1964, U.S. naval vessels were operating in the Gulf of Tonkin in support of South Vietnamese military operations against North Vietnamese military installations. On August 2, three North Vietnamese gunboats responded to one such South Vietnamese operation by attacking a supporting U.S. destroyer, the USS *Maddox*. The *Maddox*, in concert with U.S. aircraft, then sunk or damaged all three. On the night of August 4, the *Maddox* thought it was being attacked again, and responded by firing profusely at a variety of unidentified targets. There were strong indications even at the time that the August 4 "attack" was actually an overreaction to misinterpreted sonar data and that the U.S. Navy was shooting at empty ocean. In later years, this suspicion hardened to a virtual certainty.

Nonetheless, Secretary of Defense McNamara and President Johnson publicly characterized the events of August 2–4 as two unprovoked attacks on blameless U.S. naval vessels. In addition to over-hyping the probably non-existent August 4 "attack," they carefully concealed the fact that the U.S. ships came into the line of fire because they were supporting South Vietnamese assaults on the North. President Johnson sought from Congress, and got, the famous "Gulf of Tonkin Resolution," which he used as legal justification for taking the United States ever deeper into what became the Vietnam War. No less an authority than former Trump National Security Advisor H. R. McMaster concluded that Johnson and McNamara "deceived the American people and Congress" about the Gulf of Tonkin incident.[15]

The written message LBJ sent to Congress on August 5, 1964[16] might be classed as a potentially impeachable presidential falsehood. Similar falsehoods in a personal address like the annual State of the Union message might also be impeachable. There could be no doubt of the official character of either form of communication. In the first, the president is expressly asking for congressional action. In the second, the president's obligation to provide a message to Congress regarding the state of the union is written into Article 2, section 3 of the constitution.[17]

Of course, as the modern practice of "fact-checking" every presidential address has made plain, every president spins facts to his advantage at least somewhat on such occasions. It would be absurd to impeach a president for engaging in that well-understood political habit. Nonetheless, there must be some limit on presidential prevarication in official settings. It is one thing for a president to place politically advantageous interpretations on ambiguous facts, or even to cherry-pick facts a bit to support a political argument. It is quite another for a president to consciously misrepresent facts plainly germane to a congressional choice, or to consciously omit facts that, if revealed, might cause Congress to act differently.

Lies to Congress by Administration Agencies or Officials with the President's Knowledge

A second type of potentially impeachable presidential lie to Congress occurred when the Nixon administration submitted false reports about the Cambodian bombing to Congress. There the president did not personally speak, but, at least so it was alleged, he caused or authorized his subordinates to deceive Congress on his behalf.[18] Again, every administration is going to try to bend the arc of truth a bit in the direction of its ideological or policy preferences, but even in this age of relativism there must be some boundary beyond which a president cannot go when authorizing official communications to a coordinate branch of the U.S. government.

This sort of executive branch misrepresentation could become relevant to the current or future administrations. For example, by law, the executive branch must, every four years, prepare and publish a "National Climate Assessment," which is expressly designed to set out the best available science to guide Congress, executive branch regulators, and state and local governments in making decisions about how to respond to the changing global climate.[19] In 2017, government scientists and career professionals were sufficiently concerned about whether the Trump administration might either alter or suppress its findings that a draft was leaked to the press.[20] The availability of the draft may have forestalled significant meddling with the report's data or basic conclusions, but this is only one of many legally mandated reports and data compilations that, in any administration, might be subject to politically motivated censorship.

The question, for which I confess I have no easy answer, is whether there is a type and degree of suppression or distortion of reports to Congress that would properly amount to an impeachable offense. To constitute an impeachable offense, such a report would certainly have to satisfy at least three requirements: (1) it would concern a matter of genuine national significance upon which Congress is required or reasonably expected to act; (2) it would contain a significant number and degree of provably false assertions of fact; and (3) the president could be proven to have known about the report and its contents and to have been aware of its essential falsity.

CHRONIC OR PERVASIVE PRESIDENTIAL FALSEHOODS

A third category of potentially impeachable presidential falsehoods consists of lies that are neither indictable nor, strictly speaking, official, but that are so frequent as to amount to a pattern of chronic or pervasive falsehood. This category is both the easiest and hardest for those who would most like to see Mr. Trump impeached. On the one hand, whether one approves or disapproves of Mr. Trump's policies, the undeniable fact is that he lies all the time. Ceaselessly. Unrepentantly. About pretty much everything. Big things. Little things. Public matters and private ones. Both the *New York Times*[21] and the *Washington Post*[22] have published lengthy lists of

Mr. Trump's falsehoods, with the *Post* counting 6,420 false or misleading claims in less than two years in office. One can fairly quibble with the details of some of these lists, but Mr. Trump himself has largely given up denying that he is a serial, but strategic, liar.[23] Thus, proof of the factual basis for impeachment on this ground would seem easy (though as discussed below, it may prove harder than it appears).

On the other hand, the proposition that a president can be impeached, not for one specific criminal or official lie, but for *being a liar*, is not only novel, but would obviously be subject to abuse unless well-grounded in constitutional theory and carefully limited in scope. As we know, the phrase "Treason, Bribery, or other high Crimes and Misdemeanors" was introduced into the constitution to effect a moderate expansion of the acceptable class of impeachable conduct and to ensure that Congress, like Parliament, would employ a case-by-case, common law approach to defining impeachable behavior. Open-ended though the term is, the framers and ratifiers seem to have interpreted it to mean that a president should not be impeached for honest mistakes of policy, or, except in rare cases of great constitutional moment, for pursuing in good faith courses with which a majority of the legislature heartily disagreed. For example, Edmund Randolph observed at the Virginia ratifying convention that a man should not be impeached "for an opinion."[24]

That said, the framers would have distinguished between an opinion honestly held, and a knowing falsehood – a lie. Madison believed impeachment necessary because he "thought it indispensable that some provision should be made for defending the community against the incapacity, negligence, or *perfidy* of the chief magistrate."[25] By "perfidy," Madison no doubt meant to focus primarily on the larger betrayals of the nation that generally fall under the headings of treason or corruption. Still, his use of the term "perfidy" is suggestive because concern with the fundamental honesty of the president resonates with the statements and values of other founders. Theirs was a generation that placed great stock in the virtue of public men. In the *Federalist* 57, Madison maintained that, "The aim of every political constitution is or ought to be first to obtain for rulers men who possess most wisdom to discern and most virtue to pursue the common good of the society, and in the next place to take the most effectual precautions for keeping them virtuous whilst they continue to hold their public trust."[26] The term virtue conveyed a great many different concepts to the enlightened eighteenth-century mind and was scarcely limited to simple candor.[27] But the power of discernment, that is, the capacity for discovering truth, and the fortitude to convey it were certainly among the qualities of virtuous public personages – the kind of persons without whom, in Madison's mind, republican government could not flourish.

Neither Madison nor any of the other Founders were naive, of course, and as practical politicians would have had no foolish expectation that every word from an elected official's mouth would be 100 percent true. Still, one can have confidence that they would view *habitual* public dishonesty on subjects relating to the exercise of presidential power as disqualifying in a candidate and impeachable in an incumbent. As Edmund Randolph said of the president, if "he be honest, he will do what is right, if dishonest, the representatives of the people will have the power of impeaching him."[28] The evil against which the impeachment remedy was primarily aimed was presidential conduct that undermines the constitutional order. If, therefore, a pathologically dishonest chief executive undermines constitutional order, then impeachment on that ground would be consistent with the views of the founding generation.

The course of the Clinton impeachment and the evidence favoring the impeachability of lies to Congress strongly imply that a lie – or pattern of lying – is most likely to be considered impeachable if the subject is public matters and if the falsehood is uttered in connection with the president's official duties for the purpose of affecting decisions by government actors. This inference is also consistent with Hamilton's characterization of impeachable offenses as political in character.

Mr. Trump's habitual prevarication presents an unprecedented problem. The issue is not how to view one or a related series of falsehoods about one particular topic, but that Mr. Trump lies constantly about virtually all topics. Some of his untruths relate directly to particular public policy issues or proposals. Examples include claims made in connection with the debate over the future of the Affordable Care Act (ACA) that "millions of people" lost insurance coverage under the ACA and that all or portions of certain states had no insurance carrier for the ACA exchanges.[29] Likewise, he has falsely claimed that 3 million illegal aliens voted in the last election[30] and that the Obama administration tapped his telephone lines in Trump Tower.[31] And in the midst of growing tensions with North Korea, he claimed he was sending an "armada" toward Korea when in fact the carrier group in question was steaming in the opposite direction.[32] But many of his lies are about subjects – the size of his inaugural crowd or whether the head of the Boy Scouts[33] or the president of Mexico[34] called him – that in themselves are inconsequential. The question is whether numerous unrelated falsehoods, none of which would be impeachable standing alone, can be aggregated into an offense meriting removal from office.

For an ordinary president, a particular lie may be intended to affect a decision by Congress, or a court, or an agency, or a foreign government, or the electorate itself. But, for an ordinary president, what makes the lie both effective and culpable is the background assumption that presidents customarily tell the truth on important matters, and particularly in official communications. Only thus can the lie truly deceive. But what if the president lies constantly, demonstrably, and unashamedly, on such a broad array of topics that no sensible person – including his nominal political allies – accepts anything he says as true without independent corroboration? In one sense, the lies of a known chronic liar may be less damaging in a particular case precisely because the liar is less likely to be believed. But if the chronic liar is the president, his mendacity arguably undermines the operation of the government as a whole.

Chronic lying may be a political offense in the Hamiltonian sense insofar as it cripples the liar in the performance of his presidential duties. During the Clinton impeachment, it was often argued that the American president, who serves as both the operational head of government and the ceremonial and symbolic head of state, cannot function without a minimum of moral authority which is forfeit once he is proven to be a perjurer. Nonetheless, the apparent lesson of the Clinton affair is that lies about a single private matter, even if perjurious, are not enough for impeachment. The question presented by Mr. Trump is whether persistent mendacity on multiple subjects of public consequence so undermines a president's authority that lying becomes sufficient for impeachment without an accompanying criminal violation.

One can fairly conclude that the answer is yes by considering that chronic presidential lies do not merely render the president himself ineffectual, but also damage every other branch and function of American government. If the president's subordinates in the executive branch cannot believe their boss, they will be hampered both in understanding what the president's policies are and in executing them. If the legislature cannot believe what the president says, it can neither legislate with confidence that it is acting based on accurate information nor be confident that its directives will be honestly executed once enacted. If the judiciary becomes convinced that the president cannot be trusted, it will be less disposed to accept government lawyers' explanations of executive actions and more inclined to meddle in matters in which it has traditionally deferred to executive branch discretion. If foreign governments come to believe that the American president is a liar, the confidence in the fundamental reliability of the United States that is the true foundation of a sound and effective foreign policy will begin to unravel. If the American people conclude that the president is a congenital liar, their cynicism about government – already sadly advanced – will increase, making the successful operation of participatory democracy even more doubtful.

In sum, pervasive lying *by a president* tends to undermine the entire constitutional order. Accordingly, I have little hesitation in concluding that, *in theory*, pervasive presidential lies can properly constitute an impeachable offense. That said, the practical and political obstacles to impeaching a president for his mendacity alone are formidable.

First, one would have to decide which falsehoods and prevarications should count. For example, should we count only statements made after a president's inauguration? Or, since the point is to prove a pattern of lying, should statements made prior to assumption of office, for example, during the presidential campaign, be considered?

Likewise, one would have to decide how to define the statements includable in the pattern of falsehood. Should we include only statements that would qualify as perjury if made under oath – that is, statements of present or past fact that are wholly false and known by the speaker to be so when made? Or could notable exaggerations be included?

What would be the required mental state? Would one have to show that the president was consciously aware of the absolute falsity of a statement when made? Or would it be sufficient to show that the president made a statement without making any effort to determine its truth? In short, could a president be impeached for a pattern of reckless disregard for the truth?

Since the essence of the offense would be a pattern of lies, how many lies of what type would be required to make a pattern? How consequential would any particular statement have to be to be included in the pattern? Could one include, for example, a lie about whether the president received a phone call from the head of the Boy Scouts about the reception of his speech to the Boy Scout Jamboree? Or would a lie have to be about a subject directly related to an issue of public policy? If the latter, how consequential would the statement have to be?

Moreover, sometimes presidents must lie for the public good. To be entirely candid about, say, pending military operations might be unforgivable, not laudable. How would one distinguish between necessary and culpable lies?

Second, given that all presidents lie at least sometimes, there would have to be some comparative standard or every president would be impeachable for dishonesty. How would one set such a comparative standard?

Third, the proof problems would be formidable and the process of collecting evidence would necessarily involve significant intrusions into the ordinary operations of the White House. Proving that the president either knew that a particular statement was untrue or was reckless about its falsity would require discovery of all his own personal investigations into the matter and all the information and advice provided to him on the subject. Recall the extraordinarily protracted process of investigating the single question of whether President Clinton lied about sex with Monica Lewinsky and multiply that by the dozens of alleged falsehoods that would be necessary to establish a pattern of presidential lying.

Finally, any impeachment is a fool's errand unless the overwhelming majority of the public – including a solid plurality of a president's own political party – can be convinced that the allegedly impeachable offense occurred *and* is a legitimate basis for removing a president. Mr. Trump occupies the White House today as both beneficiary and inciter of a culture of distrust of "establishment" institutions and disbelief in the very existence of objective truth. To a distressing degree, many, perhaps most, people who are at all politically aware tend to receive their information from sources broadly congenial to their own settled views and tend to disbelieve information from sources they associate with "the other side." There are few, if any, widely recognized neutral arbiters of public fact.

This manifests itself directly in the electorate's views of Mr. Trump's honesty. In multiple polls taken in 2017 and 2018, only about 32–37 percent of all respondents said Mr. Trump is honest.[35] But the partisan breakdown of this view is stark. Only 5–6 percent of Democrats found him honest. Among independents, 27–35 percent did so. But on September 27, 2017, after nine months of his presidency, 79 percent of Republicans said they viewed Mr. Trump as honest, and a year later in September 2018, 72 percent of Republicans still agreed. Moreover, so cynical have we become about all elected officials past and present, that a significant fraction of the population do not believe that Mr. Trump is materially more or less honest than his predecessors. Leaving to one side the sociological and psychological explanations for these astounding figures, they mean that any effort to impeach Mr. Trump for dishonesty alone would inevitably be viewed by many, perhaps most, Republican voters as an unsubstantiated, purely partisan endeavor. That, in turn, means that Republican legislators – however dishonest they personally believe Mr. Trump to be – would cooperate with such an effort only at the peril of losing their offices.

In the end, although I am convinced that impeachment exclusively on the ground of pervasive dishonesty would be entirely constitutional, I am unconvinced that any such project is politically feasible, or perhaps even desirable. That said, lack of presidential candor might prove to be a significant feature of other impeachable offenses, and, if more concrete grounds for impeachment should ever be advanced by the House, an additional, carefully considered and crafted, count for pervasive dishonesty should at least be explored.

14

Impeachment for Corruption: Schemes of Peculation, the Emoluments Clauses, and the Avaricious President

One invariable theme in eight centuries of Anglo-American impeachment practice has been corruption. Beginning with the first true impeachments, those of lords Latimer and Neville in 1376[1] and the Earl of Suffolk in 1386,[2] through the numerous impeachments of the Stuart era,[3] and right down to the failed effort to impeach Warren Hastings in the 1780s, virtually every British impeachment alleged corruption in some form, even when the true ground of parliamentary ire was disagreements over policy. The same pattern often obtained in early American impeachments. The impeachment of Judge William Moore in Benjamin Franklin's colonial Pennsylvania was motivated by disagreements between the colony's proprietary and anti-proprietary parties, but the charges against Moore included a grab-bag of allegations such as taking double fees and failing to pay debts.[4] The famous 1774 impeachment of Massachusetts Chief Justice Oliver was a purely political move by colonists determined to ensure local control of their judiciary, but even there the charge that Oliver improperly agreed to take wages offered by the crown was ludicrously framed as acceptance of a "continual bribe."[5] Almost all of the state impeachments between 1776 and 1788 were for ordinary corruption – bribery, extortion, and misuse of public funds.[6]

It is therefore unsurprising that, at the Constitutional Convention of 1787, the one ground of presidential impeachment on which everyone agreed was corruption. Among the formulations provisionally approved by the convention before it arrived at the final language were "treason, bribery, or corruption" and then "treason or bribery."[7] And, as we know, the addition of "high Crimes and Misdemeanors" incorporated by implication the large body of British and early American corruption precedents. Moreover, the framers repeatedly mentioned corruption as being, next to overt treason, the most necessary ground for presidential impeachment.[8]

That said, corruption is a term of many meanings.[9] The narrowest is simple bribery in which a government officer accepts or demands things of value in return for the performance (or non-performance) of official duties.[10] A great many American judicial impeachments, as well as the impeachment of Secretary of War Belknap, were based on elementary corruption of this kind. In today's money-saturated political culture, identifying impeachably corrupt behavior is a good deal harder than it would have been in the founding era. Until after the Civil War, presidents, at least, did not "campaign" at all (either for themselves or their parties), but let their surrogates do the talking.[11] There was no such thing as "paid media," at least beyond fliers, handbills, pamphlets, buttons, banners, and silly hats – and the cost of that sort of thing was modest even by the standards of the time.[12] That world is long dead. The massive cost of modern, media-driven political campaigns and the general abandonment of the idea of public financing of that cost in favor of elections financed through private contributions has meant that national candidates must raise truly vast sums of money. Judicial acceptance of this system has meant that the transfer of millions of dollars to politicians by individuals and corporations interested in influencing government decisions is treated, not as the transparent bribery that, at least in ordinary language, it is, but instead as an inescapable incident of democratic politics. Therefore, while accepting money to assist one's political operation might, in an extraordinary case involving either a provable *quid pro quo* or truly egregious violations of campaign finance laws, constitute an impeachable offense, such a circumstance would be surpassingly rare.

The easier case of impeachable corruption given modern political assumptions would be one where a president (or a member of his or her family with the president's knowledge) received money, things of value, services, or valuable privileges for *personal* benefit or enjoyment. Situations of this sort could include direct *quid pro quo* arrangements in which the president demands or agrees to accept payment in return for performance of or abstention from some particular official action, or, having performed or abstained from an official action, knowingly accepts a reward for doing so.[13] Alternatively, and of particular relevance at the time of this writing, a president might accept valuable benefits beyond his governmental compensation that are not provably connected to any *quid pro quo* arrangement, but that nonetheless create concern about whether the bestowal of the benefit will distort the president's official judgment in favor of its giver.

THE EMOLUMENTS CLAUSES

A desire to forestall both kinds of behavior was the reason the framers wrote the two emoluments clauses into the constitution. Article 1, section 9, the so-called "foreign emoluments clause," states that, "no Person holding any Office of Profit or Trust under [the United States], shall, without the Consent of the Congress, accept of any present, Emolument, Office, or Title, of any kind whatever, from any King, Prince, or foreign State." Article 2, section 7, the "domestic emoluments clause," declares that: "The President shall, at stated Times, receive for his Services, a Compensation, which shall neither be encreased [sic] nor diminished during the Period for which he shall have been elected, and he shall not receive within that Period any other Emolument from the United States, or any of them."

These two clauses, particularly when read together with the provisions in Articles 1 and 3 for the salaries of members of Congress and judges, express a particular understanding about the compensation, probity, and allegiance of federal officials. First, by mandating that federal officers be salaried, the constitution rejects any idea that public service is a volunteer commitment, affordable only by the wealthy. In addition to the provision for presidential salary, Article 1, section 6, provides that, "The Senators and Representatives shall receive a Compensation for their Services, to be ascertained by Law, and paid out of the Treasury of the United States." Article 2, section 1, assures judges that they "shall, at stated Times, receive for their Services, a Compensation, which shall not be diminished during their Continuance in Office." In short, public officials are to be paid out of the public purse salaries ample for their subsistence. Second, the prohibitions on increase or decrease of presidential salary during a single term, and on decrease of judicial salary ever, were designed to ensure that Congress could not try to control the executive or judicial branch through financial rewards or punishments.

The constitutional compensation model rejects the practice long prevalent in Great Britain in which officials were paid, not with regular salaries, but by grants of land, commercial monopolies, or rights to streams of revenue from taxes, fees, or the Church.[14] The crown employed this approach in large part because it was easier to secure public servants by granting them privileges to eat what they could kill than to secure a steady national revenue stream and pay officials regular salaries from it. However, the conflict between fiscal self-interest and the public good was ever-present. The corruption engendered by the British model often provided either a reason or an excuse for British impeachments.

In order to eliminate the conflicts created for government officials by gifts or outside revenue streams, the framers also barred federal officers from receiving certain benefits or income in addition to their salaries. No federal employee "holding any Office of Profit or Trust under" the United States may accept "any present, Emolument, Office, or Title, of any kind whatever, from any King, Prince, or foreign State." Presidents are barred from getting any "emolument" in addition to salary from either the federal government or any state government. The obvious point of the foreign emoluments clause was to insulate all American officeholders from the temptation to betray their country to another nation. The dual purpose of the special bar on domestic *presidential* emoluments was, first, to prevent congressional factions or executive departments from buying the president's special affection, and, second, to ensure that the president was not bribed by states into favoring one state or region over the interests of the nation. Note that the prohibition on emoluments is not conditional on any corrupt bargain by the public official. Likewise, emoluments are barred regardless of whether the official takes or refrains from any act whatever. The framers understood that, even for the most virtuous, receipt of favors creates a predisposition to do favors in return. Once that disposition exists, it is only a tiny step to corrupt action.

It is a curious fact that our forefathers understood something about human nature that our modern Supreme Court apparently does not. Consider, for example, the case of Virginia Governor Robert McDonnell. He was convicted in federal court of Hobbs Act bribery based on evidence that he and his wife had received some $175,000 in personal gifts from the CEO of a nutritional supplement company who wanted to enlist the governor's assistance in: (a) convincing the University of Virginia to perform scientific studies on a new product; (b) influencing a state agency to provide grant money for such studies; and (c) convincing the health insurance provider for state employees to include one of the company's products as a covered drug. The evidence showed that McDonnell did a great many things – making phone calls, hosting events, arranging meetings – to signal to other state actors that he wanted them to assist his benefactor. They plainly understood they were being pressured, even though they never yielded to that pressure. But McDonnell never gave a direct order; all the signaling was indirect. The Supreme Court reversed the conviction, not because McDonnell had not taken the gifts and not because he offered no help in return, but because the court concluded that his help did not include performing an "official act."[15]

The Supreme Court's opinion in *McDonnell* has been roundly criticized, and properly so, because, as one observer put it, the court "ultimately accepts that money should be able to buy access and influence" with public officials.[16] However, the point for our purposes is not whether the Supreme Court was right or wrong on the narrow statutory question presented, but that, had Governor McDonnell been a federal executive branch official, Congress would have been entirely within its rights to impeach him despite the reversal of his conviction.

Taken as a package, the emoluments clauses represent an important facet of what one scholar has identified as a general constitutional anti-corruption principle.[17] As discussed in the section on presidential falsehoods in Chapter 13, the founding generation was simultaneously convinced of the necessity of virtue in public characters and the probability of public corruption absent checking mechanisms.[18] The emoluments clauses prescribe particular aspects of a norm of republican virtue. The impeachment power is the enforcement mechanism for that norm. Congress has the authority to decide that accepting money and favors from persons or nations who have a natural desire to ingratiate themselves with an American president is not only a technical violation of the emoluments clauses, but constitutes corruption of a type embraced by the phrase "high Crimes and Misdemeanors."

At the Philadelphia Convention, Gouverneur Morris several times spoke of the need for impeachment in the case of a president in the pay of a foreign power.[19] At the Virginia ratifying convention, Edmund Randolph said explicitly that, "There is another provision against the danger … of the President receiving emoluments from foreign powers. If discovered, he may be impeached."[20]

The emoluments clauses, particularly the foreign one, have been excavated from desuetude by the presidency of Donald Trump. The most troubling possibility is that

President Trump might have received, while in office, direct payments or financial benefits such as loans, loan forgiveness, or loan extensions from foreign governments, such as Russia, or their private agents. Such direct payments or benefits would seemingly count as emoluments whether or not they were bestowed for the explicit purpose of currying favor or buying influence. The trickiest question would be this: since the payments or benefits would undoubtedly have come from nominally private persons or entities, how close would the nexus between those persons or entities and the foreign government have to be in order to count as emoluments "from" the government? Plainly, the proper answer should not be a formalistic one, particularly if the country involved were one like contemporary Russia in which the boundary between the government and the private sector is so blurry. My sense is that payments or benefits provided by nominally private persons or entities, but at the instance of the government, should count.

Another issue might arise if it were to be proven that such payments or benefits were conferred while Mr. Trump was a candidate or during his period as president-elect. The constitutional text is pretty clearly limited to the period when an official is actually in office, an implication reinforced by the requirement of congressional permission to receive otherwise prohibited emoluments. It would be very odd to require that mere candidates ask congressional permission to receive foreign gifts or payments. The case of a president-elect seems a bit closer. Certainly, the anti-corruption concerns that underlie the foreign emoluments clause would apply just as strongly to the period just before the president took the oath of office as to the period thereafter. Nonetheless, it seems doubtful that the constitutional text could be stretched so far.

As of this writing, no evidence has emerged that Mr. Trump has received while in office the sort of payments, loans, or benefits from foreign agents or governments that would be of most concern. Should it do so, that could raise a colorable argument for impeachment. The argument would be strengthened if the sums involved were large enough to suggest that they materially affected Mr. Trump's solvency or the financial health of his business structure, and if Mr. Trump kept these troubling facts hidden by virtue of his violation of the previous norm of fairly full disclosure by presidents and presidential candidates of their financial holdings and liabilities.[21]

What we do know is that, during Mr. Trump's presidency, foreign governments or entities closely affiliated with foreign governments have paid large sums to Mr. Trump's businesses, particularly his hotel and resort properties, for lodging, food, entertainment, meeting services, and the like. Mr. Trump has not sought the constitutionally required "consent of Congress" to receive a foreign emolument. Mr. Trump's business operations also raise questions under the domestic emoluments clause because his hotel and hospitality businesses routinely receive money from state and federal employees who patronize those businesses. Moreover, it has been argued that Mr. Trump received a significant benefit from the federal government when the General Services Administration waived the provision of the lease on the Trump hotel in Washington, D.C. that barred ownership by a federal officer or employee. As a result, three groups of plaintiffs have sued challenging foreign governmental payments to Trump's businesses as violations of the emoluments clauses. One lawsuit was brought by a public interest organization and businesses and employees of businesses who claim to have suffered competitive disadvantage from preferential treatment afforded Trump's hospitality businesses.[22] A second was filed by the governments of the District of Columbia and the state of Maryland.[23] And a third was brought by a group of Democratic senators and congressmen.[24]

Three issues have predominated public discussion of these cases: the standing of the plaintiffs to sue;[25] the available remedy should they succeed on the merits;[26] and, most importantly, whether payments to a president or his business count as a prohibited emolument if received as part of an ordinary business transaction.[27] Space does not permit detailed discussion of the first two questions. Nor is the success or failure of the these actions entirely germane to a discussion of impeachment except insofar as, like the plaintiff's lawyers in the Paula Jones civil litigation, the emoluments plaintiffs might unearth evidence that the House of Representatives would find useful in an impeachment inquiry. The genuinely troublesome question is whether foreign government payments to a president avoid the prohibition on emoluments as long as they take the form of a commercial exchange.

President Trump's constitutional argument is that an arm's-length business transaction is not a "present" or "emolument." To this he adds the more general plaint that a businessman should not have to surrender his or her business (or even abandon its active management) to be president.[28] Both contentions are flawed. In the founding period, the word "emolument" was used to mean not only salary, but far more commonly, "profit," "gain," "advantage," or "benefit."[29] Even an arm's-length commercial transaction implies mutual benefit. The seller provides a good or service and receives in return value exceeding the cost of the good or service – a profit. When a foreign government buys from a president, it confers on him a profit, gain, advantage, or benefit he would not otherwise receive. It matters not at all for emoluments purposes that there is no corrupt intention on either side. The point of the emoluments prohibition is to eliminate the need to prove such things. It is the conferring of the benefit that is prohibited, and the constitution is emphatic in its ban on foreign emoluments "of any kind whatever."[30]

Likewise, the premise that a president should not have to alter his or her profit-making activities in any way to enter public office is simply wrong. The framers wrote the salary and emoluments provisions into the constitution in part to ensure that not only the wealthy could afford to serve the country. Trump's basic posture is that wealthy people like himself should be able to occupy the presidency while surrendering absolutely no private advantages. However, the tradeoff built into the constitution is that public servants will be paid for their work, but that they have to forgo certain other kinds of benefit they might have received had they stayed private citizens. Among the benefits presidents must forgo are foreign emoluments. Payments, commercial or otherwise, from foreign governments inherently risk distortion of the recipient president's judgment or at least risk the perception that the president's judgment might be distorted, which in the case of the country's chief representative in foreign affairs is nearly as bad. Moreover, the constitution does not ban foreign emoluments absolutely; it merely requires that Congress must consent to them. A businessman/woman president who wants both to serve and to continue his or her foreign commercial connections simply has to ask for permission, and in doing so, provide the people's representatives with sufficient information to assure them that giving permission does not impinge on larger national interests.

All this having been said, the issues presented by Mr. Trump's circumstances are novel. That novelty impacts the calculation of whether, if payments to Trump's hotel and resort businesses are found to be emoluments, the resultant violation of the foreign emoluments clause should constitute an impeachable offense. My sense is that the very novelty of the question should probably preclude impeachment, at least if that were the only ground, and absent some additional events. Even if one disapproves of both Mr. Trump's handling of his financial disclosures and his cavalier dismissal of the potential for emoluments clause violations, a president generally should not be removed *solely* for pursuing an honestly debatable constitutional theory. That said, if emoluments questions were decided definitively against Trump by the courts (or less probably by both Houses of Congress), and Trump either refused to seek permission to continue accepting emoluments, or defied an express congressional refusal to grant permission, then impeachment would seem entirely proper.

"SCHEME OF PECULATION"

The larger problem with President Trump's business activities is not so much that they may violate the letter of the emoluments clauses, but that they violate the principle – the idea of government service – underlying the emoluments clauses. When arguing for the inclusion of a vigorous impeachment provision, Madison worried that a president "might pervert his administration into a *scheme of peculation* . . ."[31] In its most restrictive sense, peculation means something akin to embezzlement, that is, taking or using money, particularly public money, one is responsible for managing.[32] Here, however, I think Madison uses the term in a broader sense of taking advantage of the perquisites and powers of office for self-enrichment.

In *Federalist* 72, Alexander Hamilton employed "peculation" in just that way. Arguing in favor of the constitution's provisions permitting a president to seek re-election, Hamilton contended that an "avaricious" president limited to a single term would be tempted to make hay while the sun shone. He wrote:

Another ill effect [of limiting a president to one term], would be the temptation to sordid views, to *peculation*, and, in some instances, to usurpation. An avaricious man, who might happen to fill the office, looking forward to a time when he must at all events yield up the advantages he enjoyed, would feel a propensity, not easy to be resisted by such a man, to make the best use of his opportunities, while they lasted; and might not scruple to have recourse to the most corrupt expedients to make the harvest as abundant as it was transitory . . .[33]

The notion of impeaching a president for using his office for self-enrichment is not merely a quaint conceit born of the American Founders' idiosyncratic fascination with republican virtue and honest government. Impeachment on that ground was a consistent theme of British parliamentary action. As noted in Chapter 2, the essence of many British impeachments was misuse of office for private gain. Moreover, the official conduct that triggered these impeachments was quite commonly neither criminal nor a violation of any law. Even in a system where public office was often compensated through private profit, violation of either formal rules or informal norms in aid of excessive self-enrichment was unacceptable and impeachable.[34]

More importantly, an insistence on the probity of government officials is a central tenet of modern American law and public life. At all levels of government, civil service rules tightly regulate the activities and compensation of government employees. The core prescription of these rules is contained in the federal regulation that states, "An employee shall not use his public office for his own private gain, for the endorsement of any product, service or enterprise, or for the private gain of friends, relatives, or persons with whom the employee is affiliated in a nongovernmental capacity . . ."[35] Of course, the president is not an "employee" under these laws, and some latitude must be allowed for an official with such wide-ranging political duties, but the basic principle that office must not be employed to enrich oneself or one's relatives, friends, and associates applies no less to presidents than to government accountants, case managers, or janitors.

Since his entry into office, President Trump has shattered every convention discouraging presidential self-enrichment. He and his family have used the presidency as an extended opportunity both to enhance their private commercial brand and to reap immediate cash windfalls from his occupancy of the presidency.[36] As of July 2018, he had spent 170 of his 543 days in office at a Trump property.[37] While there could hardly be an objection to a president spending time on his own ground if the ground in question were his private home, these are hospitality businesses, primarily hotels and golf courses, for which publicity translates directly into profits. On a state visit to Great Britain, Trump even made a detour for a heavily publicized stop at his Turnberry golf course in Scotland.[38] Moreover, the affiliation of these properties with the president has undoubtedly produced direct cash inflows. As one watchdog group noted, during Mr. Trump's first year in office, over one hundred federal or state government officials visited Trump Organization properties; Mr. Trump or White House staff "promoted the Trump brand by mentioning or referring to one of the president's private businesses on at least fifty-four different occasions"; and numerous special interest groups, political groups, and foreign governments have held functions at Trump properties or "paid Trump-owned entities."[39] Even when Trump visits his own properties purely for personal relaxation, he necessarily brings a huge entourage of aides and security personnel whose stays result in government payments to Trump's coffers.

One might continue with even more disconcerting examples involving Trump's immediate family – the curiously timed award of multiple trademarks to Ivanka Trump by China;[40] the attempt to encourage foreign investment in real estate held by Trump's son-in-law Jared Kushner's family by pushing the presidential connection and suggesting the availability of investor visas;[41] the efforts by Trump children to parlay the presidential association into real estate deals abroad;[42] and so forth. In the end, the point is that, in stark contradiction to over two centuries of American law and practice, Mr. Trump is openly seeking to monetize the presidency. If he continues to do so with no consequence, the corrosive effect on American political and governmental norms is likely to be real and enduring. As has been emphasized throughout this book, the ultimate function of impeachment is preservation of sound constitutional norms. It would be entirely appropriate, and entirely constitutional, for the House of Representatives to conclude that persistent and pervasive disregard of the immemorial Anglo-American norm against official self-enrichment is an impeachable offense. The case for acting on that conclusion would be strongest if it combined proof of an unrepentant violation of one or both of the emoluments clauses with proof of a pattern of conduct that was, in Hamilton's word, avaricious even when not overtly illegal.

15

The Twenty-fifth Amendment as an Alternative to Impeachment

Just around the time that I began thinking about writing this book, I was browsing in a gift shop and came across a refrigerator magnet for which I immediately overpaid. It shows the iconic Howard Chandler Christy painting of the signing of the constitution, with Washington dominating the dais and Franklin seated at his ease down at the front, Alexander Hamilton whispering in his ear. Superimposed over the assembly is a cartoon speech balloon that says, "I still think we should include something in the constitution in case the people elect a friggin' moron." However crudely put, the magnet captures the sentiments and frustrations of President Donald Trump's harshest critics. Roughly half the country believes him to be intellectually, morally, and temperamentally unfit for the presidency.[1] But even if one accepts the most negative assessment of his capacities, it is at best doubtful that essential unfitness for the office can, by itself, be framed as an impeachable offense. "Treason, Bribery, or other high Crimes and Misdemeanors" requires conduct, rather than incapacity, or at least conduct in addition to incapacity. The difficulty of articulating how Mr. Trump's conduct has constituted one or more impeachable offenses, together with a growing appreciation of the political difficulties of the impeachment process, caused a flood of interest among Mr. Trump's critics in the provisions of the Twenty-fifth Amendment which outlines procedures for replacing a president who is deemed "unable to discharge the powers and duties of his office."[2]

The Twenty-fifth Amendment, for some, seems like a quick fix, a way of circumventing the requirement of investigating and proving particular charges to a reluctant Congress, and instead focusing on what they see as the obvious, and manifest, incapacity of a president. It has been reported that even Trump administration insiders have toyed with invoking the amendment.[3] This chapter examines the genesis and particulars of the Twenty-fifth Amendment. It will attempt to dispel the notion that the amendment is likely to prove of any practical utility in the case of a president who enters upon the office saddled with a set of personal deficiencies that perhaps ought to have, but have not, rendered him unacceptable to the electorate.

THE CONSTITUTION OF 1788 AND THE PROBLEM
OF PRESIDENTIAL INCAPACITY

Midway through the constitutional summer of 1787, James Madison summed up his case for the importance of an impeachment mechanism. Impeachment, he said, is "indispensable . . . for defending the Community against the *incapacity*, negligence or perfidy of the chief Magistrate. The limitation of the period of service was not a sufficient security. He might lose his *capacity* after his appointment. He might pervert his administration into a scheme of peculation or oppression. He might betray his trust to foreign powers."[4] The impeachment mechanism ultimately crafted by the framers addressed all but one of Madison's concerns.

The phrase "Treason, Bribery, or other high Crimes and Misdemeanors" plainly covers corruption ("perfidy" and "scheme[s] of peculation"), abuses of power ("oppression"), and betrayal of the national interest to foreign powers. Moreover, contrary to the views of some commentators, it also covers the more egregious forms of "negligence" and mismanagement of the office.[5] However, "incapacity" (whatever Madison meant by that word) does not easily fit into a common-sense reading of "high crimes and misdemeanors."[6] The term implies an inability to perform one's functions rather than a choice to perform them corruptly or oppressively or unconstitutionally, or even a choice not to perform them at all.

The constitution in its original form did address one part of the problem of presidential incapacity. Article 2, section 1, states:

> In case of the removal of the President from office, or of his death, resignation, or *inability* to discharge the powers and duties of the said office, the same shall devolve on the Vice President, and the Congress may by law provide for the case of removal, death, resignation or inability, both of the President and Vice President, declaring what officer shall then act as President, and such officer shall act accordingly, until the disability be removed, or a President shall be elected.[7]

This section provides a succession mechanism in case of presidential incapacity. If the presidency is vacated, the vice president takes the president's place. If both the presidency and vice presidency are vacated, Congress is to decide which officer will step in to "act as President." Interestingly, some question later arose about the status of a vice president or other officer who steps into the vacated place of the president. When, in 1841, William Henry Harrison died a month into his term, his vice president, John Tyler, assumed his powers. Nonetheless, John Quincy Adams grumbled at Tyler's presumption in styling himself "President." Adams thought that the constitution made Tyler "acting president" only.[8] Inasmuch as there is no constitutional provision according an elected president's successor upon death any fewer powers than the original incumbent, the point was one of protocol rather than substance. When Vice President Millard Fillmore took over from President Zachary Taylor upon the latter's death in 1850, he seems to have assumed both title and powers without contemporary comment.[9] Still, the imputation of diminished legitimacy carried enough sting that, during Andrew Johnson's impeachment struggle, Congressman Ashley opened his resolution of impeachment this way: "I do impeach Andrew Johnson, *Vice President and acting President of the United States*, of high crimes and misdemeanors."[10]

In 1792, Congress accepted the textual invitation to specify a line of succession after the vice president by enacting a statute that designated the president *pro tempore* of the Senate and the Speaker of the House of Representatives as next in line.[11] This was the law that made Ben Wade the heir apparent of Andrew Johnson had he been impeached in 1868.[12] Since then, Congress has altered the line of succession several times. In 1886, a new statute replaced the congressional leaders with cabinet officers,[13] a dispensation replaced in its turn by a 1947 enactment that put the succession back in the Congress, albeit with the order reversed – the first successor now being the Speaker of the House, followed by the president *pro tempore* of the Senate.[14]

None of these laws solved the most difficult question left open by the constitution – exactly when the presidency is to be deemed empty. Article 2, section 1 mentions four means by which the presidency might be vacated: death, resignation, removal, and "inability to discharge the powers and duties of the office." Death and resignation are straightforward. "Removal" plainly alludes to the contingency of impeachment. "Inability to discharge the powers and duties of the said office" – the situation that troubled Madison in the impeachment debates – is covered insofar as the constitution says that inability to perform is the equivalent of death, resignation, or removal. However, what is conspicuously missing is either a definition of what "inability" means or any mechanism for determining when it has occurred, not to speak of any provision for a situation in which a president becomes disabled, but then is restored to full function.

HISTORICAL EXAMPLES OF PRESIDENTIAL DISABILITY

Some vagaries in constitutional language prove inconsequential because no situation ever arises requiring a precise construction. This was not the case for presidential incapacity. The mid-nineteenth century was a rough period for American presidents. William Henry Harrison died in 1841. Zachary Taylor passed on in 1850, supposedly from a combination of exhaustion, poor Washington public sanitation, and lousy medical care.[15] Lincoln was assassinated in 1865. And, in 1881, President James A. Garfield, too, was shot. Unlike Lincoln and his other prematurely deceased predecessors, Garfield lingered. The medicine of the time could not save him. After a struggle of nearly three bedridden months, he died, and was succeeded by Vice President Chester Arthur.[16] During his final convalescence, Garfield received few visitors and it seems reasonably plain that he was in no condition to carry out even the most rudimentary official actions. He was, by any ordinary definition, unable "to discharge the powers and duties" of the presidency. Yet, rather like the situation in an hereditary monarchy, there could be no other ruler while he lived and the public business languished.[17]

Garfield's sad fate naturally stirred considerable national discussion, which produced the new 1886 succession statute referenced above, but no answer to the questions of who is to adjudge a president disabled and by what standard.[18] The problem of sick presidents did not abate. In 1919, President Woodrow Wilson suffered a stroke, which caused paralysis on his left side, blindness in one eye and partial blindness in the other. He was bedridden for weeks and largely disabled from his presidential functions for months, during which time his wife and close aides tried to hide his condition from the public.[19]

During most of the four months of his unprecedented, and truncated, fourth term, Franklin Delano Roosevelt was a dying man, highly functional at times, but failing rapidly. As a polio survivor effectively crippled by the disease, he had been hiding his true physical condition from the public for his entire political career, but at the end his condition was far more dire and the concealment more consequential.[20]

In 1955, during his first term, President Eisenhower suffered a heart attack that put him in the hospital for six weeks.[21] This was followed by major intestinal surgery in 1956,[22] and a stroke in 1957. During these periods, he worked out informal arrangements for temporary transfer of authority to Vice President Nixon. But these were, by their nature, non-binding gentlemen's agreements.[23] We know, of course, that two federal judges have been impeached wholly or in part for personal incapacity arising from insanity (Pickering) or alcoholism (Delahay).[24] Yet applying these precedents to the case of presidential incapacity arising from illness or accident seems never to have been seriously pursued.

Then came the assassination of President Kennedy in 1963, which revived graphically the concern following President Garfield's murder. Suppose Kennedy had lived, but due to his head wound had been substantially incapacitated? Moved at last to action, in 1965, Congress approved the Twenty-fifth Amendment.

TWENTY-FIFTH AMENDMENT

Before considering the particulars of the Twenty-fifth Amendment, it behooves us to focus on the impetus for its passage. The perceived problem was how to deal with a president who entered office in fine, or at least acceptable, mental and physical shape, but thereafter suffered an illness or injury that dramatically reduced his baseline function. In short, the amendment was conceived to be about diminution of capacity – physical, but more particularly mental. At least in conception, it was not imagined to address flaws, however grievous, in the substance of the president's judgments, or to offer an opportunity to second-guess the judgment of the electorate about the fundamental qualifications of a president. Of course, the constitution must be interpreted primarily according to its text, and interpretations of the constitution are not always bound by the imagination of its framers. Still, the history of the Twenty-fifth Amendment suggests that its language is unlikely to run as far as some would now like.

The main points of the amendment are these:

- Section 1 eliminates all doubt about the status of a vice president who assumes office upon the removal, death, or resignation of the president. It states unequivocally that in such cases "the Vice President shall become President."[25]
- Section 2 addresses the question of whether, and if so how, to fill a vacancy in the vice presidency. This issue can arise when a vice president assumes the presidency due to presidential vacancy or if the vice president dies, resigns, or is removed. The only historical instance of the latter was the resignation of Vice President Agnew due to pending corruption charges.[26] In either event, the amendment prescribes that "the President shall nominate a Vice President who shall take office upon confirmation by a majority vote of both Houses of Congress."[27] Gerald Ford became vice president via this mechanism following the Agnew resignation.[28]
- Section 3 deals with voluntary relinquishment of authority by the president. It provides that the vice president will assume the duties of the presidency as "acting president" whenever the president transmits a written declaration to the president *pro tempore* of the Senate and the Speaker of the House that "he is unable to discharge the powers and duties of his office." The suspension of the president's authority lasts until he or she transmits to the same officers "a written declaration to the contrary."[29] This section is plainly conceived as a measure short of resignation to be employed either when a president becomes disabled but is sufficiently in control of his or her faculties to recognize the impairment, or when the president anticipates that he or she will become temporarily disabled for some period, as, for example, due to an upcoming major surgery. In either case, section 3 supposes that the president, having relinquished authority for an interval, has the option of reclaiming that authority upon recovery of his or her faculties.
- Section 4 addresses involuntary declarations of presidential incapacity, that is, a situation in which the president is disabled, but is unable or unwilling to acknowledge the fact.

The provisions of section 4 are quite convoluted. Here they are in full:

> Whenever the Vice President and a majority of either the principal officers of the executive departments or of such other body as Congress may by law provide, transmit to the President *pro tempore* of the Senate and the Speaker of the House of Representatives their written declaration that the President is unable to discharge the powers and duties of his office, the Vice President shall immediately assume the powers and duties of the office as Acting President.

Thereafter, when the President transmits to the President *pro tempore* of the Senate and the Speaker of the House of Representatives his written declaration that no inability exists, he shall resume the powers and duties of his office unless the Vice President and a majority of either the principal officers of the executive department or of such other body as Congress may by law provide, transmit within four days to the President *pro tempore* of the Senate and the Speaker of the House of Representatives their written declaration that the President is unable to discharge the powers and duties of his office. Thereupon Congress shall decide the issue, assembling within forty-eight hours for that purpose if not in session. If the Congress, within twenty-one days after receipt of the latter written declaration, or, if Congress is not in session, within twenty-one days after Congress is required to assemble, determines by two-thirds vote of both Houses that the President is unable to discharge the powers and duties of his office, the Vice President shall continue to discharge the same as Acting President; otherwise, the President shall resume the powers and duties of his office.[30]

What does all this mean? First, a president can be declared incapacitated if the "Vice President and a majority of either the principal officers of the executive departments or of such other body as Congress may by law provide" transmit to Congress a declaration that "the President is unable to discharge the power and duties of his office."[31] At present, Congress has not designated any other body to join with the vice president, so a majority of cabinet officers would be required. As soon as the declaration is transmitted, "the Vice President shall immediately assume the powers and duties of the office as Acting President."[32]

Second, if the situation that prompted the declaration of incapacity were a non-fatal illness or injury so sudden or severe that it prevented the president from acting in advance to voluntarily pass authority to the vice president pending recovery, the president could nonetheless resume office once recovered by transmitting to Congress "his written declaration that no inability exists." This same language allows a president who simply disagrees with the judgment of the vice president and the cabinet about his disability to contest their assessment. For example, if the vice president and cabinet were to declare to Congress that a president was insane and therefore incapable of holding office, the president could fire right back with his own declaration that he was not insane, but quite able to perform his functions.

Third, once a president formally declares either that he has been restored to competence or that he was never disabled in the first place, the president immediately resumes his powers, *unless* within four days the vice president and a majority of the cabinet send *another* declaration to Congress reiterating their opinion that the president is not able to perform his duties. If that happens, Congress has to decide the matter. However, in order to remove the president for incapacity, two-thirds of both houses of Congress must vote to do so. (Even then the question is not wholly settled, because the effect of such a vote is not to expel the president from office, but merely to install the vice president as acting president until such time, if ever, as Congress agrees that the president is restored to competence.)

Insofar as this discussion relates to President Trump, it is plain that the conversation could stop here. However low the majority of the country may rate his capabilities, at least as of this writing, the members of his own party seem to think he is doing just fine. His approval ratings among Republicans consistently top 80 percent, and have trended upward as his term progresses.[33] Moreover, those approval ratings have tended to translate into primary election support for Republican candidates who support Trump and rejection of those who do not.[34] Accordingly, as matters stand, no vice president with an eye to a future in Republican electoral politics is in the least bit likely to initiate the effort to remove Mr. Trump, nor is there likely to be a plentitude of cabinet members eager to join such a movement.

Even supposing that the vice president and the cabinet acted, Mr. Trump would never take it lying down. He would certainly contest the declaration and throw the question to Congress. Both houses of Congress are now divided almost evenly between the parties. Perhaps more critically, the congressional parties are now radically polarized.[35] There is now almost no ideological overlap between Democratic and Republican members and the impetus to cooperation and compromise is dwindling, if not positively extinct, in both groups. Possession of the majority in one house or the other may shift in upcoming elections, but the basic narrow division is unlikely to be altered either in Mr. Trump's first term or in a hypothetical second one. As long as political polarization remains high, Congress remains roughly evenly split, and Mr. Trump retains the loyalty of his party's voters, the chances of achieving a two-thirds vote in either chamber of Congress to declare him incapable of continued service as president are as near to zero as anything can be in an uncertain universe. The only event at all likely to change this bedrock reality would be physical collapse by Mr. Trump or a major, and public, psychotic breakdown so severe that even Trump loyalists would accede to medical reality.

In short, leaving the merits to one side, from a political perspective, invoking the Twenty-fifth Amendment would be roughly three times as difficult as impeachment. Impeachment requires no concurrence from a president's own cabinet. Impeachment can be initiated by a simple majority of the House. Only in the Senate is a two-thirds majority required to convict. The latter procedural obstacle has proven to be consistently daunting since the first impeachment of Senator Blount in 1797, as we have discussed throughout this book. But at least in impeachment the Senate is called upon to judge the merits of particular charges of presidential misbehavior, rather than to engage in the doubtful exercise of declaring a physically robust, sentient, voluble president "unable" to serve.

BEYOND THE POLITICS OF TRUMP

If we leave to one side the political calculations of the present moment, Mr. Trump's case helps to illustrate the inherent uncertainties in the process created by the Twenty-fifth Amendment. It is an excellent addition to the constitution that serves the country well in the easy cases of presidential or vice presidential death, impeachment, or resignation. It is also a plus insofar as it provides a formal mechanism for temporary transfers of authority in cases of presidential incapacity due to illness or injury. Perhaps unsurprisingly, however, the amendment does not do a particularly great job of handling situations in which those around a president recognize crippling deficiencies in capacity, but the president does not.

The most obvious recent case was that of President Ronald Reagan, who served two terms from 1981 to 1989. Reagan died in 2004 of the complications of Alzheimer's disease, but it was plain to anyone who watched his public speeches and appearances in the later stages of his presidency that he was suffering marked cognitive decline. Even his own aides apparently considered invoking the amendment.[36] The Reagan situation illustrates a perhaps unavoidable weakness in the Twenty-fifth Amendment or any likely substitute – the people closest to a president, and thus the people most able to assess the true state of his health and mental powers, are his or her White House staff. They, just like the retainers of a monarch, rely for their offices and thus their continuance in power on the continued presence in office of the president who appointed them. Even though, since the advent of the Twelfth Amendment in 1804,[37] presidents are elected in tandem with a vice president who (with the rare exception of a case like Andrew Johnson) will be a member of the same party, a new president will invariably bring new staff. Thus, from the White House staff perspective, if the president goes, so too in all probability will they. Consequently, every president's staff has a powerful incentive to minimize the boss's mental and physical insufficiency or decline.

Reagan's case nonetheless differs from Trump in important respects. The issue with Reagan was not whether he entered the presidency with faculties adequate to the job, but whether age and a degenerative neurological disease gradually robbed him of his capacity. Although, given Mr. Trump's age, the Reagan problem could re-emerge, he presents two other issues. First, many of Trump's critics question whether he was mentally unfit from the moment he took office. Second, some have wondered whether the Twenty-fifth Amendment is limited to disability arising from organic physical or mental conditions, or might also apply to a president whose overall behavior, even if not constituting a diagnosable mental disease, nonetheless demonstrates a generalized unfitness for office.

In theory, there would seem to be no obstacle to employing the Twenty-fifth Amendment, even for a newly elected president, if those politically closest to him – the vice president and the cabinet – perceived crippling mental deficiency or instability. In such a case, it would be a mistake to insist that action could be taken only if the president presented a clearly categorized and diagnosable mental disease recognized as such by the psychiatric profession. That is not what either the constitutional language or common sense requires. Nor should anyone be comfortable in delegating this quintessentially political judgment to a body of unaccountable experts. Nonetheless, in the modern world, any such extraordinary effort would almost certainly have to be bolstered by medical opinion.

Mr. Trump has been repeatedly, if controversially, assessed by psychological professionals observing him from afar as suffering from an extreme form of narcissistic personality disorder,[38] a diagnostic category in the American Psychiatric Association's *Diagnostic and Statistical Manual of Mental Disorders* (DSM-V).[39] According to DSM-V, a diagnosis of narcissistic personality disorder is supported if the subject displays:

> A pervasive pattern of grandiosity (in fantasy or behavior), need for admiration, and lack of empathy, beginning by early adulthood and present in a variety of contexts, as indicated by five (or more) of the following:
> 1. Has a grandiose sense of self-importance (e.g., exaggerates achievements and talents, expects to be recognized as superior without commensurate achievements).
> 2. Is preoccupied with fantasies of unlimited success, power, brilliance, beauty, or ideal love.
> 3. Believes that he or she is "special" and unique and can only be understood by, or should associate with, other special or high-status people (or institutions).
> 4. Requires excessive admiration.
> 5. Has a sense of entitlement (i.e., unreasonable expectations of especially favorable treatment or automatic compliance with his or her expectations).
> 6. Is interpersonally exploitative (i.e., takes advantage of others to achieve his or her own ends).
> 7. Lacks empathy: is unwilling to recognize or identify with the feelings and needs of others.
> 8. Is often envious of others or believes that others are envious of him or her.
> 9. Shows arrogant, haughty behaviors or attitudes.

Given Mr. Trump's long-standing patterns of public behavior, one understands the conclusions of the armchair psychologists. Nonetheless, the difficulty with such claims, even if they were sustained by a treating physician, is that all of the manifestations of the mental disease identified by Trump's critics were entirely, indeed notoriously, evident during his campaign and his long prior life in the public eye. One might even say he was elected because of, not in spite of, them. Under these circumstances, it would be more difficult to justify acting under the Twenty-fifth Amendment than if the president's asserted deficiencies were hidden from the electorate and observable only by his personal or professional intimates. The ultimate question in Mr. Trump's case may not be whether he is a clinically diagnosable narcissist, but whether the condition materially impairs his functioning as president. If it does, then the remedy of the Twenty-fifth Amendment (however politically improbable) is, in theory, constitutionally available.

The final Twenty-fifth Amendment question presented by Mr. Trump is whether its mechanism is available where a president is not certifiable by a medical or psychiatric professional as disabled, but is simply catastrophically unsuited for the job. My sense of the matter is that the Twenty-fifth Amendment provides no help in such a case.[40] The amendment was pretty plainly designed with organic physical or mental dysfunction in mind, and was not intended to substitute the judgment either of medical professionals or of the political class about the minimum requirements of presidential effectiveness for the electoral verdict of the populace. In any event, demonstrated unfitness requires conduct. A pattern of presidential conduct so probative of unfitness as to trigger serious talk of Twenty-fifth Amendment inability to perform would almost surely fall into one of the traditionally accepted categories of impeachable behavior: corruption; abuse of power; heinous personal criminal acts; betrayal of the nation's foreign policy interests; serious forms of maladministration; or undermining the norms of constitutional order. Put simply, impeachment already provides a remedy for the curse of a genuinely dreadful president, as long as Congress has the collective will to employ it.

16

Impeaching Donald Trump

The paramount lesson of this book is that impeachment is, and was always intended to be, a means of protecting the constitution in the broad sense, by which I mean not only the particular governmental arrangements and personal rights specified in the written document, but, equally importantly, the distinctively American institutions and norms that have grown, flourished, and solidified around the written core. Recognizing as they did the impossibility of defining in advance the precise nature of the threats to constitutional order that an uncertain national future might produce, the Founders wrote and ratified a flexible standard for impeachable conduct and delegated the choice of how to apply it to the most democratic, politically accountable branch of the national government. The result, as observed earlier, is that we can impeach a president whenever we should. The language of the impeachment clauses, the British and pre-constitutional American practices so influential in shaping that language, and the precedents created by American impeachments since 1788 impose virtually no absolute limits on what Congress may do, but all help us think about what should be done for the good of the republic in any new case.

This chapter will apply what we have learned to the case of Donald Trump. The first half of the chapter will consider whether, based on the facts publicly known when this book was finalized in early 2019, there is a constitutionally sound case for impeaching and removing Mr. Trump from the office of president of the United States. The second half will briefly survey the formidable impediments to successful impeachment of Mr. Trump or any other president in the current era.

THE CASE FOR IMPEACHMENT

The key to framing a strong impeachment case against Donald Trump is recognizing the unique character of the threat he presents to constitutional order. Every American impeachment case to date has centered on a discrete set of acts, or at least a pattern of conduct with an identifiable set of objectives or exemplifying particular disqualifying traits. Senator Blount tried to give Florida to the British. Justice Chase was alleged to have used his judicial authority for partisan purposes. Judges Pickering and Delahay were alcoholics (or in Pickering's case possibly insane). Secretary of War Belknap and a number of judges took bribes. Even the three presidential impeachment cases had straight-forward themes. Andrew Johnson violated the Tenure of Office Act, and did so as part of a general pattern of usurping congressional authority to define the course of post-Civil War Reconstruction. Bill Clinton lied about adulterous sex and obstructed justice to conceal the sex and the lies. Richard Nixon's offenses seem more various, but the charges against him nonetheless centered on three closely interrelated themes: first, his campaign organization committed crimes to gain electoral advantage and he orchestrated a cover-up of those crimes; second, he engaged in a larger pattern of abuse of power, including misuse of government agencies, for the purpose of helping his friends, hurting his perceived enemies, and gaining political advantage; and, third, he unjustifiably resisted congressional power to investigate impeachable conduct.

By contrast, the list of Trump's offenses against constitutional propriety and reasonable expectations of presidential behavior is dishearteningly diverse and includes conduct in virtually all the categories of conduct historically identified as "high Crimes and Misdemeanors." His potential offenses include those addressed in Chapters 11–14: obstruction of justice both narrowly and broadly defined; abusing (or at least thoughtlessly misusing) the pardon power; ceaseless prevarication; and using his office to enrich himself and his family while violating the emoluments clauses in the process. They run on to include varying forms of electoral misconduct; culpable maladministration of various kinds, most notably deconstruction of America's trade, diplomatic, and security architecture; persistent attacks on the legitimacy of other branches of government and of the free press; regular abuse of the norms of civil discourse; and perhaps, bizarre though it seems even to consider it, being in thrall to a hostile foreign power.

WHAT IF DONALD TRUMP HAS BEEN COMPROMISED BY RUSSIA?

Before turning to the other grave, but less fantastic, items on the list of potentially impeachable behavior, one must reckon with the last one, the possibility that Donald Trump has been compromised by and is under the influence of Russia and its president, Vladimir Putin. When I began writing this book in early 2018, such a suggestion seemed outlandish, either the product of liberal political paranoia or a wish-fulfillment dream of anti-Trump Democrats and Never Trump Republicans. So outrageous did the idea appear that even mentioning the possibility carried the risk of being labeled a crank. Now, in early 2019, the state of publicly available information has changed to such an extent that any fair-minded observer has to concede that there exists at least a non-trivial possibility that the president of the United States is subject to some type of inappropriate Russian influence.

This is not the place to lay out in detail the state of the evidence, which at present is suggestive[1] but will not be complete until Special Counsel Robert Mueller releases his report and any congressional investigations that take up the question are concluded. However, one cannot help but note that: (a) there is unanimous agreement among U.S. intelligence agencies that Russia intervened, or at least vigorously attempted to do so, on Mr. Trump's behalf in the 2016 election;[2] (b) Mr. Trump has adopted a pro-Russian, pro-Putin tone in his personal statements unprecedented in an American president; (c) Mr. Trump has consistently espoused policy positions consistent with those of Russia, but contrary to the long-established consensus of the American foreign policy establishment and to the advice of his senior counselors, as well as, on occasion, over the strongly expressed bipartisan objections of Congress; and (d) astonishingly, Mr. Trump has held at least five private meetings with Vladimir Putin attended by no other American official, or in several cases, not even by an American interpreter, and has taken extraordinary measures to prevent even his own advisors from finding out what was said.[3]

Troubling as these facts appear, they might indicate nothing more than a president's idiosyncratic personal affinity for Mr. Putin and the Kremlin's point of view. However, there is a growing body of publicly reported information that suggests the possibility of Russian leverage over Mr. Trump. This story is still developing and may in the end prove to be nothing more than unprovable speculation. That said, the possibility of Russian leverage over the president seems real.

First, the Russians may know facts about Mr. Trump's personal life and business career before he took office that he does not want revealed. These could range from the merely embarrassing to the overtly criminal. At the embarrassing end of the spectrum would be possibilities like proof that, as alleged in the famous Steele dossier, Mr. Trump paid Moscow prostitutes to urinate on a bed once occupied by President and Mrs. Obama,[4] or simply evidence that Trump is not the self-made, rich-as-Croesus, business genius he claims to be, but is instead a rather incompetent, multiply-bankrupt, developer-turned-reality-TV-star who largely squandered an inherited fortune and was then bailed out by infusions of cash from Russian sources.[5]

The latter possibility is presented by the fact that around 2006 Trump stopped his career-long practice of using debt to acquire property and turned, massively, to cash.[6] Although Trump's children maintain that the money came from the Trump Organization's operating profits,[7] this assertion is unverified and seems at least questionable given Trump's long record of business misjudgments. Moreover, the turn to cash coincided with a collective refusal by American banks to continue loaning money to Trump following his repeated defaults and successful efforts to avoid liability through bankruptcy. There is apparently significant evidence that a primary source of Trump's cash infusions was persons and entities associated with Russia.[8]

Revelation of the details of Russian sources of capital for Trump's business could be merely embarrassing in that it would deflate the Trump origin myth. Still, the idea that Trump would persistently kowtow to Putin merely to avoid this kind of humiliation seems far-fetched. The more disturbing possibility is that the complete story of Trump's involvement with Russian money includes genuinely nefarious activities. These might fall into two broad categories: first, crimes or civil wrongs before Trump's presidency; or, second, continuing financial involvement with Russian government proxies or affiliates after Trump became a candidate and then the president. The first category might include tax evasion or even Trump's complicity in laundering criminal proceeds from Russian oligarchs. The second might include revelations that, since Trump became a candidate, Russians have made large loans to him or made or promised large purchases of Trump property, or that Russians have promised Trump commercial benefits such as forbearance on existing debts or favorable terms on extensions of credit, or that Russians have dangled advantageous investment opportunities following Trump's presidency.

One must hasten to repeat that none of these informed speculations about Trump's Russian business connections may prove to be true. However, if *any* of them are accurate, then Mr. Trump is deeply compromised by Russia. Whatever dealings Trump has or once had with Russians, we can be reasonably assured that Vladimir Putin knows about them. Therefore, if Trump's pre-presidential activities had any tinge of criminality, he knows that Putin can expose him. Moreover, Putin is the undisputed master of Russia and is fully capable of either further enriching or destroying the oligarchs who sit atop modern Russia's hierarchy.[9] Therefore, if Trump's business structure is now financially reliant on Russian money, Trump knows that Putin can, through his control of the wealthy Russians whose continued prosperity depends on him, ruin Trump, or in the course of time make Trump even richer. Critically, if Trump's business now relies on Russian capital or if the Russians have provably promised valuable concessions in the future, then the mere disclosure of such facts could destroy Trump's presidency and he would know that to be true. And, of course, there remains the possibility that Mueller will show active cooperation between Russian actors or proxies and the Trump campaign during the 2016 election.

Should Special Counsel Mueller or congressional investigators prove the existence of sources of Russian leverage over Mr. Trump, then the impeachment calculus would be immediately transformed. Not even the most convincing demonstration that Trump was acting under Russian influence would amount to "treason," inasmuch as the constitutional definition of that term is effectively limited to actively assisting an enemy in wartime. However, as we have seen throughout this book, since the invention of the impeachment device in the fourteenth century, it has always extended to officials who subordinate the interests of their own nation to those of foreign powers.[10] If it can be shown that Mr. Trump has been making policy choices or even presidential statements under the influence of Russian leverage, that is impeachable conduct. Even if no direct causal connection could be shown between facts that gave Russia leverage and particular presidential actions, concealment of such facts by a president ought itself to be impeachable. The country cannot tolerate a chief executive whose fundamental loyalty is suspect.

All this having been said, the remainder of this chapter will set aside the disheartening possibility that Mr. Trump is under Russian influence and confine the discussion to those points on which the evidence is now reasonably plain.

A BILL OF PARTICULARS

Absent proof of subordination to Russia, Trump's true offense, the thing that would justify his impeachment and removal, is not any single act or pattern of behavior, but the totality of his multifaceted assault on the norms of American constitutional government. The unifying feature of all his offenses, large and small, is self-aggrandizement. His project is to draw as much power, money, and adulation to himself, and secondarily to his family, as he can. His invariable method is to attack any person, institution, law, rule, custom, or norm that might impede him from whatever he happens to want at the moment. His objective is government according to the will of the one. What he seeks, whether as some deep-laid plan or more likely because it is simply his nature, is autocracy. And there is solid, venerable precedent for impeachment on that ground.

The most important, constitutionally formative, impeachments in British history were those in which Parliament brought down ministers who "endeavoured to subvert the ancient and well established form of government in this kingdom, and instead thereof to introduce an arbitrary and tyrannical way of government."[11] This was the fundamental danger against which the framers sought to guard when they incorporated the impeachment power into the American constitution. Those opposing impeachment in particular cases are apt to emphasize language from the founding generation and others suggesting that the impeachment power should be reserved for "great occasions."[12] While that may be so, by the same principle, impeachment is a power that *reaches* the greatest of occasions and ought to be used if the republic is not to fail. We happy Americans have never before been confronted by a presidential personality that posed a real risk of degeneration into autocracy. We are loath to recognize the danger or to act on it.

Let us consider the bill of particulars against President Trump.

Obstruction of Justice

As discussed in Chapter 11, a president may properly be impeached for obstruction of justice in the narrow sense of seeking to stop or impede particular legal proceedings for a corrupt purpose, and for obstructing justice in the broader sense of undermining the integrity and operational effectiveness of the entire legal system. A case for obstruction in the narrow sense would, at present, be based on Mr. Trump's conduct in relation to the investigation into Russian meddling in the 2016 election.

The fact that Mr. Trump has sought to hinder and impede that investigation is notorious, but the lengths to which he is prepared to go remain unclear at the time of this writing. Considering only what is presently known, I judge that the case for impeachment based *purely* on obstruction of the Russia investigation is as yet incomplete. However, that judgment could be radically altered by Special Counsel Mueller's findings, or if Mr. Trump attempted to suppress those findings without adequate cause, an act that would itself merit serious consideration of impeachment.

Subversion of Justice System

If the case for obstruction of justice in the narrow sense remains uncertain, the conclusion that Mr. Trump has systematically sought to corrupt and subvert the justice system as a whole is ironclad. Throughout his pre-presidential career in business, Mr. Trump viewed the law from two perspectives. As the operator of multiple businesses some aspects of which, at best, skirted the edges of legality,[13] Mr. Trump viewed the government's civil and criminal enforcement agencies as opponents to be thwarted or circumvented. Conversely, he learned early to use his money to employ private civil litigation as a weapon against personal and business adversaries. As of 2016, he and his businesses had been involved in more 3,500 lawsuits.[14] He has carried his prior attitude toward the law into the White House. Early in his presidency, exasperated by the pertinacious refusal of James Comey to back off the Russia investigation and by Attorney General Sessions' decision to recuse himself from that investigation, Trump famously asked, "Where is my Roy Cohn?"[15] The reference being to the notoriously hard-nosed and questionably ethical lawyer who acted as Trump's legal fixer and attack dog early in his career. As discussed in Chapter 11, Mr. Trump conceives of the Department of Justice and the rest of the federal law enforcement establishment as his private lawyers and investigators who should both defend him against legal inquiries and stand ready to use the law to discredit or even imprison his critics and opponents.

The essence of Mr. Trump's defensive approach has been to appoint justice officials chosen for personal loyalty (e.g., Jeff Sessions and Matthew Whitaker) and simultaneously to attack any official, whether political appointee or career civil servant, who pursues matters that might implicate Trump, his family, or his supporters. Before finally firing him, Trump called Attorney General Sessions "weak," "disgraceful," and an "idiot."[16] He has characterized the FBI as "in tatters" and the Justice Department itself as "an embarrassment to our country."[17] His personal assaults have even reached down into the middle levels of the Justice Department bureaucracy.[18] The unifying theme of his assaults on all the men and women doing their duty by investigating matters that might implicate or inconvenience Mr. Trump is that they are corrupt members of the "criminal deep state."[19]

Trump's denigration of the integrity of his critics is not restricted to officials and employees of the executive branch he heads, but notoriously extends to the federal judiciary. Trump routinely attacks any judge or judicial panel that rules against him or an administration initiative. The examples are too numerous to mention them all, but include the following: During his 2016 candidacy, Trump said of U.S. District Judge Gonzalo Curiel, then presiding over suits against Trump University, that he should be disqualified because, as a person of Mexican heritage, he would necessarily be biased against Trump.[20] When U.S. District James Robart enjoined Trump's travel ban on persons from certain Muslim countries, Trump tweeted, "The opinion of this so-called judge, which essentially takes away law enforcement from our country, is ridiculous and will be overturned."[21] When U.S. District Judge William H. Orrick enjoined Trump's executive order attempting to punish so-called "sanctuary cities," Trump called the order "ridiculous," and the White House put out a statement declaring, "The San Francisco judge's erroneous ruling is a gift to the criminal gang and cartel element in our country, empowering the worst kind of human trafficking and sex trafficking, and putting thousands of innocent lives at risk. This case is yet one more example of egregious overreach by a single, unelected district judge."[22] When U.S. District Judge Brian Morris of Montana enjoined implementation of President Trump's order to proceed on the Keystone XL oil pipeline, Trump said, "It was a political decision made by a judge. I think it's a disgrace."[23]

This persistent pattern of questioning the integrity of the courts is not merely distasteful, but overtly dangerous. In his dissent from the Ninth Circuit's order upholding the injunction against Trump's so-called "Muslim ban," Court of Appeals Judge Jay Bybee (a Republican appointee of impeccable conservative credentials) wrote:

> Even as I dissent from our decision not to vacate the panel's flawed opinion, I have the greatest respect for my colleagues. The personal attacks on the distinguished district judge and our colleagues were out of all bounds of civic and persuasive discourse – particularly when they came from the parties. It does no credit to the arguments of the parties to impugn the motives or the competence of the members of this court; *ad hominem* attacks are not a substitute for effective advocacy. Such personal attacks treat the court as though it were merely a political forum in which bargaining, compromise, and even intimidation are acceptable principles. The courts of law must be more than that, or we are not governed by law at all.[24]

Moreover, as noted in Chapter 11, Mr. Trump's abandonment of critical norms of presidential behavior in relation to the law have not been limited to questionable appointment decisions or ceaseless rhetorical denigration of legal officers, but has extended to placing pressure on the Justice Department and law enforcement agencies to open criminal investigations into his critics and opponents. Systematic verbal assault on the justice system is bad enough because it risks creeping corrosion of the public trust essential to the rule of law. Employing the vast powers of the federal criminal apparatus against opponents directly places this or any country on a straight road to autocratic rule. The fact that the federal law enforcement apparatus has, so far, largely resisted Trump's calls for retaliatory investigations does not alter the impeachment calculus. As we saw in Chapter 8, federal agencies for the most part resisted Richard Nixon's efforts to enlist them in efforts to obstruct justice or punish his enemies, but the House Judiciary Committee included Nixon's unsuccessful efforts along with his more successful ones as grounds for his impeachment.

Abuse of the Pardon Power

As discussed in Chapter 12, misuse of the pardon power is unquestionably impeachable. The issue is what kinds of misuse should count for that purpose. Two plain cases would be: (a) pardons issued or offered as part of an attempt to obstruct or impede an investigation into wrongdoing by the president, his family, friends, or business or political associates; or (b) pardons issued as part of a corrupt bargain pursuant to which the president or some associate received a bribe or other improper benefit. Mr. Trump has clearly hinted at use of the pardon power for the first purpose with his repeated coy references to pardons in relation to the prosecutions of his former campaign manager, Paul Manafort[25] and his former National Security Advisor, Michael Flynn,[26] and also, as discussed in Chapter 12, through the unspoken signals sent to all his former associates facing legal jeopardy by the few pardons he has so far issued.[27] But it is doubtful that hints of either sort would be sufficient in an impeachment case. The closest analogue in American precedent was Richard Nixon's dangling of possible pardons to Watergate defendants; however, in that case, Nixon was on tape orchestrating the offers and making explicit that the offers were for the purpose of keeping his former aides and employees quiet.[28] That said, the moment Trump issues a pardon to any person who is a witness, target, or defendant in any investigation of Trump, his administration, his businesses, or his family, the picture transforms immediately and impeachment on that ground becomes entirely supportable.

The more difficult case would be simple misuse of the pardon power for arbitrary or capricious reasons.[29] One can imagine inclusion of pardon practices of this sort in an article of impeachment charging either gross maladministration or abuse of power, but, standing alone, such allegations would carry little constitutional weight.

Electoral Misconduct

As noted in Chapter 10, the political legitimacy of any president who ascends to the office by election, rather than operation of constitutional or statutory succession mechanisms, rests primarily on success in winning an election. Even a vice president who succeeds to the office after the removal or death of a predecessor receives a slightly attenuated version of the same kind of democratic legitimacy by having run as the vice presidential partner of the predecessor. More broadly, the entire federal government is legitimated by regular elections of both Congress and the president. In consequence, presidential misconduct of two types related to elections may constitute an impeachable offense.

The first type is any presidential behavior that casts doubt on the essential validity of the president's own election. The framers made a particular point of noting that misconduct of that type would be impeachable. George Mason maintained that a president who "procured his appointment" by corrupting the "electors" must be impeachable.[30] Gouverneur Morris made the same point.[31] By "electors" they meant members of the Electoral College because that regrettable institution was envisioned by the Founders as a body of illustrious men selected by the states who would exercise their independent judgment in selecting a proper president for the nation. As originally designed, the process of picking a president had no necessary place for voting by the citizenry. The "electors" made the choice.

To the Founders, the only obvious way of corrupting the presidential selection process was to corrupt the tiny circle of eligible voters – the electors. Today, of course, electors exercise no independent judgment. They merely transmit the preference of the voters of their state. Presidential elections are now supposed to be essentially, if sometimes imperfectly, democratic exercises that reflect the will of the people. Therefore, practical modern electoral corruption (other than outright ballot box stuffing or its modern computerized equivalents) must take the form of distorting the judgment of the electo*rate*, rather than the elect*ors*.

That sort of corruption, *if of sufficient magnitude*, might be impeachable – with this significant caveat: the arts of voter persuasion inevitably have some aspects of flim-flam. Political spinning, concealment of one's own flaws, factually questionable slurs on an opponent's record or character, appeals to emotion rather than logic – all could be said to distort reasoned voter choice. But just being an ordinary politician cannot be an impeachable offense. Even concealment of a disreputable fact about one's past surely cannot alone be impeachable. Everybody has skeletons. Impeachments on this ground would permit re-litigation in Congress of every presidential election. Therefore, an impeachment on grounds of corrupting the electorate would have to be based on behavior so far outside the elastic norms of modern political conduct that it both demonstrated the successful candidate's contempt for the democratic process and put the fair operation of democracy at risk.

Something like this is among the subjects of Special Counsel Mueller's Russia investigation. There seems little doubt, for example, that members of Mr. Trump's family and campaign apparatus sought negative information about Democratic nominee Hillary Clinton from representatives of the Russian government, most particularly at a meeting between Donald Trump, Jr., Jared Kushner, Paul Manafort, and various Russians at Trump Tower in July 2016.[32] Whether they received such information or, alternatively, encouraged Russian operatives to release it secretly through the WikiLeaks platform, remains to be seen.[33] The mere act of seeking negative information about a political opponent, even from a foreign source, is neither criminal (contrary to some breathless suggestions in the media) nor in itself a violation of any democratic norm.[34] After all, if a candidate is informed that important, potentially election-changing, negative information about the opposition is held by some person or institution that happens to be "foreign," it would hardly seem appropriate, or even constitutional, to prohibit that candidate from asking the foreign source to provide the information. Depending on the nature of the information, one can argue that a failure to ask would itself be a dereliction. What makes Trump's case more questionable is that it would have been plain to his representatives (and to Trump himself if, as seems likely, he knew about the meeting[35]) that any information would be coming from the intelligence services of a hostile foreign state and, because the information was initially touted as Secretary Clinton's emails, it would have to have been stolen or hacked by those services. Whether such behavior is illegal or not, it is certainly far outside the historical norms of American democratic politics.

A second issue relating to Russia and the 2016 election is the, by now undisputed,[36] fact that Russia attempted to intervene in the election against Hillary Clinton and for Donald Trump. Critically, it did so, not by open declarations of its government's preferences (which is thought bad form in the international community, but is hardly illegal by any standard), but by surreptitious proliferation of anti-Clinton/pro-Trump social media content.[37] Whether this conduct is in any degree chargeable to Mr. Trump depends on whether he knew about it and condoned or encouraged it. He has obstinately denied that any Russian meddling occurred and denied with even greater vehemence that he knew about or encouraged whatever the Russians may have done.[38]

As of this writing, it is plain that Mr. Trump was perfectly willing to accept secret electoral help from a traditionally hostile foreign power. More cannot yet be said. The position of these events in a possible impeachment effort is, at present, too difficult to determine.

However, Mr. Trump has consistently engaged in a more general effort to subvert the integrity of the U.S. electoral process. This has taken the form of relentless, and entirely unsubstantiated, claims of individual voter fraud or corruption on the part of election officials. This pattern began before the 2016 election with Trump's warnings that, should he lose, it would only be because of election fraud.[39] It continued after the election with Trump's repeated – and totally baseless – claim that 3–5 million illegal votes were cast in 2016 by non-citizen immigrants.[40] This was followed by Trump's appointment of a short-lived, tragicomic, commission to investigate the existence of vote fraud; the commission disbanded after eight months, partly due to the incompetence of its Republican principals, but even more directly due to the complete absence of any evidence to support its animating premise.[41]

Mr. Trump's dogged adherence to the voter fraud fantasy can be explained in large measure by his well-documented insecurity over the fact that Secretary Clinton received about 2.9 million more popular votes than Mr. Trump in the 2016 election, even though he won the Electoral College.[42] However, his assaults on the integrity of the election system have not been limited by this personal idiosyncrasy. In the days following the midterm elections of 2018, when a number of races in Arizona and Florida were so close that recounts seemed likely, Mr. Trump immediately began charging – without any evidence – that election officials were corrupt and that the elections were being stolen.[43]

The American democracy will only survive as long as the people have confidence that their votes will be counted and honored. A president who incessantly questions the essential integrity of elections cannot be excused on the ground that he is merely salving his tender ego. Nor is a persistent pattern of questioning electoral integrity any part of traditional American political discourse. It is deeply dangerous, deeply subversive of the constitutional order, and for that reason could properly be considered as part of a larger pattern supporting impeachment and removal from office.

Corruption

Some have speculated that Mr. Trump decided to run for president in the 2016 cycle not because he expected or even much wanted to win, but because making the race would raise his international profile and improve his corporate brand.[44] Whether that is the case or not, since his unexpected victory, he and his family have persistently treated the presidency as a commercial opportunity. As discussed at length in Chapter 14, use of high office for self-enrichment was an impeachable offense in Britain for four centuries prior to the founding, the framers wrote prohibitions of the particular type of self-enrichment known as emoluments into the constitutional text, and the founding generation was in universal agreement that corrupt self-enrichment generally and violation of the emoluments clauses in particular were proper grounds for impeachment.

The evidence is clear that, at a minimum, Trump has monetized the presidency in defiance of an immemorial norm against such behavior. It may yet prove that his misbehavior has gone beyond brand-building and raking in cash from those eager to curry his favor by staying at his hostelries. A variety of other suspect transactions require further inquiry. Notable among these is Mr. Trump's intervention in the contract for relocation of the FBI headquarters in downtown Washington, D.C., which appears to have led to the cancellation of an agreement to move the headquarters to a suburb and sell the site to developers who planned to put in a hotel that would compete with the Trump hotel several blocks down the street.[45]

In addition, the legal case that President Trump has violated the foreign emoluments clause through receipt of foreign governmental payments to his hospitality businesses is compelling, if not yet final. As noted in Chapter 14, it would be inappropriate to base an impeachment *purely* on the ground that the president adopted an inappropriately aggressive interpretation of a never-before-enforced constitutional provision. From the impeachment perspective, violation of the emoluments clauses is important primarily insofar as it illustrates the violation of the long-standing norm against self-enrichment. In addition, there remains the possibility discussed at the outset of this chapter that Mr. Trump has received large payments, loans, or other benefits from the Russian government or its proxies and remains under obligation to Russian investors or creditors. That would both violate the foreign emoluments clause and be solid ground for impeachment. Evidence of significant fiscal obligation to a traditional foreign enemy, particularly if that obligation had been concealed by a president, would raise crippling doubts about both the president's personal integrity and whether he could be relied upon to place the interests of the United States above his private financial interests.

Gross Maladministration, Abuse of Power, Injury to Foreign Policy Interests

As we saw in Chapter 4, the framers and the founding generation plainly contemplated that really severe instances of neglect of duty, incompetence, or maladministration would be impeachable. A strong case can be made for Mr. Trump's general managerial inefficacy – his refusal to read briefing documents or to engage in detailed consultation with officials or subject-matter experts before making reflexive decisions,[46] the persistence of critical vacancies in the upper levels of government,[47] the pattern of high-level appointees manifestly unqualified for office or plagued by ethical lapses,[48] the hollowing out of critical elements of the federal bureaucracy,[49] and so forth. But, distressing as these developments are to many, particularly those on the left, Mr. Trump and his defenders can claim that, far from being impeachable, these are merely manifestations of his managerial style or conscious choices to cut down a bloated federal work force.[50] In any event, there remains stout resistance to the idea that a president may be impeached merely for being lousy at the job.

However, if ineptitude is paired with other traditional grounds for impeachment such as abuse of power or significant injury to foreign policy interests, impeachment on such grounds is a far more palatable notion. A number of Mr. Trump's official actions can be argued to be abuses of power. Among those Trump's critics might list would be a long series of executive orders that seem ill-considered and have been held by courts to be violative either of the procedural requirements for executive action or the constitution itself. One might also argue that Trump's decision to deploy some 5,000 regular Army troops at the southern border days before the 2018 midterm election to combat the, frankly non-existent, threat that a caravan of refugees then some 800 miles south in Mexico would somehow storm the border and bring death, disease, and Middle Eastern terrorists to America was a fiscally imprudent, transparently political, abuse of the commander-in-chief power of Article 2, section 2.[51] However, I will leave arguments about these matters to others.

What does deserve serious consideration here is Mr. Trump's rolling destruction of American foreign policy. To summarize, in the seventy-odd years since the Second World War, generations of American presidents, legislators, soldiers, and diplomats have labored to create a world order of multilateral institutions and agreements with the United States at its center. That order has averted nuclear annihilation, prevented conventional war between the major powers, secured a stable, democratic Europe and an increasingly prosperous and stable East Asia, managed the fall of Soviet communism, and overseen a fairly universal rise in human material welfare, all while maintaining the United States as the single indispensable world power. All has not been wine and roses for everybody, of course. Humanity is on the verge of destroying the world's ecosystem through climate change, pollution, and habitat destruction. And global overpopulation and income inequality pose continuing threats to individual well-being and regional peace. However, the looming existential crises of the age can only be addressed (if they can be at all) through increased collaboration and cooperation across borders. Most importantly for present purposes, whatever else one may think about the current world order, it is hugely advantageous for the United States, placing this country at the center of all important decisions about international trade, finance, technology, and security.

Since his election, Mr. Trump has moved steadily in the direction of unilaterally dismantling the United States' foreign policy, trade, and security architecture[52] by formally abandoning or denigrating every form of multilateral engagement from the Paris Climate Accords, to the Trans-Pacific Partnership, to the Iran Nuclear Accord, to the World Trade Organization,[53] to a nuclear weapons treaty with Russia,[54] to the United Nations, not to speak of our most fundamental military alliance, NATO.[55] He has consistently quarreled with our oldest democratic allies, while cozying up to autocracies across the globe: Duterte's Philippines, Crown Prince Mohammed bin Salman's Saudi Arabia, Viktor Orban's Hungary, and, of course, Vladimir Putin's Russia.[56] The result is that, if allowed to continue, Trump will, singlehandedly, transform America's position among the nations, from being the leader (however imperfect) of the free world and indispensable fulcrum in every realm of hard and soft power to a diminished, cranky, ungenerous, avowedly self-absorbed friend of tyrants and oligarchs.

It is of particular moment that Trump is taking the country down this path singlehandedly. The policies he is pursuing are not the policies of the party under whose banner he ran. They are not the policies recommended to him by the vast bulk of civilian and military leaders and experts in his administration. Indeed, they are often undertaken against the explicit opposition of those persons.[57] They do not emerge from any process of study or consultation. They proceed from his personal whims, abetted by a very small coterie of courtiers. Trump's position on foreign policy is "l'état c'est moi." When this country was young, James Madison insisted that a president who made a treaty that "violated the interest of the nation" and convinced the Senate to ratify it could be impeached.[58] If, in the considered opinion of the architect of the American constitution, a president can be impeached for inveigling the Senate into one bad treaty, we ought to be able to impeach a president for heedlessly shattering a basket of good treaties and the entire intricate web of foreign relationships they support without so much as a by-your-leave.

President Trump can do these things in part because Congress has, over the years, and quite unwisely, acquiesced in the doubtful doctrine that, while two-thirds of the Senate must vote to ratify a treaty, a president may withdraw from it without consent of Congress or anyone else.[59] As pernicious as this legislative timidity has always been in principle, one could excuse it on the ground that Congress has assumed with some justice that presidents would be cautious, judicious, and consultative before taking so drastic a step. While that confidence has not always been justified, it generally has. However, in Mr. Trump, the country has for the first time a president who combines a near-complete lack of understanding of history, finance, trade, military affairs, or diplomacy with supreme confidence that he, and no one else, knows exactly how to arrange matters in all these arenas. In short, the electoral system has placed in the White House the ignorant demagogue that the framers feared at a time when the system of institutional checks they installed to deal with such an eventuality has atrophied so far as to be nearly useless. Catastrophe looms *unless* Congress recognizes the danger and reasserts the powers the constitution gave it.

I do not assert that impeachment is the first tool to which Congress should turn. To the contrary, it should, if possible, legislate lesser restrictions on Mr. Trump's regrettable impulses. That said, there is little question that the constitutional impeachment power includes a situation in which a president is inflicting irreparable harm on the nation's position in the world and will not be dissuaded. Parliament repeatedly impeached royal ministers on that ground, asserting for itself the ultimate authority over national foreign policy.[60] The framers were well aware of those precedents when they adopted the phrase "high Crimes and Misdemeanors."

Attacks on the Press and Norms of Civil Discourse

Among the norms that bind the American constitutional order are a respect for civil discourse and an appreciation of the role of the free press that makes informed public discussion possible. As to the first, we are a rowdy people, and the First Amendment protects every citizen's right to say most anything. However, even at law the right of free speech has some limitations, notably those against advocating or inciting violence. In any case, a *president* must be held to a higher standard than a political agitator or drunk at the corner bar. It is not acceptable for a president, expressly or by winking implication, to suggest that some members of the national community are less worthy of respect and the protection of the law than others. It is certainly not acceptable for a president to intimate that force is an acceptable part of political interchange. This kind of rhetoric, dangerous in every setting, is particularly intolerable when directed at members of the press. The press enjoys the particular protection of the First Amendment's dictate that "Congress shall make no law abridging . . . the freedom of the press."[61] But the principle underlying that amendment extends beyond a prohibition on formal legislation to an insistence that the press be allowed to investigate and question government without fear. A president, of course, has a reciprocal right to criticize members of the press, pungently and with vigor, as long as those criticisms do not place the imprimatur of the presidency on any suggestion that the press may not criticize those in power. To say, as Mr. Trump repeatedly has, that the media (or at least all the media who will not fawn on him) are "the enemy of the people" is intolerable.[62] As are expressions of approval of assaults on reporters.[63] Those are the incitements of the strongman, the would-be autocrat. They cannot be accepted from a sitting president.

Dishonesty

It may seem odd to close with reference to Mr. Trump's ceaseless dishonesty. As discussed in Chapter 13, lying alone, even when under oath, has not always been found impeachable. Given the preceding accounting of Mr. Trump's manifold infractions, prevarication may seem to be the least among them. However, I return to the notion, with which I think the Founders would heartily concur, that no man or woman can function as president, or at least function in any way the constitution would sanction, unless, with all the appropriate allowances for the inevitable hedging and maneuvering of high politics, he or she is fundamentally honest. At the least, I think the Founders would agree that no man who is *never* honest should be elected president, or if elected, maintained in office. Mr. Trump's essential falsity is his most disqualifying characteristic. Properly framed, it could be part of a legitimate case for his impeachment.

Mr. Trump or his defenders can say that some of the items in the foregoing sections are (a) not plainly criminal, (b) not clearly unconstitutional, or (c) merely more extreme forms of something that others do now, or have done in the past. As to any individual point, such objections may be fair. But the thing that distinguishes Donald Trump from every president who has come before him is *that no one has ever done all these things at the same time*. It is the totality of his misbehavior and its coherence into a pattern of self-aggrandizement and assaults on constitutional norms designed to prevent presidential excess that renders President Trump a plausible candidate for impeachment.

In the terms suggested in Chapter 10, an impeachment of Mr. Trump would be both prophylactic and definitional. Removing him would be prophylactic in the sense that it would prevent him from doing further damage to both the domestic political fabric of the United States and its position in the world. Trump's impeachment would also be definitional, in both a defensive and creative sense. It would be defensively definitional insofar as it would declare the country's continued allegiance to liberal democracy at home and its continued commitment to an America supportive of democracy, human rights, and simple decency abroad, while proclaiming its rejection of the Trumpist model of personal rule at home and selfish, and inevitably self-defeating, isolationism abroad. To impeach Mr. Trump could also be creatively definitional inasmuch as it would require Congress to reassert itself as the hub of democratic power the framers intended it to be.

COUNTING TO SIXTY-SEVEN IN A TRIBAL AGE, OR WHY IMPEACHMENT IS UNLIKELY

Whether one finds the case for impeaching Donald Trump compelling or not, the chances of his removal from office by that mechanism are low, for reasons ancient and modern. Let us consider them.

The most obvious obstacle to any impeachment is the one erected by the Founders – the requirement of a two-thirds majority for conviction in the Senate. In adopting the open-ended "high Crimes and Misdemeanors" standard for impeachable offenses, the framers gave Congress the power to remove a president whenever his or her continued presence in office presents a serious constitutional danger. However, by setting the conviction threshold so high, they simultaneously required that Congress be absolutely sure in its judgment of the necessity of removal. Their primary concern was that presidents should not become subservient to Congress, and most particularly that impeachment should not be employed as a tool of partisan warfare to the detriment of the stability of the government. The entirety of the famous passage in *Federalist* 65 in which Hamilton describes impeachable offenses as political highlights this concern:

> [Impeachable offenses] are of a nature which may with peculiar propriety be denominated POLITICAL, as they relate chiefly to injuries done to the society itself. The prosecution of them, for this reason, will seldom fail to agitate the passions of the whole community, and to divide it into parties more or less friendly to the accused. In many cases it will connect itself to pre-existing factions, and will enlist all their animosities, partialities, influence, and interest on one side or the other; and in such cases there will always be the greatest danger that the decision will be regulated more by the comparative strength of the parties than by the real demonstrations of innocence or guilt.[64]

The other side of the coin, however, is that factions can as easily be deployed to protect an unqualified or dangerous president as to bring down a worthy one. Indeed, that is the likeliest consequence of the two-thirds barrier. All a president, even a genuinely obnoxious president, has to do to escape removal is maintain the allegiance of a trifling one-third-plus-one of the Senate. In a reasonably closely divided Congress, this will amount to no more than roughly 60–70 percent of the members of his or her own party. For example, the Senate's party alignment during the second half of President Trump's first term is fifty-three Republicans and forty-seven Democrats.[65] If Mr. Trump were to be impeached by the House, conviction in the Senate would require guilty votes from every Democrat *and twenty Republicans*. That would be tough a hill to climb in any period. It is far steeper at present.

The framers, Madison in particular, imagined that allegiance to partisan factions would be counteracted among congressmen and senators by attachment to the institutional prerogatives of their branch. The framers may therefore have supposed that in clear cases of presidential misconduct, and particularly misconduct that threatened congressional authority, Congress would protect Congress, rather than the interests of the factions of which it was composed. To the extent that was ever the case, it has not been for a long time. Members of Congress have long tended to support the actions of presidents from their own party and oppose those of the other party, with decreasing regard for the effects of presidential action on the power of Congress as an institution. The tendency to align with faction rather than institution has become even more acute in the past thirty years or so as the parties became more ideological and less regional. Indeed, as many have observed, party alignment has now moved beyond questions of ideology and become tribal.[66] This is not the place to dissect all the reasons for this phenomenon. The point is simply that political tribalism makes governance exquisitely difficult. In today's Congress, tribalism has made even ordinary legislative functions nearly impossible because legislation requires compromise, compromise requires that both sides gain something, and any result that permits gain to the other side is anathema in an environment in which both sides stigmatize the other as intrinsically evil, or at least irredeemably wrongheaded and ignorant.

In the present political environment, convincing any significant number of senators to abandon their partisan allegiance to protect what will seem to some as ephemeral constitutional values would be immensely difficult. The difficulty is enhanced by the personality and modus operandi of Donald Trump himself. To the dismay of ideological conservatives, Trump has transformed the Republican Party from a conservative party to a populist party.[67] More importantly, he has attempted, with considerable success, to transform the Republican Party at large into something not far from a cult of personality, and the congressional Republican Party into a group of personal loyalists. Republican Trump critics like John McCain, Jeff Flake, and Bob Corker have died or left the Senate,[68] and the 2018 midterm elections added only one likely Trump adversary, Mitt Romney of Utah.[69] With few exceptions, those who remain have either bowed to Trump's party supremacy or gone quiet. The bottom line is that the aspect of Trump's personality and governing style that makes him most dangerous, the persistent tendency to personal rule, now stands as the largest obstacle to impeachment.

Trump's capture of the Republican Party is particularly important given the nature of the case for impeachment outlined above. In the two presidential impeachment controversies of the recent past – Nixon and Clinton – the argument for impeachment turned largely on the discovery of hidden misconduct by the president. With Nixon in particular, once the prosecutors, the press, and congressional investigators unearthed what Nixon had done, what he had known, and when he had known it, almost no one in the political world doubted that he should be impeached. With Trump, key components of the impeachment case against him rest on things he has done and said openly, notoriously, even proudly. And, so far at least, his party has effectively endorsed or tacitly acquiesced in all of it.

This is not to say that the Mueller investigation, state lawsuits, private litigation, or inquiries by the Democratic House majority elected in 2018 might not reveal new facts that would turn Republican opinion against Mr. Trump. It could happen. However, two other aspects of the contemporary American scene diminish the chance that any revelation, no matter how sordid, will change the views of dedicated partisans.

The first of these is the changed place of the media. As we noted in Chapter 8's discussion of the Nixon affair, the press of the period played a critical role because it was not divided into partisan camps, was generally committed to a journalistic ethic of discovering and reporting facts regardless of their political ramifications, and was generally trusted by the public to perform that job. That world is now as dead as the wooly mammoths and sabre-tooth tigers interred in the La Brea Tar Pits. Beginning with the invention of Fox News in the 1990s, the media landscape has fractured, with some outlets like CNBC attempting to imitate Fox's success on the left, and others trying to maintain allegiance to older notions of journalistic neutrality. Even more important has been the rise of specialized ideological outlets like Breitbart (right) and Huffington Post (left), and the general explosion of largely uncurated social media. The result is that people increasingly consume information from sources that tend to confirm their ideological predispositions or tribal allegiances and distrust sources that challenge those predispositions and allegiances.[70] The percentage of the populace that has considerable confidence in news from traditional media outlets like newspapers and television has plummeted. According to Gallup, the percentage of those with a great deal or quite a lot of confidence in television news fell from 46 percent in 1993 to 20 percent in 2018; in the same period the percentage of those with very little or no confidence in TV news jumped from 18 percent to 45 percent. Gallup also reports that the level of high confidence in newspapers fell from 51 percent in 1979 to 23 percent in 2018.[71] As a result, there is no set of commonly accepted authorities for deciding what is "true."

The second, and closely related, point is the general decline of public trust in public institutions. Whereas in the post-Second World War era, people generally trusted the government to provide reliable information and do the right thing, that trust has declined to perilously low levels. One survey finds that public confidence in the federal government to do the right thing "just about always" or "most of the time" fell from 73 percent in 1958 to less than 20 percent in 2015.[72] Notably, confidence in Congress has collapsed. Gallup reports that the percentage of persons with a high degree of confidence in Congress fell from 42 percent in 1973 (in the heart of the Watergate affair when an additional 35 percent expressed "some confidence" in Congress) to 11 percent in 2018.[73] Thus, the public is likely to be less disposed to accept factual conclusions either from law enforcement agencies or from a congressional impeachment investigation, particularly if those conclusions run contrary to their partisan predispositions.

Mr. Trump has consciously exacerbated this problem. He candidly admitted his motive for persistent attacks on the press: "You know why I do it? I do it to discredit you all and demean you all so when you write negative stories about me no one will believe you."[74] Similarly, his persistent assault on the Justice Department and the FBI as being dominated by nefarious members of the "deep state," and on the Mueller investigation as a partisan "witch hunt," has convinced an increasing proportion of Republicans that Mueller may not be fair, while having the reverse effect among Democrats.[75] In sum, the very presidential attacks on the justice system and the press that form a part of the indictment against Mr. Trump raise exponentially the difficulty of convincing the public at large – but more particularly his increasingly tribalized electoral base – that there exists a body of verifiable truth upon which a fair impeachment judgment could be made. Unless a significant fraction of Republican voters are convinced of facts that would justify impeachment, no Republican senator, still less the twenty that would be required for conviction, is likely to commit electoral suicide by voting for that verdict.

This is a pretty grim conclusion, whatever one thinks of Mr. Trump. If true, it means that our political polarization has run so far that a critical constitutional bulwark against executive dysfunction or even incipient tyranny may no longer be available. Of course, the country is not wholly without recourse. The Founders, after all, assumed that the primary remedy of an outraged public confronted by a rogue president is simply to vote the offender out of office. And 2020 is only next year.

Nonetheless, we do not yet know all that there is to be known about Mr. Trump's past, nor is he finished offending the letter and spirit of American constitutionalism. One can at least hope that, if revelations about his past are sufficiently heinous or his future actions are sufficiently dangerous, the country – Democrats, Republicans, and those of no party – will rise to the occasion and defend the constitution by impeaching him and expelling him from the presidency. In that spirit, I will leave the last word to the unassuming hero of the Nixon impeachment proceedings, House Judiciary Chair Peter Rodino. In a conversation with reporter Theodore White, Rodino mused:

> To me, "high crimes and misdemeanors" were never precise. The way I read them, they aren't meant to spell out anything but a President's performance in office. I see

it as the kind of conduct that brings the whole office into scandal and disrepute, the kind of abuse of power that subverts the system we live in, that brings about in and of itself a loss of confidence in this system . . . I guess, all in all, it's behavior which in its totality is not good for the Presidency, nor any part of the system. I got to agree this is an effort to overturn the election . . . but if this country can't stand a crisis, something has happened I don't understand.[76]

Amen.

Appendix: United States Impeachments, 1789 to Present

What follows is a synopsis of articles of impeachment adopted in each of the eighteen impeachments in the nation's history, as well as the Senate's votes on each of these articles. For quicker reference, this information is further condensed into a chart at the end.[*]

WILLIAM BLOUNT: U.S. SENATOR (TN)

House Vote to Impeach: July 7, 1797
    Articles of Impeachment Adopted: January 29, 1798
    Senate Action: January 11, 1799

Article 1:   In 1797, while the United States was officially neutral in the war between Spain and Great Britain, Blount, "designing and intending to disturb the peace and tranquility of the United States, and to violate and infringe the neutrality thereof," conspired to conduct a hostile military expedition against Spanish territory in Florida and Louisiana and to conquer such territory for Great Britain.

Article 2:   Despite a treaty between the United States and Spain by which both nations agreed to "maintain peace and harmony among the several Indian nations" inhabiting the Floridas, and to restrain the Indian nations within their borders from attacking the subjects or natives of the other, Blount conspired to "excite the Creek and Cherokee nations of Indians ... to commence hostilities against Spanish subjects and territory."

Article 3:   To accomplish the criminal designs described in Articles 1 and 2, Blount conspired and contrived "to alienate and divert the confidence" of the Indian nations from Benjamin Hawkins, the lawfully appointed federal agent for Indian affairs.

Article 4:   To accomplish the criminal designs described in Articles 1 and 2, Blount conspired and contrived to seduce James Carey, the official federal interpreter to the Cherokee nation, from the duty and trust of his office and to engage him to assist in the promotion and execution of Blount's criminal designs.

Article 5: To accomplish the criminal designs described in Articles 1 and 2, Blount conspired and contrived to diminish and impair the confidence of the Cherokee nation in the government of the United States, and to foment discontent and disaffection between them, in relation to treaties by which the two agreed to ascertain and mark a boundary line between them.[1]

On July 8, 1797, after receiving a message from President Adams describing Senator Blount's conduct, the Senate expelled him by a vote of 25:1.[2] Although the House had voted the previous day to impeach Senator Blount, it did not adopt the articles of impeachment necessary to pursue the matter until the following year. The Senate ultimately dismissed the case by a vote of 14:11, probably on the ground that a senator is not a civil officer subject to impeachment.[3]

JOHN PICKERING: JUDGE FOR THE DISTRICT OF NEW HAMPSHIRE

House Vote to Impeach: March 2, 1803
   Articles of Impeachment Adopted: December 30, 1803
   Senate Action: March 12, 1804

Article 1: Pickering, with the intent to evade a federal law, ordered the ship *Eliza*, its contents, and some cables to be delivered to a claimant of such property despite the claimant's failure to provide a certificate that the applicable tonnage duties had been paid.

Article 2: Pickering, with the intent to defeat the just claims of the United States, refused to hear testimony of witnesses offered to show that the ship *Eliza* and its contents were properly forfeited to the United States, and instead ordered the property returned to the private claimant.

Article 3: Pickering, "disregarding the authority of the laws and wickedly meaning and intending to injure the revenues of the United States and thereby impair their public credit" refused to allow an appeal of his ruling regarding ownership of the ship *Eliza* and its contents.

Article 4: Pickering appeared on the bench "in a state of total intoxication, produced by the free and intemperate use of intoxicating liquors," and "in a most profane and indecent manner, [did] invoke the name of the Supreme Being, to the evil example of the good citizens of the United States."[4]

Judge Pickering did not appear at the impeachment trial, but his son sent a letter to the Senate suggesting and offering to prove that the judge was insane at the time of the *Eliza* case and remained so.[5] After the Senate received evidence as to both guilt and insanity,[6] it voted on the articles of impeachment. Five senators "retired from the court" and refused to vote on the articles because they believed the form of the question posed to be an unfair one, because it precluded them from expressing judgment on what they considered the most important issues: Judge Pickering's sanity and whether the conduct charged rose to the level of an impeachable offense.[7] The Senate then convicted Judge Pickering on each count by a vote of 19:7.[8] After that, it voted 20:6 to remove Pickering from office.[9]

SAMUEL CHASE: ASSOCIATE JUSTICE OF THE SUPREME COURT OF THE UNITED STATES

House Vote to Impeach: March 12, 1804[10]
  Articles of Impeachment Adopted: December 4, 1804
  Senate Action: March 1, 1805

Article 1: During the treason trial of John Fries, Chase "conduct[ed] himself in a manner highly arbitrary, oppressive, and unjust" by: (1) delivering a written legal opinion tending to prejudice the jury against the defendant before defense counsel had been heard; (2) prohibiting defense counsel from citing to English authorities and United States statutes counsel deemed illustrative; and (3) barring defense counsel from addressing the jury on the law. This conduct deprived Fries of his constitutional rights and disgraced the character of the American bench.

Article 2: "Prompted by a similar spirit of persecution and injustice" during the libel trial of James Callender, and with the intent to oppress and procure a conviction, Chase overruled an objection to seating as a juror a person who had already made up his mind that the defendant was guilty.

Article 3: During the Callender trial, "with the intent to oppress and procure a conviction," Chase excluded testimony of a material defense witness on the pretense that the witness could not prove the truth of the whole of the allegedly libelous material, even though the charge embraced more than one fact.

Article 4: Chase's conduct throughout the Callender trial was marked by "manifest injustice, partiality, and intemperance" by: (1) requiring defense counsel to submit in writing to the court all questions they planned to ask a witness; (2) refusing to postpone the trial despite a proper request based on the absence of a material defense witness; (3) being rude and contemptuous of defense counsel and falsely insinuating that they wished to excite public fears; (4) making repeated and vexatious interruptions of defense counsel, inducing them to abandon their cause and their client;

and (5) expressing undue concern, "unbecoming even a public prosecutor," for the conviction of the accused.

Article 5: Chase illegally ordered the arrest of Callender even though he was not charged with a capital offense.

Article 6: Chase illegally tried Callender during the same term in which he was indicted.

Article 7: Disregarding the duties of his office, Chase "did descend from the dignity of a judge and stoop to the level of informer" by refusing to discharge a grand jury and advising it of allegedly libelous publications with the intention of procuring the prosecution of the printer, "thereby degrading his high judicial functions and tending to impair the public confidence" in the tribunals of justice.

Article 8: Disregarding the duties and dignity of his judicial character, Chase delivered to a Maryland grand jury "an intemperate and inflammatory political harangue, with the intent to excite the fears and resentment" of the grand jury against their state government and constitution.[11]

The Senate voted as follows: Article 1, 16 guilty:18 not guilty; Article 2, 10:24; Article 3, 18:16; Article 4, 18:16; Article 5, 0:34; Article 6, 4:30; Article 7, 10:24; Article 8, 19:15.[12]

Because the two-thirds majority required for conviction was lacking on all counts, Justice Chase was acquitted.

JAMES H. PECK: JUDGE FOR THE DISTRICT OF MISSOURI

House Vote to Impeach: April 24, 1830
  Article of Impeachment Adopted: May 1, 1830
  Senate Action: January 31, 1831

Article: In December 1825, Judge Peck issued a decree resolving a dispute to certain territorial lands. While the matter was on appeal to the Supreme Court, Judge Peck caused to be published in a local newspaper the reasons for his decision. Counsel for the appellants responded by getting another newspaper to print a letter in which he identified the errors in Judge Peck's opinion. In response, Judge Peck, "with intention wrongfully and unjustly to oppress, imprison, and otherwise injure" appellant's counsel, had counsel arrested, held him in contempt, ordered him imprisoned for twenty-four hours, and suspended him from practicing before the court for eighteen months, all "to the great disparagement of public justice, the abuse of judicial authority, and to the subversion of the liberties of the people of the United States."[13]

The Senate vote was 21 guilty:22 not guilty. Judge Peck was therefore acquitted.[14]

WEST H. HUMPHREYS: JUDGE FOR THE DISTRICT OF TENNESSEE

House Vote to Impeach: May 6, 1862
  Articles of Impeachment Adopted: May 19, 1862
  Senate Action: June 26, 1862

Article 1: On December 29, 1860, in Nashville, Tennessee, Humphreys endeavored by public speech to incite revolt and rebellion against the constitution and government of the United States.

Article 2: In 1861, "with the intent to abuse the high trust reposed in him as a judge," Humphreys openly and unlawfully supported and advocated the secession of the state of Tennessee.

Article 3: In 1861 and 1862, Humphreys organized an armed rebellion against the United States and levied war against them.

Article 4: With Jefferson Davis and others, Humphreys conspired to oppose by force the authority of the government of the United States.

Article 5: With intent to prevent the due administration of the laws of the United States, Humphreys neglected and refused to hold court, as by law he was required to do.

Article 6: With intent to subvert the authority of the government of the United States, Humphreys unlawfully acted as judge of an illegally constituted tribunal within Tennessee. In connection with this, Humphreys: (1) caused the arrest of one Perez Dickinson, and required him to swear allegiance to the Confederacy, and when Dickinson refused, Humphreys ordered him to leave the state; (2) ordered the confiscation of property of citizens of the United States, especially the property of one Andrew Johnson; and (3) caused the arrest and imprisonment of citizens of the United States because of their fidelity to their obligations as citizens and their resistance to the Confederacy.

Article 7: Humphreys, as a judge of the Confederate States of America and with the intent to injure one William G. Brownlow, ordered his unlawful arrest and imprisonment.[15]

Judge Humphreys offered no defense and made no appearance either in person or through counsel.[16] The Senate voted as follows: Article 1, 39 guilty:0 not guilty; Article 2, 36:1; Article 3, 33:4; Article 4, 28:10; Article 5, 39:0; Article 6(1), 36:1; Article 6(2), 12:24; Article 6(3), 35:1; Article 7, 35:1.[17]

Based on the guilty verdicts, the Senate then voted 38:0 to remove Judge Humphreys from office and 36:0 to disqualify him from holding in the future any office under the United States.[18]

ANDREW JOHNSON: PRESIDENT OF THE UNITED STATES

House Vote to Impeach: February 24, 1868

  Articles of Impeachment Adopted: March 2, 1868

  Senate Action: May 16, 1868

President Johnson was the only southern senator not to leave Congress when the South seceded. Later, as president, he obstructed many of the Radical Reconstruction efforts of Congress. He removed every military commander in the South who was committed to carrying out the spirit of the Reconstruction Acts. He also denounced black suffrage and claimed that some of the Reconstruction Acts, passed over his veto, were unconstitutional. Others, such as the Confiscation Act 1862, he effectively nullified by issuing a great number of pardons.[19]

Beginning in late 1866, and in response to Johnson's opposition to their political agenda, some members of the House tried to impeach the president. They charged him with, among other things, corruption in the use of his powers of appointment, pardon, and veto.[20] Some even suggested that Johnson was guilty of complicity in the murder of President Lincoln.[21] In March 1867, while the House Judiciary Committee was investigating these charges, and apparently fearing that Johnson would remove Secretary of War Stanton, the only Republican left in the cabinet after the 1866 congressional elections, Congress passed the Tenure of Office Act. This Act was designed to limit the president's power to remove subordinate officials without the Senate's consent. It required that all executive officials appointed with senatorial approval hold office until a successor had been appointed and confirmed. Thus, until the Senate agreed to a successor, senior executive officials could not be fired. A partial exception was made for cabinet officers, who were to hold office only during the term of the president who appointed them and for one month thereafter.

In August, while Congress was out of session, Johnson suspended Stanton. Although it was far from clear whether Stanton, who had been appointed by President Lincoln, was truly covered by the Act, when Congress reconvened in December, Johnson sent to the Senate his reasons for suspending Stanton. He thus implicitly acknowledged that Stanton was protected by the Act. The Senate declined to concur and Stanton returned to his post. In December, the House of Representatives rejected by a vote of 57:108 the long-pending effort to impeach President Johnson.[22]

On January 30, 1868, Congressman Schofield of Pennsylvania took the floor of the House. He proclaimed that area newspapers had reported Supreme Court Justice Stephen J. Field to have openly announced that the Tenure of Office Act was unconstitutional, and that the court would be sure to pronounce it so.[23] In response, the House of Representatives began an impeachment investigation against Justice Field.[24] This investigation dropped well into the background when, on February 21, President Johnson fired Secretary Stanton. Three days later, the House impeached President Johnson by a vote of 128:47.[25]

Article 1: On February 21, 1868, Johnson unlawfully issued an order for the removal of Edwin Stanton from his office as Secretary of War.

Article 2: On February 21, 1868, Johnson unlawfully issued a letter to Major General Lorenzo Thomas authorizing him to act as Secretary of War *ad interim*, despite the lack of a vacancy in that office.

Article 3: On February 21, 1868, while the Senate was in session, Johnson unlawfully appointed Lorenzo Thomas as Secretary of War *ad interim* without the advice and consent of the Senate.

Article 4: On February 21, 1868, Johnson illegally conspired with General Thomas to hinder and prevent Secretary of War Stanton from holding his office.

Article 5: On February 21, 1868, Johnson illegally conspired with General Thomas to prevent and hinder the Tenure of Office Act.

Article 6: On February 21, 1868, Johnson conspired with General Thomas to take possession of United States Department of War property, in violation of an 1861 Act to define and punish certain conspiracies.

Article 7: On February 21, 1868, Johnson conspired with General Thomas to take possession of United States Department of War property, in violation of the Tenure of Office Act.

Article 8: On February 21, 1868, with the intent unlawfully to control the disbursements of the Department of War, and in violation of the Tenure of Office Act, Johnson delivered a letter to General Thomas authorizing him to take charge of the Department of War.

Article 9: On February 22, 1868, as Commander in Chief of the armed forces, Johnson instructed Major General William Emory to disregard and treat as unconstitutional the Tenure of Office Act, particularly that portion that required all military orders to be issued through the General of the Army, and to obey such orders as Johnson may give directly.

Article 10: Johnson attempted "to bring into disgrace, ridicule, hatred, contempt, and reproach the Congress of the United States" by delivering loud, intemperate, inflammatory, and scandalous harangues against the Congress.

Article 11: On August 18, 1866, Johnson delivered a public speech in which he declared that the 39th Congress was not a lawful Congress of the United States, but a Congress of only some of them, in an effort to deny the validity of congressional legislation and the validity of proposed amendments to the Constitution.[26]

On May 16, the Senate voted on Article 11. The vote was 35 guilty:19 not guilty, one vote short of the two-thirds majority needed for conviction.[27] The Senate then adjourned. On May 26, the Senate voted on Articles 2 and 3. Again the vote was 35:9,[28] whereupon the Senate voted to adjourn the impeachment trial and the chief justice announced, without objection, a judgment of acquittal.[29]

One commentator has noted that "if one argues that Johnson's conviction would have resulted from votes motivated by political considerations, one must concede that the same considerations secured his acquittal."[30] This conclusion is based on evidence suggesting that at least three of the seven Republicans who broke ranks and voted to acquit did so in part for political reasons. Senators Fessenden and Grimes apparently informed Johnson's counsel that they would feel freer to vote against conviction if they were assured that the president would stop interfering with Reconstruction. They suggested that Johnson appoint General Schofield as Secretary of War. Johnson did. Senator Ross suggested he would vote for acquittal if the president accepted the new constitutions of Arkansas and South Carolina. Johnson did that too.

In early 1875, Johnson was elected to the Senate by the Tennessee legislature. He served there until his death in July 1875.

WILLIAM W. BELKNAP: FORMER SECRETARY OF WAR

House Vote to Impeach: March 2, 1876

    Articles of Impeachment Adopted: April 3, 1876

    Senate Action: August 1, 1876

    On March 2, 1876, William Belknap resigned as secretary of war. Nevertheless, later that day the House proceeded to impeach him for his alleged misconduct while in office.[31]

Article 1: On October 8, 1870, Belknap appointed Caleb P. Marsh to maintain a trading post at Fort Sill. On the same day, Marsh contracted with John S. Evans for Evans to fill the commission as post trader at Fort Sill in exchange for a yearly payment to Marsh of $12,000. On October 10, at the request of Marsh, Belknap appointed Evans to maintain the trading establishment at Fort Sill. On November 2, 1870, and on four more occasions over the next year, Belknap unlawfully received $1,500 payments from Marsh in consideration of allowing Evans to maintain a trading establishment at Fort Sill.

Article 2: Belknap, after "willfully, corruptly, and unlawfully" taking $1,500 from Marsh to permit Evans to maintain a trading post at Fort Sill, corruptly allowed Evans to maintain that trading post.

Article 3: From October 1870 to December 1875, Belknap received half of every payment Evans made to Marsh, during which period Belknap, "basely prostituting his high office to his lust for private gain" continued to allow Evans to serve as post trader, all to the great injury of the officers and soldiers of the Army of the United States.

Article 4: This article details, in seventeen separate specifications, the seventeen separate payments, ranging from $750 to $1,700, Belknap received from Marsh in consideration of allowing Evans to remain post trader.

Article 5: Belknap permitted Evans to remain post trader until March 2, 1876, despite knowing that Evans had contracted to pay Marsh for his influence in securing the appointment; and that, in order to make sure that the payments to Marsh would continue, Belknap received or caused his wife to receive large sums of money.[32]

On April 17, former Secretary Belknap appeared in person and urged the Senate to take no further cognizance of the articles of impeachment on the grounds that as a private citizen he was not subject to impeachment.[33] However, on May 29, by a vote of 37:29, the Senate resolved that Belknap was amenable to trial by impeachment, notwithstanding his resignation before the House impeached him.[34] It then gave him ten days to file a plea. Belknap refused to enter a plea, and instead continued to challenge the Senate's jurisdiction.[35] The Senate proceeded with the trial as if Belknap had pleaded not guilty, and Belknap's counsel cross-examined the House manager's witnesses and then presented the defendant's case.[36] After trial, the Senate voted as follows: Article 1, 35 guilty:25 not guilty; Article 2, 36:25; Article 3, 36:25; Article 4, 36:25, Article 5, 37:25.[37]

As a result, Mr. Belknap was acquitted. Twenty-two of the senators who voted to acquit (as well as two who voted to convict and one who did not vote) believed the Senate lacked jurisdiction.[38]

CHARLES H. SWAYNE: JUDGE FOR THE NORTHERN DISTRICT OF FLORIDA

House Vote to Impeach: December 13, 1904
  Articles of Impeachment Adopted: January 18, 1905
  Senate Action: February 27, 1905

Article 1: On April 20, 1897, knowing that a far smaller sum was due, and for the purpose of obtaining payment, Swayne made a false claim in the amount of $230 against the United States for travel expenses relating to holding court in Waco, Texas. In doing so, he signed a false certificate.

Article 2: Swayne, knowing the rules on reimbursement for expenses, falsely certified that his expenses in traveling to, holding court in, and returning from Tyler, Texas, in December 1900 were $10 per day for 31 days, for which he received $310, when in fact his actual expenses were less.

Article 3: Swayne, knowing the rules on reimbursement for expenses, falsely certified that his expenses in traveling to, holding court in, and returning from Tyler, Texas, in January 1903 were $10 per day for 41 days, for which he received $410, when in fact his actual expenses were less.

Article 4: In 1893, for the purpose of transporting himself, his family, and his friends from Delaware to Florida, Swayne unlawfully appropriated to his own use a railroad car owned by a railroad company that was under receivership in his court. In addition, and without paying therefor, Swayne was supplied by the receiver with provisions which he and his friends consumed, as well as the services of a conductor. Then, in his capacity as judge, Swayne allowed the receiver to claim these expenses as part of the necessary costs of operating the railroad company.

Article 5: In 1893, for the purpose of transporting himself, his family, and his friends from Florida to California, Swayne unlawfully appropriated to his own use a railroad car owned by a railroad company which was under receivership in his court. In addition, and without paying therefor, Swayne was supplied by the receiver with provisions which he and his friends consumed, as well as the services of a conductor. Then, in his capacity as judge, Swayne allowed the receiver to claim these expenses as part of the necessary costs of operating the railroad company.

Article 6: When Congress altered the boundaries of the northern district of Florida in 1894 in a way that removed Swayne's residence from the district, Swayne did not acquire a new residence within the district for more than six years, in violation of a law requiring judges to reside in the district in which they sit.

Article 7: "Totally disregarding his duty" to reside within the newly defined district, Swayne did not do so for a period of about nine years.

Article 8: On November 12, 1901, Swayne "did maliciously and unlawfully" hold an attorney named E. T. Davis in contempt of court, for which Swayne fined him $100 and imprisoned him for ten days.

Article 9: On November 12, 1901, Swayne "did knowingly and unlawfully" hold an attorney named E. T. Davis in contempt of court, for which Swayne fined him $100 and imprisoned him for ten days.

Article 10: On November 12, 1901, Swayne "did maliciously and unlawfully" hold an attorney named Simeon Belden in contempt of court, for which Swayne fined him $100 and imprisoned him for ten days.

Article 11: On November 12, 1901, Swayne "did knowingly and unlawfully" hold an attorney named Simeon Belden in contempt of court, for which Swayne fined him $100 and imprisoned him for ten days.

Article 12: On December 9, 1902, Swayne "did unlawfully and knowingly" hold W. C. O'Neal in contempt of court, for which Swayne imprisoned him for sixty days.[39]

Judge Swayne was acquitted after the Senate voted as follows: Article 1, 33 guilty:49 not guilty; Article 2, 32:50; Article 3, 32:50; Article 4, 13:69; Article 5, 13:69; Article 6, 31:51; Article 7, 19:63; Article 8, 31:51; Article 9, 31:51; Article 10, 31:51; Article 11, 31:51; Article 12, 31:51.[40]

ROBERT W. ARCHBALD: JUDGE FOR THE COURT OF APPEALS FOR THE THIRD CIRCUIT

Articles of Impeachment Adopted: July 11, 1912[41]
  Senate Action: January 13, 1913

  Article 1: On March 31, 1911, while assigned to the United States Commerce Court, Archbald induced the Erie Railroad Company, which was a litigant in several cases before the Commerce Court, to sell him and a partner certain property owned by a subsidiary corporation. In doing this, Archbald "willfully, unlawfully, and corruptly took advantage of his official position of a judge" in order to profit for himself.

  Article 2: In August 1911, Archbald willfully, unlawfully, and corruptly used his influence as a judge of the Commerce Court to induce parties in litigation pending before the court and before the Interstate Commerce Commission to settle their dispute by having one party sell two-thirds of its stock to another party.

  Article 3: In October 1911, Archbald unlawfully and corruptly used his official position and influence as a judge of the Commerce Court to cause a litigant before that court to lease him a culm dump containing large coal deposits.

  Article 4: In late 1911 and early 1912, Archbald communicated secretly with the attorney for one party in a case before the Commerce Court and advised the attorney to see one of the witnesses and get an explanation and interpretation of the testimony given by the witness. He then secretly informed the attorney of the court's discovery of evidence contrary to the statements of the attorney and advised the attorney to submit additional arguments. Archbald did this all without the knowledge or consent of the Commerce Court.

  Article 5: In 1904, Archbald wrongfully attempted to use his influence to assist Frederick Warnke in obtaining a lease of a culm dump owned by Philadelphia & Reading Coal & Iron Co., a company which also owned a railroad engaged in interstate commerce. After Archbald's efforts proved to be unsuccessful, he accepted a promissory note for $500 from Warnke for making the attempt and for other favors.

Article 6:   In 1911, Archbald unlawfully, improperly, and corruptly attempted to use his influence as a judge to induce the officers of Lehigh Valley Coal Co. to purchase an interest in an 800-acre tract of coal land.

Article 7:   In 1908, Archbald wrongfully and corruptly agreed to purchase the stock in a gold-mining scheme in Honduras with W. W. Rissinger, who owned the Old Plymouth Coal Co., a plaintiff in several cases pending before Archbald. Archbald later ruled for the Old Plymouth on several legal issues, resulting in settlements by which Old Plymouth recovered approximately $28,000.

Article 8:   In 1909, Archbald drew a promissory note for $500 in his favor and had it signed by John Henry Jones. At that time, Christopher and William Boland owned a coal company engaged in litigation involving a large sum of money and over which Archbald was presiding. Archbald agreed that the note, bearing his name and endorsement, should be presented to the Bolands in an effort to get them to discount it. This was done with the intent that Archbald's name on the note would coerce or induce them to do so.

Article 9:   In 1909, Archbald drew another promissory note in his favor for $500 and had it signed by John Henry Jones. Knowing that his own endorsement was not sufficient to secure money in normal commercial channels, Archbald wrongfully permitted the endorsed note to be presented for discount at the office of C. H. Von Storch, in whose favor Archbald had recently ruled in a lawsuit. Von Storch did discount the note. The note was never paid.

Article 10:   On May 1, 1910, Archbald received a large sum of money from Henry W. Cannon for the purpose of defraying the cost of a pleasure trip to Europe. At that time, Cannon was a stockholder and officer of various interstate railway companies that in due course were likely to be interested in litigation pending in the Commerce Court and presided over by Archbald. Accepting this money was improper and brought Archbald's office into disrepute.

Article 11:   In May 1910, Archbald received more than $500 from attorneys who practiced before him, the money having been solicited by court officers appointed by Archbald.

Article 12:   On April 9, 1901, Archbald appointed J. B. Woodward, an attorney for Lehigh Valley Railroad Co., as jury commissioner for his district court. While serving as jury commissioner, Woodward continued to act as attorney for the railroad, which Archbald well knew.

Article 13:   During his time as a district judge and as a judge assigned to the Commerce Court, Archbald wrongfully sought to obtain credit from and through persons who were interested in litigation over which he presided. He speculated for profit in the purchase and sale of various coal properties, and unlawfully used his position as judge to influence officers of various railroad companies to enter into contracts in which he had a financial interest, which such companies had litigation pending in his court.[42]

The Senate voted as follows: Article 1, 68 guilty:5 not guilty; Article 2, 46:25; Article 3, 60:11; Article 4, 52:20; Article 5, 66:6; Article 6, 24:45; Article 7, 29:36; Article 8, 22:42; Article 9, 23:39; Article 10, 1:65; Article 11, 11:51; Article 12, 19:46; Article 13. 42:20.[43]

After the guilty verdict was announced, the Senate voted to remove Judge Archbald from office. Then, by a vote of 39:35, it disqualified him from holding any office under the United States in the future.[44]

GEORGE ENGLISH: JUDGE FOR THE EASTERN DISTRICT OF ILLINOIS

Articles of Impeachment Adopted: April 1, 1926
  Senate Action: December 13, 1926

Article 1: English abused his office through tyranny and oppression, thereby bringing the administration of justice in his court into disrepute, by (1) disbarring Thomas Webb and later Charles A. Karch without proffering charges against either, without prior notice to either, and without permitting either to be heard in his own defense; (2) unlawfully and deceitfully summoning several state and local officials to appear before him in an imaginary case, placing them in a jury box, and then in a loud, angry voice and using profane and indecent language, denouncing them without naming any act of misconduct and threatening to remove them from their offices; (3) intending to coerce the minds of certain jurymen by telling them that he would send them to jail if they did not convict a defendant whom the judge said was guilty; (4) unlawfully summoning an editor of the *East St. Louis Journal* and a reporter for the *St. Louis Post-Dispatch* and in angry and abusive language threatening them with imprisonment if they published truthful facts relating to the disbarment of Karch; and (5) unlawfully summoning the publisher of the Carbondale Free Press and threatening to imprison him for printing an editorial and some handbills.

Article 2: English engaged in a course of unlawful and improper conduct, "filled with partiality and favoritism," in connection with bankruptcy cases within the district. He did this by, among other things: (1) appointing Charles B. Thomas as the referee for all such cases; (2) unlawfully changing the rules of bankruptcy for the district to allow Thomas both to appoint friends and relatives as receivers and to charge the cost of expensive office space to the United States and the estates in bankruptcy;

and (3) allowing Thomas to hire English's son at a large compensation to be paid out of funds of the estates in bankruptcy.

Article 3: English corruptly extended partiality and favoritism, bringing the administration of justice into disrepute, by refusing to appoint the temporary receivers suggested by counsel for the parties in interest in a major case unless Charles Thomas was appointed attorney for such receivers. When they agreed, he retroactively increased the salary for Thomas, producing a total charge of $43,350, even though Thomas' services were not necessary. English did similar things in other cases. In a criminal case, English sentenced the convicted defendant to four months and a $500 fine. When the defendant's counsel withdrew and was replaced by Thomas, English vacated the sentence of imprisonment. For this, the defendant paid Thomas $2,500. English acted on the matter without the presence of Thomas in the court and without investigation, in order to show favoritism to Thomas, to whom English was under financial obligation. English then received $1,435 from Thomas in return for the favoritism extended.

Article 4: In conjunction with Thomas, English corruptly and improperly deposited, transferred, and used bankruptcy funds for the pecuniary benefit of himself and Thomas.

Article 5: English repeatedly treated members of the bar in a coarse, indecent, arbitrary, and tyrannical manner, so as to hinder them in their duties and deprive their clients of the benefits of counsel. He wickedly and illegally refused to allow parties the benefit of trial by jury. He conducted himself in making decisions and issuing orders so as to inspire the widespread belief that matters in his court were not decided on their merits, but with partiality and favoritism.[45]

Judge English resigned his office on November 4, 1926.[46] On December 11, the House managers of the impeachment reported that Judge English's resignation "in no way affects the right of the Senate" to hear and determine the impeachment charges. Nevertheless, they recommended that the impeachment proceedings against him be discontinued.[47] The House then passed a resolution indicating its desire not to urge the articles of impeachment before the Senate.[48] On December 13, the Senate concurred by a vote of 70:9.[49]

HAROLD LOUDERBACK: JUDGE FOR THE NORTHERN DISTRICT OF CALIFORNIA

Articles of Impeachment Adopted: February 24, 1933
   Amended: April 17, 1933
   Senate Action: May 24, 1933

Article 1: Louderback abused the power of his office through tyranny, oppression, favoritism, and conspiracy, and brought the administration of justice within the district into disrepute. In particular, on March 11, 1930, he discharged Addison G. Strong as receiver in a case after he attempted to coerce Strong to hire Douglas Short as attorney for the receiver by promising to allow large fees and threatening to reduce fees if Short were not appointed. He then appointed Short, who had been suggested by Sam Leake, to whom Louderback was under personal obligation. Leake had previously conspired with Louderback to rent lodgings for Louderback in San Francisco under Leake's name, so that Louderback could reside in San Francisco while maintaining a fictitious residence in Contra Costa County, so that a lawsuit Louderback expected to be filed against him could be removed to Contra Costa County. Short did receive exorbitant fees for his services as attorney for the receiver, and Leake received a kickback from Short.

Article 2: Louderback, filled with partiality and favoritism, improperly granted excessive and exorbitant allowances to the receiver and attorney he had appointed in a case over which he had improperly acquired jurisdiction. When his orders in the case were reversed on appeal, and Louderback was directed to order the receiver to turn the property over to the state insurance commissioner, Louderback improperly and illegally conditioned that order on the commissioner's agreement not to appeal the award of fees Louderback had granted to the receiver and attorney. This allowed Louderback to favor and enrich his friends at the expense of the litigants and parties in interest in the case.

Article 3: Louderback misbehaved in office, resulting in expense, annoyance, and hindrance to the litigants, by appointing Guy H. Gilbert as receiver in a case, knowing that Gilbert was incompetent and unqualified for that position. He then refused the litigants a hearing on the appointment and caused them to be misinformed of his actions.

Article 4: For the sole purpose of enriching his friends, Louderback appointed a receiver on an improper application in a case involving Prudential Holding Co. Louderback then refused to give proper consideration to Prudential's petition to remove the receiver. When Prudential became the subject of a bankruptcy case, Louderback improperly and illegally took jurisdiction over the case, and appointed the receiver as receiver in bankruptcy, causing Prudential unnecessary expense and depriving it of the right to fair and impartial consideration of its rights.

Article 5: During his tenure as judge and in the manner in which he issued orders, appointed receivers, and appointed attorneys for receivers, Louderback displayed "a high degree of indifference to the litigants" and inspired the widespread belief that matters in his court were not decided on their merits, but with partiality and favoritism, all of which is prejudicial to the dignity of the judiciary.[50]

In response to a motion from Judge Louderback's counsel for a more definite statement of Article 5B the House later amended it to make it more detailed.[51] The Senate acquitted Judge Louderback by voting as follows: Article 1, 34 guilty:42 not guilty; Article 2, 23:47; Article 3, 11:63; Article 4, 30:47.[52]

HALSTEAD L. RITTER: JUDGE FOR THE SOUTHERN DISTRICT OF FLORIDA

Articles of Impeachment Adopted: March 2, 1936
  Amended: March 30, 1936
  Senate Action: April 17, 1936

Article 1: In July 1930, Ritter awarded his former law partner an advance of $2,500 for his services in a receivership proceeding. Ritter, aware of the appearance of impropriety, then asked another judge in the district to fix the final fee allowance. The other judge did so, setting the fee at $15,000. Nevertheless, Ritter then allowed an additional $75,000. When the amount was paid, the former partner in turn paid Ritter $4,500 in cash, which Ritter corruptly and unlawfully accepted for his own use and benefit.

Article 2: In 1929, Ritter conspired with his former law partner and others to place a hotel into receivership in proceedings before Ritter. The former partner then filed the action without authorization from and contrary to the instructions of the parties in interest. When the matter came before Ritter, he refused the parties' request to dismiss the action and appointed one of the other conspirators receiver. Then follow the facts alleged in Article 1. Ritter willfully failed to perform his duty to conserve the assets of the company in receivership. Instead, he permitted their waste and dissipation, and personally profited thereby.

Article 3: Ritter violated the Judicial Code of the United States by continuing to work on a case after he became a judge, and he solicited and accepted an additional $2,000 in fees for such work.

Article 4: Ritter violated the Judicial Code of the United States by working on another case after he became a judge, for which he received $7,500.

Article 5: Ritter violated federal law by willfully attempting to evade federal tax on income earned in 1929. Specifically, he received $12,000 in unreported income, $9,500 of which relates to matters described in Articles 3 and 4.

Article 6: Ritter violated federal law by willfully attempting to evade federal tax on income earned in 1930. Specifically, he received $5,300 in unreported income, $2,000 of which relates to matters described in Article 1.

Article 7:   The reasonable and probable consequences of Ritter's actions were "to bring his court into scandal and disrepute," to the prejudice of the court and public confidence in the administration of justice therein. Specifically, in addition to the conduct in Articles 1–6, when one of his decisions came under public criticism, Ritter agreed to recuse himself from the case if the city commissioners of Miami passed a resolution expressing confidence in his integrity. Ritter thereby bartered his judicial authority for a vote of confidence.[53]

The Senate voted on the articles of impeachment as follows: Article 1, 55 guilty:29 not guilty; Article 2, 52:32; Article 3, 44:39; Article 4, 36:48; Article 5, 36:48; Article 6, 46:37; Article 7, 56:28.[54]

As a result, Judge Ritter was acquitted on the first six articles, each of which charged specific wrongdoing, but was convicted on the final, general article charging Ritter with bringing his court into scandal and disrepute. The chair ruled that conviction carries with it removal from office, without a further vote being necessary.[55] The Senate then voted 76:0 not to disqualify Ritter from holding future office.[56]

HARRY CLAIBORNE: JUDGE FOR THE DISTRICT OF NEVADA

Articles of Impeachment Adopted: July 22, 1986
   Senate Action: October 9, 1986

Article 1:   In June 1980, in violation of federal law, Claiborne willfully and knowingly filed a federal income tax return for the year 1979 that failed to report a substantial amount of income.

Article 2:   In June 1981, in violation of federal law, Claiborne willfully and knowingly filed a federal income tax return for the year 1980 that failed to report a substantial amount of income.

Article 3:   On August 10, 1984, Claiborne was found guilty of making and subscribing a false income tax return for the calendar years 1979 and 1980.

Article 4:   By willfully and knowingly falsifying his income on his federal tax returns for 1979 and 1980, Claiborne "betrayed the trust of the people of the United States and reduced confidence in the integrity and impartiality of the judiciary, thereby bringing disrepute on the federal courts and the administration of justice by the courts."[57]

After a trial committee received the evidence, the entire Senate voted on the articles of impeachment as follows: Article 1, 87 guilty:10 not guilty, 1 present; Article 2, 90:7, 1 present; Article 3, 46:17, 35 present; Article 4, 89:8, 1 present.[58]

Judge Claiborne was therefore convicted on counts 1, 2, and 4, but acquitted on count 3.[59]

ALCEE L. HASTINGS: JUDGE FOR THE SOUTHERN
DISTRICT OF FLORIDA

Articles of Impeachment Adopted: August 3, 1988
  Senate Action: October 20, 1989

Article 1: In 1981, Hastings and William Borders, an attorney, engaged in
a corrupt conspiracy to obtain $150,000 from defendants in *United
States v. Romano*,[60] a case tried before Judge Hastings, in return
for the imposition of sentences which would not require
incarceration.

Article 2: In 1983, while Hastings was a defendant in a criminal case and under
oath, Hastings knowingly and falsely stated that he and Borders never
made any agreement to solicit a bribe from defendants in the *Romano*
case.

Article 3: In 1983, while Hastings was a defendant in a criminal case and under
oath, Hastings knowingly and falsely stated that he and Borders never
agreed to modify the sentences of defendants in the *Romano* case in
return for a bribe from those defendants.

Article 4: In 1983, while Hastings was a defendant in a criminal case and
under oath, Hastings knowingly and falsely stated that he and
Borders never agreed that, in return for a bribe, Hastings would
modify an order he previously issued that property of the *Romano*
defendants be forfeited.

Article 5: In 1983, while Hastings was a defendant in a criminal case and under
oath, Hastings knowingly and falsely stated that his appearance at the
Fontainebleau Hotel on September 16, 1981, was not part of a plan to
demonstrate his participation in a bribery scheme and that he had not
expected to meet Borders there.

Article 6: In 1983, while Hastings was a defendant in a criminal case and under
oath, Hastings knowingly and falsely stated that he did not expect
Borders to appear at his room at the Sheraton Hotel on September 12,
1981.

Article 7: In 1983, while Hastings was a defendant in a criminal case and under
oath, Hastings knowingly and falsely stated that his motive for instructing his law clerk to prepare a new forfeiture order in the *Romano* case
was based on his concern that the order be revised before the law clerk's
scheduled departure, when in fact the instruction was in furtherance of
a bribery scheme.

Article 8: In 1983, while Hastings was a defendant in a criminal case and under
oath, Hastings knowingly and falsely stated that his October 5, 1981,
telephone conversation with Borders was about writing letters to solicit
assistance for Hemphill Pride, when in fact it was a coded conversation

in furtherance of a conspiracy with Borders to solicit a bribe from defendants in the *Romano* case.

Article 9: In 1983, while Hastings was a defendant in a criminal case and under oath, Hastings knowingly and falsely stated that three documents that purported to be drafts of letters to assist Hemphill Pride had been written by Hastings on October 5, 1981, and were the letters referred to by Hastings in his October 5 telephone conversation with Borders.

Article 10: In 1983, while Hastings was a defendant in a criminal case and under oath, Hastings knowingly and falsely stated that on May 5, 1981, he talked to Hemphill Pride by placing a telephone call to 803-758-8825.

Article 11: In 1983, while Hastings was a defendant in a criminal case and under oath, Hastings knowingly and falsely stated that on August 2, 1981, he talked to Hemphill Pride by placing a telephone call to 803-782-9387.

Article 12: In 1983, while Hastings was a defendant in a criminal case and under oath, Hastings knowingly and falsely stated that on September 2, 1981, he talked to Hemphill Pride by placing a telephone call to 803-758-8825.

Article 13: In 1983, while Hastings was a defendant in a criminal case and under oath, Hastings knowingly and falsely stated that 803-777-7716 was a telephone number through which Hemphill Pride could be contacted in July 1981.

Article 14: In 1983, while Hastings was a defendant in a criminal case and under oath, Hastings knowingly and falsely stated that on October 9, 1981, he called his mother and Patricia Williams from his hotel room at the L'Enfant Plaza Hotel.

Article 15: In 1983, while Hastings was a defendant in a criminal case and under oath, Hastings knowingly made a false statement concerning his motives for taking a plane on October 9, 1981, from Baltimore-Washington International Airport rather than from Washington National Airport.

Article 16: On September 6, 1985, Hastings revealed highly confidential information that he learned as the judge supervising a wiretap. As a result of this improper disclosure, certain investigations then being conducted by law enforcement agents of the United States were thwarted and ultimately terminated.

Article 17: Hastings, through a corrupt relationship with Borders, giving false testimony under oath, fabricating false documents, and improperly disclosing confidential information acquired by him as the supervisory judge of a wiretap, undermined confidence in the integrity and impartiality of the judiciary and betrayed the trust of the people of the United States, thereby bringing disrepute on the Federal courts and the administration of justice by the Federal courts.[61]

Prior to Senate action, Hastings had been acquitted in a criminal trial for bribery and conspiracy, but his alleged co-conspirator, Borders, had been convicted in a separate trial. During the impeachment trial, a committee of the Senate received the evidence. Prior to voting on the articles of impeachment, and with the consent of both the House managers and counsel for Judge Hastings, the entire Senate decided that if it acquitted on Article 1, no vote should be taken on Articles 2–5, 7 or 8.[62] Instead, a judgment of acquittal on those charges should be automatically entered. The Senate then began to vote. After voting on the first six articles, the Senate decided it would be unnecessary to vote on Articles 10–15. The votes were as follows: Article 1, 69 guilty:26 not guilty; Article 2, 68:27; Article 3, 69:26; Article 4, 67:28; Article 5, 67:28; Article 6, 48:47; Article 7, 69:26; Article 8, 68:27; Article 9, 70:25; Article 16, 0:95; Article 17, 60:35.[63]

Judge Hastings was therefore deemed removed from office. In 1992, Hastings was elected to and became a member of the House of Representatives. As of 2018, he was serving his thirteenth term.

WALTER L. NIXON: JUDGE FOR THE SOUTHERN DISTRICT OF MISSISSIPPI

Articles of Impeachment Adopted: May 10, 1989
   Senate Action: November 3, 1989

Article 1: On July 18, 1984, Nixon testified before a federal grand jury investigating his business relationship with Wiley Fairchild and the handling of the criminal prosecution of Fairchild's son for drug smuggling. In doing so, he falsely denied ever having discussed the Fairchild case with District Attorney Paul Holmes.

Article 2: On July 18, 1984, Nixon testified before a federal grand jury investigating his business relationship with Wiley Fairchild and the handling of the criminal prosecution of Fairchild's son for drug smuggling. In doing so, he falsely asserted that he had nothing whatsoever to do with the Fairchild case and had never influenced anybody with respect to it.

Article 3: Nixon "has raised substantial doubt as to his judicial integrity, undermined confidence in the integrity and impartiality of the judiciary, betrayed the trust of the people of the United States, disobeyed the laws of the United States and brought disrepute on the Federal courts and the administration of justice by the Federal courts." He did this, after entering into an investment with Wiley Fairchild, by concealing from federal investigators and from a grand jury conversations Nixon had with Fairchild, the District Attorney, and others about the prosecution of Fairchild's son.[64]

In 1986, Nixon was convicted on federal criminal charges for the conduct described in Articles 1 and 2. At the time of his impeachment trial, he had exhausted his appeals and was serving a five-year sentence. The Senate appointed a committee to receive the evidence at trial. The whole Senate then voted on the articles of impeachment as follows: Article 1, 89 guilty:8 not guilty; Article 2, 78:19; Article 3, 57:40.[65]

As a result of the conviction on Articles 1 and 2, Nixon was removed from office, without a separate vote.

WILLIAM J. CLINTON: PRESIDENT OF THE UNITED STATES

Articles of Impeachment Adopted: December 19, 1998
  Senate Action: February 12, 1999

Article 1:   On August 17, 1998, President Clinton gave perjurious, false, and mis-
             leading testimony to a grand jury concerning one or more of the follow-
             ing: (1) the nature and details of his relationship with a subordinate
             government employee; (2) prior perjurious testimony he gave in
             a federal civil rights action brought against him; (3) prior false and
             misleading statements he allowed his attorney to make to the judge in
             that civil rights action; and (4) his corrupt efforts to influence the testi-
             mony of witnesses and to impede the discovery of evidence in that civil
             rights action.[66]

Article 2:   Clinton obstructed the administration of justice, personally and through
             subordinates, by engaging in a course of conduct designed to conceal the
             existence of evidence and testimony related to a civil rights action
             brought against him. Clinton did this by: (1) on or about December 17,
             1997, corruptly encouraging a witness in a federal civil rights action
             brought against him to execute a sworn affidavit that he knew to be
             perjurious; (2) on or about December 17, 1997, corruptly encouraging
             a witness in a civil rights action brought against him to give perjurious
             testimony if and when called to testify in that proceeding; (3) on or
             about December 28, 1997, corruptly engaging in a scheme to conceal
             evidence that had been subpoenaed in the civil rights action brought
             against him; (4) from December 7, 1997, through January 14, 1998,
             endeavoring to secure a job for a witness in the civil rights action brought
             against him in order to corruptly prevent the truthful testimony of that
             witness in that proceeding; (5) on or about January 17, 1998, at his
             deposition in the civil rights action, corruptly allowing his attorney to
             make false and misleading statements to the judge, in order to prevent
             questioning deemed relevant by the judge; (6) on or about January 18 and
             20–21, 1998, relating a false account of events relevant to the civil rights

action to a potential witness, in order to corruptly influence the testimony of that witness; and (7) on or about January 21, 23 and 26, 1998, making false statements to potential witnesses in a grand jury proceeding in order to corruptly influence the testimony of those witnesses.[67]

Both articles of impeachment sought not only Clinton's removal from office, but also his disqualification from holding any federal office in the future. After trial, the Senate voted as follows: Article 1, 45 guilty:55 not guilty; Article 2, 50:50.

As a result, President Clinton was acquitted.

SAMUEL B. KENT: JUDGE FOR THE SOUTHERN DISTRICT OF TEXAS

Articles of Impeachment Adopted: June 19, 2009
Senate Action: July 22, 2009

Article 1: On one or more occasions between 2003 and 2007, Judge Kent sexually assaulted Cathy McBroom, an employee of the Office of the Clerk of the Court for the Southern District of Texas assigned to Judge Kent's courtroom, by touching her private areas directly and through her clothing against her will and by attempting to cause her to engage in a sexual act with him.

Article 2: On one or more occasions between 2001 and 2007, Judge Kent sexually assaulted Donna Wilkerson, an employee of the Southern District of Texas, by touching her in her private areas against her will and by attempting to cause her to engage in a sexual act with him.

Article 3: Kent corruptly obstructed, influenced, or impeded an official proceeding by lying to a Special Investigative Committee as follows: (a) Judge Kent falsely stated to the Committee that the extent of his unwanted sexual contact with Donna Wilkerson was one kiss, when in fact and as he knew he had engaged in repeated sexual contact with Donna Wilkerson without her permission; (b) Judge Kent falsely stated to the Committee that when told by Donna Wilkerson his advances were unwelcome no further contact occurred, when in fact and as he knew, Judge Kent continued such advances even after she asked him to stop.

Article 4: Kent made material false and misleading statements about the nature and extent of his non-consensual sexual contact with Cathy McBroom and Donna Wilkerson to agents of the Federal Bureau of Investigation on or about November 30, 2007, and to agents of the Federal Bureau of Investigation and representatives of the Department of Justice on or about August 11, 2008.[68]

Kent was indicted, pleaded guilty and was sentenced to imprisonment for the felony of obstruction of justice in violation of section 1512(c)(2) of title 18,

United States Code, on the basis of false statements made to the Special Investigative Committee described in Article 3. The sentencing judge described his conduct as "a stain on the justice system itself."

Judge Kent resigned from office on June 30, 2009.[69] Following his resignation, the House agreed not to further pursue the articles of impeachment against him. On July 20, 2009, the House passed a resolution asking the Senate to end Kent's trial.[70] On July 22, 2009, the Senate dismissed the articles.[71]

G. THOMAS PORTEOUS, JR.: JUDGE FOR THE EASTERN DISTRICT OF LOUISIANA

Articles of Impeachment Adopted: March 11, 2010
    Senate Action: December 8, 2010

Article 1: Porteous declined to recuse himself from a case despite his corrupt relationship with a law firm representing one of the parties in the action. While a state court judge in Louisiana in the 1980s, Porteous had appointed a partner in the firm as a "curator" in hundreds of cases and thereafter requested and accepted from the firm a portion of the curatorship fees that had been paid to the firm. Porteous received approximately $20,000 during the period of the scheme. Porteous also made intentionally misleading statements at the recusal hearing intended to minimize the extent of his personal relationship with the law firm, which "deprived the parties and the public of the right to the honest services of his office." Porteous also engaged in corrupt conduct after the case by soliciting and accepting things of value from the law firm, including a payment of thousands of dollars in cash. Without disclosing his corrupt relationship with the law firm, Porteous ruled in favor of their client.

Article 2: Porteous, while a state court judge and continuing while he was a Federal judge, engaged in a corrupt relationship with a bail bondsman, Louis M. Marcotte, III, and his sister Lori Marcotte. Porteous solicited and accepted numerous things of value, including meals, trips, home repairs, and car repairs, for his personal use and benefit, while at the same time taking official actions that benefited the Marcottes. The official actions included improperly setting aside or expunging felony convictions for two Marcotte employees. Porteous used the power and prestige of his office to assist the Marcottes in forming relationships with state judicial officers and individuals important to the Marcottes' business. As Judge Porteous well knew and understood, Louis Marcotte also made false statements to the Federal Bureau of Investigation in an effort to assist Judge Porteous in being appointed to the Federal bench.

Article 3: While a Federal judge, Porteous knowingly and intentionally made material false statements and representations under penalty of perjury related to his personal bankruptcy filing and repeatedly violated a court order in his bankruptcy case. Judge Porteous did so by: (1) using a false name and a post office box address to conceal his identity as the debtor in the case; (2) concealing assets; (3) concealing preferential payments to certain creditors; (4) concealing gambling losses and other gambling debts; and (5) incurring new debts while the case was pending, in violation of the bankruptcy court's order.

Article 4: In 1994, in connection with his nomination to be a Federal judge, Porteous knowingly made material false statements about his past to both the United States Senate and the Federal Bureau of Investigation in order to obtain the office of United States District Court Judge. Porteous denied that there was anything in his personal life that could be used by someone to coerce or blackmail him, or that there was anything in his life that could cause an embarrassment to himself or the president if publicly known. Porteous also falsely told the Federal Bureau of Investigation on two separate occasions that he was not concealing any activity or conduct that could be used to influence, pressure, coerce, or compromise him in any way or that would impact negatively on his character, reputation, judgment, or discretion. On the Senate Judiciary Committee's "Questionnaire for Judicial Nominees," Porteous stated he did "not know of any unfavorable information that may affect [his] nomination."[72]

The Senate voted as follows: Article 1, 96 guilty:0 not guilty; Article 2, 69:27; Article 3, 88:8; Article 4, 90:6.[73]

The Senate then voted 94:2 to forever disqualify Porteous from holding an office of honor, trust or profit under the United States.[74]

United States Impeachments, 1789 to Present

Official	Office	Dates	Grounds	Result
William Blount	U.S. Senator (TN)	1798–99	Conspiracy to aid a foreign power despite official U.S. neutrality	Expelled; impeachment case then dismissed for lack of jurisdiction
John Pickering	Judge (D. NH)	1803–4	Improper rulings, drunkenness and blasphemy	Convicted and removed from office
Samuel Chase	Supreme Court Justice	1804–5	Bias in charging a grand jury and delivering an inflammatory political harangue to another	Acquitted
James H. Peck	Judge (D. MO)	1830–31	Improperly holding in contempt a lawyer who had criticized his rulings	Acquitted
West H. Humphreys	Judge (D. TN)	1862	Incitement to revolt and rebellion	Convicted, removed, and disqualified from future office
Andrew Johnson	President	1868	Violation of the Tenure of Office Act by firing Secretary of War Stanton	Acquitted
William W. Belknap	Secretary of War	1876	Bribery	Acquitted after resignation largely on jurisdictional grounds
Charles H. Swayne	Judge (N.D. FL)	1905	Falsifying expense accounts and using property held in a receivership	Acquitted
Robert W. Archbald	Judge (3d Cir.)	1912–13	Bribery and hearing cases in which he had a financial interest	Convicted, removed, and disqualified from future office
George English	Judge (E.D. IL)	1926	Habitual malperformance	No action taken by Senate after his resignation
Harold Louderback	Judge (N.D. CA)	1933	Using favoritism in appointing receivers	Acquitted
Halstead L. Ritter	Judge (S.D. FL)	1936	Taking kickbacks, tax evasion, and bringing his court into scandal and disrepute	Convicted only of last charge and removed from office

Name	Position	Year	Charge	Outcome
Harry Claiborne	Judge (D. NV)	1986	Tax evasion	Convicted after committee trial and removed from office
Walter L. Nixon	Judge (D. MS)	1989	Perjury and obstruction of justice	Convicted of two articles and removed
William J. Clinton	President	1998–99	Perjury and obstruction of justice	Acquitted
Samuel B. Kent	Judge (S.D. TX)	2009	Sexual assault, obstruction of justice, and making false statements	Following his resignation, House and Senate agreed not to further pursue impeachment
G. Thomas Porteous, Jr.	Judge (E.D. LA)	2010	Taking kickbacks, making false statements, and using the power and prestige of his office to engage in corrupt relationships with counsel and others	Convicted on all charges and removed from office; forever disqualified from holding federal office
Near-Impeachments				
Mark W. Delahay	Judge (D. KS)	1873	Questionable financial dealings	Resigned after House voted to impeach but before articles of impeachment were adopted
Richard M. Nixon	President	1974	Obstruction of justice	Resigned after Judiciary Committee voted to impeach but before whole House voted
Robert Collins	Judge (E.D. LA)	1993	Bribery	Resigned following his criminal conviction
Robert P. Aquilar	Judge (N.D. CA)	1996	Obstruction of justice	Retired with full pension as part of deal to avoid impeachment

Notes

INTRODUCTION

1. The blog can be found at: https://impeachableoffenses.net.
2. WILLIAM SHAKESPEARE, HAMLET, Act I, sc. 5.

1 HOW TO INTERPRET THE CONSTITUTION'S IMPEACHMENT CLAUSES

1. *See America's Founding Documents: The Constitution of the United States*, NATIONAL ARCHIVES, at: www.archives.gov/founding-docs/constitution, last accessed Nov. 7, 2018.
2. Article VII of the constitution provides that ratification by nine of the then-existing thirteen states put the new constitution into effect between the states ratifying it. On June 21, 1788, New Hampshire became the ninth state to ratify the document. THE CONSTITUTION OF THE UNITED STATES AND AMENDMENTS THERETO 24 (James J. Kilpatrick ed., 1961).
3. DAVID C. HENDRICKSON, PEACE PACT: THE LOST WORLD OF THE AMERICAN FOUNDING 3, 200 (2003).
4. Some of these constitutions are recorded in a work by the school of Aristotle which contains descriptions of the constitutions of some 170 Greek city-states. PSEUDO-ARISTOTLE, CONSTITUTION OF THE ATHENIANS (Horace Rackham trans., 1935); ARISTOTLE, THE ATHENIAN CONSTITUTION (Frederic G. Kenyon trans., 1891).
5. THE FEDERAL AND STATE CONSTITUTIONS, COLONIAL CHARTERS, AND OTHER ORGANIC LAWS OF THE STATES, TERRITORIES AND COLONIES NOW OR HERETOFORE FORMING THE UNITED STATES OF AMERICA, VOLS. 1–7 (Francis Newton Thorpe ed., 1906).
6. President Abraham Lincoln, Gettysburg Address (Nov. 19, 1863).
7. It has been argued that the anti-Federalists decried the absence of a bill of rights mostly as a tactic to prevent adoption of the constitution in any form, and that, once the constitution was ratified and the bill of rights was under consideration by the first Congress, they no longer cared very much about its substance. Robert Bork, *Neutral Principles: First Amendment Problems, in* INTERPRETING THE CONSTITUTION: THE DEBATE OVER ORIGINAL INTENT 214 (Jack Rakove ed., 1990).

8. U.S. CONST. amend. VIII.

9. U.S. CONST. amend. V.

10. U.S. CONST. amend. IV.

11. The first ten amendments were approved and sent to the states for ratification by the 1st Congress in 1789. James Madison, then a member of the House of Representatives, originally proposed that the charter of rights be integrated into appropriate parts of the constitution. The final decision was to make the amendments free-standing codicils to the constitution. William Michael Treanor, *Against Textualism*, 103 NW. U. L. REV. 983, 1001–2 (2009).

12. OLIVER WENDELL HOLMES, JR., THE COMMON LAW 35–37 (1881).

13. D. C. M. YARDLEY, INTRODUCTION TO BRITISH CONSTITUTIONAL LAW 45 (1960).

14. THEODORE F. T. PLUCKNETT, A CONCISE HISTORY OF THE COMMON LAW 59 (4th ed., 1948).

15. YARDLEY, INTRODUCTION TO BRITISH CONSTITUTIONAL LAW, *supra* note 13, at 27.

16. *Ibid.*, at 25.

17. KEITH E. WHITTINGTON, CONSTITUTIONAL INTERPRETATION: TEXTUAL MEANING, ORIGINAL INTENT, AND JUDICIAL REVIEW 50 (1999): "The power of the British legislature increasingly came to be seen as absolute, both by itself and its observers, until no checks on its authority could be distinguished in the latter half of the eighteenth century."

18. W. R. Lederman, *The Independence of the Judiciary*, 34 CAN. B. REV. 1139, 1142 (1956).

19. Joseph H. Smith, *An Independent Judiciary: The Colonial Background*, 124 U. PENN. L. REV. 1104, 1105 (1976).

20. U.S. CONST. Art. III, § 1.

21. The question of federal judicial supremacy over state court interpretations of federal law was resolved in Martin v. Hunter's Lessee, 1 Wheat. 304 (1816), in which the U.S. Supreme Court rejected the highest Virginia court's challenge to the constitutionality of section 25 of the Judiciary Act of 1789, which gave the Supreme Court the power to review final decisions of state courts resting on federal law.

22. *See, e.g.*, THE FEDERALIST NO. 78 (Alexander Hamilton). Hamilton argued that a power of judicial review of statutes for their constitutionality is implied from the status of the constitution as fundamental law, and, in any case, need not be feared because judges will be constrained by application of the tried and true Anglo-American common law method of deciding cases. *See also* ARCHIBALD COX, THE COURT AND THE CONSTITUTION 55, 68–69 (1987).

23. Marbury v. Madison, 5 U.S. (1 Cranch) 137, 177, 180 (1803).

24. *Ibid.*, at 177.

25. In a letter to Abigail Adams in 1804, Jefferson sputtered, "Nothing in the Constitution has given [federal judges] a right to decide for the Executive, more than for the Executive to decide for them ... The opinion which gives to the judges the right to decide what laws are constitutional and what not, not only for themselves, in their own sphere of action, but for the Legislature and the Executive also in their spheres, would make the Judiciary a despotic branch."

Letter from Thomas Jefferson to Abigail Smith Adams, September 11, 1804, NATIONAL ARCHIVES, available at: https://founders.archives.gov/?q=Project%3A %22Jefferson%20Papers%22%20Dates-To%3A1804-09–12%20Dates-From% 3A1804-09–11&s=1511311111&r=1, last accessed Nov. 7, 2018.

26. *Letter from Thomas Jefferson to Edward Livingston, 25 March 1825,* NATIONAL ARCHIVES, available at: https://founders.archives.gov/?q=Project%3A% 22Jefferson%20Papers%22%20Dates-From%3A1825-03–01%20Dates-To% 3A1825-03–31&s=1511311111&r=70, last accessed Nov. 7, 2018. *See also Thomas Jefferson on Judicial Tyranny* (Robert A. J. Gagnon ed.), available at: www.robga gnon.net/JeffersonOnJudicialTyranny.htm (assembling Jefferson quotations), last accessed Nov. 7, 2018.

27. Nor need we tarry here examining the degree to which Justice Marshall's work in *Marbury v. Madison* was as path-breaking as has long been assumed. Alexander Bickel thought *Marbury* novel in proclaiming the doctrine of judicial review of the constitutionality of statutes. ALEXANDER M. BICKEL, THE LEAST DANGEROUS BRANCH: THE SUPREME COURT AT THE BAR OF POLITICS 1 (1962). Later scholars maintain that other judges had employed judicial review in the early years of the Republic. William Michael Treanor, *Judicial Review before Marbury,* 58 STAN. L. REV. 455 (2005). The point for our purposes is that judicial review of the constitutionality of federal statutes was a contestable, and con-tested, component of the constitutional authority of the federal judiciary until the *Marbury* case declared the doctrine openly, and by virtue of its gradual acceptance in ensuing years settled the question.

28. MICHAEL J. GERHARDT & THOMAS D. ROWE, JR., CONSTITUTIONAL THEORY: ARGUMENTS AND PERSPECTIVES 39 (1993).

29. In her confirmation hearing, Justice Elena Kagan remarked that, "we are all originalists." *The Nomination of Elena Kagan to be an Associate Justice of the Supreme Court of the United States: Hearing before the S. Comm. on the Judiciary,* 111th Cong. 62 (2010). But, of course, what Kagan means by original-ism is quite different from how Justice Antonin Scalia and like-minded thinkers on the right interpret the term. *See* Jamal Greene, *How Constitutional Theory Matters,* 72 OHIO St. L.J. 1183, 1194 (2011): "The open-ended and progressive conception [of originalism] that scholars like Jack Balkin and lawyers like Doug Kendall support may share a name and a conceptual origin with the narrow, results-oriented conception that has entered public discourse, but it is no more related than Barack Obama is to Dick Cheney"; James E. Fleming, *Living Originalism and Living Constitutionalism as Moral Readings of the American Constitution,* 92 B.U. L. REV. 1171, 1173: "[W]e are witnessing the 'Balkanization' of originalism (when originalism splits into warring camps) along with the 'Balkinization' of originalism (when even Balkin, hitherto a progressive, prag-matic, living constitutionalist, becomes an originalist)"; JACK BALKIN, LIVING ORIGINALISM (2011).

30. ANTONIN SCALIA & BRYAN A. GARNER, READING LAW: THE INTERPRETATION OF LEGAL TEXTS (2012).

31. *See* Frederick Schauer, *Easy Cases,* 58 S. CAL. L. REV. 399, 407 (1985).

32. U.S. Const. Art. I, § 2.
33. U.S. Const. Art. I, § 3.
34. U.S. Const. Art. II, § 1.
35. Of course, this kind of whole-document textualism can generate widely divergent interpretive techniques and substantive results. Justice Scalia's textualism is a very different animal than John Hart Ely's "non-clause-bound interpretivism." John Hart Ely, Democracy and Distrust: A Theory of Judicial Review 11–12 (1980).
36. U.S. Const. Art. I, § 2.
37. U.S. Const. amend. VIII.
38. *See, e.g.,* Richard A. Posner, *The Incoherence of Antonin Scalia,* New Republic (Aug. 23, 2012), available at: https://newrepublic.com/article/106441/scalia-garner-reading-the-law-textual-originalism, last accessed Jan. 2, 2019.
39. Steven G. Calabresi & Sakrishna B. Prakash, *The President's Powers to Execute the Law,* 104 Yale L.J. 541, 553 (1994).
40. U.S. Const. Art. II, § 1.
41. *See generally* Whittington, Constitutional Interpretation, *supra* note 17, at 35–37 (describing the originalist project); Daniel A. Farber, *The Originalism Debate: A Guide for the Perplexed,* 49 Ohio St. L.J. 1085 (1989); Robert W. Bennett & Lawrence B. Solum, Constitutional Originalism: A Debate 1–4 (2011).
42. 404 U.S. 71, 76 (1971) (holding that the equal protection clause of the Fourteenth Amendment bars giving "a mandatory preference to members of either sex over members of the other"). *See generally Reed v. Reed at 40: Equal Protection and Women's Rights,* 20 J. Gender, Soc'y Pol'y & L. 315 (2011).
43. Adam Cohen, *Justice Scalia Mouths Off on Sex Discrimination,* Time (Sept. 22, 2010), available at: http://content.time.com/time/nation/article/0,8599,2020667,00.html, last accessed Jan. 2, 2019.
44. Ruth Bader Ginsburg, *Sexual Equality Under the Fourteenth and Equal Rights Amendments,* 1979 Wash. U. L. Rev. 161, 161 (1979): "Boldly dynamic interpretation, departing radically from the original understanding, is required to tie to the fourteenth amendment's equal protection clause a command that government treat men and women as individuals equal in rights, responsibilities, and opportunities."
45. Steven G. Calabresi & Julia T. Rickert, *Originalism and Sex Discrimination,* 90 Tex. L. Rev. 1 (2011).
46. *Ibid.,* at 2.
47. *See, e.g.,* Steven G. Calabresi & Livia Fine, *Two Cheers for Professor Balkin's Originalism,* 103 Nw. U. L. Rev. 663, 668–69 (2009).
48. *But see* Whittington, Constitutional Interpretation, *supra* note 17, at 187–95.
49. David Strauss, The Living Constitution (Oxford University Press 2010); David Strauss, *Common Law Constitutional Interpretation,* 63 U. Chi. L. Rev. 877 (1996): "[W]hen people interpret the Constitution, they rely not just on the text but also on the elaborate body of law that has developed, mostly through judicial decisions, over the years."

50. *Ibid.*, at 879.
51. Missouri v. Holland, 252 U.S. 416, 433 (1920).
52. 1 THE RECORDS OF THE FEDERAL CONVENTION OF 1787, at 15 (Max Farrand ed., 1911) [hereinafter FARRAND'S RECORDS] (Journal, May 29, 1787) (noting that the convention resolved "[t]hat nothing spoken in the House be printed, or otherwise published, or communicated without leave").
53. FARRAND'S RECORDS, *supra* note 52, at 6 (Yates' Notes, May 25, 1787); xi–xiv (describing the journal).
54. *Ibid.*, *supra* note 52, at xiv.
55. They were Alexander Hamilton, Rufus King, George Mason, James McHenry, William Paterson, William Pierce, Robert Yates, and James Madison. Gregory E. Maggs, *A Concise Guide to the Records of the Federal Constitutional Convention of 1787 as a Source of the Original Meaning of the Constitution*, 81 GEO. WASH L. REV. 18 (2012).
56. FARRAND'S RECORDS, *supra* note 52, at xii.
57. *Ibid.*, at xiv.
58. The first compilation was a five-volume work assembled from 1894 to 1905 by the Bureau of Rolls and Library of the U.S. State Department, THE DOCUMENTARY HISTORY OF THE CONSTITUTION OF THE UNITED STATES OF AMERICA, 1786–1870 (1894–1905) (five vols.). *See* Maggs, *Concise Guide*, *supra* note 55, at 19.
59. FARRAND'S RECORDS, *supra* note 52.
60. Maggs, *Concise Guide*, *supra* note 55, at 481.
61. THE DEBATES IN THE SEVERAL STATE CONVENTIONS, ON THE ADOPTION OF THE FEDERAL CONSTITUTION, AS RECOMMENDED BY THE GENERAL CONVENTION AT PHILADELPHIA, IN 1787 (1827–1830) (Jonathan Elliot ed., 1836) [hereinafter ELLIOT'S DEBATES], available at: http://memory.loc.gov/ammem/amlaw/lwed.html.
62. COX, THE COURT AND THE CONSTITUTION, *supra* note 22, at 68–69.
63. Notably the abolition of slavery, the establishment of universal male suffrage, and the due process and equal protections in the post-Civil War amendments, the requirement of direct election of senators (Seventeenth Amendment), the establishment of female suffrage (Nineteenth Amendment), and the reduction of the national voting age to eighteen (Twenty-sixth Amendment).
64. McCulloch v. Maryland, 17 U.S. (4 Wheat.) 316 (1819).
65. COX, THE COURT AND THE CONSTITUTION, *supra* note 22, at 72–78.
66. Gibbons v. Ogden, 221 U.S. (9 Wheat.) 1 (1824).
67. COX, THE COURT AND THE CONSTITUTION, *supra* note 22, at 84–91 (discussing *Gibbons v. Ogden* and subsequent commerce clause cases).
68. Brown v. Board of Education of Topeka, 347 U.S. 483 (1954).
69. Loving v. Virginia, 388 U.S. 1 (1967).
70. U.S. CONST. Art. I, § 8.
71. Following the Pearl Harbor attack, the United States declared war on Japan on December 8, 1941. Declarations of war against Germany and Italy followed on December 11, 1941, and in 1942, the United States declared war against German allies Bulgaria, Hungary, and Rumania. *Official Declarations of War by Congress*, U.S. SENATE, available at: www.senate.gov/pagelayout/history/h_mul

ti_sections_and_teasers/WarDeclarationsbyCongress.htm, last accessed Nov. 7, 2018.

72. *See Major Military Operations Since World War II,* INFOPLEASE, available at: www.infoplease.com/timelines/major-military-operations-world-war-ii, last accessed Nov. 7, 2018.

73. The two largest post-Second World War American wars received either no congressional authorization at all (the Korean Conflict, 1950–53) or equivocal authorization of debatable legitimacy (the Vietnam War, 1961–73, authorized, if authorization it can be called, only by the infamous Gulf of Tonkin Resolution). Since Vietnam, presidents have nominally been bound by the 1973 War Powers Resolution, 50 U.S.C. § 1541 et seq., obliging them to consult with Congress prior to introducing U.S. forces into hostilities, to make reports to Congress when U.S. forces become involved in hostilities, and to withdraw those forces within a stated period unless Congress acts to approve the military action. Compliance with the War Powers Resolution has been spotty. Geoffrey S. Corn, *Clinton, Kosovo, and the Final Destruction of the War Powers Resolution,* 42 WM. & MARY L. REV. 1149, 1152 (2001).

74. *See, e.g.,* Gary Lawson, *The Rise and Rise of the Administrative State,* 107 HARV. L. REV. 1231 (1994).

75. Nixon v. United States, 506 U.S. 224, 226 (1993) (holding that an objection to the Senate's rules for receiving evidence in impeachment trials is a non-justiciable political question).

76. *See, e.g.,* 3 DESCHLER'S PRECEDENTS OF THE UNITED STATES HOUSE OF REPRESENTATIVES 2236 (1994), available at: www.gpo.gov/fdsys/pkg/GPO-HPREC-DESCHLERS-V3/pdf/GPO-HPREC-DESCHLERS-V3-5–5-5.pdf (remarks of the presiding officer in the Senate trial of Judge Halsted Ritter, April 3, 1936: "Precedents in proceedings of this character are rare and not binding upon [the Senate] in any course that it might desire to pursue.").

77. A petition seeking the impeachment of President John Tyler was introduced in the House of Representative in July 1842, but was first tabled and later rejected and the matter went no further. OLIVER PERRY CHITWOOD, JOHN TYLER: CHAMPION OF THE OLD SOUTH 303 (1964).

78. THE FEDERALIST NO. 65 (Alexander Hamilton).

79. BICKEL, THE LEAST DANGEROUS BRANCH, *supra* note 27 (coining the term "counter-majoritarian difficulty"). Some argue that judicial invalidation of legislatively created laws is illegitimate or at least constitutionally suspect. Others contend that the judiciary is by constitutional design counter-majoritarian in the sense that it is supposed to constrain popular majorities when they invade the rights and liberties of disfavored minorities.

2 BRITISH IMPEACHMENTS, 1376–1787

1. JAMES C. HOLT, MAGNA CARTA 13–14 (3d ed. 2015).

2. The class of "free men" was smaller than might be supposed because it excluded those bound to service, the unfree peasantry or "villeins." THEODORE F. T.

PLUCKNETT, A CONCISE HISTORY OF THE COMMON LAW 507–8 (4th ed. 1948) [hereinafter PLUCKNETT, CONCISE HISTORY]; T. F. T. PLUCKNETT, TASWELL– LANGMEAD'S ENGLISH CONSTITUTIONAL HISTORY 177–83 (1960) [hereinafter PLUCKNETT, TASWELL–LANGMEAD].

3. Magna Carta, clause 21, provides that "[e]arls and barons shall be fined only by their equals, and in proportion to the gravity of their offence." *English Translation of Magna Carta*, BRIT. LIBR. (Jul. 28, 2014), available at: www.bl .uk/magna-carta/articles/magna-carta-english-translation, last accessed Jan. 2, 2019.

4. *Ibid.*, at cls. 39, 52.

5. *Ibid.*, at cl. 50. For a discussion on why the barons so disliked Athée, see Margaret Caroline Rickaby, Girard d'Athee and the Men from the Touraine: Their Roles under King John (July 21, 2011) (unpublished doctoral thesis, Durham University), available at: http://etheses.dur.ac.uk/901.

6. S. T. Ambler, *Magna Carta: Its Confirmation at Simon de Montfort's Parliament of 1265*, 130 ENG. HIST. REV. 801 (2015).

7. D. A. CARPENTER, THE MINORITY OF HENRY III 407–12 (1990) (discussing the determination of upper nobility to influence the choice of royal ministers).

8. T. F. T. Plucknett, *The Origin of Impeachment*, 24 TRANS. ROYAL HIST. SOC. 47, 48 (1942) [hereinafter Plucknett, *Origin*].

9. *Ibid.*, at 56–58.

10. T. F. T. Plucknett, *State Trials Under Richard II*, 2 TRANS. ROYAL HIST. SOC. 159, 159 (1952), noting that by the reign of Richard II (1377–99): "[t]he principle had . . . been accepted that parliament was the proper jurisdiction for the trial of eminent or official persons who were accused of misconducting public affairs."

11. *See, e.g.*, PLUCKNETT, TASWELL–LANGMEAD, *supra* note 2, at 184–93.

12. 1 T. B. HOWELL, A COMPLETE COLLECTION OF STATE TRIALS AND PROCEEDINGS FOR HIGH TREASON AND OTHER CRIMES AND MISDEMEANORS FROM THE EARLIEST PERIOD TO THE YEAR 1783, WITH NOTES AND OTHER ILLUSTRATIONS 91–112 (1816) [hereinafter HOWELL, VOL. I]. Suffolk was first impeached in 1386 by the House of Commons and convicted by the House of Lords on a set of charges not apparently denominated as treason. *Ibid.*, at 90–91. The impeachment removed Suffolk from office. *Ibid.* Later, in 1388, a set of "appeals" (in essence, criminal charges) alleging treason were filed by certain lords in the House of Lords. Suffolk was convicted, but by that time had prudently decamped to France. *Ibid.*, at 97–98.

13. *See* RAOUL BERGER, IMPEACHMENT: THE CONSTITUTIONAL PROBLEMS 2 (1974).

14. PLUCKNETT, CONCISE HISTORY, *supra* note 2, at 194–95, 418–19, 675 (describing varieties of forfeitures as punishment for treason and in cases of attainder). The penalty of drawing and quartering for treason was only abolished by the Forfeiture Act of 1870. A. B. KEITH, RIDGES' CONSTITUTIONAL LAW OF ENGLAND 412 (6th ed. 1937).

15. 1 WILLIAM BLACKSTONE, COMMENTARIES ON THE LAWS OF ENGLAND: IN FOUR BOOKS 46 (15th ed. 1809): "Here it is impossible that the party could foresee that an action, innocent when it was done, should be afterwards converted to

guilt by a subsequent law: he had therefore no cause to abstain from it; and all punishment for not abstaining must of consequence be cruel and unjust. All laws should be therefore made to commence in futuro, and be notified before their commencement."

16. T. F. T. Plucknett, *The Impeachments of 1376*, 1 TRANS. ROYAL HIST. SOC. 153, 154 (1951) [hereinafter Plucknett, *Impeachments of 1376*]; 1 W. S. HOLDSWORTH, A HISTORY OF ENGLISH LAW 378 (3d ed. 1931) [hereinafter HOLDSWORTH, VOL. I].

17. HOLDSWORTH, VOL. I, *supra* note 16, at 380; PLUCKNETT, TASWELL–LANGMEAD, *supra* note 2, at 164; Plucknett, *Origin*, *supra* note 8, at 69; 1 JAMES FITZJAMES STEPHEN, A HISTORY OF THE CRIMINAL LAW OF ENGLAND 148–49 (1883); KEITH, RIDGES' CONSTITUTIONAL LAW, *supra* note 14, at 215.

18. STEPHEN, CRIMINAL LAW OF ENGLAND, *supra* note 17, at 149.

19. Plucknett, *Impeachments of 1376*, *supra* note 16, at 156–57, 162.

20. *Ibid.*, at 160.

21. *Ibid.*, at 163.

22. *Ibid.*, at 164.

23. *Ibid.*, at 158.

24. NIGEL SAUL, RICHARD II 12, 24 (1997).

25. HOWELL, VOL. I, *supra* note 12, at 90–94.

26. *Ibid.*, at 94; N. B. Lewis, *Article VII of the Impeachment of Michael de la Pole in 1386*, 42 ENG. HIST. REV. 402, 402 (1927).

27. PLUCKNETT, TASWELL–LANGMEAD, *supra* note 2, at 170–71.

28. *Ibid.*, at 171–72; *see also* Stanley B. Chrimes, *Richard II's Questions to the Judges, 1387*, 72 L.Q. REV. 365, 370 (1956); T. F. T. Plucknett, *Impeachments and Attainder*, 3 TRANS. ROYAL HIST. SOC. 145, 145 (1953) [hereinafter Plucknett, *Impeachments and Attainder*].

29. PLUCKNETT, TASWELL–LANGMEAD, *supra* note 2, at 172–73.

30. *Ibid.*, at 173; Plucknett, *Impeachments and Attainder*, *supra* note 28, at 146–47.

31. The duke of Gloucester and the earls of Warwick and Arundel were charged by appeal. Plucknett, *Impeachments and Attainder*, *supra* note 28, at 149. Sir Thomas Mortimer and Sir John Cobham were impeached, *Ibid.*, at 151–52. PLUCKNETT, TASWELL–LANGMEAD, *supra* note 2, at 175–76. *See also* HOWELL, VOL. I, *supra* note 12, at 125.

32. PLUCKNETT, TASWELL–LANGMEAD, *supra* note 2, at 175–76.

33. Plucknett, *Impeachment and Attainder*, *supra* note 28, at 153.

34. Anthony Tuck, *Richard II (1367–1400)*, *in* OXFORD DICTIONARY OF NATIONAL BIOGRAPHY (2009), available at: www.oxforddnb.com/view/10.1093/ref:odnb/9780198614128.001.0001/odnb-9780198614128-e-23499, last accessed Jan. 4, 2019.

35. PLUCKNETT, TASWELL–LANGMEAD, *supra* note 2, at 194.

36. *Ibid.*; HOWELL, VOL. I, *supra* note 12, at 272–73.

37. *Ibid.*, at 274–76.

38. *Ibid.*, at 275–76.

39. *See, e.g.*, STEPHEN, CRIMINAL LAW OF ENGLAND, *supra* note 17, at 158.

40. MAURICE ASHLEY, CHARLES I AND OLIVER CROMWELL: A STUDY IN CONTRASTS AND COMPARISONS 141 (1987).

41. *Ibid.*, at 141–42.

42. KEITH, RIDGES' CONSTITUTIONAL LAW, *supra* note 14, at 216: "Attainder served as a means of proceeding against a person when no real charge could be substantiated"; PLUCKNETT, TASWELL–LANGMEAD, *supra* note 2, at 232–34. *But see* BERGER, IMPEACHMENT, *supra* note 13, at 30–31 (asserting that an attainder "is only by courtesy labelled 'legislative', for it is a judgment of individual guilt in everything but name"); Matthew Steilen, *Bills of Attainder*, 3 HOUS. L. REV. 767 (2016) (arguing that bills of attainder should be considered forms of summary legal process, rather than legislative acts).

43. *See* J. R. Lander, *Attainder and Forfeiture, 1453 to 1509*, 4 HIST. J. 119 (1961), available at: www.cambridge.org/core/journals/historical-journal/article/i-attainder-and-forfeiture-1453-to-15091/1EA8D0EFB954878797B941400045B969, last accessed Jan. 4, 2019.

44. Alison Reppy, *The Slayer's Bounty: History of Problem in Anglo-American Law*, 19 N.Y.U. L.Q. REV. 229, 233 (1942).

45. *See generally* DAVID GRUMMITT, A SHORT HISTORY OF THE WARS OF THE ROSES (2013).

46. HOLDSWORTH, VOL. I, *supra* note 16, at 381; PLUCKNETT, TASWELL–LANGMEAD, *supra* note 2, at 233; KEITH, RIDGES' CONSTITUTIONAL LAW, *supra* note 14, at 216–17.

47. Stanford E. Lehmberg, *Parliamentary Attainder in the Reign of Henry VIII*, 18 HIST. J. 675, 681 (1975).

48. *Ibid.*, at 692–94.

49. *Ibid.*, at 694–97.

50. PLUCKNETT, TASWELL–LANGMEAD, *supra* note 2, at 233; EDWARD COKE, THE FOURTH PART OF THE INSTITUTES OF THE LAWS OF ENGLAND: CONCERNING THE JURISDICTION OF COURTS 37 (1644).

51. STEILEN, *Bills of Attainder*, *supra* note 42, at 821–22.

52. *Ibid.*, at 880–89 (describing postwar events in Pennsylvania).

53. U.S. CONST. Art. I, § 9: "No Bill of Attainder or *ex post facto* Law shall be passed."

54. PAULINE CROFT, KING JAMES 11 (2003).

55. *Ibid.*, at 6.

56. DAVID NORTON, A TEXTUAL HISTORY OF THE KING JAMES BIBLE (2005).

57. CHARLES E. HATCH, JR., THE FIRST SEVENTEEN YEARS: VIRGINIA, 1607–1624 (1957).

58. KING JAMES I, THE TRUE LAW OF FREE MONARCHIES: OR THE RECIPROCAL AND MUTUAL DUTY BETWIXT A FREE KING AND HIS NATURAL SUBJECTS (1616) [hereinafter THE TRUE LAW]. THE TRUE LAW was a treatise, possibly written to counteract emerging contractarian theories of government. The work was first published in Scotland in 1598 and later in England upon James' accession to the English throne.

59. KING JAMES I, BASILIKON DORON (1603). The BASILIKON DORON was a sort of ruler's manual addressed to James' eldest son Henry and, after Henry's premature death, passed on to his second son Charles, who followed James as next king of England. ASHLEY, CHARLES I AND OLIVER CROMWELL, *supra* note 40, at 21.

60. 6 W. S. HOLDSWORTH, A HISTORY OF ENGLISH LAW 11–12 (2d ed. 1937) [hereinafter HOLDSWORTH, VOL. VI].

61. *Ibid.*, at 20–23, 71; CHRISTOPHER HIBBERT, CHARLES I, at 100–1 (1968).

62. KING JAMES I, THE TRUE LAW OF FREE MONARCHIES: AND, BASILIKON DORON 69 (Daniel Fischlin & Mark Fortier eds., 1996).

63. CROFT, KING JAMES, *supra* note 54, at 75–81, 93.

64. ASHLEY, CHARLES I AND OLIVER CROMWELL, *supra* note 40, at 143.

65. *Ibid.*, at 144–47.

66. J. J. SCARISBRICK, HENRY VIII (1968).

67. EAMON DUFFY, FIRES OF FAITH: CATHOLIC ENGLAND UNDER MARY TUDOR 79 (2009); DAVID M. LOADES, MARY TUDOR: A LIFE (1989).

68. HOLDSWORTH, VOL. VI, *supra* note 60, at 128.

69. *Ibid.*, at 84; 5 W. S. HOLDSWORTH, A HISTORY OF ENGLISH LAW 428, 430, 453–54 (1931) [hereinafter HOLDSWORTH, VOL. V].

70. Damien X. Powell, *Why was Sir Francis Bacon Impeached? The Common Lawyers and the Chancery Revisited: 1621*, 81 HIST. 511 (1996).

71. *Ibid.*, at 515–16.

72. BENJAMIN FARRINGTON, THE PHILOSOPHY OF FRANCIS BACON: AN ESSAY ON ITS DEVELOPMENT FROM 1603 TO 1609 (1964).

73. *See generally* JOHN BOWLE, CHARLES I: A BIOGRAPHY 58–59 (1975).

74. 2 T. B. HOWELL, A COMPLETE COLLECTION OF STATE TRIALS AND PROCEEDINGS FOR HIGH TREASON AND OTHER CRIMES AND MISDEMEANORS FROM THE EARLIEST PERIOD TO THE YEAR 1783, WITH NOTES AND OTHER ILLUSTRATIONS 1086–120 (1816) [hereinafter Howell, Vol. II]. Note that the dates in Howell are different than those cited in the text. It appears that Howell used the dates noted in the original records, and does not adjust for the official change to the Gregorian Calendar, which occurred in 1752. I. M. Kerzhner, *Converting Dates from the Julian (Old Style) or French Republican (Revolutionary) Calendars to the Gregorian (New Style) Calendar*, 33 TAXON 410 (1984).

75. HOWELL, VOL. II, *supra* note 74, at 1120–32.

76. BOWLE, CHARLES I, *supra* note 73, at 59.

77. HOWELL, VOL. II, *supra* note 74, at 1112–14.

78. BOWLE, CHARLES I, *supra* note 73, 79–80; PLUCKNETT, TASWELL–LANGMEAD, *supra* note 2, at 354.

79. R. H. TAWNEY, BUSINESS AND POLITICS UNDER JAMES I: LIONEL CRANFIELD AS MERCHANT AND MINISTER (1958).

80. HOLDSWORTH, VOL. VI, *supra* note 60, at 17.

81. BOWLE, CHARLES I, *supra* note 73, at 280–81.

82. ASHLEY, CHARLES I AND OLIVER CROMWELL, *supra* note 40, at 216.

83. HIBBERT, CHARLES I, *supra* note 61, at 29–32.

84. *Ibid.*, at 31.

85. BOWLE, CHARLES I, *supra* note 73, at 99–100 (describing some among the older aristocracy complaining about "abuse of honor" by arrivistes who gained titles through royal favor or purchase).

86. PEREZ ZAGORIN, THE COURT AND THE COUNTRY: THE BEGINNING OF THE ENGLISH REVOLUTION 63 (1969).
87. BOWLE, CHARLES I, *supra* note 73, at 95–96.
88. *Ibid.*, at 100.
89. HOWELL, VOL. II, *supra* note 74, at 1308.
90. *Ibid.*, at 1307–21.
91. 1 PEREZ ZAGORIN, REBELS AND RULERS 1500–1660: SOCIETIES, STATES AND EARLY MODERN REVOLUTION 100 (1982); Douglas W. Allen, *Purchase, Patronage, and Professions: Incentives and the Evolution of Public Office in Pre-Modern Britain*, 161 J. INSTITUTIONAL THEORETICAL ECON. 57 (2003), available at: www.sfu.ca/ ~allen/venality.pdf; John Miller, *The Potential for 'Absolutism' in Later Stuart England*, 69 HIST. 187 (1984).
92. HOLDSWORTH, VOL. I, *supra* note 16, at 382.
93. *Parliaments, 1604–1629: The Reigns of James I and* Charles, HIST. OF PARLIAMENT, available at: www.historyofparliamentonline.org/research/parliaments/parlia ments-1604–1629, last accessed July 18, 2018; *Parliaments, 1640–1660: Civil War, Commonwealth and Protectorate*, HIST. OF PARLIAMENT, available at: www.historyof parliamentonline.org/research/parliaments/parliaments-1640–1660, last accessed July 18, 2018. However, in 1637, Parliament did impeach a group of judges for ruling that it was lawful for the king to collect the so-called ship money tax without the consent of Parliament. D. L. Keir, *The Case of Ship Money*, 52 L.Q. REV. 546 (1936); 3 T. B. HOWELL, COMPLETE COLLECTION OF STATE TRIALS AND PROCEEDINGS FOR HIGH TREASON AND OTHER CRIMES AND MISDEMEANORS FROM THE EARLIEST PERIOD TO THE YEAR 1783, WITH NOTES AND OTHER ILLUSTRATIONS 1260 (1816) [here-inafter HOWELL, VOL. III].
94. BOWLE, CHARLES I, *supra* note 73, at 177–78.
95. Craig S. Lerner, *Impeachment, Attainder, and a True Constitutional Crisis: Lessons from the Strafford Trial*, 69 U. CHI. L. REV. 2057, 2062 (2002).
96. HOLDSWORTH, VOL. VI, *supra* note 60, at 112–14, 135–36.
97. CATHARINE DRINKER BOWEN, THE LION AND THE THRONE: THE LIFE AND TIMES OF SIR EDWARD COKE: 1552–1634 (1990).
98. Edward P. Cheyney, *The Court of Star Chamber*, 18 AM. HIST. REV. 727, 746–50 (1913).
99. JOHN SOUTHERDEN BURN, THE HIGH COMMISSION: NOTICES OF THE COURT AND ITS PROCEEDINGS (1865), available at: https://babel.hathitrust.org/cgi/pt? id=hvd.hx3iig;view=1up;seq=5, last accessed Jan. 3, 2019.
100. HOLDSWORTH, VOL. VI, *supra* note 60, at 31.
101. Cheyney, *Court of Star Chamber, supra* note 98, at 750; SAMUEL RAWSON GARDINER, *The Act for the Abolition of the Court of Star Chamber, in* THE CONSTITUTIONAL DOCUMENTS OF THE PURITAN REVOLUTION, 1625–1660 (Samuel Rawson Gardiner ed., 1906), available at: http://oll.libertyfund.org/ pages/1641-the-act-for-the-abolition-of-the-court-of-star-chamber; SAMUEL RAWSON GARDINER, 35.: *The Act for the Abolition of the Court of High Commission, in* THE CONSTITUTIONAL DOCUMENTS OF THE PURITAN REVOLUTION, 1625–1660 (Samuel Rawson Gardiner ed., 1906), available at:

http://oll.libertyfund.org/pages/1641-the-act-for-the-abolition-of-the-court-of-high-commission.

102. STEPHEN, CRIMINAL LAW OF ENGLAND, *supra* note 17, at 159.
103. HOLDSWORTH, VOL. VI, *supra* note 60, at 73–77; C. V. WEDGWOOD, THOMAS WENTWORTH: FIRST EARL OF STRAFFORD, 1593–1641: A REVALUATION (1961).
104. *See generally* Harold Hulme, *Opinion in the House of Commons on the Proposal for a Petition of Right, 6 May, 1628*, L. ENG. HIST. REV. 302 (1935); HOLDSWORTH, VOL. VI, *supra* note 60, at 74–75.
105. LERNER, *Impeachment, Attainder, supra* note 95, at 2064–65.
106. HUGH F. KEARNEY, STRAFFORD IN IRELAND, 1633–41: A STUDY IN ABSOLUTISM (2d ed. 1989).
107. CHARLES CARLTON, ARCHBISHOP WILLIAM LAUD 77–80 (1987).
108. BOWLE, CHARLES I, *supra* note 73, at 149–50.
109. *Letter of Wm. Laud to Thomas Wentworth, Lord Deputy, Sept. 9, 1633, in* GEORGE RADCLIFFE, THE EARL OF STRAFFORDE'S LETTERS AND DISPATCHES 111 (1739).
110. G. M. TREVELYAN, ILLUSTRATED HISTORY OF ENGLAND 396 (1956); 1 RICHARD BAGWELL, IRELAND UNDER THE STUARTS AND DURING THE INTERREGNUM 192 (1909).
111. HOWELL, VOL. III, *supra* note 93, at 1385–86 (this is a quote from Article 1 of the first summary articles of impeachment levied against Strafford).
112. *Ibid.*, at 1386. This is the essence of Article 3 of the first summary articles of impeachment, expanded on at length in supplemental articles seemingly filed later, particularly Articles 9–14. *Ibid.*, at 1391–94.
113. *Ibid.*, at 1386.
114. *Ibid.*
115. This charge has always been controversial because it turned on the interpretation of an ambiguous statement by Strafford that could have meant either that the Irish army should be used to confront the Scots force mustered in the north, or that it should be used to suppress dissidents in England itself. The first reading would have been entirely unobjectionable, and, as noted, even the second was treason only if one believed that a king may not use force against his own rebellious subjects.
116. HOWELL, VOL. III, *supra* note 93, at 1388–89.
117. "Essentially, Strafford stood trial for his role in Charles I's personal rule of 1629–40 . . ." D. ALAN ORR, TREASON AND THE STATE: LAW, POLITICS AND IDEOLOGY IN THE ENGLISH CIVIL WAR 61 (2002), available at: https://ens9004-mza.infd.edu.ar/sitio/upload/12-%20ORR,%20D.%20-%20LIBRO%20-%20Treason%20and%20The%20State.pdf#page=75.
118. BERGER, IMPEACHMENT, *supra* note 13, at 33.
119. 8 JOHN RUSHWORTH, HISTORICAL COLLECTIONS OF PRIVATE PASSAGES OF STATE, WEIGHTY MATTERS IN LAW, REMARKABLE PROCEEDINGS IN FIVE PARLIAMENTS 666, 669 (1721).
120. *See generally* ORR, TREASON AND THE STATE, *supra* note 117, at 62.
121. Lord Birkenhead observed: "Was Strafford guilty of treason? The answer in strict law must clearly be in the negative. Treason is an offence against the allegiance

due to the Sovereign in aid and counsel. The underlying theory of the Commons that there were fundamental laws, and that to aim at overturning them was treason, is erroneous. In legal theory there are in this country no laws, not even the Act of Settlement or the Act of Union, which Parliament may not alter as easily as a Statute providing for by-laws in a country parish. To break the law is a crime. To break the laws upon which civil liberty depends is a high crime. But to call treason that which falls clearly outside the terms of the Statute of Treason does not justify a conviction. He was charged with treason, but at best the evidence proved offences, heinous indeed to the last degree, but not treasonable. Nevertheless, if one sets aside the purely legal aspect of the case and regards it from the wider standpoint, there can be little doubt that Charles and his advisors were working to substitute arbitrary government for the rule of law. Strafford had shown himself to be a grave menace to the constitution, and in that untechnical sense he was a traitor." F. E. SMITH, EARL OF BIRKENHEAD, FAMOUS TRIALS OF HISTORY 44–45 (1926). More recent commentators have taken the opposite view. *See, e.g.,* ORR, TREASON AND THE STATE, *supra* note 117, at 61–100.

122. ORR, TREASON AND THE STATE, *supra* note 117, at 98.

123. 4 T. B. HOWELL, COMPLETE COLLECTION OF STATE TRIALS AND PROCEEDINGS FOR HIGH TREASON AND OTHER CRIMES AND MISDEMEANORS FROM THE EARLIEST PERIOD TO THE YEAR 1783, WITH NOTES AND OTHER ILLUSTRATIONS 315 (1816) [hereinafter HOWELL, VOL. IV]; CARLTON, ARCHBISHOP WILLIAM LAUD, *supra* note 107, at 200–1.

124. CARLTON, ARCHBISHOP WILLIAM LAUD, *supra* note 107, at 214.

125. Apparently, there is some doubt about the exact terms of the articles, due in part to the absence of contemporaneous records and in part to the fact that Laud's trial did not occur for five years after his arrest and multiple sets of charges seem to have been drawn against him. CARLTON, ARCHBISHOP WILLIAM LAUD, *supra* note 107, at 217.

126. HOWELL, VOL. IV, *supra* note 123, at 321–30 (articles passed by the Commons in December 1640); *ibid.,* at 332–36 (additional articles were passed in October 1643). He was also accused of subverting the Protestant faith in England and promoting Catholicism, as well as bribery.

127. ORR, TREASON AND THE STATE, *supra* note 117, at 101–2.

128. HOWELL, VOL. IV, *supra* note 123, at 585; CARLTON, ARCHBISHOP WILLIAM LAUD, *supra* note 107, at 218, 222.

129. HOWELL, VOL. IV, *supra* note 123, at 599; CARLTON, ARCHBISHOP WILLIAM LAUD, *supra* note 107, at 223.

130. HOWELL, VOL. IV, *supra* note 123, at 600; CARLTON, ARCHBISHOP WILLIAM LAUD, *supra* note 107, at 223.

131. RICHARD CUST, CHARLES I: A POLITICAL LIFE (2005); *see also* HIBBERT, CHARLES I, *supra* note 61.

132. 6 T. B. HOWELL, COMPLETE COLLECTION OF STATE TRIALS AND PROCEEDINGS FOR HIGH TREASON AND OTHER CRIMES AND MISDEMEANORS FROM THE EARLIEST PERIOD TO THE YEAR 1783, WITH NOTES AND OTHER ILLUSTRATIONS 330–34 (1816) [hereinafter HOWELL, VOL. VI]. Clarendon was also charged

with the by-then customary allegations of corruption and official incompetence. *Ibid.*

133. Clayton Roberts, *The Impeachment of the Earl of Clarendon*, 13 CAMBRIDGE HIST. J. 1, 15 (1957); HOLDSWORTH, VOL. VI, *supra* note 60, at 174–78.

134. 11 T. B. HOWELL, COMPLETE COLLECTION OF STATE TRIALS AND PROCEEDINGS FOR HIGH TREASON AND OTHER CRIMES AND MISDEMEANORS FROM THE EARLIEST PERIOD TO THE YEAR 1783, WITH NOTES AND OTHER ILLUSTRATIONS 600–18 (1816) [hereinafter HOWELL, VOL. XI].

135. *Ibid.*, at 619–21.

136. *Ibid.*, at 620–27.

137. BERGER, IMPEACHMENT, *supra* note 13, at 45.

138. PLUCKNETT, CONCISE HISTORY, *supra* note 2, at 59; HOLDSWORTH, VOL. VI, *supra* note 60, at 193–94.

139. PLUCKNETT, CONCISE HISTORY, *supra* note 2, at 59; *see generally* J. R. JONES, THE REVOLUTION OF 1688 IN ENGLAND (1988).

140. HOLDSWORTH, VOL. VI, *supra* note 60, at 240–43; KEITH, RIDGES' CONSTITUTIONAL LAW, *supra* note 14, at 8–9 (enumerating the provisions of the Bill of Rights of 1689).

141. Mary died of smallpox in 1694. Abbas M. Behbehani, *The Smallpox Story: Life and Death of an Old Disease*, 47 MICROBIOLOGICAL REV. 455, 458 (1983), available at: www.ncbi.nlm.nih.gov/pmc/articles/PMC281588/pdf/micro rcv00019-0005.pdf. William continued to reign until his death in 1702 after a fall from a horse. RICHARD LODGE, 8 THE HISTORY OF ENGLAND FROM THE RESTORATION TO THE DEATH OF WILLIAM III, at 450 (1910).

142. ANDREW C. THOMPSON, GEORGE II: KING AND ELECTOR 95 (2011).

143. 15 T. B. HOWELL, COMPLETE COLLECTION OF STATE TRIALS AND PROCEEDINGS FOR HIGH TREASON AND OTHER CRIMES AND MISDEMEANORS FROM THE EARLIEST PERIOD TO THE YEAR 1783, WITH NOTES AND OTHER ILLUSTRATIONS 1129, 1159 (1816) [hereinafter HOWELL, VOL. XV].

144. *Ibid.*, at 762, 806; ALEXANDER SIMPSON, JR., A TREATISE ON FEDERAL IMPEACHMENTS 150–51 (1916).

145. SIMPSON, JR., TREATISE ON FEDERAL IMPEACHMENTS, *supra* note 144 at 151–62; BERGER, IMPEACHMENT, *supra* note 13, at 71–72. The charges against Oxford and Bolingbroke were couched as both treason and high crimes and misdemeanors. Strafford's charges were labeled high crimes and misdemeanors. Bolingbroke was attainted and later pardoned. SIMPSON, JR., TREATISE ON FEDERAL IMPEACHMENTS, *supra* note 144, at 152. Strafford was never tried. *Ibid.*, at 156. Oxford was tried and acquitted. *Ibid.*, at 162. In addition, in 1715, the duke of Ormond was impeached for treasonous collusion with French forces while acting as commander of British forces in the Netherlands during the war. HOWELL, VOL. XV, *supra* note 143, at 1007.

146. In 1725, the earl of Macclesfield was impeached, convicted, fined, and imprisoned for corruption during his term as Lord Chancellor. 16 T. B. HOWELL, COMPLETE COLLECTION OF STATE TRIALS AND PROCEEDINGS FOR HIGH TREASON AND OTHER CRIMES AND MISDEMEANORS FROM THE EARLIEST PERIOD TO THE YEAR

1783, WITH NOTES AND OTHER ILLUSTRATIONS 767–68 (1816) [hereinafter HOWELL, VOL. XVI]. The impeachment procedure was also employed in 1746 to try to execute Simon Fraser, Lord Lovat, for his role in the Scottish rebellion of 1745. 18 T. B. HOWELL, COMPLETE COLLECTION OF STATE TRIALS AND PROCEEDINGS FOR HIGH TREASON AND OTHER CRIMES AND MISDEMEANORS FROM THE EARLIEST PERIOD TO THE YEAR 1783, WITH NOTES AND OTHER ILLUSTRATIONS 529–857 (1816). Lovat's demise differed from the sort of impeachment that concerns us here because the choice of the impeachment vehicle had nothing to do with imposing legislative constraint on crown policy or removing a corrupt minister. Lord Lovat was a peer of the realm who had taken up arms against the king and, according to the law of the time, could only be condemned to death by trial in the House of Lords. Hence, his impeachment.

147. Perhaps Burke's most famous written work was EDMUND BURKE, REFLECTIONS ON THE REVOLUTION IN FRANCE (1790).

148. SAMUEL B. GRIFFITH, IN DEFENSE OF THE PUBLIC LIBERTY 102, 161–62 (1976); CHARLES R. RITCHESON, EDMUND BURKE AND THE AMERICAN REVOLUTION (1976), available at: www.questia.com/read/11097739/edmund-burke-and-the-ameri can-revolution.

149. SMITH, FAMOUS TRIALS OF HISTORY, *supra* note 121, at 168–69.

150. *Ibid.*, at 169.

151. PATRICK TURNBULL, WARREN HASTINGS 205 (1975).

152. 4 SPEECHES OF THE MANAGERS AND COUNSEL IN TRIAL OF WARREN HASTINGS, at lxiv–lxviii (E. A. Bond ed., 1861).

153. THE HERITAGE GUIDE TO THE CONSTITUTION: FULLY REVISED 293 (David F. Forte & Matthew Spalding eds., 2d ed. 2014).

154. KEITH, RIDGES' CONSTITUTIONAL LAW, *supra* note 14, at 512–13. *See generally* JOHN KEAY, THE HONORABLE COMPANY: A HISTORY OF THE ENGLISH EAST INDIA COMPANY (1993).

155. SMITH, FAMOUS TRIALS OF HISTORY, *supra* note 121, at 164.

156. *Ibid.*, at 164–68. *See also The East India Company: The Company that Ruled the Waves*, THE ECONOMIST (Dec. 17, 2011), available at: www.economist.com/ christmas-specials/2011/12/17/the-company-that-ruled-the-waves, last accessed Jan. 7, 2019.

157. SMITH, FAMOUS TRIALS OF HISTORY, *supra* note 121, at 165–76.

158. SIMPSON, JR., TREATISE ON FEDERAL IMPEACHMENTS, *supra* note 144, at 167–88.

159. *E.g.*, the seventh article alleges that Hastings violated company policy in favor of securing goods and services through publicly advertised solicitations with the "most reasonable proposal" to be accepted when he entered into a contract with George Templer for draught animals and provisions at rates 30 percent higher than a competing proposal. *Ibid.*, at 173. Articles 10 and 11 allege other violations of company contracting policies. *Ibid.*, at 174–75. Articles 9 and 10 also relate to Hasting's alleged disregard of instructions from the company board. *Ibid.*, at 174.

160. Articles 5 and 16 allege mismanagement of the affairs of the provinces of Farruckabad and Oude. *Ibid.*, at 177.

161. Articles 2–6, as well as Articles 14, 16–18, and 22, fall generally in this category. *Ibid.*, at 168–73, 176, 177–81, 185–88.
162. Article 1 alleges that Hastings violated instructions not to engage in "any offensive war whatever" by instigating and employing British troops in a war against the Rohilla people. *Ibid.*, at 167–68. Article 14 relates to a war between Ranna of Gohud and Madajee Scindia. *Ibid.*, at 176. Article 20 concerns a war with the Mahrattas. *Ibid.*, at 182–84.
163. Articles 8 and 16 allege personal or collective corruption. *Ibid.*, at 174, 177.
164. EDMUND BURKE, ON EMPIRE, LIBERTY, AND REFORM: SPEECHES AND LETTERS 388 (David Bromwich ed., 2000).
165. Chris Monaghan, *In Defence of Intrinsic Human Rights: Edmund Burke's Controversial Prosecution of Warren Hastings, Governor-General of Bengal*, 2 LAW, CRIME AND HIST. 58, 63–64 (2011), available at: http://lawcrimehistory.org/journal/vol.1%20issue2%202011/Monaghan.pdf.
166. P. J. MARSHALL, THE IMPEACHMENT OF WARREN HASTINGS 15–16 (1965). *See generally* THOMAS BABINGTON MACAULAY, WARREN HASTINGS (1886); JOHN MORLEY, EDMUND BURKE: A HISTORICAL STUDY (1924).
167. This phrase also appears in some American impeachments of the colonial and post-Revolution but pre-Constitution periods discussed below in Chapter 3.
168. Among the numerous instances of this phenomenon are: (1) the statement of Charles I when he went to the House of Lords to intercede on behalf of Lord Strafford that, "I cannot condemn him of High-Treason; yet I cannot say I clear him of Misdemeanor." HOWELL, VOL. III, *supra* note 93, at 1513; 2 WILLIAM COBBETT, PARLIAMENTARY HISTORY OF ENGLAND 755 (1807); 5 JAMES MCINTOSH, HISTORY OF ENGLAND 253 (1835); (2) the statement of the bishop of Lincoln, a member of the House of Lords during the 1715 impeachment trial of the earl of Oxford for treason, that, "To high crimes and misdemeanours I could readily agree, and I hoped, and therefore wished, that their prosecution might have stopped there. The H[ouse] of Commons have gone further." Clyve Jones, *The Opening of the Impeachment of Robert Harley, Earl of Oxford, June to September 1715: The 'Memorandum' of William Wake, Bishop of Lincoln*, 4 ELECTRONIC BRIT. LIBR. J. 4, 7 (2015).
169. BERGER, IMPEACHMENT, *supra* note 13, at 35–52 (1973).
170. *Ibid.*, at 7–52.
171. Clayton Roberts, *The Law of Impeachment in Stuart England: A Reply to Raoul Berger*, 84 YALE L. J. 1419, 1427 (1975).
172. *Ibid.*, at 1423–27.
173. *Ibid.*, at 1426.
174. Roberts' argument about treason seems misconceived on one other point. He contends that the House of Lords acted as judges and was empowered to find treason only by reference to preexisting statutes or common law precedents, but he seems to misconceive the nature of common law judging. Even in the modern United States where courts have expressly disavowed the power to create new common law crimes, the power to interpret statutes, regulations, and the constitution itself is *de facto* the power to make new law. *See, e.g.,*

Brown v. Board of Education, 347 U.S. 483 (1954) (finding in the Equal Protection Clause of the Fourteenth Amendment a previously unknown prohibition against racially segregated education facilities in the United States).

In England of the Stuart period, this was even more the case because the "common law" was judge-made law – an evolving set of principles and particular rules created by judges ruling by analogy to prior decisions. To say that the Lords could not declare new treasons because they had only the power of common law judges is a contradiction in terms. Common law judges created "new" crimes all the time (even if they did not give their creations new names) by beginning with old principles and precedents and using logic or the exigencies of changed circumstances to expand the law.

175. The great British judge Sir Matthew Hale in his monumental work, THE HISTORY OF THE PLEAS OF THE CROWN (1736), was extremely critical of what he called "constructive treasons," decrying the danger of departing from the precise terms of treason statutes "to multiply and inhanfe crimes into treafon by ambiguous and general words, as *accroaching of royal power, fubverting of fundamental laws*, and the like." 1 MATTHEW HALE, HISTORIA PLACITORUM CORONÆ: THE HISTORY OF THE PLEAS OF THE CROWN 86 (1736) [hereinafter HALE, PLEAS OF THE CROWN]. However, the point of his criticism was to express disapproval of parliamentary practice, not to deny its existence. Indeed, he seems to grudgingly admit the power of Parliament to adjudge new treasons in particular cases, while resisting the inference that such judgments create precedent for future cases outside the parliamentary setting. *Ibid.*, at 262–64.

176. U.S. CONST. Art. I, § 9.

177. *Ibid.*, § 3.

178. *See supra* notes 83–93 and accompanying text.

179. As noted above, *supra* note 145 and accompanying text, Strafford was impeached along with the earl of Oxford and Viscount Bolingbroke for essentially the same offenses, but Strafford's charges were labeled high crimes and misdemeanors only, while Oxford and Bolingbroke were also charged with treason. SIMPSON, JR., TREATISE ON FEDERAL IMPEACHMENTS, *supra* note 144, at 151–62; BERGER, IMPEACHMENT, *supra* note 13, at 71–72.

180. *See supra* notes 146–66 and accompanying text.

181. HOWELL, VOL. IV, *supra* note 123, at 160–63. Several other men, including George Benyon and Sir Edward Dering, were impeached around the same time for promoting a "false, dangerous, and seditious petition" impugning Parliament. HOWELL, VOL. IV, *supra* note 123, at 141–43, 151–52.

182. HOWELL, VOL. IV, *supra* note 123, at 159–63.

183. *Ibid.*, at 165–66. The articles contain no general descriptor of the charges. One source says that the Speaker of the House of Commons informed Gurney that he was charged with "High Crimes and Misdemeanors." Gurney's various pleadings in answer to the charges refer to them as "crimes and misdemeanors" or as "offences, practices, contempts, and misdemeanors." *Ibid.*, at 163–64.

184. HOWELL, VOL. VI, *supra* note 132, at 865–67. *See also* THE HISTORY OF PARLIAMENT: THE HOUSE OF COMMONS 1660–1690 (B. D. Henning ed., 2006),

available at: www.historyofparliamentonline.org/volume/1660–1690/member/
pett-peter-1610–1672.

185. *Ibid.*, at 144–49. Whether Kidd was really a pirate is disputed. RICHARD ZACKS, THE PIRATE HUNTER: THE TRUE STORY OF CAPTAIN KIDD (2003).

186. HOWELL, VOL. XV, *supra* note 143, at 1–35.

187. *Ibid.*, at 29.

188. Parliament occasionally impeached private persons who held no official position. For example, in 1698, John Goudet and nine other merchants were impeached for violating wartime trade restrictions by doing business with France; most pled guilty and were fined. SIMPSON, JR., TREATISE ON FEDERAL IMPEACHMENTS, *supra* note 144, at 141–43. But consideration of those cases is omitted here as irrelevant to the influence of British impeachment practice on the American institution of impeachment.

189. Levying war against the king in his realm was undoubtedly a capital treason. HALE, PLEAS OF THE CROWN, *supra* note 175, at 130.

190. *See supra* notes 143–45 and accompanying text.

191. *See supra* note 146 and accompanying text.

192. *John Mordaunt, 1st Viscount Mordaunt, 1626–75*, BCW-PROJECT, available at: http://bcw-project.org/biography/john-mordaunt, last accessed July 19, 2018. Mordaunt was saved from judgment when Charles II prorogued Parliament. HOWELL, VOL. VI, *supra* note 132, at 785–806.

193. *See supra* notes 18–23 and accompanying text.

194. *See supra* notes 146–66 and accompanying text.

195. In addition to those mentioned above, consider the cases of the Lord Treasurer Middlesex (1624), HOWELL, VOL. II, *supra* note 74, at 1184; Sir William Penn (1668), HOWELL, VOL. VI, *supra* note 132, at 869–78, SIMPSON, JR., TREATISE ON FEDERAL IMPEACHMENTS, *supra* note 144, at 132; Edward Seymour, Treasurer of the Navy, 8 T. B. HOWELL, COMPLETE COLLECTION OF STATE TRIALS AND PROCEEDINGS FOR HIGH TREASON AND OTHER CRIMES AND MISDEMEANORS FROM THE EARLIEST PERIOD TO THE YEAR 1783, WITH NOTES AND OTHER ILLUSTRATIONS 127 (1816) [hereinafter HOWELL, VOL. VIII]; and the earl of Macclesfield (1725), HOWELL, VOL. XVI, *supra* note 146, at 767.

196. U.S. CONST. Art. I, § 9, para. 8: "No Title of Nobility shall be granted by the United States: And no Person holding any Office of Profit or Trust under them, shall, without the Consent of the Congress, accept of any present, Emolument, Office, or Title, of any kind whatever, from any King, Prince, or foreign State"; U.S. CONST. Art. II, § 1, para. 6 (prohibiting the president from receiving any "Emolument" from the federal government or the states beyond "a Compensation" for his "Services" as chief executive).

197. On the anti-corruption norm in the U.S. constitution, *see generally* Zephyr Teachout, *The Anti-Corruption Principle*, 94 CORNELL L. REV. 341 (2009).

198. Edmund Randolph was a delegate to both the Constitutional Convention in Philadelphia and the Virginia ratification convention. During the Virginia convention, he observed: "There is another provision against the danger, mentioned by the honorable member, of the President receiving emoluments

from foreign powers. If discovered, he may be impeached." 3 JONATHAN ELLIOT, THE DEBATES IN THE SEVERAL STATE CONVENTIONS OF THE ADOPTION OF THE FEDERAL CONSTITUTION 326 (1827).

199. HOWELL, VOL. II, *supra* note 74, at 1136.

200. HOWELL, VOL. VIII, *supra* note 195, at 127.

201. *See supra* note 192 and accompanying text.

202. BERGER, IMPEACHMENT, *supra* note 13, at 249.

203. PLUCKNETT, TASWELL–LANGMEAD, *supra* note 2, at 194.

204. *See supra* notes 145, 179 and accompanying text. Other cases include the impeachments of the earl of Middlesex (1624); the duke of Buckingham, charged with helping the Catholic French king against the Protestant French Huguenots (1626); and the earl of Danby, impeached for his role in negotiating British neutrality in the Franco-Dutch War (1678). *See supra* notes 134–37 and accompanying text.

205. The impeachment of Senator Blount will be discussed at length in Chapter 5.

206. *See supra* notes 131–37 and accompanying text.

207. *See supra* notes 146–66 and accompanying text.

3 AMERICAN IMPEACHMENTS BEFORE 1787

1. PETER CHARLES HOFFER & N. E. H. HULL, IMPEACHMENT IN AMERICA, 1635–1805, at 15–56 (1984). Hoffer and Hull are the pre-eminent authorities on the impeachments of this period. The depth of their research is breathtaking and anyone who writes on this subject stands on their shoulders.

2. Of course, both the Dutch and the French had a role in the European settlement of North America, but their story has no direct relevance to the issue of impeachment. *See, e.g.,* JAAP JACOBS, THE COLONY OF NEW NETHERLAND: A DUTCH SETTLEMENT IN SEVENTEENTH-CENTURY AMERICA (2010); W. J. ECCLES, THE FRENCH IN NORTH AMERICA, 1500–1783 (1998).

3. KAREN ORDAHL KUPERMAN, THE JAMESTOWN PROJECT 1 (2007); BERNARD BAILYN, THE BARBAROUS YEARS: THE PEOPLING OF BRITISH NORTH AMERICA: THE CONFLICT OF CIVILIZATIONS, 1600–1675, at 11–12 (2012).

4. North and South Carolina were originally a single colony, founded in 1663, which was eventually divided into two. There is some disagreement as to when it was divided. Some believe it was in 1712 when independent governors were appointed for the north and south. Others say it was in 1729 when the property was sold to the royal crown. JOHN SPENCER BASSETT, THE CONSTITUTIONAL BEGINNINGS OF NORTH CAROLINA (1663–1729) 9, 11 (1894).

5. Martin Kelly, *Chart of the 13 Original Colonies*, THOUGHTCO. (Aug. 28, 2018), available at: www.thoughtco.com/chart-of-thirteen-original-colonies-4059705.

6. NATHANIEL PHILBRICK, MAYFLOWER 35–47 (2006).

7. *Ibid.,* at 41.

8. THE FUNDAMENTAL ORDERS OF CONNECTICUT (1639), *reprinted in* 43 HARVARD CLASSICS, AMERICAN HISTORICAL DOCUMENTS: 1000–1904 (1909–1914), available at: www.bartleby.com/43/7.html, last accessed Jan. 7, 2019.

9. Samuel Eliot Morison, The Oxford History of the American People 64 (1965); *see generally* Charles Edward Banks, The Winthrop Fleet of 1630: An Account of the Vessels, the Voyage, the Passengers, and Their English Homes from Original Authorities (Genealogical Publishing Company 1968) (1930).

10. Charter of Connecticut (1662), available at: http://avalon.law.yale.edu/ 17th_century/cto3.asp, last accessed Jan. 7, 2019.

11. Richard Ross, *Legal Communications and Imperial Governance, in* 1 The Cambridge History of Law in America 129 (Michael Grossberg & Christopher Tomlins eds., 2008).

12. Herbert L. Osgood, *The Proprietary Province as a Form of Colonial Government*, 2 Am. Hist. Rev. 644, 647–48 (1897).

13. *Ibid.*, at 648.

14. *Ibid.*, at 655–60.

15. *Ibid.*, at 653.

16. *Ibid.*, at 650.

17. Herbert L. Osgood, *England and the American Colonies in the Seventeenth Century*, 17 Pol. Sci. Q. 206 (1902).

18. Alan Taylor, American Colonies 130 (2002).

19. C. Albert White, A History of the Rectangular Survey System 8–9 (1926). Georgia became a royal colony in 1752. *See* Taylor, American Colonies, *supra* note 18, at 241–42.

20. The affairs of Britain's overseas possessions were first overseen by the Privy Council, from 1675 to 1696 by a committee of the Council called the Lords of Trade and Plantations, and from 1696 to 1768 by the Board of Trade. Winfred T. Root, *The Lords of Trade and Plantations, 1675–1696*, 23 Am. Hist. Rev. 20–41 (1917); *see also* Osgood, *England and the American Colonies, supra* note 17, at 206, 208 (noting that all corporate colonies were effectively royal by the end of the seventeenth century and describing mechanisms of English governmental control).

21. One exception to this general pattern was Connecticut, where the governor was always elected. *See generally* Dwight Loomis & Joseph Gilbert Calhoun, The Judicial and Civil History of Connecticut (1895).

22. C. Albert White, A History of the Rectangular Survey System 8–9 (1926).

23. *See generally* Erwin C. Surrency, *The Courts in the American Colonies*, 11 Am. J. Legal Hist. 253 (1967).

24. Andrew Robertson & Michael Tilbury, *Unity, Divergence, and Convergence in the Common Law of Obligations, in* The Common Law of Obligations: Divergence and Unity 2 (Andrew Robertson & Michael Tilbury eds., 2016).

25. Peter C. Hoffer & N. E. H. Hull, *The First American Impeachments*, 53 Wm. & Mary Q. 653, 654–55 (1978).

26. Among the first were John Rushworth, Historical collections of private passages of state, weighty matters in law, remarkable proceedings in five parliaments: beginning the sixteenth year of King James, anno 1618, and ending the fifth year of King Charles, anno 1629 (1680) (eight-volume

collection of parliamentary and royal documents), and JOHN SELDEN, OF THE
JUDICATURE IN PARLIAMENTS, A POSTHUMOUS TREATISE (1681). Hoffer & Hull, *First
American Impeachments, supra* note 25, at 655.

27. SIR MATTHEW HALE, THE HISTORY OF THE PLEAS OF THE CROWN (1736).
28. Hoffer & Hull, *First American Impeachments, supra* note 25, at 654; *see* Ross,
    Legal Communications and Imperial Governance, supra note 11, at 135–37 (dis-
    cussing the informal mechanisms of legal information flow within colonies and
    between colonies and the mother country).
29. MORISON, OXFORD HISTORY OF THE AMERICAN PEOPLE, *supra* note 9, at 65;
    FRANCIS J. BREMER, THE PURITAN EXPERIMENT: NEW ENGLAND SOCIETY FROM
    BRADFORD TO EDWARDS 77 (Univ. Press of New England rev. ed. 1995) (1976);
    Virginia Dejohn Anderson, *Migrants and Motives: Religion and the Settlement
    of New England, 1630–1640,* 58 NEW ENG. Q. 339, 344, 375–76 (1985); PETER
    OLIVER, ORIGIN AND PROGRESS OF THE AMERICAN REBELLION: A TORY VIEW 14–15
    (Douglass Adair & John A. Schultz eds., 1961).
30. On Laud's impeachment, see *supra* Chapter 2, notes 123–30 and accompanying
    text.
31. Harvard University was founded in 1636, the College of William & Mary in 1693,
    St. John's College in 1696, Yale in 1701, the University of Pennsylvania in 1740,
    and Princeton in 1746. *10 of the Oldest Universities in the US,* TOP UNIVERSITIES,
    available   at: www.topuniversities.com/blog/10-oldest-universities-us,   last
    accessed June 6, 2018; *see generally* FREDERICK RUDOLPH, THE AMERICAN
    COLLEGE AND UNIVERSITY: A HISTORY (2d ed. 1990).
32. Hoffer & Hull, *First American Impeachments, supra* note 25, at 658–59. Hoffer
    and Hull characterize the actions of the Virginia House of Burgesses in seeking
    the removal of Governor John Harvey in 1635 as an impeachment in form, if not
    in name. *Ibid.,* at 656–57. In their account of the affair, the burgesses framed a
    "petition of grievances" complaining of Harvey's Indian land grant and trade
    policies, and his relations with the Maryland colony, with which a portion of the
    governor's council apparently agreed, the result being the detention of Harvey
    and his transportation back to Britain for resolution of the matter. This looks like
    an impeachment inasmuch as it begins with complaints by a lower house
    followed by a sort of adjudication or affirmation by an upper house. However,
    at least one other historian says that the council acted first, arresting Harvey and
    then calling on the burgesses to ratify their actions; a sequence that makes the
    affair look more like a rebellion than an impeachment. J. Mills Thornton, III,
    The Thrusting Out of Governor Harvey: A Seventeenth-Century Rebellion, 76 VA.
    MAG. HIST. BIOG. 11, 12 (1968). Absent a resolution of this discrepancy, the better
    course seems to exclude Harvey's case from the list of proper colonial
    impeachments.
33. Hoffer & Hull, *First American Impeachments, supra* note 25, at 658–59.
34. MARYLAND STATE ARCHIVES, 2 PROCEEDINGS AND ACTS OF THE GENERAL ASSEMBLY,
    APRIL 1666–JUNE 1676, at 172–73 [hereinafter MARYLAND STATE ARCHIVES,
    PROCEEDINGS OF THE GENERAL ASSEMBLY, VOL. 2], available at: http://aomol
    .msa.maryland.gov/megafile/msa/speccol/sc2900/sc2908/000001/000002/html/

am2–173.html. Morris, the instigator of the business, was also ordered to pay the huge fine of £1,422. *Ibid.*, at 173.

35. *Ibid.*, at 485–86; Hoffer & Hull, *First American Impeachments*, *supra* note 25, at 660.

36. Maryland State Archives, Proceedings of the General Assembly, Vol. 2, *supra* note 34, at 475–76.

37. *Ibid.*, at 493. The managers included the attorney general and two other gentlemen. *Ibid.*

38. *Ibid.*, at 494, 500–1, 503–4; Hoffer & Hull, *First American Impeachments*, *supra* note 25, at 661.

39. For details of these impeachments, see *supra* Chapter 2 notes 23 (Latimer), 25–30 (Suffolk), 87–90 (Buckingham), 112–15 (Strafford), 184 (Pett) and accompanying text.

40. Maryland State Archives, Proceedings of the General Assembly, Vol. 2, *supra* note 34, at 490–91; Hoffer & Hull, *First American Impeachments*, *supra* note 25, at 662.

41. Hoffer & Hull, *First American Impeachments*, *supra* note 25, at 662.

42. Maryland State Archives, 7 Proceedings and Acts of the General Assembly, April 1666–June 1676, at 380, 386, 531, 558, 559, 564, 591, available at: https://msa.maryland.gov/megafile/msa/speccol/sc2900/sc2908/000001/000002/html/am2–494.html; Hoffer & Hull, *First American Impeachments*, *supra* note 25, at 663.

43. 5 The Federal and State Constitutions, Colonial Charters, and Other Organic Laws of the States, Territories and Colonies Now or Heretofore Forming the United States of America 3051 (Francis Newton Thorpe ed., 1906), available at: https://catalog.hathitrust.org/Record/001140815 [hereinafter Federal and State Constitutions, Vol. V].

44. 6 T. B. Howell, Complete Collection of State Trials and Proceedings for High Treason and Other Crimes and Misdemeanors from the Earliest Period to the Year 1783, with Notes and other Illustrations 869–78 (1816) [hereinafter Howell, Vol. VI]; Alexander Simpson, Jr., A Treatise on Federal Impeachments 132 (1916).

45. 1 Minutes of the Provincial Council of Pennsylvania from the Organization to the Termination of the Proprietary Government 83–86 (1838), available at: https://babel.hathitrust.org/cgi/pt?id=wu.89066115874; view=1up;seq=144 [hereinafter Minutes of Pennsylvania Provincial Council].

46. Hoffer & Hull, *First American Impeachments*, *supra* note 25, at 664.

47. Minutes of Pennsylvania Provincial Council, *supra* note 45, at 84–85.

48. *Ibid.*, at 87.

49. Hoffer & Hull, *First American Impeachments*, *supra* note 25, at 665–66.

50. *Ibid.*, at 665.

51. *Penn Biographies: James Logan (1674–1751)*, Penn. U. Archives & Rec. Center, available at: www.archives.upenn.edu/people/1700s/logan_jas.html, last accessed August 8, 2018; *see generally* E. Gordon Alderfer, *James Logan: The*

Political Career of a Colonial Scholar, 24 PA. HIST. 34 (1957), available at: https://journals.psu.edu/phj/article/viewFile/22512/22281.

52. Peter C. Hoffer & N. E. H. Hull, *Power and Precedent in the Creation of an American Impeachment Tradition: The Eighteenth-Century Colonial Record*, 36 WM. & MARY Q. 51, 54–56 (1979) [hereinafter Hoffer & Hull, *Power and Precedent*]; 1 *Votes and Proceedings of the House of Representatives of the Province of Pennsylvania (Dec. 4, 1682–June 11, 1707)* [hereinafter *Votes and Proceedings, Vol. I*] *in* 1 PENNSYLVANIA ARCHIVES, EIGHTH SERIES 652, 715–19 (Gertrude McKinney ed., 1931), available at: https://babel.hathitrust.org/cgi/pt?id=mdp.39015035580011;view=1up;seq=5.

53. For discussion of the impeachment of the duke of Buckingham, see *supra* Chapter 2, note 178 and accompanying text.

54. *Votes and Proceedings, Vol. I, supra* note 52, at 715–16.

55. FEDERAL AND STATE CONSTITUTIONS, VOL. V, *supra* note 43, at 3076–81.

56. MINUTES OF PENNSYLVANIA PROVINCIAL COUNCIL, *supra* note 45, at 355–58.

57. *Votes and Proceedings, Vol. I, supra* note 52, at 715, 718–19.

58. Lord Strafford was accused in 1640 of seeking to "subvert the fundamental laws and government of the realms of England and Ireland, and instead thereof, to introduce an arbitrary and tyrannical government against law." 3 T. B. HOWELL, COMPLETE COLLECTION OF STATE TRIALS AND PROCEEDINGS FOR HIGH TREASON AND OTHER CRIMES AND MISDEMEANORS FROM THE EARLIEST PERIOD TO THE YEAR 1783, WITH NOTES AND OTHER ILLUSTRATIONS 1385–86 (1816). In 1678, the earl of Danby was alleged to have "endeavoured to subvert the ancient and well-established form of government in this kingdom, and instead thereof to introduce an arbitrary and tyrannical way of government." 11 T. B. HOWELL, COMPLETE COLLECTION OF STATE TRIALS AND PROCEEDINGS FOR HIGH TREASON AND OTHER CRIMES AND MISDEMEANORS FROM THE EARLIEST PERIOD TO THE YEAR 1783, WITH NOTES AND OTHER ILLUSTRATIONS 625 (1816). In 1642, the Commons impeached Sir Richard Gurney, Lord Mayor of London, with striving to "bring in an arbitrary and tyrannical government." 4 T. B. HOWELL, COMPLETE COLLECTION OF STATE TRIALS AND PROCEEDINGS FOR HIGH TREASON AND OTHER CRIMES AND MISDEMEANORS FROM THE EARLIEST PERIOD TO THE YEAR 1783, WITH NOTES AND OTHER ILLUSTRATIONS 159–61 (1816).

59. *See supra* Chapter 2, notes 54–137 and accompanying text (describing themes of parliamentary impeachments during the Stuart dynasty).

60. *See generally* Hoffer & Hull, *Power and Precedent, supra* note 52, at 62–65; *see also* William Renwick Riddell, *Libel on the Assembly: A Prerevolutionary Episode*, 52 PA. MAG. HIST. BIOG. 176, available at: https://journals.psu.edu/pmhb/article/viewFile/28131/27887.

61. Riddell, *Libel on the Assembly, supra* note 60, at 177–78; Hoffer & Hull, *Power and Precedent, supra* note 52, at 63; 6 *Votes and Proceedings of the House of Representatives of the Province of Pennsylvania (Dec. 4, 1682–June 11, 1707), in* PENNSYLVANIA ARCHIVES, EIGHTH SERIES 652, 4682 (Gertrude McKinney ed., 1931), available at: https://babel.hathitrust.org/cgi/pt?id=mdp.39015035580011;view=1up;seq=5 [hereinafter *Votes and Proceedings, Vol. VI*].

62. *See generally* FRED ANDERSON, CRUCIBLE OF WAR: THE SEVEN YEARS' WAR AND THE FATE OF EMPIRE IN BRITISH NORTH AMERICA, 1754–1766 (2000).

63. William Smith Mason, *Franklin and Galloway: Some Unpublished Letters*, 34 PROC. AM. ANTIQUARIAN SOC. 227, 228–29 (1924), available at: www.american antiquarian.org/proceedings/44806731.pdf.

64. ANDERSON, CRUCIBLE OF WAR, *supra* note 62, at 160–63. At one point the governor refused to sign a tax bill that would raise £60,000 because it did not exempt the proprietary estates. Sanderson Beck, *English, French, and Indian Wars 1754–63*, available at: www.san.beck.org/13-3-AngloFrenchWar1754-63.html, last accessed October 22, 2018. For contemporary observations of the dispute, *see From Richard Jackson: Private Sentiments and Advice on Pennsylvania Affairs (April 24, 1758)*, *in* 8 THE PAPERS OF BENJAMIN FRANKLIN, 1758–1759, at 22 (Leonard W. Labarce ed., 1965) [hereinafter FRANKLIN PAPERS], available at: http://franklinpapers.org/framedVolumes.jsp, and *From Isaac Norris (June 15, 1758)*, *ibid.*, at 101.

65. *See, e.g.*, *Votes and Proceedings, Vol. VI*, *supra* note 61, at 4897–98.

66. *Ibid.*

67. *See* HOFFER & HULL, IMPEACHMENT IN AMERICA, *supra* note 1, at 42.

68. *Ibid.*, at 43; *Moore's Address to Governor Denny, October 19, 1757*, *in* SMITH FAMILY PAPERS, HIST. SOC. PHILADELPHIA.

69. *Votes and Proceedings, Vol. VI*, *supra* note 61, at 4683–90.

70. Ralph L. Ketcham, *Benjamin Franklin and William Smith: New Light on an Old Philadelphia Quarrel*, 88 PA. MAG. HIST. BIOG. 142, 155 (1964).

71. *Ibid.*

72. 7 *Votes and Proceedings of the House of Representatives of the Province of Pennsylvania (Dec. 4, 1682–June 11, 1707)*, *in* PENNSYLVANIA ARCHIVES, EIGHTH SERIES 4691–93 (Gertrude McKinney ed., 1931) [hereinafter *Votes and Proceedings, Vol. VII*], available at: https://babel.hathitrust.org/cgi/pt?id=mdp.39015035580011;view=1up;seq=5.

73. Peter C. Hoffer, *Law and Liberty: In the Matter of Provost William Smith of Philadelphia, 1758*, 38 WM. & MARY Q. 681, 693–701 (1981); William Smith Mason, *Franklin and Galloway: Some Unpublished Letters*, 34 PROC. AM. ANTIQUARIAN SOC. 227, 248–50 (1924), available at: www.americanantiquarian.org/proceedings/44806731.pdf; *Votes and Proceedings, Vol. VII*, *supra* note 72, at 5091–92.

74. *See, e.g.*, HOFFER & HULL, IMPEACHMENT IN AMERICA, *supra* note 1, at 44.

75. *E.g.*, in his January 24, 1758, letter to the Assembly, Denny complains of the legislators' "sudden and unexpected Determination of changing the late Assembly's Address to remove Mr. Moore into Articles of Impeachment, and your confinement of his person . . ." *Votes and Proceedings, Vol. VII*, *supra* note 72, at 4713.

76. *Letter to Lieutenant Governor from Assembly Speaker Thomas Leech, Jan. 10, 1758*, *in Votes and Proceedings, Vol. VII*, *supra* note 72, at 4684; *Letter to Lieutenant Governor from Assembly Speaker Thomas Leech, Jan. 17, 1758*, *in Votes and Proceedings, Vol. VII*, *supra* note 72, at 4702.

77. *Votes and Proceedings, Vol. VII, supra* note 72, at 4684, 4699, 4813–22.

78. *Ibid.*, at 4713.

79. Joseph H. Smith, Appeals to the Privy Council From the American Colonies 646–49 (1950).

80. *Votes and Proceedings, Vol. VII, supra* note 72, at 4699.

81. Frank O. Bowman III, *British Impeachments (1376–1787) and the Present American Constitutional Crisis*, 46 Hastings Constitutional Law Qtrly __ (2019), available at: https://papers.ssrn.com/sol3/papers.cfm?abstract_id=3221676.

82. *Biographical Index of the Framers of the Constitution*, National Archives, available at: www.archives.gov/founding-docs/founding-fathers, last accessed Aug. 9, 2018.

83. Charles Rappleye, Robert Morris, Financier of the American Revolution 13 (2010); *see also Robert Morris*, National Archives & Rec. Admin., available at: http://law2.umkc.edu/faculty/projects/ftrials/conlaw/marrypenn.html, last accessed Aug. 9, 2018.

84. William Smith Mason, *Franklin and Galloway: Some Unpublished Letters*, 34 Proc. Am. Antiquarian Soc. 227, 240 (1924): "The Moore–Smith affair caused much interest in Great Britain."

85. Philip S. Klein & Ari Arthur Hoogenboom, History of Pennsylvania 82 (1980).

86. In February 1758, Isaac Norris, Speaker of the Assembly, wrote to Franklin to tell him that Smith had been jailed. *Letter of Isaac Norris (Feb. 21, 1758)*, in 7 Franklin Papers 223, available at: http://franklinpapers.org/frank lin//framedVolumes.jsp. In April 1759, Franklin wrote to Joseph Galloway, a member of the Assembly and political ally, noting that Smith was in London for his appeal and vowing to do what he could to thwart it. *Letter to Galloway (April 7, 1759)*, in 8 Franklin Papers 309, available at: http:// franklinpapers.org/franklin//framedVolumes.jsp. See also *Letter from Hugh Roberts to Franklin (June 1, 1758)*, in 8 Franklin Papers 81, available at: http://franklinpapers.org/franklin//framedVolumes.jsp (noting that "the confining of Smith and Moor [sic]" had quieted certain noisy opposition factions). Likewise, Franklin had two letters from David Hall, the printer involved in publishing Moore's alleged libel on the Assembly, pouring out his troubles. *Letter from Franklin to David Hall (June 10, 1758)*, in 8 Franklin Papers 97, available at: http://franklinpapers.org/franklin// framedVolumes.jsp.

87. Franklin's papers contain multiple documents about the Smith appeal indicating his personal involvement, including a copy of Smith's petition annotated by Franklin. *Documents on the Hearing of William Smith's Petition, (April 27, 1758)*, in 8 Franklin Papers 28–49, available at: http://franklinpapers.org/frank lin//framedVolumes.jsp.

88. In May 1758, Franklin reported to the Assembly's leaders about the April Privy Council hearing. In the same letter, Franklin noted the particular interest of Judge Moore's brother, a member of the House of Commons, in the proceedings. *Franklin's Letter to Thomas Leech and the Pennsylvania Assembly*

Committee of Correspondence (May 13, 1758), in 8 FRANKLIN PAPERS 60, available at: http://franklinpapers.org/franklin//framedVolumes.jsp. Franklin wrote to the Assembly about Smith and Moore again in June 1758. *Franklin Letter to Thomas Leech and the Pennsylvania Assembly Committee of Correspondence (June 10, 1758), in* 8 FRANKLIN PAPERS 87, available at: http://franklinpapers.org/franklin//framedVolumes.jsp.

89. *See generally* AN HISTORICAL REVIEW OF THE CONSTITUTION AND GOVERNMENT OF PENNSYLVANIA (1759), available at: https://books.google.com/books?id=uTAmAAAAMAAJ&printsec=frontcover&source=gbs_ge_summary_r&cad=o#v=onepage&q&f=false.

90. *Ibid.*, at 71. The book at one point states: "Against Logan, the Proprietary's Minister, stand upon record, still unanswered, Thirteen Articles of Malversation, by way of Impeachment, which the governor (Evans) found means to evade, against the repeated Offers of the Assembly to produce their witnesses and fasten their proofs upon him." *Ibid.* That Franklin had made a careful study of British parliamentary practice is suggested not only by the many references to that subject in the *Historical Review*, but also by his possession at the time of his death of a twenty-four-volume set of books on parliamentary history. George Simpson Eddy, *Dr. Benjamin Franklin's Library*, 34 PROC. AM. ANTIQUARIAN SOC. 211, 215 (1924), available at: www.americanantiquarian.org/proceedings/44806730.pdf.

91. William Smith Mason, *Franklin and Galloway: Some Unpublished Letters*, 34 PROC. AM. ANTIQUARIAN SOC. 227, 255 (1924).

92. *See generally* JAMES FALKNER, THE WAR OF THE SPANISH SUCCESSION 1701–1714 (2015).

93. For discussion of the Oxford, Bolingbroke, and Strafford impeachments of 1715, see *supra* Chapter 2, note 145.

94. Hoffer & Hull, *Power and Precedent, supra* note 52, at 53–54.

95. *Ibid.*, at 54. Vetch went on to other Canadian adventures, heading a royally sponsored military expedition against Nova Scotia in 1710 and being twice named its provincial governor for his trouble. However, he botched the job, overextended his finances, and died in an English debtors prison in 1732. GEORGE WALLER, SAMUEL VETCH: COLONIAL ENTERPRISER (1960).

96. *See generally* Barbara Aronstein Black, *Massachusetts and the Judges: Judicial Independence in Perspective*, 3 LAW & HIST. REV. 101, 103–12 (1985).

97. *William III, 1700 & 1701: An Act for the further Limitation of the Crown and Better Securing the Rights and Liberties of the Subject, in* 7 STATUTES OF THE REALM: 1695–1701, at 636–38 (John Raithby ed., 1820), available at: www.british-history.ac.uk/statutes-realm/vol7.

98. Black, *Massachusetts and the Judges, supra* note 96, at 108–10.

99. THOMAS WESTON, JR., PETER OLIVER, THE LAST CHIEF JUSTICE OF THE SUPERIOR COURT OF JUDICATURE OF THE PROVINCE OF MASSACHUSETTS BAY 23 (1855), available at: https://archive.org/stream/peteroliverlastcoowest/peteroliverlastcoowest_djvu.txt (a paper read before the New England Historical Genealogical Society and the Bostonian Society).

100. 3 The Federal and State Constitutions, Colonial Charters, and Other Organic Laws of the States, Territories and Colonies Now or Heretofore Forming the United States of America 1886–88 (Francis Newton Thorpe ed., 1906) [hereinafter Federal and State Constitutions, Vol. III], available at: https://catalog.hathitrust.org/Record/001140815 (composition of legislature).

101. Oliver, Origin and Progress, *supra* note 29, at 107–11.

102. *Thomas Hutchinson*, Encyclopedia Britannica, available at: www.britannica.com/biography/Thomas-Hutchinson, last accessed August 9, 2018; Bernard Bailyn, The Ordeal of Thomas Hutchinson 31 (1974).

103. Weston, Peter Oliver, the Last Chief Justice, *supra* note 99, at 20–21; *Communication by John Noble, in* 5 Publications of the Colonial Soc. of Mass. 70–71 (1902). For Justice Oliver's view of the affair, written during his post-Revolutionary exile in Britain, see Oliver, Origin and Progress, *supra* note 29.

104. *Letter of Peter Oliver (Jan. 26, 1774), in* 50 J. Mass. Leg. 133–35 (1981) [hereinafter Journal of Massachusetts Legislature, Vol. 50], available at: https://babel.hathitrust.org/cgi/pt?id=mdp.39015070562999;view=1up;seq=219.

105. *Ibid.*, at 136.

106. *Ibid.*, at 146–48. The vote was not close. There were only 9 nays to nearly 100 ayes. *Ibid.*

107. *Ibid.*, at 159.

108. *Ibid.*, at 167–68.

109. *Ibid.*, at 162.

110. *Ibid.*, at 172–73.

111. *Ibid.*, at 182–83.

112. *Ibid.*, at 183.

113. *Ibid.*, at 194–99.

114. *Ibid.*, at 195–96.

115. *Ibid.*, at 199.

116. *Ibid.*, at 198–99.

117. Black, *Massachusetts and the Judges*, *supra* note 96, at 128.

118. Oliver, Origin and Progress, *supra* note 29, at 31.

119. Massachusetts Colony Superior Court, Suffolk, ss, at the Superior Court, &c. August 1774 (1774), available at: www.loc.gov/resource/rbpe.03703400/?st=text.

120. Oliver, Origin and Progress, *supra* note 29, at xii.

121. Oliver was a relative by marriage of the governor, and arguably the beneficiary of nepotism, but there seem to have been no allegations of corruption. Oliver, Origin and Progress, *supra* note 29, at xi.

122. Black, *Massachusetts and the Judges*, *supra* note 96, at 150: "It is also fair enough to see colonial impeachment in the large as illustrative of the colonial drive for greater autonomy, but the Oliver impeachment was part of a Massachusetts drive to achieve restoration of a traditional constitutional balance."

123. Adams reported that he first suggested impeachment at a dinner with members of the General Court, and that he later showed one or more members treatises discussing parliamentary impeachment precedents, in particular Hale's *Pleas of the Crown* and John Selden, *Of the Judicature of Parliaments*. 2 JOHN ADAMS, DIARY AND AUTOBIOGRAPHY OF JOHN ADAMS 299–301 (L. H. Butterfield, Leonard C. Faber, & Wendell D. Garrett eds., 1962); John Adams, Entry of March 2, 1774, *in* DIARY OF JOHN ADAMS 20 (1774), available at: www.masshist.org/digita ladams/archive/doc?id=D20&bc=%2Fdigitaladams%2Farchive%2Fbrowse% 2Fdiaries_by_date.php. One writer in the 1850s claimed that a copy of Oliver's articles of impeachment survived in Adams' own handwriting. WESTON, PETER OLIVER, THE LAST CHIEF JUSTICE, *supra* note 99, at 26. Adam's claim of priority is discussed in HOFFER & HULL, IMPEACHMENT IN AMERICA, *supra* note 1, at 51 and Black, *Massachusetts and the Judges*, *supra* note 96, at 149.

124. Josiah Quincy, Jr., *Quincy on the Impeachment of Public Officers*, BOSTON GAZETTE, Jan. 4, 1768, *reprinted in* JOSIAH QUINCY, JR., REPORTS OF CASES ARGUED AND ADJUDGED IN THE SUPERIOR COURT OF JUDICATURE OF THE PROVINCE OF MASSACHUSETTS BAY BETWEEN 1761 AND 1772, at 580–84 (Samuel H. Quincy ed., 1865), available at: https://babel.hathitrust.org/cgi/pt?id=uc1 .b5187680;view=1up,seq=9.

125. MASS. CONST. of 1780, pt. I, ch. I, § 2, Art. 8; *ibid.*, § 3, Art. 6.

126. *See* JOHN ADAMS, THOUGHTS ON GOVERNMENT (1776), available at: www.nps.gov/ inde/upload/Thoughts-on-Government-John-Adams-2.pdf.

127. DARREN STALOFF, HAMILTON, ADAMS, JEFFERSON: THE POLITICS OF ENLIGHTENMENT AND THE AMERICAN FOUNDING 195, 229 (2005).

128. The Massachusetts ratifying convention convened on Jan. 9, 1788, and voted to adopt the constitution on Feb. 6, 1788. DEBATES IN THE CONVENTION OF THE COMMONWEALTH OF MASSACHUSETTS ON THE ADOPTION OF THE FEDERAL CONSTITUTION (1788) [hereinafter MASSACHUSETTS DEBATES], available at: www.constitution.org/rc/rat_ma.htm. Adams returned from Great Britain in March 1788. *Timeline: Chronological Events in the Life of John Adams*, JOHN ADAMS HIST. SOC., available at: www.john-adams-heritage.com/timeline, last accessed Aug. 9, 2018.

129. JOURNAL OF MASSACHUSETTS LEGISLATURE, VOL. 50, *supra* note 104, at 200.

130. *Ibid.*, at 199.

131. MASSACHUSETTS DEBATES, *supra* note 128. Hancock was elected president on the first day. *Ibid.*

132. Those who both voted on Oliver's impeachment and attended the Massachusetts ratifying convention included William Phillips, William Heath, Benjamin Lincoln (U.S. Secretary of War under the Articles of Confederation), Jabez Fisher, Dr. Samuel Holton (who did not vote at the Massachusetts convention, but was a committee appointee), Michael Farley, Aaron Wood, Daniel Thurston (or Thruston), Abraham Fuller, John Turner, Joseph Cushing, David Thatcher (or Thacher), Stephen Maynard, Dr. John Taylor, and Jeremiah Learned. *Compare* JOURNAL OF MASSACHUSETTS LEGISLATURE, VOL. 50, *supra* note 104, at 200 *with* MASSACHUSETTS DEBATES,

supra note 128. As an aside, among these fifteen, at least three – William Phillips, Dr. Samuel Holton, and David Thatcher – were also involved in drafting the Massachusetts constitution of 1780, with its impeachment provisions. JOURNAL OF THE CONVENTION FOR FRAMING A CONSTITUTION OF GOVERNMENT FOR THE STATE OF MASSACHUSETTS BAY, FROM THE COMMENCEMENT OF THEIR FIRST SESSION, SEPTEMBER 1, 1779, TO THE CLOSE OF THEIR LAST SESSION, JUNE 16, 1780, at 9–11 (1832), available at: https://babel .hathitrust.org/cgi/pt?id=uc1.$b47249;view=1up;seq=7.

133. MASSACHUSETTS DEBATES, *supra* note 128.

134. *James Bowdoin*, TEACHING AM. HIST., available at: http://teachingamericanhis tory.org/static/ratification/people/bowdoin.html, last accessed Aug. 9, 2018.

135. MASSACHUSETTS DEBATES, *supra* note 128.

136. Massachusetts Bar Association, *The Constitutional History of the Supreme Judicial Court of Massachusetts*, 2 MASS. L. Q. 408, 421 (1916), available at: https://books.google.com/books?id=1DkbAAAAYAAJ&dq=%22william% 20cushing%22%20judge%20refuse%20royal%20charter&pg=PA408#v=onepag e&q=cushing&f=false.

137. Reports of the Oliver impeachment appeared in at least the following British newspapers: LONDON CHRON. (May 24–26, 1774), available at: www.rarenewspa pers.com/view/568861?imagelist=1, last accessed Jan. 9, 2019; KENTISH GAZETTE (May 28, 1774), www.britishnewspaperarchive.co.uk/viewer/bl/0000235/ 17740528/008/0004; CALEDONIAN MERCURY (May 30, 1774) (London), www .britishnewspaperarchive.co.uk/viewer/bl/0000045/17740530/003/0002; *On a Remonstrance for Removing Chief Justice Oliver*, THE SCOTS MAG. (May 1, 1774), www.britishnewspaperarchive.co.uk/viewer/BL/0000545/17740501/006/ 0022, later three last accessed Jan. 9, 2019.

138. Among the American newspapers publishing reports of the Oliver impeachment were: THE BOSTON GAZETTE (March 7, 1774), available at: www.rarenews papers.com/view/568861?imagelist=1, last accessed Jan. 9, 2019; THE PROVIDENCE GAZETTE AND COUNTRY J., March 2, 1774, at 1; *Province of Massachusetts Bay*, THE N. H. GAZETTE AND HIST. CHRON., March 11, 1774, at 1; *Province of Massachusetts Bay*, THE CONN. COURANT, March 8, 1774, at 2.

139. SAMUEL B. GRIFFITH II, IN DEFENSE OF THE PUBLIC LIBERTY 156–71 (1976).

140. Indeed, the First Continental Congress advised the newly independent states to set up new governing arrangements. 4 JOURNALS OF THE CONTINENTAL CONGRESS, 1774–1789, at 342 (Worthington C. Ford ed., 1904). On the process of constitution-making in the new states, *see generally* Gordon S. Wood, *Forward: State Constitution-Making in the American Revolution*, 24 RUTGERS L. J. 911 (1993).

141. 1 THE FEDERAL AND STATE CONSTITUTIONS, COLONIAL CHARTERS, AND OTHER ORGANIC LAWS OF THE STATES, TERRITORIES AND COLONIES NOW OR HERETOFORE FORMING THE UNITED STATES OF AMERICA, at iii–xiv (Francis Newton Thorpe ed., 1906) [hereinafter FEDERAL AND STATE CONSTITUTIONS, VOL. I], available at: https://catalog.hathitrust.org/Record/001140815. This count includes Vermont, which declared its independence in 1777 and wrote a constitution the same

year; however, New York maintained claims to Vermont territory which remained unresolved until after the Revolution and prevented Vermont's admission into the new United States until 1791. P. Jeffrey Potash et al., Freedom and Unity: A History of Vermont (2004). New Hampshire wrote a very brief constitution during the war, in 1776. It wrote a new one in 1784 after the peace, but before the federal Constitutional Convention, and it is the later one that includes impeachment provisions. 4 The Federal and State Constitutions, Colonial Charters, and Other Organic Laws of the States, Territories and Colonies Now or Heretofore Forming the United States of America 2451, 2453 (Francis Newton Thorpe ed., 1906) [hereinafter Federal and State Constitutions, Vol. IV], available at: https://catalog.hathitrust.org/Record/001140815.

142. The states with straightforward impeachment provisions were: Virginia, New Jersey, Delaware, Pennsylvania, North Carolina, New York, Vermont, South Carolina, Massachusetts, and New Hampshire. The relevant text is set out in Appendix A at the end of this chapter. *See supra* Appendix A: Impeachment Provisions of State Constitutions, 1776–87.

143. Maryland's constitution is unusually long and detailed. Article XXX provides that judges enjoy tenure "during good behavior" and are removable either for a conviction (presumably in a regular court) or by address to the governor supported by a vote of 2/3rds of both houses of the legislature. Federal and State Constitutions, Vol. III, *supra* note 100, at 1689. Article X makes the lower house (the House of Delegates) the "grand inquest of the State" authorized to inquire into virtually any complaint and to commit persons to jail for "any crime" subject to later release. *Ibid.*, at 1692. This provision seems to permit the House of Delegates to act as a sort of investigative grand jury, but implies that final adjudication of any criminal charges it might lodge would rest elsewhere. The Maryland constitution does not provide for a legislative power of removing executive branch officers.

144. The fourteen delegates to the federal Constitutional Convention who had also been delegates to state constitutional conventions that adopted impeachment provisions were: George Read (DE), Richard Bassett (DE), Nathaniel Gorham (MA), Caleb Strong (MA), David Brearly (NJ), William Paterson (NJ), Robert Yates (NY), George Clymer (PA), Gouverneur Morris (PA), John Rutledge (SC), James Madison (VA), George Mason (VA), Edmund Randolph (VA), and John Blair (VA). *Biographical Index of the Framers of the Constitution*, National Archives, available at: www.archives.gov/founding-docs/founding-fathers, last accessed Aug. 9, 2018.

145. William F. Swindler, *"Rights of Englishmen" since 1776: Some Anglo-American Notes*, 124 U. Pa. L. Rev. 1083, 1091 (1976).

146. Wood, *State Constitution-Making, supra* note 140, at 914: "The revolutionaries' central aim was to prevent power, which they identified with the governors, from encroaching on liberty, which was the possession of the people or their representatives in the legislatures."

147. Federal and State Constitutions, Vol. V, *supra* note 43, at 3058.

148. 6 The Federal and State Constitutions, Colonial Charters, and Other Organic Laws of the States, Territories and Colonies Now or Heretofore Forming the United States of America 3744 (Francis Newton Thorpe ed., 1906) [hereinafter Federal and State Constitutions, Vol. VI], available at: https://catalog.hathitrust.org/Record/001140815.

149. U.S. Const. Art. I, § 3.

150. However, South Carolina's provision for removing judges by "joint address" of the house and senate implies that impeachment might not apply, or at least always be necessary, for the judiciary. *S.C. Const. of 1778, art. XXVII, reprinted in* Federal and State Constitutions, Vol. VI, *supra* note 148, at 3254.

151. Pennsylvania's constitution says that the general assembly has the power to impeach "state criminals," at ch. 2, section 9. Federal and State Constitutions, Vol. V, *supra* note 43, at 3084–85; but a later clause, ch. 2, section 22, states that a state official "shall be liable to be impeached by the general assembly, either when in office, or after his resignation, or removal for mal-administration." *Ibid.*, at 3088. This is a very odd bit of drafting. The question is what the phrase "for mal-administration" modifies. If it modifies only the word "removal," then the entire passage seems to be about *when* the general assembly can impeach – when in office, after resignation, or after removal for "mal-administration." But if this is the proper reading, it implies removal for "mal-administration" by some mechanism other than impeachment, and no such mechanism is obvious. If, instead, "for mal-administration" modifies not "removal" but "impeached," then the passage is about both the timing and grounds of impeachment. The acceptable times for impeachment would be (a) when in office, or (b) after resignation or removal. The acceptable grounds for impeachment would be maladministration, thus limiting the phrase "state criminals" in ch. 2, section 9.

152. *See supra* notes 45–50 and accompanying text (Moore), and notes 51–59 and accompanying text (Logan).

153. Vt. Const. of 1786, ch. 2, art. XVII, *reprinted in* Federal and State Constitutions, Vol. VI, *supra* note 148, at 3757.

154. Va. Const. of 1776, *reprinted in* 7 The Federal and State Constitutions, Colonial Charters, and Other Organic Laws of the States, Territories and Colonies Now or Heretofore Forming the United States of America 3818 (Francis Newton Thorpe ed., 1906) [hereinafter Federal and State Constitutions, Vol. VII], available at: https://catalog.hathitrust.org/Record/001140815.

155. Del. Const. of 1776, art. XXIII, *reprinted in* Federal and State Constitutions, Vol. I, *supra* note 141, at 566.

156. N.C. Const. of 1776, art. XXIII, *reprinted in* Federal and State Constitutions, Vol. V, *supra* note 43, at 2792.

157. *See supra* note 112 and accompanying text (noting that the article of impeachment against Justice Oliver categorized his offenses as "high crimes and misdemeanors").

158. Hoffer & Hull, Impeachment in America, *supra* note 1, at 79.

159. *Ibid.*, at 79.
160. *Ibid.*, at 83.
161. *See, e.g.*, the 1783 Vermont impeachment of Justice of the Peace John Barret. *Ibid.*, at 80; *see also* the 1787 New Hampshire impeachment of Justice of the peace Moody Moriss. *Ibid.*, at 86.
162. *Ibid.*, at 85–86
163. *Ibid.*, at 87–91.
164. *Ibid.*, at 95.
165. 1 THE PAPERS OF GEORGE MASON, 1725–1792, at 295–98 (Robert A. Rutland ed., 1970); Notice of Madison's Death, *in* THE PAPERS OF JAMES MADISON iii–v (Henry D. Gilpin ed., 1840).
166. *See, e.g.*, GA. CONST. OF 1777, *art. XI, reprinted in* 2 THE FEDERAL AND STATE CONSTITUTIONS, COLONIAL CHARTERS, AND OTHER ORGANIC LAWS OF THE STATES, TERRITORIES AND COLONIES NOW OR HERETOFORE FORMING THE UNITED STATES OF AMERICA 780 (Francis Newton Thorpe ed., 1906) [hereinafter FEDERAL AND STATE CONSTITUTIONS, VOL. II], available at: https://catalog.hathitrust.org/Record/001140815 (barring any person holding or claiming a title of nobility from voting or holding public office); MD. CONST. OF 1776, *art. XXXII, reprinted in* FEDERAL AND STATE CONSTITUTIONS, VOL. III, *supra* note 100, at 1689 (prohibiting holding multiple offices without express "approbation of this State"); MD. CONST. OF 1776, *art. XL, reprinted in* FEDERAL AND STATE CONSTITUTIONS, VOL. III, *supra* note 100, at 1690 ("no title of nobility, or hereditary honours, ought to be granted in this State").
167. *See, e.g.*, MD. CONST. OF 1776, *art. XXX, reprinted in* FEDERAL AND STATE CONSTITUTIONS, VOL. III, *supra* note 100, at 1689 ("salaries, liberal, but not profuse, ought to be secured to the Chancellor and the Judges").
168. VA. CONST. *of 1776, reprinted in* FEDERAL AND STATE CONSTITUTIONS, VOL. VII, *supra* note 154, at 3818.
169. *Ibid.*
170. N.J. CONST. *of 1776, art. XII, reprinted in* FEDERAL AND STATE CONSTITUTIONS, VOL. V, *supra* note 43, at 2596.
171. DEL. CONST. *of 1776, art. XXIII, reprinted in* FEDERAL AND STATE CONSTITUTIONS, VOL. I, *supra* note 141, at 566.
172. PA. CONST. *of 1776, ch. 2, § 9, reprinted in* FEDERAL AND STATE CONSTITUTIONS, VOL. V, *supra* note 43, at 3085.
173. PA. CONST. *of 1776, ch. 2, § 22, reprinted in* FEDERAL AND STATE CONSTITUTIONS, VOL. V, *supra* note 43, at 3088.
174. PA. CONST. *of 1776, ch. 2, § 23, reprinted in* FEDERAL AND STATE CONSTITUTIONS, VOL. V, *supra* note 43, at 3088.
175. The General Assembly of North Carolina consisted of a Senate and a House of Commons. The implication of this language is that impeachment by the General Assembly would involve houses.
176. N.C. CONST. *of 1776, art. XXIII, reprinted in* FEDERAL AND STATE CONSTITUTIONS, VOL. V, *supra* note 43, at 2792.

177. N.Y. CONST. of 1777, *art. XXXII, reprinted in* FEDERAL AND STATE CONSTITUTIONS, VOL. V, *supra* note 43, at 2635.

178. N.Y. CONST. of 1777, *art. XXXIII, reprinted in* FEDERAL AND STATE CONSTITUTIONS, VOL. V, *supra* note 43, at 2635.

179. VT. CONST. of 1777, *ch. 2, § 8, reprinted in* FEDERAL AND STATE CONSTITUTIONS, VOL. VI, *supra* note 148, at 3742–43. The language of this provision remained unchanged in the revised Vt. Constitution of 1786. VT. CONST. of 1786, *ch. 2, § IX, reprinted in* FEDERAL AND STATE CONSTITUTIONS, VOL. VI, *supra* note 148, at 3755.

180. VT. CONST. of 1777, *ch. 2, § 20, reprinted in* FEDERAL AND STATE CONSTITUTIONS, VOL. VI, *supra* note 148, at 3745. The language of this provision remained unchanged in the revised Vt. Constitution of 1787. VT. CONST. of 1786 *ch. 2, § XXI, reprinted in* FEDERAL AND STATE CONSTITUTIONS, VOL. VI, *supra* note 148, at 3758.

181. VT. CONST. of 1786, *ch. 2, art. XVII, reprinted in* FEDERAL AND STATE CONSTITUTIONS, VOL. VI, *supra* note 148, at 3757.

182. S.C. CONST. OF 1778, *art. XXIII, reprinted in* FEDERAL AND STATE CONSTITUTIONS, VOL. VI, *supra* note 148, at 3253–54.

183. S.C. CONST. OF 1778, *art. XXVII, reprinted in* FEDERAL AND STATE CONSTITUTIONS, VOL. VI, *supra* note 148, at 3254.

184. MASS. CONST. of 1780, *pt. I, ch. I, § 3, art. 6, reprinted in* FEDERAL AND STATE CONSTITUTIONS, VOL. III, *supra* note 100, at 1897.

185. XIV T.B. HOWELL, COMPLETE COLLECTION OF STATE TRIALS AND PROCEEDINGS FOR HIGH TREASON AND OTHER CRIMES AND MISDEMEANORS FROM THE EARLIEST PERIOD TO THE YEAR 1783, WITH NOTES AND OTHER ILLUSTRATIONS 233–349 (1816). *See generally* Chester Kirby, *The Four Lords and the Partition Treaty,* 52 AM. HIST. REV. 477 (1947). Whether Kidd was really a pirate is disputed. *See* RICHARD ZACKS, THE PIRATE HUNTER: THE TRUE STORY OF CAPTAIN KIDD (2003).

186. N.H. CONST. of 1784, *pt. II, reprinted in* FEDERAL AND STATE CONSTITUTIONS, VOL. IV, *supra* note 141, at 2462.

187. *Ibid.,* at 2461.

188. MD. CONST. of 1776, *Declaration of Rights XXX, reprinted in* FEDERAL AND STATE CONSTITUTIONS, VOL. III, *supra* note 100, at 1689.

189. MD. CONST. of 1776, *art. X, reprinted in* FEDERAL AND STATE CONSTITUTIONS, VOL. III, *supra* note 100, at 1692.

4 THE FOUNDERS' IMPEACHMENT

1. SAMUEL B. GRIFFITH II, IN DEFENSE OF THE PUBLIC LIBERTY 309, 525–26 (1976); 2 PAGE SMITH, A NEW AGE BEGINS 1642 (1976); SAMUEL ELIOT MORISON, THE OXFORD HISTORY OF THE AMERICAN PEOPLE 279 (1965).

2. ARTICLES OF CONFEDERATION of 1781, Art. II, available at: www.gpo.gov/fdsys/pkg/SMAN-107/pdf/SMAN-107-pg935.pdf.

3. *Ibid.,* Art. III.

4. All Congress could do was set the necessary level of national expenditures and then appeal to the states legislatures to appropriate the funds required to make those expenditures. *Ibid.,* Art. VIII.

5. Congress thereafter created five executive departments – foreign affairs, finance, war, admiralty, and a post office – but these operated under

congressional authority. MORISON, OXFORD HISTORY OF THE AMERICAN PEOPLE, *supra* note 1.

6. ARTICLES OF CONFEDERATION of 1781, Arts. IX, X, available at: www.gpo.gov/fdsys/pkg/SMAN-107/pdf/SMAN-107-pg935.pdf.

7. *Ibid.*, Art. IX.

8. NOAH FELDMAN, THE THREE LIVES OF JAMES MADISON: GENIUS, PARTISAN, PRESIDENT 40–43 (2017); SMITH, A NEW AGE BEGINS, *supra* note 1, at 1147, 1762–78; MORISON, OXFORD HISTORY OF THE AMERICAN PEOPLE, *supra* note 1, at 300, 304.

9. MORISON, OXFORD HISTORY OF THE AMERICAN PEOPLE, *supra* note 1, at 301–5; 6 DOUGLAS SOUTHALL FREEMAN, GEORGE WASHINGTON: PATRIOT AND PRESIDENT 71–72 (1954) (describing George Washington's reaction to Shay's Rebellion).

10. DAVID C. HENDRICKSON, PEACE PACT: THE LOST WORLD OF THE AMERICAN FOUNDING 4, 199–207 (2003).

11. MORISON, OXFORD HISTORY OF THE AMERICAN PEOPLE, *supra* note 1, at 304. The Annapolis meeting emerged from a call by Virginia for a national conference on trade and regulation of commerce sent out on Jan. 21, 1786. 2 THE PAPERS OF GEORGE MASON, 1725–1792, at 843–44 (Robert A. Rutland ed., 1970) [hereinafter GEORGE MASON PAPERS, VOL. II]. The states represented were New Jersey, New York, Pennsylvania, Delaware, and Virginia. ROBERT K. WRIGHT, JR. & MORRIS J. MCGREGOR, JR., SOLDIER-STATESMEN OF THE CONSTITUTION, app. A at 266 (1987), available at: https://history.army.mil/books/RevWar/ss/appa.htm. Massachusetts, Rhode Island, New Hampshire, and North Carolina appointed delegates, but they showed up too late. Connecticut, South Carolina, Georgia, and (incredibly given the location) Maryland did not even appoint delegates. BROADUS MITCHELL, ALEXANDER HAMILTON: A CONCISE BIOGRAPHY 142–43 (1976).

12. FELDMAN, THREE LIVES OF JAMES MADISON, *supra* note 8, at 73–80 (describing the Annapolis Convention); SHIRLEY VLASAK BALTZ, A CLOSER LOOK AT THE ANNAPOLIS CONVENTION, SEPTEMBER 1786 (1986); Louis Ottenberg, A *Fortunate Fiasco: The Annapolis Convention of 1786*, 45 ABA J. 834, 837 (1959).

13. ANNAPOLIS CONVENTION RESOLUTION of 1786 para. 4, available at: http://teachingamericanhistory.org/library/document/annapolis-convention-resolution.

14. MORISON, OXFORD HISTORY OF THE AMERICAN PEOPLE, *supra* note 1, at 305.

15. MITCHELL, ALEXANDER HAMILTON, *supra* note 11, at 154–55.

16. FREEMAN, GEORGE WASHINGTON, *supra* note 9, at 87.

17. HENDRICKSON, PEACE PACT, *supra* note 10, at 127–37; MERRILL JENSEN, THE ARTICLES OF CONFEDERATION: AN INTERPRETATION OF THE SOCIAL-CONSTITUTIONAL HISTORY OF THE AMERICAN REVOLUTION, 1774–1781, at 177–84 (1959); MILTON E. FLOWER, JOHN DICKINSON: CONSERVATIVE REVOLUTIONARY (1983).

18. Mason's original draft of the Declaration of Rights states: "That the legislative and executive Powers of the State should be separate and distinct from the judicative ..." THE VIRGINIA DECLARATION OF RIGHTS (*c.* May 20–26, 1776) (first draft), *in* 1 THE PAPERS OF GEORGE MASON, 1725–1792, at 276–78 (Robert A. Rutland ed., 1970) [hereinafter GEORGE MASON PAPERS, VOL. I].

19. *Ibid.*, at 287.

20. *Ibid.*, at 295–98.

21. *Ibid.*, at 276 (noting assessments of later American scholars and the effusive praise of French intellectuals Jacques Pierre Brissot and the Marquis de Condorcet).

22. Maryland, Massachusetts, New Hampshire, North Carolina, Pennsylvania, and Vermont each adopted declarations of rights. 3 THE FEDERAL AND STATE CONSTITUTIONS, COLONIAL CHARTERS, AND OTHER ORGANIC LAWS OF THE STATES, TERRITORIES AND COLONIES NOW OR HERETOFORE FORMING THE UNITED STATES OF AMERICA 1686 (Francis Newton Thorpe ed., 1909) [hereinafter FEDERAL AND STATE CONSTITUTIONS, VOL. III] (Maryland); 4 THE FEDERAL AND STATE CONSTITUTIONS, COLONIAL CHARTERS, AND OTHER ORGANIC LAWS OF THE STATES, TERRITORIES AND COLONIES NOW OR HERETOFORE FORMING THE UNITED STATES OF AMERICA 2453 (Francis Newton Thorpe ed., 1909) [hereinafter FEDERAL AND STATE CONSTITUTIONS, VOL. IV] (New Hampshire); 5 THE FEDERAL AND STATE CONSTITUTIONS, COLONIAL CHARTERS, AND OTHER ORGANIC LAWS OF THE STATES, TERRITORIES AND COLONIES NOW OR HERETOFORE FORMING THE UNITED STATES OF AMERICA 2787 (Francis Newton Thorpe ed., 1909) [hereinafter FEDERAL AND STATE CONSTITUTIONS, VOL. V] (North Carolina); 6 THE FEDERAL AND STATE CONSTITUTIONS, COLONIAL CHARTERS, AND OTHER ORGANIC LAWS OF THE STATES, TERRITORIES AND COLONIES NOW OR HERETOFORE FORMING THE UNITED STATES OF AMERICA 3749 (Francis Newton Thorpe ed., 1909) [hereinafter FEDERAL AND STATE CONSTITUTIONS, VOL. VI] (Vermont).

23. The failure to include a declaration of rights in the original constitution was a primary reason that Mason ultimately refused to vote in favor of its adoption, and went on to oppose its ratification by Virginia. GEORGE MASON, *Objections To This Constitution of Government* (c. Sept. 16, 1787), *in* 3 THE PAPERS OF GEORGE MASON 1725–1792, at 991 (Robert A. Rutland ed., 1970) [hereinafter GEORGE MASON PAPERS, VOL. III].

24. LANCE BANNING, THE SACRED FIRE OF LIBERTY: JAMES MADISON AND THE FOUNDING OF THE FEDERAL REPUBLIC 113–15 (1995).

25. 1 JONATHAN ELLIOT, THE DEBATES IN SEVERAL STATE CONVENTIONS OF THE ADOPTION OF THE FEDERAL CONSTITUTION 121, 143 (1827) [hereinafter 1 ELLIOT].

26. The United Kingdom first created a Supreme Court separate from the House of Lords in 2005. Constitutional Reform Act 2005, c. 4 (UK), available at: www .legislation.gov.uk/ukpga/2005/4/contents.

27. GLENN DYMOND, THE APPELLATE JURISDICTION OF THE HOUSE OF LORDS 2–5, HOUSE LORDS LIBR. (2009), available at: www.parliament.uk/documents/lords-library/lln2009-010appellate.pdf.

28. As Madison observed in *The Federalist* No. 47, "On the slightest view of the British Constitution, we must perceive that the legislative, executive, and judiciary departments are by no means separate and distinct from each other." THE FEDERALIST NO. 47, at 302 (James Madison) (Clinton Rossiter ed., 1961).

29. *See* Robert G. Hazo, *Montesquieu and the Separation of Powers*, 54 ABA J. 665 (1968) (the traditional, somewhat hagiographical version, of Montesquieu's separation doctrine); Robert Shackleton, *Montesquieu, Bolingbroke, and the Separation of Powers*, 3 FRENCH STUDIES 25 (1949).

30. Montesquieu, *Book XI: On the Laws That Form Political Liberty in its Relation with the Constitution, in* The Spirit of the Laws (Anne M. Cohler et al. eds. & trans., Cambridge University Press 1989) (1748). Madison was sufficiently sensitive to Montesquieu's great authority in American constitutional thought that he devoted several lengthy paragraphs in *The Federalist* No. 47 to contending that the Frenchman's doctrine of separation of powers did not imply the absence of any control or influence by one branch over the actions of another. The Federalist No. 47, at 302–3 (James Madison) (Clinton Rossiter ed., 1961).

31. The Virginia Declaration of Rights (c. May 20–26, 1776) (first draft), *in* George Mason Papers, Vol. I, *supra* note 18, at 276–78. The final draft adopted the same language. *Ibid.*, at 287.

32. *Ibid.*, at 276. Maryland, Massachusetts, New Hampshire, North Carolina, Pennsylvania, and Vermont each adopted Declarations of Rights. Federal and State Constitutions, Vol. III, *supra* note 22, at 1686 (Maryland); *ibid.*, at 1888 (Massachusetts); Federal and State Constitutions, Vol. IV, *supra* note 22, at 2453 (New Hampshire); Federal and State Constitutions, Vol. V, *supra* note 22, at 2787 (North Carolina); *ibid.*, at 3081 (Pennsylvania); Federal and State Constitutions, Vol. VI, *supra* note 22, at 3749 (Vermont). All these except Pennsylvania included in their declarations of rights an express endorsement of the separation of powers. Georgia had no declaration of rights, but the first article of its 1777 constitution stated that: "The legislative, executive, and judiciary departments shall be separate and distinct, so that neither exercises the powers properly belonging to the other." 2 The Federal and State Constitutions, Colonial Charters, and Other Organic Laws of the States, Territories and Colonies Now or Heretofore Forming the United States of America 778 (Francis Newton Thorpe ed., 1909) [hereinafter Federal and State Constitutions, Vol. II].

33. David Hendrickson notes that the national government under the articles "had no distinct executive, judicial, or administrative departments" and might best be considered a "plural Executive" or "deliberating Executive assembly." Hendrickson, Peace Pact, *supra* note 10, at 136.

34. Vt. Const. *of 1786, in* Federal and State Constitutions, Vol. VI, *supra* note 22, at 3754–61.

35. Pa. Const. *of 1776, in* Federal and State Constitutions, Vol. V, *supra* note 22, at 3084–92.

36. *Ibid.*, § 19, at 3087.

37. *See Sketch of Pinckney's Plan for a Constitution*, 1787, 9 Am. Hist. Rev. 735 (1904).

38. 1 Elliot, *supra* note 25, at 121, 143 (Randolph Resolutions); *ibid.*, at 145 (Pinckney Plan).

39. 1 Elliot, *supra* note 25, at 121, 175–77; 1 The Records of the Federal Convention of 1787, at 242–45 (Max Farrand ed., 1911) [hereinafter 1 Farrand's Federal Convention Records].

40. 1 Elliot, *supra* note 25, at 179; 1 Farrand's Federal Convention Records, *supra* note 39, at 291–93.

41. The point recurs throughout the *Federalist Papers. See* THE FEDERALIST NO. 48, at 306–7 (James Madison) (Clinton Rossiter ed., 1961) (explaining the "superiority" of the "legislative department"); THE FEDERALIST NO. 51, at 322 (James Madison) (Clinton Rossiter ed., 1961): "In republican government, the legislative authority necessarily predominates"; THE FEDERALIST NO. 71, at 433 (Alexander Hamilton) (Clinton Rossiter ed., 1961) (discussing "the tendency of the legislative authority to absorb every other"); and THE FEDERALIST NO. 73, at 444 (Alexander Hamilton) (Clinton Rossiter ed., 1961) (noting "the superior weight and influence of the legislative body in a free government and the hazard to the executive in a trial of strength with that body").

42. HENDRICKSON, PEACE PACT, *supra* note 10, at 221–22; MORISON, OXFORD HISTORY OF THE AMERICAN PEOPLE, *supra* note 1, at 307.

43. MORISON, OXFORD HISTORY OF THE AMERICAN PEOPLE, *supra* note 1, at 308.

44. The constitutions of New Jersey, Delaware, Massachusetts, and New Hampshire all provided for impeachment by the lower house of the legislature and trial by an upper house, variously denominated the council or the senate. *NJ CONST. of 1776, Art. XII, in* FEDERAL AND STATE CONSTITUTIONS, VOL. V, *supra* note 22, at 2596; *DEL. CONST. of 1776, Art. XXIII, in* 1 THE FEDERAL AND STATE CONSTITUTIONS, COLONIAL CHARTERS, AND OTHER ORGANIC LAWS OF THE STATES, TERRITORIES AND COLONIES NOW OR HERETOFORE FORMING THE UNITED STATES OF AMERICA 566 (Francis Newton Thorpe ed., 1909) [hereinafter FEDERAL AND STATE CONSTITUTIONS, VOL. I], available at: https://babel.hathitrust.org/cgi/pt?id=mdp.39015005892172;view=2up;seq=6; *MASS. CONST. of 1780, pt. I, ch. I, § 3, Art. 6, in* FEDERAL AND STATE CONSTITUTIONS, VOL. III, *supra* note 22, at 1897; *NH CONST. of 1784, pt. II, in* FEDERAL AND STATE CONSTITUTIONS, VOL. IV, *supra* note 22, at 2462.

45. Hamilton would have preferred a monarchy. MITCHELL, ALEXANDER HAMILTON, *supra* note 11, at 152. His proposal for the constitution would have placed the president (whom he styled the "governor"), the senate, and the judges in office "during good behavior," which is to say, effectively for life barring removal by impeachment. 1 ELLIOT, *supra* note 25, at 179–80.

46. *See, e.g.,* 1 FARRAND'S FEDERAL CONVENTION RECORDS, *supra* note 39, at 48 (statement of Elbridge Gerry at Constitutional Convention, May 31, 1787: "The evils we experience flow from the excess of democracy." *See also* MORISON, OXFORD HISTORY OF THE AMERICAN PEOPLE, *supra* note 1, at 309 (describing the constitution as a "'mixed government,' in which the democratic aristocratic, and authoritarian elements were balanced").

47. The original Virginia Plan and the Pinckney Plan both created an upper house selected by members of the lower house. Hamilton proposed something like the system ultimately adopted for the president, in which senators would be chosen by "electors" who had been selected for this purpose by the people. 1 ELLIOT, *supra* note 25, at 179.

48. U.S. CONST. Art. II, § 3.

49. MORISON, OXFORD HISTORY OF THE AMERICAN PEOPLE, *supra* note 1, at 306; THE FEDERALIST NO. 62 (James Madison).

50. 1 FARRAND'S FEDERAL CONVENTION RECORDS, *supra* note 39, at 288–89 (Hamilton's speech of June 18, 1787) (saying that "the British government was the best in the world," and on the design of the executive, "The English model was the only good one on this subject"); MITCHELL, ALEXANDER HAMILTON, *supra* note 11, at 152; BANNING, SACRED FIRE OF LIBERTY, *supra* note 24, at 150.

51. 1 ELLIOT, *supra* note 25, at 179–80; 1 FARRAND'S FEDERAL CONVENTION RECORDS, *supra* note 39, at 289, 292.

52. 1 FARRAND'S FEDERAL CONVENTION RECORDS, *supra* note 39, at 300.

53. The motion to have the chief executive serve "during good behavior" was made by Dr. McClurg on July 17, 1787, and failed the same day. 2 THE RECORDS OF THE FEDERAL CONVENTION OF 1787, at 33–36 (Max Farrand ed., 1911) [hereinafter 2 FARRAND'S FEDERAL CONVENTION RECORDS].

54. 1 FARRAND'S FEDERAL CONVENTION RECORDS, *supra* note 39, at 85.

55. 1 ELLIOT, *supra* note 25, at 175–76.

56. *Ibid.*, at 148: "The executive power of the United States shall be vested in a President of the United States, which shall be his style; and his title shall be His Excellency. He shall be elected for __ years; and shall be re-eligible."

57. *Ibid.*, at 144: "A national executive shall be instituted, to be chosen by the national legislature for the term of __ years . . . to be ineligible a second time; and that, besides the general authority to execute the national laws, *it* ought to enjoy the executive rights vest in Congress by the Confederation" (emphasis added).

58. U.S. CONST. Art. II, § 1. The present two-term limit was not adopted until the Twenty-Second Amendment of 1951.

59. The states with annual elections for chief executive were Georgia, FEDERAL AND STATE CONSTITUTIONS, VOL. II, *supra* note 32, at 778 (Art. II); Maryland, FEDERAL AND STATE CONSTITUTIONS, VOL. III, *supra* note 22, at 1695 (Art. XXV); Massachusetts, *ibid.*, at 1900; New Hampshire, FEDERAL AND STATE CONSTITUTIONS, VOL. IV, *supra* note 22, at 2462–63; New Jersey, FEDERAL AND STATE CONSTITUTIONS, VOL. V, *supra* note 22, at 2596 (Art. VII); North Carolina, *ibid.*, at 2791 (Art. XV); Pennsylvania, *ibid.*, at 3087 (§ 19); Vermont, FEDERAL AND STATE CONSTITUTIONS, VOL. VI, *supra* note 22, at 3755–56 (Arts. VIII, X); and Virginia, 7 THE FEDERAL AND STATE CONSTITUTIONS, COLONIAL CHARTERS, AND OTHER ORGANIC LAWS OF THE STATES, TERRITORIES AND COLONIES NOW OR HERETOFORE FORMING THE UNITED STATES OF AMERICA 3816 (Francis Newton Thorpe ed., 1909) [hereinafter FEDERAL AND STATE CONSTITUTIONS, VOL. VII].

60. FEDERAL AND STATE CONSTITUTIONS, VOL. VI, *supra* note 22, at 3249 (Art. III).

61. FEDERAL AND STATE CONSTITUTIONS, VOL. I, *supra* note 44, at 563 (Delaware); FEDERAL AND STATE CONSTITUTIONS, VOL. V, *supra* note 22, at 2632 (New York) (Art. XVII).

62. *See supra* Chapter 3, Table 3.2.

63. Madison makes precisely this connection in *Federalist* 39 by recounting the short tenures of governors under existing state constitutions and the absence of impeachment provisions in some states, and concluding with the reassurance that, although the president enjoys a term of four years, he is impeachable

throughout. THE FEDERALIST NO. 39, at 241–42 (James Madison) (Clinton Rossiter ed., 1961).

64. 2 FARRAND'S FEDERAL CONVENTION RECORDS, *supra* note 53, at 497–98.

65. U.S. CONST. Art. II, § 1.

66. In explaining the rationales of the Committee of Eleven for creating a system of electors, Gouverneur Morris listed "the indispensable necessity of making the Executive independent of the Legislature." 2 FARRAND'S FEDERAL CONVENTION RECORDS, *supra* note 53, at 500.

67. THE FEDERALIST NO. 68, at 302 (Alexander Hamilton) (Clinton Rossiter ed., 1961).

68. One historian expressed the point oracularly by characterizing the Electoral College as "designed to create a bulwark between the aroused passions of the people and the office of chief executive." JAMES MCGREGOR BURNS, THE VINEYARD OF LIBERTY 38 (1982).

69. 2 FARRAND'S FEDERAL CONVENTION RECORDS, *supra* note 53, at 500 (statement of Gouverneur Morris explaining the rationales of the Committee of Eleven for Electoral College). Not everyone bought the Committee's rationale. Charles Pinckney apparently thought that, inasmuch as both senators and electors would be chosen by state legislatures, they would likely be the same people or at least answerable to the same interests, and thus the people responsible for selecting and impeaching presidents would be substantially the same. *Ibid.*, at 501.

70. U.S. CONST. Art. II, § 1.

71. *See* STEVEN G. CALABRESI & CHRISTOPHER S. YOO, THE UNITARY EXECUTIVE: PRESIDENTIAL POWER FROM WASHINGTON TO BUSH (2008).

72. U.S. CONST. Art. II, § 2.

73. U.S. DEPARTMENT OF DEFENSE, NUMBER OF MILITARY AND DOD APPROPRIATED FUND (APF) CIVILIAN PERSONNEL PERMANENTLY ASSIGNED (December 31, 2017), available at: www.dmdc.osd.mil/appj/dwp/rest/download?fileName=DMDC_Website _Location_Report_1712.xlsx&groupName=milRegionCountry (Excel document).

74. It appears that from 1783 to 1789, there were never more than a few hundred men in the United States service. JOHN R. MASS, DEFENDING A NEW NATION, 1783–1811, at 9–13 (2013). By 1789, the total number was 718. U.S. DEPARTMENT OF DEFENSE, SELECTED MANPOWER STATISTICS FISCAL YEAR 1997, at 48 table 2–11, available at: www.alternatewars.com/BBOW/Stats/DOD_SelectedStat s_FY97.pdf.

75. For example, Elbridge Gerry and Luther Martin urged a constitutional provision limiting the size of the U.S. army to 3,000 men in peacetime. MORISON, OXFORD HISTORY OF THE AMERICAN PEOPLE, *supra* note 1, at 308.

76. Louis Jacobson, *Taking the Measure of the Federal Workforce under Donald Trump*, POLITIFACT (Jan. 22, 2018), available at: www.politifact.com/truth-o-meter/article/2018/jan/22/taking-measure-federal-workforce.

77. *The Cabinet*, THE WHITE HOUSE: PRESIDENT BARACK OBAMA, available at: https://obamawhitehouse.archives.gov/administration/cabinet.

78. A quarter of a century later, in 1816, there were still only 6,327 federal employees. Bureau of the Census, Historical Statistics of the United States, 1789–1945, at 294 (1949), available at: www2.census.gov/prod2/statcomp/documents/HistoricalStatisticsoftheUnitedStates1789-1945.pdf.

79. U.S. Const. Art. II, § 2.

80. *Ibid.*

81. *See Removal by the President. – Bill for establishing an executive department, to be denominated the Department of Foreign Affairs, House of Representatives, June 16, 1789, in* 4 Jonathan Elliot, The Debates in Several State Conventions of the Adoption of the Federal Constitution 350–404 (1827) [hereinafter 4 Elliot]. *E.g.*, James Madison argued that the power of appointment implied the power of removal, *ibid.*, at 378–83, while Roger Sherman and Elbridge Gerry argued the reverse, *ibid.*, at 393–94, 403–4.

82. U.S. Const. Art. II, § 2.

83. *Ibid.*

84. *Ibid.*, § 3.

85. *See, e.g.*, 1 Farrand's Federal Convention Records, *supra* note 39, at 107 (debates of Constitutional Convention, June 4, 1787, including remarks of Mssrs. Gerry, King, Wilson, Hamilton, Madison, and Mason).

86. U.S. Const. Art. I, § 7.

87. The assumption that Congress might not be in session all that much is revealed in the curious provision of Article I, section 4, that Congress "shall assemble at least once in every year, and such meeting shall be on the first Monday in December, unless they shall by law appoint a different day." Apparently, the framers thought that the country might get along fine without Congress for eleven months of the year. *See, e.g.*, 5 Jonathan Elliot, The Debates in Several State Conventions of the Adoption of the Federal Constitution 383 [hereinafter 5 Elliot] In remarks made at the Constitutional Convention on Aug. 7, 1787, Rufus King said he "could not think there would be a necessity for a meeting every year. A great vice in our system was that of legislating too much." In 1933, the mandatory meeting date was changed to January 3 by the Twentieth Amendment.

88. U.S. Const. Art. II, § 3.

89. *Ibid.*, § 2.

90. *See, e.g.*, 1 Farrand's Federal Convention Records, *supra* note 39, at 73 (remark of James Wilson on June 1, 1787: "The great qualities in the several parts of the Executive are vigor and dispatch").

91. *Randolph's Propositions, in* 1 Elliot, *supra* note 25, at 144 (§ 9).

92. *Charles Pinckney's Draft, in* 1 Elliot, *supra* note 25, at 149 (Art. IX): "One of these courts shall be termed the Supreme Court, whose jurisdiction shall extend to all cases arising under the laws of the United States, or affecting ambassadors, other public ministers, and consuls; to the trial of impeachment of officers of the United States; to all cases of admiralty and maritime jurisdiction."

93. *Colonel Hamilton's Plan of Government, in* 1 Elliot, *supra* note 25, at 180 (§ 9): "The governors, senators, and all officers of the United States to be liable to

impeachment for real and corrupt conduct; and, upon conviction, to be removed from office, and disqualified for holding any place of trust or profit."

94. *Patterson's Propositions, in* 1 ELLIOT, *supra* note 25, at 176 (§ 4): "That the United States in Congress be authorized to elect a federal executive ... removable on impeachment and conviction for malpractices or neglect of duty, by Congress, on application by a majority of the executives of the several states."

95. 5 ELLIOT, *supra* note 87, at 341–42 (Statement of Rufus King, Constitutional Convention, July 20, 1787).

96. Charles Pinckney shared the separation of powers concern, 5 ELLIOT, *supra* note 87, at 341, as did Gouverneur Morris, although he was especially hesitant if impeachment in the House were to result in suspension of presidential power during the trial (which has not been the practice), *ibid*.

97. 5 ELLIOT, *supra* note 87, at 342 (Statement of Rufus King, Constitutional Convention, July 20, 1787): "The president ought not to be impeachable unless he held his office during good behavior."

98. *Ibid.*, at 339 (Statement of Gouverneur Morris, Constitutional Convention, July 19, 1787), Morris "was for a short term, in order to avoid impeachments, which would be otherwise necessary."

99. Gunning Bedford of Delaware objected to a proposed presidential term of seven years because the country would be in woeful shape if saddled for so long a period with a president who proved unqualified or lost his capacities after election. Bedford argued that even impeachment would be insufficient in such a case because it "would reach misfeasance only, not incapacity." 1 FARRAND'S FEDERAL CONVENTION RECORDS, *supra* note 39, at 68–69.

100. 5 ELLIOT, *supra* note 87, at 343 (Statement of Charles Pinckney, Constitutional Convention, July 20, 1787), Pinckney: "presumed that [the president's] power would be so circumscribed as to render impeachments unnecessary."

101. 5 ELLIOT, *supra* note 87, at 335 (Statement of Gouverneur Morris, Constitutional Convention, July 19, 1787); *see also* 2 FARRAND'S FEDERAL CONVENTION RECORDS, *supra* note 53, at 54 (Morris supposed that, "Without these ministers, the executive can do nothing of consequence").

102. 1 ELLIOT, *supra* note 25, at 146, 149 (Pinckney Plan, Arts. III, IX).

103. *Ibid.*, at 176 (Paterson Plan, § 4).

104. *Ibid.*, at 180 (Hamilton Plan, § 9).

105. *Ibid.*, at 89–90 (emphasis added).

106. *See, e.g.,* 1 FARRAND'S FEDERAL CONVENTION RECORDS, *supra* note 39, at 226 (formulas advanced and debated on June 13); 2 FARRAND'S FEDERAL CONVENTION RECORDS, *supra* note 53, at 61 (July 20); *ibid.*, at 116 (July 26); *ibid.*, at 367 (Aug. 22) (proposing to make the judges of the Supreme Court "triable by the Senate, on impeachment by the House of representatives"); *ibid.*, at 495 (Sept. 4) (proposing removal of the president "on impeachment by the house of representatives, and conviction by the Senate").

107. 1 FARRAND'S FEDERAL CONVENTION RECORDS, *supra* note 39, at 85, 87, 92 (records of Federal Convention, June 2, 1787).

108. *See, e.g.*, 2 Farrand's Federal Convention Records, *supra* note 53, at 422 (approval on Aug. 25 of proposal that the president be removable "on impeachment by the House of representatives, and conviction in the supreme Court").

109. *See, e.g., ibid.*, at 551 (remarks of Roger Sherman, Sept. 8, 1787).

110. 1 Farrand's Federal Convention Records, *supra* note 39, at 292–93. Edmund Randolph revived Hamilton's suggestion in July, but it got no traction. 2 Farrand's Federal Convention Records, *supra* note 53, at 67. Hamilton's original suggestion was qualified by the proviso that all such state judges must have the measure of political independence granted by a permanent salary and appointment during good behavior. 1 Farrand's Federal Convention Records, *supra* note 39, at 292–93.

111. *See, e.g.*, 2 Farrand's Federal Convention Records, *supra* note 53, at 551 (comments of Charles Pinckney, Sept. 8, 1787). Madison had this concern to the end, raising it on Sept. 8, *ibid.*, at 551, and again on Sept. 14 as an argument against the proposal to suspend impeached officers pending trial, *ibid.*, at 612: "The President is made too dependent already on the Legislature, by the power of one branch to try him in consequence of an impeachment by the other. This intermediate suspension, will put him in the power of one branch only – They can at any moment, in order to make way for the functions of another who will be more favorable to their views, vote a temporary removal of the existing magistrate."

112. *Ibid.*, at 551 (Sept. 8, 1787).

113. *E.g.*, George Mason listed the power of the Senate as one of his reasons for declining to vote for the constitution at the close of the convention. *Ibid.*, at 638.

114. U.S. Const. Art. II, § 3. Assignment of impeachment trials to the Senate was first formally proposed by the Committee of Eleven on Sept. 4. 2 Farrand's Federal Convention Records, *supra* note 53, at 493.

115. U.S. Const. Art. II, § 4.

116. *Ibid.*, § 3.

117. *Ibid.*

118. *Ibid.*

119. Professors McGinnis and Rappaport have argued that "the central principle underlying the Constitution is governance through supermajority rules." John O. McGinnis & Michael B. Rappaport, *Our Supermajoritarian Constitution*, 80 Tex. L. Rev. 703, 705 (2002).

120. U.S. Const. Art. II, § 2.

121. *Ibid.*, § 5.

122. *Ibid.*, Art. I, § 7.

123. *Ibid.*, Art. V.

124. *Ibid.*

125. 2 Farrand's Federal Convention Records, *supra* note 53, at 497 (recommendations of the Committee of Eleven, Sept. 4, 1787).

126. As noted *supra* in Chapter 3, Maryland had provisions for the removal of judges by the governor upon the "address" of the legislature that were very similar to impeachment.

127. South Carolina and New York had two-thirds requirements for both impeachment and conviction. Federal and State Constitutions, Vol. V, *supra* note 22, at 2635 (NY); Federal and State Constitutions, Vol. VI, *supra* note 22, at 3253–54 (SC). Maryland, which had an impeachment-like mechanism limited to judges in which a governor could remove a judge upon the "address" of the legislature, required a two-thirds vote in both houses to authorize an address. Federal and State Constitutions, Vol. II, *supra* note 32, at 1689.

128. Peter Charles Hoffer & N. E. H. Hull, Impeachment in America, 1635–1805, at 106 (1984).

129. Feldman, Three Lives of James Madison, at xiii–xiv (2017).

130. "[Impeachment] will seldom fail to agitate the passions of the whole community, and to divide it into parties more or less friendly or inimical to the accused. In many cases it will connect itself with the pre-existing factions, and will enlist all their animosities, partialities, influence, and interest on one side or on the other; and in such cases there will always be the greatest danger that the decision will be regulated more by the comparative strength of parties, than by the real demonstrations of innocence or guilt." The Federalist No. 65, at 396–97 (Alexander Hamilton) (Clinton Rossiter ed., 1961).

131. The Virginia and Delaware constitutions provided that impeachment would result in removal "or ... such pains or penalties as the laws shall direct." Va. Const. *of 1776, in* Federal and State Constitutions, Vol. VII, *supra* note 59, at 3818; *Del. Const. of 1776, Art. XXIII, in* Federal and State Constitutions, Vol. I, *supra* note 44, at 566. However, it is unclear whether those pains could follow automatically or only after regular courts performed their function "as the laws shall direct."

132. U.S. Const. Art. I, § 3.

133. *Ibid.,* § 9.

134. *See supra* Chapter 2, notes 42–53, 121–22, 128–29, 174–76 and accompanying text.

135. 2 Farrand's Federal Convention Records, *supra* note 53, at 69.

136. Curiously, Hoffer and Hull seem to think that the framers' divergence from parliamentary practice on the matter of punishment indicates that English precedent was of "disputable relevance." Hoffer & Hull, Impeachment in America, *supra* note 128, at 97. I think they have it backwards. The fact that the Americans did not ape the English in every detail of impeachment design hardly means that English practice did not affect them. That is rather like saying that, since the framers chose an elective president rather than a hereditary king, the English experience of constitutional monarchy did not influence their choice. Of course it did. It is simply that the Americans drew different lessons from English experience than the English did.

137. The remaining two (Pennsylvania and Vermont) said only that "state criminals" might be impeached. Pa. Const. *of 1776, ch. 2, § 9, in* Federal and State Constitutions, Vol. V, *supra* note 22, at 3085; *Vt. Const. of 1786 ch. 2, § IX, in* Federal and State Constitutions, Vol. VI, *supra* note 22, at 3755.

138. 1 Farrand's Federal Convention Records, *supra* note 39, at 78–79, 88. Also on June 2, John Dickinson of Delaware suggested impeachment for "malconduct or neglect in the execution of his office," a phrase nearly indistinguishable from the Williamson and Davie formulation. *Ibid.*, at 89–90.

139. *Ibid.*, at 74.

140. NC. Const. *of* 1776, Art. XXIII, *in* Federal and State Constitutions, Vol. V, *supra* note 22, at 2792.

141. Va. Const. *of* 1776, *in* Federal and State Constitutions, Vol. VII, *supra* note 59, at 3818 (Virginia); Del. Const. of 1776, Art. 23, *in* Federal and State Constitutions, Vol. I, *supra* note 44, at 566 (Delaware); SC. Const. *of* 1778, Art. XXIII, *in* Federal and State Constitutions, Vol. VI, *supra* note 22, at 3253 (South Carolina); NY. Const. *of* 1777, Art. XXXIII, *in* Federal and State Constitutions, Vol. V, *supra* note 22, at 2635 (New York); Mass. Const. *of* 1780, ch. 1, § II, Art. VIII, *in* Federal and State Constitutions, Vol. III, *supra* note 22, at 1897 (Massachusetts); NH. Const. *of* 1784, *pt.* II, *in* Federal and State Constitutions, Vol. IV, *supra* note 22, at 2461 (New Hampshire).

142. It appears in multiple drafts and received favorable votes on June 13, 1 Farrand's Federal Convention Records, *supra* note 39, at 226, 230, 236, and July 20, 2 Farrand's Federal Convention Records, *supra* note 53, at 61, 64. It also appears in three of the first four reports of the Committee of Detail. 2 Farrand's Federal Convention Records, *supra* note 53, at 132, 134, 145.

143. *Report of Committee of Detail, IV, in* 2 Farrand's Federal Convention Records, *supra* note 53, at 145. The original phrase "malpractice or neglect of duty" was in the handwriting of Edmund Randolph, while the new phrase "treason, bribery, or corruption" is in the hand of John Rutledge. *Ibid.*, at 137.

144. SC. Const. *of* 1778, Art. XXIII, *in* Federal and State Constitutions, Vol. VI, *supra* note 22, at 3253–54.

145. In mid-August, it was proposed to create a Council of State to advise the president consisting of the chief justice and secretaries of domestic affairs, commerce and finance, foreign affairs, war, marine, and state, all serving at the president's pleasure, but also impeachable for "neglect of duty, malversation, or corruption." 2 Farrand's Federal Convention Records, *supra* note 53, at 337. Inasmuch as "malversation" means corrupt behavior in a position of public trust, inclusion of that term seems redundant and the term did not reappear.

146. 2 Farrand's Federal Convention Records, *supra* note 53, at 422, 427.

147. *Ibid.*, at 499.

148. *Ibid.*, at 550–52.

149. George Mason Papers, Vol. I, *supra* note 18, at 295, 301 (Mason's first draft of the Virginia constitution providing for retention of judges on "good behavior" and impeachment of the governor, privy councilors, and other officers "for maladministration, or corruption"); *ibid.*, at 308 (final draft of Virginia constitution expanding grounds for impeachment to "mal-administration, corruption, or other means by which the safety of the state may be endangered").

150. Hoffer & Hull, Impeachment in America, *supra* note 128, at 74.

151. 1 FARRAND'S FEDERAL CONVENTION RECORDS, *supra* note 39, at 74 (statement of James Madison, June 1, 1787): "To prevent a man from holding an office longer than he ought, he may for malpractice be impeached"; *ibid.*, at 92 (statement of James Madison, June 2, 1787): "Mr. Madison said it was far from being his wish that every executive Officer should remain in Office, without being amenable to some Body for his conduct"; 2 FARRAND'S FEDERAL CONVENTION RECORDS, *supra* note 53, at 86 (statement of George Mason, June 2, 1787).
152. 2 FARRAND'S FEDERAL CONVENTION RECORDS, *supra* note 53, at 65.
153. *Ibid.*, at 65–66.
154. *Ibid.*, at 86.
155. *Ibid.*, at 339.
156. *Ibid.*, at 345.
157. 2 WILLIAM BLACKSTONE, COMMENTARIES ON THE LAWS OF ENGLAND: IN FOUR BOOKS, bk. IV, ch. 7, § 17 (1893).
158. 2 FARRAND'S FEDERAL CONVENTION RECORDS, *supra* note 53, at 550.
159. *See supra* Chapter 2, notes 42–53 and accompanying text.
160. *See, e.g.*, Clayton Roberts, *The Law of Impeachment in Stuart England: A Reply to Raoul Berger*, 84 YALE L.J. 1419, 1427 (1975).
161. *See supra* Chapter 3, Appendix A, Impeachment Provisions of State Constitutions, 1776–1787.
162. 2 FARRAND'S FEDERAL CONVENTION RECORDS, *supra* note 53, at 550.
163. One is even tempted to wonder if the entire interchange was not prearranged to produce the outcome it did. Against that supposition is the fact that, by September, Mason was beginning to harden into his ultimate opposition to the crystallizing final draft, while Madison was its most prominent architect and cheerleader. Whether in the penultimate moments of the convention the two would have coordinated quite this closely is questionable.
164. LAWRENCE TRIBE & JOSHUA MATZ, TO END A PRESIDENCY: THE POWER OF IMPEACHMENT 39 (2018).
165. *See, e.g.*, RAOUL BERGER, IMPEACHMENT: THE CONSTITUTIONAL PROBLEMS 86 (1973): "Manifestly, [Mason's substitution of 'high Crimes and Misdemeanors' for his original proposal of 'maladministration'] was made for the purpose of limiting, not expanding, the initial Mason proposal." Cass Sunstein refers to "high Crimes and Misdemeanors" as Mason's "seemingly narrower phrase," which leaves ambiguous whether he thinks it *is* narrower or was just meant to *look* narrower, or perhaps is not narrower, but merely seems so. CASS R. SUNSTEIN, IMPEACHMENT: A CITIZEN'S GUIDE 48 (2017).
166. BERGER, IMPEACHMENT, *supra* note 165, at 54, 87 (1973). Berger opened his discussion by asserting that: "To understand what the Framers had in mind we must begin with English law, for nowhere did they more evidently take from that law than in drafting impeachment provisions." His conclusion was that "high crimes and misdemeanors" was a term of art with an "ascertainable content," and therefore "that content furnishes the boundaries of the [impeachment] power."

167. In the five years before the American Revolution, British booksellers exported 120,000 books and pamphlets per year to America. JAMES RAVEN, THE BUSINESS OF BOOKS: BOOKSELLERS AND THE ENGLISH BOOK TRADE 1450–1850, at 144 (2007).

168. The U.S. Supreme Court has called Blackstone "the preeminent authority on English law for the founding generation," Alden v. Maine, 527 U.S. 706, 715 (1999), and used him as a guide to founding era American understanding of the law in cases as widely separated in time and subject matter as Marbury v. Madison, 5 U.S. 137, 147, 163 (1803) (power of judicial review), and District of Columbia v. Heller, 554 U.S. 570, 583 (2008) (individual right to bear arms under Second Amendment).

169. 1 JOHN RUSHWORTH, HISTORICAL COLLECTIONS OF PRIVATE PASSAGES OF STATE, WEIGHTY MATTERS IN LAW, REMARKABLE PROCEEDINGS IN FIVE PARLIAMENTS (1680), available at: https://babel.hathitrust.org/cgi/pt?id=nyp.33433004875773 ;view=1up;seq=11. Among the impeachments covered are the duke of Buckingham in 1626, *ibid.*, at 303 *et seq.*; Roger Manwaring in 1628, *ibid.*, at 593 *et seq.*; John Lilburne in 1637, 2 JOHN RUSHWORTH, HISTORICAL COLLECTIONS OF PRIVATE PASSAGES OF STATE, WEIGHTY MATTERS IN LAW, REMARKABLE PROCEEDINGS IN FIVE PARLIAMENTS 468 (1680); Judge Berkley in 1637, *ibid.*, at 600 *et seq.*; and the earl of Strafford in 1640.

170. EDWARD HYDE, THE HISTORY OF THE REBELLION AND CIVIL WARS IN ENGLAND, BEGUN IN THE YEAR 1641 (1731) (a history in four volumes in which impeachments make a regular appearance).

171. DAVID HUME, HISTORY OF ENGLAND: FROM THE INVASION OF JULIUS CAESAR TO THE END OF THE REIGN OF JAMES II (first published 1754–62).

172. MATTHEW HALE, THE HISTORY OF THE PLEAS OF THE CROWN (1736).

173 JOHN SELDEN, OF THE JUDICATURE OF PARLIAMENTS (1681).

174. JOHN RUSHWORTH, THE TRYAL OF THOMAS EARL OF STRAFFORD, LORD LIEUTENANT OF IRELAND, UPON AN IMPEACHMENT OF HIGH TREASON (1680), available at: https://babel.hathitrust.org/cgi/pt?id=mdp.35112204867180; view=1up;seq=11.

175. EDWIN WOLF AND KEVIN J. HAYES, THE LIBRARY OF BENJAMIN FRANKLIN (2006). Franklin had pamphlets on all these impeachments in his library; they appear under the following catalogue numbers: Strafford, 1304; Danby, 1388; Oxford, 2499; Scroggs, 3037; Sacheverell, 2976, 2977; and Torrington, 3261.

176. Several such works appeared soon after the turn of the century. *See* WILLIAM COBBETT, THE PARLIAMENTARY HISTORY OF ENGLAND FROM THE EARLIEST PERIOD TO THE YEAR 1803 (1806); T. B. HOWELL, A COMPLETE COLLECTION OF STATE TRIALS AND PROCEEDINGS FOR HIGH TREASON AND OTHER CRIMES AND MISDEMEANORS FROM THE EARLIEST YEAR TO 1783, WITH NOTES AND OTHER ILLUSTRATIONS (1816) (21 vols.).

177. Tribe and Matz simply wave aside the historical origins of "high crimes and misdemeanors" with this breezy passage: "Unlike some scholars, we don't assign any further meaning to this choice of language. While 'high Crimes and Misdemeanors' was a term of art dating to 1386, and thus had accumulated centuries of intellectual baggage, there's no reason to think the Framers had all

that in mind." TRIBE AND MATZ, TO END A PRESIDENCY, *supra* note 164, at 40. This combines a linguistic evasion with disregard of plentiful historical evidence. Of course, the framers did not have "all" of the British parliamentary history of impeachment in mind when they wrote the constitution. As noted above, not all of it was available in 1787 and none of the framers would have known all the details even of the material then extant. But as indicated here, the framers had access to a *lot* of information about British impeachments, and even a cursory reading of the convention's proceedings demonstrates that many of the framers, particularly those like Mason, Madison, and Franklin who were most involved in the impeachment discussions, knew a great deal of parliamentary history and employed their knowledge at every turn.

178. For discussion of the details of all these impeachments, see *supra* Chapter 2, notes 75–77, 103–66 and accompanying text.

179. *See, e.g.*, James Otis, *The Rights of the British Colonies Asserted and Proved, in* TRACTS OF THE AMERICAN REVOLUTION, 1763–1776, at 19–40 (Merrill Jensen ed., 1967); William Hicks, *The Nature and Extent of Parliamentary Power Considered, in* TRACTS OF THE AMERICAN REVOLUTION, 1763–1776, at 164–84 (Merrill Jensen ed., 1967); JAMES WILSON, CONSIDERATIONS ON THE NATURE AND EXTENT OF THE LEGISLATIVE AUTHORITY OF THE BRITISH PARLIAMENT (1774) (a widely circulated pamphlet by a delegate to the Constitutional Convention).

180. These included Oliver Ellsworth (CT), William Samuel Johnson (CT), Roger Sherman (CT), Richard Bassett (DE), Gunning Bedford, Jr. (DE), John Dickinson (DE), George Read (DE), Abraham Baldwin (GA), William Few (GA), William Houston (GA), Luther Martin (MD), Nathaniel Gorham (MA), Rufus King (MA), Caleb Strong (MA), David Brearly (NJ), Jonathan Dayton (NJ), William C. Houston (NJ), William Livingston (NJ), William Paterson (Patterson) (NJ), Alexander Hamilton (NY), John Lansing, Jr. (NY), Robert Yates (NY), William Richardson Davie (NC), Alexander Martin (NC), Jared Ingersoll (PA), Gouverneur Morris (PA), Charles Pinckney (SC), Charles Cotesworth Pinckney (SC), John Rutledge (SC), John Blair (VA), Edmund Randolph (VA), and George Wythe. *Biographical Index of the Framers of the Constitution*, NATIONAL ARCHIVES, available at: www.archives.gov/founding-docs/founding-fathers, last accessed Oct. 20, 2018. Roscoe Pound put the count at thirty-one. Roscoe Pound, *The Legal Profession in America*, 19 NOTRE DAME L. REV. 334, 339 (1944), available at: https://scholarship.law.nd.edu/ndlr/vol19/iss4/2.

181. Those who had served as judges by the time of the 1787 Convention included William Samuel Johnson (CT), Roger Sherman (CT), George Read (DE), Nathaniel Gorham (MA), David Brearly (NJ), Robert Yates (NY), Alexander Martin (NC), John Rutledge (SC), John Blair (SC), and George Wythe (VA). *Biographical Index of the Framers of the Constitution*, NATIONAL ARCHIVES, *supra* note 180.

182. "Four had studied in the Inner Temple, five in the Middle Temple." CHARLES E. HUGHES, THE SUPREME COURT OF THE UNITED STATES 11 (1928). Those who studied at the Middle Temple were John Dickinson (DE), Charles Cotesworth

Pinckney (SC), John Rutledge (SC), John Blair (SC), and Jared Ingersoll (PA). Among those who studied at the Inner Temple was William Houston (GA). *Biographical Index of the Framers of the Constitution*, National Archives, *supra* note 180.

183. Delegates whose libraries contained works that discuss parliamentary impeachments include at least the following: (1) Benjamin Franklin, whose library contained Blackstone, a wide variety of materials on English history and parliamentary practice, and pamphlets on multiple impeachments, including those of Strafford and Danby, Edwin Wolf & Kevin J. Hayes, The Library of Benjamin Franklin (2006) (catalogue numbers: Strafford, 1304; Danby, 1388; earl of Oxford, 2499; Sacheverell, 2976; Scroggs 3037; earl of Torrington, 3261); (2) Alexander Hamilton, *see Legacy Library of Alexander Hamilton*, available at: www.librarything.com/profile/AlexanderHamiltonI, last accessed Oct. 20, 2018 (multiple); (3) Roger Sherman, *see Legacy Library of Roger Sherman*, available at: www.librarything.com/catalog/RogerSherman, last accessed Oct. 20, 2018 (trial of Rev. Sacheverell); (4) Elbridge Gerry (George Philips, Lex Parliamentaria (1689)); (5) James Madison, *see Legacy Library of James Madison*, available at: www.librarything.com/catalog/JamesMadisonLibrary, last accessed Oct. 20, 2018 (Blackstone); and (6) possibly George Washington, who owned a "History of England" that may have been a portion or abridgement of David Hume's history, *see Legacy Library of George Washington*, available at: www.librarything.com/catalog/GeorgeWashington, last accessed Oct. 20, 2018.

184. Jack P. Greene, The Intellectual Heritage of the Constitutional Era: The Delegates' Library 5 (1986).

185. Edward Hyde, The History of the Rebellion and Civil Wars in England, Begun in the Year 1641 (1731) (a history in four volumes in which impeachments make a regular appearance).

186. Greene, Intellectual Heritage of the Constitutional Era, *supra* note 184, at 19–22. In addition to the titles listed in the text, the Library Company had dozens of others on British law, parliamentary history, and governmental practice. Libr. Co. of Philadelphia, A Catalogue of the Books Belonging to The Library Company of Philadelphia (1789). For its holding on politics see *ibid.*, at 176–216, and on law, see *ibid.*, at 222–35.

187. *See, e.g.*, William Hamilton Bryson, Census of Law Books in Colonial Virginia (1978) (noting that in the period 1676–1776, Virginia lawyers and others with legal interests owned books on state trials generally, *ibid.*, at 13–16, 43; the impeachment trials of the Rev. Sacheverell, *ibid.*, at 13; the earl of Strafford, *ibid.*, at 13; the earl of Danby, *ibid.*, at 6; and Archbishop Laud, *ibid.*, at 15; as well as Blackstone, *ibid.*, at 34; Coke's *Institutes*, *ibid.*, at 41–42; Hale's *Pleas of the Crown*, *ibid.*, at 53; Hawkins' *Pleas of the Crown*, *ibid.*, at 54; Rushworth's *Historical Collections*, *ibid.*, at 73; and Selden's *Of the Judicature of Parliaments*, *ibid.*, at 74).

188. The particulars of Hastings' case and the fact that he was charged with "high crimes and misdemeanors" were widely available in American newspapers. *See, e.g.*, Columbian Herald (Charleston, SC), June 12, 1786, at 2

(referring to the "nine charges of high crimes and misdemeanors brought against Warren Hastings"); COLUMBIAN HERALD (Charleston, SC), June 15, 1786, at 2 (referring to "high crimes and misdemeanors" and listing the headings of nine articles); INDEPENDENT JOURNAL (New York, NY), June 3, 1786, at 2 (same); AMERICAN RECORDER (Boston, MA), June 9, 1786, at 3 (same); MARYLAND CHRONICLE (Frederick, MD), June 19, 1786, at 2 (reporting Hastings' impeachment for "high crimes and misdemeanors"); INDEPENDENT JOURNAL (New York, NY), Aug. 30, 1786, at 2 (enumerating "some leading particulars respecting the Impeachment of Mr. Hastings"); MASSACHUSETTS GAZETTE (Boston, MA), Sept. 1, 1786, at 3 (reporting the vote to impeach Hastings "of high crimes and misdemeanors"); AMERICAN RECORDER (Boston, MA), Sept. 8, 1786, at 2 (reporting particulars of Hastings' dealings in Benares, India); FREEMAN'S JOURNAL (Philadelphia, PA), Sept. 20, 1786, at 2 (reporting Hastings' impeachment for "high crimes and misdemeanors"); AMERICAN HERALD (Boston, MA), June 4, 1787, at 1 (full speech of Richard Brinsley Sheridan in favor of impeaching Hastings); NEW JERSEY JOURNAL (Elizabethtown, NJ), June 6, 1787, at 3 (reporting Hastings' impeachment for "high crimes and misdemeanors"); FREEMAN'S JOURNAL (Philadelphia, PA), June 13, 1787, at 2 (same); INDEPENDENT GAZETTEER (Philadelphia, PA), June 23, 1787, at 2 (reporting on proceedings regarding the eighth article of impeachment against Hastings); BOSTON GAZETTE (Boston, MA), July 2, 1787, at 2 (same); NEW HAMPSHIRE GAZETTE (Portsmouth, NH), July 21, 1787, at 2 (reprinting account from London papers of Hastings' impeachment); CONNECTICUT JOURNAL (New Haven, CT), July 25, 1787, at 2 (accounts of May 11, 1787 proceedings in House of Commons on Hastings' impeachment for "high crimes and misdemeanors"); PENNSYLVANIA EVENING HERALD (Philadelphia, PA), Aug. 8, 1787, at 3 (reprinting verbatim the introduction to Hastings' articles of impeachment) (each of the foregoing articles is accessible at: https://info web.newsbank.com).

189. This episode is discussed *supra* in Chapter 2 notes 28–31 and accompanying text. *See also* Stanley B. Chrimes, *Richard II's Questions to the Judges*, 1387, 72 L. Q. REV. 365, 370 (1956); T. F. T. Plucknett, *Impeachments and Attainder*, 3 TRANS. ROYAL HIST. SOC. 145, 146–47 (1953).

190. Thomas Jefferson, *A Summary View of the Rights of British North America, in* TRACTS OF THE AMERICAN REVOLUTION, 1763–1776, at 270 (Merrill Jensen ed., 1967). The person to whom Jefferson alludes was Sir Robert Tresilian. *See* John L. Leland, *Sir Robert Tresilian*, OXFORD DICTIONARY OF NATIONAL BIOGRAPHY (2011), available at: www.oxforddnb.com/view/10.1093/ref:odnb/978019 8614128.001.0001/odnb-9780198614128-e-27715;jsessionid=BB2982CB6E42150B 14C96BF76BA1A47D. He was convicted, condemned, and executed in 1388. CLEMENTINE OLIVER, PARLIAMENT AND POLITICAL PAMPHLETEERING IN FOURTEENTH-CENTURY ENGLAND 160–65 (2010).

191. *E.g.*, the oppressions of Archbishop Laud in aid of Charles I's "despotic" reign were mentioned by Patrick Dollard in the South Carolina ratification

convention. And, of course, Josiah Quincy specifically mentioned Strafford's impeachment in his famous disquisition on the subject in 1768. JOSIAH QUINCY, JR., REPORTS OF CASES ARGUED AND ADJUDGED IN THE SUPERIOR COURT OF JUDICATURE OF THE PROVINCE OF MASSACHUSETTS BAY, BETWEEN 1761 AND 1772, app. IV at 581, 583, 584 (Samuel M. Quincy ed., 1865).

192. 50 J. MASS. LEGISLATURE 1773–1774, at 200 (1981).

193. These were George Read (DE), Richard Bassett (DE), Nathaniel Gorham (MA), Caleb Strong (MA), David Brearly (NJ), William Paterson (NJ), Robert Yates (NY), George Clymer (PA), Gouverneur Morris (PA), John Rutledge (SC), James Madison (VA), George Mason (VA), Edmund Randolph (VA), and John Blair (VA). *Biographical Index of the Framers of the Constitution*, NATIONAL ARCHIVES, *supra* note 180.

194. Convention delegates William Richardson Davie, Alexander Martin, and Richard Dobbs Spaight were all in the North Carolina legislature when in January 1787 it considered impeachment of the judges of the superior court, HOFFER & HULL, IMPEACHMENT IN AMERICA, *supra* note 128, at 89, as were Spaight and Davie in 1786 during an impeachment of justices of the peace in Franklin County, 18 STATE RECORDS OF NORTH CAROLINA 41, 81–82, 272 (photo. reprint 1900) (Walter Clark ed., 1786), available at: https://babel.hathitrust.org/cgi/pt?id=mdp.39015074315873;view=1up;seq=5. George Clymer and Robert Morris were members of the Pennsylvania legislature during the impeachment inquiry of Francis Hopkinson, and Jared Ingersoll defended Hopkinson. HOFFER & HULL, IMPEACHMENT IN AMERICA, *supra* note 128, at 81. William Paterson and William Livingston of New Jersey would have been quite familiar with their own state's impeachment processes. Between 1776 and 1787, while Paterson was the attorney general and Livingston the governor, New Jersey impeached at least eight justices of the peace and magistrates. *Ibid.*, at 79–80, 84. Neither would have participated directly in the proceedings, but both would have had intimate familiarity with the cases.

195. Another indicator of the extent of Madison's study of British parliamentary history is his reference during an Aug. 13 debate over the origination of money bills to parliamentary practice in the reign of Queen Anne. 2 FARRAND'S FEDERAL CONVENTION RECORDS, *supra* note 53, at 275.

196. *Ibid.*, at 345. *See also* Treason Act 1351, c. 2 (UK), available at: www.legislation.gov.uk/aep/Edw3Stat5/25/2.

197. *See, e.g.*, 5 ELLIOT, *supra* note 87, at 342–43 (during the impeachment debate of Sept. 20, 1787, Franklin alludes to an incident in the career of William of Orange).

198. This term evokes the scholarly debates over whether, *e.g.*, Parliament could impeach for treason when the conduct did not fit within existing statutes by invoking the *lex parliamentaria*. *See, e.g.*, BERGER, IMPEACHMENT, *supra* note 165, at 50. Resolving these particular erudite disagreements is unnecessary for our purposes. The point is simply that the framers would have understood that Parliament used the phrase "high crimes and misdemeanors," but defined its reach on a case-by-case basis.

199. *See supra* Chapter 2 text accompanying notes 188–205.
200. John Viscount Mordaunt was impeached for unlawful imprisonment and rape. *John Mordaunt, 1st Viscount Mordaunt, 1626–75*, BCW-PROJECT, available at: http://bcw-project.org/biography/john-mordaunt, last accessed July 19, 2018. 6 T. B. HOWELL, COMPLETE COLLECTION OF STATE TRIALS AND PROCEEDINGS FOR HIGH TREASON AND OTHER CRIMES AND MISDEMEANORS FROM THE EARLIEST PERIOD TO THE YEAR 1783, WITH NOTES AND OTHER ILLUSTRATIONS 785–806 (1816) [hereinafter HOWELL, VOL. VI].
201. U.S. CONST. Art. I, § 9 (barring grants of titles of nobility by the United States and receipt by federal officeholders of foreign titles).
202. *Ibid.*, § 3, cl. 7.
203. *See supra* Chapter 2, notes 83–187 and accompanying text discussing the impeachments of the duke of Buckingham, the earl of Stafford, Sir Richard Gurney, Peter Pett, the earl of Oxford, Lord Somers, Lord Halifax, the Rev. Sacheverell, and Warren Hastings. *See also* BERGER, IMPEACHMENT, *supra* note 165, at 62 (in sum, "'high crimes and misdemeanors' appear to be words of art confined to impeachments, without roots in the ordinary criminal law and which ... had no relation to whether an indictment would lie in the particular circumstances"); *ibid.*, at 67–68 (listing cases of impeachment for non-criminal conduct).
204. 1 T. B. HOWELL, A COMPLETE COLLECTION OF STATE TRIALS AND PROCEEDINGS FOR HIGH TREASON AND OTHER CRIMES AND MISDEMEANORS FROM THE EARLIEST PERIOD TO THE YEAR 1783, WITH NOTES AND OTHER ILLUSTRATIONS 89, 91 (1816).
205. 2 BLACKSTONE, COMMENTARIES, *supra* note 157, at 259.
206. Raoul Berger says that he "found no English impeachment for 'high crimes and misdemeanors' in which it appeared that the impeachment must fail for lack of an indictable crime." BERGER, IMPEACHMENT, *supra* note 165, at 55. Nor have I.
207. Hoffer and Hull suggest that the term misdemeanors had an independent significance, meaning "that the House of Representatives was permitted to charge officials with minor breaches of ethical conduct, misuse of power, and neglect of duty, as well as more prolonged, egregious or financially rapacious conduct." HOFFER & HULL, IMPEACHMENT IN AMERICA, *supra* note 128, at 102. This seems clearly incorrect. "High crimes and misdemeanors" was introduced by Mason as a unified term of art meaning roughly "the kind of offenses traditionally punished in impeachment trials in England." In that phrase, the word "high" modifies both crimes and misdemeanors. Nothing in British or prior American practice suggested impeachment for low or minor offenses. Moreover, such an approach would run contrary to the purposes of both Mason and Madison to fashion an impeachment remedy that protected against significant risks to the constitutional order without making the president subject to legislative caprice.
208. 3 JONATHAN ELLIOT, THE DEBATES IN SEVERAL STATE CONVENTIONS OF THE ADOPTION OF THE FEDERAL CONSTITUTION 500 (1827) [hereinafter 3 ELLIOT] (statement of James Madison) (emphasis added).

209. 4 ELLIOT, *supra* note 81, at 109.

210. Frank O. Bowman, III, *"High Crimes and Misdemeanors"*: *Defining the Constitutional Limits on Presidential Impeachment*, 72 S. CAL. L. REV. 1517, 1528 n. 38 (1999); TRIBE & MATZ, TO END A PRESIDENCY, *supra* note 164, at 38.

211. *See, e.g., supra* Chapter 2 text accompanying notes 83–92 (impeachment of the duke of Buckingham).

212. In addition to the examples cited in the text, when "malpractice or neglect of duty" was dropped as the definition of impeachable conduct, John Rutledge's original substitute was "treason, bribery, or corruption." 2 FARRAND'S FEDERAL CONVENTION RECORDS, *supra* note 53, at 145, 137. Likewise, when the idea of a council of state was floated, it was accompanied by a special provision for impeachment of council members for "neglect of duty, malversation, or corruption." *Ibid.*, at 335–37, 343–44.

213. 1 FARRAND'S FEDERAL CONVENTION RECORDS, *supra* note 39, at 86.

214. 2 FARRAND'S FEDERAL CONVENTION RECORDS, *supra* note 53, at 65.

215. *Ibid.*, at 67.

216. *Ibid.*, at 65–66.

217. 11 T. B. HOWELL, COMPLETE COLLECTION OF STATE TRIALS AND PROCEEDINGS FOR HIGH TREASON AND OTHER CRIMES AND MISDEMEANORS 600–18 (1816).

218. 2 FARRAND'S FEDERAL CONVENTION RECORDS, *supra* note 53, at 68–69.

219. *Ibid.*, at 103.

220. U.S. CONST. Art. 1, § 9, cl. 8.

221. 3 ELLIOT, *supra* note 208, at 326.

222. Recall the impeachment of William de la Pole in part for his role in arranging the marriage of Henry VI to Margaret of Anjou, T. F. T. PLUCKNETT, TASWELL–LANGMEAD'S ENGLISH CONSTITUTIONAL HISTORY 194 (1960), and the 1715 impeachments of Oxford, Bolingbroke, and Strafford for their advocacy of the Treaty of Utrecht, ALEXANDER SIMPSON, JR., A TREATISE ON FEDERAL IMPEACHMENTS 62 (1916). *See also supra* Chapter 2 text accompanying notes 201–2.

223. 2 FARRAND'S FEDERAL CONVENTION RECORDS, *supra* note 53, at 66.

224. 3 ELLIOT, *supra* note 208, at 346.

225. 4 ELLIOT, *supra* note 81, at 126.

226. *See supra* Chapter 2 text accompanying notes 199–205.

227. 2 BLACKSTONE, COMMENTARIES, *supra* note 157, 120–21.

228. 1 FARRAND'S FEDERAL CONVENTION RECORDS, *supra* note 39, at xiv.

229. 3 ELLIOT, *supra* note 208, at 18–19.

230. 2 JONATHAN ELLIOT, THE DEBATES IN SEVERAL STATE CONVENTIONS OF THE ADOPTION OF THE FEDERAL CONSTITUTION 168–69 (1827).

231. Cassius II: Letter to Richard Henry Lee, Esquire (April 9, 1788), available at: https://archive.csac.history.wisc.edu/Cassius_II(1).pdf, last accessed October 21, 2018.

232. 1 ANNALS OF CONG. 498 (1789) (Joseph Gales ed., 1834).

233. Hoffer and Hull maintain that, in Mason's mind, "high crimes and misdemeanors" always included "maladministration." HOFFER & HULL, IMPEACHMENT IN

America, *supra* note 128, at 101. Chancellor James Kent wrote in the early 1800s that "the constitution has . . . rendered [the President] amenable by law for maladministration." 1 James Kent, Commentaries on American Law 289 (6th ed. 1848). However, his definition of the term seems to be focused on violations of "the constitution or the law of the land," rather than on bad management.

234. 15 T. B. Howell, Complete Collection of State Trials and Proceedings for High Treason and Other Crimes and Misdemeanors from the Earliest Period to the Year 1783, with Notes and other Illustrations 1–35 (1816).

235. Bowman, *Defining the Constitutional Limits on Presidential Impeachment*, *supra* note 210, at 1526.

236. U.S. Const. Amend. XXV, § 4.

237. 2 Farrand's Federal Convention Records, *supra* note 53, at 65–66.

238. U.S. Const. Amend. XXV.

239. *See supra* Chapter 2 text accompanying notes 111–27.

240. The Federalist No. 65, at 396 (Alexander Hamilton) (Clinton Rossiter ed., 1961).

241. 4 Elliot, *supra* note 81, at 113.

242. 2 Farrand's Federal Convention Records, *supra* note 53, at 550 (emphasis added).

243. 8 John Rushworth, Historical Collections of Private Passages of State, Weighty Matters in Law, Remarkable Proceedings in Five Parliaments 666, 669 (1721). *See supra* Chapter 2 text accompanying notes 111–27.

244. Clayton Roberts, *The Impeachment of the Earl of Clarendon*, 13 Cambridge Hist. J. 1, 15 (1957); 6 W. S. Holdsworth, A History of English Law 174–78 (2d ed. 1937).

245. T. B. Howell, Complete Collection of State Trials and Proceedings for High Crimes and Misdemeanors from the Earliest Period to the Year 1783, with Notes and other Illustrations 625 (1816).

246. Edmund Burke, On Empire, Liberty, and Reform: Speeches and Letters 388 (David Bromwich ed., 2000).

5 IMPEACHING LEGISLATORS AND LESSER EXECUTIVE BRANCH OFFICIALS

1. U.S. Const. Art. II, § 4.

2. The constitution is silent on the question of whether impeachment is the only legal method of removing a presidential subordinate who does not want to go – a point that became critical in the impeachment of Andrew Johnson – which we will examine in Chapter 7.

3. U.S. Const. Art. I, § 3, cl. 7. I say "can disqualify" rather than "will disqualify" because, although this point, too, is textually unclear, the current consensus seems to be that the Senate must take a separate, post-conviction vote to disqualify an accused from future federal office. Alcee Hastings, impeached for bribery while a federal judge, won election as a congressman thereafter because the

Senate did not take the additional vote. See discussion of Hastings' impeachment in Chapter 6.

4. 1 MAX FARRAND, THE RECORDS OF THE FEDERAL CONVENTION OF 1787, at 292 (1911).

5. 2 MAX FARRAND, THE RECORDS OF THE FEDERAL CONVENTION OF 1787, at 67 (1911).

6. *Ibid.*, at 68.

7. 3 JONATHAN ELLIOT, THE DEBATES IN SEVERAL STATE CONVENTIONS OF THE ADOPTION OF THE FEDERAL CONSTITUTION 402 (1827) [hereinafter 3 ELLIOT].

8. *Ibid.*, at 397.

9. *Ibid.*, at 202.

10. Letter from Richard Henry Lee to Edmund Randolph (Oct. 16, 1787), *in* 1 JONATHAN ELLIOT, THE DEBATES IN SEVERAL STATE CONVENTIONS OF THE ADOPTION OF THE FEDERAL CONSTITUTION 503 (1827).

11. 3 ELLIOT, *supra* note 7, at 661.

12. 2 JONATHAN ELLIOT, THE DEBATES IN SEVERAL STATE CONVENTIONS OF THE ADOPTION OF THE FEDERAL CONSTITUTION 477 (1827) [hereinafter 2 ELLIOT]. Curiously, Michael Gerhardt reads this statement as indicating that Wilson did not think that legislators were impeachable. MICHAEL GERHARDT, THE FEDERAL IMPEACHMENT PROCESS: A CONSTITUTIONAL AND HISTORICAL ANALYSIS 18 (2d ed. 2000). That reading does not seem supportable. Wilson is not arguing that senators cannot be impeached, only that convincing two-thirds of their colleagues, some of whom may also have been implicated in their misconduct, would be difficult. Wilson concedes the practical difficulty, but says that the remedy lies in the fact that senators who escape judgment by their colleagues are indictable after leaving office.

13. 4 JONATHAN ELLIOT, THE DEBATES IN SEVERAL STATE CONVENTIONS OF THE ADOPTION OF THE FEDERAL CONSTITUTION 131 (1827) (Spencer); *ibid.*, at 265 (Pinckney). *See also ibid.*, at 276 (remark of Edward Rutledge of South Carolina: "If the President or the senators abused their trust, they were liable to impeachment and punishment").

14. *Ibid.*, at 246.

15. THE FEDERALIST NO. 66 (Alexander Hamilton).

16. Hamilton wrote: "And so far even as might concern the corruption of leading members, by whose arts and influence the majority may have been inveigled into measures odious to the community, if the proofs of that corruption should be satisfactory, the usual propensity of human nature will warrant us in concluding that there would be commonly no defect of inclination in the body to divert the public resentment from themselves by a ready sacrifice of the authors of their mismanagement and disgrace." *Ibid.*

17. 2 ELLIOT, *supra* note 12, at 168.

18. 7 ANNALS OF CONG. 39 (1797). Many of the facts in the following account are drawn from Buckner Melton's exhaustive study of the Blount impeachment. BUCKNER F. MELTON, JR., THE FIRST IMPEACHMENT: THE CONSTITUTION'S FRAMERS AND THE CASE OF SENATOR WILLIAM BLOUNT (1998).

19. *Ibid.*, at 61–66.

20. One source characterizes him as a "chronically overextended landjobber." PETER CHARLES HOFFER & N .E. H. HULL, IMPEACHMENT IN AMERICA, 1635–1805, at 152 (1984).

21. The conflict was the so-called War of the Pyrenees. WILL DURANT & ARIEL DURANT, STORY OF CIVILIZATION XI: THE AGE OF NAPOLEON 53, 97 (1975).

22. Louisiana had been claimed by France beginning in 1682, but was ceded to Spain under the Treaty of Paris in 1763. Spain ceded Louisiana back to France in the secret Treaty of San Ildefonso in 1800. Napoleon then sold it to the United States in 1803 – the famous Louisiana Purchase. LIGHT TOWNSEND CUMMINGS ET AL., LOUISIANA: A HISTORY (Bennett H. Wall & John C. Rodrigue eds., 6th ed. 2014); J. CHRISTOPHER HEROLD, THE AGE OF NAPOLEON 141, 208 (1985).

23. MELTON, THE FIRST IMPEACHMENT, *supra* note 18, at 95.

24. *Ibid.*, at 97.

25. *Ibid.*, at 98–107; HOFFER & HULL, IMPEACHMENT IN AMERICA, *supra* note 20, at 152; 2 PAGE SMITH, JOHN ADAMS, 1784–1826, at 939 (1962).

26. 2 PAGE SMITH, *supra* note 25, at 939–40; MELTON, THE FIRST IMPEACHMENT, *supra* note 18, at 107–8; 7 ANNALS OF CONG. 34 (1797).

27. MELTON, THE FIRST IMPEACHMENT, *supra* note 18, at 109–10.

28. 7 ANNALS OF CONG. 38–39 (1797).

29. *Ibid.*, 43–44.

30. MELTON, THE FIRST IMPEACHMENT, *supra* note 18, at 127.

31. 7 ANNALS OF CONG. 38 (1797).

32. *The Founding Fathers: Pennsylvania*, U.S. NATIONAL ARCHIVES & RECORDS ADMIN., available at: www.archives.gov/founding-docs/founding-fathers-pennsyl vania#ingersoll, last accessed Oct. 20, 2018 (see section on Jared Ingersoll); WILLIAM MONTGOMERY MEIGS, THE LIFE OF CHARLES JARED INGERSOLL (1897).

33. MELTON, THE FIRST IMPEACHMENT, *supra* note 18, at 118; RAYMOND WALTERS, JR., ALEXANDER JAMES DALLAS: LAWYER, POLITICIAN, FINANCIER, 1759–1817 (1943).

34. 7 ANNALS OF CONG. 948–51 (1798).

35. *Ibid.*, 948–49.

36. Act of June 5, 1794, 3d Cong., 1 Stat. 381, 384 (1794); Act of March 2, 1797, 4th Cong., 1 Stat. 497 (1797).

37. Treaty of Friendship, Limits, and Navigation Art. V, Oct. 27, 1795, available at: www.loc.gov/law//help/us-treaties/bevans/b-es-ust000011-0516.pdf.

38. 8 ANNALS OF CONG. 2247, 2291 (1799).

39. *Ibid.*, 2249–51 (see remarks of House manager Bayard).

40. In early 1798, Senator Henry Tazewell presented a formal bill that would have required a jury for impeachments; it failed 26:3. 7 ANNALS OF CONG. 508 (1798). When Blount's counsel raised the issue again in their answer, it received short shrift.

41. *See, e.g.,* Argument of Mr. Ingersoll, 8 ANNALS OF CONG. 2286–87. The same point had been raised by Congressman Albert Gallatin in the House debates. 7 ANNALS OF CONG. 450–52 (1797).

42. 8 ANNALS OF CONG. 2316 (1799). *See also* the arguments to the same effect of Congressman Samuel Dana during the House debates. 7 ANNALS OF CONG. 453 (1797).

43. It is in *Federalist 65* that Hamilton famously described impeachable offenses as "of a nature which may with peculiar propriety be denominated POLITICAL, as they relate chiefly to injuries done immediately to the society itself." THE FEDERALIST NO. 65, at 396 (Alexander Hamilton) (Clinton Rossiter ed., 1961).

44. *See generally* WAYNE R. LAFAVE, CRIMINAL LAW 649 (5th ed. 2010) (on the common law of conspiracy).

45. NEW LETTERS OF ABIGAIL ADAMS, 1788–1801, at 100–1 (Stewart Mitchell ed., 1947).

46. HOFFER & HULL, IMPEACHMENT IN AMERICA, *supra* note 20, at 156–57.

47. *Ibid.*, at 158–59.

48. 8 ANNALS OF CONG. 2318 (1799).

49. *Ibid.*, 2319.

50. *See, e.g.*, Buckner F. Melton, Jr., *Let Me Be Blunt: In Blount, the Senate Never Said that Senators Aren't Impeachable*, 33 QUINNIPIAC L. REV. 33 (2014). The question of the impeachability of former officials seems to have been definitively resolved by the case of Secretary of War Belknap, of which more momentarily.

51. Raoul Berger makes the best case, but he relies perhaps too heavily on evidence from the records of the Philadelphia and ratifying conventions without accounting for the strength of the contrary textual arguments. RAOUL BERGER, IMPEACHMENT: THE CONSTITUTIONAL PROBLEMS 214–23 (1973).

52. Gregory E. Maggs, *A Concise Guide to the Records of the Federal Constitutional Convention of 1787 as a Source of the Original Meaning of the Constitution*, 80 GEO. WASH. L. REV. 1707, 1725 (2012).

53. *Ibid.*

54. THE FEDERALIST: A COLLECTION OF ESSAYS, WRITTEN IN FAVOUR OF THE NEW CONSTITUTION, AS AGREED UPON BY THE FEDERAL CONVENTION, SEPTEMBER 17, 1787, IN TWO VOLUMES (1788).

55. 8 ANNALS OF CONG. 2251–53 (1799).

56. *Ibid.*, 2266–67.

57. DAVID HUME, THE HISTORY OF ENGLAND (Liberty Fund, Inc. ed., 1985) (1754–61).

58. RICHARD WOODDESON, SYSTEMATICAL VIEW OF THE LAWS OF ENGLAND AS TREATED OF IN A COURSE OF VINERIAN LECTURES (1792).

59. 8 ANNALS OF CONG. 2279–88 (1799). In his first appearance before the Senate on Blount's behalf, on July 8, 1796, Ingersoll mentioned the 1321 case against the father and son named Hugh le Despenser that was a precursor to later parliamentary impeachment practice. PHILADELPHIA GAZETTE, July 10, 1796, at 2. The newspaper account refers only to a case of "Le Despenser" and gives the date as 1301, but the reference can only be to the 1321 affair.

60. 8 ANNALS OF CONG. 2280 (1799). For the text of the Treason Act 1351, *see* 1351 c.2 (Regnal 25_Edw_3_Stat_5), available at: www.legislation.gov.uk/aep/Edw3Stat5/25/2.

61. *Ibid.*, 2287.

62. *Ibid.*, 2296–99 (1799). Harper was absolute, saying: "It cannot . . . be doubted that the term 'impeachment' in our Constitution has, and was intended by the

framers of the Constitution to have, precisely the same meaning, force, and extent as in English law." *Ibid.*, 2298–99.

63. SAMUEL ELIOT MORISON, THE OXFORD HISTORY OF THE AMERICAN PEOPLE 346 (1965) (Washington's Farewell Address of Sept. 17, 1796); *ibid.*, at 350 (describing Adams' policy of "armed neutrality"); DAVID MCCULLOUGH, JOHN ADAMS 444–45, 483–84 (2001) (describing neutrality policy shared by Washington and Adams).

64. Although the Spaniards seem to have regretted making these promises and hoped to find some excuse to break out of the treaty. 2 PAGE SMITH, *supra* note 25, at 935–36.

65. *Belknap's Sudden Death*, N.Y. TIMES (Oct. 14, 1890), available at: https://time smachine.nytimes.com/timesmachine/1890/10/14/103272326.pdf.

66. WILLIAM S. MCFEELY, GRANT: A BIOGRAPHY 427–28 (1981).

67. *Ibid.*, at 428–29.

68. STAFF OF H. COMM. ON THE JUDICIARY, 93D CONG., IMPEACHMENT: SELECTED MATERIALS ON PROCEDURE, 609 (Comm. Print 1974) [hereinafter IMPEACHMENT PROCEDURE].

69. *Ibid.*, at 613, 615–20.

70. PROCEEDINGS OF THE SENATE SITTING FOR THE TRIAL OF WILLIAM W. BELKNAP, LATE SECRETARY OF WAR (1876), available at: https://archive.org/stream/procee dingssenaoohousgoog#page/n4/mode/2up.

71. *Ibid.*, at 1095.

72. Senator George Wright of Iowa seems to have been nearly the lone dissenter on this point. He believed that only violation of the bribery statute would constitute an impeachable offense in this case, and he concluded (quite remarkably) that Belknap lacked the requisite culpable mental state. *Ibid.*, at 1119–22.

73. *Ibid.*, at 1105 (opinion of Senator Stevenson).

74. *See, e.g., ibid.*, at 1097–117 (the opinions of senators Thomas Norwood (D-GA), John W. Stevenson (D-KY), and Bainbridge Wadleigh (R-NH).

75. U.S. CONST. Art. I, § 3, cl. 7.

76. IMPEACHMENT PROCEDURE, *supra* note 68, at 884–92.

77. *Ibid.*, at 891.

78. *See supra* Chapter 4 note 101 and accompanying text.

79. *See* Myers v. United States, 272 U.S. 52 (1926) (holding that the president has exclusive power to remove appointed executive branch officials), and Humphrey's Executor v. United States, 295 U.S. 602 (1935) (limiting the president's power to remove members of independent agencies). The parameters of the presidential removal power remain unclear.

80. *See, e.g.*, Frank Bowman, *He's Impeachable, You Know*, N.Y. TIMES (May 3, 2007), available at: www.nytimes.com/2007/05/03/opinion/03bowman .html (the case of Attorney General Alberto Gonzales); Frank Bowman, *The Icing is Iglesias: His Firing is Reason Alone for Congress to Impeach Gonzales*, SLATE (May 17, 2007), available at: https://slate.com/news-and-politics/2007/05/how-to-impeach-gonzales.html. Mr. Gonzales resigned effective Sept. 17, 2007. Steven Lee Myers & Philip Shenon, *Embattled*

Attorney General Resigns, N.Y. TIMES (Aug. 27, 2007), available at: www
.nytimes.com/2007/08/27/washington/27cnd-gonzales.html.

6 IMPEACHMENT OF JUDGES

1. *See supra* Chapter 3 notes 96–106 and accompanying text.
2. U.S. CONST. Art. III, § 1.
3. *Ibid.*, Art. II, § 4 (emphasis added).
4. 2 THE RECORDS OF THE FEDERAL CONVENTION OF 1787, at 66–67 (Max Farrand ed., 1911) [hereinafter 2 FARRAND'S FEDERAL CONVENTION RECORDS].
5. It consisted of John Rutledge (SC), Edmund Randolph (VA), Nathaniel Gorham (MA), Oliver Ellsworth (CT), and James Wilson (PA). John R. Vile, *The Critical Role of Committees at the U.S. Constitutional Convention of 1787*, 48 AM. J. LEGAL HIST. 147, 163 (2006).
6. 2 FARRAND'S FEDERAL CONVENTION RECORDS, *supra* note 4, at 337.
7. *Ibid.*, at 186.
8. *Ibid.*, at 428.
9. *Ibid.*
10. *Ibid.*
11. *Ibid.*, at 429.
12. *Ibid.*
13. The Report of the House Judiciary Committee proposing impeachment of Judge George English expressly indicated that the constitutional provision limiting the tenure of federal judges to their good behavior should be considered along with the Article 2, § 4 standard applicable to all other civil officers. The Report continued: "good behavior is the essential condition on which the tenure of judicial office rests, and any act committed or omitted by the incumbent in violation of this condition necessarily works a forfeiture of the office." HOUSE COMM. ON THE JUDICIARY, 93D CONG., IMPEACHMENT: SELECTED MATERIALS ON PROCEDURE 886 (Comm. Print 1974) [hereinafter IMPEACHMENT PROCEDURE], available at: https://babel.hathitrust.org/cgi/pt?id=mdp.39015078700823; view=1up;seq=3.
14. MICHAEL GERHARDT, THE FEDERAL IMPEACHMENT PROCESS: A CONSTITUTIONAL AND HISTORICAL ANALYSIS 83–102 (2d ed. 2000) (opining that impeachment is the only mechanism for removing federal judges and that the standard for impeaching judges is "treason, bribery, or other high crimes and misdemeanors"). *But see* RAOUL BERGER: IMPEACHMENT: THE CONSTITUTIONAL PROBLEMS 122–77 (1973) (arguing at length that the good behavior standard implies a separate and broader power of judicial removal).
15. Among the best and most perceptive accounts of the Chase affair is that of former Chief Justice William Rehnquist, from which many of the following details are drawn. *See generally* WILLIAM H. REHNQUIST, GRAND INQUESTS: THE HISTORIC IMPEACHMENTS OF JUSTICE SAMUEL CHASE AND PRESIDENT ANDREW JOHNSON (1992). *See also* Richard B. Lillich, *The Chase Impeachment*, 4 J. LEGAL HIST. 49 (1960).

16. JOHN SEDGWICK, WAR OF TWO: ALEXANDER HAMILTON, AARON BURR, AND THE DUEL THAT STUNNED THE NATION 359–60 (2015).

17. REHNQUIST, GRAND INQUESTS, *supra* note 15, at 20–21; DAVID MCCULLOUGH, JOHN ADAMS 123–24 (2001) (describing Chase's efforts to secure votes for independence from Maryland's delegates to the Continental Congress).

18. *Samuel Chase, 1796–1811*, SUP. CT. HIST. SOC., available at: http://supreme courthistory.org/timeline_samuelchase.html.

19. ROBERT HARVEY, THE WAR OF WARS: THE EPIC STRUGGLE BETWEEN BRITAIN AND FRANCE: 1789–1815, at 117, 904–7 (2006).

20. *See generally* TODD ESTES, THE JAY TREATY DEBATE, PUBLIC OPINION, AND THE EVOLUTION OF EARLY AMERICAN POLITICAL CULTURE (2006); JERALD A. COMBS, THE JAY TREATY: POLITICAL BATTLEGROUND OF THE FOUNDING FATHERS (1970).

21. MCCULLOUGH, JOHN ADAMS, *supra* note 17, at 493–98.

22. *Ibid.*, at 503–5.

23. *See generally* David Jenkins, *The Sedition Act of 1798 and the Incorporation of Seditious Libel into First Amendment Jurisprudence*, 45 AM. J. LEGAL HIST. 154 (2001) (discussing contemporary and later scholarly views of the Sedition Act).

24. PAUL DOUGLAS NEWMAN, FRIES'S REBELLION: THE ENDURING STRUGGLE FOR THE AMERICAN REVOLUTION (2004); MCCULLOUGH, JOHN ADAMS *supra* note 17, at 540; REHNQUIST, GRAND INQUESTS, *supra* note 15, at 60–61.

25. Kathryn Turner, *Federalist Policy and the Judiciary Act of 1801*, 22 WM. & MARY Q. 3, 3 (1965).

26. Jane Shaffer Elsmere, *The Trials of John Fries*, 103 PA. MAG. HIST. & BIOGRAPHY 432, 437–38 (1979).

27. REHNQUIST, GRAND INQUESTS, *supra* note 15, at 63–70.

28. MCCULLOUGH, JOHN ADAMS, *supra* note 17, at 540–41.

29. 3 ASHER C. HINDS, *The Impeachment and Trial of Samuel Chase, in* HINDS' PRECEDENTS OF THE HOUSE OF REPRESENTATIVES OF THE UNITED STATES 711, 722–24 (§ 2346) (1907) [hereinafter HINDS' PRECEDENTS], available at: https://babel .hathitrust.org/cgi/pt?id=uc1.c3241708;view=1up;seq=729.

30. In his book on the Chase impeachment, Justice Rehnquist mentions the Hemmings allegation with obvious distaste as an example of the sort of low muckraker Callender was. REHNQUIST, GRAND INQUESTS, *supra* note 15, at 75. Muckraking it might have been, but it was also true. *See* ANNETTE GORDON-REED, THOMAS JEFFERSON AND SALLY HEMMINGS: AN AMERICAN CONTROVERSY (1997); Laef Smith, *Tests Link Jefferson, Slave's Son*, WASH. POST, Nov. 1, 1998, at A01.

31. REHNQUIST, GRAND INQUESTS, *supra* note 15, at 75.

32. HINDS' PRECEDENTS, *supra* note 29, at 722 (Art. 2 of Chase articles of impeachment).

33. *Ibid.*, at 722–23 (Art. 3 of Chase articles of impeachment).

34. *Ibid.*, at 723 (Art. 4 of Chase articles of impeachment).

35. *Ibid.*

36. *Ibid.* (Art. 5 of Chase articles of impeachment).

37. *Ibid.* (Art. 4 of Chase articles of impeachment).

38. *Ibid.*
39. *Ibid.*
40. Wayne R. LaFave, Jerold H. Israel, Nancy J. King, & Orin S. Kerr, Criminal Procedure 1087–88 (5th ed. 2009) (§ 22.3(c) Challenges for Cause).
41. Fed. R. Evid. 401.
42. Rehnquist, Grand Inquests, *supra* note 15, at 86–87.
43. Samuel Eliot Morison, The Oxford History of the American People 363 (1965).
44. *Powers of Federal Grand Juries*, 4 Stan. L. Rev. 68, 71–74 (1951).
45. Hinds' Precedents, *supra* note 29, at 723–24 (Art. 7 of Chase articles of impeachment).
46. Modern practices differ from jurisdiction to jurisdiction. In federal courts, the judge convening the grand jury will customarily address them orally and also provide written instructions in the form of a manual or handbook. *See Handbook for Federal Grand Jurors*, available at: www.ndd.uscourts.gov/jury/jury_handbook_grand_jurors.pdf.
47. Rehnquist, Grand Inquests, *supra* note 15, at 94–96.
48. *Ibid.*, *supra* note 15, at 93–94
49. Letter of Thomas Jefferson to Joseph H. Nicholson (May 13, 1803), *in* 2 Nathan Schachner, Thomas Jefferson: A Bibliography 778 (1951).
50. *See, e.g.*, Robert D. Bair and Robin D. Coblentz, *The Trials of Mr. Justice Samuel Chase*, 27 Md. L. Rev. 365, 366 (1967); Jerry W. Knudson, *The Jeffersonian Assault on the Federalist Judiciary, 1802–1805; Political Forces and Press Reaction*, 14 Am. J. Leg. Hist. 55 (1970).
51. 1 John Quincy Adams, Memoirs of John Quincy Adams 322 (Charles Francis Adams ed., 1874). *See also* Hinds' Precedents, *supra* note 29, at 739, 753.
52. *Ibid.*, at 771.
53. U.S. Senate, *Party Division*, available at: www.senate.gov/history/partydiv.htm.
54. 5 U.S. (1 Cranch) 137 (1803).
55. Rehnquist, Grand Inquests, *supra* note 15, at 115, 130.
56. Hinds' Precedents, *supra* note 29, at 771; Impeachment Procedure, *supra* note 13, at 472.
57. *Code of Conduct for United States Judges*, Canon 5, available at: www.uscourts.gov/judges-judgeships/code-conduct-united-states-judges#f.
58. House Comm. on the Judiciary, Impeachment: Selected Materials, H.R. Doc. No. 93–7, at 140–42 (1973) [hereinafter Impeachment Materials], available at: https://babel.hathitrust.org/cgi/pt?id=pur1.32754068870819;view=2up;seq=2; Impeachment Procedure, *supra* note 13, at 514–15, 522.
59. 134 Cong. Rec. 20208–9, 20221 (1988); 135 Cong. Rec. 25329, 25330–35 (1989) (Hastings).
60. Michael A. Memoli, *Senate Convicts Louisiana Federal Judge in Impeachment Trial*, L.A. Times (Dec. 9, 2010), available at: http://articles.latimes.com/2010/dec/09/news/la-pn-senate-impeachment-20101209; Jennifer Steinhauer, *Senate, for Just the 8th Time, Votes to Oust a Federal Judge*, N.Y. Times (Dec. 8, 2010), at A27. For the articles of impeachment and evidence against Judge Porteous, *see*

House Comm. on the Judiciary, Impeachment of G. Thomas porteous, Jr., Judge of the United States District Court for the Eastern District of Louisiana, H.R. Rep. No. 111–427 (2010), available at: www.congress.gov/con gressional-report/111th-congress/house-report/427/1. For pleadings in the Senate, see U.S. Senate, Impeachment of Judge G. Thomas Porteous, Jr., S. Doc. No. 111–13, at 15–23 (2010), available at: https://babel.hathitrust.org/cgi/pt?id=mdp .39015085436601;view=1up;seq=1.

61. *Jury Convicts Federal Judge of Bribery*, UPI (June 29, 1991), available at: www .upi.com/Archives/1991/06/29/Jury-convicts-federal-judge-of-bribery/ 3180678168000; John McQuaid, *Impeachment Proceedings OK'd*, Times-Picayune (June 24, 1993), available at: www.tulanelink.com/tulanelink/collin simpeach_08b.htm; John McQuaid, *Collins Resigns Federal Judgeship*; *Resignation Letter is Given to Clinton*, Times-Picayune (Aug. 7, 1993), available at: www.tulanelink.com/tulanelink/collinsimpeach_08b.htm. By interesting coincidence, Judge Porteous had taken over the seat vacated by Judge Collins when he resigned to avoid impeachment.

62. *The Impeachment and Trial of Charles Swayne, in* Hinds' Precedents, *supra* note 29, at 948–79, available at: www.gpo.gov/fdsys/pkg/GPO-HPREC-HINDS-V3/pdf/GPO-HPREC-HINDS-V3-27.pdf.

63. *The Impeachment and Trial of Robert W. Archbald, in* Impeachment Procedure, *supra* note 13, at 795–818. For the complete records of the Archbald proceedings, *see Proceedings of the United States Senate and the House of Representatives in the Trial of Impeachment of Robert W. Archbald* (1913) (three volumes), available at: https://babel.hathitrust.org/cgi/pt? id=mdp.35112101597203;view=1up;seq=9.

64. Impeachment Materials, *supra* note 58, at 164–73.

65. *Impeachment of Judge Ritter, in* 3 Lewis Deschler, Precedents of the U.S. House of Representatives: Deschler's Precedents 2205, 2205–46 (photo. reprint 2013) (1976) [hereinafter Deschler's Precedents], available at: www .gpo.gov/fdsys/pkg/GPO-HPREC-DESCHLERS-V3/pdf/GPO-HPREC-DESCHLERS-V3-5-5-5.pdf.

66. *Impeachment of Judge Louderback, in* 3 Deschler's Precedents, *supra* note 65, at 2198–204, available at: www.gpo.gov/fdsys/pkg/GPO-HPREC-DESCHL ERS-V3/pdf/GPO-HPREC-DESCHLERS-V3-5-5-4.pdf; *see also* 80 Cong. Rec. 4597–99 (1936).

67. None of the articles of impeachment against judges Archbald, English, Ritter, or Louderback alleged a statutory crime. *See* Impeachment Materials, *supra* note 58, at 176–83 (Archbald); *Impeachment of Judge English, in* 3 Deschler's Precedents, *supra* note 65, at 2195–98, available at: www.gpo.gov/fdsys/pkg/ GPO-HPREC-DESCHLERS-V3/html/GPO-HPREC-DESCHLERS-V3-5-5-3.htm; *Impeachment of Judge Ritter, supra* note 65; Impeachment Procedure, *supra* note 13, at 823–26 (Louderback).

68. Impeachment Procedure, *supra* note 13, at 665.

69. 3 Deschler's Precedents, *supra* note 65, at 2220–23, available at: www.gpo.gov/ fdsys/pkg/GPO-HPREC-DESCHLERS-V3/pdf/GPO-HPREC-DESCHLERS-

V3-5-5-5.pdf (Articles of Impeachment of Halsted Ritter, Art. IV, para. 1); 80 CONG. REC. 4597–99 (1936).

70. IMPEACHMENT MATERIALS, *supra* note 58, at 133–35. Congressional sensitivity to judicial vulgarity continued into the twentieth century when Judge English was charged with (among other things) using profane and indecent language. *Ibid.*, at 164–73.

71. IMPEACHMENT PROCEDURE, *supra* note 13, at 409.

72. *Ibid.*, at 713–16. The oddity here was dispatching the investigative committee to Kansas. Informing the Senate of the fact of a vote to impeach before drawing up formal articles has not been uncommon, either in Great Britain or the United States.

73. Simon Rifkind, representing Justice William O. Douglas during the attempt by the House to impeach him in 1970, claimed that Pickering's charges amounted to three counts of violating a federal statute "relating to the posting of bond in certain attachment situations, and misdemeanors of public drunkenness and blasphemy." U.S. HOUSE SPECIAL COMM. ON H.R. RES. 920 OF THE HOUSE COMM. ON THE JUDICIARY, 91ST CONG., LEGAL MATERIALS ON IMPEACHMENT 20 (Comm. Print 1970). Later commentators disagreed, denying that violations of the act on posting bonds were a crime, and noting that drunkenness and blasphemy were both minor and not federal offenses. Charles Morgan Jr., Hope Eastman, Mary Ellen Gale, & Judith Areen, *Impeachment: An Historical Overview*, 5 SETON HALL L. REV. 689, 698 (1974). I think Morgan, Jr. et al. have the better of the argument. *See generally* MICHAEL J. GERHARDT, THE FEDERAL IMPEACHMENT PROCESS 50–51 (2d ed. 2000).

74. IMPEACHMENT PROCEDURE, *supra* note 13, at 713–16.

75. REHNQUIST, GRAND INQUESTS, *supra* note 15, at 127–28.

76. Lynn W. Turner, *The Impeachment of John Pickering*, 54 AM. HIST. REV. 485, 487 (1949).

77. *Ibid.*, at 493–94

78. *Ibid.*, at 498–99.

79. *See* JOSHUA DRESSLER, UNDERSTANDING CRIMINAL LAW 336–42 (7th ed. 2015).

80. Turner, *Impeachment of John Pickering*, *supra* note 76, at 500.

81. IMPEACHMENT PROCEDURE, *supra* note 13, at 409.

82. On July 20, 1787, Madison urged the necessity of "defending the Community against the incapacity, negligence or perfidy" of the president, and worried that, "He might lose his capacity after his appointment." 2 FARRAND'S FEDERAL CONVENTION RECORDS, *supra* note 4, at 65. On the same day, Morris said that, "Corrupting [the president's] electors, and incapacity were other causes of impeachment." *Ibid.*, at 69.

83. 1 THE RECORDS OF THE FEDERAL CONVENTION OF 1787, at 69 (Max Farrand ed., 1911) [hereinafter 1 FARRAND'S FEDERAL CONVENTION RECORDS].

84. REHNQUIST, GRAND INQUESTS, *supra* note 15, at 99–100.

85. IMPEACHMENT PROCEDURE, *supra* note 13, at 713–16.

86. IMPEACHMENT MATERIALS, *supra* note 58, at 136–39; IMPEACHMENT PROCEDURE, *supra* note 13, at 506.

87. Impeachment Procedure, *supra* note 13, at 667–68.

88. *Ibid.*, at 506 (Peck); *ibid.*, at 684 (Swayne).

89. *Ibid.*, at 823–26.

90. *Ibid.*, at 713–16.

91. *Ibid.*, at 886.

92. *Ibid.*, at 667–68.

93. It may not be quite correct to say that Judge Ritter was convicted for tax evasion. The Senate voted to acquit him on the two articles that specifically alleged tax evasion, but to convict him on a final summary article (Art. 7) that included the tax evasions among his "high crimes and misdemeanors." 80 Cong. Rec. 5602–6 (1936).

94. House Comm. on the Judiciary, Impeachment of Judge Samuel B. Kent, H.R. Rep. No. 111–59 (2009), available at: www.congress.gov/111/crpt/hrpt159/CRPT-111hrpt159.pdf; Skip Hollandsworth, *Perversion of Justice*, Tex. Monthly (Dec. 2009), available at: www.texasmonthly.com/articles/perversion-of-justice.

95. 134 Cong. Rec. 20208–9 & 20221 (1988); 135 Cong. Rec. 25330–35 (1989).

96. 135 Cong. Rec. 8814–24 (1989); 135 Cong. Rec. 27102–4 (1989).

97. House Comm. on the Judiciary, Impeachment of G. Thomas Porteous, Jr., Judge of the United States District Court for the Eastern District of Louisiana, H.R. Rep. No. 111–427 (2010), available at: www.congress.gov/congressional-report/111th-congress/house-report/427/1.

98. H.R. Rep. No. 111–59, *supra* note 91, at 2–4.

99. 5 U.S. (1 Cranch) 137 (1803).

100. Robert Barnes, *Impeachment Calls Part of Life for a Supreme Court Justice, But Few Get Very Far*, Wash. Post (Oct. 31, 2010), available at: www.washingtonpost.com/wp-dyn/content/article/2010/10/31/AR2010103103379.html.

101. *Justice Douglas Impeachment*, CQ Almanac (1970), available at: https://library.cqpress.com/cqalmanac/document.php?id=cqal70-1292316.

102. Impeachment Procedure, *supra* note 13, at 886.

103. The staff of the House Judiciary Committee in the Nixon presidential impeachment took the view that the standard for impeachment of judges is no different than the standard for presidents, but agreed with this reading of the judicial impeachment cases insofar as it takes them to involve "an assessment of the conduct of the officer in terms of the constitutional duties of his office." Staff of the Impeachment Inquiry of the House Comm. on the Judiciary, 93d Cong., Constitutional Grounds for Presidential Impeachment 17 (Comm. Print 1974).

7 THE IMPEACHMENT OF ANDREW JOHNSON

1. David Herbert Donald, Lincoln 596–99 (1996); Stephen B. Oates, With Malice Toward None: The Life of Abraham Lincoln 468–71 (1977).

2. Donald, Lincoln, *supra* note 1.

3. Annette Gordon-Reed, Andrew Johnson 18–19, 22–23 (2011).

4. Hans L. Trefousse, Andrew Johnson: A Biography 20–36 (1989) [hereinafter Trefousse, Biography].

5. *Ibid.*, at 53–62.

6. The Compromise of 1850 was a package of bills designed to address the perennial difficulties posed by the combination of western territorial expansion and the desire of southern states to extend slavery into the new lands. In addition to the act to ban the slave trade in the District of Columbia, the bills provided for admission of California to the Union as a free state, resolution of the borders of Texas, determination about slavery in the Utah and New Mexico territories by referendum of their residents, rejection of the Wilmot Proviso barring slavery in new territories, and a strengthened Fugitive Slave Act.

7. Trefousse, Biography, *supra* note 4, at 82–88.

8. *Ibid.*, at 98, 107; Gordon-Reed, Andrew Johnson, *supra* note 3, at 51–62.

9. Gordon-Reed, Andrew Johnson, *supra* note 3, at 63–68; Trefousse, Biography, *supra* note 4, at 128–43.

10. Trefousse, Biography, *supra* note 4, at 143–47.

11. *Ibid.*, at 152; Oates, With Malice Toward None, *supra* note 1, at 360, 399.

12. Eric Foner, Reconstruction: America's Unfinished Revolution, 1863–1877, at 43 (1988); Trefousse, Biography, *supra* note 4, at 155.

13. 1 Shelby Foote, The Civil War: A Narrative 656–57 (1958).

14. Abraham Lincoln, President of the United States of America, The Emancipation Proclamation (Jan 1, 1863), available at: www.ourdocuments .gov/doc.php?flash=false&doc=34&page=transcript, last accessed Oct. 20, 2018). The proclamation was issued in September 1862, but gave the rebel states three months to return to the Union before the order became effective. It freed slaves in all of Arkansas, Texas, Mississippi, Alabama, Florida, Georgia, South Carolina, North Carolina, and parts of Louisiana and Virginia.

15. Trefousse, Biography, *supra* note 4, at 165–66.

16. 2 Shelby Foote, The Civil War: A Narrative 859, 865 (1963); Trefousse, Biography, *supra* note 4, at 159–61.

17. Aaron Astor, *When Andrew Johnson Freed His Slaves*, N.Y. Times (Aug. 9, 2013), available at: https://opinionator.blogs.nytimes.com/2013/08/09/when-andrew-johnson-freed-his-slaves.

18. Foner, Reconstruction, *supra* note 12, at 44.

19. Donald, Lincoln, *supra* note 1, at 328.

20. Doris Kearns Goodwin, Team of Rivals: The Political Genius of Abraham Lincoln 603–9 (2005).

21. Donald, Lincoln, *supra* note 1, at 192–93.

22. *See generally* Harold Holzer, Lincoln at Cooper Union: The Speech That Made Abraham Lincoln President 119–46 (2004).

23. Goodwin, Team of Rivals, *supra* note 20, at 623.

24. *Ibid.*, at 623–24.

25. *Ibid.*; Donald, Lincoln, *supra* note 1, at 503–6.

26. Goodwin, Team of Rivals, *supra* note 20, at 625–26.

27. *Ibid.*

28. Trefousse, Biography, *supra* note 4, at 183; Foner, Reconstruction, *supra* note 12, at 44; *Andrew Johnson*, National Park Serv. (Apr. 14, 2015), available at: www .nps.gov/anjo/learn/historyculture/moses-speech.htm. For a skeptical take on Johnson's posture toward emancipation and the rights of freedmen, see Gordon-Reed, Andrew Johnson, *supra* note 3, at 78–81.

29. *See Tennessee State Convention: Slavery Declared Forever Abolished*, N.Y. Times (Jan. 15, 1865), available at: www.nytimes.com/1865/01/15/archives/tennessee-state-convention-slavery-declared-forever-abolished.html.

30. *Sketch of Hon. Andrew Johnson's Louisville Speech*, N.Y. Times (Oct. 19, 1864), available at: www.nytimes.com/1864/10/19/archives/sketch-of-hon-andrew-john sons-louisville-speech.html (summarizing Johnson's speech delivered Oct. 13, 1864, in Louisville, KY).

31. On another occasion, Johnson is reported to have said "[d]amn the Negroes, I am fighting those traitorous aristocrats, their masters." Foner, Reconstruction, *supra* note 12, at 44. During the presidential campaign of 1864, one of Johnson's public arguments against southern slavery was that "the blood of the South, once pure [had] become contaminated by negro . . . blood." Trefousse, Biography, *supra* note 4, at 182.

32. *Sketch of Hon. Andrew Johnson's Louisville Speech*, *supra* note 30.

33. Roger H. Ransom, *The Economics of the Civil War*, Econ. Hist. Assoc., available at: https://eh.net/encyclopedia/the-economics-of-the-civil-war, last accessed Oct. 20, 2018.

34. Foner, Reconstruction, *supra* note 12, at 105–7.

35. *See* Lacy K. Ford, Deliver Us From Evil: The Slavery Question in the Old South 507–8 (2009) (describing the transformation of the southern view of slavery from an economically necessary moral evil to, in the words of John C. Calhoun, "the most safe and stable basis for free institutions in the world").

36. Religious justifications for slavery were a staple of southern clerical and political discourse. *See, e.g.*, William Lee Miller, Arguing About Slavery: The Great Battle in the United States Congress 139 (1996) (describing the 1836 speech of Congressman James Henry Hammond reciting a common trope of such presentations, the "doom of Ham"); George Fitzhugh, Sociology for the South or the Failure of Free Society 82–104, 175–82 (1854) (enumerating historical and religious justifications for slavery, including in the latter category the Old Testament story of Hagar and the New Testament writings of St. Paul).

37. Foner, Reconstruction, *supra* note 12, at 222.

38. *Andrew Johnson*, *supra* note 28.

39. Foner, Reconstruction, *supra* note 12, at 179.

40. *Interview with Delegation of Blacks*, Wash. Morning Chron., Feb. 8, 1866, reprinted in 10 The Papers of Andrew Johnson, 48 n. 3 (Paul H. Bergeron ed., 1992) [hereinafter Bergeron] (citing LaWanda Cox & John H. Cox, Politics, Principle, and Prejudice, 1865–1866: Dilemma of Reconstruction America 163 (1963)).

41. Andrew Johnson, *Third Annual Message* (Dec. 3, 1867), *in* 9 A Compilation of the Messages and Papers of the Presidents, 1789–1897, at 3763 (James D. Richardson ed., 1898).

42. J. David Hacker, *A Census-Based Count of the Civil War Dead*, 57 Civ. War Hist. 307 (2011).

43. 3 Shelby Foote, The Civil War: A Narrative 1040 (1974) [hereinafter 3 Foote].

44. Ransom, *Economics of the Civil War*, *supra* note 33 (noting, e.g., that the direct cost of the war amounted to 1.5 times the entire gross national product of the United States in 1860).

45. 3 Foote, *supra* note 43, at 1002–6.

46. *Ibid.*, at 1022–23; Anthony Arthur, General Jo Shelby's March 61–75 (2010).

47. James M. McPherson, Abraham Lincoln and the Second American Revolution 27 (1991).

48. The Confederate constitution contained multiple provisions guaranteeing the perpetuation of slavery, notably including Article I, section 9(4), which barred the Confederate Congress from passing any "bill of attainder, *ex post facto* law, or law denying or impairing the right of property in negro slaves[.]" Const. of Confederate States, Art. I, § 9(4) (1861), available at: http://avalon.law.yale.edu/19th_century/csa_csa.asp.

49. Foner, Reconstruction, *supra* note 12, at 220; Sven Beckert, Empire of Cotton: A Global History 274–75, 280–82 (2014).

50. One northern commercial newspaper editorialized that the economic mobility of freed blacks "cannot be deemed anything more than a temporary state of affairs, to be corrected by the joint agency of the vagrancy laws and the necessity of the vagrants." Beckert, Empire of Cotton, *supra* note 49, at 284.

51. U.S. Const. Art. I, § 4. The Twentieth Amendment, enacted in 1993, changed the mandatory meeting date to Jan. 3.

52. *Dates of Sessions of the Congress*, United States Senate, available at: www.senate.gov/reference/Sessions/sessionDates.htm, last accessed Oct. 20, 2018.

53. The last major Confederate units surrendered in the Trans-Mississippi Department (essentially Texas and parts of Arkansas) on June 3, 1865. Richard L. Aynes, *The 39th Congress (1865–1867) and the 14th Amendment: Some Preliminary Perspectives*, 42 Akron L. Rev. 1019, 1032 (2009).

54. U.S. Const. Art. I, § 3.

55. Presidential Proclamation No. 11, 13 Stat. 737 (Dec. 8, 1863).

56. Foner, Reconstruction, *supra* note 12, at 182.

57. *Ibid.*, at 187–89; Ryan A. Swanson, *Andrew Johnson and His Governors: An Examination of Failed Reconstruction Leadership*, 71 Tenn. Hist. Q. 16, 27–29 (2012).

58. Michael Les Benedict, The Impeachment and Trial of Andrew Johnson 6 (1973).

59. Foner, Reconstruction, *supra* note 12, at 188–89.

60. *Ibid.*, at 199–201; Trefousse, Biography, *supra* note 4, at 230; James M. McPherson & James K. Hogue, Ordeal by Fire: The Civil War and Reconstruction 511–12 (1982).

61. Foner, Reconstruction, *supra* note 12, at 203–5.

62. McPherson & Hogue, Ordeal by Fire, *supra* note 60, at 510.

63. FONER, RECONSTRUCTION, *supra* note 12, at 180, 190; HANS L. TREFOUSSE, IMPEACHMENT OF A PRESIDENT: ANDREW JOHNSON, THE BLACKS, AND RECONSTRUCTION 29 (1975) [hereinafter TREFOUSSE, IMPEACHMENT]: "While Andrew Johnson was President he would utilize the entire resources of his high office to keep the South a white man's country."

64. BENEDICT, IMPEACHMENT AND TRIAL, *supra* note 58, at 36, 39–40.

65. FONER, RECONSTRUCTION, *supra* note 12, at 225.

66. *Ibid.* (quoting Charles A. Dana); MCPHERSON & HOGUE, ORDEAL BY FIRE, *supra* note 60, at 502–3.

67. *See, e.g.*, TREFOUSSE, BIOGRAPHY, *supra* note 4, at 233: "That Johnson had made any effective Reconstruction impossible was recognized at the time ... [H]e reanimated Southern resistance and fatally undermined efforts to integrate freedmen into society."

68. Aynes, *The 39th Congress*, *supra* note 53, at 1022 nn. 17–18 (basing his numbers on WILLIAM H. BARNES, HISTORY OF THE THIRTY-NINTH CONGRESS OF THE UNITED STATES 577–624 (1868)). The number in the text is the final tally at the end of the session. Tennessee's readmission sent eight Unconditional Unionist members to the House in July 1866. Nebraska's admission produced a single Republican representative in March 1867.

69. *Party Division*, UNITED STATES SENATE, available at: www.senate.gov/history/partydiv.htm, last accessed Oct. 20, 2018. The Senate website lists thirty-nine Republicans, eleven Democrats, three Unconditional Unionists, and one Unionist. But these numbers include Tennessee and Nebraska and the two flavors of Unionist were Republican in sympathy. *See also* S. JOURNAL, 39th Cong., 1st Sess. 3–5 (1865) (enumerating states represented in the Senate at the start of the session).

70. U.S. CONST. Art. I, § 5; U.S. CONST. Art. V.

71. David P. Currie, *The Reconstruction Congress*, 75 U. CHI. L. REV. 383, 383–86 (2008).

72. *See, e.g.*, S. JOURNAL, 39th Cong., 1st Sess. 9 (1865) (noting that on Dec. 5, 1865, William Sharkey and James Alcorn of Mississippi had presented their credentials for admission to the Senate and tabling them for later action).

73. MCPHERSON & HOGUE, ORDEAL BY FIRE, *supra* note 60, at 503.

74. U.S. CONST. Art. I, § 5: "Each House shall be the Judge of the Elections, Returns and Qualifications of its own Members ..."

75. FONER, RECONSTRUCTION, *supra* note 12, at 239; DAVID O. STEWART, IMPEACHED: THE TRIAL OF PRESIDENT ANDREW JOHNSON AND THE FIGHT FOR LINCOLN'S LEGACY 43 (2009).

76. RAOUL BERGER, IMPEACHMENT: THE CONSTITUTIONAL PROBLEMS 255 n. 28 (1973) (citing, *inter alia*, Powell v. McCormack, 395 U.S. 486 (1969)).

77. Luther v. Borden, 48 U.S. 1, 42 (1849).

78. Currie, *The Reconstruction Congress*, *supra* note 71, at 386–90 (discussing the merits of the congressional claim of right to reject proposed southern representatives).

79. S. JOURNAL, 39th Cong., 1st Sess. 10–23 (1865); JAMES E. SEFTON, ANDREW JOHNSON AND THE USES OF CONSTITUTIONAL POWER 118 (1980): "In tone [Johnson's December 1865] message was mild and moderate."

80. Aynes, *The 39th Congress, supra* note 53, at 1024.

81. MCPHERSON & HOGUE, ORDEAL BY FIRE, *supra* note 60, at 509–10. *See generally* PAUL A. CIMBALA, THE FREEDMEN'S BUREAU: RECONSTRUCTING THE AMERICAN SOUTH AFTER THE CIVIL WAR (2005).

82. An Act to Establish a Bureau for the Relief of Freedmen and Refugees, 13 Stat. 507 (1865).

83. *Ibid*.

84. *Ibid*. For a general discussion of the second Freedmen's Bureau Bill, see Mark A. Graber, *The Second Freedmen's Bureau Bill's Constitution*, 94 TEX. L. REV. 1361 (2016).

85. Message of the President of the United States, returning Bill (S. 60) to amend an act entitled "An act to establish a Bureau for the relief of Freedmen and Refugees," and for other purposes, with his objections thereto, Feb. 19, 1866, *in* 8 A COMPILATION OF THE MESSAGES AND PAPERS OF THE PRESIDENTS, 1789–1897, 3598–99 (James D. Richardson ed., 1901).

86. For a discussion of the Civil Rights Act 1866 and the maneuvering that led to its final approval, see Currie, *The Reconstruction Congress, supra* note 71, at 394–99.

87. Civil Rights Act 1866, 14 Stat. 27 (1866).

88. *Ibid*.

89. Wilson said: "[The Act] provides for the equality of citizens of the United States in the enjoyment of 'civil rights and immunities.' What do these terms mean? Do they mean that in all things civil, social, political, all citizens, without distinction of race or color, shall be equal? By no means can they be so construed. Do they mean that all citizens shall vote in the several States? No; for suffrage is a political right which has been left under the control of the several States, subject to the action of Congress only when it becomes necessary to enforce the guarantee of a republican form of government (protection against a monarchy). Nor do they mean that all citizens shall sit on the juries, or that their children shall attend the same schools. The definition given to the term 'civil rights' in Bouvier's Law Dictionary is very concise, and is supported by the best authority. It is this: 'Civil rights are those which have no relation to the establishment, support, or management of government.'" CONG. GLOBE, 39th Cong., 1st Sess. 1117 (1866).

90. U.S. CONST. Art. 1, § 8, cl. 4.

91. *See, e.g.*, Naturalization Act 1790, 1 Stat. 103 (1790); Naturalization Act 1795, 1 Stat. 414 (1795); Naturalization Act 1798, 1 Stat. 566 (1798); Naturalization Act 1802, 2 Stat. 153 (1802).

92. S. JOURNAL, 279–80 (1866).

93. The slogan originated with Indiana Democrat Thomas Hendricks. Ralph D. Gray, *Thomas A. Hendricks: Spokesman for the Democracy*, GENTLEMEN FROM INDIANA: NATIONAL PARTY CANDIDATES, 1836–1940 (1977).

94. FONER, RECONSTRUCTION, *supra* note 12, at 250–51.
95. CONG. GLOBE, 39th Cong., 1st Sess. 2545 (passage by House), 3042 (passage by Senate), 3149 (reconciliation).
96. As the more far-sighted legislators of the period recognized, the Fourteenth Amendment could (and ultimately did) have far-reaching effects on the basic balance of authority between states and the federal government that extended far beyond the particular controversies of the Reconstruction period.
97. U.S. CONST. Art. I, § 2, cl. 3.
98. U.S. CONST. Amend. XIV.
99. TREFOUSSE, BIOGRAPHY, *supra* note 4, at 274–75.
100. SEFTON, ANDREW JOHNSON, *supra* note 79, at 135–36, 144; MCPHERSON & HOGUE, ORDEAL BY FIRE, *supra* note 60, at 521 (noting that Johnson dissuaded the legislatures of Virginia and Alabama from ratifying the Fourteenth Amendment).
101. James Gilbert Ryan, *The Memphis Riots of 1866: Terror in a Black Community During Reconstruction*, 62 J. NEGRO HIST. 243 (1977).
102. MCPHERSON & HOGUE, ORDEAL BY FIRE, *supra* note 60, at 520; STEWART, IMPEACHED, *supra* note 75, at 68; TREFOUSSE, BIOGRAPHY, *supra* note 4, at 258–59.
103. Act of Jul. 16, 1866, 14 Stat. 173, 177 (overriding presidential veto).
104. FONER, RECONSTRUCTION, *supra* note 12, at 267.
105. STEWART, IMPEACHED, *supra* note 75, at 67–69; TREFOUSSE, BIOGRAPHY, *supra* note 4, at 262–66.
106. *See generally* BENEDICT, IMPEACHMENT AND TRIAL, *supra* note 58, at 45 n. 37 (citations omitted).
107. STEWART, IMPEACHED, supra note 75, at 69.
108. TREFOUSSE, BIOGRAPHY, *supra* note 4, at 270–71.
109. *Party Divisions of the House of Representatives, 1789–Present*, U.S. HOUSE OF REPRESENTATIVES, available at: http://history.house.gov/Institution/Party-Divisions/Party-Divisions, last accessed Oct. 21, 2018.
110. *Party Divisions*, U.S. SENATE, available at: www.senate.gov/history/partydiv .htm, last accessed Oct. 21, 2018.
111. SEFTON, ANDREW JOHNSON, *supra* note 79, at 145; FONER, RECONSTRUCTION, *supra* note 12, at 272.
112. *President Johnson's Amnesty Proclamation*, N.Y. TIMES (May 30, 1865); Circular, Attorney General's Office, June 7, 1865, *in* 8 A COMPILATION OF THE MESSAGES AND PAPERS OF THE PRESIDENTS, 1789–1897, *supra* note 85, at 3539–40 (emphasizing that applicants for presidential pardons under the February 1865 proclamation must make a personal written application accompanied by the required oath).
113. TREFOUSSE, IMPEACHMENT, *supra note* 63, at 11.
114. FONER, RECONSTRUCTION, *supra* note 12, at 274–76.
115. An Act to Provide for the More Efficient Government of the Rebel States, 14 Stat. 428, 429 (1867).
116. FONER, RECONSTRUCTION, *supra* note 12, at 276; TREFOUSSE, IMPEACHMENT, *supra note* 63, at 46.

117. Second Reconstruction Act, 15 Stat. 2, 2–5 (1867). *See also* MCPHERSON & HOGUE, ORDEAL BY FIRE, *supra* note 60, at 524; BENEDICT, IMPEACHMENT AND TRIAL, *supra* note 58, at 18.

118. Veto message from President Andrew Johnson to the House of Representatives (Mar. 23, 1867), *supra* note 41, at 3729–33; TREFOUSSE, IMPEACHMENT, *supra* note 63, at 68–69.

119. MCPHERSON & HOGUE, ORDEAL BY FIRE, *supra* note 60, at 523.

120. 14 Stat. 430 (1867).

121. TREFOUSSE, IMPEACHMENT, *supra* note 63, at 43–45, 145, 173; BERGER, IMPEACHMENT, *supra* note 76, at 259–60, 274–78.

122. MCPHERSON & HOGUE, ORDEAL BY FIRE, *supra* note 60, at 527.

123. *Ibid.*, at 527–28.

124. An Act Supplementary to an Act Entitled "An Act to Provide for the More Efficient Government of the Rebel States," 15 Stat. 14 (1867); SEFTON, ANDREW JOHNSON, *supra* note 79, at 156.

125. Order from President Andrew Johnson to the Hon. Edwin M. Stanton (Aug. 12, 1867), *supra* note 41, at 3754.

126. TREFOUSSE, IMPEACHMENT, *supra* note 63, at 81–82, 100.

127. MCPHERSON & HOGUE, ORDEAL BY FIRE, *supra* note 60, at 528–30.

128. Andrew Johnson, *By the President of the United States of America. A Proclamation* (Sept. 7, 1867), *supra* note 41, at 3745–47.

129. STEWART, IMPEACHED, *supra* note 75, at 18.

130. TREFOUSSE, IMPEACHMENT, *supra* note 63, at 50–53.

131. CONG. GLOBE, 39th Cong., 2d Sess. 320 (1867).

132. TREFOUSSE, IMPEACHMENT, *supra* note 63, at 107–8; MCPHERSON & HOGUE, ORDEAL BY FIRE, *supra* note 60, at 526, 530; *Impeachment Efforts Against President Andrew Johnson*, U.S. HOUSE OF REPRESENTATIVES, available at: http://history.house.gov/Historical-Highlights/1851–1900/Impeachment-efforts-against-President-Andrew-Johnson. last accessed Oct. 21, 2018.

133. BENEDICT, IMPEACHMENT AND TRIAL, *supra* note 58, at 26–36 (discussing the contemporary arguments about scope of impeachment).

134. Asher C. Hinds, *United States House of Representatives*, 3 HINDS' PRECEDENTS 821–43 (1907).

135. MCPHERSON & HOGUE, ORDEAL BY FIRE, *supra* note 60, at 529–30.

136. Johnson, *Third Annual Message* (Dec. 3, 1867), *supra* note 41, at 3764.

137. *Ibid.*, at 3766–67.

138. MCPHERSON & HOGUE, ORDEAL BY FIRE, *supra* note 60, at 530–31.

139. CONG. GLOBE, 40th Cong., 2d Sess. 1400 (1868); CONG. GLOBE SUPP., 40th Cong., 2d Sess., THE TRIAL OF ANDREW JOHNSON 3–5 (1868) [hereinafter JOHNSON TRIAL].

140. BERGER, IMPEACHMENT, *supra* note 76, at 267.

141. JOHNSON TRIAL, *supra* note 139, at 3–4.

142. *Ibid.*, at 4.

143. *Ibid.*, at 6.

144. *Ibid.*, at 29.

145. BERGER, IMPEACHMENT, *supra* note 76, at 274–78; TREFOUSSE, IMPEACHMENT, *supra* note 63, at 173 (noting reservations of some Republican senators about whether the Tenure of Office Act covered members of the cabinet).

146. Section 1 of the Tenure of Office Act stated: "That every person holding any civil office to which he has been appointed by and with the advice and consent of the Senate, and every person who shall hereafter be appointed to any such office, and shall become duly qualified to act therein, is, and shall be entitled to hold such office until a successor shall have been in like manner appointed and duly qualified, except as herein otherwise provided: Provided, That the Secretaries of State, of the Treasury, of War, of the Navy, and of the Interior, the Postmaster-General, and the Attorney General, shall hold their offices respectively for and during the term of the President by whom they may have been appointed and for one month thereafter, subject to removal by and with the advice and consent of the Senate." An Act Regulating the Tenure of Certain Civil Offices, 14 Stat. 430, 430 (1876).

147. TREFOUSSE, IMPEACHMENT, *supra* note 63, at 43–45, 145, 173; BERGER, IMPEACHMENT, *supra* note 76, at 259–60, 274–78.

148. *See supra* note 131 and accompanying text.

149. Debate on bill for establishing an executive department, to be denominated the Department of Foreign Affairs (Jun. 16, 1789), *in* 4 DEBATES ON THE ADOPTION OF THE FEDERAL CONSTITUTION 378–83 (Madison), 393–94 (Sherman), 403–4 (Gerry) (Jonathan Elliot ed., 1836).

150. The precise question put to the House was whether, in a bill creating certain cabinet offices, the words "to be removable by the president" should remain in the Act. *Ibid.*, at 404. Those like Madison who held that the Senate had no right to disapprove presidential removals voted for the language. However, one could also vote for this language on the theory that, although the Senate has a general right to advise and consent to removals, Congress could by legislation create offices for which the president had unfettered powers of removal.

151. LANCE BANNING, THE SACRED FIRE OF LIBERTY: JAMES MADISON AND THE FOUNDING OF THE FEDERAL REPUBLIC 276–78 (1995).

152. BERGER, IMPEACHMENT, *supra* note 76, at 280–83.

153. Letter from James Madison to Edmund Randolph (May 31, 1789), *in* 12 PAPERS OF JAMES MADISON 189–91 (Charles F. Hobson & Robert A. Rutland eds., 1979), available at: https://founders.archives.gov/documeniits/Madison/01–12–02–0122, last accessed Oct. 21, 2018. *See also* THE FEDERALIST NO. 48 (James Madison).

154. CONG. GLOBE, 39th Cong., 2d Sess. 1966 (1867) (recording votes of senators Fessenden, Fowler, Grimes, Henderson, Ross, Van Winkle, and Trumbull to override veto of Tenure of Office Act).

155. *See, e.g., Excerpt from James W. Grimes Opinion on the Trial of Andrew Johnson 1868,* FROM REVOLUTION TO RECONSTRUCTION & BEYOND PROJECT, available at: www.let.rug.nl/usa/documents/1851–1875/exerpt-from-james-w-grimes-opi nion-on-the-trial-of-andrew-johnson-1868.php, last accessed Oct. 21, 2018; EDMUND G. ROSS, HISTORY OF THE IMPEACHMENT OF ANDREW JOHNSON,

President of the United States, by the House of Representatives, and his Trial by the Senate for High Crimes and Misdemeanors in Office, 1868, at 202 (1896).

156. Schenck v. United States, 249 U.S. 47, 52 (1919) (analogizing provocative speech to "falsely shouting fire in a theater and causing a panic").

157. Johnson Trial, *supra* note 139, at 42.

158. *Ibid.*, at 44.

159. *Ibid.*, at 45–49.

160. *Ibid.*, at 290.

161. *Ibid.*, at 290–94. Defense counsel Benjamin R. Curtis made a weak version of this argument in his opening. Ibid., at 134.

162. William H. Rehnquist, Grand Inquests: The Historic Impeachments of Justice Samuel Chase and President Andrew Johnson 233–34 (1992); McPherson & Hogue, Ordeal by Fire, *supra* note 60, at 533.

163. Trefousse, Impeachment, *supra* note 63, at 166–67.

164. Trefousse, Biography, *supra* note 4, at 332–34.

165. U.S. Const. Amend. XXV.

166. Rehnquist, Grand Inquests, *supra* note 162, at 211.

167. *Ibid.*, at 246. *See generally* Hans L. Trefousse, Benjamin Franklin Wade: Radical Republican from Ohio (1963).

168. Trefousse, Impeachment, *supra* note 63, at 148–49.

169. *See, e.g.*, the remarks of Congressman John Roy Lynch, a black congressman of the Reconstruction period. John R. Lynch, The Facts of Reconstruction, ch. 1 (1913), available at: www.gutenberg.org/files/16158/16158-h/16158-h.htm#CHAPTER_I, last accessed Oct. 22, 2018.

170. Trefousse, Biography, *supra* note 4, at 309.

171. Rehnquist, Grand Inquests, *supra* note 162, at 246–47; Trefousse, Impeachment, *supra* note 63, at 175–78; Benedict, Impeachment and Trial, *supra* note 58, at 133–36; Sefton, Andrew Johnson, *supra* note 79, at 182; McPherson & Hogue, Ordeal by Fire, *supra* note 60, at 533; Stewart, Impeached, *supra* note 75, at 317.

172. Benedict, Impeachment and Trial, *supra* note 58, at 137–39; Sefton, Andrew Johnson, *supra* note 79, at 180–81; McPherson & Hogue, Ordeal by Fire, *supra* note 60, at 533.

173. Cong. Globe, 40th Cong., 2d Sess. 1400 (1868).

174. Georgia v. Stanton, 73 U.S. 50 (1867); Mississippi v. Johnson, 71 U.S. 475 (1866) (denying request for injunction against President Johnson to prevent him from enforcing reconstruction legislation).

175. Cong. Globe, 39th Cong., 2d Sess. 320 (1867).

176. U.S. Const. Art. II, § 3.

177. U.S. Const. Art. II, § 1.

178. Johnson Trial, *supra* note 139, at 283 (noting that it had proven hard to collect evidence on the general allegations in Art. 11, because Johnson spoke candidly mostly to white southerners who agreed with him, and because army officers and civil servants under him were reluctant to speak).

179. *See, e.g.*, 3 DEBATES ON THE ADOPTION OF THE FEDERAL CONSTITUTION 268–69 (Jonathan Elliot ed., 1836). (At the Virginia ratifying convention of 1788, Edmund stated, "no man ever thought of impeaching a man for an opinion.")
180. *See supra* Chapters 2, 3, and 4.
181. JOHNSON TRIAL, *supra* note 139, at 50 (brief of William Lawrence written for the House of Representatives and introduced by Congressman Butler).
182. THE FEDERALIST NO. 65 (Alexander Hamilton).
183. JOHN F. KENNEDY, PROFILES IN COURAGE 107 (1955).
184. BERGER, IMPEACHMENT, *supra* note 76, at 295.

8 THE FALL OF PRESIDENT RICHARD NIXON

1. THEODORE H. WHITE, BREACH OF FAITH: THE FALL OF RICHARD NIXON, 28, 32, app. B (Nixon's resignation speech) (1975). Other accounts of the meeting between Nixon and the Republican leadership omit Goldwater's detailed discussion of particular articles of impeachment, but agree on the essence of the conversation and Goldwater's message that he himself might vote to impeach. *See, e.g.*, BOB WOODWARD & CARL BERNSTEIN, THE FINAL DAYS 414–15 (1976).
2. *Ibid.*, at 59–63; H. LOWELL BROWN, HIGH CRIMES AND MISDEMEANORS IN PRESIDENTIAL IMPEACHMENT 64–65 (2010).
3. WHITE, BREACH OF FAITH, *supra* note 1, at 63.
4. *See generally*, RICHARD H. ROVERE, SENATOR JOE MCCARTHY (1996).
5. JOHN EARL HAYNES & HARVEY KLEHR, VENONA: DECODING SOVIET ESPIONAGE IN AMERICA 167–73 (1999).
6. BROWN, HIGH CRIMES AND MISDEMEANORS, *supra* note 2, at 65.
7. *E.g.*, in 1954, Nixon joined in calls for American military intervention in support of the French in Indochina. ARTHUR M. SCHLESINGER, ROBERT KENNEDY AND HIS TIMES 128 (1978). Similarly, the so-called "kitchen debate" with Soviet leader Nikita Khrushchev during a 1959 visit to Russia promoted his image as a steady voice in foreign policy, and reputedly helped Nixon secure the 1960 Republican presidential nomination.
8. *See generally* THEODORE H. WHITE, THE MAKING OF THE PRESIDENT 1960 81–82 (1961).
9. BROWN, HIGH CRIMES AND MISDEMEANORS, *supra* note 2, at 65.
10. Richard Nixon, Press Conference (Nov. 7, 1962), available at: http://language log.ldc.upenn.edu/myl/RichardNixonConcession.html.
11. TAYLOR BRANCH, PARTING THE WATERS: AMERICA IN THE KING YEARS 1954–1963, at 128–29, 143–205 (1988).
12. TAYLOR BRANCH, AT CANAAN'S EDGE: AMERICA IN THE KING YEARS 1965–1968 (2007); *Civil Rights Martyrs*, SOUTHERN POVERTY LAW CTR, available at: www .splcenter.org/what-we-do/civil-rights-memorial/civil-rights-martyrs, last accessed Oct. 30, 2018.
13. WILLIAM MANCHESTER, THE GLORY AND THE DREAM 1123–50 (describing events of 1968); DAVID FARBER, CHICAGO '68 (1988).

14. James Boyd, *Nixon's Southern Strategy*, N.Y. TIMES (May 17, 1970), available at: www.nytimes.com/1970/05/17/archives/nixons-southern-strategy-its-all-in-the-charts.html.
15. Boyd, *Nixon's Southern Strategy*, *supra* note 14.
16. JOE ESZTERHAS & MICHAEL D. ROBERTS, THIRTEEN SECONDS: CONFRONTATION AT KENT STATE (1970).
17. By 1970, two-thirds of Americans believed the war to have been a mistake. William L. Lunch & Peter W. Sperlich, *American Public Opinion and the War in Vietnam*, 32 W. POL. Q. 21 (1979).
18. MARGARET MACMILLAN, NIXON AND MAO: THE WEEK THAT CHANGED THE WORLD (2007).
19. ROBERT S. LITWAK, DÉTENTE AND THE NIXON DOCTRINE: AMERICAN FOREIGN POLICY AND THE PURSUIT OF STABILITY, 1969–1976 (1986).
20. WILLIAM SHAWCROSS, SIDESHOW: KISSINGER, NIXON, AND THE DESTRUCTION OF CAMBODIA (1979).
21. H.R. REP. NO. 93-1305, at 146–50 (1974) (Judiciary Committee Report on the Impeachment of Richard M. Nixon, President of the United States) [hereinafter "Impeachment Report"]; ROBERT DALLEK, NIXON AND KISSINGER: PARTNERS IN POWER 117–123 (2007). *See generally* SHAWCROSS, SIDESHOW, *supra* note 20.
22. Impeachment Report, *supra* note 21, at 150; WHITE, BREACH OF FAITH, *supra* note 1, at 121–22 (describing a wiretap on journalist Joseph Kraft).
23. Impeachment Report, *supra* note 21, at 151–52; BROWN, HIGH CRIMES AND MISDEMEANORS, *supra* note 2, at 64, 66 n. 23; WHITE, BREACH OF FAITH, *supra* note 1, at 134–35.
24. WHITE, BREACH OF FAITH, *supra* note 1, at 151–52.
25. Impeachment Report, *supra* note 21, at 157; WHITE, BREACH OF FAITH, *supra* note 1, at 146–51.
26. New York Times Co. v. United States, 403 U.S. 713 (1971).
27. WHITE, BREACH OF FAITH, *supra* note 1, at 149–51; Impeachment Report, *supra* note 21, at 157–65; BROWN, HIGH CRIMES AND MISDEMEANORS, *supra* note 2, at 67–68.
28. BROWN, HIGH CRIMES AND MISDEMEANORS, *supra* note 2, at 69; WHITE, BREACH OF FAITH, *supra* note 1, at 155–58.
29. BROWN, HIGH CRIMES AND MISDEMEANORS, *supra* note 2, at 70–72; WHITE, BREACH OF FAITH, *supra* note 1, at 158–60.
30. For a decent, if compressed, timeline of the Watergate scandal, *see* WOODWARD & BERNSTEIN, FINAL DAYS, *supra* note 1, at 13–17.
31. JOHN M. ORMAN, PRESIDENTIAL SECRECY AND DECEPTION: BEYOND THE POWER TO PERSUADE 126 (1980).
32. WHITE, BREACH OF FAITH, *supra* note 1, at 161.
33. *Ibid.*, 163–68; WOODWARD & BERNSTEIN, FINAL DAYS, *supra* note 1, at 34–35; JOHN W. DEAN, THE NIXON DEFENSE: WHAT HE KNEW AND WHEN HE KNEW IT 122–23 (2014).
34. Nixon won 60.8 percent of the popular vote and 97 percent of the electoral votes. WOODWARD & BERNSTEIN, FINAL DAYS, *supra* note 1, at 14.

35. Max Frankel, *President Won 49 States and 521 Electoral Votes*, N.Y. Times (Nov. 9, 1972), available at: www.nytimes.com/1972/11/09/archives/new-jersey-pages-president-won-49-states-and-521-electoral-votes.html.

36. Lawrence Meyer, *Last Two Guilty in Watergate Plot*, Wash. Post (Jan. 31, 1973), available at: www.washingtonpost.com/politics/last-two-guilty-in-watergate-plot/2012/06/04/gJQAQQdHJV_story.html?utm_term=.e4ab43a6e3d7.

37. Woodward & Bernstein, Final Days, *supra* note 1, at 14; Dean, The Nixon Defense, *supra* note 33, at 317–25.

38. Impeachment Report, *supra* note 21, at 92.

39. White, Breach of Faith, *supra* note 1, at 220–21.

40. *Ibid.*, at 230.

41. *Ibid.*, at 235; Staff of S. Select Comm. on Presidential Campaign Activities, 93d Cong., Final Report (Comm. Print 1974), available at: https://archive.org/details/FinalReportOfTheSenateSelectCommitteeOnPresidentialCampaignActivities/page/111.

42. Impeachment Report, *supra* note 21, at 122–23; Woodward & Bernstein, Final Days, *supra* note 1, at 15.

43. White, Breach of Faith, *supra* note 1, at 264–71; David E. Kyvig, The Age of Impeachment: American Constitutional Culture since 1960 151 (2008).

44. Impeachment Report, *supra* note 21, at 123–25; Kyvig, The Age of Impeachment, *supra* note 43, at 154.

45. According to one count, on October 23–24, 1974, twenty-two bills were introduced in Congress calling for an impeachment investigation. Woodward & Bernstein, Final Days, *supra* note 1, at 15.

46. John R. Labovitz, Presidential Impeachment 180–82 (1978).

47. Impeachment Report, *supra* note 21, at 187.

48. Stephen Bates, Jack Goldsmith, & Benjamin Wittes, *Jaworski Road Map to be Mostly Unsealed*, Lawfare (Oct. 15, 2018), available at: www.lawfareblog.com/jaworski-road-map-be-mostly-unsealed.

49. Carl Bernstein & Bob Woodward, All the President's Men (1974).

50. Impeachment Report, *supra* note 21, at 187–88.

51. Woodward & Bernstein, Final Days, *supra* note 1, at 133–46.

52. Impeachment Report, *supra* note 21, at 126; United States v. Nixon, 418 U.S. 683 (1974).

53. Impeachment Report, *supra* note 21, at 227 (analyzing the technical report on the 18½-minute gap).

54. White, Breach of Faith, *supra* note 1, at 236.

55. Richard Lyons & William Chapman, *Judiciary Committee Approves Article to Impeach President Nixon, 27 to 11: 6 Republicans Join Democrats to Pass Obstruction Charge*, Wash. Post, July 28, 1974, at A01.

56. Impeachment Report, *supra* note 21, at 213–17, 219–220.

57. Woodward & Bernstein, Final Days, *supra* note 1, at 303–21.

58. Impeachment Report, *supra* note 21, at 1–4.

59. STAFF OF H.R. COMM. OF THE JUDICIARY, STAFF OF THE IMPEACHMENT INQUIRY, 93D CONG., CONSTITUTIONAL GROUNDS FOR PRESIDENTIAL IMPEACHMENT (Comm. Print 1974) [hereinafter "Staff Report"].

60. *Ibid.*, at 17–18.

61. James D. St. Clair et al., *An Analysis of the Constitutional Standard for Presidential Impeachment*, 10 WEEKLY COMP. OF PRES. DOC. 270–83 (Feb. 28, 1974), available at: https://catalog.hathitrust.org/Record/000037961 (brief by president's legal team); Samuel Garrison III et al., *The Argument for Criminality as a Necessary Element of Impeachable Conduct* (March 1974) [hereinafter "Minority Staff Report"] (unpublished) (cited in LABOVITZ, PRESIDENTIAL IMPEACHMENT, *supra* note 46, at 96 n. 8).

62. St. Clair, *Constitutional Standard for Presidential Impeachment*, *supra* note 61, at 51.

63. LABOVITZ, PRESIDENTIAL IMPEACHMENT, *supra* note 46, at 96 (quoting Minority Staff Report).

64. Impeachment Report, *supra* note 21, at 359, 371.

65. These particular terms are drawn from the Model Penal Code, but these terms or others with roughly equivalent meanings are ubiquitous in both state and federal law. *Compare* MODEL PENAL CODE § 2.02 General Requirements of Culpability, *with* COLO. REV. STAT. § 18-1-501 (defining mental states of intentionally, knowingly or willfully, recklessly, and with criminal negligence), *and* U.S. Court of Appeals for the Eleventh Circuit, Criminal Pattern Jury Instructions 2016, Instruction B9.1A (defining knowingly and willfully).

66. OLIVER WENDELL HOLMES, THE COMMON LAW 47–48 (1881).

67. Indeed, the congressmen were wrong when they asserted that the constitution bars criminal liability without proof of a culpable mental state; to the contrary, strict liability offenses are common and have never been held unconstitutional by the Supreme Court. Joshua Dressler, Understanding Criminal Law 7th ed. § 11.03 (2015).

68. Minority Staff Report, *supra* note 61, at 24.

69. Impeachment Report, *supra* note 21, at 289.

70. *Ibid.*, at 327 (Statement of Congresswoman Holtzman, joined by Congressmen Kastenmeier, Edwards, Hungate, Conyers, Waldie, Drinan, Owens, and Mezvinsky).

71. *Ibid.*, at 297 (emphasis added).

72. *Ibid.*, at 341 (Statement of Congressman Wayne Owens).

73. *Ibid.*, at 287 (Supplemental Views of Congressman Don Edwards).

74. *Ibid.*, at 349 (McClory was joined by Congressmen Danielson and Fish).

75. *Ibid.*, at 26–27.

76. Impeachment Report, *supra* note 21, at 8.

77. *Ibid.*, at 2 (quoting Article I of the Nixon articles of impeachment).

78. *Ibid.*, at 2–3.

79. *See, e.g.,* 18 U.S.C. § 1001 (false statements); 18 U.S.C. §§ 1621 & 1623 (perjury); 18 U.S.C. § 201 (bribery of public officials or witnesses); 18 U.S.C. § 1512 (witness tampering); and 18 U.S.C. § 2 (aiding and abetting).

80. President Nixon conveyed promises or suggestions of the possibility of clemency to Howard Hunt, John Mitchell, Jeb Magruder, and John Dean. Impeachment Report, *supra* note 21, at 75–81.
81. Impeachment Report, *supra* note 21, at 133–36, §§ 13, 20, 29 (summary of evidence in support of Art. I).
82. *Ibid.*, at 135, § 30.
83. *See supra* Chapter 4 notes 81–82 and accompanying text.
84. Impeachment Report, *supra* note 21, at 3, 139.
85. *Ibid.*, at 141–45.
86. *Ibid.*, at 146–56.
87. *Ibid.*, at 157–70.
88. *Ibid.*, at 171.
89. *Ibid.*
90. *Ibid.*, at 177 (added emphasis).
91. *Ibid.*, at 139.
92. *Ibid.* (quoting Gilchrist v. Collector of Charleston, 1 Hall L.J. 429 (C.C.D.S.C, 1808)).
93. Labovitz, Presidential Impeachment, *supra* note 46, at 121, 130.
94. Impeachment Report, *supra* note 21, at 188.
95. U.S. Const. Art. I, § 2, cl. 5.
96. Impeachment Report, *supra* note 21, at 206 (quoting Kilbourn v. Thompson, 103 U.S. 168, 190 (1881)).
97. *Ibid.*, at 213.
98. The minority cited Watkins v. United States, 354 U.S. 178 (1957), for the proposition that the subpoena power of congressional committees is limited by the subject matter of the committee's jurisdiction. Whether that be true or not, it seems largely irrelevant in the case of impeachment. Not only is the definition of impeachable conduct undecided, but it is almost surely non-justiciable. In other words, a court could hardly rule on the relevance of material requested in an impeachment inquiry without first deciding what constitutes impeachable conduct – and that is a task for Congress, not the courts.
99. Impeachment Report, *supra* note 21, at 485–87.
100. Impeachment Report, *supra* note 21, at 217–19.
101. *Ibid.*, at 218.
102. 50 U.S.C. §§ 1541–48.
103. Impeachment Report, *supra* note 21, at 218–19.
104. *Ibid.*, at 220–23.
105. Carrie Johnson, *Long-Secret Watergate "Road Map" May Soon Be Public. Could It Guide Mueller's Team?* NPR (Oct. 15, 2018), available at: www.npr .org/2018/10/15/656897281/long-secret-watergate-road-map-may-soon-be-public-could-it-guide-mueller-s-team.
106. Pub. L. No. 95-521, tit. VI, § 601(a), 92 Stat. 1867 (1978); 28 U.S.C. §§ 591–99.
107. Fed. R. Crim. P. 6(e)(2)(B).

108. There is a type of "special grand jury" authorized by 18 U.S.C. § 3333 to issue reports in cases involving organized crime; however, the Watergate grand jury was not of this type.

109. FED. R. CRIM. P. 6(e)(3).

110. In re Report & Recommendation of June 5, 1972 Grand Jury Concerning Transmission of Evidence to House of Representatives, 370 F. Supp. 1219, 1230 (D.D.C. 1974).

111. Haldeman v. Sirica, 501 F.2d 714, 715 (D.C. Cir. 1974).

112. 370 F. Supp., at 1221.

113. *Ibid.*, at 1231 n. 51.

114. 418 U.S. 683 (1974).

115. The subpoena was issued pursuant to Federal Rule of Criminal Procedure 17 (c), which provided: "A subpoena may also command the person to whom it is directed to produce the books, papers, documents or other objects designated therein. The court on motion made promptly may quash or modify the subpoena if compliance would be unreasonable or oppressive. The court may direct that books, papers, documents or objects designated in the subpoena be produced before the court at a time prior to the trial or prior to the time when they are to be offered in evidence and may upon their production permit the books, papers, documents or objects or portions thereof to be inspected by the parties and their attorneys." FED. R. CRIM. P. 17(c).

116. 418 U.S., at 700.

117. In *Nixon* v. *United States*, the Supreme Court did not address the applicability and reach of executive privilege in the grand jury setting. This question was presented during the Clinton impeachment investigation and will be addressed in Chapter 9.

118. 487 F.2d 700 (D.C. Cir. 1973).

119. 498 F.2d 725 (D.C. Cir. 1974).

120. *Ibid.*, at 732.

121. *Ibid.*

122. In the *Senate Select Committee* case, Judge Wilkey concurred in the result, but expressed his view that the question presented implicated the constitutional principle of separation of powers and was thus a non-justiciable political question. *Id.* at 734.

9 THE STRANGE CASE OF WILLIAM JEFFERSON CLINTON

1. *See generally* RAYMOND GARTHOFF, THE GREAT TRANSITION: AMERICAN–SOVIET RELATIONS AND THE END OF THE COLD WAR (1994).

2. RICK ATKINSON, CRUSADE: THE UNTOLD STORY OF THE PERSIAN GULF WAR 488–500 (1993).

3. Dylan Matthews, *The Clinton Economy, in Charts*, WASH. POST (Sept. 5, 2012), available at: www.washingtonpost.com/news/wonk/wp/2012/09/05/the-clinton-economy-in-charts/?utm_term=.8d3aed7e7298.

4. Some of Clinton's legislative victories enacted policies of debatable merit, as, for example, the financial deregulation that arguably contributed to the financial crisis and Great Recession beginning in 2007–8. But those future events played no role in the calculus that led to his impeachment.

5. JEFFREY TOOBIN, A VAST CONSPIRACY: THE REAL STORY OF THE SEX SCANDAL THAT NEARLY BROUGHT DOWN A PRESIDENT 81 (1999).

6. *Bill Clinton's Vietnam Test*, N.Y. TIMES (Feb. 14, 1992), available at: www.nytimes .com/1992/02/14/opinion/bill-clinton-s-vietnam-test.html.

7. GARRY WILLS, REAGAN'S AMERICA: INNOCENTS AT HOME 339–42 (1987).

8. *Ibid.*, at 341–42 (describing presidents Kennedy, Johnson, Nixon, Ford, and Reagan as "second lieutenant presidents" because they were all junior officers in the Second World War). Truman had served in the First World War, and, of course, Eisenhower commanded Allied Forces in Europe in the Second World War. And Roosevelt had at least been Assistant Secretary of the Navy. JEAN EDWARD SMITH, FDR 97–101 (2007).

9. *See, e.g.*, JOE CONASON & GENE LYONS, THE HUNTING OF THE PRESIDENT: THE TEN-YEAR CAMPAIGN TO DESTROY BILL AND HILLARY CLINTON 325 (2000) (describing, albeit from a distinctly pro-Clinton angle, the attitude of some older Republicans about the Clintons).

10. *See, e.g.*, FLOYD G. BROWN, SLICK WILLIE: WHY AMERICA CANNOT TRUST BILL CLINTON (1992) (a campaign season hitpiece by an anti-Clinton operative earlier responsible for the Willie Horton advert in the Bush–Dukakis campaign of 1988 – but the nickname was prevalent beyond the precincts of the far right).

11. RICHARD A. POSNER, AN AFFAIR OF STATE: THE INVESTIGATION, IMPEACHMENT, AND TRIAL OF PRESIDENT CLINTON 204–5 (1999).

12. *John Mordaunt, 1st Viscount Mordaunt, 1626–75*, BCW-PROJECT, available at: http://bcw-project.org/biography/john-mordaunt, last accessed July 19, 2018; 6 T. B. HOWELL, A COMPLETE COLLECTION OF STATE TRIALS AND PROCEEDINGS FOR HIGH TREASON AND OTHER CRIMES AND MISDEMEANORS FROM THE EARLIEST PERIOD TO THE YEAR 1783, WITH NOTES AND OTHER ILLUSTRATIONS 785–806 (1816).

13. BILL CLINTON, MY LIFE 673, 680–84 (2004).

14. TOOBIN, A VAST CONSPIRACY, *supra* note 5, at 85–86; U.S. HOUSE COMMITTEE ON THE JUDICIARY, IMPEACHMENT OF WILLIAM JEFFERSON CLINTON, PRESIDENT OF THE UNITED STATES, H.R. REP. 105–830, at 7–8 (1998) [hereinafter "Judiciary Report"].

15. KENNETH W. STARR, THE STARR REPORT: THE FINDINGS OF INDEPENDENT COUNSEL KENNETH W. STARR ON PRESIDENT CLINTON AND THE LEWINSKY AFFAIR 48–74 (1998) [hereinafter "STARR REPORT"]; CLINTON, MY LIFE, *supra* note 13, at 773.

16. CONASON AND LYONS, HUNTING OF THE PRESIDENT, *supra* note 9, at 280–81.

17. *Ibid.*, at 290, 323–32; BOB WOODWARD, SHADOW: FIVE PRESIDENTS AND THE LEGACY OF WATERGATE 359 (1999).

18. H. LOWELL BROWN, HIGH CRIMES AND MISDEMEANORS IN PRESIDENTIAL IMPEACHMENT 92 (2010); Complaint, Jones v. Clinton, 858 F. Supp. 902 (E.D. Ark. 1994), available at: www.washingtonpost.com/wp-srv/politics/special/ pjones/docs/complaint.htm.

19. *Ibid.*
20. Clinton v. Jones, 500 U.S. 681 (1997). The court did not address the question of whether a court could compel the president to appear at a particular time or place to respond to questions. *Ibid.*, at 689–92.
21. *Ibid.*, at 702.
22. Toobin, A Vast Conspiracy, *supra* note 5, at 11, 35–37.
23. Brown, High Crimes and Misdemeanors, *supra* note 18, at 209 n. 9 (internal source citations omitted). *See also,* Toobin, A Vast Conspiracy, *supra* note 5, at 26–28 (Jones' Feb. 11, 1994, appearance at CPAC meeting); 125–28 (rejection of settlement and resignation of lawyers).
24. *See* Jones v. Clinton, 990 F. Supp. 657 (E.D. Ark. 1998) (dismissing Jones' case on summary judgment).
25. Brown, High Crimes and Misdemeanors, *supra* note 18, at 93; Judiciary Report, *supra* note 14, at 8–9.
26. Judiciary Report, *supra* note 14, at 10–11.
27. *Ibid.*, at 17–19; Brown, High Crimes and Misdemeanors, *supra* note 18, at 94.
28. *Ibid.*
29. Judiciary Report, *supra* note 14, at 15–17.
30. *Ibid.*, at 19.
31. As modified by the judge, the final definition used in Clinton's interrogation was as follows: "For the purposes of this deposition, a person engages in 'sexual relations' when the person knowingly engages in or causes – contact with the genitalia, anus, groin, breast, inner thigh, or buttocks of any person with the intent to arouse or gratify the sexual desire of any person." Toobin, A Vast Conspiracy, *supra* note 5, at 218–19. For a clever person (like Bill Clinton) looking for a way to avoid admitting adultery without committing perjury, the reference to "person" can be read to mean the deponent (Clinton), while the phrase "any person" can be read to refer only to the deponent's sexual partner (Ms. Lewinsky), and not to the deponent himself.
32. Pub. L. 95-521 (1978); 28 U.S.C. §§ 591–99.
33. For a good description of the Act and its deficiencies, see Julie R. O'Sullivan, *The Independent Counsel Statute: Bad Law, Bad Policy*, 33 Am. Crim. L. Rev. 463 (1996).
34. Morrison v. Olson, 487 U.S. 654 (1988).
35. *See, e.g.,* O'Sullivan, *Independent Counsel Statute, supra* note 33; Stephen L. Carter, *The Independent Counsel Mess*, 102 Harv. L. Rev. 105 (1988).
36. *See* Lawrence E. Walsh, Final Report of the Independent Counsel for Iran/Contra Matters (1993), available at: https://fas.org/irp/offdocs/walsh; Malcolm Byrne, Iran-Contra: Reagan's Scandal and the Unchecked Abuse of Presidential Power (2014).
37. Jim Mokhiber, *A Brief History of the Independent Counsel Law*, Frontline (May 1998), available at: www.pbs.org/wgbh/pages/frontline/shows/counsel/office/history.html.
38. *Ibid.*

39. *Whitewater Timeline*, WASH. POST (1998), available at: www.washingtonpost.com /wp-srv/politics/special/whitewater/timeline.htm.

40. *Ibid.*

41. David Von Drehle & Howard Schneider, *Foster's Death a Suicide*, WASH. POST, July 1, 1994, at A1.

42. Pub. L. 103-270 (1994).

43. Judge Sentelle's involvement in the dismissal of Fiske and appointment of Starr was widely criticized due to his long history as a Republican activist in North Carolina and protégé of Senator Jesse Helms, not to speak of a curiously timed lunch with Helms and Senator Lauch Faircloth (R.N.C.), both outspoken Clinton opponents, just before Starr was appointed. Marilyn W. Thompson, *Lunch Among "Old Friends" Causes Latest Whitewater Ripple*, WASH. POST (Aug. 24, 1994), available at: www.washingtonpost.com/archive/politics/1994/ 08/24/lunch-among-old-friends-causes-latest-whitewater-ripple/6ce8bbc8-8d7e-410a-828e-43837514a197/?utm_term=.cc919325b29a; TOOBIN, A VAST CONSPIRACY, *supra* note 5, at 72–73.

44. TOOBIN, A VAST CONSPIRACY, *supra* note 5, at 75–78.

45. *E.g.*, Foster's death was investigated by the Justice Department before Fiske looked at the matter. They concluded it was suicide. Fiske agreed. The Republican-controlled House Committee on Government Operations then did its own investigation, concluding on Aug. 12, 1994, that it was suicide. The Senate Banking Committee also got in the act. On Jan. 3, 1995, it, too, concluded suicide. The OIC would spend nearly three more years looking at the matter before, at last, conceding in Oct. 1997 that it was suicide. TOOBIN, A VAST CONSPIRACY, *supra* note 5, at 189.

46. *Travelgate to Furnituregate: A Guide to the Clinton Scandals of the 90s*, GUARDIAN (U.S. edition) (May 27, 2016), available at: www.theguardian.com/ us-news/2016/may/27/hillary-clinton-bill-clinton-scandals; Neil A. Lewis, *Final Report by Prosecutor on Clintons is Released*, N.Y. TIMES (March 21, 2001), available at: www.nytimes.com/2002/03/21/us/final-report-by-prosecutor-on-clin tons-is-released.html.

47. TOOBIN, A VAST CONSPIRACY, *supra* note 5, at 192–96.

48. *Ibid.*, at 203–6; BROWN, HIGH CRIMES AND MISDEMEANORS, *supra* note 18, at 95.

49. Robert W. Gordon, *Imprudence and Partisanship: Starr's OIC and the Clinton– Lewinsky Affair*, 68 FORDHAM L. REV. 639 (1999).

50. Jones v. Clinton, 993 F. Supp. 1217, 1219, 1222 (E.D. Ark. 1998).

51. Jones v. Clinton, 990 F. Supp. 657 (E.D. Ark. 1998); TOOBIN, A VAST CONSPIRACY, *supra* note 5, at 295–96.

52. TOOBIN, A VAST CONSPIRACY, *supra* note 5, at 251–52.

53. *Ibid.*, at 307–8, 322–25.

54. *Ibid.*, at 312–14.

55. *Ibid.*, at 318.

56. 28 U.S.C. § 595(c).

57. TOOBIN, A VAST CONSPIRACY, *supra* note 5, at 328–30.

58. The road map consisted of a two-page summary of evidence, fifty-three witness statements, and ninety-seven supporting documents. *In re Petition for Order Directing Release of Transcripts of Testimony Before Watergate Grand Juries*, Case No. 11-mc-44 (BAH), at 2 (D.D.C. Oct. 11, 2018), available at: www.politico .com/f/?id=00000166-65b1-d0b1-a57e-edbb7ecc0001. Much of it is now publicly available. *See* Benjamin Wittes, *Watergate Road Map Unsealed*, Lawfare (Oct. 31, 2018), available at: www.lawfareblog.com/watergate-road-map-unsealed.

59. *E.g.*, the report contains no description of the initial contacts with Ms. Lewinsky and her mother on the eve of the Clinton deposition. Relatedly, the explanation of the OIC's decision to seek authority to investigate the Lewinsky affair is particularly tendentious. In effect, it alleges that Linda Tripp was a witness in "three ongoing OIC investigations" – a doubtful, if not outright false, assertion – and that the Lewinsky affair "had parallels to" another matter with OIC jurisdiction because Vernon Jordan was involved. Starr Report, *supra* note 15 (Scope of Referral/Background of Investigation).

60. *Ibid.*

61. This is the entirety of the OIC's treatment of this vexed constitutional question: "The Presidency is more than an executive responsibility. It is the inspiring symbol of all that is highest in American purpose and ideals." When he took the Oath of Office in 1993 and again in 1997, President Clinton swore that he would "faithfully execute the Office of President." As the head of the executive branch, the president has the constitutional duty to "take Care that the Laws be faithfully executed." The president gave his testimony in the Jones case under oath and in the presence of a federal judge, a member of a co-equal branch of government; he then testified before a federal grand jury, a body of citizens who had themselves taken an oath to seek the truth. In view of the enormous trust and responsibility attendant to his high Office, the president has a manifest duty to ensure that his conduct at all times complies with the law of the land. In sum, perjury and acts that obstruct justice by any citizen – whether in a criminal case, a grand jury investigation, a congressional hearing, a civil trial, or civil discovery – are profoundly serious matters. When such acts are committed by the president of the United States, we believe those acts "may constitute grounds for an impeachment" (citations omitted). *Ibid.*

62. In later testimony before the House Judiciary Committee, Starr expanded slightly on the constitutional analysis. However, even then, the analysis was anemic, and tellingly relied largely on expert testimony given to the committee after the referral. *See Impeachment Inquiry: William Jefferson Clinton, Hearing Before the H. Comm. on the Judiciary*, 105th Cong. 53–54 (1998) (prepared statement of Kenneth Starr given Nov. 19, 1998).

63. Toobin, A Vast Conspiracy, *supra* note 5, at 330–31.

64. *Ibid.*, at 337.

65. Brown, High Crimes and Misdemeanors, *supra* note 18, at 97–104. I was one of the contributors to the committee record. *Background and History of Impeachment: Hearing Before the Subcomm. on the Constitution of the House*

Comm. on the Judiciary, 105th Cong. 342–72 (Nov. 9, 1999) (statement of Frank O. Bowman, III and Stephen L. Sepinuck).

66. For discussion of the 2018 status of this norm, *see* Quinta Juricic, *About That 60-Day Rule*, Lawfare (Sept. 3, 2018), available at: www.lawfareblog.com/about-60-day-rule. On the question of whether Starr sought to avoid affecting the election, or hoped to damage Clinton and the Democrats, *see* Toobin, A Vast Conspiracy, *supra* note 5, at 305–7.

67. Frank Newport, *Presidential Approval Ratings: Bill Clinton's High Ratings in the Midst of Crisis, 1998*, Gallup (June 1999), available at: https://news.gallup .com/poll/4609/presidential-job-approval-bill-clintons-high-ratings-midst.aspx.

68. Alison Mitchell & Eric Schmitt, *The 1998 Elections: Congress – The Overview; GOP in Scramble Over Blame for Poor Showing at the Polls*, N.Y. Times (Nov. 5, 1998).

69. Judiciary Report, *supra* note 14, 32–106.

70. 144 Cong. Rec. 12040–42 (1998); Toobin, A Vast Conspiracy, *supra* note 5, at 367.

71. *See, e.g.*, Bruce Ackerman, The Case Against Lameduck Impeachment (1999).

72. 1 U.S. Senate, Proceedings of the United States Senate in the Impeachment Trial of President William Jefferson Clinton, S. Doc. No. 106-4, at 17–20 (2000) [hereinafter Senate Trial].

73. Newport, *Presidential Approval Ratings, supra* note 67.

74. 2 Senate Trial, *supra* note 72, at 1582–83, 1687–797; 3 Senate Trial, *supra* note 72, at 2027–533.

75. 2 Senate Trial, *supra* note 72, at 1188–92 (arguments of Rep. Henry Hyde).

76. Howard Kurtz, *Report of Hyde Affair Stirs Anger*, Wash. Post (Sept. 17, 1998), at A17; Eric Pianin, *Livingston Quits as Speaker-Designate*, Wash. Post (Dec. 20, 1998), at A1; Eric Randall, *Past Adulterer Newt Gingrich Promises Not to Cheat on His Current Wife*, Atlantic (Dec. 12, 2011), available at: www.theatlantic .com/politics/archive/2011/12/past-adulterer-newt-gingrich-pledges-not-cheat-his-latest-wife/334406.

77. David G. Savage, *Hyde View on Lying is Back Haunting Him*, L. A. Times (Dec. 4, 1998), available at: http://articles.latimes.com/1998/dec/04/news/mn-50567.

78. 2 Senate Trial, *supra* note 72, at 1358 (remarks of Charles Ruff).

79. *Ibid.*, at 1402–3, 1410–11.

80. 4 Senate Trial, *supra* note 72, at 1994–2000.

81. *See, e.g.*, Michael Gerhardt, The Federal Impeachment Process 106 (1996): "Not all statutory crimes demonstrate unfitness for office"; U.S. Senate, Impeachment Inquiry: William Jefferson Clinton, President of the United States, Presentation on Behalf of the President, 105th Cong. 20 (1998) (statement of Prof. Sean Wilentz): "Above all, the scholars agreed that not all criminal acts are necessarily impeachable acts," available at: www.gpo.gov/fdsys/pkg/CHRG-105hhrg52320/pdf/CHRG-105hhrg52320 .pdf. The Clinton affair did not change the consensus. *See, e.g.*, Posner, An Affair of State, *supra* note 11, at 119 (observing that it must be admitted

"that impeachable offenses are not limited to crimes and that not all crimes are impeachable offenses").

82. *See generally* discussion in Chapter 4 *supra*.

83. 18 U.S.C. § 41.

84. LAWRENCE TRIBE, AMERICAN CONSTITUTIONAL LAW 294 (2d ed. 1988) (jaywalking or speeding "obviously would not be an adequate basis for presidential impeachment and removal").

85. 18 U.S.C. § 112(a) (foreign official); 18 U.S.C. § 153(a) (destroying document); 18 U.S.C. § 342 (operating bus or train); 18 U.S.C. § 501 (counterfeiting postage stamp); 18 U.S.C. § 511 (obliterating VIN).

86. *See, e.g.*, H.R. REP. NO. 93-1305, at 356 (concurring views of Congressman Hamilton Fish, Jr.: "At the very least [the President] is bound not to violate the law; not to order others to violate the law; and not to participate in the concealment of evidence respecting violations of law of which he is made aware").

87. *See* 2 Senate Trial, *supra* note 72, at 1191 (closing remarks of Rep. Henry Hyde, Chair of the House Judiciary Committee: "The rule of law is what stands between all of us and the arbitrary exercise of power by the state").

88. THE FEDERALIST PAPERS NO. 65 (Alexander Hamilton).

89. Regardless of whether one believes a president can be indicted while in office, *see, e.g.*, Eric M. Freedman, *The Law as King and the King as Law: Is a President Immune from Criminal Prosecution Before Impeachment?* 20 HASTINGS CONST. L. Q. 7 (1992), there can be no doubt of the power to indict once his or her term is concluded.

90. *See supra* Chapter 4, text accompanying notes 50–246.

91. As noted *supra* in Chapter 5, Judge Halstead Ritter, in 1936, and Judge Harry Claiborne, in 1986, were both impeached for income tax evasion. Of course, as discussed in *supra* Chapter 8, rejection of the Nixon impeachment article regarding personal tax evasion may be explainable as a tactical choice by those favoring the president's removal to focus on the more serious and more "political" first three articles, rather than as a judgment that presidential tax evasion is never an impeachable offense.

92. For an emphatic conclusion to the contrary, see POSNER, AN AFFAIR OF STATE, *supra* note 11, at 46–51.

93. *See* Trial Memorandum of President William Jefferson Clinton, *In re Impeachment of William Jefferson Clinton, President of the United States*, available at: http://movies2.nytimes.com/library/politics/011499impeach-text-contents.html.

94. 18 U.S.C. § 1623; *see, e.g.*, United States v. Reilly, 33 F.3d 1396, 1419 (3d Cir. 1994); United States v. Barrett, 111 F.3d 947, 953 (D.C. Cir. 1997).

95. Of course, the discombobulated character of the federal criminal code makes any very precise ranking of seriousness nearly impossible. For a time, the Federal Sentencing Guidelines promulgated by the U.S. Sentencing Commission and approved by Congress could be said to have provided a more exact seriousness measurement, but even that yardstick is now in doubt

inasmuch as the Guidelines were rendered advisory in 2005 by United States v. Booker, 543 U.S. 220 (2005).

96. *See* WASH. REV. CODE § 9A.56.020(1)(a), (c); WASH. REV. CODE § 9A.56.030(1)(a).

97. *See, e.g.,* WILLIAM RAWLE, A VIEW OF THE CONSTITUTION OF THE UNITED STATES (2d ed. 1829) (excerpted in 2 THE FOUNDERS' CONSTITUTION 169 (Philip B. Kurland & Ralph Lerner eds., 1987)): "In general those offences which may be committed equally by a private person as a public officer, are not the subjects of impeachment. Murder, burglary, robbery, and indeed all offenses not immediately connected with the office, except the two expressly mentioned, are left to the ordinary course of judicial proceeding."

98. *E.g.,* a group of 400 historians styling themselves "Historians in Defense of the Constitution" signed a letter asserting that the Constitution authorizes presidential impeachment only "for high crimes and misdemeanors in the exercise of executive power." *Background and History of Impeachment: Hearing Before the Subcomm. on the Constitution of the House Comm. on the Judiciary,* 105th Cong. 334 (1998) (statement of Historians in Defense of the Constitution). Similarly, more than four hundred law professors wrote to the Speaker of the House and argued that, while private crimes might in some circumstances merit impeachment, the crimes alleged against President Clinton were not impeachable because they did not "involve the derelict exercise of executive powers." Letter from professors of law to Speaker Gingrich and House Leaders (Nov. 6, 1998); *see also* Bernard J. Hibbitts, *More Than 430 Law Professors Send Letter to Congress Opposing Impeachment,* JURIST, available at: www.law.jurist .org/wayback/petit1.htm, last accessed Nov. 5, 2018.

99. *Background and History of Impeachment: Hearing Before the Subcomm. on the Constitution of the House Comm. on the Judiciary,* 105th Cong. 89 (1998) (statement of Cass R. Sunstein).

100. *Ibid.,* at 90.

101. *See* 145 CONG. REC. S933-02, S948 (statement of Rep. Henry Hyde, Chair of the House Judiciary Comm.).

102. For a general account of the conventional justifications of criminal punishment, *see* ANDREW VON HIRSCH, DOING JUSTICE: THE CHOICE OF PUNISHMENTS 9–55 (1976).

103. *See* JOSEPH STORY, COMMENTARIES ON THE CONSTITUTION § 799 (1833): "an impeachment is a proceeding of a purely political nature. It is not so much designed to punish an offender, as to secure the state against gross official misdemeanors. It touches neither his person nor his property, but simply divests him of his political capacity."

104. Impeachment achieves both specific and general deterrence. Specific deterrence (deterrence of the offender him- or herself) is accomplished because once a president is impeached and removed, he or she is unable to return to the office of the presidency and commit more of the transgressions from which we wish to deter him or her. The law would prevent return if the Senate imposed that penalty in addition to removal; practical politics would almost certainly prevent re-election even in the absence of the Senate bar. Impeachment should

also produce general deterrence (deterrence of persons other than the offender) in the impeached president's successors.

105. STORY, COMMENTARIES ON THE CONSTITUTION, at § 799.

106. Henry M. Hart, Jr., *The Aims of the Criminal Law*, 23 LAW & CONTEMPORARY PROBLEMS 404 (1958).

107. JOSHUA DRESSLER, UNDERSTANDING CRIMINAL LAW 18–19 (6th ed. 2012).

108. WAYNE R. LaFAVE, CRIMINAL LAW 25–26 (3d ed. 2000).

109. FRANKLIN ZIMRING, PERSPECTIVES ON DETERRENCE 4–5 (1971).

110. The refusal of the full House to impeach for perjury in the Jones lawsuit is most readily explained as a judgment that the lies were not "high Crimes or Misdemeanors" either because no lie about sex in a private civil lawsuit could ever be impeachable, or because these lies concerned issues so peripheral to this lawsuit that the president's falsehoods were either legally immaterial or nearly so. Article IV, approved by the Judiciary Committee but rejected by the full House, which proposed impeaching President Clinton for incomplete, misleading, or false answers to interrogatories from the Judiciary Committee, can easily be viewed as failing at all three levels of prosecutorial analysis. First, there was a real factual issue about whether the responses were false and misleading, or merely permissibly narrow and unforthcoming. Second, even if one concluded that the answers were impermissibly narrow or downright deceptive, there was a genuine issue about whether slippery responses to Congress, as opposed to outright defiance, constitute a "high Crime or Misdemeanor." Finally, even those ordinarily disposed to defend congressional powers of impeachment inquiry undoubtedly questioned whether the violation here, even if impeachable in theory, was of sufficient magnitude to warrant exercising discretion in favor of bringing down a president.

111. Morrison v. Olson, 487 U.S. 654, 705–15 (Scalia, J., dissenting).

112. At least it would have been in 1998. Given the extreme polarization of American politics in 2018, as this book is written, one can no longer be so sure.

113. CHARLES DICKENS, OLIVER TWIST 338 (1838).

114. *See* Richard M. Pious, *Impeaching the President: The Intersection of Constitutional and Popular Law*, 43 ST. LOUIS U. L. J. 859, 883–86 (1999) (discussing the consensus among senatorial investigators of the Iran-Contra matter that "we don't want to go after the President," and "the country didn't need another Watergate," as well as other indications that Democrats "had bound themselves publicly and privately with what games theorists refer to as a 'pre-commitment rule' barring the ultimate sanction").

10 THE SCOPE OF IMPEACHABLE PRESIDENTIAL CONDUCT: GENERAL PRINCIPLES

1. *See supra* Chapter 4 notes 103–14 and accompanying text.

2. MO. CONST. Art. VII, §§ 1–2. When the defendant is either the governor or a member of the Supreme Court, the trial is conducted by a specially selected panel of lower court judges. *Ibid.*, Art. VII, § 2.

3. Matter of Impeachment of Judith K. Moriarty, 902 S.W.2d 273, 277 (Mo. 1994).

4. Mo. Const. Art. VII, § 1.
5. For extensive discussion of Missouri impeachment law, *see* Frank O. Bowman, III, *Impeachment in the States: Missouri Governor Edition, Part I*, Impeachable Offenses? (Jan. 19, 2018), available at: https://impeachableoffenses.net/2018/01/19/impeachment-in-the-states-missouri-governor-edition-part-i. See also Frank O. Bowman, III, *Impeachment in the States: Missouri Governor Edition, Part 2*, Impeachable Offenses? (Jan. 20, 2018), available at: https://impeachableoffenses.net/2018/01/20/impeachment-in-the-states-missouri-governor-edition-part-2; Frank O. Bowman, III, *Impeachment in the States: Missouri Governor Edition, Part 6 – Pre-Inaugural Crime*, Impeachable Offenses? (April 12, 2018), available at: https://impeachableoffenses.net/2018/04/12/impeachment-in-the-states-missouri-edition-part-6-pre-inaugural-crime.
6. *See supra* Chapter 1 note 81 and accompanying text.
7. Nixon v. U.S., 506 U.S. 224 (1993) (rejecting a challenge by U.S. District Judge Nixon to the Senate's procedure of assigning a committee to hear evidence and report to the full Senate, which then voted on the articles of impeachment). Some scholars have argued that *Nixon* was wrongly decided and that congressional decisions on at least some aspects of the impeachment process should be justiciable. I think the better argument is to the contrary, at least in any but the most extreme and unlikely case. For perhaps the best exposition of this view, *see* Michael Gerhardt, The Federal Impeachment Process: A Constitutional and Historical Analysis 118–46 (Univ. of Chi. Press, 2d ed. 2000). Several of the justices in *Nixon* suggested that truly egregious deviations from basic constitutional norms of fairness and procedural due process might warrant judicial intervention in an impeachment proceeding, but even if one accepts this premise, it does not affect the central issue addressed in this chapter, that of interpreting "Treason, Bribery, or other high Crimes and Misdemeanors." *See Nixon*, 506 U.S. 224.
8. The first Pennsylvania and Vermont constitutions grant the legislature the power to "impeach state criminals." This phrase seems to limit impeachable conduct to indictable crimes, but as discussed in Chapter 3, that does not seem to have been the meaning ascribed to it since officials were impeached for non-criminal conduct. As observed in Chapter 3, the best reading of the phrase "state criminals" was probably something like "persons who have gravely offended against the state, especially in some official capacity." *See supra* Chapter 3 notes 152–53 and accompanying text.
9. *See supra* Chapter 4 note 198 and accompanying text.
10. 116 Cong. Rec. H3114 (1970) (statement of Rep. Gerald Ford).
11. Frank O. Bowman, III & Stephen L. Sepinuck, *"High Crimes & Misdemeanors": Defining the Constitutional Limits on Presidential Impeachment*, 72 So. Cal. L. Rev. 1517, 1564–65 (1999).
12. Dennis Overbye, *On the Other Side Now, But Still Spurring Debate*, N.Y. Times (Oct. 30, 2018), at D6.
13. U.S. Const. Art. III, § 3.

14. *See generally* Charles Warren, *What Is Giving Aid and Comfort to the Enemy?*, 27 YALE L.J. 331 (1918); *see also* JAMES WILLARD HURST, THE LAW OF TREASON IN THE UNITED STATES: COLLECTED ESSAYS (1971).

15. THE FEDERALIST NO. 43 (James Madison).

16. *See supra* Chapter 4 notes 155–63 and accompanying text.

17. Madison, *Saturday September 8th. In Convention, in* 2 THE RECORDS OF THE FEDERAL CONVENTION OF 1787, at 550–52 (Max Farrand ed., 1911) [hereinafter 2 FARRAND'S FEDERAL CONVENTION RECORDS].

18. COMM. ON THE JUDICIARY, H.R., 93RD CONGRESS, IMPEACHMENT: SELECTED MATERIALS 140–42 (Comm. Print 1973) [hereinafter IMPEACHMENT MATERIALS].

19. 4 WILLIAM BLACKSTONE, COMMENTARIES ON THE LAWS OF ENGLAND: IN FOUR BOOKS 139 (1765–69).

20. ROLLIN M. PERKINS & RONALD N. BOYCE, CRIMINAL LAW 527 (The Found. Press, 3d ed. 1982).

21. Act of July 31, 1789, ch. 5, § 35, 1 Stat. 29 (1789).

22. Crimes Act of 1790, ch. 9, § 21, 1 Stat. 112 (1790).

23. 18 U.S.C. § 201(b) (1994) (bribery); 18 U.S.C. § 201(c) (1994) (unlawful gratuity).

24. 18 U.S.C. § 666 (1994) (federal program bribery).

25. Commercial bribery may in some instances be prosecuted as a form of wire or mail fraud under 18 U.S.C. §§ 1341, 1343 (2008).

26. Foreign Corrupt Practices Act 1977 § 104, 15 U.S.C. § 78dd-1 (1998).

27. *E.g.*, in United States v. Sun-Diamond Growers of California, the Supreme Court found that the unlawful gratuities statute, 18 U.S.C. § 201(c), requires proof of a nexus between the gratuity and an official action, but not a *quid pro quo*. 526 U.S. 398 (1999).

28. *See supra* Chapter 6 note 61 and accompanying text.

29. *See supra* Chapter 2 notes 178–87 and accompanying text.

30. *See supra* Chapter 3 notes 59, 80–81, 113–16, 152–53 and accompanying text.

31. *See supra* Chapter 4 notes 200–10 and accompanying text.

32. *See supra* Chapter 4 note 209 and accompanying text.

33. *See supra* Chapter 5 notes 43–46 and accompanying text; *see also supra* Chapter 6 notes 67–69, 70–73, 84–86 and accompanying text.

34. *See, e.g.*, LAWRENCE H. TRIBE, AMERICAN CONSTITUTIONAL LAW: A STRUCTURE FOR LIBERTY 220 (1978): "A showing of criminality is neither necessary nor sufficient for the specification of an impeachable offense"; RAOUL BERGER, IMPEACHMENT: THE CONSTITUTIONAL PROBLEMS 56–57 (1973); CHARLES L. BLACK, JR., IMPEACHMENT: A HANDBOOK 33–35 (1974); GERHARDT, FEDERAL IMPEACHMENT PROCESS *supra* note 7, at 103; H. LOWELL BROWN, HIGH CRIMES AND MISDEMEANORS IN PRESIDENTIAL IMPEACHMENT 118–19 (2010). For a lonely dissenting view, *see* Nikolas Bowie, *High Crimes Without Law*, 132 HARV. L. REV. F. 59 (2018); for my response, *see* Frank O. Bowman, III, *Crime is NOT a prerequisite for impeachment, Impeachable Offenses?*, available at: https://impeacha bleoffenses.net/2019/01/03/crime-is-not-a-prerequisite-for-impeachment.

35. TRIBE, AMERICAN CONSTITUTIONAL LAW, *supra* note 34.

36. As noted in Chapter 7, the Tenure of Office Act categorizes any violation of its provisions as a "high misdemeanor," a label affixed to justify impeachment if President Johnson dared defy it. *See supra* Chapter 7 note 120 and accompanying text. Nonetheless, the penalties designated in the statute would make it a felony in modern criminal taxonomy, which ordinarily designates as felonies those crimes for which a defendant may be imprisoned for more than one year.

37. *See supra* Chapter 7 note 155 and accompanying text. Of course, as discussed in Chapter 7, the motives for acquittal in Johnson's case were numerous and varied.

38. *See supra* Chapter 9 notes 94–95 and accompanying text.

39. *See supra* Chapter 5 notes 52–62 and accompanying text.

40. *See supra* Chapter 2 notes 189–207 and accompanying text; *see also supra* Chapter 3 notes 152–59 and accompanying text; *see also supra* Chapter 4 notes 199–239 and accompanying text.

41. *See supra* Chapter 4 notes 240–41 and accompanying text.

42. 2 Farrand's Federal Convention Records, *supra* note 16, at 550–52; *also supra* Chapter 4 notes 240–47 and accompanying text.

43. *See supra* Chapter 4 notes 140, 143, 212–16, 239 and accompanying text.

44. At the Virginia ratifying convention, Edmund Randolph said that if the president is discovered "receiving emoluments from foreign powers ... he may be impeached." 3 Jonathan Elliot, The Debates in the Several State Conventions of the Adoption of the Federal Constitution 486 (1827) [hereinafter 3 Elliot]. At the Constitutional Convention, Gouverneur Morris made the same point, though he couched it in terms of bribery. 5 Jonathan Elliot, The Debates in the Several State Conventions of the Adoption of the Federal Constitution 343 (1827) [hereinafter 5 Elliot].

45. *See* remarks of James Madison at Virginia ratifying convention on July 18, 1787, *in* 3 Elliot, *supra* note 44, at 498.

46. *See* remarks of James Iredell at North Carolina ratifying convention on July 28, 1788, *in* 4 Jonathan Elliot, The Debates in the Several State Conventions of the Adoption of the Federal Constitution 118 (1827).

47. *See* remarks of George Mason and Gouverneur Morris at Constitutional Convention on July 20, 1787. 5 Elliot, *supra* note 44, at 323–24 (1827).

48. *See supra* Chapter 6 notes 58–91 and accompanying text.

49. *See supra* Chapter 6 notes 92–95 and accompanying text.

50. *See supra* Chapter 6 notes 17–51 and accompanying text.

51. *See supra* Chapter 5 notes 63–64 and accompanying text.

52. U.S. Const. Art. II, § 1.

11 IMPEACHMENT FOR OBSTRUCTION OF JUSTICE

1. U.S. Const. Art. II, § 3.

2. Staff of the Impeachment Inquiry, Comm. on the Judiciary, House of Representatives, 93d Cong., Constitutional Grounds for Presidential Impeachment 19–20 (Comm. Print 1974), available at: https://democrats-judi

ciary.house.gov/sites/democrats.judiciary.house.gov/files/
1974ImpeachmentInquiryReport.pdf.

3. Daniel J. Hemel & Eric A. Posner, *Presidential Obstruction of Justice*, 106 CAL. L. REV. 1277, 1279 (2018).

4. *See supra* Chapter 2 notes 75–77 and accompanying text.

5. *See supra* Chapter 6 notes 59–61, 65 and accompanying text.

6. Jim Rutenberg & Rebecca R. Ruiz, *Ex-Playboy Model Karen McDougal Sues to Speak on Alleged Trump Affair*, N.Y. TIMES (March 20, 2018), available at: www.nytimes.com/2018/03/20/us/ex-playboy-model-sues-to-break-silence-on-trump.html; Scott Pilutik, *The Stormy Daniels Lawsuit is Convoluted to the Point of Paradox*, SLATE (March 7, 2018), available at: https://slate.com/news-and-politics/2018/03/the-stormy-daniels-lawsuit-is-convoluted-to-the-point-of-paradox.html. One of the alleged girlfriends also sued President Trump unsuccessfully over his alleged defamation of her. Rebecca R. Ruiz, *Stormy Daniels Told to Pay Trump Legal Fees after Defamation Suit*, N.Y. TIMES (Oct. 15, 2018), available at: www.nytimes.com/2018/10/15/admin/stormy-daniels-lawsuit-dismissed-trump.html.

7. *See infra* Chapter 14 notes 21–30 and accompanying text.

8. Hemel & Posner, *Presidential Obstruction of Justice*, *supra* note 3, at 1284.

9. 2 WILLIAM BLACKSTONE, COMMENTARIES ON THE LAWS OF ENGLAND: IN FOUR BOOKS 126, 139–40 (1769) (book four). Blackstone also recorded the offense of "obstructing the execution of lawful process," which sounds like our obstruction of justice, but seems to have been nothing more than interfering with an arrest made pursuant to a lawful warrant. *Ibid.*, at 126.

10. *Ibid.*, at 140.

11. *See* U.S. Department of Justice, *Criminal Resource Manual § 1704: Protection of Government Processes – Omnibus Clause – 18 U.S.C. § 1503*, available at: www .justice.gov/jm/criminal-resource-manual-1724-protection-government-pro cesses-omnibus-clause-18-usc-1503.

12. *See, e.g.*, United States v. Neal, 951 F.2d 630 (5th Cir. 1992); United States v. Guzzino, 810 F.2d 687 (7th Cir. 1987); United States v. Capo, 791 F.2d 1054, 1070 (2d Cir. 1986), *reh'g granted on other grounds*, 817 F.2d 947 (2d Cir. 1987) (en banc); United States v. Johnson, 605 F.2d 729, 730 (4th Cir. 1979); United States v. Baker, 494 F.2d 1262, 1265 (6th Cir. 1974).

13. United States v. Aguilar, 515 U.S. 593 (1995); United States v. Wood, 958 F.2d 963, 975 n. 18 (10th Cir. 1992); United States v. Campanale, 518 F.2d 353, 356 (9th Cir. 1975) (*per curiam*). Any federal criminal investigation will, if successful in securing evidence sufficient to establish probable cause of a federal felony, eventually involve a grand jury, if only because a grand jury indictment is a constitutional prerequisite to a federal felony prosecution. *Ex parte* Wilson, 114 U.S. 417 (1885).

14. United States v. Nelson, 852 F.2d 706 (3d Cir. 1988). Even if Justice Department attorneys have issued subpoenas under the authority of and returnable to a particular grand jury, but have not yet informed the grand jurors of these actions, a judicial proceeding may be deemed pending for purposes of section 1503.

United States v. Steele, 241 F.3d 302, 305 (3d Cir. 2001); United States v. Simmons, 591 F.2d 206, 209–10 (3d Cir. 1979); United States v. Nelson, 852 F.2d 706 (3d Cir. 1988).

15. United States v. Aguilar, 515 U.S. 595 (1995).

16. United States v. Frankhauser, 80 F.3d 641 (1st Cir. 1996) (FBI); United States v. Fassenacht, 332 F.3d 440 (7th Cir. 2003).

17. United States v. Quattrone, 441 F.3d 153 (2d Cir. 2006).

18. It is unclear whether "official proceeding" would include a federal criminal investigation limited only to agent inquiries that did not involve a grand jury or judge. United States v. Ramos, 537 F.3d 439, 463 (5th Cir. 2008).

19. United States v. Reich, 479 F.3d 179 (2d Cir. 2007).

20. Section 1515(b) limits this definition to use of the term in 18 U.S.C. § 1505 (Obstruction of proceedings before departments, agencies, and committees). It nonetheless seems reasonable to assume that this definition has at least persuasive force when construing the same term in §§ 1503 and 1512. *See* Hemel & Posner, *Presidential Obstruction of Justice, supra* note 3, at 1287.

21. United States v. Carson, 560 F.3d 566, 573 (6th Cir. 2009).

22. United States v. Reich 479 F.3d 179 (2d Cir. 2007). Such forgery is independently prosecutable under 18 U.S.C. § 505.

23. United States v. Farrell, 126 F.3d 484, 488 (3d Cir. 1997).

24. United States v. Petruk, 781 F.3d 438 (8th Cir. 2015); United States v. Khatami, 280 F.3d 907 (9th Cir. 2002).

25. 544 U.S. 696 (2005).

26. United States v. Doss, 630 F.3d 1181, 1189–90 (9th Cir. 2011).

27. United States v. Coppin, 569 Fed. App. 326 (5th Cir. 2014).

28. Eyder Peralta, *Obama Goes it Alone, Shielding up to 5 Million Immigrants from Deportation*, NPR (Nov. 20, 2014), available at: www.npr.org/sections/thetwo-way/2014/11/20/365519963/obama-will-announce-relief-for-up-to-5-million-immigrants.

29. Jeremy Berke, *Obama: It's "Untenable" for Government to Enforce "a Patchwork of Laws" on Marijuana*, Bus. Insider (Nov. 30, 2016), available at: www.businessinsider.com/obama-on-weed-legalization-2016–11.

30. Public Citizen, *Corporate Impunity: "Tough on Crime" Trump is Weak on Corporate Crime and Wrongdoing* (July 2018), available at: www.citizen.org/sites/default/files/corporate-enforcement-public-citizen-report-july-2018.pdf.

31. United States v. Matthews, 505 F.3d 698, 704–8 (7th Cir. 2007). *E.g.*, a lawyer representing a criminal client has been found guilty of obstruction for using legal maneuvers to expose and frustrate an FBI undercover investigation into gambling activities in which both the lawyer and his client had large financial stakes. United States v. Cueto, 151 F.3d 620 (7th Cir. 1998).

32. Sari Horwitz & Philip Rucker, *A Bold New Legal Defense for Trump: Presidents Cannot Obstruct Justice*, Wash. Post (Dec. 4, 2017), available at: www.washingtonpost.com/world/national-security/a-bold-new-legal-defense-for-trump-presidents-cannot-obstruct-justice/2017/12/04/b95cb262-d91c-11e7-a841-2066faf731ef_s

tory.html?utm_term=.b1aee55949ba (describing claims by defenders of President Trump).

33. A real-life instance of this principle arose when President Andrew Jackson ordered a federal prosecutor to drop a case involving jewelry stolen from a Dutch princess. Roger Taney, then attorney general, responded to a request for legal advice from the secretary of state with an opinion concluding that the president was within his rights. The Jewels of the Princess of Orange, 2 Op. Att. Gen. 482 (1831).

34. As an example of the distinction drawn in the text, consider the requirement of Federal Rule of Criminal Procedure 7(c)(1) that, to be valid, an indictment "must be signed by an attorney for the government." Suppose a president wanted a particular indictment approved by a grand jury to be filed, but the U.S. attorney in the district did not. Under ordinary circumstances, we would not consider the president to be a lawyer for the government, even if he or she happened to be an attorney. Therefore, to get the indictment legally filed, the president would presumably have to order someone who qualified as an attorney for the government to sign the document.

35. Hemel & Posner, *Presidential Obstruction of Justice, supra* note 3, at 1312 (emphasis in original).

36. The Hemel and Posner article, *ibid.*, is the most scholarly, thorough, and even-handed assessment of presidential obstruction of justice now available. It explores many nuances impossible to discuss in the space available here.

37. *See supra* Chapter 8 note 33 and accompanying text.

38. Michael D. Shear & Matt Apuzzo, *FBI Director James Comey is Fired by Trump*, N.Y. Times (May 9, 2017), available at: www.nytimes.com/2017/05/09/us/poli tics/james-comey-fired-fbi.html, last accessed Jan. 24, 2019.

39. Peter Baker, Katie Benner, & Michael D. Shear, *Jeff Sessions is Forced Out as Attorney General as Trump Installs Loyalist*, N.Y. Times (Nov. 7, 2018), available at: www.nytimes.com/2018/11/07/us/politics/sessions-resigns.html.

40. *See supra* Chapter 8 notes 82, 88–90 and accompanying text.

41. *See, e.g.*, Rebecca Morin, *Trump Revives His Attack on Mueller*, Politico (Nov. 7, 2018), available at: www.politico.com/story/2018/11/07/trump-attacks-mueller-971062.

42. *See, e.g.*, Samuel W. Buell, *Open and Shut: The Obstruction Case Against Trump is Already a Slam Dunk*, Slate (July 6, 2017), available at: https://slate .com/news-and-politics/2017/07/the-obstruction-of-justice-case-against-trump-is-already-a-slam-dunk.html.

43. Katie Benner, Nicholas Fandos & Katie Rogers, *Trump Denounces Justice Department as Investigations Swirl Around Him*, N.Y. Times (Aug. 23, 2018), available at: www.nytimes.com/2018/08/23/us/politics/trump-flipping-cohen-manafort.html.

44. *Ibid.* (quoting Tweets by President Trump calling for the Justice Department to investigate Hillary Clinton, the Clinton Foundation, James Comey, and a litany of people connected with the Russian collusion investigation).

45. Natasha Bertrand, *Trump Wants Sessions to Investigate "Anonymous." But There Was No Crime*, ATLANTIC (Sept. 7. 2018) (describing President Trump's request for a criminal investigation of an anonymous opinion article in the *New York Times* critical of the president purportedly written by a government official close to the White House).

46. Jeet Heer, *Trump Incites a "Lock Her Up" Chant Against Women Who Make Sexual Harassment Allegations*, NEW REPUBLIC (Nov. 5, 2018), available at: https://newrepublic.com/minutes/152046/trump-incites-lock-up-chant-women-make-sexual-harassment-accusations.

47. David Wright, *Mukasey Rips Trump Threat: "It Would be Like a Banana Republic,"* CNN (Oct. 11, 2016), available at: www.cnn.com/2016/10/11/politics/michael-mukasey-interview-trump-banana-republic/index.html.

48. The criminal investigation of former FBI Deputy Director Andrew McCabe for misleading his former employers about the source of leaks to the media during the 2016 presidential campaign is concerning. *See* Sonam Sheth, *Prosecutors Are Using a Grand Jury to Investigate Whether Former FBI Deputy Director Andrew McCabe Misled the Bureau*, BUS. INSIDER (Sept. 6, 2018), available at: www.businessinsider.com/grand-jury-investigates-andrew-mccabe-2018–9. It is unsurprising that McCabe might be fired for "lack of candor" in interviews with internal investigators, but transforming that kind of dispute into a full-blown criminal investigation is very unusual. Even though the referral emanated from the respected Department of Justice Office of Inspector General, the fact that McCabe was under sustained public attack by President Trump before the criminal referral is troublesome. *See* Emma Stefansky, *Trump Doubles Down on McCabe Attacks Amid Reports of Memos in Mueller's Hands*, VANITY FAIR (March 18, 2018), available at: www.vanityfair.com/news/2018/03/mccabe-memos-trump-attacks-tweets.

49. *See supra* Chapter 8, note 91.

50. Michael E. Miller, *Nixon Had an Enemies List. Now So Does Trump*, WASH. POST (Aug. 19, 2018), available at: www.washingtonpost.com/news/retropolis/wp/2018/08/17/nixon-had-an-enemies-list-now-so-does-trump. *See also*, Chapter 8, notes 24–28 and accompanying text.

51. *Ibid.*, at note 90 and accompanying text.

52. *See, e.g.*, Heidi M. Przybyla, *Trump Calls on Justice Dept. to Investigate "Rigged" Dem Primary in Series of Morning Tweets*, USA TODAY (Nov. 3, 2017), available at: www.usatoday.com/story/news/politics/2017/11/03/trump-calls-justice-dept-investigate-rigged-dem-primary-series-morning-tweets/828704001; Tucker Higgins, *President Trump: Comey is "Criminal," and IG Report "Totally Exonerates Me,"* CNBC (June 15, 2018), available at: www.cnbc.com/2018/06/15/trump-doj-watchdog-report-totally-exonerates-me-comeys-actions-criminal.html; Katie Benner, Nicholas Fandos, & Katie Rogers, *Trump Denounces Justice Department as Investigations Swirl Around Him*, N.Y. TIMES (Aug. 23, 2018), available at: www.nytimes.com/2018/08/23/us/politics/trump-flipping-cohen-manafort.html; Amanda Sakuma, *Trump is Peddling Conspiracy Theories to*

Try to Undercut Roger Stone's Indictment, Vox (Jan. 26, 2019), available at: www
.vox.com/2019/1/26/18198456/trump-conspiracy-roger-stone-indictment.
53. *See* Frank O. Bowman, III, *A Reality Check for Impeachment Enthusiasts: House
Judiciary Committee Republicans,* Impeachable Offenses? (Aug. 3, 2017), available at: https://impeachableoffenses.net/2017/08/03/a-reality-check-for-impeach
ment-enthusiasts-house-judiciary-committee-republicans.

12 IMPEACHMENT FOR ABUSE OF THE PARDON POWER

1. U.S. Const. Art. II, § 2.
2. Professor Martin Redish has argued that pardons might be reviewable and
   voidable by the courts on due process grounds. This claim is analyzed and
   disputed *in* Frank O. Bowman, III, *A Due Process Challenge (Almost
   Certainly Fruitless) to the Arpaio Pardon,* Impeachable Offenses?, available
   at: https://impeachableoffenses.net/2017/08/30/a-challenge-almost-certainly-
   fruitless-to-the-arpaio-pardon. Dean Erwin Chemerinsky, Michael Tigar,
   and Jane Tigar have contended that pardons in contempt cases are reviewable
   and voidable on separation of powers grounds. Their theory is analyzed and
   disputed *in* Frank O. Bowman, III, *The Arpaio Pardon: Dean Chemerinsky's
   Separation of Powers Argument is Clever, Learned … and Wrong,*
   Impeachable Offenses?, available at: https://impeachableoffenses.net/2017/
   09/24/the-arpaio-pardon-dean-chemerinskys-separation-of-powers-argument-is-
   clever-learned-and-wrong.
3. U.S. Const. Art. II, § 2.
4. 3 Jonathan Elliot, The Debates in Several State Conventions on the
   Adoption of the Federal Constitution 497 (1827). Recall that, despite his
   exertions at the Philadelphia Constitutional Convention, Mason decided in the
   end that he could not support the final document. He went back to Virginia and
   became a vociferous opponent of ratification.
5. *Ibid.,* at 498.
6. *Ibid.,* at 17.
7. Hamilton's way of expressing the thought was elliptical, even by his standards, but
   the point is clear enough. He wrote: "A President … though he may even pardon
   treason, when prosecuted in the ordinary course of law, could shelter no offender,
   in any degree, from the effects of impeachment and conviction. Would not the
   prospect of a total indemnity for all the preliminary steps be a greater temptation
   to undertake and persevere in an enterprise against the public liberty, than the
   mere prospect of an exemption from death and confiscation, if the final execution
   of the design, upon an actual appeal to arms, should miscarry? Would this last
   expectation have any influence at all, when the probability was computed that
   the person who was to afford that exemption might himself be involved in the
   consequences of the measure, and might be incapacitated by his agency in it
   from affording the desired impunity?" The Federalist No. 69 (Alexander
   Hamilton).
8. *See supra* Chapter 8 notes 77 and 79 and accompanying text.

9. U.S. Const. Art. II, § 3.

10. U.S. Const. Art II, § 1.

11. Eric Lichtblau & Davan Maharaj, *Clinton Pardon of Rich a Saga of Power, Money*, Chi. Tribune (Feb. 19, 2001), available at: www.chicagotribune.com/sns-clinton-pardons-analysis-story.html.

12. One can fairly argue that the Rich pardon was precisely the kind of sleazy maneuver that lent credence to the often overhyped accusations against both Clintons and left an indelible taint on the Clinton "brand" – a taint that more than any other factor defeated Hillary Clinton and produced the Donald Trump presidency.

13. Among other considerations, there remain serious questions about whether a federal official can be impeached after leaving office. *See supra* Chapter 5 notes 70–77 and accompanying text (discussing impeachments of Secretary of War Belknap and Judge George English).

14. The Federalist No. 74 (Alexander Hamilton). *See also* Margaret Colgate Love, *The Twilight of the Pardon Power*, 100 J. Crim. Law & Criminology 1169, 1172 (2010).

15. *See supra* Chapter 7 notes 111, 156 and accompanying text.

16. Love, *Twilight of the Pardon Power*, *supra* note 14, at 1173–75.

17. *Ibid.*, at 1174 n. 17.

18. U.S. Dept. of Justice, *Pardons Granted by President Barack Obama*, available at: www.justice.gov/pardon/obama-pardons.

19. Peter Baker, *Dinesh D'Souza, Pardoned by Trump, Claims Victory over Obama Administration*, N.Y. Times (June 1, 2018), available at: www.nytimes.com/2018/06/01/us/politics/trump-pardon-dsouza.html.

20. Julie Hirschfeld Davis & Maggie Haberman, *Trump Pardons Joe Arpaio, Who Became Face of Immigration Crackdown*, N.Y. Times (Aug. 25, 2017), available at: www.nytimes.com/2017/08/25/us/politics/joe-arpaio-trump-pardon-sheriff-arizona.html.

21. Peter Baker, *Trump Pardons Scooter Libby in a Case that Mirrors His Own*, N.Y. Times (Apr. 13, 2018), available at: www.nytimes.com/2018/04/13/us/politics/trump-pardon-scooter-libby.html.

22. *Trump Pardons, Congratulates Navy Sailor Who Took Illegal Submarine Photos*, CBS News (March 10, 2018), available at: www.cbsnews.com/news/trump-pardons-congratulates-kristian-saucier-navy-sailor-illegal-submarine-photos.

23. *See* Baker, *Scooter Libby Pardon*, *supra* note 21.

24. *See* Love, *Twilight of the Pardon Power*, *supra* note 14, at 1190–200.

13 IMPEACHMENT FOR LYING

1. *See supra* Chapter 6 notes 92–95 and accompanying text (judges); Chapter 8 note 77 and accompanying text (Nixon); and Chapter 9 notes 69–70 and accompanying text (Clinton).

2. 18 U.S.C. § 1623 (false declarations before a grand jury or court).

3. 18 U.S.C. § 1621 (perjury generally).

4. 18 U.S.C. § 1001 (false statements).
5. *See, e.g.*, 18 U.S.C. § 1341 (mail fraud).
6. Neil A. Lewis, *Senate Convicts U.S. Judge, Removing Him from Bench*, N.Y. TIMES (Nov. 4, 1989), available at: www.nytimes.com/1989/11/04/us/senate-convicts-us-judge-removing-him-from-bench.html.
7. *How the Senators Voted on Impeachment*, CNN.COM (Feb. 12, 1999), available at: www.cnn.com/ALLPOLITICS/stories/1999/02/12/senate.vote.
8. Here, too, there is a seriousness element. Presumably, a president would not be impeachable for lying to protect a family member or political associate from prosecution for jaywalking or speeding, or minor possessory drug crimes and the like.
9. *See supra* Chapter 8 notes 76–77 and accompanying text.
10. 18 U.S.C. § 1001(c)(2) (false statements in the course of "any investigation or review, conducted pursuant to the authority of any committee, subcommittee, commission or office of the Congress, consistent with applicable rules of the House or Senate").
11. The full quotation runs as follows: "The President must certainly be punishable for giving false information to the Senate. He is to regulate all intercourse with foreign powers, and it is his duty to impart to the Senate every material intelligence he receives. If it should appear that he has not given them full information, but has concealed important intelligence which he ought to have communicated, and by that means induced them to enter into measures injurious to their country, and which they would not have consented to had the true state of things been disclosed to them – in this case, I ask whether, upon an impeachment for a misdemeanor upon such an account, the Senate would probably favor him." 4 JONATHAN ELLIOT, THE DEBATES IN SEVERAL STATE CONVENTIONS ON THE ADOPTION OF THE FEDERAL CONSTITUTION 127 (1827).
12. *See supra* Chapter 8 note 99 and accompanying text.
13. Frank O. Bowman, III, *"High Crimes & Misdemeanors": Defining the Constitutional Limits on Presidential Impeachment*, 72 SO. CAL. L. REV. 1517, 1546 (1999).
14. Lt. Cmdr. Pat Paterson, U.S. Navy, *The Truth about Tonkin*, 22 NAVAL HIST. MAG. (Feb. 2008), available at: www.usni.org/magazines/navalhistory/2008–02/truth-about-tonkin.
15. H. R. MCMASTER, DERELICTION OF DUTY 108 (1997).
16. Lyndon Baines Johnson, President's Message to Congress, Aug. 5, 1964, available at: www.mtholyoke.edu/acad/intrel/tonkinsp.htm.
17. U.S. CONST. Art. II, § 3.
18. Seymour Hersh, *The Pentagon*, N.Y. TIMES (July 22, 1973), available at: www.nytimes.com/1973/07/22/archives/falsifying-military-records-the-pentagon.html?mcubz=1.
19. *What is the National Climate Assessment?* NAT'L OCEANIC & ATMOSPHERIC AGENCY, available at: www.climate.gov/teaching/what-national-climate-assessment-nca.

20. Michael D. Shear & Brad Plumer, *Climate Report Could Force Trump to Choose Between Science and His Base*, N.Y. TIMES (Aug. 17, 2017), available at: www .nytimes.com/2017/08/08/us/politics/climate-trump-scientists-supporters.html.

21. David Leonhardt & Stuart A. Thompson, *Trump's Lies*, N.Y. TIMES (Dec. 14, 2017), available at: www.nytimes.com/interactive/2017/06/23/opinion/trumps-lies.html.

22. *Fact Checker: 100 Days of Trump's Claims*, WASH. POST (2017), available at: www.washingtonpost.com/graphics/politics/trump-claims/?noredirect=o n&utm_term=.31a8acd8b1cc. *See also, All False Statements Involving Donald Trump*, POLITIFACT, available at: www.politifact.com/personalities/donald-trump/statements/byruling/false.

23. John Wagner, *"When I Can, I Tell the Truth": Trump Pushes Back Against His Peddling of Falsehoods*, WASH. POST (Nov. 1, 2018), available at: www.washing tonpost.com/politics/when-i-can-i-tell-the-truth-trump-pushes-back-against-his-peddling-of-falsehoods/2018/11/01/e8278d68-ddbe-11e8-85df-7a6b4d25cfbb_ story.html?utm_term=.9ec555fe8aa0. *See also Trump and the Truth*, THE NEW YORKER (2016), available at: www.newyorker.com/topics/trump-truth-fact-checking-investigation (essays fact-checking assertions made by President Trump during the 2016 campaign).

24. 3 JONATHAN ELLIOT, THE DEBATES IN SEVERAL STATE CONVENTIONS OF THE ADOPTION OF THE FEDERAL CONSTITUTION 401 (1827) [hereinafter 3 ELLIOT].

25. 2 THE RECORDS OF THE FEDERAL CONVENTION OF 1787, at 65 (Max Farrand ed., 1911).

26. THE FEDERALIST NO. 57 (James Madison).

27. "Virtue" played a particularly central role in the thinking of Montesquieu, whose political philosophy so heavily influenced the constitutional modeling of the framers. For a discussion of his complex thought about virtue, *see* Carole Dornier, *Virtue, in* A MONTESQUIEU DICTIONARY, available at: http://diction naire-montesquieu.ens-lyon.fr/en/article/1376475883/en. Among the attributes of the virtuous is a disposition to truth-telling, particularly when candor would be personally disadvantageous.

28. 3 ELLIOT, *supra* note 24, at 368.

29. *See Fact Checker: 100 Days of Trump Claims, supra* note 22.

30. Michael D. Shear & Emmarie Huetteman, *Trump Repeats Lie about Popular Vote in Meeting with Lawmakers*, N.Y. TIMES (Jan. 23, 2017), available at: www .nytimes.com/2017/01/23/us/politics/donald-trump-congress-democrats.html.

31. Michael D. Shear & Michael S. Schmidt, *Trump, Offering No Evidence, Says Obama Tapped His Phones*, N.Y. TIMES (March 4, 2017), available at: www .nytimes.com/2017/03/04/us/politics/trump-obama-tap-phones.html.

32. Phil Stewart, *As Trump Warned North Korea, His "Armada" was Headed Toward Australia*, REUTERS (April 18, 2017), available at: https://uk.reuters.com/article/ uk-northkorea-usa-carrier-idUKKBN17L039.

33. David Crary, *Boy Scouts Deny Trump Claim that Top Leader Called Him to Praise Speech*, CHI. TRIBUNE (Aug. 2, 2017), available at: www.chicagotribune .com/news/nationworld/ct-trump-boy-scouts-20170802-story.html.

34. Kevin Liptak, *Trump's Call History Called into Question*, CNN (Aug. 2, 2017), available at: www.cnn.com/2017/08/02/politics/trump-phone-calls/index.html.

35. Frank Newport, *Americans Evaluate Trump's Character Across 13 Dimensions*, GALLUP (June 25, 2018), available at: https://news.gallup.com/poll/235907/amer icans-evaluate-trump-character-across-dimensions.aspx; *Trump Is Not Fit to be President, American Voters Say*, QUINNIPIAC UNIV. POLL (Sept. 27, 2017), available at: https://poll.qu.edu/national/release-detail?ReleaseID=2487; *Poll on President Trump*, CNN (Sept. 10, 2018), available at: http://cdn.cnn.com/cnn/2018/images/09/10/rel8a.-.trump.pdf.

14 IMPEACHMENT FOR CORRUPTION: SCHEMES OF PECULATION, THE EMOLUMENTS CLAUSES, AND THE AVARICIOUS PRESIDENT

1. *See supra* Chapter 2 notes 18–23 and accompanying text.
2. *See supra* Chapter 2 notes 25–26 and accompanying text.
3. *See supra* Chapter 2 notes 73–137 and accompanying text.
4. *See supra* Chapter 3 notes 60–61 and accompanying text.
5. *See supra* Chapter 3 notes 96–116 and accompanying text.
6. *See supra* Chapter 3 note 158 and accompanying text.
7. *See supra* Chapter 4 notes 140–47 and accompanying text.
8. *See supra* Chapter 4 notes 211–16 and accompanying text.
9. Professor Zephyr Teachout argues that the framers saw political corruption as "self-serving use of public power for private ends, including, without limitation, bribery, public decisions to serve private wealth made because of dependent relationships, public decisions to serve executive power made because of dependent relationships, and use by public officials of their positions of power to become wealthy." Zephyr Teachout, *The Anti-Corruption Principle*, 94 CORNELL L. REV. 341, 373–74 (2009).
10. *See supra* Chapter 10 notes 18–27 and accompanying text.
11. *See supra* Chapter 7 notes 15–16 and accompanying text (discussing Lincoln's declination even to attend the Republican Party convention of 1864, and President Andrew Johnson's abandonment of the campaigning norm in the midterm elections of 1866).
12. This is not, of course, to suggest that money played no role in the elections of the early republic. Simple voter bribery was not unheard of, and stories of local politicians and political organizations fueling voter turnout with free whiskey are legend. Even George Washington got in on the act. Paul Bedard, *George Washington Plied Voters with Booze*, U.S. NEWS & WORLD REP. (Nov. 8, 2011), available at: www.usnews.com/news/blogs/washington-whispers/2011/11/08/george-washington-plied-voters-with-booze. *See also* DENNIS J. POGUE, FOUNDING SPIRITS: GEORGE WASHINGTON AND BEGINNINGS OF THE AMERICAN WHISKEY INDUSTRY (2011). Nonetheless, expenditures for this sort of thing would have been minuscule by modern standards.

13. In federal criminal law, these two kinds of misbehavior are customarily labeled bribery in the first case, 18 U.S.C. § 201(b)(1), and accepting an illegal gratuity in the second, 18 U.S.C. § 201(c).
14. *See supra* Chapter 2 notes 76, 84, 91 and accompanying text.
15. McDonnell v. United States, 136 S.Ct. 2355 (2016). For a discussion of the opinion, *see Leading Case: McDonnell v United States*, 130 HARV. L. REV. 467 (2016).
16. *Leading Case: McDonnell v United States*, 130 HARV. L. REV. 467 (2016).
17. Teachout, *The Anti-Corruption Principle, supra* note 9.
18. *See supra* Chapter 13 notes 25–28 and accompanying text.
19. *See supra* Chapter 4 notes 218–19 and accompanying text.
20. 3 JONATHAN ELLIOT, THE DEBATES IN THE SEVERAL STATE CONVENTIONS OF THE ADOPTION OF THE FEDERAL CONSTITUTION 486 (1827).
21. *See, e.g.*, Brett Samuels, *Trump Says He Will Refuse to Release Tax Returns as Long as They are Under Audit*, THE HILL (Nov. 7, 2018), available at: https://thehill.com/homenews/administration/415526-trump-says-he-will-refuse-to-release-tax-returns-as-long-as-they-are (noting that, "The president broke with decades of precedent when he opted not to release his tax returns during the 2016 presidential campaign").
22. Citizens for Responsibility and Ethics in Washington v. Trump, 276 F. Supp. 3d 174 (S.D.N.Y. 2017).
23. District of Columbia v. Trump, 291 F. Supp. 3d 725, 737 (D. Md. 2018).
24. Blumenthal v. Trump, No. CV 17-1154 (EGS), 2018 WL 4681001 (D.D.C. Sept. 28, 2018).
25. As of this writing, one district court has found that the public interest group and private plaintiffs lacked standing to bring an emoluments claim. Citizens for Responsibility and Ethics in Washington v. Trump, 276 F. Supp. 3d 174 (S.D.N.Y. 2017). A second district court found that the governments of the state of Maryland and the District of Columbia do have standing. District of Columbia v. Trump, 291 F. Supp. 3d 725, 737 (D. Md. 2018). The congressional group was also found to have standing. Blumenthal v. Trump, No. CV 17-1154 (EGS), 2018 WL 4681001 (D.D.C. Sept. 28, 2018).
26. It is somewhat difficult to imagine a district court ordering a sitting president to divest large business holdings, for example. More likely the relief would come in the form of a declaratory judgment finding a violation of the foreign emoluments clause, perhaps accompanied by a directive that the president seek permission from Congress to continue in his present courses. But what a court would do if the president refused to ask for permission or Congress refused to grant it is anybody's guess.
27. A fourth issue has been raised by several energetic controversialists who have argued that the foreign emoluments clause does not apply to the president because he or she does not "hold an Office of Profit or Trust under" the United States. The argument is ingenious, but ultimately frivolous. It was rejected in District of Columbia v. Trump, 315 F. Supp. 3d 875, 883 (D. Md. 2018). *See also* Frank O. Bowman, III, *Foreign Emoluments, the President &*

Professor Tillman, Impeachable Offenses? (Oct. 27, 2017), available at: https://impeachableoffenses.net/2017/10/27/foreign-emoluments-the-president-profes sor-tillman.

28. At the outset of his presidency, Mr. Trump refused to divest himself of his business or to make more than cosmetic changes in its management. He said, "I could actually run my business and run government at the same time. I don't like the way that looks, but I would be able to do that if I wanted to." Andy Sullivan, Emily Stephenson, & Steve Holland, *Trump Says won't Divest from His Business While President*, Reuters (Jan. 11, 2017), available at: www.reuters .com/article/us-usa-trump-finance/trump-says-wont-divest-from-his-business-while-president-idUSKBN14V21I.

29. For a brilliant scholarly proof of this point, see John Mikhail, *The Definition of "Emolument" in English Language Dictionaries, 1523–1806* (2017), available at: https://papers.ssrn.com/sol3/papers.cfm?abstract_id=2995693.

30. U.S. Const. Art. I, § 9. At the time of this writing, one district court has found that commercial payments can constitute a prohibited emolument. District of Columbia v. Trump, 315 F. Supp. 3d 875, 883 (D. Md. 2018). For contrasting views on this point, *compare* Norman L. Eisen, Richard Painter, & Laurence H. Tribe, *The Emoluments Clause: Its Text, Meaning, and Application to Donald J. Trump*, Governance Studies at Brookings (December 16, 2016) (arguing that commercial transactions are within the ban on foreign emoluments); *and* Marissa L. Kibler, *The Foreign Emoluments Clause: Tracing the Framers' Fears about Foreign Influence Over the President*, 74 N.Y.U. Ann. Surv. Am. L. (forthcoming Mar. 2019) (working draft 9/18/18) (same), *with* Amandeep S. Grewal, *The Foreign Emoluments Clause and the Chief Executive*, 102 Minn. L. Rev. 639 (2017).

31. 2 The Records of the Federal Convention of 1787, at 65–66 (Max Farrand ed., 1911) (emphasis added).

32. *See* Cambridge Dictionary, available at: https://dictionary.cambridge.org/us/dictionary/english/peculation, last accessed Jan 25, 2019. Samuel Johnson defined peculation as, "Robbery of the publick; theft of publick money." Samuel Johnson, A Dictionary of the English Language (3d ed. 1768). Webster's dictionary of 1828 defined "peculate" as "to defraud the public of money or goods entrusted to one's care by appropriating the property to one's own use; to defraud by embezzlement." Noah Webster, An American Dictionary of the English Language (1828).

33. The Federalist No. 72 (Alexander Hamilton) (emphasis added).

34. *See supra* Chapter 2 notes 193–95 and accompanying text.

35. Use of Public Office for Private Gain, 5 C.F.R. § 2635.702.

36. As the president's son, Eric Trump boasted in 2018, "I think our brand is the hottest it has ever been." Karen Yourish & Troy Griggs, *Tracking the President's Visits to Trump Properties*, N.Y. Times (July 16, 2018), available at: www.nytimes .com/interactive/2017/04/05/us/politics/tracking-trumps-visits-to-his-branded-properties.html?mtrref=www.google.com.

37. *Ibid.*

38. Katie Rogers, *In Trump's U.K Visit, Some See "Infomercial" for Money-Losing Golf Resort*, N.Y. TIMES (July 14, 2018), available at: www.nytimes.com/2018/07/14/world/europe/uk-trump-scotland-golf.html. Similarly, on the way back from a tour of Asia, he stopped in Honolulu and took a side trip to the Trump Hotel in Waikiki, assertedly to thank the employees for a "tremendously successful project." Lindsay Gibbs, *Trump Interrupts Foreign Trip to Promote Trump-Branded Hotel*, THINKPROGRESS (Nov. 4, 2017), available at: https://thinkprogress.org/trump-hawaii-hotel-stop-f3d6265c0e9d.

39. *Profiting from the Presidency: A Year's Worth of President Trump's Conflicts of Interest*, CITIZENS FOR RESPONSIBILITY AND ETHICS IN WASHINGTON (CREW), available at: www.citizensforethics.org/profitingfromthepresidency.

40. Austin Ramzy, *China Grants Ivanka Trump Initial Approval for New Trademarks*, N.Y. TIMES (Nov. 6, 2018), available at: www.nytimes.com/2018/11/06/business/china-ivanka-trump-trademarks.html.

41. Javier C. Hernández, Cao Li, & Jesse Drucker, *Jared Kushner's Sister Highlights Family Ties in Pitch to Chinese Investors*, N.Y. TIMES (May 6, 2017), available at: www.nytimes.com/2017/05/06/world/asia/jared-kushner-sister-nicole-meyer-china-investors.html.

42. Annie Gowen, *Trump Jr. to Give Foreign Policy Speech While on "Unofficial" Business Trip to India*, WASH. POST (Feb. 19, 2018), available at: www.washingtonpost.com/world/trump-jr-to-give-foreign-policy-speech-while-on-unofficial-business-trip-to-india/2018/02/19/37d00c37-d9e8-40c4-934b-0a26b8160dcd_story.html?utm_term=.2fd8f2fa27d6.

15 THE TWENTY-FIFTH AMENDMENT AS AN ALTERNATIVE TO IMPEACHMENT

1. Emily Goldberg, *Poll: Majority of Voters Say Trump isn't Fit to be President*, POLITICO (Sept. 27, 2017), available at: www.politico.com/story/2017/09/27/trump-poll-fit-to-be-president-243219; Josh Delk, *Majorities in New Poll Say Trump Not Level-Headed or Fit for Office*, THE HILL (Jan. 10, 2018), available at: https://thehill.com/blogs/blog-briefing-room/368343-majorities-in-new-poll-say-trump-not-level-headed-fit-for-office.

2. U.S. CONST. Amend. XXV.

3. Maureen Groppe, *Eight Things to Know About the 25th Amendment*, USA TODAY (Sept. 5, 2018), available at: www.usatoday.com/story/news/politics/2018/09/05/could-25th-amendment-used-remove-trump-office/1012979001.

4. 2 THE RECORDS OF THE FEDERAL CONVENTION OF 1787, at 65–66 (Max Farrand ed., 1911) [hereinafter FARRAND'S FEDERAL CONVENTION RECORDS] (emphasis added).

5. *See supra* Chapter 2 notes 199–200 and accompanying text; *see also supra* Chapter 3 notes 152–58 and accompanying text; Chapter 4 notes 226–35 and accompanying text; Chapter 6 notes 70–91 and accompanying text.

6. This point was not lost on the framers. Gunning Bedford of Delaware objected to a proposed presidential term of seven years because the country would be in woeful shape if saddled for so long a period with a president who proved to be

unqualified or lost his capacities after election. Bedford argued that even impeachment would be insufficient in such a case because it "would reach misfeasance only, not incapacity." 1 FARRAND'S FEDERAL CONVENTION RECORDS, *supra* note 4, at 68–69.

7. U.S. CONST. Art. II, § 1 (emphasis added).
8. 12 JOHN QUINCY ADAMS, THE MEMOIRS OF JOHN QUINCY ADAMS, COMPRISING PORTIONS OF HIS DIARY FROM 1795 TO 1848, at 176 (Charles Francis Adams ed., 1877).
9. SAMUEL ELIOT MORISON, THE OXFORD HISTORY OF THE AMERICAN PEOPLE 573 (1965).
10. CONG. GLOBE, 39th Cong., 2d Sess. 320 (1867) (emphasis added).
11. John D. Feerick, *The Twenty-Fifth Amendment: An Explanation and Defense*, 30 WAKE FOREST L. REV. 481, 484 (1995).
12. *See supra* Chapter 7 note 166 and accompanying text.
13. Feerick, *Twenty-Fifth Amendment*, *supra* note 11, at 486.
14. *Ibid.*, at 488.
15. MORISON, OXFORD HISTORY OF THE AMERICAN PEOPLE, *supra* note 9, at 573.
16. *Ibid.*, at 735.
17. Feerick, *Twenty-Fifth Amendment*, *supra* note 11, at 485.
18. *Ibid.*, at 485–86.
19. Arthur S. Link, *Woodrow Wilson: A Cautionary Tale*, 30 WAKE FOREST L. REV. 585, 586–89 (1995); E. A. WEINSTEIN, WOODROW WILSON: A MEDICAL AND PSYCHOLOGICAL BIOGRAPHY 260–70 (1981); HERBERT HOOVER, THE ORDEAL OF WOODROW WILSON 271–78 (1958).
20. WILLIAM MANCHESTER, THE GLORY AND THE DREAM: A NARRATIVE HISTORY OF AMERICA, 1932–1972, at 321–27, 334–35, 347–50 (1973); JOHN GUNTHER, ROOSEVELT IN RETROSPECT: A PROFILE IN HISTORY 272–74 (1950).
21. CLARENCE G. LASBY, EISENHOWER'S HEART ATTACK: HOW IKE BEAT HEART DISEASE AND HELD ON TO THE PRESIDENCY 57–113 (1997).
22. Anthony Leviero, *President Undergoes Surgery on Intestine Block at 2:59 AM: Doctors Pronounce it Success: Condition is Good: Operation Lasts Hour and 53 Minutes – 13 Attend Him*, N.Y. TIMES, June 9, 1956, at 1.
23. Feerick, *Twenty-Fifth Amendment*, *supra* note 11, at 489, 492.
24. *See supra* Chapter 6 notes 70–83 and accompanying text.
25. U.S. CONST. Amend. XXV, § 1.
26. THEODORE H. WHITE, BREACH OF FAITH: THE FALL OF RICHARD NIXON 258–59 (1975).
27. U.S. CONST. Amend. XXV, § 2.
28. WHITE, BREACH OF FAITH, *supra* note 26, at 258, 271.
29. U.S. CONST. Amend. XXV, § 3.
30. U.S. CONST. Amend. XXV, § 4.
31. *Ibid.*
32. *Ibid.*
33. *Presidential Approval Ratings – Trump*, GALLUP, available at: https://news .gallup.com/poll/203198/presidential-approval-ratings-donald-trump.aspx, last accessed Oct. 29, 2018.

34. *See, e.g.*, Meredith Conroy, Nathaniel Rakich, & Mai Nguyen, *We Looked at Hundreds of Endorsements. Here's Who Republicans are Listening To*, FIVETHIRTYEIGHT (Sept. 24, 2018), available at: https://fivethirtyeight.com/fea tures/we-looked-at-hundreds-of-endorsements-heres-who-republicans-are-listen ing-to (noting that, during the 2018 midterm primary season, Republican candidates backed by Donald Trump had a high success rate but adding the caveat that other factors may also have been at work).

35. *See generally* Cynthia R. Farina, *Congressional Polarization: Terminal Constitutional Dysfunction?* 115 COLUM. L. REV. 1689 (2015).

36. Jack Nelson, *Aide's '87 Memo Raised Question of Removing Reagan from Office*, WASH. POST (Sept. 15, 1988), available at: www.washingtonpost.com/archive/ politics/1988/09/15/aides-87-memo-raised-question-of-removing-reagan-from-office/a9ec7c98-2783-4362-8d9c-af41664af057/?utm_term=.6774443f8984; Jane Mayer, *Worrying About Reagan*, THE NEW YORKER (Feb. 24, 2011), available at: www.newyorker.com/news/news-desk/worrying-about-reagan.

37. U.S. CONST. Amend. XII.

38. *See e.g.*, Alex Morris, *Trump's Mental Health: Is Pathological Narcissism the Key to Trump's Behavior?*, ROLLING STONE (April 5, 2017), available at: www .rollingstone.com/politics/politics-features/trumps-mental-health-is-pathologi cal-narcissism-the-key-to-trumps-behavior-126354.

39. AM PSYCHIATRIC ASS'N, DIAGNOSTIC AND STATISTICAL MANUAL OF MENTAL DISORDERS § 301.81 (5th ed. 2013).

40. For other discussions of the Twenty-fifth Amendment arriving at roughly the same conclusion about its possible applications to the current president, *see* LAURENCE TRIBE AND JOSHUA MATZ, TO END A PRESIDENCY: THE POWER OF IMPEACHMENT 221–31 (2018); CASS R. SUNSTEIN, IMPEACHMENT: A CITIZEN'S GUIDE 135–48 (2017); GENE HEALY, INDISPENSABLE REMEDY: THE BROAD SCOPE OF THE CONSTITUTIONAL IMPEACHMENT POWER 39–46 (Cato Institute 2018).

16 IMPEACHING DONALD TRUMP

1. Max Boot, *Here are 18 Reasons Trump Could be a Russian Asset*, WASH. POST (Jan. 13, 2019), available at: www.washingtonpost.com/opinions/here-are-18-reasons-why-trump-could-be-a-russian-asset/2019/01/13/45b1b250-174f-11e9-88fe-f9f77a3bcb6c_story.html?utm_term=.6c7c2bfec565.

2. Mary Clare Jalonick & Deb Reichmann, *Senate Panel Backs Intelligence Agencies Findings on Russian Meddling in 2016 Election*, PBS (May 16, 2018), available at: www.pbs.org/newshour/politics/senate-panel-backs-intelligence-agencies-findings-on-russian-meddling-in-2016-election.

3. Peter Baker, *Trump and Putin Have Met Five Times. What Was Said Is a Mystery*, N.Y. TIMES (Jan. 15, 2019), available at: www.nytimes.com/2019/01/15/us/politics/ trump-putin-meetings.html; Matt Steib, *Report: Trump Had Second Private Meeting with Putin in 2018*, N.Y. MAGAZINE (Jan. 30, 2019), available at: http:// nymag.com/intelligencer/2019/01/report-trump-had-second-private-meeting-with-putin-in-2018.html; Greg Miller, *Trump has Concealed Details of His Face-*

to-Face Encounters with Putin from Senior Officials in Administration, WASH. POST (Jan. 13, 2019), available at: www.washingtonpost.com/world/national-secur ity/trump-has-concealed-details-of-his-face-to-face-encounters-with-putin-from-senior-officials-in-administration/2019/01/12/65f6686c-1434-11e9-b6ad-9cfd62dbb0a8_story.html?noredirect=on&utm_term=.99d02d55af1a.

4. Aaron Blake, *Why We Should All be Careful About the Lewd Trump–Russian Prostitute Allegation*, WASH. POST (April 14, 2018), available at: www.washington post.com/news/the-fix/wp/2018/04/15/why-the-lewd-trump-russian-prostitute-alle gation-is-a-distraction-and-we-should-all-be-careful/?utm_term=.e48636d392a7.

5. For a detailed description of Mr. Trump's business career, *see* David Barstow, Suzanne Craig, & Russ Buettner, *Trump Engaged in Suspect Tax Schemes as He Reaped Riches from His Father*, N.Y. TIMES (Oct. 2, 2018), available at: www .nytimes.com/interactive/2018/10/02/us/politics/donald-trump-tax-schemes-fred-trump.html.

6. Jonathan O'Connell, David A. Fahrenthold, & Jack Gillum, *As the "King of Debt," Trump Borrowed to Build His Empire. Then He Began Spending Hundreds of Millions in Cash*, WASH. POST (May 5, 2018), available at: www .washingtonpost.com/politics/as-the-king-of-debt-trump-borrowed-to-build-his-empire-then-he-began-spending-hundreds-of-millions-in-cash/2018/05/05/ 28te54b4-44c4-11e8-8569-26fda6b404c7_story.html?utm_term=.a9be51de6265.

7. *Ibid.*

8. Michael Hirsch, *How Russian Money Helped Save Trump's Business*, FOREIGN POLICY (Dec, 21, 2018), available at: https://foreignpolicy.com/2018/12/21/how-russian-money-helped-save-trumps-business.

9. Alan Cullison, *A Trio of Wealthy Russians Made an Enemy of Putin. Now They're All Dead*, WALL ST. J. (Oct. 10, 2018), available at: www.wsj.com/articles/a-trio-of-wealthy-russians-made-an-enemy-of-putin-now-theyre-all-dead-1539181416; Masha Gessen, *The Wrath of Putin*, VANITY FAIR (Apr. 2012), available at: www .vanityfair.com/news/politics/2012/04/vladimir-putin-mikhail-khodorkovsky-russia.

10. *See supra* Chapter 2, notes 178–79, 203–5.

11. *See supra* Chapter 2 notes 204–5 and accompanying text.

12. The classic quotation in this vein is from Lord Chancellor Somer, who said in 1691 that "the power of impeachment ought to be, like Goliath's sword, kept in the temple, and not used but on great occasions." 5 NEW PARL. HIST. 678 (1691).

13. *See* David A. Graham, *The Many Scandals of Donald Trump: A Cheat Sheet*, ATLANTIC (Jan. 23, 2017), available at: www.theatlantic.com/politics/archive/ 2017/01/donald-trump-scandals/474726.

14. Nick Penzenstadler & Susan Page, *Exclusive: Trump's 3,500 Lawsuits Unprecedented for a Presidential Nominee*, USA TODAY (June 1, 2016), available at: www.usatoday.com/story/news/politics/elections/2016/06/01/donald-trump-lawsuits-legal-battles/84995854.

15. Ron Elving, *President Trump Called for Roy Cohn, But Roy Cohn Was Gone*, NPR (Jan. 7, 2018), available at: www.npr.org/2018/01/07/576209428/president-trump-called-for-roy-cohn-but-roy-cohn-was-gone.

16. *Ibid.*

17. *Ibid.*

18. Michael D. Shear, Katie Benner, & Nicholas Fandos, *Embracing Conspiracy Theory, Trump Escalates Attack on Bruce Ohr*, N.Y. TIMES (Aug. 17, 2018), available at: www.nytimes.com/2018/08/17/us/politics/trump-conspiracy-bruce-nellie-ohr.html (describing Trump's attacks on Bruce Ohr, a mid-level Justice Department official).

19. Jonathan Allen, *Trump Weaponizes "Deep State" to Investigate His Investigators*, NBC NEWS, available at: www.nbcnews.com/politics/white-house/trump-weap onizes-deep-state-investigate-his-investigators-n876551 (quoting Tweet by President Trump after his allies in the House introduced a resolution calling for investigations of alleged irregularities in the Russia investigation: "Look how things have turned around on the Criminal Deep State. They go after Phony Collusion with Russia, a made up Scam, and end up getting caught in a major SPY scandal the likes of which this country may never have seen before! What goes around, comes around!"). *See generally* Evan Osnos, *Trump vs. The Deep State: How the Administration's Loyalists are Quietly Reshaping American Governance*, THE NEW YORKER (May 21, 2018), available at: www.newyorker .com/magazine/2018/05/21/trump-vs-the-deep-state.

20. Brent Kendall, *Trump Says Judge's Mexican Heritage Presents "Absolute Conflict*," WALL ST. J. (June 3, 2016), available at: www.wsj.com/articles/ donald-trump-keeps-up-attacks-on-judge-gonzalo-curiel-1464911442?mg=id-wsj.

21. Eugene Scott & Allie Malloy, *Trump Attacks Another Federal Judge*, CNN (Feb. 5, 2017), available at: www.cnn.com/2017/02/04/politics/donald-trump-attacks-federal-judge-travel-ban/index.html.

22. Kristine Philips, *All the Times Trump Personally Attacked Judges – and Why His Tirades are "Worse than Wrong*," WASH. POST (April 26, 2017), available at: www .washingtonpost.com/news/the-fix/wp/2017/04/26/all-the-times-trump-person ally-attacked-judges-and-why-his-tirades-are-worse-than-wrong/?utm_term=.e2e d55d42285 (also enumerating Trump attacks on other courts and judges).

23. Lisa Friedman & Coral Davenport, *Judge's Decision Blocks Work on Keystone XL in a Setback for Trump*, N.Y. TIMES (Nov. 10, 2018), available at: www .nytimes.com/2018/11/09/climate/judge-blocks-keystone-pipeline.html.

24. Washington v. Trump, 858 F.3d 1168, 1185 (9th Cir. 2017) (en banc) (Bybee, J., dissenting).

25. *Donald Trump Says He's Considering Pardon for Paul Manafort*, THE TELEGRAPH (Aug. 23, 2018), available at: www.telegraph.co.uk/news/2018/08/23/ donald-trump-says-considering-pardon-paul-manafort; Mark Moore, *Giuliani Says Trump Sought Advice on Pardoning Manafort*, N.Y. POST (Aug. 23, 2018), available at: www.marketwatch.com/story/giuliani-says-trump-sought-advice-on-pardoning-manafort-report-2018–08-23.

26. Max Kutner, *Will Trump Pardon Michael Flynn? "We'll See," He Says*, NEWSWEEK (Dec. 15, 2017), available at: www.newsweek.com/trump-pardon-michael-flynn-special-counsel-investigation-749382.

27. *See supra* Chapter 12 notes 19–23 and accompanying text.

28. *See supra* Chapter 8 note 80 and accompanying text.

29. *See supra* Chapter 12 notes 20–23 and accompanying text.

30. 2 The Records of the Federal Convention of 1787, at 65 (Max Farrand ed., 1911).

31. *Ibid.*, at 69.

32. Jo Becker, Adam Goldman, & Matt Apuzzo, *Russian Dirt on Clinton? "I Love It," Donald Trump Jr. Said*, N.Y. Times (July 11, 2017), available at: www.nytimes .com/2017/07/11/us/politics/trump-russia-email-clinton.html.

33. *See, e.g.*, Natasha Bertrand, A *Timeline of Trump Associates Asking for Dirt on Clinton*, Atlantic (May 27, 2018), available at: www.theatlantic.com/politics/ archive/2018/05/a-timeline-of-trump-associates-asking-for-dirt-on-clinton/ 561350. The possibility of Trump campaign involvement in the release of the Clinton campaign emails seems somewhat enhanced by the allegations in the indictment of Roger Stone. Quinta Jurecic, *Document: Indictment of Roger Stone*, Lawfare (Jan. 25, 2019), available at: www.lawfareblog.com/document-indictment-roger-stone.

34. Frank O. Bowman, III, *The Russian Lawyer Meeting and Election Law Crimes: The Experts Weigh In*, Impeachable Offenses? (July 13, 2017), available at: https://impeachableoffenses.net/2017/07/13/the-russian-lawyer-meeting-and-election-law-crimes-the-experts-weigh-in.

35. Philip Bump, *What We Know about the Trump Tower Meeting*, Wash. Post (Aug. 7, 2018), available at: www.washingtonpost.com/news/politics/wp/2018/08/ 07/what-we-know-about-the-trump-tower-meeting/?utm_term=.d7408cbb5d93.

36. Karen Yourish & Troy Griggs, *Eight Intelligence Groups Blame Russia for Meddling, but Trump Keeps Clouding the Picture*, N.Y. Times (Aug. 2, 2018), available at: www.nytimes.com/interactive/2018/07/16/us/elections/russian-inter ference-statements-comments.html.

37. Scott Shane & Mark Mazetti, *The Plot to Subvert an Election: Unraveling the Russia Story So Far*, N.Y. Times (Sept. 20, 2018), available at: www .nytimes.com/interactive/2018/09/20/us/politics/russia-interference-election-trump-clinton.html.

38. *See, e.g.*, Chuck Todd, Mark Murray, & Carrie Dann, *Trump Continues to Deny Russia Interfered in 2016. Here's Why That's a Problem*, NBC News (July 2, 2018), available at: www.nbcnews.com/politics/first-read/trump-continues-deny-russia-interfered-2016-here-s-why-s-n888206.

39. Ashley Parker, *Donald Trump, Slipping in Polls, Warns of "Stolen Election,"* N.Y. Times (Oct. 13, 2016), available at: www.nytimes.com/2016/10/14/us/poli tics/trump-election-rigging.html.

40. Aaron Blake, *Trump and Kobach Say Illegal Vote May Have Given Clinton the Popular Vote. The Math Disagrees*, Wash. Post (July 19, 2017), available at: www.washingtonpost.com/news/the-fix/wp/2017/07/19/the-white-house-still-thinks-illegal-votes-may-have-given-clinton-the-popular-vote-basic-logic-and-math-disagree/?utm_term=.c3baf130faf9; Miles Parks, *Fact Check: Trump Repeats Voter Fraud Claims About California*, NPR (Apr. 5, 2018), available at: www.npr.org/2018/04/05/599868312/fact-check-trump-repeats-voter-fraud-

claim-about-california: "In many places, like California, the same person votes many times – you've probably heard about that," Trump said. "They always like to say 'oh that's a conspiracy theory' – not a conspiracy theory folks. Millions and millions of people"; Ledyard King, *Trump's Claims of Massive Voter Fraud are Baseless, Election Integrity Panel Member Says*, USA TODAY (Aug. 4, 2018), available at: www.usatoday.com/story/news/politics/2018/08/04/donald-trumps-widespread-voter-fraud-claim-untrue-election-official/905262002.

41. Michael Tackett & Michael Wines, *Trump Disbands Commission on Voter Fraud*, N.Y. TIMES (Jan. 3, 2018), available at: www.nytimes.com/2018/01/03/us/politics/trump-voter-fraud-commission.html.

42. Jon Sharman, *Hillary Clinton Wins 2,864,974 More Votes than Donald Trump, Final US Election Count Shows*, INDEPENDENT (Dec. 21, 2016), available at: www.independent.co.uk/news/world/americas/hillary-clinton-3-million-popu lar-vote-donald-trump-us-election-a7487901.html.

43. Michelle Fox, *Trump Doubles Down on Unsubstantiated Claims of Election "Stealing" in Florida*, CNBC (Nov. 10, 2018) (quoting Trump Tweet: "Trying to STEAL two big elections. We are watching closely!"), available at: www.cnbc .com/2018/11/10/trump-doubles-down-on-claims-of-election-stealing-in-florida .html; Jesus Rodriguez, *Trump Floats Senate Race Do-over in Arizona*, POLITICO (Nov. 9, 2018) (quoting President Trump as alleging "electoral corruption"), available at: www.politico.com/story/2018/11/09/trump-arizona-senate-election-981676.

44. *See, e.g.*, Sally Persons, *Trump Did Not Expect, Want to Win the Presidency*, WASH. TIMES (Jan. 3, 2018), available at: www.washingtontimes.com/news/2018/jan/3/president-trump-did-not-expect-want-win-presidency.

45. See Matthew Barakat, *Emails Show Trump Intervened Personally to Stop FBI Headquarters from Moving Out of DC, Democrats, Say*, CHI. TRIBUNE (Oct. 18, 2018), available at: www.chicagotribune.com/news/nationworld/politics/ct-trump-fbi-headquarters-20181018-story.html; Jonathan O'Connell, *Trump Intervenes in FBI Headquarters Project*, WASH. POST (July 30, 2018), available at: www.washingtonpost.com/business/2018/07/30/trump-intervenes-fbi-head quarters-project/?utm_term=.03a9c8efb793.

46. David A. Graham, *The President Who Doesn't Read*, ATLANTIC (Jan. 5, 2018), available at: www.theatlantic.com/politics/archive/2018/01/americas-first-post-text-president/549794.

47. Juliet Eilperin, Josh Dawsey, & Seung Min Kim, *"It's Way Too Many": As Vacancies Pile Up in Trump Administration, Senators Grow Concerned*, WASH. POST (Feb. 4, 2019), available at: www.washingtonpost.com/national/health-science/its-way-too-many-as-vacancies-pile-up-in-trump-administration-sena tors-grow-concerned/2019/02/03/c570eb94-24b2-11e9-ad53-824486280311_story.ht ml?utm_term=.f2010f3d3da8&wpisrc=nl_most&wpmm=1; John W. Schoen, *After 500 Days, Hundreds of White House Jobs Remain Unfilled by Trump Administration*, CNBC (June 4, 2018), available at: www.cnbc.com/2018/06/04/after-500-days-dozens-of-white-house-jobs-remain-unfilled.html.

48. *Trump Team's Conflicts and Scandals*, Bloomberg (Nov. 1, 2018), available at: www.bloomberg.com/graphics/trump-administration-conflicts.

49. *See, e.g.*, Robbie Gramer, Dan De Luce, & Colum Lynch, *How the Trump Administration Broke the State Department*, Foreign Policy (July 31, 2017), available at: https://foreignpolicy.com/2017/07/31/how-the-trump-administration-broke-the-state-department.

50. James Freeman, *Could Trump Really Be Draining the Swamp?* Wall Street J. (June 30, 2017), available at: www.wsj.com/articles/could-trump-really-be-draining-the-swamp-1498850264.

51. Thomas Gibbons-Neff & Helene Cooper, *Deployed Inside the United States: The Military Waits for the Migrant Caravan*, N.Y. Times (Nov. 10, 2018), available at: www.nytimes.com/2018/11/10/us/deployed-inside-the-united-states-the-military-waits-for-the-migrant-caravan.html.

52. Melvyn P. Leffler, *The Strategic Thinking That Made America Great*, Foreign Affairs (Aug. 10, 2018), available at: www.foreignaffairs.com/articles/2018-08-10/strategic-thinking-made-america-great.

53. *See, e.g.*, Philip Bump, *Where the U.S. Has Considered Leaving or Left International Agreements Under Trump*, Wash. Post (June 29, 2018), available at: www.washingtonpost.com/news/politics/wp/2018/06/29/where-the-u-s-has-considered-leaving-or-left-international-agreements-under-trump/?utm_term=.a590dae9faeo; Simon Nixon, *Trump Puts WTO on the Ropes*, Wall Street J. (July 11, 2018), available at: www.wsj.com/articles/trump-puts-the-wto-on-the-ropes-1531340083.

54. Deirdre Shesgreen, *Trump Administration Withdraws from Nuclear Weapons Treaty, Accuses Russia of Violations*, USA Today (Feb. 1, 2019), available at: www.usatoday.com/story/news/world/2019/02/01/trump-administration-withdraws-u-s-russia-nuclear-weapons-treaty/2737306002; W. J. Hennigan, *Trump Plans to Tear Up a 31-year-old Nuclear Weapons Treaty. Now What?* Time (Oct. 21, 2018), available at: http://time.com/5430388/donald-trump-nuclear-weapons-treaty-inf-withdrawal.

55. Kathryn Watson, *"What Good Is NATO?": Trump Criticizes Germany and Other Allies at Summit*, CBS News (July 11, 2018), available at: www.cbsnews.com/news/trump-criticizes-nato-allies-germany-at-summit.

56. Domenico Montanaro, *6 Strongmen Trump Has Praised and the Conflicts It Presents*, NPR (May 2, 2017), available at: www.npr.org/2017/05/02/526520042/6-strongmen-trumps-praised-and-the-conflicts-it-presents; Richard Wolffe, *As Trump Cozies up to Saudi Arabia, the Rule of Law Collapses Further*, The Guardian (Oct. 18, 2018), available at: www.theguardian.com/world/commentisfree/2018/oct/18/as-trump-cozies-up-to-saudi-arabia-the-rule-of-law-collapses-further.

57. Helene Cooper, *Jim Mattis, Defense Secretary, Resigns in Rebuke of Trump's Worldview*, N.Y. Times (Dec. 20, 2018), available at: www.nytimes.com/2018/12/20/us/politics/jim-mattis-defense-secretary-trump.html.

58. 3 Jonathan Elliot, The Debates in Several State Conventions of the Adoption of the Federal Constitution 500 (1827).

59. Russell Feingold, *Donald Trump Can Unilaterally Withdraw from Treaties Because Congress Abdicated Its Responsibility*, NBC News (May 7, 2018), available at: www.nbcnews.com/think/opinion/donald-trump-can-unilaterally-withdraw-treaties-because-congress-abdicated-responsibility-ncna870866.

60. *See supra* Chapter 4 notes 203–5 and accompanying text.

61. U.S. Const. Amend. I.

62. John Wagner, *Trump Renews Attacks on Media as "The True Enemy of the People,"* Wash. Post (Oct. 29, 2018), available at: www.washingtonpost.com/politics/trump-renews-attacks-on-media-as-the-true-enemy-of-the-people/2018/10/29/9ebc62ee-db60-11e8-85df-7a6b4d25cfbb_story.html?utm_term=.da3066e47ef5.

63. Kate Sullivan, Jim Acosta, Betsy Klein, & Kevin Liptak, *Trump Says He Has No Regrets About Praising Congressman for Assaulting Reporter*, CNN (Oct. 19, 2018), available at: www.cnn.com/2018/10/18/politics/trump-rally-gianforte-my-guy/index.html.

64. The Federalist No. 65 (Alexander Hamilton).

65. Technically, there are two independents, Angus King of Maine and Bernie Sanders of Vermont, but both caucus with the Democrats.

66. *See, e.g.*, *The Primeval Tribalism of American Politics*, The Economist (May 24, 2018), available at: www.economist.com/united-states/2018/05/24/the-primeval-tribalism-of-american-politics; Gillian Tett, *Us Versus Them: America Divided into Tribes*, Financial Times (Feb. 20, 2018), available at: www.ft.com/content/f4e18952-157b-11e8-9e9c-25c814761640; Scott Beauchamp, *Tribal Passions, Totalitarian Parties*, The American Conservative (Oct. 25, 2018), available at: www.theamericanconservative.com/articles/tribal-passions-totalitarian-political-parties.

67. As Max Boot, former Republican, memorably put it, the Republican Party used to be "a conservative party with a white-nationalist fringe. Now it's a white-nationalist party with a conservative fringe." Max Boot, *I Left the Republican Party. Now I Want Democrats to Take Over*, Wash. Post (July 4, 2018), available at: www.washingtonpost.com/opinions/i-left-the-republican-party-now-i-want-democrats-to-take-over/2018/07/03/54a4007a-7e38-11e8-boef-fffcabeff946_story.html?utm_term=.5e4686ceebc9.

68. Megan Keneally, *"No Room for … Trump Critics" Among Republican Candidates Now: Sen. Jeff Flake*, ABC News (Oct. 23, 2018), available at: https://abcnews.go.com/Politics/room-trump-skeptics-trump-critics-republican-primaries-now/story?id=58686592; Jordain Carney, *McCain's Death Marks Decline of Trump's GOP Senate Critics*, The Hill, available at: https://thehill.com/homenews/senate/403895-mccains-death-marks-decline-of-trumps-gop-senate-critics.

69. Isaac Stanley-Becker, *Utah sends Mitt Romney, 2012 GOP Nominee for President, to the Senate*, Wash. Post (Nov. 6, 2018), available at: www.washingtonpost.com/politics/2018/live-updates/midterms/midterm-election-updates/utah-sends-mitt-romney-2012-gop-nominee-for-president-to-the-senate/?utm_term=.423c99cad276.

70. *Political Polarization in the American Public*, PEW RES. CTR. (June 12, 2014), available at: www.people-press.org/2014/06/12/section-1-growing-ideological-consistency.
71. *Confidence in Institutions*, GALLUP (2018), available at: https://news.gallup.com/poll/1597/confidence-institutions.aspx.
72. *Beyond Distrust: How Americans View Their Government*, PEW RES. CTR. (Nov. 23, 2015), available at: www.people-press.org/2015/11/23/1-trust-in-government-1958–2015.
73. GALLUP, *Confidence in Institutions, supra* note 57.
74. Ian Schwartz, *Leslie Stahl: Trump Told Me He Uses Term "Fake News" to Discredit the Media*, REAL CLEAR POLITICS (May 23, 2018), available at: www.realclearpolitics.com/video/2018/05/23/leslie_stahl_trump_told_me_he_uses_term_fake_news_to_discredit_the_media.html.
75. Alec Tyson, *Views of Mueller's Investigation – and Trump's Handling of the Probe – Turn More Partisan*, PEW RES. CTR. (Sept. 24, 2018), available at: www.pewresearch.org/fact-tank/2018/09/24/views-of-muellers-investigation-and-trumps-handling-of-the-probe-turn-more-partisan.
76. THEODORE H. WHITE, BREACH OF FAITH: THE FALL OF RICHARD NIXON 285 (1967).

APPENDIX: UNITED STATES IMPEACHMENTS, 1789 TO PRESENT

* The bulk of this Appendix is drawn from a similar attachment to an article written during the Clinton impeachment controversy, Frank O. Bowman, III & Stephen L. Sepinuck, *"High Crimes & Misdemeanors": Defining the Constitutional Limits on Presidential Impeachment*, 72 S. CAL. L. REV. 1517 (1999). The appendix to the article was the work of my colleague, Steve Sepinuck. Professor Sepinuck and the Southern California Law Review have both graciously consented to the slight modification and reuse of his work here. Summaries of the two most recent judicial impeachments are courtesy of my superb research assistant, Taylor Payne.
1. House Comm. on the Judiciary, Impeachment: Selected Materials, H.R. Doc. No. 93-7, at 126–28 (1973) [hereinafter Impeachment Materials].
2. *See* 7 Annals of Cong. 43–44 (1797). *See also* House Comm. on the Judiciary, 93d Cong., Impeachment: Selected Materials on Procedure 343–47 (Comm. Print 1974) [hereinafter Impeachment Procedure].
3. *See* IMPEACHMENT PROCEDURE, *supra* note 2, at 378.
4. IMPEACHMENT MATERIALS, *supra* note 1, at 133–35.
5. *See* IMPEACHMENT PROCEDURE, *supra* note 2, at 397–99.
6. *See ibid.*, at 403–4.
7. *See ibid.*, at 409.
8. *See ibid.*
9. *See ibid.* Note: Professor Gerhardt has suggested that "the Senate has construed the Constitution to make removal automatic upon a two-thirds vote on at least one article of impeachment." MICHAEL J. GERHARDT, THE FEDERAL IMPEACHMENT PROCESS 60 (1996). It is true that the Senate has removed every impeached official whom it has convicted. Moreover, in the impeachment trial of Judge Ritter, the

chair ruled that conviction carries with it automatic removal. *See infra* text accompanying note 55. The Senate's action here in voting separately on conviction and removal, as it also did in the impeachment trials of judges Humphreys and Archbald, *see infra* text accompanying notes 18 and 44, suggests that the two need not be inexorably linked; however, I think Professor Gerhardt is correct that the modern consensus is that conviction equates to removal.

10. The vote to impeach Justice Chase apparently came less than one hour after the Senate convicted and removed Judge Pickering. *See* Daniel H. Pollitt, *Sex in the Oval Office and Cover-up Under Oath: Impeachable Offense?* 77 N.C. L. Rev. 259, 270 (1998).

11. Impeachment Materials, *supra* note 1, at 133–35.

12. *See* Impeachment Procedure, *supra* note 2, at 472.

13. Impeachment Materials, *supra* note 1, at 136–39.

14. *See* Impeachment Procedure, *supra* note 2, at 506.

15. *See* Impeachment Materials, *supra* note 1, at 140–42.

16. *See* Impeachment Procedure, *supra* note 2, at 518.

17. *See ibid.*, at 522.

18. *See ibid.*, at 523–24. Senator Solomon Foot of Vermont, the President *pro tempore* of the Senate who presided over the trial, ruled that removal and disqualification were separate issues, and divided the vote on them. Cf. *supra* note 9.

19. *See* Michael Les Benedict, The Impeachment and Trial of Andrew Johnson 41–43 (1973).

20. *See* Impeachment Procedure, *supra* note 2, at 526–34.

21. *See ibid.*, at 528.

22. *See ibid.*, at 547.

23. *See* Irving Bryant, Impeachment: Trials and Errors 136–37 (1972).

24. *See ibid.*, at 137.

25. *See* Impeachment Procedure, *supra* note 2, at 555.

26. *See* Impeachment Materials, *supra* note 1, at 154–60.

27. *See* Impeachment Procedure, *supra* note 2, at 602–3.

28. *See ibid.*, at 605.

29. *See ibid.*

30. Benedict, Impeachment and Trial, *supra* note 19, at 126.

31. *See* Impeachment Procedure, *supra* note 2, at 608–9.

32. *See* Impeachment Materials, *supra* note 1, at 143–48.

33. *See* Impeachment Procedure, *supra* note 2, at 624–25.

34. *See ibid.*, at 639.

35. *See ibid.*, at 641–42.

36. *See ibid.*, at 644–46.

37. *See ibid.* at 651.

38. *See ibid.*

39. Impeachment Materials, *supra* note 1, at 149–53.

40. *See* Impeachment Procedure, *supra* note 2, at 684.

41. Beginning with the impeachment of Judge Archbald, the House voted on impeachment only after specific articles of impeachment were presented to it, usually by the Judiciary Committee.

42. *See* IMPEACHMENT MATERIALS, *supra* note 1, at 177–83.

43. *See* IMPEACHMENT PROCEDURE, *supra* note 2, at 817.

44. *See ibid.* With regard to the Senate's separately voting on guilt and removal, compare *supra* note 9.

45. *See* IMPEACHMENT MATERIALS, *supra* note 1, at 164–73.

46. *See* IMPEACHMENT PROCEDURE, *supra* note 2, at 890.

47. *Ibid.*, at 891.

48. *See ibid.*

49. *See ibid.*

50. IMPEACHMENT MATERIALS, *supra* note 1, at 184–87.

51. *See* IMPEACHMENT PROCEDURE, *supra* note 2, at 835–39.

52. *See ibid.*, at 850.

53. IMPEACHMENT MATERIALS, *supra* note 1, at 188–202.

54. *See* 80 CONG. REC. 5602–6 (1936).

55. *See ibid.*, at 5607. Cf. *supra* note 9.

56. *See ibid.*

57. 132 CONG. REC. 17295–305 (1986).

58. *See* 132 CONG. REC. 29870–72 (1986).

59. Although more than two-thirds of those voting voted to convict, fewer than two-thirds of those present voted to convict. *See* U.S. CONST. Art. I, § 3. This issue apparently also arose in the impeachment trial of Judge Ritter. After the Senate voted 56:28 on the last article of impeachment, the chair pronounced Ritter guilty. Senator Austin made a point of order suggesting, among other things, that the required two-thirds majority was lacking because two-thirds of those present had not voted to convict. *See* 80 CONG. REC. 5606 (1986). The point of order was overruled. *See ibid.* In doing so, the President *pro tempore* commented briefly on Senator Austin's other arguments, but made no reference to the requirement of a two-thirds majority of those present.

60. 523 F. Supp. 1209 (S.D. Fla. 1981).

61. *See* 134 CONG. REC. 20208–9 & 20221 (1988).

62. *See* 135 CONG. REC. 25239 (1989).

63. *See* 135 CONG. REC. 25330–35 (1989).

64. *See* 135 CONG. REC. 8814–24 (1989).

65. *See* 135 CONG. REC. 27102–4 (1989).

66. It is interesting to compare the specificity of this charge to the articles of impeachment against judges Hastings and Nixon, both of whom were also charged with perjury. In both of the prior cases, the articles of impeachment identified very specific perjurious statements that the judges allegedly made, whereas the charge against President Clinton was entirely general.

67. *See* 144 CONG. REC. H11774–75 (daily ed. Dec. 18, 1998). Article 1 was adopted by a vote of 228:206. Article 3 was adopted by a vote of 221:212. *See* 144 CONG. REC. H12040–42 (daily ed. Dec. 19, 1998). The House rejected two other proposed

articles of impeachment. One of these, rejected by a vote of 205:229, concerned giving false responses to interrogatories and false deposition testimony in the Paula Jones suit. The other, rejected by a vote of 148:285, concerned the president's refusal to respond to some requests for admission and his providing false responses to other requests for admission presented to him by the House Judiciary Committee in connection with the impeachment investigation. *See ibid.*

68. House Comm. on the Judiciary, Impeachment of Judge Samuel B. Kent, H.R. Rep. No. 111–159, at 2–3 (2009).
69. 155 Cong. Rec. S7833 (daily ed. July 22, 2009).
70. H.R. Res. 661, 111th Cong. (2009).
71. 155 Cong. Rec. S7832–33 (daily ed. July 22, 2009).
72. House Comm. on the Judiciary, Impeachment of G. Thomas Porteous, Jr., Judge of the United States District Court for the Eastern District of Louisiana, H.R. Rep. No. 111-427, at 2–3 (2010).
73. 156 Cong. Rec. S8607–10 (daily ed. July 22, 2009).
74. 156 Cong. Rec. S8611 (daily ed. July 22, 2009).

Index